The Politics of the Rope

the campaign to abolish capital punishment in Britain 1955-1969

The author, Neville Twitchell, has a BA in history from Birkbeck College, University of London, an MA in twentieth century historical studies from the University of Westminster, and a PhD in British political history from London Metropolitan University, for a thesis on the campaign to abolish hanging in Britain, of which this book is essentially an outgrowth.

GW00566759

The Politics of The Rope

the campaign to abolish capital punishment in Britain 1955-1969

Neville Twitchell

Arena Books

First published in 2012 by Arena Books

Arena Books
6 Southgate Green
Bury St. Edmunds
IP33 2BL

www.arenabooks.co.uk

Distributed in America by Ingram International, One Ingram Blvd., PO Box
3006, La Vergne, TN 37086-1985, USA.

Neville Twitchell
The Politics of the Rope the campaign to abolish capital punishment in
Britain 1955-1969
1.Capital punishment – Great Britain – History – 20th century. 2.Capital punishment
- Great Britain – Public opinion – History – 20th century. 3.Public opinion - Great
Britain – History – 20th century.
I.Title
364.6'6'0941'09045-dc23

ISBN-13 978-1-906791-98-8

BIC classifications:- JKV, JPP, HBTB, JK.

Printed and bound by Lightning Source UK

Cover design
By Jason Anscomb

Typeset in
Times New Roman

CONTENTS

Illustrations of Home Secretaries, judges, churchmen, journalists, campaigners, and hangmen, featured in this book will be found between pages 194 & 195.

ACKNOWLEDGEMENTS

My list of acknowledgements is a lengthy one because I have had the assistance in one form or another of a great many people in a wide variety of organizations and establishments over a very long period of time. Alas some of this goes back such a very long time that I cannot recall all of them. My apologies to the (doubtless) many people whom I have overlooked in the following, or whose names I have misspelled, or who are no longer in the positions they occupied then.

This book is an outgrowth of my PhD thesis at London Metropolitan University, or London Guildhall University as it still was when I started (I have spent so long on this work that the ground has often shifted from under my feet) or more precisely it is one of the longer versions of it; the original having had to be cut down on a draconian basis to come in under the stipulated and exacting maximum word count, much to my vexation. First and foremost I should thank Professor Stephen Haseler of London Metropolitan University and the Global Policy Institute, my PhD supervisor, for his advice and encouragement and indeed forbearance, because he must often have despaired of me ever finishing the project (as I sometimes did myself). I should thank also Professor Peter Laugharne, my second supervisor, Professor Robert Self, my internal examiner, and Dr Wendy Stokes of London Metropolitan, all of whom, at one time or another, made valuable comments on my thesis, as did likewise Professor Philip Murphy of Reading University, my external examiner. I thank also Professor Peter Dorey of Cardiff University and Professor Mel Read, now of Queen's University, Belfast for supplying me with an interesting conference paper relating to my research.

I should express my gratitude particularly to those people who agreed to be interviewed by me for the purposes of my research; namely Shirley Williams (Lady Williams of Crosby), Professor Terence Morris and Louis Blom-Cooper, QC, and Stan Newens, MEP (all face to face), and Braham Murray and Michael Elwyn (over the telephone), all of whom were able to give me valuable insights into historical matters which I hope enriched my understanding of them.

The following list of thanks is in no particular order. I should like to acknowledge the assistance of the staff of the British Library, including the Humanities Reading Room who were able to supply me with a seemingly never-ending stream of books very swiftly, the Historical Manuscripts Section where I was able to peruse the Gerald Gardiner papers which were central to my thesis, the Sound Recording Centre and Ike Egbetola and Yadley Day and their excellent facilities, and the Newspaper Reading Rooms at Colindale. I should acknowledge the staff of the National Archives (or the Public Records Office as I think it still was when I started my research – another area where the ground has shifted) for access to governmental papers, especially Home Office documents and Cabinet minutes.

I should thank the Modern Records Centre at the University of Warwick (Coventry) and Richard Temple for giving me sight of the Gollancz papers and the papers of the NCADP; the Howard League and Frances Crook for permission to view the papers of the NCACP at their premises; and the Centre for Capital Punishment Studies at the University of Westminster and Professor Peter Hodgkinson and Seema Kandelia for their assistance in my research and for allowing me to rummage around in their library and offices. I should thank Andrew Riley of the Churchill Archives Centre, Churchill College, University of Cambridge, and the executors of the estate of Lord Duncan-Sandys for permitting to view the Duncan Sandys papers, particularly those relating to his campaign to re-introduce hanging. My thanks to the Bodleian Library, Oxford, and Jeremy McIlwaine, for permitting me to view the Conservative Party archives including shadow cabinet minutes; the Manchester Peoples History Museum, the National Museum of Labour History and Darren Treadwell for permitting me to view Labour Party archives including, the General Secretaries papers; and the LSE, and Sue Donnelly, for sight of the C H Rolph papers and Liberal Party papers.

I am grateful to the Church of England Library at Lambeth Palace for permitting to view the papers of various senior clergy, and particularly Matti Watton who was very helpful in guiding me through all the material, and Philip Gale of the CERC for providing me with the Canon Collins papers. I thank the Catholic National Library at Farnborough, and Tony Martin and Joan Bond there for their assistance in enabling me to view documents, and Fr Nicholas Schofield of the Roman Catholic Diocesan Archives, Westminster, for his help in my viewing of material. I thank the Friends Meeting House in Euston Road for their assistance and for enabling me to view the archives of the Society of Friends Penal Reform Committee. I thank the London Metropolitan Archives for giving me sight of the Jakobovits papers and the papers of the Board of Deputies of British Jews, and Sandra Clark of said Board for giving me permission to view their papers. I thank Sussex University for my viewing of the Mass Observation archive at Falmer, and Nick Moon and NOP for giving me sight of original polling data and poll findings at their London offices. I thank Liz Davies of the Haldane Society of Socialist Lawyers at Garden Court, Lincolns Inn Fields for permitting me to view the records of that society. I thank Steven Towndrow and Lee Sands, of the BMA Public Information Unit, for giving me sight of the records and archives of the BMA at their London offices, and Francis Maunze, archivist of the Royal College of Psychiatrists, for supplying me with material from the Council of the Royal Medico-Psychological Association.

I should acknowledge the British Film Institute, particularly Kathleen Dickson, for enabling me to view films and television programmes there, and Phil Wickham, their archivist of the TV Curatorial Unit, for helpful information about the existence or non-existence of TV recordings. I should thank the BBC Written Archives Centre at Caversham Park, Reading for permitting me to view their programme files and microfiche records, particularly David McGowan and Louise North, who was endlessly patient with me when I had to call upon her technical expertise with exasperating frequency to rescue me from the devilish microfilm reading device. I thank especially Braham Murray and Michael Elwyn for giving me background information about the play "Hang down your head and die" and David Wood for supplying me with a script of the play and other interesting information.

Finally I should thank James Farrell and Arena Books for agreeing to publish the book, and allowing this work which has occupied fully a quarter of my life, finally to see the light of day.

Of course any errors of fact are my own responsibility and the historical judgements and misjudgements are entirely mine.

Neville Twitchell
Harlow, Essex
August 2012

CHAPTER 1

INTRODUCTION

On Thursday, 13th August 1964 the fifth and final Test match between England and Australia commenced at the Oval, ending in a predictably dour draw five days later. During the course of it Fred Trueman took his long-awaited 300th Test wicket, Colin Cowdrey passed 5,000 Test runs and Geoffrey Boycott scored his maiden Test century. Six weeks earlier the first *Beatles* film, *A Hard Day's Night*, directed by Richard Lester, was released to popular and critical acclaim with its frenetic and innovative style. The song of the same name released as a single a few days later was enjoying its third consecutive week at number one in the charts, jostling with the Rolling Stones *It's All Over Now* which it succeeded and Manfred Mann's *Du Wah Diddy Diddy* which it preceded in that position. That week the first coloured matron was appointed in the NHS and the May road casualty figures were released being the worst on record and highlighting fears over road safety. Ian Fleming, the author of the James Bond novels, had died the previous day. The news was dominated by the escape from prison of the Great Train Robber Charles Wilson, the activities of 'mods and rockers' at seaside resorts and the libel action threatened by Lord Boothby against the Sunday Mirror in respect of a story concerning himself and his association with the Krays, East London gangsters. Politically Britain looked toward the next general election, due in October at the latest, and Harold Wilson's opposition Labour Party currently enjoyed a 6.5% lead in the Gallup polls. Internationally there was growing tension in Vietnam as American involvement heightened after the Tonkin incident.

Amidst all of this, and attracting surprisingly little attention, a strange ritual was being played out. At a few minutes before eight o'clock in the morning, in two separate prisons several miles apart, two men were led from their respective prison cells with their hands pinioned behind their backs; marched into an adjoining cell through a door, the presence of which had been hitherto concealed from them by a wardrobe; were positioned over the chalk marks drawn on a wooden trap door; had their ankles strapped together and a white hood placed over their heads; had a noose attached to a rope suspended from the ceiling placed round their necks, held in place around their neck by a rubber washer with the metal eyelet situated under the left angle of the jaw. A cotter pin was swiftly removed from the trap door and a lever pulled causing the doors beneath them to bang open. At this they instantly fell a distance of about six feet through the air until their drop was arrested by the rope causing their heads to jerk sharply backwards, breaking one or more cervical vertebrae and severing or crushing the spinal cord. Death was instantaneous. The whole exercise from the parties' entry to the cell up to the moment of death had taken about twelve seconds.[1] Peter Anthony Allen and Gwynne Owen Evans had become the last men to be hanged in England under the jurisdiction of the English criminal law.[2]

The grisly pantomime that had been staged time and again was never to be repeated. This last hanging was the final episode of a struggle that had consumed the passions of generations of politicians and Parliamentarians, lawyers, judges, churchmen, writers, journalists, novelists and campaigners and had been the cockpit of a furious battle for the previous twenty years in which all the machinery of the British Parliamentary system had been enlisted. The object of this struggle was an archaic punishment, still practised with the trappings of antiquity and clung about with the musty odours of former centuries.[3] Just over a year later an Act was passed into law that abolished the practice. Capital punishment had come to an end and was never to be restored.

Almost everyone had a view on hanging. Opinion polls showed, whatever else they might indicate, that nearly everyone had a view one way or the other. It was a simple issue. It didn't involve complex economic arguments or political calculations. It didn't have awkward ramifications. It was a straight choice - an 'eye for an eye' or 'turning the other cheek'. This simplistic view was reflected, on a slightly more sophisticated plane of argument, at the level of party and pressure group politics. Here the pros and cons of hanging had been thrashed out time and again in sometimes thrilling set-piece House of Commons debates, in 1948, in 1953, 1955 and 1956 and then in 1964-65, and 1969, and then many times again in the years after abolition. It is an issue that never quite goes away, no matter how much hanging seems now to have receded into the mists of time. It remains one of the most contentious of all of the 'peripheral' questions of British politics.

This work seeks to answer some basic questions about hanging and the campaign to end it, that, for all the heat generated by the debate, seem not yet to have been answered in any satisfactory way. It asks why the issue generated so

---

[1] This account is based on that given in Block, Brian P and John Hostettler, *Hanging in the Balance: A History of the Abolition of Capital Punishment in Britain* (Winchester: Waterside, 1997), p. 15, which was culled partly from Pierrepoint, Albert, *Executioner: Pierrepoint* (London: Harrap, 1974); see also Jones, Elwyn, *The Last Two to Hang* (London: Macmillan, 1966)

[2] It is a widespread fallacy that James Hanratty was the last man to be hanged in Britain, for in fact he had seven successors, of which these were the last. Eddleston, John J, *The Encyclopaedia of Executions* (London: John Blake, 2002)

[3] In fact executions had once invariably been in public, and it was only in 1868 that this practice ceased and they were confined within prison walls.

much controversy. It asks why abolition succeeded when it did, and not earlier or later. Why did it culminate in the period 1964-65? Why did it take twenty years for a Commons majority for abolition, which had existed since 1945, to translate itself into an Abolition Act, given that hanging was, and is, traditionally a question that is decided on a free vote of the House? Or, to put the question in a very different way, how did abolition manage to triumph against the combined opposition of the massed ranks of the establishment and of popular opinion in the country, and to do it so soon after it had been decisively rejected? Was it the *zeitgeist* of the early sixties? If someone who knew a lot about British politics, but, by some quirk, knew nothing about the capital punishment issue, was asked to guess when abolition took place he might well hazard the early sixties, and perhaps even, if he was particularly well informed he might come up with the precise year of 1965. Perhaps his knowledge of election results would stand him in good stead here, together with an understanding of the propensities and sympathies of the membership of the parties, and the sort of time-scales that are involved in bringing to fruition a controversial measure such as that of abolition. Perhaps, also, received ideas about the 'permissive society' and the 'swinging sixties', associated with a *melange* of measures to do with homosexual law reform, abortion liberalization, easier divorce, abolition of theatre censorship etc. would enable him to make an informed guess.

In retrospect it seems curiously fitting that abolition took place when it did. It is hard to imagine the England of earlier periods *not* still having the death penalty, even if only as a lingering vestige sparingly used. Equally, it is difficult to conceive of the England of the mid-sixties forwards still *having* the death penalty. It belongs quintessentially, it seems at this distance, to sterner, fustier times shrugged off in the social revolution of the 1960s. Some events seem to be so right for their times that it is almost impossible to imagine them not happening when they did or of them happening at some other time. Abolition seems to be one such. But for all that, abolition happened when it did because of the mechanics of Parliamentary procedure, the results of elections, and the actions of individuals. Politics was the vehicle of abolition, sailing on a liberal tide.

Abolition raised some intriguing counterfactual questions. Suppose that abolition had not been brought about when it was? How would the subsequent course of English political history have differed? How would the question of terrorism, which was virtually re-invented in the late sixties, have been handled if the gallows was still in action?[4] Would terrorists, of whatever stamp and in

---

[4] Curiously, though hanging for murder had been abolished in 1965 in respect of England, Wales and Scotland it remained on the statute book in Northern Ireland until abolished by the Northern Ireland (Emergency Powers) Act of 1973 at the height of 'The Troubles'. In practice, after 1965, the Home Secretary always exercised the prerogative of mercy to reprieve convicted murderers in Northern Ireland, the Isle of Man and the Channel Islands. It

whatever cause, have been executed and what would the consequences have been of that for any peace process? High political considerations would probably have precluded the use of the rope in terrorist cases, but if so then it could scarcely have been used in 'ordinary' murder cases. It would therefore have fallen into abeyance, and if in abeyance would that merely have presaged its abolition anyway? But can one then conceive of abolition happening in the much more violent climate of the terrorist era? As it was, abolition had to be driven through the narrow aperture of Parliamentary procedure, and once thus driven, the process was almost organic in that it could hardly have been reversed. But if the process had not taken place then could an even narrower aperture have been traversed later?

What of the party political scene in the early to mid-sixties? By then the Labour Party had moved from being preponderantly abolitionist to being overwhelmingly abolitionist. The Conservative Party was still predominantly retentionist, though the abolitionist rump of the fifties had swelled to about a quarter to a third of the party by 1964-65. Why was abolition so very much an obsession within the Labour Party, and the left and centre of British politics, and why did the question divide along party lines to the extent that it did, given the supposedly non-partisan nature of the issue? Labour had always been the abolitionist party going back to the inter-war years, and the abolitionist campaigners had always reposed their hopes in Labour. Yet there was nothing intrinsically socialist or left-wing about abolition, and the hanging question and penal policy generally was tangential to the main arena of partisan conflict over economic and social questions. Part of the answer must lie with Labour's Christian/humanist origins which naturally indicated an 'enlightened' and 'progressive' penal policy, with the stress on reform and rehabilitation rather than punishment and deterrence.

Also, many of the founders and early leaders of the party were pacifists. Abolition was, arguably, the penal equivalent of pacifism. The values that drove men to refuse to serve in the armed forces, and to incite others to do likewise, clearly informed opinion about penal questions. Labour has always seen itself as the 'progressive' party, by contrast with the 'outmoded' values promoted by the Tories, and not merely as the party of socialism, trade unionism or the working class. Abolition was clearly 'progressive' in the historical sense of being in accord with the general trend of policy over the decades and centuries, which was towards a softening of the harshness of judicial punishments and the search for more humane methods of correction. There has not been the same degree of concern in Labour's ranks with the maintenance of law and order and the defence of property that has traditionally driven the Tories to favour a tougher stance on penal issues. Again there is a reflexive streak of anti-establishmentism

---

is interesting, in retrospect, to speculate on the possible ramifications for Northern Irish politics of the execution of an IRA or Loyalist terrorist at that time.

in the Labour ranks, and nowhere were establishment attitudes more evident and more deeply entrenched than in the ranks of the judiciary and the legal profession. Furthermore the judiciary, for most of the century had been deeply Conservative in its political hue, and notoriously anti-Labour, a further goad to the left to abolish one of its most cherished institutions - one that conferred upon its higher echelons the power of life and death.

For the Conservative Party these considerations were less significant, but nonetheless a substantial minority of its MPs had, by the 1950s, moved to an abolitionist stance, arising mostly from the same humanistic values that drove Labour abolitionists. Finally, though capital punishment was nearly always subject to a free vote in the House of Commons it would be naive to suppose that MPs were thereby free of pressures. The lash of the whips was replaced by the blandishments of pressure groups and fellow MPs, and the admonishments of constituents and constituency parties. It is uncertain whether such pressures operated within the Labour Party on this issue, but it is clear that they did within the Conservative Party and that many abolitionist Conservative MPs at the height of the controversy, in the mid-fifties, were under strong pressure to fall into line with the bulk of their party, and that they very often succumbed to the pressure.[5]

Much has been said about the supposedly liberal spirit of the era, but public opinion throughout the controversy, at least as measured by the polls, showed consistently large majorities in favour of hanging, whatever liberal sentiments might have been expressed on other issues of the day. Though the trend was towards abolition, even by 1964-65 there was still a majority for hanging. It is plain that whatever *zeitgeist* moved the abolitionists it was not that of the bulk of the population. Why the consistent pro-hanging stance of the public? What differences were evident here, if any, on the basis of age, sex, class, income, level of education, views on other matters, religious beliefs, party political affiliation, and even personality factors? What changes in opinion were evident as a function of events in the courtroom and the political arena, and did factors such as these operate differently with different types of people? Did the chance occurrence of a series of horrific murders at a particular time cause a resurgence in the popularity of hanging, and, conversely, did disquiet over miscarriages cause a shift towards abolitionism? To what extent did public opinion influence the politicians, if at all, or were opinion polls, like crime statistics, used by the politicians in the manner that the drunkard uses the lamp-post - for support rather than illumination? Finally, why did public opinion fail to follow the lead given by the politicians, as it has in so many other areas of policy?

How was the party political fight affected by the issue? Since Labour was

---

[5] Noteworthy is the case of Nigel Nicolson, but he was only the most prominent. See especially Nicolson, Nigel, *People and Parliament* (London: Weidenfeld and Nicolson, 1958)

by 1964 almost wholly abolitionist, and was effectively the sponsor of the Silverman Abolition Bill in all but name, did this adversely affect its fortunes at the polls in the 1964 and 1966 general elections, or in subsequent by-elections, or in subsequent general elections? Did the issue have any salience amongst the general public; were they aware of the stance of the parties, and did it weigh with them when they entered the polling booth? Though Labour did not seem to have suffered to any significant degree, it is interesting that at the 1966 general election a pro-hanging candidate, the uncle of a murdered child, garnered a very large number of votes standing against the leading abolitionist, and though not unseating him gained more votes than any genuinely independent candidate since the end of the Second World War.[6] Nonetheless a 'capital punishment party' has never emerged. Why not?

Consideration of public opinion, and its interplay with politics, leads on naturally to a consideration of the role played by the various pressure groups that sprang up to advance the cause of abolition; most notably, from 1955 onwards, the National Campaign for the Abolition of Capital Punishment (NCACP), and to a lesser extent, the Howard League for Penal Reform, which from the early fifties began to devote itself increasingly to the cause. From where did they draw the bulk of their support, and what motivated them? How effective was their campaign, what methods did they use, to what audience did they pitch, and how well did they liaise with the parties and politicians who carried their banner? On the other side of the debate there was initially no 'Campaign for the Retention of Capital Punishment', and no major figures in public life propagating for retention. Thus it may seem that it was an unequal struggle, and yet the retentionists had much of the establishment on their side in the form of the judiciary, the police force and its influential mouthpieces, the prison service and its associations, the House of Lords, and the bulk of the general public. It was, for much of the time, a contest between two evenly matched, but disparately organized and led bodies of opinion. A condition of dynamic equilibrium had been established. But it would be misleading to suppose that this was a contest between idealists and pragmatists. The retentionists were often portrayed, and often portrayed themselves, as hard-headed realists standing out against the sickly sentimentality of the abolitionists. Yet given the uncertainty of the deterrent value of hanging, and the extreme unlikelihood of anyone of their number being the victim of murder, it seems that the attitude of the pro-hangers was in many ways just as ideologically motivated as that of the anti-hangers. It was a contest between two sets of ideologues over what was for both of them, and for nearly everyone else, an almost abstract concept.

---

[6] Patrick Downey, uncle of Lesley Downey, a victim of the Moors Murderers. Downey stood on an expressly pro-hanging platform and gained 5,000 votes, a post-war record for a genuinely independent, non former MP, standing in a general election. See Hughes, Emrys, *Sydney Silverman: Rebel in Parliament* (London: Charles Skilton, 1969) pp.182-92

Much has been written about the supposed effects on the murder rate, and on crime generally, of abolition, and adduced as evidence, given the appropriate gloss, by both sides. No doubt the number of murders has risen dramatically in the years since abolition, but this arguably reflects the increasingly violent nature of society and may have little or nothing to do with the effects of abolition. The murder rate had been rising steadily, along with other forms of violent crime, for years and decades before abolition, and it is a moot point whether the *rate* of increase steepened from the mid-sixties, or merely continued on a smooth upward parabola.[7] What is the comparison with the figures for other countries where abolition has taken place?

What was the effect of the various miscarriages of justice, real or supposed, that littered the period from Timothy Evans in 1950 to Hanratty in 1962? How did these influence the debate and shift public opinion? Many books have been written about Timothy Evans and John Christie, Derek Bentley and Christopher Craig, Ruth Ellis and James Hanratty, as well as numerous other less well-publicized cases. Did the drama and unease about these cases begin to move public opinion away from hanging, as is often supposed? Is there opinion poll evidence on these specific points? Was Hanratty the final straw, or were these cases largely irrelevant; convenient fodder for abolitionist propaganda, but not the reason for anyone to change his mind about hanging? Plainly there was public disquiet, and the much-vaunted power of the Home Secretary to reprieve, so often adduced by retentionists in support of the contention that innocent men were never hanged, was much dented by the failure of successive Home Secretaries to issue a reprieve in the two cases (Bentley and Ellis) that cried out for it.

What of the role of the media in all of this? The press was sharply divided on the merits of abolition, with the divide roughly shadowing the political divide. The Conservative press tended to be pro-hanging, and most of the Labour or Liberal press abolitionist. Was this co-incidence, or did the papers follow the lead of the politicians and parties they generally supported, and what was the nature of the interplay between the parties and the press? And how influential was the press in massaging public opinion? Was the press as uninfluential as it generally is in the realm of politics?

What of the rest of the media? Given the salience of the capital punishment issue it was naturally a frequent topic of debate on television and radio, with many news items, current affairs programmes and documentaries devoted to the question. How influential were these in shaping public opinion and the nature of the debate? What was the extent of their influence by

---

[7] During the currency of the abolition provisions of the Homicide Act from 1957-1965 when there were, uniquely in English criminal history, two classes of murder it rather seems that the rate of increase in non-capital murder was not significantly greater than that of capital murder.

comparison with that of the press? And did the cinema, the theatre and the literature of the time take up the theme; and if so what was their stance, how did they interpret the debate and weave it into the fabric of popular culture, and how influential were they in conditioning political and public perceptions?

Given the salience of the capital punishment question there is no dearth of literature on the history of hanging and of the numerous abolition campaigns.[8] There is, however, no work dedicated specifically to the period of the consummation of the campaign from 1955 to 1969, which culminated in the passage of Sydney Silverman's Murder (Abolition of Death Penalty) Act in 1965 and its confirmation in 1969, and this work seeks to fill that lacuna. It should be pointed out that of course capital punishment was technically only abolished, in 1965, for the crime of murder, and that it remained theoretically in force for the crimes of treason, arson in government dockyards, piracy on the high seas, and mutiny in the armed forces.[9] This is very much a technicality since, even when the death penalty was still in common use, only three men had been hanged for treason (or for any crime other than murder) this century, and all of these were during, or in the immediate aftermath, of war.[10]

---

[8] The chief works that deal, *inter alia*, with the period in question, or part of the period, are: - Tuttle, Elizabeth Orman, *The Crusade against Capital Punishment in Great Britain* (London: Stevens 1961); Christoph, James B, *Capital Punishment and British Politics: The British Movement to Abolish the Death Penalty 1945-1957* (London: Allen and Unwin, 1962); Potter, Harry *Hanging in Judgment: Religion and the Death Penalty in England from the Bloody Code to Abolition* (London: SCM 1993); and Block and Hostettler, op cit.

[9] Capital punishment was formally abolished for these other crimes in May 1998.

[10] Roger Casement, John Amery and William Joyce. This excepts a total of nineteen executions of American servicemen that took place during the Second World War under the jurisdiction of USA military courts.

CHAPTER 2

A BRIEF HISTORY OF THE CAPITAL PUNISHMENT
CONTROVERSY

This chapter traces the long history of capital punishment in England and the numerous attempts to abolish it, or restrict its application, up to the 1950s, culminating in the Homicide Act of 1957, and the partial abolition embodied therein. It draws heavily on the excellent accounts already cited in Christoph; Tuttle; Potter; and Block and Hostettler, as well as works dealing specifically with the history of hanging in the eighteenth and nineteenth centuries.[11]

Capital Punishment Down the Ages

Hanging as a punishment seems to have originated in Anglo-Saxon times and to have been continued under the Normans. In the thirteenth century hanging replaced mutilation as the standard punishment for all serious crimes, and up until the early nineteenth century its propriety went largely unchallenged.[12] It seems that numerous executions took place, and the number of offences for which hanging was mandatory was very extensive. In fact during the eighteenth century the number of capital crimes increased substantially from about fifty in 1700 to between 220 and 230 by 1800. This was the so-called *Bloody Code*, and embraced offences as diverse (and innocuous) as stealing turnips, consorting with gypsies, damaging a fishpond, writing threatening letters, impersonating out-pensioners at Greenwich Hospital, being found armed or disguised in a forest, park or rabbit warren, cutting down a tree, poaching, forging, picking pockets and shoplifting.[13] This trend was in stark contrast to

---

[11]There are many works dealing with the history of the death penalty in this country, especially in the eighteenth and nineteenth centuries. Prominent among them are: Radzinowicz, Leon, *A History of English Criminal Law and its Administration from 1750, vol 1: The Movement for Reform 1750-1833* (London: Stevens and Sons, 1948); Hay, Douglas, Peter Linebaugh, John G Rule, E P Thompson and Cal Winslow, *Albion's Fatal Tree: Crime and Society in Eighteenth Century England* (Harmondsworth: Penguin, 1975); Thompson, E P, *Whigs and Hunters: The Origins of the Black Act* (London: Allen Lane, 1975); Linebaugh, Peter, *The London Hanged: Crime and Civil Society in the Eighteenth Century* (Harmondsworth: Penguin, 1993); Gatrell, V A C, *The Hanging Tree: Execution and the English People, 1770-1868* (Oxford: OUP, 1994); and Brooke, Alan and David Brandon, *Tyburn: London's Fatal Tree* (Stroud: Sutton 2004)
[12]This section summarizes the issue up to the advent of the Labour government of 1945 and is based on Christoph, op cit, pp.13-34; Tuttle, op cit, pp.1-54; Block and Hostettler, op cit, pp. 18-101; and Potter, op cit, pp 1-141, *inter alia*
[13] Koestler, Arthur *Reflections on Hanging* (London 1956) p.13, quoted by Christoph, ibid, p.14

that in most other European countries at the time which were moving towards a reduction in the use of capital punishment and the divergence can probably be attributed to the social upheavals caused by the Industrial Revolution.[14] Also there was at that time no proper police force. The judiciary enthusiastically expanded the range of hanging offences, as guardians of the common law. Executions were carried out in public, and indeed were treated as holidays for some workers. People 'flocked to Tyburn Tree as to the music hall or a sporting event.'[15] It was not unusual for children to be hanged. Attempts to reform the law met with implacable opposition from the House of Lords and the Bench. Nonetheless crime rates soared.

By the early nineteenth century a minority of people emerged who agitated for reform of the criminal law. In 1810 a 'Society for the Diffusion of Knowledge upon the Punishment of Death' sprang into being supported by reformers in the House of Commons such as Sir Samuel Romilly and Sir James Mackintosh.[16] Numerous bills passed the Commons to eliminate hanging as the penalty for minor offences, but they were all defeated in the Lords, spurred on by the Law Lords and especially the hard-line Lord Chancellor Eldon and Lord Chief Justice Ellenborough.[17] Romilly's bill to abolish hanging as the sentence for shoplifting of goods of five shillings was passed by the Commons and scuppered by the Lords six times; in 1810, 1811, 1813, 1816, 1818 and 1820. However, reform gradually came, partly as a response to the increasing tendency of juries to refuse to convict people of petty offences which carried the death penalty. Thus it was both savage and ineffective at the same time and businessmen began to agitate for milder, and enforceable, penalties. Parliament was bombarded with petitions on the subject. A Select Committee of the Commons was set up and recommended the abolition of hanging as the penalty for crimes against property. Though initially resisted by the Lords, they gradually gave way, and the number of capital crimes was steadily reduced. Hanging was abolished for cattle, horse and sheep stealing in 1832; for housebreaking in 1833; for sacrilege and stealing letters by post office employees in 1835; for coinage and forgery in 1836; and for burglary and stealing in dwelling houses in 1837. By the accession of Victoria in 1837 the number of capital offences had dwindled to fifteen. From 1840 to 1860 this number was further reduced to a hard core of four which lasted for another

---

[14] Austria under the Emperor Joseph, for example, abolished capital punishment in the 1780s.
[15] Christoph, op cit, p.15
[16] Sir Samuel Romilly (1757-1818) Whig politician, lawyer and legal reformer. Solicitor-general 1806-7, MP for, successively, Queenborough, Horsham, Wareham, Arundel and Westminster. Influenced by the Italian jurist and philosopher, Beccaria. Sir James Mackintosh (1765-1832) Scots Whig politician, jurist and historian. Recorder of Bombay 1804. MP for, successively, Nairn and Knaresborough.
[17] John Scott, 1st Earl of Eldon, PC, KC (1751-1838) Lord Chancellor 1801-1806 and 1807-1827; Sir Edward Law, 1st Baron Ellenborough (1750-1818) Lord Chief Justice 1802-1818

century:- murder, treason, piracy with violence and arson in government dockyards and arsenals. The number of hangings steadily declined partly because of this reduction in the range of capital crimes, and partly because of an increased use of the reprieve power.

The Derby Government set up a Royal Commission to look into the question of capital punishment in 1864, and it recommended the creation of two degrees of murder on the American model; the creation of a separate offence of infanticide; and the abolition of public hangings. Five members, including John Bright, recommended complete abolition, though they were a small minority.[18] Only the last of these recommendations was given immediate effect, whilst numerous bills to differentiate between different classes of murder failed of passage.

The Children's Act of 1908 abolished the death penalty for persons under sixteen (later raised to eighteen) and the Infanticide Act of 1922 reduced the offence of a mother killing her child soon after birth from murder to manslaughter. In 1921 the Howard League for Penal Reform came into being with the abolition of the death penalty for murder as one of its central planks. In 1925 the National Council for the Abolition of the Death Penalty was founded as an umbrella organisation for abolitionist groups.

The emergence of the Labour Party as a serious political force in the 1920s also gave heart to the abolitionists, who had had little impact upon the older parties. After the Labour victory in the general election of 1929 a resolution of the House of Commons proposed the abolition of capital punishment. There was no vote on the main question, but the debate led to the appointment of a Select Committee to look at the question, consisting of seven Labour MPs, six Conservatives and two Liberals. It reported in 1930 and recommended that capital punishment be abolished for an experimental period of five years.[19] The Conservative members of the committee, however, refused to sign the report and indeed withdrew from the committee two weeks before it was published, thus imparting a partisan flavour to the report which was not conducive to its acceptance.[20] Shortly after the Committee reported the government fell, and with it went the Committee's recommendations. During the 1930s a number of attempts were made to translate the Select Committee's recommendations into law by means of private member's bills, but they got nowhere. In 1938 the National Government introduced a Criminal Justice Bill, sponsored by the Home Secretary, Sir Samuel Hoare; a mixed bag of measures

---

[18] John Bright (1811-1889) Liberal politician. Founded Anti-Corn Law League 1839; supported repeal of the Corn Laws 1846, opposed Crimean War 1854-1856, instrumental in passage of Second Reform Bill 1867; President of the Board of Trade in Gladstone's First Ministry 1868-1870; Chancellor of the Duchy of Lancaster in same 1873-74 and 1880-82 in Gladstone's Second Ministry; resigned over the use of force in Egypt 1882.

[19] Report of the Select Committee on Capital Punishment (HMSO,1931).

[20] Christoph, op cit p.20.

for law reform which did not, unsurprisingly, include any proposal to abolish the death penalty.[21] Hoare, a subsequent convert to the cause of abolition (along with several Home Secretaries who usually waited until after they had vacated the office before announcing their conversion) said that he didn't want to jeopardise the passage of the bill by including such a contentious measure.[22] Abolitionists put down a motion welcoming legislation for the suspension of the death penalty for an experimental five-year period, which was passed on a free vote by 114-89, but the government refused to amend the bill accordingly. Ten future ministers in Labour governments were counted among the abolitionists.

Though hanging was the mandatory sentence for murder, other than for defendants under eighteen or for pregnant women, the rigidity of the law was sometimes tempered by the jury who might return an acquittal or a verdict of manslaughter unwarranted by the evidence, or accompany a murder verdict with a recommendation of mercy (though this option was unprompted by any mention in the judges summing up to the jury). In the period 1900-1949 such a recommendation was given in 39% of all cases of a murder conviction, and of these 74% were granted reprieves, as against only 28% of convictions not thus accompanied.[23]

A successful defence of insanity, under the McNaghten rules of 1843, was another means of cheating the hangman. The Scottish law of murder differed from the English in at least two key respects. It did not recognize the English common law doctrine of constructive malice (felony murder) which might render a defendant liable to a conviction for murder if the act were committed in pursuit of a serious felony, even where there was no intent to kill or cause grievous bodily harm. Also, it recognised diminished responsibility, as distinct from insanity, as a partial defence. Finally there was the Royal Prerogative of Mercy exercised by the Home Secretary (or Secretary of State for Scotland if the conviction were under Scottish law) as a long-stop. All capital convictions were reviewed by the Home Secretary, and a reprieve commuted the sentence of death to one of penal servitude for life (life imprisonment after the Criminal Justice Act of 1948). Home Secretaries could draw upon the expertise of their civil servants, the words of the judge and any jury recommendation, and precedents set by their predecessors, as well as ordering medical reports in the case of defendants suspected of insanity. The power of

---

[21] Sir Samuel John Gurney Hoare (Viscount Templewood) (1880-1959) Conservative politician. MP for Chelsea 1910-1944; Secretary for Air 1922-24, 1924-29; Secretary for India 1931-35; Foreign Secretary 1935; First Lord of the Admiralty 1936-37; Home Secretary 1937-39; Lord Privy Seal 1939-40; Secretary for Air 1940; British Ambassador to Spain 1940-44; Created 1st Viscount Templewood 1944.

[22] Viscount Templewood (Sir Samuel Hoare) *The Shadow of the Gallows* (London: Gollancz, 1951) p.10, quoted by Christoph, op cit, p.20

[23] Report of the Royal Commission on Capital Punishment HMSO (1953). Quoted by Christoph, op cit, p.23

reprieve was commonly exercised, and in the period 1900-1949 1,210 people were sentenced to death in Great Britain of whom 553, or 45.7%, had their sentences commuted or respited. Given all of these factors it is readily explicable that though on average ninety people were arrested for murder each year since 1900, only thirteen on average were executed each year.

Several organizations came into being dedicated to the complete abolition of the death penalty, such as the 'Society for the Abolition of Capital Punishment' led chiefly by Quakers, which lasted until the First World War, though it was largely ineffective. Two bodies were pre-eminent in this regard. One was the Howard League for Penal Reform, a small but prestigious organization formed in 1921 and dedicated to 'an open-minded study of the causes and treatment of crime and penal administration'. Though its concerns range across all penal questions it has been a consistent supporter of abolition, albeit that it has traditionally campaigned in a discreet manner (given its need to maintain good relations with the prison service). The other was the National Council for the Abolition of the Death Penalty (NCADP), founded by a young Quaker, E Roy Calvert. He formed the 'Central Consultative Council for the Abolition of Capital Punishment' in 1925 composed of representatives from ten religious and reform societies, and this evolved into the National Council for the Abolition of the Death Penalty. Its membership never rose above 1,200 and it was essentially a one-man organization. His campaign concentrated on collecting and disseminating statistics on the crime figures of countries where abolition had taken place to buttress his belief in the inefficacy of the deterrent. In due course this issued in *Capital Punishment in the Twentieth Century* published in 1927, the first really scientific tract arguing for abolition.[24]

This in turn had much to do with the matter being raised in Parliament and the appointment of the aforementioned Select Committee in 1929. It produced numerous tracts and pamphlets in the 1930s, including the writings of William Temple, Archbishop of York (and later of Canterbury).[25] It published a periodical called *The Penal Reformer*, and *Notes for Speakers*, but despite its activity it enjoyed little success at the highest level, and the abolition movement stayed in the doldrums for many years. Calvert died in 1933 and was replaced by John Paton. Both Paton and his wife were elected as Labour MPs in 1945, and Paton's place was taken by Frank Dawtry, a former prison welfare officer and Howard League member. It was a small, intensely motivated but very un-typical body of people, and despite its high profile it was acutely conscious of its inability to achieve anything without a substantial shift of opinion in the country, and more significantly, in Parliament.

---

[24] E Roy Calvert, *Capital Punishment in the Twentieth Century* (London: Putnam, 1927)
[25] William Temple (1881-1944) Churchman; Archbishop of York 1929-1942; Archbishop of Canterbury 1942-44.

The Labour Government 1945 and the Criminal Justice Act 1948

The election of a Labour government with a very large majority in 1945 transformed the political panorama and gave renewed hope to the abolitionists.[26] Given that abolition was technically Labour Party policy (because the 1934 party conference had passed, unopposed, a resolution for abolition) it was hoped that the new government would soon introduce legislation.[27] Furthermore it was an earlier Labour government (of 1929-31) that had appointed a Select Committee on the question, and in 1938 ten future Labour ministers, including James Chuter Ede, by now Home Secretary, had supported the backbench motion urging abolition.[28] On the other hand there had been nothing in the party's 1945 election manifesto to that effect. There was intense lobbying of the government to introduce a Criminal Justice Bill embodying an abolition clause. Given the long queue of proposed legislation it was not until the third session of that Parliament, in 1947-48, that such a bill duly appeared, and then to the intense disappointment of the NCADP and abolitionists generally, it contained no such provision. The bill followed closely the bill of 1938, which had been lost due to the war, and its only controversial provision was the abolition of corporal punishment.

The omission of a clause abolishing capital punishment may have been due to many factors. There was the 'official' line given by Chuter Ede on the second reading, and subsequent occasions, that hanging was a deterrent that could not justifiably be dispensed with. There was the desire to ensure the smooth passage of the bill, which could have been delayed for up to two years by the House of Lords (then still possessed of the powers delineated by the 1911 Parliament Act to veto Commons bills twice) during which time the next election would have fallen due. There was the belief in some quarters that Chuter Ede, as many a Home Secretary before and after him, was the prisoner of his senior officials, or if not them, then the police and prison officers through their influential mouthpieces. Finally there may have been a fear of offending public opinion, then as always, deeply hostile to abolition, particularly at a time when the government's popularity may have been waning. The Cabinet considered the question of capital punishment on six occasions between June

---

[26] This section is largely based on Christoph, op cit, pp.35-75; Tuttle, op cit, pp. 55-83; Block and Hostettler, op cit, pp 102-126; and Potter, op cit, pp 142-152.

[27] *The Annual Report of the Howard League for Penal Reform 1946-47* stated that: 'it is surely unthinkable that a Government which contains such distinguished champions of abolition, when they were out of office, should make any effort to prevent the House from obeying the dictates of humanity and profiting from the experience of other countries' pp.5-6, quoted in Christoph, ibid, p.70

[28] James Chuter Ede, Baron Chuter Ede (1882-1965) Labour politician; MP for Mitcham 1923, MP for South Shields 1929-1931 and 1935-64; Home Secretary 1945-1951; Leader of the House of Commons 1951.

1947 and July 1948 but didn't budge from the collective view that it should be retained, at least for the time being.[29]

The government decided against imposing the whips to defeat an abolitionist amendment, or conversely of promising a separate abolition bill, and opted to allow a free vote on any abolitionist amendment to the bill (which would only be allowed at the report stage after the bill had been considered by standing committee). The government may have underestimated the strength of abolitionist feeling on its own backbenches or failed to think through the consequences. Abolitionist (and retentionist) supporters organised themselves in the Commons, the former under the leadership of Sydney Silverman, left-wing Labour MP for Nelson and Colne, who was rapidly emerging as their chief spokesman.[30] The NCADP lobbied members, and organised both inside and outside Parliament. Public opinion polls consistently showed large majorities against abolition, across age, sex, class, religious and party political affiliation. The press was restrained on the issue. The *Times*, the *Manchester Guardian* and the *Observer* pressed for experimental abolition; the *Daily Telegraph* found abolition inopportune; the mass circulation dailies were evenly split; and the provincial papers were vocal in opposition to abolition. A number of brutal murders committed at the time, and highlighted by the retentionist press, may have hardened popular feeling against abolition. The government decided to limit the free vote to backbenchers, and to prohibit ministers and junior ministers from supporting the Silverman abolitionist amendment (though they might abstain). This was the cause of much acrimony within the Parliamentary Labour Party (PLP), especially at the party meeting convened on the day of the vote when this decision was announced.

---

[29] Cabinet Minutes (47) 89th Conclusions, quoted in Lord Windlesham, *Responses to Crime, volume 2, Penal Policy in the Making* (Oxford: Oxford University Press, 1993) pp.58-9. Windlesham mentions that Keith Morgan estimated that the Cabinet was split 11-5 in favour of retention. All this is cited in Hodgkinson, Peter and Andrew Rutherford *Capital Punishment: Global Issues and Perspectives* (Winchester: Waterside Press, 1996) pp. 262-3

[30] Sydney Silverman (1895-1968) Solicitor and politician, born in Liverpool of Jewish Rumanian parentage; unsuccessfully fought Liverpool Exchange by-election 1933; Labour MP for Nelson and Colne 1935-1968; diminutive and pugnacious left-winger; master of parliamentary tactics and a prominent figure on the Labour left throughout his career; imprisoned as a conscientious objector during the First World War; successfully defended John Braddock on charge of incitement to riot 1932 (prosecuted by David Maxwell-Fyfe); deprived of the Labour whip 1954 for voting against German re-armament; and again in 1961-1963 for voting against the defence estimates; in both cases in defiance of a PLP decision to abstain; strongly critical of Harold Wilson after his 'dog licence' speech to the PLP in 1967; the leading parliamentary campaigner for the abolition of the death penalty throughout the post-war period, co-ordinating the campaigns of 1948, 1956-57 and 1964-65; unsuccessfully challenged at the 1966 general election by Patrick Downey, uncle of murdered Lesley Ann Downey, victim of the 'Moors Murderers' Ian Brady and Myra Hindley. See Hughes, Emrys *Sydney Silverman: Rebel in Parliament* op cit., pp. 95-112, 144-156 and 171-192.

The debate on the report stage of the bill took place on 14th April 1948, amid intense media and public interest. The abolitionist clause (for the death penalty for murder to be abolished for an experimental five-year period) was moved by Silverman and Christopher Hollis, the chief spokesman for the Conservative abolitionists in the Commons.[31] It was sponsored also by Lady Megan Lloyd George (daughter of the former prime minister), Reginald Paget, John Paton (all Labour), and by Derick Heathcoat-Amory (Conservative). It rehearsed the familiar arguments for abolition, citing the experience of other countries and pointing out the inconsistency of abolishing corporal, but not capital, punishment.[32] The clause was opposed by Sir John Anderson, a former Home Secretary, who advanced the view that no innocent person had been hanged this century.[33]

The debate was remarkable for the cross-bench nature of the two coalitions. The thirteen abolitionist speakers were comprised of eight Labour members, three Conservatives and two Independents, whilst the ten retentionist speakers were composed of seven Conservatives and three Labourites. It was noticeable that none of the four law officers took part in the debate. The clause was passed by 245-222.[34] Labour members supported the amendment by a margin of 3-1, but Conservatives opposed it by 10-1. A large number of ministers abstained rather than oppose the amendment (44 out of 72) and amongst Cabinet ministers with seats in the Commons only nine out of fourteen voted against (including Attlee, Morrison, Ernest Bevin and Chuter Ede).[35]

---

[31] (Maurice) Christopher Hollis. (1902-1977) Conservative MP for Devizes 1945-1955. Brother of Sir Roger Hollis, director-general of MI5 1956-65.

[32] Hughes, Emrys, op cit, pp.100-107

[33] Sir John Anderson, 1st Viscount Waverley (1882-1958) Civil servant and politician, National MP for the Scottish Universities 1938-1950, Lord Privy Seal 1938-9; Home Secretary 1939-40; Chancellor of the Duchy of Lancaster 1940-43 and Chancellor of the Exchequer 1943-5. Anderson shelters are named after him.

[34] HC Deb, vol 449, cols. 979-1103 (15th April 1948), Templewood, op cit, pp.112-121. Hughes, op cit, p.108

[35] Clement Richard Attlee (1883-1967). Labour politician. Mayor of Stepney 1919-1920. MP for Limehouse 1922-1950. MP for Walthamstow West 1950-1955. PPS to Ramsay MacDonald 1922-24. Under Secretary for War 1924. Chancellor of Duchy of Lancaster 1930-1931. PMG 1931. Deputy Leader of Labour Party 1931-35. Leader of Labour Party 1935-1955. Lord Privy Seal 1940-1942. Dominions Secretary 1942-43. Lord President of the Council 1943-45. Deputy PM 1942-1945. PM 1945-1951. Leader of the Opposition 1951-55. Created Earl Attlee 1955. Herbert Stanley Morrison (1888-1965) Labour politician. Secretary of the London Labour Party 1915-1945. Member of LCC 1922-1945. MP for Hackney South 1923-24, 1929-1931, 1935-45, for Lewisham East 1945-50, for Lewisham South 1950-59. Minister of Transport 1929-1931, Minister of Supply 1940, Home Secretary 1940-45. Deputy PM 1945-1951. Lord President of the Council and Leader of the Commons 1945-51, Foreign Secretary 1951. Deputy Leader of Labour Party 1951-1955. Created Baron Morrison of Lambeth (Life Peer) 1959. Ernest Bevin (1881-1951). Labour politician. General Secretary of TGWU 1921-1940. Member of General Council of TUC. 1925-40. MP for Wandsworth

Stafford Cripps, Aneurin Bevan and Harold Wilson were present but abstained, along with all four of the law officers in the Commons.[36] Chuter Ede had promised to abide by the result and now had to facilitate the passage of a piece of legislation he had opposed and had advised against.

The House of Lords, too, now had to consider its position. The Lords, at that time, was still very heavily retentionist in spirit, partly or largely because of its huge built-in Conservative majority. The Law Lords, too, were almost unanimous for retention, and quite a few of the ecclesiastical contingent of the Upper House. Though it was reluctant to exercise its power of veto, particularly at a time when its constitutional position was under review, it was conscious that on this issue at least it was in accord with public opinion, whereas the Commons was very much at odds with it. Furthermore the government itself was opposed to abolition, as it had made clear, and so paradoxically the Lords, by opposing the new clause, would have been rescuing the Labour government from its own backbenchers.[37] The government, for its part, was seeking to curtail the powers of the Lords, but for that very reason was reluctant to pick a fight on the one issue where the Lords could reasonably have presented themselves as guardians of the popular will against an 'unrepresentative' Commons.

The second reading in the Lords was moved by the Lord Chancellor, Viscount Jowitt, in a speech that was rich in paradox in that he stoutly defended the death penalty whilst moving a bill that contained the abolitionist clause.[38]

Central 1940-1950, Woolwich East 1950-51. Minister of Labour and National Service 1940-45. Foreign Secretary 1945-51. Lord Privy Seal 1951.

[36] Sir (Richard) Stafford Cripps (1889-1952). Labour politician. MP for Bristol East 1931-50, Bristol South-East 1950-1951. Solicitor-General 1930-31. British Ambassador to Soviet Union 1940-42. Lord Privy Seal and Leader of the Commons 1942. Minister of Aircraft Production 1942-45. President of Board of Trade 1945-47. Minister for Economic Affairs 1947. Chancellor of the Exchequer 1947-1950. Aneurin Bevan (1897-1960). Labour politician. MP for Ebbw Vale 1929-1960. Minister of Health 1945-1951. Minister of Labour and National Service 1951. Resigned from government April 1951 over health service charges. Figurehead of Labour left for most of the 1950s. Resigned from Labour front bench 1954 over SEATO. Nearly expelled from party 1955. Partly reconciled with front bench from 1956. Party Treasurer 1956-60. Deputy Leader of Party 1959-60. Abolitionist Cabinet abstainer 1948. Interceded with Home Secretary on behalf of Derek Bentley 1953. (James) Harold Wilson (1916-1997). Labour politician. MP for Ormskirk 1945-50, Huyton 1950-1983. PPS to Minister of Works 1945-47. Secretary for Overseas Trade 1947. President of Board of Trade 1947-51. Resigned with Nye Bevan April 1951 over health service charges. Took Bevan's place on front bench 1954. Party leader 1963-1976. Leader of Opposition 1963-64. PM 1964-70. Leader of Opposition 1970-74. PM 1974-76. KG 1976. Baron Wilson of Rievaulx (Life Peer) 1983. Enthusiastic abolitionist.

[37] Bromhead, P A *The House of Lords and Contemporary Politics, 1911-1957* (London: Routledge and Kegan Paul, 1958) p.217. Quoted by Christoph, op cit, p.58

[38] William Allen Jowitt, 1st Earl Jowitt (1885-1957) Liberal and Labour politician and lawyer. Liberal MP for The Hartlepools 1922-4, Labour MP for Preston 1929-31, Labour MP

The balance of the speeches was retentionist in character. Goddard, the Lord Chief Justice, in a maiden speech, argued strongly for its retention, alluding to a series of grisly cases.[39] He was supported by Salisbury, Simon and Samuel.[40] Templewood (as Samuel Hoare had become) argued for abolition. The ecclesiastical bench was divided with the Bishop of Chichester (Bell) abolitionist, Truro (Hunkin) retentionist (and indeed wanting to extend hanging to lesser offences) and the Archbishop of Canterbury (Fisher) favouring degrees of murder. The clause was defeated by 181-28, the minority consisting of 23 Labour peers, three Conservatives, one Liberal and the Bishop of Chichester.[41]

The bill, minus the Silverman clause, returned to the Commons. The government responded by unveiling a compromise clause, establishing degrees of murder, that they hoped would satisfy both the abolitionist majority in the Commons, and the retentionist majority in the Lords. The criteria distinguishing the two proposed classes of murder were necessarily somewhat arbitrary, and attracted the ridicule of the press, whilst satisfying nobody. The Commons then voted by 307-209 to disagree with the Lords deletion of the Silverman clause but to substitute the new compromise clause. The compromise clause then returned once more to the Lords, which defeated it by 99-19. It returned once again to the Commons minus both the original Silverman clause and the government compromise clause. The government was reluctant to press the matter further since the whole bill might be lost and, given the tightness of their timetable, it could ill afford the bill to spill over into the next session. Furthermore it could not use the Parliament Act, 1911, to override the Lords because the amended form of the clause had not been in the bill when it initially went to the Lords. The government thus acquiesced in the Lords deletion, but

---

for Ashton-under-Lyne 1939-45. Attorney-general 1929-32, Solicitor-general 1940-42, Lord Chancellor 1945-51, Leader of the Labour Party in the House of Lords 1952-55

[39] Rayner Goddard, Baron Goddard of Aldbourne (1877-1971) Lord Chief Justice 1946-58. Trial judge in the Craig-Bentley case of 1952.

[40] Robert Arthur James Gascoyne-Cecil, 5th Marquis of Salisbury, KG, PC (1893-1972) Grandson of the Conservative Prime Minister, the 3rd Marquis, Conservative politician, MP for Dorset South 1929-41, holder of numerous offices of state, Leader of the House of Lords 1942-45 and 1951-57, resigned from Macmillan Cabinet 1957 in protest at release of Archbishop Makarios, founder president of the Monday Club 1961. Sir John Allsebrook Simon (1873-1954). Liberal and National Liberal politician. MP for Walthamstow (Liberal) 1906-18, Spen Valley (Liberal) 1922-31, Spen Valley (National Liberal) 1931-40. Solicitor-General 1910-13, Attorney-General 1913-15, Home Secretary, 1915-16. Resigned over conscription. Foreign Secretary 1931-35. Leader of National Liberal Party 1931-40. Home Secretary and Deputy Leader of Commons 1935-37. Chancellor of Exchequer 1937-1940. Lord Chancellor 1940-45. Herbert Louis Samuel, 1st Viscount Samuel (1870-1963) Liberal politician and diplomat, MP for Cleveland 1902-1918, MP for 1929-35, holder of numerous offices of state, High Commissioner of Palestine 1920-25, Leader of the Liberal Party 1931-35, Leader of the Liberal Party in the House of Lords 1944-55, delivered the first ever televised party political broadcast in the 1951 general election.

[41] H L Deb, vol 155, col 398 (27th April 1948). Hughes, Emrys, op cit, pp.108-110

sugared the pill for the abolitionists by promising that the whole question would be subject to review. The Labour abolitionists felt betrayed, though Tory abolitionists were prepared to go along with things. On a whipped vote the Commons accepted the Lords deletion of the compromise clause by 215-34, Silverman and Paget being amongst the minority protest vote. They had sought in vain to get the government to give a promise to bring in a separate abolition bill.[42]

Thus abolition had been defeated for the moment but the issue had been brought to the forefront of public consciousness. Clearly the matter was not going to rest there, and the abolitionists were confident that though they had lost the battle they had not lost the war. Outside Parliament the NCADP, exhausted of funds, merged with the Howard League which set up a special sub-committee on the death penalty. In November 1948 the government announced the setting up of a Royal Commission on the death penalty.

The Gowers Commission 1949-1953

The issue fell briefly into abeyance but re-surfaced in the mid-fifties due to the confluence of several factors:- the persistence of the abolitionists in Parliament; the influx of new, sometimes abolitionist, Tory MPs in the 1950, 1951 and 1955 general elections; the report of the Royal Commission in 1953; the creation of a new umbrella organization in the shape of the National Campaign for the Abolition of Capital Punishment (NCACP); and the effect of several highly publicized and controversial murder cases in the courts.[43]

Royal Commissions are often set up by governments more as a means of delaying making a decision than as a means of arriving at solutions.[44] This may well have been the case with the Royal Commission set up here, given the intractable nature of the problem and the government's desire to push it to one side. The chairman was a retired civil servant Sir Ernest Gowers, and the membership consisted of a wide range of distinguished figures from relevant fields, none of whom had declared themselves publicly one way or the other on the abolition controversy.[45] Its terms of reference were to investigate the possibilities of creating degrees of murder, but not to arrive at a decision on whether there should be outright abolition or not, though 'the uninvited guest made its presence known frequently in the deliberations'.[46] Gowers himself

---

[42] Hughes, Emrys, op cit, p.112

[43] This section draws heavily on Christoph, op cit, pp.76-95; Tuttle, op cit, pp. 84-99; Block and Hostettler, op cit, pp. 127-135; and Potter, op cit, pp. 153-9.

[44] Wheare, K C, *Government by Committee: An essay on the British Constitution* (Oxford: Clarendon Press, 1955) pp.88-93. Quoted by Christoph, ibid p.77

[45] Sir Ernest Arthur Gowers (1880-1966).Civil servant and author of *The Complete Plain Words,* a style guide for the civil service and of *A Life for a Life?.*

[46] Christoph, op cit, p.82

became converted to the abolitionist cause as a result of his work on the Commission, publishing a book on the subject two years after it had reported.[47] The Commission took oral and written evidence from a very wide range of bodies, and visited prisons and penal institutions in several countries. Evidence given to the Commission was often a departmental view, and it was not always easy to determine the extent to which testimony was personal or official. The Howard League certainly felt that much of the evidence was heavily coloured by establishment desires to maintain the status quo. The Commission finally reported to Parliament in September 1953, almost five years after it had been formed.[48] Meanwhile there had been two general elections, and the Conservatives, less receptive to abolition and penal reform generally, had returned to power.

The Commission in its recommendations came close to advocating abolition, stating that: 'It is therefore important to view the question in a just perspective and not to base a penal policy in relation to murder on exaggerated estimates of the uniquely deterrent force of the death penalty.'[49] It suggested that the doctrine of constructive malice should be abolished; that the definition of provocation should be widened; that one who assists a suicide should not be convicted of murder; that the minimum age of liability to hang should be raised from eighteen to twenty-one (by a majority of 6-5); and it questioned the satisfactoriness of the McNaghten Rules. The really crucial question to which the Commission had been referred, however, was that of the satisfactoriness of the Royal Prerogative of Mercy. It suggested that any statutory re-definition of murder to limit the scope of hanging would be impractical, as would likewise a statutory attempt to create degrees of murder, given the wide variation in the extent of culpability. It recommended that the *trial jury* should be empowered to decide whether a sentence of life imprisonment should be substituted for one of hanging, bearing in mind any extenuating circumstances. It had found this a satisfactory method where it had been employed in other countries, and saw it as a preferable means of correcting 'the rigidity which is the outstanding defect of the existing law.'

The Howard League, and its death penalty sub-committee, offered lukewarm support, perhaps conscious that a more limited application of hanging might only serve to entrench and legitimize the institution.[50] Nonetheless it felt that it had to support the proposals in the absence of anything better on offer, and because it would necessarily bring the debate back before Parliament and the public. A debate in the Lords to register disapproval of the jury discretion

---

[47] Gowers, Sir Ernest, *A Life for A Life? The Problem of Capital Punishment* (London: Chatto and Windus, 1956)

[48] Report of the Gowers Commission on Capital Punishment, Cmnd.8932 (hereafter Gowers). See *The Times* for 24th September 1953.

[49] Gowers, ibid

[50] Annual Report of the Howard League,1953-54 pp.4-5

idea took place in December 1953, moved by Viscount Simon.[51] Disapproval was registered by several speakers, and the point was made by Asquith of Bishopstone that this was a backdoor attempt to abandon the rope altogether by whittling it down to almost nothing.[52] Though Gowers did not have any direct effect on government action, it did serve to keep the debate alive.

The *Causes Celebre* of the Mid-Fifties

There was a definite mood change in the period 1948-1956 caused not so much by the Gowers Report or by Parliamentary activity, as by events in the courtroom and in the press.[53] Whilst the murders of the late forties, and the press reporting of them, were such as to reinforce the public and establishment hostility to abolition, the murders of the fifties were, as Christoph says, rather more of a mixed bag. Three cases, in particular, occurred in the early to mid-fifties which aroused widespread public concern, and cast serious doubt upon the much vaunted claims of the retentionists that 'no innocent person has been hanged this century' to quote Sir John Anderson in the 1948 Commons debate.

The first such case, at any rate in terms of the order in which the cases attained notoriety, was that of Derek Bentley and Christopher Craig, two youths who were convicted of the murder of a policeman in November 1952.[54] The circumstances of the case were highly controversial from the legal standpoint because the conviction of the nineteen year-old Bentley rested upon the judicial doctrine of common purpose, whereby all parties to a crime are deemed equally responsible for anything that occurs in the course of the commission of that crime. The mentally defective Bentley had been in police custody for fifteen minutes before the fatal shot was fired by Craig, but the latter as a sixteen year-old was too young to hang. The jury recommended mercy, but this was not acted upon by the Home Secretary, Sir David Maxwell Fyfe.[55] It is perhaps the only case in English legal history where someone hanged, though only vicariously responsible, where the principal did not hang. The feeling persisted that Bentley had been denied a reprieve because it was deemed necessary that someone should hang for the murder of a policeman. Attempts to raise the

---

[51] HL.Deb. 137-188 (16th December 1953)
[52] Cyril Asquith, Baron Asquith of Bishopstone (1890-1954) Fourth son of the former Liberal Prime Minister. Barrister and judge.
[53] This section draws heavily on Christoph, op cit, pp.96-108; Tuttle, op cit, pp. 90-93; and Block and Hostettler, op cit, pp.137-158.
[54] See particularly Paget, Reginald and Silverman, Sydney, *Hanged - and Innocent?* (London: Gollancz, 1953) pp. 89-110. The Bentley/Craig case occurred after that of Timothy Evans but before that of John Christie, and because the latter case(s) only achieved notoriety due to Christie's trial and conviction Bentley and Craig has been put first.
[55] Sir David Patrick Maxwell Fyfe, 1st Earl Kilmuir (1900-1967) Lawyer, judge and Conservative politician. Prosecutor at the Nuremberg trials. Home Secretary 1951-54; Lord Chancellor 1954-62. Victim of Macmillan's 'Night of the Long Knives'.

matter in Parliament by Silverman and others were quashed by the Speaker, under the quaint (and absurd) tradition that a death sentence could not be discussed until it had been carried out.[56] Motions, petitions and deputations were unavailing and the sentence was duly carried out in Wandsworth Prison, whilst crowds, half angry and half curious, milled around outside.

The second such notorious case (or cases) was that of Timothy Evans and John Christie, perhaps the most bizarrely sinister in English criminal history.[57] Timothy Evans was convicted in 1950 of the murder of his child the previous year, largely on the basis of several mutually contradictory confessions that he had made to the police. He was hanged in March 1950, after having been denied a reprieve by Home Secretary Chuter Ede. A chief witness against him was the man who lived in the flat below, John Christie, whom he had in one of his (discounted) statements accused of being the actual murderer. Three years later the bodies of six dead women were discovered in Christie's flat and backyard, including that of his wife. Christie was arrested and confessed. He also admitted to the murder of Evans' wife, but he denied murdering his baby (the murder of which Evans had actually been convicted). He pleaded guilty but insane, but was found guilty and sane, and was hanged in June 1953. It had been assumed at the Evans trial that the murderer of Evans' wife and baby was one and the same person. If Evans had really been guilty of the murder of his baby, then it assumed a fantastic set of coincidences, centring on there being two murderers living under the same roof at the same time, operating independently of each other (and presumably without knowledge of each other), murdering people in an almost identical fashion, and disposing of their bodies in an almost identical fashion.

There followed demands for an enquiry into the whole affair, and an attempt under the Ten Minute Rule to introduce a bill to suspend capital punishment for a five year period. The Home Secretary, Maxwell Fyfe, responded by agreeing to an enquiry under John Scott Henderson, QC, to take place immediately (July 1953) and to report before Christie had been hanged, on the question whether there had been any miscarriage in respect of Evans. The enquiry reported in a week and concluded that Evans had been properly convicted, that the case against him was an overwhelming one, that he had been guilty of both the murder of his wife and child and that Christie's confession to the murder of Mrs Evans was both unreliable and untrue. The day following the report's publication Christie was hanged at Pentonville Prison. Two weeks later a debate on the report was held in Parliament, in which left-wing Labour

---

[56] H.C Deb, vol 517, cols 1897-1905 (14th July 1953)

[57] See Paget, Reginald and Sydney Silverman, op cit; Eddowes, Michael, *The Man on Your Conscience: An Investigation of the Evans Murder Trial* (London: Cassell, 1955); Altrincham, Lord (John Grigg) and Ian Gilmour *The Case of Timothy Evans: An Appeal to Reason* (London: The Spectator, 1956); Kennedy, Ludovic, *10 Rillington Place* (London: Gollancz, 1961); and the Scott Henderson Report of Enquiry Cmnd.8896 (HMSO 1953).

abolitionists such as Silverman, Michael Foot, Aneurin Bevan and Geoffrey Bing accused the report of being a whitewash, designed to exonerate the authorities.[58]

The third significant case of the fifties was that of Ruth Ellis, who in April 1955 shot her lover in a fit of jealousy, and pleaded not guilty on the basis of extreme provocation (having, she claimed, been assaulted by him a few days earlier causing a miscarriage). The judge instructed the jury that her defence was insufficient to reduce the charge to one of manslaughter, and she was duly convicted of murder and sentenced to hang. There was widespread fascination with the case in the press, and amongst the public, and there were demands from many quarters for the Home Secretary, Gwilym Lloyd George, to reprieve her, which he disregarded.[59] She was executed at Holloway Prison in July 1955, amid scenes of public disturbance. Within a month of her hanging a new abolitionist movement was born - the National Campaign for the Abolition of Capital Punishment (NCACP). Just as some of the retentionists had made the utmost use of grisly murders of the late forties to thwart the abolition campaign, so by the mid-fifties the abolitionists were making the most of these three cases to propagate their own cause.

Renewal of the Parliamentary Campaign 1955

The tide of public sentiment was moving, albeit rather sluggishly, in the direction of abolition, partly as a result of the notorious cases mentioned above.[60] The abolitionists now renewed the Parliamentary campaign which had been on the backburner since 1948. Nonetheless public opinion as measured by the polls still showed a majority of the nation for retention by very substantial margins.

It was not until 1955 that the government permitted a debate on the Gowers Commission which had reported two years previously, and then only to 'take note' of its findings.[61] Silverman moved an amendment to suspend the

---

[58] HC Deb col. 1469 (29th July 1953). Michael Mackintosh Foot (1913-2010) Labour politician, journalist and author. MP for Plymouth Devonport 1945-55, Ebbw Vale 1955-83, Blaenau Gwent 1983-1992. Secretary for Employment 1974-76, Lord President of Council and Leader of Commons 1976-79. Deputy Leader of Labour Party 1976-80, Leader of the Labour Party 1980-83.Geoffrey Henry Cecil Bing (1909-1977) Lawyer and Labour politician. MP for Hornchurch 1945-55. Active in the Haldane Society and the NCCL.

[59] Gwilym Lloyd George, 1st Viscount Tenby (1894-1967) Younger son of David Lloyd George. Liberal and National Liberal politician. Liberal MP for Pembrokeshire 1922-24 and 1929-50; National Liberal/Independent Liberal/Liberal Conservative MP for Newcastle upon Tyne, North 1951-57. Minister for Fuel and Power 1942-45; Minister of Food 1951-54; Home Secretary 1954-57.

[60] This section draws on Christoph, op cit, pp.109-125; Tuttle, op cit, pp.100-122; Block and Hostettler, op cit, pp. 159-185; and Potter, op cit, pp. 167-180

[61] HC Deb, vol 536, cols. 2064-2180 (19th February 1955)

death penalty for a five year period.[62] This was opposed by the government. The Home Secretary, Gwilym Lloyd George (who had been an abolitionist in 1948 but had now changed sides) rehearsed the arguments that had been deployed by Chuter Ede in 1948 to the effect that the death penalty was an effective deterrent; that life imprisonment as an alternative was impractical; and that public opinion was not ready for a change. Paradoxically while Major Lloyd George had switched from abolitionist to retentionist so Chuter Ede had switched sides in the opposite direction. Lloyd George's professed reason was that he had been misled in 1948 by Paget's false assertion that Sir Alexander Paterson, the distinguished Prison Commissioner, had become a convert to abolition before his death.[63] The declared reason for Chuter Ede's change of heart was that he had been the unfortunate Home Secretary who had signed Timothy Evans' death warrant, and he poignantly hoped that no future Home Secretary would be put in a comparable position.[64] The Silverman amendment was defeated by 245-214 on a free vote. It was supported by 194 Labourites, seventeen Conservatives and three Liberals, and opposed by 239 Conservatives, five Labourites and one Liberal.

Once again, as in 1948, despite the supposedly non-partisan character of the debate and the fact of a free vote the question nonetheless divided the House very largely along party lines. The Labour Party had moved from being preponderantly abolitionist in 1948 to being overwhelmingly so by 1955, the Labour retentionists dropping from 74 to five. Interesting is the voting behaviour of former Labour ministers, who had been prohibited from supporting the Silverman clause in 1948. Though Attlee and Morrison abstained in 1955, former retentionists such as Chuter Ede and George Isaacs now voted for abolition, as did 1948 abstainers such as Aneurin Bevan, Hugh Gaitskell, James Griffiths, John Strachey, George Strauss and Kenneth Younger.[65] Abolitionists knew that for their cause to succeed they had either to await a Labour victory at the polls or convert a few more Tories. The Conservatives, however, were returned to power at the May 1955 general election with an increased majority.

The campaign was joined by noted figures from outside Parliament such as Victor Gollancz, the left-wing publisher, Arthur Koestler, and Canon Collins, a radical clergyman. Gollancz became chairman of the nascent NCACP, and its

---

[62] Hughes, Emrys op cit, pp.145-148

[63] Sir Alexander Henry (Alec) Paterson (1884-1947) penologist. Commissioner of Prisons and Director of Convict Prisons 1922-1946, when he introduced many humane reforms to the prison system.

[64] Hughes, Emrys op cit, pp.148-9

[65] Hugh Todd Naylor Gaitskell (1906-1963) Labour politician. MP Leeds South 1945-63. PS Ministry of Fuel and Power 1946-47. Min of Fuel and Power 1947-50; Min of State for Economic Affairs 1950; Chancellor of the Exchequer 1950-51; Leader of the Labour Party 1955-1963.

Executive Committee consisted of Koestler, Collins, Gerald Gardiner (a liberal barrister, treasurer of the Howard League and subsequently Lord Chancellor in the 1964-1970 Labour Government) and an MP from each of the three major parties - Christopher Hollis (Conservative), Reginald Paget (Labour) and Frank Owen (Liberal). It also formed a Committee of Honour drawn from many walks of life and including Benjamin Britten, Prof Cecil Day-Lewis, the Earl of Listowel, Henry Moore, Lord Pakenham, J.B. Priestley, Canon Raven, Moira Shearer and Dr. Donald Soper.[66] It campaigned sedulously for abolition from its inception in 1955. Straws in the wind that year were the Liberal Party Council's resolution to urge the Parliamentary Liberal Party to press for abolition, and an Oxford Union debate that came out heavily for abolition by 378-161. A Mass Observation Poll of January 1956 showed that though a large majority was still for hanging a substantial minority favoured an experimental period of abolition, and there was clearly movement in the abolitionist direction. Also there were indications that the recent *causes celebre* (especially Ruth Ellis) had been a factor in the shift of opinion for abolitionists, whereas retentionists tended to be more influenced by murder cases generally.

The Homicide Act 1957

Given the developments of the mid-fifties the abolitionists once again tested the Parliamentary waters in the new session of November 1955.[67] There were further attempts to bring in a private members bill which met with no success. The government had announced its intention not to act upon any of the recommendations of the Gowers Report. Silverman again attempted to bring in a bill under the Ten Minute Rule in November.[68] The government decided to allow a debate on the question in January 1956, and conscious of the growing restiveness of Tory abolitionists decided to adopt the recommendations of the Heald Report, which had been prepared a few months earlier by the Inns of Court Conservative and Unionist Society headed by a former Attorney-General Sir Lionel Heald.[69] The government proposed to amend the law of murder by incorporating the Heald recommendations relating to constructive malice, provocation and diminished responsibility, seeing it as a way of placating its own backbench abolitionists. Thus it was effectively adopting the measures it had earlier rejected *vis a vis* Gowers. The abolitionists were sceptical, seeing the proposals as a way of heading off complete abolition, and were determined not

---

[66] See Thompson, Douglas, *Donald Soper: A Biography* (Nutfield, Surrey: Denholm House, 1971) He wanted the Royal Commission to consider complete abolition, (p.158)

[67] This section draws on Christoph, op cit, pp.126-168; Tuttle, op cit, pp. 123-139; Block and Hostettler, op cit, pp 186-198; and Potter, op cit, pp.167-180.

[68] Hughes, Emrys op cit, p.149

[69] Heald, Sir Lionel, *Murder: Some Suggestions for the Reform of the Law Relating to Murder in England* (London: Inns of Court Conservative and Unionist Society, 1956)

to be deflected. There was a massive propaganda campaign in the country orchestrated by the NCACP, and several books came off the presses, including most notably that by Sir Ernest Gowers announcing his conversion.

The debate took place in February 1956 on the government motion that 'while the death penalty should be retained, the law relating to the crime of murder should be amended'.[70] Silverman had tabled an amendment calling for total abolition. There was again a free vote, which extended to ministers. The abolitionist amendment was passed by 293-262, to the ecstasy of the abolitionists. The majority consisted of 242 Labourites, 48 Conservatives and five Liberals, and the minority comprised 256 Conservatives, eight Labourites and no Liberals.[71] The 48 Tory abolitionists included seventeen who had either abstained or voted against the abolitionist motion of a year before, as well as eighteen members who had entered the House in May 1955. Prime Minister Eden and ten other Cabinet ministers voted for retention, but nine ministers known to be abolitionists, including three of Cabinet rank (Selwyn Lloyd, Derick Heathcoat-Amory and Iain Macleod) abstained.[72]

The government had promised to abide by the result, and was now confronted with the same dilemma with which the Labour government had been confronted in 1948. Rather than bring forth a government bill to enact abolition, to which it had stated its vehement opposition, it decided to circumvent the problem by resurrecting Silverman's Ten Minute Rule abolition bill which had gone to the bottom of the queue, and to give it government time to pass the Commons. This smacked of duplicity to most of the abolitionists, because obviously a private members bill stood less chance than a government bill. Furthermore some of the Tory abolitionists were known to be waverers, and

---

[70] HC Deb, vol 548, cols. 2544-2664 (16th February 1956)

[71] As with all Parliamentary division lists given in this volume the numbers include the tellers, hence the extra two votes on each side.

[72] Sir (Robert) Anthony Eden (1897-1977). Conservative politician. MP for Warwick and Leamington 1923-1957. PPS to Austen Chamberlain 1926-29. Under Secretary for Foreign Affairs 1931-33. Lord Privy Seal 1933-35. Minister without Portfolio for League of Nations Affairs 1935. Foreign Secretary 1935-38. Resigned February 1938 over appeasement. Secretary for Dominions 1939-40. Secretary for War 1940. Foreign Secretary 1940-45. Foreign Secretary 1951-55. PM 1955-57. (John) Selwyn Brooke Lloyd (1904-78). Conservative politician. MP for Wirral 1945-76. Min of State, Foreign Office 1951-54, Min of Supply 1954-55, Min of Defence 1955, Foreign Secretary 1955-60, Chancellor of the Exchequer 1960-62, Lord Privy Seal and Leader of Commons 1963-64. Speaker 1971-76. Derick Heathcoat-Amory (1899-1981) Conservative politician. MP for Tiverton 1945-60. Min of Pensions 1951-53. Min of State for Board of Trade 1953-54. Min of Agg 1954-58. Chancellor of Exchequer 1958-60. Iain Norman Macleod (1913-1970) Conservative politician. Con MP for Enfield West 1950-70. Min of Health 1952-55, Min of Labour 1955-59, Sec of State for Colonies 1959-61, Chancellor of Duchy of Lancaster and Leader of Commons 1961-63. Chmn of party 1961-63. Editor of Spectator 1963-65, Chancellor of Exchequer 1970.

several were coming under pressure from their constituency parties.[73]

The Silverman bill passed its second reading by 286-262 in March 1956, with Tory abolitionist support remaining solid.[74] The committee stage was to be taken on the floor of the House. Unofficial whipping was organized for the committee stage, led by Kenneth Robinson for the Labour abolitionists; Peter Kirk and Angus Maude for the Conservative abolitionists; John Eden and Oliver Crosthwaite-Eyre for the Tory retentionists; and Sir Hugh Lucas-Tooth for a Tory retentionist splinter group favouring the bill but subject to amendments.[75] The retentionists swamped the committee stage with amendments, designed to neuter the bill in various ways, by delaying its implementation, retaining hanging for various classes of murder, or limiting its application in some way. Consideration of these amendments occupied four days spread over two months from April onwards. Only one was successful, that to retain hanging for murders committed by those already serving a life sentence, and was due to a failure of whipping by the abolitionists, and was subsequently deleted at the report stage by some neat Parliamentary tactics. Silverman was masterly in his navigation of the bill through the House.

In June 1956 Silverman, seconded by Nigel Nicolson, a prominent Tory abolitionist, successfully moved the third reading by 152-133. It proceeded to the Lords, where there was also to be a free vote on both sides. Though still strongly retentionist in composition, the Lords and especially its Leader, Salisbury, were sensitive to Labour's known desire to reform the Upper House and were anxious not to upset the Labour Party too much lest draconian measures might be brought in when Labour eventually returned to power. Furthermore it was conscious that it was now dealing with a measure which had, in effect, been passed twice in the Commons, once in 1948 and once in 1956 under both a Labour government and a Conservative government. The Commons could, anyway, under the 1949 Parliament Act, now force it through

---

[73] Nicolson, Nigel, *People and Parliament* op cit. pp. 84-105 and passim

[74] Hughes, Emrys, op cit, p.150

[75] (Sir) Kenneth Robinson (1911-1996) Labour politician. MP for St Pancras North 1949-70. Minister of Health 1964-68; (Sir) Peter Michael Kirk (1928-1977) Conservative politician. MP for Gravesend 1955-1964, MP for Saffron Walden 1965-1977, Under-Secretary of State for War 1963-64; Under-Secretary of State for the Navy 1970-73; Leader of first Tory delegation to the European Parliament 1973. Angus Edmund Upton Maude, Baron Maude of Stratford-upon-Avon (1912-1993) Conservative politician and journalist. MP for Ealing South 1950-56; MP for Stratford-upon-Avon 1963-1983; Paymaster General in the first Thatcher Cabinet 1979-1981; John Benedict Eden, Baron Eden of Winton (1925-) Nephew of Sir Anthony Eden; Conservative politician; MP for Bournemouth West 1954-83; Oliver Eyre Crosthwaite-Eyre (1913-1978) Conservative politician, MP for the New Forest and Christchurch 1945-50; MP for the New Forest 1950-1968; Sir Hugh Vere Huntly Duff Munro-Lucas-Tooth, Bt (1903-1985) Conservative politician. First man born in the twentieth century to be elected to Parliament. MP for Isle of Ely 1924-29, MP for Hendon South 1945-70.

the Lords after the lapse of only one year. In the event the Lords threw out the bill by 238-95.[76] However, it was noteworthy that the number of abolitionists in the Lords had increased dramatically compared to 1948, and that it included a lot of Conservatives, four out of eight Law Lords, both archbishops, and eight bishops (with only one voting against).

The bill returned to the Commons, and the government had to choose between invoking the Parliament Act and returning it to the Lords, or withdrawing the bill and bringing in its own measure to amend the law whilst retaining hanging. During the summer recess some of the Tory abolitionists had been subject to much pressure from their local parties, especially Nigel Nicolson at Bournemouth East and Christchurch.[77] There was also pressure from the party whips, headed by Chief Whip Edward Heath, at Westminster who were anxious for them not to resist the impending government legislation.[78] A substantial proportion of them started to waver. The Conservative Party conference in the autumn was dominated by motions resisting abolition and urging either retention in the present form or only partial abolition. On the eve of the conference Nicolson became the first of the Tory abolitionists to recant or modify his views, announcing that he would support a government compromise measure.[79]

In October 1956 Eden declared that the government would definitely introduce a bill to limit but not abolish hanging in the coming session, and that as a corollary to this it could not find time to re-introduce the Silverman bill (which, if it were to proceed at all, would have to do so in its original colours as a private members bill). The abolitionists saw this as a betrayal of the government's original promise to support the Silverman bill (extending to a second session if necessary in order to overcome the Lords veto). The government's Homicide Bill was a two-pronged measure that followed the Gowers and Heald Reports by proposing to abolish the doctrine of constructive malice and import the concept of diminished responsibility on the one hand, and on the other proposed to create two degrees of murder only one of which would attract the death penalty.[80] This latter part of the bill was in effect the Silverman bill plus most of the amendments that had been defeated in the spring. The government, by combining the widely agreed upon reforms with partial abolition, had neatly wrong-footed the abolitionists, who were now in a

---

[76] Hughes, Emrys op cit, p.151

[77] Nicolson, Nigel, op cit

[78] (Sir) Edward Richard George Heath, KG, MBE, PC (1916-2005) Conservative politician. MP for Bexley 1950-74, MP for Sidcup 1974-. Conservative whip 1951-55; Chief Whip 1955-59; Minister of Labour 1959-60; Lord Privy Seal 1960-63; Sec. of State for Trade and Industry 1963-64; Leader of Conservative Party 1965-1975; Leader of the Opposition 1965-70; PM 1970-74; and Leader of the Opposition 1974-75.

[79] Nicolson, op cit, p.141

[80] Hughes, Emrys, op cit, pp.152-153

quandary as to whether to support the bill or not. Furthermore because the bill was substantially different from the Silverman bill it would be exempted from the provisions of the Parliament Act 1949 (which required that bills be presented in essentially the same form) and the Commons would not be able to invoke the Act to force the bill through over a Lords veto. Labour MPs also did badly in the balloting for private members bills, and though Alice Bacon drew eighth place and chose to sponsor a bill basically the same as Silverman's it would not be debated until February by which time the government's Homicide Bill would be well under way.[81]

The government chose to put the whips on for the Homicide Bill. There was widespread support for the first part of the bill, but deep division over the second part to create two degrees of murder, capital and non-capital. The Home Secretary Gwilym Lloyd George summed up the government's position by saying that the intention was to remove from the purview of hanging those cases about which there was unease, whilst retaining it as a deterrent to the professional criminal and as protection for public servants.[82] He calculated that the effect of the legislation would be to reduce the number of capital sentences by about three-quarters. Anthony Greenwood and Silverman attacked the government for what they saw as a breach of faith.[83] They derided the attempt to graft onto the legal system the concept of degrees of murder, which had been characterized as unfeasible by Gowers, the Lord Chief Justice (Goddard), various law lords and many jurists.[84] Nonetheless, all attempts to amend the bill were defeated in a committee of the whole House, with most former Tory abolitionists now supporting the government or, even if speaking for the amendments, still only abstaining.[85] Then a Conservative filibuster in February 1957 prevented Alice Bacon's bill from getting a second reading. Five days later the Homicide Bill got its third reading by 217-131.[86]

The main provisions of the bill were:

1) The abolition of capital punishment for murder with the exception of a) murders of police officers in the execution of their duty; b) murders of prison officers in the

---

[81] Alice Martha Bacon, Baroness Bacon (1909-1993) Labour politician, MP for Leeds NE 1945-55, MP for Leeds SE 1955-1970, member of the party NEC 1941-70, party chairman 1950-51, Minister of State at the Home Office 1964-67, Minister of State at the Department of Education and Science 1967-70.

[82] HC Deb, vol 560, cols. 1146-1261 (15th November 1956)

[83] Arthur William James Anthony Greenwood, Baron Greenwood of Rossendale (1911-82) Labour politician, MP for Heywood and Radcliffe 1946-50, MP for Rossendale 1950-1970, chairman of the party 1963-4, Secretary of State for the Colonies 1964-5, Minister of Overseas Development 1965-6, Minister of Housing and Local Government 1966-9.

[84] Hughes, Emrys, op cit, p.153

[85] Hughes, Emrys, ibid p.154

[86] HC Deb, vol 564, cols. 454-568 (6th February 1957).

execution of their duty; c) murder in the course or furtherance of theft; d) murder by shooting or causing an explosion; and e) murder to assist an escape from lawful custody - all of which were re-designated 'capital murder' and which had to be indicted as such. In addition a person convicted of committing murder on separate occasions was still liable to capital punishment.

2) The importation into English law of the Scots law concept of diminished responsibility - which acted as a partial defence, reducing murder to manslaughter.

3) Murder committed as part of a suicide pact also to be a partial defence.

4) The partial defence of provocation to be expanded to include things said as well as things done, and for provocation to be a jury question (a judge could not withdraw a provocation defence from the jury once raised).

5) The abolition of the doctrine of constructive malice (whereby an accidental killing committed in the course of crime became murder for legal purposes).

Thus for the first time in English law there were two classes of murder - capital and non-capital - of which only the former attracted the death penalty. There were three partial defences to murder:- provocation, diminished responsibility and suicide pact killing all of which reduced murder to manslaughter. In addition murder had been to some extent re-defined.

The new Home Secretary, R.A. (Rab) Butler, hailed the bill as a victory for majority opinion, and as a step towards a more humane legal system.[87] Silverman sought an assurance from him that as the price for the support of the Tory abolitionists the government had promised them that the existing moratorium on hangings would continue indefinitely. This was vehemently denied by Butler, who insisted that all future capital cases would, as before the moratorium, be dealt with on their merits. Labour members used the occasion of the final stages of the bill to issue warnings that, so far as they were concerned, the whole question of capital punishment was very much unfinished business. The Lords, this time, accepted the government's bill with alacrity. On 21st March 1957 the Homicide Act, 1957 received the Royal Assent, the first major piece of legislation dealing with capital punishment for ninety years.[88]

Crucial to the whole course of Parliamentary events was the role of the Tory abolitionists. It was they who forced the government to bring in its own bill and it was their decision to support the government bill that dashed the hopes of the Silverman abolitionists. Why did this group change its stance from voting for the Silverman bill in February 1956 to supporting the government's compromise measure in November 1956? Christoph identifies five probable factors. Firstly, some of the milder abolitionists probably thought that the

---

[87] Richard Austen Butler (1902-1982) Conservative politician, MP for Saffron Walden 1929-65, Under-Secretary for India 1932-37, Parliamentary Secretary at the Ministry of Labour 1937-38, Under-Secretary, Foreign Office 1938-41, President of Board of Education 1941-44, Minister of Education 1944-45, Minister of Labour 1945, Chancellor of the Exchequer 1951-55, Leader of the House of Commons 1955-61, Lord Privy Seal 1955-59, Home Secretary 1957-62, First Secretary of State 1962-63, Foreign Secretary 1963-64.

[88] Hughes, Emrys, op cit, p.155

government's proposals were quite satisfactory and represented a victory for the abolitionist standpoint. Secondly, they were under strong pressure from constituency parties, constituents and the party whips throughout 1956. Thirdly, the Homicide Act was a whipped government bill, unlike the Silverman bill which was a backbench measure subject to a free vote. Fourthly the unity of the Conservative Party was under pressure as a result of Suez, and there was a strong desire to close ranks over a subordinate issue such as capital punishment. And fifthly, by the end of 1956 the whole subject had become more than a little wearisome. Also, whereas 1955-56 had been a quiet session the session of 1956-57 was chock-full of other controversies, over foreign policy, the Rent Act, a change of premiership etc, and MPs were keen to put the whole imbroglio behind them.

Conclusion

The social and political landscape of mid twentieth century England was utterly unrecognizable from that of the late eighteenth and early nineteenth and a huge distance had been traversed in legal terms from the *Bloody Code* to the Homicide Act of 1957. From well over two hundred capital offences there were now only four, and hangings were now wholly different affairs from the raucous and licentious public carnivals that they were then. Murder had been effectively re-cast in such a way as to exclude certain categories of unlawful homicide from its scope, such as infanticide (by virtue of the Infanticide Act of 1922) and the range of defences had been enlarged from the crude one of insanity under the old McNaghten rules to include diminished responsibility, provocation (now very liberally defined) and acting as part of a suicide pact (by virtue of the Homicide Act). Persons under the age of eighteen could no longer be hanged, where once even young children were liable. Yet, looked at from a different perspective nothing much had really changed between the 1860s and the 1950s. There had been no further reduction in the number of capital offences and the battle over hanging for murder had been inconclusive.

After a period of very intensive campaigning by the abolitionists both inside and outside Parliament lasting for two years, itself a chapter in a much longer running but relatively low intensity war against hanging that had lasted for more than a century, a significant but limited victory had been gained. A large measure of abolition had been enacted; many murders would now no longer fall within the purview of the death penalty; the number and scope of partial defences to the law of murder had been increased and the law of murder had been redefined at the margins. Yet this provided most abolitionists, certainly within the hard core of the movement, with little satisfaction. Their aim had always been complete and total abolition and anything short of that was a failure in their eyes. The Homicide Act was objectively speaking a partial success, but generally they would not have seen it that way, especially given that they had come so tantalisingly close (as they might have believed) to the full prize. It might even have been regarded as a defeat in the sense that reform could 're-legitimize' hanging by eliminating the possibility of some of the miscarriages that had so bedevilled the last decade. No longer might the movement be provided with the propaganda value to be extracted from cases such as Evans/Christie, Craig/Bentley and Ruth Ellis.

It should be noted that the effect of the various provisions of the Act, if they had been in force at the relevant time, were that Evans would not be liable to hang, the murder for which he was indicted being non-capital but that Christie would be liable in respect of the several murders for which he was indicted, they being committed on separate occasions. Bentley would not hang because, although the murder of a police officer was still capital, the doctrine of felony murder was no longer in operation. Ruth Ellis could hang, committing her murder by shooting but, given the anguished public reaction to that event, a future Home Secretary in a comparable case might be more persuaded of the wisdom of a reprieve. Not only were the abolitionists unlikely to be supplied with such ready propaganda ammunition again, but future Home Secretaries, especially if they were believers in the death penalty, would be rather less likely to 'blunder' in the manner of Chuter Ede, Maxwell Fyfe and Gwilym Lloyd George, by refusing reprieves in such controversial cases.

Moreover, hangings were soon to resume, albeit at a lesser frequency than before the Act and the moratorium that had preceded it, and any illusions that the abolitionists may have harboured to the effect that the government had really enacted abolition by stealth, were rapidly dispelled. It was clear from both words and actions that the government fully intended to operate the new Act in accordance with its provisions. Hanging had been restricted and curtailed but emphatically not abolished.

To the NCACP and others it was very much unfinished business, and the campaign was soon to be renewed and battle rejoined. The next chapter looks at the abolition campaign and pressure group activity.

CHAPTER 3

ABOLITIONIST PRESSURE GROUPS

This chapter examines pressure group activity and its influence on the debate. The great weight of such activity was, inevitably, on the abolitionist side, at least until 1965, because it was they who were seeking to effect change. The active retentionists, by contrast, were located chiefly within pre-existing institutional bodies such as the Police Federation, the prison service, the judiciary, the Conservative Party (or elements of it) and the House of Lords. After 1965, when abolition had become a reality, retentionist bodies began to emerge and flourish. These are examined in a separate chapter.

Easily the largest and most significant of the abolitionist bodies was the National Campaign for the Abolition of Capital Punishment (NCACP), which was far and away the most influential of such bodies and effectively incorporated within itself most pre-existing abolitionists and abolitionist movements. The great weight of abolitionist sentiment was articulated through the organs of the NCACP, which had some claim to be an 'insider' group in that it often had the ear of those in power, and because its membership was sufficiently high-level for it to have some leverage with government, though it was not institutionally an insider group in the sense of enjoying a regular forum with government ministers or departments.

The NCACP: Inception and Early Successes

By 1955 the feeling within progressive circles was that circumstances were propitious for a renewed drive towards abolition. The Royal Commission on Capital Punishment had reported in September 1953 and had come as close as its terms of reference allowed to recommending complete abolition.[89] Several prominent figures had declared themselves for abolition, most notably Viscount Templewood, who, as Samuel Hoare, had been Home Secretary in the National government in the 1930s, and who was not in any sense a radical.[90] There had been several egregious miscarriages and injustices, especially those of Timothy Evans and Derek Bentley, and to a lesser extent, Ruth Ellis, the cumulative effect of which was to shake the faith of many in the infallibility of British

---

[89] Gowers, Sir Ernest, *Report of the Royal Commission on Capital Punishment*, Cmnd 8932 (HMSO, 1953)
[90] Templewood, Viscount, *The Shadow of the Gallows* op cit.
Five years later Sir Ernest Gowers, the chairman of the Commission, came down for abolition in Gowers, Ernest, *A Life for a Life?: The Problem of Capital Punishment* op cit.

justice and the impossibility of hanging an innocent person.[91] Public opinion, which had been extremely hostile to abolition a few years before was beginning to move. A more liberal climate was emerging in the Britain of the mid-1950s, with memories of the war and post-war austerity receding into the past, and a greater willingness to consider measures of social reform. Against this background leading supporters of abolition began to coalesce around figures such as Victor Gollancz who had long been a champion of such causes.[92]

The NCACP was founded in the late summer of 1955 by three men who thereafter formed the nucleus of the group:- the wealthy publisher and campaigner Victor Gollancz, the philosopher and academic Arthur Koestler and the radical cleric Canon John Collins. It was effectively the successor body to the National Council for the Abolition of the Death Penalty (NCADP) which had been set up in 1925 by E Roy Calvert.[93] The earlier body, after heavy activity in the 1920s and 1930s, rather faded in the late 1940s after the failure of the 1948 abolition drive and merged with the Howard League later that year. There was little overlap of membership, and no carry-over of funds or organization, though Gollancz, Gardiner and Frank Dawtry were active in both bodies, and their aims and methods were of course largely identical. The Howard League acted as a kind of midwife, with its secretary Hugh Klare being active on the Executive of the NCACP. The later body enjoyed much greater success in that it was able to carry its campaign through to a victorious conclusion, arguably because its leadership had a much higher profile but also perhaps because it operated in an era much more receptive to social reform.

Gollancz was a tireless campaigner on behalf of numerous humanitarian causes and his abolitionist instincts extended even to an appeal to the Israeli government not to execute Eichmann.[94] His involvement with the cause of abolition dated back well before the formation of the NCACP for he had been closely involved with several reprieve campaigns in the early post-war period. In 1953 a Kitty Lamb wrote to him asking him to speak at a meeting at Conway Hall regarding abolition.[95] This clearly signalled the crystallization of a new abolition movement around Gollancz and others to replace the defunct NCADP and revive its campaign. Hugh Klare of the Howard League wrote to Gollancz

---

[91] David Maxwell Fyfe (Conservative MP and later Home Secretary in the Churchill government of 1951-55) had declared in the 1948 Commons debate that those who thought an innocent man could hang were 'moving in a realm of fantasy'. HC Deb vol 449, col 1077, 14th April 1948

[92] Victor Gollancz (1893-1967) publisher, writer and humanitarian. Founded the Left Book Club in the 1930s whose authors included George Orwell and Ford Madox Ford. Campaigned for reconciliation with Germany after World War II.

[93] Papers of the National Council for the Abolition of the Death Penalty, 1925-1948 (Modern Records Centre at the University of Warwick).

[94] Gollancz papers (hereafter cited as Gollancz), Modern Records Centre, University of Warwick, MS/157/3/CAP/1/6 - 18th April 1961.

[95] Gollancz, MS/157/3/CAP/3/8, Kitty Lamb to Gollancz, 9th March 1953

in 1955 about the government's rejection of a motion to suspend capital punishment that February due, he felt, to the government's belief in a lack of public support for it.[96] The Howard League was going to present a Memorial, signed by '200 leaders of public opinion', to the Home Secretary as part of its campaign, designed presumably to persuade the government of the strength of popular feeling, and naturally he wanted Gollancz to add his own name.

Gollancz was motivated to publish an article in the *News Chronicle* later that year (1955) entitled *It's Still Murder even if we all plead Innocence* which adumbrated his case against capital punishment, and apparently launched the Campaign proper, which hitherto had probably existed only in slightly inchoate and nebulous form.[97] The article bore the unmistakeable imprint of his emotive and impassioned style:-

> Imagine that you are in the death cell, with three weeks to wait…I am convinced that, on balance, it [capital punishment] is devoid of preventative value, and may even tend positively in the opposite direction. But if I believed the opposite I should still say, with undiminished conviction, that the most urgent of all tasks, for any people with a care for religious or human values, is the ending of capital punishment… Capital punishment is wrong; and that is all there is to it…it transgresses the most categorical of all imperatives - 'Thou shalt not do unspeakable cruelty to thy brother'.

Of the other leading figures Koestler was a brilliant journalist, writer, polymath and radical polemicist of long-standing, while Collins was a very prominent radical clergyman who had been active in many campaigns, founding Christian Action, which was a sort of guerrilla wing of the Church of England. A couple of years later he helped found CND, with which there was much cross-over of membership. Another very prominent figure of the NCACP from its formative years onwards was Gerald Gardiner, a liberal barrister and later Lord Chancellor in the Labour Government of 1964 (appointed to that post by Harold Wilson partly to oversee abolition, given his known views).[98] Gardiner, too, had been active in the cause for many years preceding the advent of the NCACP, and had been active in the NCADP. As early as 1946 he was engaged in correspondence with Frank Dawtry of the NCADP over the desirability of the execution of war criminals at Nuremberg.[99] A year or two later he was in

---

[96] Gollancz, MS/157/3/CAP/3/12, Klare to Gollancz, June 1955

[97] Gollancz, MS/157/3/CAP/4/10, article in the News Chronicle 10th November 1955

[98] See Box, Muriel, *Rebel Advocate: A Biography of Gerald Gardiner* (London: Gollancz, 1983) written by his wife. He had originally been a member of the Haldane Society of left-wing lawyers but left it in the late 1940s because of its increasing infiltration by Communists to join the Society of Labour Lawyers of which he was the inaugural chairman. Box, pp. 54-68

[99] Gerald Gardiner papers at the British Library (Historical Manuscripts section), hereafter cited as 'Gardiner'. Letter Dawtry to Gardiner, 2nd August 1946, enclosing a draft urging that death sentences not be carried out. Gardiner, MS: Add 56455A, vol 1 1946-1955.

correspondence with Chuter Ede, Home Secretary in the Attlee government, urging the introduction of an abolition clause in the forthcoming Criminal Justice Bill and praying in aid the findings of the 1930 Select Committee and the 1934 Party Conference resolution.[100]

The NCACP grew extraordinarily rapidly, recruiting many prominent figures, and gaining a membership of thousands within a few months of its inception. It remained in being for at least twenty years and certainly until well after abolition had been achieved in the mid-sixties.[101] It was a very high-powered organization supported by a roll-call of eminent individuals from all walks of life. It was well funded by the millionaire Gollancz as well as by subscription and donation and its leading individuals were highly influential in their respective spheres. It also gained a strong platform in the *Observer* newspaper, whose editor/proprietor, David Astor, was another prominent abolitionist, and which gave a regular column to Koestler under the pseudonym *Vigil*, in which he blasted the political and judicial establishment.

The Executive Committee, formed in August 1955 consisted initially of the three founder members: Gollancz, Collins and Koestler; plus Gerald Gardiner, QC (barrister and later co-chairman with Gollancz); Ruth Gollancz (Victor's wife); Christopher Hollis (publisher and former Conservative MP); Hugh Klare, (secretary of the Howard League); Reginald Paget, QC, (Labour MP); and Frank Owen (ex Liberal MP and journalist). Peggy Duff, an indefatigable left-wing campaigner, became secretary to the Committee. Over the next few years it was supplemented by several others including John Grigg, Lord Altrincham (writer, historian and politician); Canon Edward Carpenter (treasurer of Westminster Abbey); Julian Critchley, (Conservative MP); Frank Dawtry (secretary of the National Association of Probation Officers); John Freeman (politician and broadcaster); C R Hewitt (C H Rolph) of the *New Statesman* (an ex police inspector in the City of London force); Dr J A Hobson (psychiatrist); Peter Kirk, (Conservative MP); Sydney Silverman (Labour MP); Jeremy Thorpe (Liberal MP) and Wayland Young, Lord Kennet (Labour politician).[102] Their active participation in the affairs of the body varied considerably from person to person and over time. The Campaign, in due

---

[100] Letter from Gardiner to Chuter Ede (undated but presumably 1947), Gardiner, MS: Add 56455A

[101] The exact date of its formal dissolution is unclear, though it certainly remained in being, albeit maybe only in skeletal form, well into the 1970s long after the re-affirmation of abolition in December 1969.

[102] John Freeman, MBE (1915-) Labour MP for Watford 1945-1955, Bevanite. Resigned as junior minister in 1951 with Bevan and Wilson over prescription charges. Editor of the New Statesman 1961-5. Presenter of *Face to Face* 1960-61. High Commissioner to India 1965-8, Ambassador to USA 1969-71, Chairman of LWT 1971-84. Cecil Hewitt Rolph or Cecil Rolph Hewitt (1901-1994) policeman, author and journalist. John Jeremy Thorpe (1929-) Liberal MP for North Devon 1959-1979. Party leader 1967-1976. Wayland Hilton Young, 2nd Baron Kennet (1923-) writer and Labour and SDP politician.

course, also formed a 'Committee of Honour' of the great and the good who supported its aims which was chaired by the Earl of Harewood, a cousin of the Queen.

The inaugural meeting of the Executive was in August 1955 at its Henrietta St. headquarters, the offices of Gollancz publishing.[103] It consisted of Gollancz (chairman), Collins[104], Gardiner[105], Ruth Gollancz[106], Christopher Hollis[107], Koestler, Frank Owen[108] and Reginald Paget QC MP[109], with Peggy Duff[110] as secretary and treasurer. Hugh Klare, formerly a leading figure of the predecessor NCADP, and now secretary of the Howard League, was also present. Thus the Executive represented a broad spectrum of distinguished figures from politics, the law, the church, business, academia and journalism. It decided upon the name of the organization; resolved to inaugurate a 'Committee of Honour' and drew up a list of prospective members to be invited to join it; resolved to hold a press conference and issue a statement to the press as soon as possible; and resolved upon a plan of campaign which was to combine the conventional and the unconventional. The former was to include a press campaign, the distribution of literature, public meetings, lobbying and a comprehensive 'Memorial' to the Prime Minister. The latter was to consist of

---

[103] Executive Committee minutes, 11th August 1955. Gardiner, MS Add: 56460 (vol VI)

[104] (Lewis) John Collins (1905-1982), Anglican clergyman. Dean of St Paul's for 33 years; political campaigner for a raft of radical causes, especially the anti-apartheid movement and CND of which he was a founder member. Also a founder of Christian Action (for reconciliation with Germany after WWII), War on Want (to fight global poverty) and the Canon Collins Educational Trust for Southern Africa (CCETSA).

[105] Gerald Austin Gardiner, Baron Gardiner of Kittisford, CH KC PC (1900-1990), barrister and human rights campaigner. Labour parliamentary candidate (unsuccessful) in the general election of 1951. Defence counsel in the Lady Chatterley obscenity trial of 1960. Refused promotion to the bench because of opposition to capital punishment. Lord Chancellor 1964-70, overseeing widespread penal reform and the introduction of the Law Commission, as well as the abolition of capital punishment. Subsequently Chancellor of the Open University.

[106] Livia Ruth Gollancz, wife of Victor Gollancz.

[107] (Maurice) Christopher Hollis (1902-1977) academic, author and politician, Conservative MP for Devizes 1945-55. One of the earliest Conservative converts to abolition.

[108] (Humphrey) Frank Owen (1905-1979) journalist, broadcaster and Liberal MP for Hereford, 1929-1931. Editor of the Evening Standard 1938-41 and of the Daily Mail 1947-50. Biographer of Lloyd George.

[109] Reginald Thomas Guy Des Voeux Paget, Baron Paget of Northampton, QC PC (1908-1990). Barrister and politician. Labour MP for Northampton 1945-1974. Author of polemical work on the Bentley case.

[110] (Margaret Doreen) Peggy Duff (nee Eames) (1910-1981) journalist and political activist. Member of Common Wealth party during WWII. Associated with Gollancz's Save Europe Now campaign 1945; business manager of Tribune 1949-55; Labour councillor and chief whip on St Pancras Borough Council 1956; organizing secretary of CND 1958-65; resigned from the Labour Party 1967 in protest at Wilson's support for the US in Vietnam; wrote *Left, Left, Left: A Personal Account of Six Protest Campaigns, 1945-65* (London: Allison and Busby, 1971).

pledges not to attend places of recreation or amusement, or parties, on the night preceding an execution, services in churches from midnight until the hour of execution, the closing of shops and offices for one hour and the wearing of some form of mourning on the eve of an execution. It also resolved that no activities outside prison gates should be encouraged. Koestler and Gollancz agreed to consult together about the publication of further books on abolition, including one on the Ruth Ellis case.

A press release accompanying the formation of the body asserted that: 'It is believed that there has recently been a significant change in public opinion on capital punishment' and that a national campaign was to be launched and a 'Committee of Honour' to be formed including the name of Benjamin Britten. The campaign announced that it was to employ two methods – one educational with the publication of books, pamphlets and statements and public meetings and the other more personal with, for example, abolitionists abstaining from attending places of entertainment etc. on the eve of an execution. It emphasized that the: 'Campaign will be conducted in a reverent and indeed religious spirit; any disruptive or sensational action such as demonstrations outside prisons will be rigorously discountenanced.'[111]

Meetings continued on a regular and more or less monthly basis, as agreed, and these early meetings were staggeringly productive of ideas for publicity and campaigning, many of which, though not all, came to fruition. But for all this torrent of activity the Executive of the NCACP cannot be said to have been the most harmonious of organizations, and in fact it appeared to have been riven with internal discord, largely of a personal nature. In particular there was a giant clash of egos between Gollancz and Koestler, who had entirely different conceptions of how the Campaign should develop and whose intellectual and literary rivalry threatened to undermine the whole Campaign.[112] As Rolph has written their joint efforts were 'fruitful but stormy.'[113] They were equally passionate in their loathing of capital punishment but Koestler was for reasoned argument whereas Gollancz was for absolutist denunciation.[114] This dichotomy was evident in their respective testaments. Koestler's *Reflections on Hanging* (1956) based on extensive research displayed formidable intellectual rigour, whereas Gollancz's *Capital Punishment: the Heart of the Matter* (1955) was emotive and confessional. Koestler's masterpiece did not impress Gollancz, who started to write his book as a consciously moral and religious appeal

---

[111] Gardiner, MS Add 56460, (vol VI). This latter stressed the extent to which the newly formed body was anxious to distance itself from some of the noisier and less respectable outlets for abolitionism such as the activities of Mrs Violet van der Elst (1882-1966), a vociferous abolitionist who organized demonstrations outside prisons on the eve of an execution.

[112] Collins, John, *Faith Under Fire* (London: Leslie Frewin, 1966) p. 247

[113] C H Rolph Collection (LSE), Capital Punishment papers, File 1/4/3

[114] Dudley Edwards, Ruth, *Victor Gollancz: A Biography* (London: Gollancz, 1987) p. 638

compared to Koestler's argumentation. The two books were complementary and presented the two faces of the abolitionist rhetoric, the rational and the heartfelt.

Aside from these personal animosities another potential source of disharmony was the broad range of the political affiliations of the membership. The Campaign was of course mindful of the need to appeal to as wide a spectrum of the population as possible, and in particular not to frighten away Conservatives who might have been chary of joining a movement that drew its inspiration primarily from the left. As it was, some were clearly reluctant to make common cause with the likes of Canon Collins or Sydney Silverman. The Campaign was anxious to allay any suggestion that it was a left-wing or socialist body, and to that end it was careful to include Conservatives on the Executive. Christopher Hollis (former Conservative MP for Devizes) was there from the outset and he was joined in due course by Peter Kirk, the leading Conservative abolitionist MP, John Grigg and Julian Critchley.[115] Much later both Geoffrey Howe (founder of the Bow Group of progressive Conservatives) and Iain Macleod were invited to join. The presence of Conservatives on the Executive also assisted the vital aspect of liaising with potentially sympathetic Conservative MPs, without whose assistance the Campaign could not possibly hope to make legislative progress.

In late 1955 Gardiner set to work on his own book *Capital Punishment as a Deterrent and the Alternative* to be published by Gollancz, organized meetings, and wrote to both Sir Ian Jacobs, the then director-general of the BBC and Sidney Bernstein, head of Granada television and the Granada cinema chain (independent commercial television having just begun in 1955) urging them to make programmes on the subject of capital punishment.[116] The Campaign also set about publishing a monthly bulletin which would summarize the current activities of the organization and give a round-up of persons convicted of murder and sentenced to death. The first issue of the NCACP Bulletin was

---

[115] Sir Peter Michael Kirk (1928-77). Conservative MP for Gravesend 1955-1964. Conservative MP for Saffron Walden 1965-1977. Leading Tory abolitionist. John Edward Poynder Grigg, 2nd Baron Altrincham. Conservative politician, author and historian (1924-2001) Stood unsuccessfully for the Conservatives in 1951 and 1955. Disclaimed peerage on the day the Peerages Act received the Royal Assent in 1963. Joined the SDP in 1982. Biographer of Lloyd George. Sir Julian Michael Gordon Critchley (1930-2000) Conservative MP for Rochester and Chatham 1959-64, Aldershot 1970-1997. Strong critic of Thatcherism.

[116] Gardiner, MS: Add 56455B. Letter to Jacobs, 4th January 1956; letter to Bernstein 4th January 1956. The Bernstein letter seems to have been lobbying for a short documentary to be shown in cinemas rather than on TV. Sidney Lewis Bernstein (1899-1993), later Baron Bernstein, was the head of the Granada group and a prominent socialist millionaire. It is unclear whether anything came of this lobbying. Certainly the reply from Bernstein was not encouraging, but that from a T S Gregory of the BBC was more so. See the chapter on television.

published on 15th January 1956.[117] It trumpeted the successes of the Campaign to date; announced the setting up of a Scottish branch in Glasgow and regional committees in Birmingham, Liverpool, Manchester, Edinburgh, Glasgow and Swansea; and boasted of its roll-call of prominent supporters, both individual and corporate.

By February 1956 the Campaign had maintained its momentum of the preceding months and had continued to flourish in many ways.[118] Moreover, and far more significantly, there was to be a debate on an abolitionist motion in the Commons, and the Executive was to convene an extraordinary meeting when the precise date of this was known. Six days later the extraordinary meeting was duly held with Gollancz, Collins, Gardiner, Ruth Gollancz, Hewitt, Hobson, Hollis, Koestler and Duff.[119] In anticipation of the forthcoming Commons debate every MP had been sent a copy of Gardiner's book and a report of the *Vigil* article in *The Observer* (penned by Koestler).

The NCACP and the 1956 Parliamentary Campaign

Early 1956 saw the first fruits of the Campaign at a Parliamentary level with a Commons vote in favour of a motion to abolish or suspend capital punishment in February 1956.[120] This was assisted in large part by the presence in the abolition lobby of a substantial bloc of Conservative MPs for the first time, many of them, such as Peter Kirk, from the younger, more liberal intake that had been elected in May 1955. Though the Eden government had promised to honour the result of the motion by giving it legislative effect it eventually decided on giving government time to a private members bill introduced the previous autumn by Sydney Silverman rather than to legislate on its own account. Obviously such a bill had less chance of success than a government bill, and in particular it would have had to surmount the formidable barrier of the Upper House which had sunk the abolition clause of the 1948 Criminal Justice Bill.

Nonetheless, the passage by a good majority of the abolitionist motion seemed to persuade Gollancz that victory was already won and that the Campaign could be wound down. He wrote to Lady Squire about the: 'sensational victory in the Commons...there is no further need for a campaign

---

[117] Howard League files. *NCACP: Essays and Papers Arguing Abolition 1969-79*; Gardiner, MS Add 56455B

[118] Executive Committee minutes, 8th February 1956. Gardiner, MS Add 56455B

[119] Executive Committee minutes, 14th February 1956. Gardiner, MS Add 56455B

[120] HC Deb, vol 548, cols. 2651-6, 16th February 1956. The motion, moved by former Labour Home Secretary James Chuter Ede, called for the government to introduce legislation forthwith for the abolition or suspension of the death penalty. It passed by 292-246.

in the original sense. We shall, however, keep going as a vigilance group on a small scale...'[121] In the same vein he wrote to Nigel Nicolson, MP, one of the leading abolitionists on the Tory side, thanking him for his speech which he thought one of the: '2 decisive speeches of the evening.'[122] He had become absurdly over-optimistic about the imminence of total success, which was to cause a rupture with Koestler and others who took a more hard-headed view, and he seemed curiously oblivious to the fact that there was every probability that an Abolition Bill would founder in the House of Lords, just as the 1948 abolition clause had foundered in the Upper House eight years previously. There was no reason to suppose that the mood of the Lords was very different from that of 1948, for although the episcopal benches were notably more liberal the Archbishop of Canterbury, Fisher, was still against total abolition, and the judicial benches were still under the sway of the hard-nosed Lord Chief Justice, Goddard. The Labour contingent of the Lords was greater than it had been but was still massively under-represented.

Gollancz, Gardiner and Koestler conferred outside the House of Commons immediately after the key vote, and Gollancz expressed his conviction that the war had been won and that the Campaign should be wound down by cancelling projected meetings, whereas Koestler was well aware that they had merely won a battle and that there was still a long way to go to get a Bill through the Lords.[123] Gollancz unilaterally cancelled the forthcoming meeting at Manchester, to the annoyance of the Bishop of Middleton, telling him that he didn't think that many people would turn up to hear about a *fait accompli*![124] Rolph reports Peggy Duff as saying that Gollancz had simply become bored with the Campaign and that his fickle intellect had already moved on to other things.[125] At the next meeting a week later it was decided that all further national meetings were to be cancelled and to issue a statement that the Campaign was to be widened to take in penal reform.[126]

The Campaign now centred almost wholly on supporting the Parliamentary effort to get the Silverman Abolition Bill through the Commons and then, crucially, the House of Lords. The Lords was a key target for propaganda, especially its episcopal and judicial benches. It was decided in June to circularize all peers who had voted for the abolition clause in 1948 and all Labour and Liberal peers who were regular attenders with Campaign literature.[127]

These great efforts came to nought in Parliament with the defeat in the

---

[121] Gollancz, MS/157/3/CAP/3/19, Gollancz to Lady Squire, 17th February 1956
[122] Gollancz, MS/157/3/CAP/3/20, Gollancz to Nicolson, 17th February 1956
[123] Duff, Peggy, op cit. p. 106
[124] Dudley Edwards, op cit. p. 641
[125] Rolph, op cit. 1/4/3. Dudley Edwards, op cit. p. 646
[126] Executive Committee minutes, 21st February 1956. Gardiner, MS Add 56455B
[127] Executive Committee minutes, 7th June 1956. Gardiner, MS Add 56455B

House of Lords, by a large majority, of the Silverman Bill, in July 1956.[128] The Campaign had to move to its fallback position which was to try to persuade the government to legislate itself on abolition, but it was very unlikely that the government would attempt to carry all-out abolition given its instinctive hostility to the measure, and the opposition of the overwhelming majority of grassroots Conservatives. Moreover, it was soon to become embroiled in the Suez affair, and social reform took rather a back seat. The Campaign concentrated its energies on a 'Memorial' for presentation to the Prime Minister which would contain the names of as many distinguished figures as possible urging abolition. In the latter part of 1956 Gardiner corresponded widely with leading figures, particularly educationalists such as headmasters, masters of colleges and professors, to persuade them to add their names to the proposed Memorial.

The Homicide Act 1957 and After

In the next Parliamentary session of 1956-7 the government brought forth its own Bill which delicately attempted to steer a middle course between the total abolition of hanging demanded by a clear majority in the Commons on the one hand, and the outright hostility to abolition of any kind of a majority in the Lords (and rank and file Conservatives) on the other. It envisaged the partial abolition of hanging, along with a number of other reforms to the law of homicide, some of which had been advocated by the Gowers' Commission. Capital punishment was to be retained for only a few special classes of murder such as that of police and prison officers in the execution of their duty, murder in the course or furtherance of theft, murder by shooting or causing an explosion, and multiple murder if the murders were committed on separate occasions. The Bill also proposed a number of other changes to the law of homicide such as the introduction of a partial defence of diminished responsibility and the abolition of the doctrine of felony murder, which were on the whole welcome to the abolitionists and to progressive opinion but which in no way compensated, in their eyes, for the failure to do away with hanging altogether. The NCACP and the Labour abolitionists in the House opposed the Bill (or at any rate the provisions for two classes of murder) but the Tory abolitionists decided *en masse* to support it. With the force of the government behind it the Bill passed easily through the Lords and became law in March 1957. The moratorium on hanging, which had held since the autumn of 1955, came to an end and in July 1957 John Willson Vickers became the first man to be hanged for nearly two years. Executions continued but at a somewhat reduced rate of about half a dozen per year rather than, as before, a dozen.

---

[128] HL Deb, vol 198, col 839-42, 10th July 1956. The Bill was defeated on second reading by 238-95. Nonetheless this was a much larger number of abolitionists than in 1948.

The Homicide Act of 1957 was 'a disaster from day one'.[129] The operation of the Act was riven with anomalies which discredited the legislation from the outset and the Act was utterly friendless. Absurdities abounded such as that of a man who attempted to kill his wife with a shotgun and when that failed due to malfunction battered her to death with the butt-end. This was technically non-capital since the actual cause of death was not shooting but battery. Equally deemed non-capital was the case of a woman who had murdered three husbands by poisoning and had forged their wills to benefit herself, because the forging of the wills was not theft in the technical sense. The discrediting of the Act, together with the natural reluctance of the legal profession to go back to the position pre-1957, led ineluctably to complete abolition a few years later.

After this ferment of activity in the first year of its life there was an inevitable sense of anti-climax within the ranks of the NCACP after the defeat of the Silverman Bill in the Lords, which was scarcely appeased by the government's decision to bring in its own Bill to limit the application, but not abolish, hanging. Executive meetings became less frequent and the Campaign went off the boil. In March 1957 Gardiner wrote on behalf of the Executive to the membership outlining the Campaign's position, post Homicide Act. Executions, he said, were to recommence and there was: 'no practical prospect of getting any further in the lifetime of this Parliament'. However, they were not going to abandon the campaign until capital punishment had been finally abolished. The organization was to stay in being to maintain records and statistics, to issue information and letters to the press, to supply information to candidates and others, etc. He closed with a plea for continued funds from the membership.[130] This was a hard-headed decision based on a realistic appraisal of the situation, but it was not congenial to all members, some of whom would doubtless have preferred that the Campaign continue to be more pro-active and energetic, however remote the prospects of success in the short to medium term.

There may have been misapprehensions in some quarters, not least among abolitionists, that although hanging had not been totally abolished *de jure* by virtue of the Homicide Act it would be abolished *de facto*, or only used very sparingly indeed. In fact hanging was to continue as normal for those categories of murder deemed capital, as the government soon made clear both in words and actions by virtue of the hanging of Vickers. A key question for the Campaign was whether, and in what way, it should lobby for a reprieve in individual capital cases. One view was that it should do its utmost in any and every case so as at least to reduce to the minimum the number of executions. The alternative view was that there were many cases where little could be said for the defendant, and a reprieve campaign would not only have been futile but possibly counter-productive in that it would lessen the impact in a case where

---

[129] This was the uncompromising verdict of Terence Morris (criminologist and NCACP member), interview 6th April 2006

[130] Gardiner letter to members, March 1957. Gardiner, MS Add 56457A

there were strong grounds for a reprieve.

This difficulty is illustrated by an exchange of letters between Gardiner and Silverman in late 1958 regarding Brian Chandler, whose appeal against sentence of death had been rather cursorily dismissed by the Court of Appeal. Gardiner queried whether there was any point in writing to the Home Secretary about the case and Silverman took the view that a letter would come better from Gardiner than from himself.[131] In the event Gardiner did indeed write to the Home Secretary pressing for a reprieve.[132] This ambivalence reared its head again a month or two later respecting another case with Gardiner writing to Silverman:-

> I have as you know for some time been uncertain whether our policy of writing to the Home Secretary in nearly every case is a sound one. If one does this it necessarily weakens the effect when one does write. On the other hand if one writes in 90% of the cases, not to write would seem discrimination in the case of the other 10%. I thought that my letter in Chandler's case was a sound reasoned argument but as you know the Home Secretary refused a reprieve.

Gardiner continued to correspond with the press regarding individual cases such as that of Vickers.[133] The Marwood case was another that aroused much attention and was the subject of various pleas including from the local vicar and parish priest, as well as from Nuell, secretary of Christian Action, enclosing a petition for mercy.[134]

The government was determined to give the Act 'a chance to work' and to monitor its effects, however unsatisfactory its compromise was universally reckoned to be. The NCACP knew that it could do nothing but sit things out and wait for the return of a Labour government (whenever that would be). There were continued Parliamentary guerrilla tactics by abolitionists in the Commons led by Silverman and other sympathetic Labour members, who repeatedly took advantage of procedural niceties to call for abolition or the further reduction of hangings, and periodically protested to the Home Secretary about an upcoming execution which they felt represented a miscarriage, or a misconstruction of the intentions of the Act. The cases of Vickers, Marwood, Podola, Forsyth and Harris and Hanratty in particular were all grist to the abolitionists' mill, though other cases too aroused excitement and controversy.

---

[131] Gardiner to Silverman, 2nd December 1958. Silverman to Gardiner, nd. Gardiner, MS Add 56457B

[132] Gardiner to Home Secretary (Butler), 8th December 1958. Gardiner, MS Add 56457B

[133] Gardiner to the editor of the *Manchester Guardian*, 2nd July 1957, marked 'not for publication in the event of a reprieve' pointing out that the conviction raised questions about the meaning of malice aforethought in the new Act. Gardiner papers, MS Add 56457A

[134] F Nuell, Christian Action, to Gardiner 27th April 1959. Gardiner papers, MS Add 56457B

Outside Parliament and the offices of the NCACP the controversy raged on in other ways. There were often demonstrations outside the prison gates on the day of an execution, which intensified and sometimes degenerated into a near riot. The debate was continued in the pages of the national press and there were periodic contributions from leading public figures. In 1960 the new Lord Chief Justice, Parker, caused a storm by denouncing the Homicide Act as unworkable and indicating his conversion to abolition even if only as the lesser evil of the two. It was acutely embarrassing for the government and symbolized the gradual transformation of the judiciary from a very largely pro-hanging body to a preponderantly sceptical or anti-hanging one. Similar transformations had already taken place, or were taking place, within the episcopacy and the hierarchy of the churches generally, and these straws in the wind all spoke of the fact that abolition was not far off.

The general election of October 1959 was the next major opportunity for the Campaign to exert itself. Gardiner sent out a circular letter to all declared candidates asking them not to commit themselves to the maintenance of capital punishment until they had had the opportunity to consider all the relevant facts – including the effect of the Homicide Act. Equally there was a circular letter to all Campaign members asking them to write to all candidates in their constituency urging them to support abolition if elected.[135]

The Revival of the Campaign 1960-64

The future direction of the Campaign was uncertain, with the Executive still effectively being forced to mark time until another general election brought a less Tory-dominated House, yet having to cope with an increasingly restless grass-roots membership frustrated at the lack of progress. An attempt to revive the flagging spirits of the Campaign was made with the arranging of a major public meeting at the Royal Albert Hall scheduled for 18th April 1961 to feature speakers including Altrincham (John Grigg), Kingsley Amis, Peter Kirk, Christopher Brasher, the Bishop of Colchester, Gardiner, Gollancz and Silverman.[136] Further big meetings were planned for Manchester in October and Edinburgh in November. A new Memorial was planned which was to be sent out to 16,000 people, with 2,418 signatures gained up to that time.[137]

The next significant development was the government's stated intention to review the position of capital punishment and the working of the Homicide

---

[135] Gardiner to parliamentary candidates; Gardiner to Campaign members, September 1959.Gardiner, MS: Add 56458A

[136] Circular from Gardiner and Gollancz to the membership, 15th February 1961 regarding a meeting 'crucial' to the Campaign. Gardiner, MS Add 56459A

[137] Elizabeth Ferriday (secretary) to Gardiner, 27th June 1961. Gardiner, MS Add 56459A

Act after a five year period, which period was due to expire in March 1962.[138] The perennially optimistic Silverman was of the opinion that the following year might be a good time for another Parliamentary push. There was evidence of further activity in the Church of England with the Bishop of Southwark to propose, and Exeter to second, a motion for abolition at the forthcoming meeting of Convocation the following January (1962).[139] After Convocation had voted almost unanimously for abolition Gollancz wrote to all the bishops in both Provinces (Canterbury and York) to sign the Memorial.[140]

This second Memorial was duly presented to Prime Minister Macmillan in March 1962 by a very high-powered deputation headed by the Archbishop of York (Coggan), Harewood and Chuter Ede.[141] Macmillan said that abolition was a matter of timing, and that though it was inevitable sooner or later there was no question of the government legislating in the present Parliament.[142] Silverman reported on a deputation to the Home Secretary which had consisted of himself, Critchley, Kirk, Chuter Ede and Jeremy Thorpe. The meeting had been friendly and Butler had said that he appreciated that all the trends were towards abolition and that he was sure it would eventually come, but that the level of Conservative support for it in the House was insufficient to justify further government legislation this session. Thus Silverman advocated that a concerted drive to convert Tory MPs was desirable, particularly given that Butler had indicated that the deputation should stay in touch and report to him on any significant change in the temper of the House.

These events led to further debate as to the desirability of continuing a full-blooded campaign or resting on the oars pending another general election. Gardiner argued that there was little point in continuing a full-time campaign at this stage, and announced that the secretary, Morag Rennie, was to be retained only on a part-time basis. Altrincham by contrast argued for the maintenance of a full campaign to attempt to keep up the pressure on public opinion. It was decided that there should be no public suggestion that the Campaign was to quieten down as this might be construed as an admission of failure. Letters were to be sent out to local branches and to members urging them to contact secretaries of local organizations with a view to holding talks and debates, and the Campaign head office would continue to supply literature and speakers to such meetings on request. They would also continue the practice of replying to all letters in the press supporting retention.

---

[138] Gardiner to Pakenham, 27th September 1961. Gardiner papers, MS Add 56459A
Frank (Francis Aungier) Pakenham, 7th Earl of Longford KG PC (1905-2001). Labour politician, author and social reformer. Cabinet minister under Harold Wilson 1964-68. Resigned over failure to raise the school-leaving age.
[139] Correspondence, 12th December 1961. Gardiner, MS Add 56459A
[140] Rennie to Gardiner, 19th January 1962. Gardiner, MS Add: 56459B
[141] Gardiner and Gollancz to Macmillan, 28th March 1962. Gardiner, MS Add 56459B
[142] Executive Committee minutes, 13th September 1962. Gardiner, MS Add 56455B

The 1964 General Election – Victory in Prospect

By 1964 another general election was in the offing, expected by some in the spring, though it didn't materialize until almost the last possible moment in October. The Campaign took the view that tactically their best policy was to downplay capital punishment as an issue given that a Labour majority was likely which would probably deliver the goods for them, whilst if capital punishment had a high salience in the election Labour candidates could be embarrassed by the question.[143] Gollancz and Gardiner wrote jointly to all members in April 1964 asking them to keep abolition out of the forthcoming general election, telling them that it would not be an issue and that it would not be in the interests of the movement to make it an issue. However, they added, once the election was over they would be writing to members asking them to do what they can to ensure that a bill is introduced. Labour, they said, had made it clear they would leave it to a free vote, but whatever government was returned to power the House would be younger and there was every probability that their efforts would be crowned with success. An indication of the Campaign's confidence at this time was a letter from Paget to Gollancz saying: 'Frankly, we have only got to win the Election in order to abolish capital punishment.'[144]

After the election and the coming to power of a Labour government under Wilson events rapidly gathered momentum. The NCACP was very active and its members were in constant contact with the government and sympathetic backbenchers over the drafting of a Bill and Parliamentary tactics, but the spotlight moved to the Parliamentary theatre. After a stormy and drawn out Parliamentary passage, in both Commons and Lords, complete abolition became a fact in November 1965 with the Death Penalty (Abolition Bill) receiving the Royal Assent. The Campaign had to decide whether to remain in being or to wind itself up. Given that the Abolition Act, as passed, contained a renewal clause that had to be voted on within five years if abolition were to remain permanent, and given also that there would almost certainly be a concerted drive by retentionists to bring back hanging either then or earlier, there could not really be much doubt that they would decide to maintain the organization, even if only in reduced form.

By the late 1960s, as the date for the Parliamentary vote on the confirmation clause approached the Campaign re-awoke. By then both Gollancz and Silverman had died and Collins had been unanimously chosen as Gollancz's successor as chairman at a meeting on 20th June 1968. It was decided

---

[143] Gardiner and Gollancz to membership, April 1964. Gardiner, MS Add 56459C; Gollancz, MS/157/3/CAP/1/62

[144] Gollancz, MS/157/3/CAP/1/63 - 25th April 1964

to meet at quarterly intervals thereafter and to prepare literature and statistics for the coming struggle to be anticipated. Members were contacted as to whether they wished to remain members, which in the overwhelming majority of cases they did, and they were asked for further contributions.[145] Collins sent out letters to all members in August 1969 seeking their continued support in the light of attempts to bring back capital punishment: '...we must prepare ourselves for further action. Mr Duncan Sandys and his colleagues are already campaigning for the re-introduction of capital punishment in certain cases and it is essential...we should be ready to counter their propaganda.'

Callaghan, then Home Secretary, wrote to Collins in November 1969 regarding the timing of the debate on the confirmation resolutions.[146] He suggested they hold themselves in reserve against a retentionist campaign, though there was useful work to be done in continuing to press the cause privately and in informed circles: 'I should be grateful if before considering any wider campaign you would be good enough to discuss it with me.' After the successful negotiation of the confirmatory resolutions in 1969 abolition was entrenched and required no further Parliamentary action to become permanent. But that of course did not preclude the possibility (if not probability) of the retentionist camp making repeated attempts to re-introduce hanging, especially if the murder rate were to increase significantly. The Sandys campaign had illustrated how influential such a restoration campaign could be, though it failed at the Parliamentary level. Moreover, both the 1965 Bill and the 1969 resolution had passed through a House of Commons with a Labour majority. There was no guarantee that a future, Conservative dominated, Commons might not one day pass a restoration bill. Thus the Campaign resolved to stay in being for the foreseeable future, though it concerned itself primarily thereafter with the question of capital punishment outside Great Britain, especially in the parts of the Commonwealth that still possessed it.

On the face of it the NCACP enjoyed a remarkable degree of success, certainly if judged by the standards of pressure groups in general. Within a few months of its inception it had gained tens of thousands of adherents including leading figures in politics, the law, the church, the arts and media and had made a big impact via its highly publicized meetings, articles in the press, radio and television coverage and an outpouring of literature. A regional organization and local activities of all sorts sprang up everywhere and abolitionist sentiment seemed to be manifesting itself across the board. Not only that, but within six months or so moves were afoot in Parliament once more to bring in another abolition measure, and this, unlike its predecessors, looked as if it were to succeed. So much so that Gollancz, for one, was convinced of its success and felt able to scale down the Campaign. In the event this proved over-optimistic

---

[145] Howard League, NCACP (Committee of Honour) correspondence file 1969
[146] Howard League, ibid, NCACP correspondence 1969, Callaghan to Collins, 4th November 1969

because of the intransigence of the Upper House, and the movement had to be content with a highly unsatisfactory compromise measure embodied in the Homicide Act. After this setback the wind rather went out of its sails and it more or less reconciled itself to waiting for a more opportune political time to achieve ultimate victory. That time proved to be only eight or nine years in the future. Thus the Campaign was crowned with success within ten years of its formation. It would be difficult to think of a comparable movement around a highly contentious issue that achieved so much so rapidly.

How much of this success, however, was attributable to the efforts of the Campaign itself, and would the change in the law have happened anyway on more or less the same time scales even if the NCACP (or an equivalent movement) had not existed? Undoubtedly the Campaign focussed public attention on the question and gave a boost to those who had already been campaigning for abolition in more isolated and less well publicized ways. It provided a channel into which these pre-existing campaigns could pool their resources and enabled the abolition movement to present itself as a highly-organized and essentially respectable body, rather than merely a collection of well-intentioned cranks engaged on a futile mission.

Though several Executive members were highly influential in their respective walks of life it is hard to gauge the extent of this influence on those spheres. Collins was a very high profile figure in the Church of England, but also a highly suspect one in the eyes of many of its more orthodox communicants, and it is unclear what the effect of Christian Action propaganda was on rank and file Anglican opinion. It may well have been mixed. It is true that opinion on many subjects within the church hierarchy was evolving radically at about this time but that was chiefly a function of the changing of the guard at the top with Ramsey, Coggan, Stockwood and others replacing more conservative figures such as Fisher, and would have happened anyway. Gardiner was eminent in the legal profession, as a future chairman of the Bar Council and Lord Chancellor, and the legal and judicial profession was certainly starting to move in an abolitionist direction, but this was again a function of long-term changes in the profession. Gollancz himself was a distinguished figure but a highly controversial one and his campaign for the reprieve of Eichmann, for example, provoked a very hostile response from many within the Jewish community.

In the final analysis Parliamentary action was the *sine qua non* of bringing about a change in the law and this required the marshalling of majorities in the Commons and the Lords and preferably a sympathetic government. There had been a majority for abolition in the Commons since 1945 but this had been unable to prevail in 1948 both because of the hostility of the government and the outright opposition of the Lords. A few isolated attempts in the early 1950s had got nowhere and it was only in 1956 that an abolition bill (as distinct from an abolition clause) had been passed in the

Commons. This was a result partly of the altered arithmetic with the Labour Party (front and backbench) now overwhelmingly on the abolition side and a substantial bloc of backbench Conservatives, many of them elected in 1955, now likewise abolitionist. The Eden government, if not exactly sympathetic, was at least reluctantly acquiescent. It is difficult to believe that these Parliamentary manoeuvres would not have taken place when and how they did irrespective of external campaigns and the existence of the NCACP. Though there was a great deal of liaison between the Parliamentary and the extra-Parliamentary wings of the movement it is noticeable that Silverman, the pre-eminent abolitionist MP, was kept off the NCACP Executive for a long time apparently because of personal hostility between Gollancz and himself. The NCACP Executive had a good deal of contact with certain Conservative abolitionist MPs such as Medlicott and this may have helped stiffen the resolve of some of these who might otherwise have resiled from their position in the face of grassroots Tory hostility. But then again it is difficult to evaluate the extent of this kind of influence and it is likely that most Conservative abolitionists would have stuck to their guns anyway given the strength of feeling on the issue at the time. When, subsequently, the government put the whips on to force through the Homicide Bill, to which the Campaign was adamantly opposed, all of these Tory abolitionists fell into line behind their political masters.

In the years immediately following this, when there was no real will in the Commons for further reform, the activities of the Campaign were utterly unavailing, and it had to await the advent of a new Labour government (one that was for the first time very favourable to reform and highly pro-active) before abolition could finally be enacted. Thus, for all the great exertions of the Campaign it was ultimately necessary to have the government of the day on its side. If the government was onside then success was almost assured, and if it wasn't then it was highly improbable. The Campaign made a great deal of noise and generated an enormous amount of heat but it didn't have any power, and in the final analysis was probably less effectual than it appeared and less so than it might have liked to portray itself.

Other Abolitionist Campaigns

In addition to the Howard League and the NCACP there were naturally many organizations and individuals which had an interest in penal matters and which took an abolitionist stance, including, for example, *The Society of Labour Lawyers*, whose leading light by the early 1960s was Dingle Foot, shortly to be Solicitor-General in the 1964 Labour government, and *The Haldane Society of Socialist Lawyers*. In addition abolitionist societies were set up in academic circles, for example by Oxford University in the form of 'the University Movement for the Abolition of Capital Punishment' whose leading figure was Professor H L A Hart. Another body that appeared to take a consistently abolitionist line was *The National Secular Society*. Bodies that were associated with the NCACP from shortly after its inception included *The Ethical Union* and *The Fellowship of Reconciliation* (the former a secular body and the latter a Christian pacifist body). *The National Council for Civil Liberties* (NCCL) was another established pressure group that took an abolitionist line. In early 1956 its executive committee recommended that the Council should support abolition, chiefly because of the possibility of a miscarriage rather than because of opposition to hanging in principle.[147] It resolved that:-

> ...having considered the case of the three men who were wrongly convicted of attacking a policeman and causing him grievous bodily harm and taking into consideration other cases of wrongful conviction known to the Council, and the general doubt about the Christie-Evans case, [the Executive] have decided to recommend to the annual general meeting that in view of the errors in the administration of justice which not only can, but manifestly do occur, the NCCL should on these grounds support the abolition of capital punishment.

One might also mention, in regard to Northern Ireland (which was autonomous in penal matters and was excluded from the Abolition Act that was passed in 1965) the formation of the 'Association for the Reform of the Law on Capital Punishment in Northern Ireland' in August 1961 after one of the two executions there that year.[148]

Apart from these organized bodies there was an assortment of private individuals who campaigned, some vociferously, but whose influence was very slight. Foremost among these was Mrs Violet van der Elst, a wealthy and colourful eccentric, whose speciality was to demonstrate noisily outside prison gates during executions and who once shouted down the Archbishop of Canterbury from the public gallery while he was giving evidence before the Royal Commission.[149] She was kept at arm's length by the NCACP in the light of her exhibitionism which was probably felt to be potentially detrimental to the cause. Strangely though, Attlee is alleged to have stated to her biographer that: 'she has strong claims to be regarded as the woman who did more than anyone

---

[147] *The Times*, 16th February 1956

[148] 'Ulster on the Tightrope' by Alan Milner (lecturer in law at Queen's University, Belfast), *The Spectator,* 2nd March 1962. He mentions also the formation in September, of something 'unique in the annals of penal retrogression' – A Society for the Retention of Capital Punishment in Northern Ireland. A debate between the two bodies at Queens University led to a victory for the abolitionists by 184-26

[149] Gattey, Charles Neilson, *The Incredible Mrs Van der Elst* (London: Leslie Frewin 1972); Van der Elst, Violet *On The Gallows* (London: Doge Press, 1937)

else to secure the abolition of capital punishment in Britain.'[150]

This is almost certainly mistaken and he may have been over-impressed with her voluble methods. Her campaign began in 1935 and seems to have been inspired by her late husband who was a passionate abolitionist. She felt temperamentally unable to work as part of a team and declined to join either the NCADP or the Howard League whom she regarded as intellectuals who would disapprove of her methods (in which she was probably right). She cast herself in the role of a latter-day suffragette, and her first prison demonstration set the tone for all the others. She drove around in her yellow Rolls Royce, hired a brass band to play the Death March and got a sandwich-board man to parade up and down with placards. She toured the West End inviting signatories to her petition for reprieves. She even hired aeroplanes to fly above the prison. She also started a paper, *Humanity,* to campaign for her cause and in 1937 published *On the Gallows*, a lively indictment of capital punishment, in which she stated her belief that murderers were very often insane, or sex maniacs, or drug-addicted or the victims of poverty and unemployment and that none deserved to die. Moreover, trials were often unfair, she argued, because juries were unqualified to assess these matters. Predictably both the Derek Bentley and Ruth Ellis cases engaged her energies. When the Abolition Bill passed its second reading in March 1956 with her in the public gallery several Labour MPs in the chamber including Jennie Lee stood and applauded her. After the Lords rejection of the Bill she wanted to abolish the Lords. She died in 1966.

Conclusion

The vexed question of capital punishment generated such passion that from the nineteenth century onwards a series of pressure groups emerged to campaign for abolition, culminating in the inception of the NCACP in 1955, led by Gollancz, Koestler, Collins and Gardiner. This was a far more effective body than any of its predecessor organizations had been. It was better funded, better organized, more politically astute, had a higher profile membership, made better use of the media and generated far greater publicity than any of its predecessors, and, though it tended to be prey to internal discord, it was able to crown its efforts with success in the form of the passage of the Death Penalty (Abolition) Act of 1965 which seemed to end hanging for perpetuity. It successfully resisted a series of attempts to resurrect the gallows in 1966, 1969 and on numerous occasions thereafter. Other very small abolition groups and individuals continued to exist and to campaign separately but they were of little significance. The NCACP tended to operate in tandem with the Howard League, a longstanding and highly respected penal reform body that had the ear

---

[150] Gattey, ibid. p.7

of the Home Office, and the two organizations tended to complement each other and to supplement each others efforts, with the League providing the access to officialdom, the resources and the statistics carried over from the older NCADP, and the Campaign providing the mass membership, funding and high profile propaganda. The NCACP also developed very close relations with Parliamentary backbench abolitionists, such as Silverman and Paget, and they were able to co-ordinate their efforts to good effect. It is debatable, however, to what extent the NCACP, for all of its high profile, may be said to be chiefly responsible for the success of the abolition campaign. Ultimately it was only the existence of a large majority for abolition within Parliament (Lords as well as Commons), and a benevolent government willing and able to assist, that the Bill made its way onto the statute book.

CHAPTER 4

THE POLITICAL PARTIES

Crucial to the success of the abolition campaign was, of course, the stance of the political parties. Parties are the vehicles of political change in a democracy, and significant reform can rarely occur without at least one major party putting its weight behind the cause. Hanging was of course a 'non-partisan' issue. Technically this had always been true in the sense that no political party had ever adopted abolition (or retention/restoration) as party policy; it had never been the subject of a pledge in an election manifesto (save for Labour's 1964 promise to 'give time' for a backbench bill and to permit a free vote on the question); and Parliament had nearly always allowed a free vote on the question (at least to backbench MPs). The only real exception to this was the Conservative government's promulgation of the Homicide Act in 1957, but that was a measure to which the Eden government felt itself driven so as to appease the abolitionist majority in the Commons which had been frustrated by the veto of the Lords.

But despite the supposedly non-partisan character of the issue what is striking is the extent to which the division of opinion on hanging in the Commons (and outside) has reflected the party divide. From when the issue first emerged seriously onto the political agenda the Labour and Liberal parties have been largely abolitionist, and latterly overwhelmingly so, whilst the Conservatives have been preponderantly retentionist, initially massively so and latterly by majorities of round about two-to-one. Moreover, the Labour government of 1964 was strongly, if semi-covertly, supportive of abolition to the extent of providing time and assistance to the Silverman bill when it looked to be in trouble, and then putting through the confirmatory votes necessitated by the Act in December 1969. Thus it is necessary to qualify, rather heavily, the traditional view of the question as non-partisan, and to offer instead a modified view of it as a 'quasi-party' issue - one which, whilst the subject of free votes in the Commons, is heavily skewed on party lines. This chapter proceeds to look at each of the major parties in turn and briefly at the more prominent minor parties, and to analyze the balance of opinion within them on the issue, how it developed over time, how it was affected by the views of the party leadership, the party membership, public opinion and the institutions with which they were informally linked, and seeks to produce an ideological map of the parties in terms of capital punishment and other conscience issues.

The Labour Party

Perusal of the division lists reveals consistent differences between the parties. Most obviously the great bulk of abolitionist votes had always come from the Labour side of the House. The Labour Party had been consistently abolitionist and increasingly so over the years, and moved from being predominantly abolitionist in 1948 to being overwhelmingly so by the time of the 1964-65 Bill.

As early as 1927 the party had issued a petition against capital punishment, declaring that: 'Capital punishment revolts the moral sense of the whole community...it is a relic of barbarism which hinders the reform of our whole prison system...Our Movement is almost unanimously ranged against Capital punishment.'[151] Labour members such as Ernest Thurtle were in the forefront of the campaign to abolish the death penalty for desertion, cowardice and other military offences in the armed forces in the 1920s.[152] The MacDonald government of 1929-1931 set up an all-party Select Committee to look into the question, as previously mentioned, and the Labour Party conference of 1934 passed, unopposed, a resolution to abolish the death penalty.[153] It was thus party policy. But Labour party policy is not necessarily Labour government policy. The 1945 Labour manifesto did not make any mention of the issue, and neither did any of the Queen's speeches of the 1945-1951 Parliaments, though Labour abolitionists both inside and outside the House were hopeful that there would be an abolition measure at some point in the life of the government; either a substantive measure or as part of a portmanteau criminal justice bill. The great champion of the cause was a Labour MP, Sydney Silverman, and the former secretary of the *National Committee to Abolish the Death Penalty*, John Paton,

---

[151] Labour Party manifesto on capital punishment, January 1927. Gardiner, Add 56463B. Its signatories included both Ernest Bevin and Herbert Morrison who as Cabinet ministers in the 1945-51 Attlee government voted again the Silverman clause, as well as such names as Margaret Bondfield, H N Brailsford, Fenner Brockway, Arthur Creech Jones, F W Jowett, George Lansbury and Ellen Wilkinson.

[152] McHugh, John, 'The Labour Party and the Parliamentary Campaign to Abolish the Military Death Penalty, 1919-1930' *The Historical Journal*, Vol. 42, No. 1 (March 1999), pp. 233-249. Ernest Thurtle (1884-1954) Labour MP for Shoreditch 1923-31, 1935-50; Shoreditch and Finsbury 1950-54; George Lansbury's son-in-law. Curiously he was one of relatively few Labour members to cast a vote against abolition in a division of 1953.

[153] 'This Conference expresses its conviction that experience in this and other countries, as shown by the evidence submitted to the Select Committee of the House of Commons in 1930, has demonstrated the futility of the Death Penalty. The Conference believes that this punishment is ineffective as a deterrent, and, in its demoralizing effects, gravely prejudicial to social order and security. The Conference therefore urges the next Labour government to give legislative effect to the recommendations of the Select Committee for the Abolition of the Death Penalty for an experimental period of five years.' Labour Party Conference Reports 1934.

was now in the House also in the Labour interest, and there were many known supporters of abolition sitting on the Labour benches. The government had a very large majority, and was indeed the first Labour government to have any sort of overall majority. It was thus not unreasonable for abolitionists to suppose that their hour had come, though their optimism looks in retrospect rather naive.

However, when it came to the crunch, the Attlee government proved hostile to all-out abolition, and when it finally brought forth a criminal justice bill it contained no such provision.[154] Silverman moved an abolition clause at the report stage, much to the government's embarrassment, and the government then proceeded to advise the House against its adoption and, moreover, prohibited ministers and whips from supporting it. Nonetheless, on the vote on the clause in April 1948, it received a majority of twenty-three (245-222) in which there were 216 Labour abolitionists as against only seventy-five retentionists, a split of about 3-1 in favour of abolition.[155]

Furthermore the number of abolitionists was artificially reduced, and possibly the number of retentionists boosted, because of the Attlee government's controversial refusal to allow ministers (and presumably PPSs also) to vote for the clause. Almost certainly a substantial number of the Labour ministerial abstentionists would have voted for abolition had they been permitted to do so. Within the Cabinet, of fourteen members with seats in the Commons, nine voted against the clause (including the big guns Attlee, Bevin, Morrison and Home Secretary Chuter Ede) but five abstained (Stafford Cripps, Aneurin Bevan, Harold Wilson, Philip Noel-Baker and Arthur Creech-Jones). Some of these abstained ostentatiously, and certainly Cripps, Bevan and Wilson were all ardent abolitionists constrained by their Cabinet position. Interestingly these were probably the three most left-wing members of the Cabinet. Remarkable also was the fact that all four of the government's law officers (outside the Cabinet) chose to abstain rather than toe the government line, and indeed absented themselves from the chamber during Chuter Ede's speech deprecating the Silverman clause.[156] Among back-benchers the proportion of abolitionists

---

[154] For a full account of the manoeuvring inside the Attlee government and the PLP see Bailey, Victor, 'The Shadow of the Gallows: The Death Penalty and the British Labour Government 1945-51', *Law and History Review*, vol 18 (no 2), (Summer 2000), pp 305-349

[155] HC Deb, vol 449, cols 1093-1098 (division no 124) 14th April 1948. Figures, as for all divisions cited, include tellers on both sides. Christoph, op cit, gives the figure as 74 Labour retentionists including tellers. The slight discrepancy might be accounted for by the ambiguity of party labels in some cases.

[156] Attorney-General Hartley Shawcross, Solicitor-General Sir Frank Soskice, Lord Advocate John Wheatley and Scottish Solicitor-General Douglas Johnston. They would have been expected, in their official capacity, to sit on the government benches during the debate, and it was hard not to see their absence as a silent token of dissent from the government's anti-abolition position. See Christoph, op cit. Shawcross had been an Allied prosecutor at the Nuremberg trials and in that capacity had pressed for the execution of Nazi war criminals, but that was a special case. Shawcross himself says that he was in unhappy conflict with Attlee

was even larger. Noticeable also was the fact that the two Communists in the House both voted for abolition, as did the former Common Wealth MP Ernest Millington (now in receipt of the Labour whip), most Liberals, the one Irish Nationalist, and several Independents.

By the time of the next vote on the question in July 1953 (with Labour now in opposition) the Labour benches were even more skewed towards abolition. The number of Labour retentionists had shrunk dramatically from seventy five to fifteen, while there were 191 abolitionists.[157] Of course Labour representation in the House was much reduced as a result of the general elections of 1950 and 1951, but the ratio of abolitionists to retentionists within the Parliamentary party had changed from about 3-1 to about 9-1. There is no reason to suppose that Labour MPs who had lost their seats in those two elections, or who had retired, were disproportionately composed of retentionists, nor that the intakes of those elections were disproportionately abolitionist. Thus it followed that many Labour MPs had switched their vote from retention to abolition in the intervening period. One such was Chuter Ede, the former Home Secretary, who had been a supporter of abolition pre-war but then became antipathetic to it once in office and who had now reverted to his former position. Precisely why isn't clear, though, as suggested by Christoph he may have been captured by the 'official' Home Office view whilst in power. He had certainly been affected by the Timothy Evans case in which, as Home Secretary, he had refused a reprieve to a man now found to be almost certainly innocent.

So far as the bulk of the PLP was concerned it may have been that they were simply falling in with what was clearly the overwhelming consensus of their Parliamentary colleagues, and of the party in the country, or that (particularly in the case of former ministers) relieved of the responsibilities of office they were free to pursue and advocate a more 'experimental' course, no longer having to answer for the possible consequences of their votes in the House. Also the tide of events was encouraging the steady growth of abolitionist sentiment in the country, and the fear of alienating voters was perhaps not so acute. Certainly Chuter Ede announced his conversion (in 1956) on the basis of the Evans/Christie cases and his realization that as Home Secretary, in 1950, he had been instrumental in sending an innocent man to the gallows. The Labour front bench in general seemed to have abandoned its former antipathy to abolition by the early to mid 1950s, as evidenced by the various Parliamentary divisions of this period, and by the accession to the leadership of Gaitskell and then Wilson, both ardent abolitionists, in succession to the lukewarm Attlee.

The third post-war Commons vote on the issue came shortly afterwards in

---

and Morrison over the Bill and opposed to their decision to give way to the Lords. Shawcross, Hartley, *Life Sentence: The Memoirs of Lord Shawcross* (London: Constable, 1995) p.167

[157] HC Deb, vol 517, cols 407-418 (division no 209) 1st July 1953

February 1955 (on the report of the Gowers Commission). The Labour pro-hanging vote had dwindled even further to a mere five as against 195 abolitionists.[158] And by the next occasion in February 1956 the balance was three to 241.[159] In March 1956, on the second reading of the Silverman Abolition Bill the balance was eight to 236.[160] On the third reading in June 1956 it was three to 130 in favour of the abolitionists.[161] On the third reading of the Conservative government's Homicide Bill containing the compromise provision for partial abolition, which Labour had decided to oppose, there were only four Labour MPs going into the government lobby, all of them retentionists, as against 129 going into the lobby against the government.[162]

By 1964, and with another large new intake of younger members, the balance had shifted even further, and on the second reading of the new Silverman Abolition Bill only one Labour member voted against, while 268 voted in favour.[163] On the third reading it was 171-0 for abolition.[164] In the 1966 vote on the Sandys Bill to reintroduce hanging for the murder of police and prison officers there was some 'backsliding' in that seventeen Labour members voted for it, though 255 still opposed it, but this may have been a slight aberration in reaction to the public outcry occasioned by the recent murder of police officers.[165] When it came to the 1969 vote required to confirm abolition the former pattern of small and diminishing Labour support for hanging was resumed. Only three Labour members voted against the motion to confirm, as against 279 in favour.[166]

When it came to the various attempts to re-introduce the rope subsequent to 1969 Labour supporters of re-introduction were similarly very thin on the ground though not quite totally extinct. For example, in 1975, in the wake of IRA bombings in London there were only three Labour members for restoration as against 297 against.[167] In 1979 following the return to power of the Conservatives under Margaret Thatcher there were again only three Labour

---

[158] HC Deb, vol 536, cols 2064-2184 (division no 34) 10th February 1955

[159] HC Deb, vol 548, cols 2536-2656 (division no 111) 16th February 1956

[160] HC Deb, vol 550, cols 36-152 (division no 119) 12th March 1956

[161] HC Deb, vol 555, cols 713-840 (division no 250) 28th June 1956

[162] HC Deb, vol 564, cols 454-568 (division no 55) 6th February 1957

[163] HC Deb, vol 704, cols 870-1010 (division no 44) 21st December 1964. The solitary Labour retentionist was Frank Tomney, the very right-wing member for Hammersmith North.

[164] HC Deb, vol 716, cols 358-466 (division no 256) 13th July 1965

[165] HC Deb, vol 736, cols 1409-1418 (division no 208) 23rd November 1966

[166] HC Deb, vol 793, cols 1148-1298 (division no 39) 16th December 1969. The Labour antis were Peter Doig (Dundee West), Jack Dunnett (Nottingham Central) and David Ensor (Bury and Radcliffe) teller for the noes. In addition Desmond Donnelly, MP for Pembroke, who had resigned the Labour whip earlier that year and now sat as an independent, also voted against.

[167] HC Deb, vol 902, cols 663-728 (division no 15) 11th December 1975. The Labour restorationists were Doig and Dunnett again plus Arthur Lewis (West Ham North). The motion was to restore capital punishment for terrorist murder.

MPs for restoration, as against 256 against.[168] There were corresponding imbalances within the Labour ranks in votes on the question in the House of Lords in 1948, 1956, 1964/65 and 1969. This probably reflected, roughly, the balance of opinion among party members in the country (though hard evidence on this point is lacking because pollsters rarely if ever poll grassroots party members) but did not of course reflect the views of the great mass of ordinary Labour voters.

Table 1: Labour Party Voting on Capital Punishment 1948-1979

Vote	Abolitionist	Retentionist	Abstention	Total Labour MPs
1948	216 (54.96)	75 (19.08)	102 (25.95)	393
1953	191 (64.96)	15 (5.10)	88 (29.93)	294
1955	195 (66.32)	5 (1.70)	94 (31.97)	294
1956 (Feb)	241 (87.00)	3 (1.08)	33 (11.91)	277
1956 (March)	236 (85.19)	8 (2.88)	33 (11.91)	277
1964	267 (84.22)	1 (0.31)	49 (15.45)	317
1966	255 (70.44)	17 (4.69)	90 (24.86)	362
1969	279 (80.17)	3 (0.86)	66 (18.96)	348
1973	238 (82.92)	3 (1.04)	46 (16.02)	287
1974	302 (94.67)	3 (0.94)	14 (4.38)	319
1975	297 (93.39)	3 (0.94)	18 (5.66)	318
1979	256 (95.16)	3 (1.11)	10 (3.71)	269

Source: HC Deb. Figures in brackets are the percentages of Labour members voting for or against or abstaining. All figures include tellers on both sides.

It is abundantly clear from the above table that the Labour Party has been consistently and overwhelmingly anti-hanging, at least since the early 1950s if not before, with the number of Labour pro-hangers withering away to very small proportions by the 1960s and dying out completely by the 1980s. Noticeable also was the uniformity of abolitionism across the whole of the party spectrum with the right and centre almost as solidly abolitionist as the left. It was an issue that united the party from Sydney Silverman to Roy Jenkins. Another curiosity is that the process of moving to the right politically often seemed to result in the acquisition of pro-hanging views. For example, both

---

[168] HC Deb, vol 970, cols 2019-2126 (division no 70) 19th July 1979. The three Labour restorationists were Dunnett and Lewis again plus Leslie Spriggs (St Helens). This was the last occasion when a Labour MP went into the division lobby in support of hanging.

Alan Brown and Desmond Donnelly who resigned the Labour whip at different times and subsequently joined the Conservatives voted in a pro-hanging direction afterwards.[169]

It is unlikely that Labour members experienced any sort of pressure from their constituency parties to vote against abolition, unlike in the Conservative Party where there was undoubtedly strong pressure to do so, given that most local Labour Party members would have been likely to have been abolitionist.[170] It is possible that some Labour members voting to restore capital punishment in later years might have come under constituency pressure although there is no evidence of this. On the other hand Labour MPs and candidates certainly faced demands from voters and sometimes representations from local bodies, especially the police, to vote for hanging.[171] But there is again no evidence that these were effective, though it is possible that the relatively large Labour vote for the Sandys motion of 1966 (aiming to restore hanging for the murder of police and prison officers) may have been influenced by these factors in some cases, especially given the recency of the Shepherds Bush murders.[172]

An analysis of the very small number of Labour retentionists from the 1950s onwards is illuminating.[173] It shows that they came almost exclusively from the right of the party, and more particularly the old working class, trade union right. Only William Baxter, who voted for the Sandys motion in 1966, could remotely be characterized as a left-winger.[174] Some, such as Stanley Evans and Frank Tomney were conspicuously right-wing.[175] They were

---

[169] Alan Brown resigned the Labour whip in 1961 over defence and subsequently crossed the floor to join the Conservatives. He voted against raising the minimum age for hanging in 1961 on a party vote. Donnelly resigned the whip in 1968, sitting as an Independent and then forming his own Democratic Party, before joining the Conservatives in 1971. He voted for restoration in 1969, having previously been an abolitionist and a member of the delegation to the Home Secretary that urged a reprieve for Derek Bentley seventeen years previously.

[170] Though data is lacking on the views of constituency party members on this issue and matters in general. Affiliated trade union members were of course a different proposition.

[171] This was certainly so in the case of Stan Newens, successful Labour candidate for Epping in 1964. Interview 9th April 1999.

[172] Six of the seventeen had voted for abolition less than two years previously and four voted for abolition again in 1969.

[173] Those voting for retention in 1948 can be discounted because in many cases they were simply following front bench advice.

[174] He had been deprived of the whip in 1961 for voting against the Defence Estimates along with four other Labour members, including Silverman. Norton, Philip, *Dissension in the House of Commons: Intra-Party Dissent in the House of Commons' Division Lobbies 1945-1974* (London: Macmillan, 1975), pp.160-1; Jackson, Robert J., *Rebels and Whips: An Analysis of Dissension, Discipline and Cohesion in British Political Parties* (London: Macmillan, 1968), pp 180-1; HC Deb vol 636, col 1529-30 (division no 109) 15th March 1961.

[175] Evans had been sacked from the Attlee government for criticizing the 'featherbedding' of industry in 1951 and had been the only Labour pro-Suez rebel. He stepped down in 1956. Tomney was right-wing on most issues.

generally somewhat older than the average for Labour members at the time; seventeen out of the twenty-two who had voted for hanging at one time or another in the 1950s had been born in the nineteenth century, which made them significantly older than the great bulk of Labour MPs at that time who had entered the House in the landslide of 1945, and indeed several of these were veterans who had first been elected in the inter-war period.[176] It is difficult to escape the conclusion that they were pro-hanging, at least partly, out of tradition, having been socialized into a world where the death penalty was taken for granted.

They tended to be northern and often either Nonconformist or Roman Catholic, representing constituencies that were likewise northern and often with a large Nonconformist and/or Roman Catholic population. The influence of the church may have been felt, if not on the MP himself then on his constituents' views and on his perception of those views (much of the church hierarchy then being still fairly hostile to abolition). A majority (though slim) had had no more than elementary education. Most were working class in origins (when it was easier to differentiate the classes) and had had manual occupations and/or were trade union officials. Railwaymen were well represented among them. Very few had been ministers in the Attlee administration nor were to become so in the Wilson governments. The retentionists of the 1950s were an entirely separate group from those of the 1960s, nearly all of them having disappeared from the Commons by 1964.

As mentioned earlier, in 1948 the Labour Cabinet abstainers were chiefly from the left, and members of parties to the left of Labour such as the two Communists and one former Common Wealth member (in the 1945 Parliament) voted abolitionist, as have the smattering of Plaid Cymru, Northern Irish SDLP and Irish nationalists in various subsequent Parliaments. It is apparent that the Labour Party, and the left and centre of British politics in general, has been fiercely and steadfastly abolitionist.

The Conservative Party

More interesting, because more divided, is the case of the Conservative Party. Here the pattern is to some extent the opposite of that of Labour. The Conservatives have always been predominantly pro-hanging, with the abolitionist element an initially small but steadily growing minority within the party, though the Tory abolitionists have been, at least after 1948, a somewhat larger minority within their party than the Labour retentionists within theirs, and have tended to be a growing minority rather than a diminishing one.

---

[176] HC Deb, op cit.; Stenton, Michael and Stephen Lees, *Who's Who of British Members of Parliament, vol IV* (1945-1979) (Sussex: Harvester Press, 1981)

In 1948 there were sixteen Conservative supporters of the Silverman clause (including as Conservatives the National Liberals who were by then indistinguishable from them and the Ulster Unionists who then still took the Conservative whip), as against 145 Conservatives and allies who were against.[177] In the 1953 vote there were only four Conservative abolitionists as against 241 retentionists, superficially indicating that support for abolition was ebbing away within Tory ranks.[178] But by the 1955 vote they had rallied with seventeen abolitionists as against 239 retentionists.[179] And by 1956, reinforced by a new intake of younger members at the 1955 general election who were believed to be rather more liberal then their predecessors, their numbers had risen dramatically to forty-nine as against 245 retentionists.[180] They were now about a sixth of the party's strength in the Commons. In March 1956, on the second reading of the Silverman Bill they had stayed solid at forty-seven to 254.[181] On the third reading, with a reduced turnout, the figures were 20-130, a roughly similar balance.[182]

With the defeat of the Silverman Bill in the Lords, however, and the introduction of the Conservative government's Homicide Bill in the next session as a compromise the position changed. Whereas the Labour abolitionists were antagonistic to the Bill the Tory abolitionists by contrast fell in with the government's wishes, undoubtedly having been subject to strong pressure from the whips, and in some cases from their constituency parties (especially Nigel Nicolson at Bournemouth).[183] In the third reading on the Homicide Bill not a single Tory abolitionist joined the Labour Party in the no lobby, much to the disgust and chagrin of the Labour abolitionists, who felt that they had betrayed their principles.[184] But the Tory abolitionists may have felt, at least in some cases, that partial abolition would pave the way for greater public acceptance of full abolition at some time in the future whereas complete abolition there and then might have caused a popular backlash. Abolition in two stages may have been preferable to one.

By 1964 the ranks of the Tory abolitionists had swelled further, again with the infusion of a younger and perhaps more liberal generation of members in the recent election, and the party split almost exactly two-to-one (counting those who voted) for the new Silverman Bill on the second reading; eighty for the Bill and 168 against.[185] On the third reading it was twenty-three for the Bill

---

[177] HC Deb, vol 449, cols 1093-1098, 14th April 1948.

[178] HC Deb, vol 517, cols 407-418 (division no 209) 1st July 1953.

[179] HC Deb, vol 536, cols 2064-2184 (division no 34) 10th February 1955.

[180] HC Deb, vol 548, cols 2536-2656 (division no 111) 16th February 1956.

[181] HC Deb, vol 550, cols 36-152 (division no 119) 12th March 1956.

[182] HC Deb, vol 555, cols 713-840 (division no 250) 28th June 1956.

[183] Nicolson, Nigel, op cit; Martin, Laurence W, 'The Bournemouth Affair: Britain's First Primary Election', *The Journal of Politics*, vol 22 (no 4) (November 1960), pp. 654-681

[184] HC Deb, vol 564, cols 454-568 (division no. 55) 6th February 1957.

[185] HC Deb, vol 704, cols 870-1010 (division no 44) 21st December 1964.

and ninety-eight against.[186] In the 1969 vote the balance altered somewhat in the opposite direction with fifty voting to make abolition permanent and 180 voting against.[187] Doubtless quite a number of the Tories who had voted for abolition in 1964/1965 had done so on an experimental basis, and were now reverting to type in the light of evidence they may have regarded as indicating the failure of the experiment, though strong constituency pressures undoubtedly played a role in some cases. It is noticeable that on all of the votes up to 1969 there was a large contingent of abstainers, and though many of these would have been unavoidably absent, paired or simply undecided, it is not too fanciful to speculate that they included a substantial contingent of abolitionist inclined members who were fearful of upsetting their local parties but equally could not bring themselves to vote for hanging. At any rate it is likely that there were more abolitionists than retentionists among the abstainers.

Later votes saw a further slight tilt away from abolitionism with, in 1975 for example, the split being 47-214, reflecting probably a reaction to the rise of terrorism.[188] But by the time of the 1979 vote the abolitionists had risen again to the levels of 1964 and higher with 92 as against 227.[189] This rough balance of opinion within the party was maintained into the 1980s and 1990s until the debate finally fizzled out.

Table 2: Conservative Party Voting on Capital Punishment (1948-1979)

Year	Abolitionist		Retentionist		Non-voting		Total Con MPs
1948	17	(7.83)	146	(67.28)	54	(24.88)	217
1953	4	(1.24)	243	(75.46)	75	(23.29)	322
1955	18	(5.59)	241	(74.84)	63	(19.56)	322
1956 (Feb)	49	(14.24)	245	(71.22)	50	(14.53)	344
1964	81	(26.64)	170	(55.92)	53	(17.43)	304
1966	30	(11.85)	154	(60.86)	69	(27.27)	253
1969	53	(20.00)	181	(68.30)	31	(11.69)	265
1975	48	(17.26)	216	(77.69)	14	(5.03)	278
1979	93	(27.43)	229	(67.55)	17	(5.01)	339
1983	141	(35.51)	212	(53.40)	44	(11.08)	397

Note: Figures in brackets are the percentages of the total number of Conservative MPs. Conservative includes National Liberal and Ulster Unionist up to 1969, but for votes thereafter Ulster Unionists are excluded. The 1956 vote is the abolitionist motion of February. The voting on the second reading of the consequent abolition bill a month later was almost identical. All figures include tellers for both sides.
Source: HC Deb

As with the Labour Party the balance of Conservative opinion in the House of Commons was echoed in the Lords, though of course the picture was somewhat confused by the huge number of non-voting Tory hereditary peers

[186] HC Deb, vol 716, cols 358-466 (division no 256) 13th July 1965.
[187] HC Deb, vol 793, cols 1148-1298 (division no 39) 16th December 1969.
[188] HC Deb, vol 902, cols 663-728 (division no 15) 11th December 1975.
[189] HC Deb, vol 970, cols 2019-2126 (division no 70) 19th July 1979.

whose views were unknown and whose votes and presence in the chamber were a rarity.[190] So far as the Tory Party in the country was concerned there was an overwhelming majority against abolition, as attested to by several party conference debates, especially that at Llandudno in 1956 in the immediate wake of the first Silverman Bill. In his speech to the conference Home Secretary Gwilym Lloyd George was anxious to assert his pro-hanging credentials:-

> As the minister responsible for the maintenance of law and order in this country, I felt it my duty at the time when the Bill was before the House to urge the House to vote against abolition. My advice was not taken, but my belief that it would be a grave mistake to abolish capital punishment has not been altered.[191]

Conference resolved by an overwhelming majority: 'That this conference emphatically opposes the terms of the Death Penalty (Abolition) Bill but urges that the law of murder be amended so as to limit the imposition of the death penalty.'

The strength of feeling among grass-roots Conservative may be gauged also by the tone of the letters that flooded into Conservative Central Office around this time. Typical was that from a lady in Worthing who complained of the recent failure to hang two child murderers and talked of: 'Sloppy Home Secretaries reprieving every murderer.' and said that the public would have to 'take steps'. The birch should not have been abolished nor flogging for robbery, she went on, and for good measure she advocated castration for sex offenders and hanging for all murderers over the age of sixteen.[192] The Conservative Women's Annual Conference passed an emergency resolution by a large majority saying that it:-

> ...welcomes the amendment to the capital punishment bill [sic] which provides for the retention of the death penalty in certain circumstances...urges Conservative MPs to continue efforts...that adequate attention may be given to the views of the many women who are strongly opposed to the total abolition of the death penalty.[193]

---

[190] See Bromhead, P A, *The House of Lords and Contemporary Politics 1911-1957* (London: Routledge and Kegan Paul, 1958); and Morgan, Janet P, *The House of Lords and the Labour Government 1964-1970* (Oxford: Clarendon Press 1975). Morgan, (p.2) estimates that, in mid-1968, there were 116 Labour peers, 351 Conservative peers, 41 Liberal peers and 554 peers taking no whip, based on *Lords Reform*, Cmnd 3799, November 1968. The 554 whipless peers may have been largely Conservative by inclination but that gave no indication as to the likelihood or the direction of their voting on conscience issues.

[191] Conservative Party Conference Report, Llandudno, 12th October 1956.

[192] Conservative Party Archives, (The Bodleian Library, Oxford University) CCO 4/7/21. Mrs Blanchard to Lord Hailsham, 26th October 1957.

[193] Conservative Party Archives, ibid. CCO 4/7/21, undated.

The intensity of grass-roots feeling against some Tory abolitionists for ignoring their constituents' views is typified in a letter from a Gravesend Borough Councillor, who deprecated his MP's abolitionist stance (Peter Kirk being the offending member): 'I think it is regrettable that he should have added his name to any proposal without consulting his supporters.'[194] Another correspondent deprecated the Tory abolitionists: '..morning of disillusionment for many of us who have believed that Conservatives had the courage to put their public duty above all...cowardly self-appeasement at the expense of the community.'[195] The government's Homicide Bill did not receive a warm welcome from some correspondents either. An anonymous writer from Bury St Edmund's characterized it as the 'Murderer's Protection Bill' and asked if they were surprised at recent by-election results: '...your Tory government has passed a bill making it illegal to hang a diabolical murderer – right against public opinion – will not vote for you again.'[196]

Thus the Parliamentary party was considerably more abolitionist than the rank and file. The Conservative Party supplied nearly all of the chief Parliamentary campaigners opposed to abolition prior to 1965 such as Sir Thomas Moore, Brigadier Terence Clarke and Cyril Osborne, and nearly all the leading Parliamentarians who agitated for restoration after 1965 such as Duncan Sandys, Peter Rawlinson, Eldon Griffiths, Teddy Taylor and Jill Knight.

It is largely unsurprising that the Conservatives should have been so hostile to abolition given that they were the party of law and order and of custom and tradition, all of which might predispose them to prefer the retention of hanging. On the other hand there was nothing in Tory history and philosophy that expressly mandated support for the death penalty (just as there was nothing in Labour's ideology to mandate the opposite), and a significant minority of the party's MPs has been consistently abolitionist, notwithstanding considerable pressure, in some cases, from their constituency parties to modify or abrogate their stance.[197] Nigel Nicolson (Bournemouth), Sir Edward Boyle (Birmingham, Handsworth), Montgomery Hyde (North Belfast), Sir Frank Medlicott (Norfolk East) and Humphry Berkeley (Lancaster) are all members who at one time or another experienced difficulties with their constituency parties which derived, at least in part, from their stance on hanging; though in all of these cases, and most

---

[194] Conservative Party Archives, ibid. CCO 4/7/21, Denis A Ford to party chairman, 16th February 1956

[195] Conservative Party Archives, ibid. CCO 4/7/21, Dr G C Steel, SW15, to Central Office, 17th February 1956.

[196] Conservative Party Archives, ibid. CCO 4/7/21, anon to Central Office, 23rd March 1957

[197] See Jackson, R J, op cit; Nicolson, Nigel, op cit. In addition to the notorious Nicolson case there were other less heralded instances of constituency pressure being exerted on abolitionist Tories, sometimes successfully. Shirley Williams (Lady Williams of Crosby) feels that Edward Boyle was hounded out of politics because of his abolitionism. Interview 10th May 2007.

other such, it was compounded by other offences. In fact abolitionist votes were usually a minor count on the indictment against them and it was some other offence that formed the main count; Suez in the case of Nicolson, Boyle and Medlicott. For Hyde though, who was a *pro-Suez* rebel, it was chiefly hanging that brought him into conflict with his constituency party and led to his de-selection in 1959, and for Berkeley it was chiefly his support for homosexual law reform that enraged some of his constituents and may have led to defeat in the 1966 general election.[198]

On the other hand there were several abolitionists among the pro-Suez group who were generally on the right of the party and there is no evidence that they experienced any constituency pressure (apart from Hyde). Thus it seems that abolitionist voting was usually tolerated where the member was fundamentally 'sound', but was a convenient stick with which to beat a member when he was already 'suspect'.

It is intriguing to analyze the divisions within the party on this issue, given its totemic significance to the Tory party, and to speculate on what influenced a member's attitude. Much analysis has been devoted to the question based on a range of variables which indicates that age and religion may have been slight factors influencing opinion, but none have really attempted to analyse the effects of ideology.[199]

Given that the Labour Party was strongly abolitionist and given also the apparent left-right orientation of the divide it might have been expected that Conservative abolitionists would have come chiefly, if not exclusively, from the left or inner wing of the party - that is to say the wing that was closer to the Labour Party on issues in general. Yet curiously this isn't entirely borne out by the division lists, which have shown a fair number of right-wing Conservatives voting for abolition and some left-wing ones for retention. For example, several Suez rebels (from the right-wing pro-imperial Suez Group) such as Angus Maude and Hinchingbrooke were in the abolitionist camp in 1956-57, and the most definitively right-wing MP of recent times, Enoch Powell, had since 1955 been a consistent supporter of abolition (and opponent of restoration).[200]

---

[198] Berkeley, Humphry, *Crossing the Floor* (London: Allen and Unwin, 1972). He states (p.18) that he had had much more trouble from his constituency party than from the whips over his stance on many issues; including abolition, his introduction of a Homosexual Reform Bill in 1966 and his views on Africa (none of which necessarily put him at odds with the party leadership). At a public meeting in his Lancaster constituency a member of the City Council asked him what would be done with all the released murderers who would have hanged, and flatly refused to believe that only six had hanged in the previous three years (p.126).

[199] See Richards, Peter G, *Parliament and Conscience* (London: Allen and Unwin, 1970) pp. 179-96

[200] Heffer, Simon, *Like the Roman: The Life of Enoch Powell* (London: Weidenfeld and Nicolson, 1998), p.380, p.539, pp.664-5, p.776. See also Roth, Andrew, *Enoch Powell: Tory Tribune* (London: Macdonald, 1970) and Shepherd, Robert, *Enoch Powell: A Biography*

Conversely, Reginald Maudling, one of the most left-wing Tories on most questions, was consistently a supporter of hanging.

This may of course reflect the fact that it is notoriously more difficult to assign MPs reliably to the left or right of the Conservative Party than it is to do likewise in the Labour Party. The Conservatives have often been described as a party of tendencies rather than factions.[201] It might be more accurate to refer to a 'foreign policy right-wing', an 'economic policy right-wing' and a 'social/penal policy right-wing', which may be overlapping but not identical. One might therefore suppose that the abolitionists would have come from the 'social policy left' of the party and to have been likely to support other liberal measures such as homosexual law reform, the legalization of abortion and the relaxation of the divorce laws (which seems to have been the case) without necessarily taking up leftish positions on economics or foreign policy.[202] It may also conceal the fact that Conservative MPs may have had very different reasons from each other, and from their Labour counterparts, for favouring abolition. An exceptional case was that of Julian Amery, a consistent abolitionist, whose brother, John, had been hanged as a traitor in 1946.[203] Was this the source of his hostility to hanging?

To analyze this further it would be desirable to have a measure of where a Conservative MP stood in the party spectrum and to which, if any, ideological camp he belonged, but this is a notoriously difficult and chimerical exercise. It is well documented that there are 'liberal' Tories who tend to vote fairly consistently for measures of social and penal reform.[204] But there is little

---

(London: Hutchinson, 1996)

[201] Rose, Richard, 'Parties, factions and tendencies in Britain' *Political Studies*, vol XII (1) 1964, pp. 33-46. Tendencies constitute 'fluctuating alignments on specific issues' whereas factions represent 'a group of individuals who seek to further a broad range of policies through consciously organized political activity'. By contrast the Labour Party had a very consistent left-wing faction that was disaffected over a whole range of issues, both foreign and domestic.

[202] Richards, P G, op cit.

[203] West, Rebecca, *The Meaning of Treason* (London: Virago, 1982); Rubinstein, William D 'The Secret of Leopold Amery', *History Today*, Vol 49 (2), February 1999 pp.17-23; Weale, Adrian, *Patriot Traitors: Roger Casement, John Amery and the Real Meaning of Treason* (London: Viking, 2001); Faber, David, *Speaking for England: Leo, Julian and John Amery – The Tragedy of a Political Family* (London: Free Press, 2005). This was an extraordinary saga. John Amery was the elder son of the war-time Secretary of State for India, and long-time ardent imperialist politician, Leo Amery. A fascist sympathizer, John Amery was convicted after the war of treason chiefly for having attempted to recruit British and Allied prisoners-of-war into an autonomous 'Legion of St George' to fight alongside Nazi Germany against Soviet Russia. Even more bizarre is the fact that, as revealed by Rubinstein, Leo Amery was a closet half-Jew, and John could scarcely have been unaware of his ancestry.

[204] See for example:- Hibbing, John R and David Marsh, 'Accounting for the Voting Patterns of British MPs on Free Votes', *Legislative Studies Quarterly*, vol 12 (no 2) (May 1987), pp. 275-297; Read, Melvyn, David Marsh and David Richards, 'Why Do They Do It? Voting on

evidence of these 'liberals' voting a consistent 'left' ticket on other issues. Of course on most mainstream issues of an economic, industrial or foreign policy nature the whips would have been on and so differences would not have shown up, unless there was a backbench revolt. But it is just such a revolt that may give indicators as to a Conservative MP's general ideological position. Another such indicator is the Early Day Motion (EDM) but these are numerous, and often uninformative as to whether a signatory is genuinely in support of the motion.[205] A third indicator is membership of an ideological group within the party, such as the Bow Group, the One Nation Group, the Monday Club and the Suez Group, the chief such ginger groups within the party at the relevant time.[206] Again membership is not always easy to ascertain, sometimes fairly nebulous, and also possibly misleading. Though the Bow Group has always had the reputation of being on the left of the party there are some members who clearly belong to the right on some issues and a few MPs such as Geoffrey Rippon have been members of both the Bow Group and the Monday Club. Likewise the One Nation Group, also impliedly leftist, contained some right-wing members such as Enoch Powell and Angus Maude, the former also a member of the Suez Group.

Early attempts to map the ideological contours of the party were made by Berrington, in the early 1960s, based chiefly upon EDMs as well as votes.[207] He noted that not only were revolts less common in the Tory Party by comparison with Labour, but that they differed in scope and nature. From 1955 to 1961 there had been three major crises of disunity within the party:- over abolition in 1956, Suez 1956 and Northern Rhodesia in 1961. However, the rebels on each

---

Homosexuality and Capital Punishment in the House of Commons', *Parliamentary Affairs*, vol 47 (1994), pp. 374-386; Pattie, Charles, Edward Fieldhouse and R J Johnston, 'The Price of Conscience: The Electoral Correlates and Consequences of Free Votes and Rebellions in the British House of Commons, 1987-92',*British Journal of Political Science*, vol 24 (3) (1994), pp. 359-380; Mughan, Anthony and Roger M Scully, 'Accounting for Change in Free Vote Outcomes in the House of Commons', *British Journal of Political Science*, vol 27 (4) (1997) pp. 640-647; Cowley, Philip and Mark Stuart, 'Sodomy, Slaughter, Sunday Shopping and Seatbelts: Free Votes in the House of Commons, 1979-1996' *Party Politics*, vol 3 (no 1) 1997, pp. 119-130

[205] See Franklin, Mark N and Michael Tappin, 'Early Day Motions as Unobtrusive Measures of Backbench Opinion in Britain', *British Journal of Political Science*, vol 7 (1), (1977), pp. 49-69

[206] Critchley, Julian, 'The Intellectuals', *Political Quarterly*, vol 32, 1961, pp. 267-274 gives an account of the Conservative Political Centre, the Bow Group and the One Nation Group and their activities and influence within the Conservative Party.

[207] Berrington, Hugh, 'The Conservative Party: Revolts and Pressures 1955-1961', *Political Quarterly*, vol 32 (1961) pp. 363-373. See also: - Finer, S, H B Berrington and D J Bartholomew, *Backbench Opinion in the House of Commons, 1955-59* (London: Pergamon, 1961); Berrington, Hugh, *Backbench Opinion in the House of Commons, 1945-55* (London: Pergamon, 1973); Norton, Philip, *Conservative Dissidents: Dissent within the Parliamentary Conservative Party, 1970-74* (London: Temple Smith, 1978).

of these issues were not altogether the same people. Berrington noted that the forty-eight Conservatives who voted for abolition in 1956 were a very mixed bag who formed an *ad hoc* coalition, and that there was very little correlation with how they had voted over the Suez crisis, the Rhodesia revolt and corporal punishment in 1961. In regard to Suez, there was only a slight tendency for the abolitionists to be more left, in terms of motions signed, than for backbenchers in general. There was the same proportion of abolitionists among what he termed the 'extreme right' (15%) as among backbenchers generally. In regard to Northern Rhodesia and the Turton motion of February 1961 (regarded as critical of Colonial Secretary Macleod and his attempt to impose black majority rule) there was again very little difference in the attitude of the abolitionists and the backbenches generally, with the former only slightly less sympathetic than the whole party to the motion. Even in regard to the associated question of corporal punishment where one would reasonably have expected abolitionists to be noticeably more liberal than their retentionist colleagues there was no significant difference between the reaction of the abolitionists and the party generally. On the amendment to the Criminal Justice Bill proposing the retention of corporal punishment (April 1961) 22% of abolitionists supported it as against 28% of the backbenches generally, and 31% opposed it as against 28% of the backbenches generally. Apparently hangers are not always floggers and anti-hangers not always anti-floggers!

As Berrington comments it would be difficult to find better evidence of the very specific character of Conservative rebellions. Though he went on to argue that there were signs of a consistent right-wing faction emerging in that the Rhodesia rebels overlapped substantially with the Common Market dissidents, and to a lesser extent with the birching rebels, he felt that this may have been exceptional. Moreover he found little or no evidence of the rebel or dissident groups being identifiable by any of the obvious factors such as age, social class, occupational or educational background, type of constituency, etc, with the exception of the younger members tending to be more liberal on penal reform, as already noted. But as Berrington presciently observed the European question (the Common Market) seemed to bear the hallmarks of an issue capable of splitting the party, though subsequent Conservative divisions over Europe (by far the most deep and numerous) have borne little or no relationship to divisions over capital punishment or other policy areas.

Later and more sophisticated attempts to analyze the ideological structure of the party have tended to argue for the emergence of factions but based on two or even three dimensions of policy. Baker, Gamble and Ludlam (1993), for example, argue that simple left/right categories have never made much sense in the context of the Conservative Party and offer instead a two-dimensional analysis in which the party's MPs are arrayed on European integrationism versus nationalism in the foreign policy sphere and interventionism versus *laissez faire* in the economic; dimensions which are very largely independent of each other.[208] Thus their analysis yields four ideological quadrants in which, for example, Margaret Thatcher and Norman Lamont appear in the nationalist, *laissez faire* quadrant; Nigel Lawson and John Major in the Europeanist, *laissez faire*; Kenneth Baker and Alan Clark in the nationalist, interventionist; and Edward Heath and Michael Heseltine in the Europeanist and interventionist. It is a more satisfying topology of the party than a conventional left-right one though many MPs would be hard to place within this framework, and there is probably rather more of a tendency for the pro-Europeans to be economic interventionists than the authors allow. The analysis was of course based on the party of the early 1990s but was clearly intended to be applicable to earlier (and later) eras. Though the authors do not touch on the matter, since they are concerned pre-eminently with Europe, there is no reason to suppose that either of their hypothesized dimensions correlates with opinion on capital punishment or any social/penal question.

Another and even more recent analysis by Heppell (2002) utilizes three dimensions, essentially taking the foreign and economic policy dimensions of Baker *et al* and adding a third.[209] He postulates, following Cowley and Garry (1998), that the party can be ideologically configured in terms of economic policy (extended state versus limited state), European policy (pro-European versus Eurosceptic), and what he designates 'social/sexual/moral policy' (social liberals versus social conservatives).[210] He deploys data derived from division lists, EDMs signed, membership of party groups and public and private comments to ascertain MPs positions. His index on social, sexual and moral conservatism develops the 'Read and Marsh index' based on voting on capital punishment, abortion, homosexuality and divorce, so as to include another seven moral issues:- corporal punishment, immigration, identity cards, embryo research, voluntary euthanasia, the ordination of women priests and Sunday trading.[211] His typology yields eight different categories of Conservative MP, based on the different combinations of the three variables, to which all Conservative members of the 1992 House of Commons are assigned. Thus Michael Heseltine and Edward Heath, for example, appear as 'extended state, pro-European social liberals'; and Michael Howard and Michael Portillo are

---

[208] Baker, David, Andrew Gamble and Steve Ludlam, 1846...1906...1996? 'Conservative Splits and European Integration', *Political Quarterly*, vol 64 (1993), pp 420-434. Their terminology is slightly different but amounts to the same thing.

[209] Heppell, Timothy, 'The Ideological Composition of the Parliamentary Conservative Party 1992-97', *British Journal of Politics and International Relations*, vol 4, no 2, June 2002, pp. 299-324. See also the reply to this: Cowley, Philip and Philip Norton, 'What a ridiculous thing to say! (which is why we didn't say it): a response to Timothy Heppell', ibid, pp. 325-329.

[210] Cowley, Philip and J Garry, 'The British Conservative Party and Europe: the choosing of John Major', *British Journal of Political Science*, vol 28 (1998) pp. 473-499.

[211] Read, M and D Marsh, 'The Family Law Bill: Conservative Party splits and Labour Party cohesion', *Parliamentary Affairs*, vol 50 (1997), pp. 263-279

'limited state, anti-European social conservatives' (by far the largest category).[212]

As with Baker *et al* the analysis is peculiar to that Parliament but is clearly intended to be applicable to the party in previous and later periods. The third dimension identified by Heppell is far and away the most significant from the point of view of predicting attitude towards capital punishment which is of course a primary component of the index. Heppell's index identifies 101 'social liberals' and 230 'social conservatives'; i.e. a split of rather more than two-to-one in favour of the social conservatives - reflecting very roughly the balance of opinion at various times over capital punishment. Of course not every MP classified as a social liberal was always in the abolitionist lobby, but the great majority of those in the social conservative category would invariably have been in the pro-hanging lobby given that this was a touchstone issue of social conservatism.

Examining all the evidence of votes on capital punishment and other moral issues, and mainstream party issues, both free and whipped, as well as membership of party ginger groups, no clear picture emerges of the typical abolitionist Tory (or the typical retentionist). There is some evidence that the abolitionist is more left-wing than the retentionist, particularly if one looks at dissenting votes on mainstream issues of both a domestic and international character, but it is far from conclusive. And it is in any case often extremely difficult to place a Tory MP as being on the left or right, or to say what stance on any given issue is left or right. It is clear that within the Conservative Party it was very difficult to predict which MPs would swing which way on capital punishment; a function both of the complex ideological structure of the party and of the 'stand-alone' nature of the hanging issue itself.

The Liberal Party and minor parties

The Liberal Party has since 1945 been generally abolitionist, with the majority of its very small number of MPs going into the anti-hanging lobby in each of the major votes on the issue from 1948 onwards. It voted 7-0 for abolition in 1948, when it had twelve MPs, and in the 1950s when it was down to a mere six MPs only the then leader, Clement Davies, recorded a vote for retention in 1953, while the party voted 5-0 for abolition in the votes of 1955 and 1956. All its MPs opposed the relevant provisions of the Homicide Bill in 1957, and the new leader, Jo Grimond, protested that the Bill was 'a curious compromise between right and wrong' and merely a device for the suppression

---

[212] There are two additional categories based on those who were 'agnostic' on Europe and economics, which somewhat surprisingly includes John Major - who might have been regarded as embattled rather than agnostic.

of the Silverman Bill.[213]

In 1964 on the second reading of the Silverman bill they voted 8-1 for abolition and in 1969 on the confirmatory vote 10-2 against restoration. Alasdair Mackenzie (MP for Ross and Cromarty 1964-70) was the solitary Liberal retentionist in 1964, and only he and Wallace Lawler (Birmingham, Ladywood) among Liberals voted for hanging in 1969. Mackenzie was a supporter of the Sandys campaign to reinstate the death penalty for the murder of police and prison officers in 1966. Generally to the right of his Liberal colleagues on most issues this further reinforces the picture of the left-right orientation of the capital punishment debate. Lawler's was a perverse vote registering a protest against Home Secretary Callaghan's 'failure to offer a proper alternative', because he was in principle an abolitionist and said that had the vote looked like being close he would have abstained.[214] Peter Bessell (Bodmin), who had been a qualified retentionist, voted for abolition because he did not want to go back to the Homicide Act. After 1970 the party remained very strongly abolitionist, though a few MPs voted the other way in votes in the 1970s.[215] By 1975 the Party Council issued a statement that regretted the repeated calls for the re-introduction of capital and corporal punishment and, in anticipation of later developments, called for the new European Parliament to draw up a declaration on 'Basic Human and Civil Rights' to be ratified by member states which should make clear its opposition to the death penalty.[216]

By the mid-1950s it would be fair to say that the party was overwhelmingly abolitionist in the tenor of its pronouncements. The Liberal Party Council, the governing body of the extra-parliamentary party, resolved in September 1955, as the controversy was building, that the party should:-

> give a lead to enlightened public opinion by firmly declaring its opposition to the continuance of capital punishment in this country. It welcomes the findings of the recent Royal Commission that capital punishment is not the only effective deterrent for the crime of murder and that no increase in the murder rate has resulted in any of the countries which, for years, have lived without it. It urges the Party Executive and the Parliamentary Liberal Party to do everything in their power to secure the early removal of the death penalty from the Statute Book.[217]

---

[213] Liberal Party Papers (LSE), file 16/20/22, Information Department paper, November 1961

[214] Liberal News, no 1072, 23rd December 1969

[215] After 1970 only three Liberal MPs ever voted for restoration: - Cyril Smith (Rochdale), consistently, Stephen Ross (Isle of Wight) and David Penhaligon (Truro). Penhaligon was a curious case in that he had entered Liberal politics partly out of opposition to hanging (he had given evidence for the defence in the trial of Pascoe and Whitty in 1963), but voted for it on one occasion in 1975.

[216] Liberal Party Papers (LSE), file 16/21/133, briefing paper, 26th June 1979

[217] The Times, 26th September 1955

At a joint debate of the National Liberal Club and the Eighty Club (also a Liberal club) in February 1956 an abolitionist motion was carried by 64-26, with Gardiner and Basil Wigoder speaking for the motion and Tudor Price against.[218] This was not, however, binding on members of the Parliamentary Party, and in later years there were occasional votes registered for the return of capital punishment by Liberal MPs, and there was always a free vote on the matter, as with the other parties.

The party's full conversion to the abolitionist cause was trumpeted by an editorial in its chief organ, *Liberal News*, of 2nd March 1956, which urged that the party should put its weight behind the Silverman Bill and expressed the hope that there would be a free vote in all parties and that there would be no pressure on Conservative MPs behind the scenes.[219] It also argued that there must be a full opportunity to overcome constitutionally the opposition of the Lords, which implied the use of the Parliament Act, and insisted on a moratorium on hangings while the legislation passed. The editorial recognized, however, that there were different opinions within the party, and that it would be wrong to attempt to bind all members to an abolitionist stance. A further editorial of July 1956, after the Lords' rejection of the Bill, underlined the party's stance by recording with approval the large number of Liberal peers who had voted for the Bill, and reiterated that there must be no more hangings. The former leader Lord Samuel, it noted, had abstained on the vote but had proposed an extension of the Home Secretary's power of reprieve, whilst Lord Rea (Liberal leader in the Lords) and Lords Sherwood, Moynihan, Russell of Liverpool and Layton had all spoken and voted in favour of the Bill.[220] Generally Liberal peers followed their brethren in the Commons and voted for abolition. Samuel, as a cautious and unenthusiastic retentionist, was untypical but belonged to a much earlier and rather different generation of Liberals which had matured in the nineteenth century.[221]

Liberal party members, Liberal organizations and Liberal supporters in the country were generally also abolitionist. A Young Liberal meeting of 1962, for example, voted overwhelmingly for abolition.[222] Liberals, or Liberal supporters, were often prominent in the frontline of the capital punishment debate. In addition to Thorpe's activities on the NCACP, Ludovic Kennedy, broadcaster and journalist and Liberal Parliamentary candidate (for Rochdale in 1958) was a prominent supporter of abolition and a leading campaigner for a posthumous pardon for Timothy Evans about whose case he had written a highly influential book.

---

[218] *The Times*, 10th February 1956
[219] *Liberal News*, no. 508, 2nd March 1956, 'There Must Be No More Hanging' (editorial)
[220] *Liberal News*, 20th July 1956, 'No More Hanging' (editorial)
[221] Herbert Louis Samuel, 1st Viscount Samuel (1870-1963). Liberal Party leader 1931-5, Liberal Party leader in the House of Lords 1944-55
[222] *Liberal News*, 17th March 1962, 'End Hanging Debate' (news item)

Party documents rarely touched on the subject given its 'conscience issue' status, though a 1966 Liberal Party pamphlet dealing with legal reform briefly recapitulated the party's attitude towards hanging by pointing out that all Liberal members present had voted for the third reading of the Silverman abolition bill in 1965, and all had, at the time, opposed the distinctions introduced by the Homicide Act, 1957.[223] It went on to quote approvingly the words of Emlyn Hooson, Liberal MP for Montgomeryshire and home affairs spokesman, during the third reading debate, that: 'Let us get rid of all the cant and hypocrisy about the deterrent. The only genuine argument in favour of hanging is retribution...while that is the only genuine argument in favour of the retention of the death penalty, I suggest that in a civilised community its retention on this ground cannot be tolerated.' The document went on to criticize the Tory Home Secretaries Butler and Brooke for failing to review the working of the Homicide Act and for taking no notice of the Home Office's own Research Unit report of 1961.

Following a Council resolution of 1965 the party conference in Scarborough that year, after an impassioned speech by Ludovic Kennedy, resolved in favour of calling upon the Home Secretary to institute a new enquiry into the Timothy Evans case and to grant a posthumous free pardon if there was any doubt about his guilt.[224]

In that respect the Liberal Party was very similar to Labour in the pattern of its voting, illustrating that on social issues the Liberals were as 'liberal' as Labour if not more so (unsurprisingly). Moreover, its leadership from the mid-1950s onwards in the form of Jo Grimond (1956-1967), Jeremy Thorpe (1967-1976) and David Steel (1976-1987) was consistently abolitionist. Thorpe in fact was a member of the Executive Committee of the NCACP from the late 1950s onwards and a prominent abolitionist, and both Grimond and Steel were strong and consistent abolitionists as manifested both by their votes and utterances in the Commons and elsewhere, and would have set the tone for the rest of the party in that respect. Grimond in 1961 firmly declared himself opposed to both capital and corporal punishment as barbaric and ineffective deterrents.

Other, more minor, political parties were of very little moment as regards the capital punishment issue given their negligible, or non-existent, representation in Parliament at the relevant times, and the general lack of policy statements issuing from them on the question. So far as parties to the left of Labour were concerned the Communist Party (and other socialist or Marxist parties) were usually abolitionist, certainly so far as the inclinations of its supporters were concerned, and indeed the two Communist members in the Commons between 1945 and 1950 voted for the 1948 abolition clause, as did

---

[223] Liberal Party Papers (LSE), file 16/19/1 - Law and Order pamphlet, March 1966.
[224] Liberal Party Papers (LSE), file 16/19/4, Council minutes 27th February 1965. Party conference minutes, 24th September 1965

the solitary Common Wealth member (though by then having joined Labour).[225] At the other extreme parties to the right of the Conservatives and/or quasi-fascist parties would usually have been pro-hanging both because of their 'tough-minded' stance on law and order and because of their appeal to tradition. Support for the return of capital punishment was certainly party policy for the National Front in the 1970s.

So far as the separatist and irredentist parties are concerned Plaid Cymru has been strongly abolitionist, though having had very little representation in the House at the relevant periods, while the Scottish National Party (SNP) was for a time in the 1970s evenly split (somewhat surprisingly given their generally left-wing stance on most issues), and their Parliamentary leader Donald Stewart (Western Isles) voted consistently for restoration. In Northern Ireland the Ulster Unionists have been treated as Conservatives for the purposes of the foregoing section and took the Tory whip up to the early 1970s. In general they were consistently right-wing on most issues. They have been very largely retentionist, though Montgomery Hyde was an early and vocal supporter of abolition (and may have suffered in his Belfast North constituency as a result). The hard-line Democratic Unionist Party of the Reverend Ian Paisley has been largely retentionist, though manifested in the House of Commons for much of the time exclusively in the person of Paisley himself. The moderately republican and socialist Social Democratic and Labour Party (SDLP) again had very little representation, and its solitary MP, Gerry Fitt, voted for abolition and against restoration.

Other, very minor, parties had no representation in the Commons or Lords in the relevant periods and would have been most unlikely to have taken up any strong position on the issue given that their interests were of a highly sectional nature.

Conclusion

The parties were crucial to the success of the campaign in that party was the vehicle of change in Parliament, even in regard to a backbench issue such as that of capital punishment, and moreover a controversial private member's bill had little chance of success, no matter how large the majority for it in the Commons, unless the government of the day looked benignly upon it at the very least. It was evident from the early days of the campaign that the Labour Party was favourable to the reform and that a very large and growing majority of the PLP would support the measure, notwithstanding the tepidness of the front

---

[225] Willie Gallacher (MP for Fife, West 1935-50) and Phil Piratin (MP for Stepney, Mile End 1945-50) were the two Communists and Ernest R Millington (MP for Chelmsford 1945-50) was the solitary Common Wealth member, though he joined the Labour Party in April 1946.

bench in the immediate post-war period. By the mid-fifties the pro-hanging element within the PLP had almost withered away completely, and the leadership had passed to men passionately abolitionist such as Gaitskell and especially Wilson, while avid social reformers such as Roy Jenkins had advanced within the party and were actively promoting a reform programme. In 1964 it was generally understood that the new Labour government would provide time for a bill to be passed, and would, though perhaps more discreetly, provide assistance of other kinds. This was abundantly demonstrated when it allowed the Commons to sit in the mornings to get the committee stages through after a tactical coup by the Conservative Opposition brought the Committee back to the floor of the House. After the Bill had passed the government then organized the introduction and passage of the required confirmatory measure four years later, again incurring the wrath of the Opposition, this time by rushing it through prematurely, as the Conservatives sought to characterize it. Thus the support of the overwhelming majority of the PLP was vital to the campaign's prospects of success in that it both provided the majority and the organizational skill necessary to see the reform through.

The Conservatives moved from a position of overwhelming hostility to abolition in the late 1940s to a steadily growing acceptance of it, to the point where, in 1964-5 a third or so of the party in the Commons supported the Bill. This more or less remained the balance of opinion within the Parliamentary party for the next few years. The existence of a sizeable minority of support for abolition both on the back benches and, more importantly, on the front bench enabled the Bill to pass with a very large majority, while the emergence of the abolitionist Heath to the leadership facilitated the passage of the confirmatory vote in 1969. The bulk of the party nonetheless remained hostile to abolition and a succession of right-wing Tory backbenchers sought to reintroduce the rope by way of private member's bill or amendment to government justice bills throughout the 1970s and beyond. The Liberals tended to be very strongly abolitionist and other parties were of little account.

CHAPTER 5

OFFICIAL BODIES AND PROFESSIONAL ASSOCIATIONS

Whilst the activities of the pressure groups and the political parties were central to the campaign, somewhat less significant but still of considerable weight were the views of the associations representing bodies that were deeply involved in the criminal justice process, especially the police and the prison officers, and the judiciary and the Bar, and to a lesser extent the medical and psychiatric professions. These were often highly vocal in the campaign, with the police and the prison officers as those most closely involved being particularly unequivocal in their support for the retention of hanging – the police because they felt that the removal of the 'invisible shield' left them defenceless against the armed robber bent on escape at all costs, and the prison officers who likewise feared that they were vulnerable to the 'lifer' determined to escape by whatever means. In both cases, they argued, the removal of the death penalty meant that an armed robber or a potential escaper had nothing to lose by killing to achieve his ends. These fears were strongly articulated, publicly and privately, through their respective mouthpieces:- the Police Federation representing the rank and file of the force, and the Prison Officers Association (POA).

This chapter looks in turn at the legal profession, the police, the prison officers and the medical and psychiatric profession, and assesses the extent and nature of their influence.

The Legal Profession

Judges were drawn, then as now, almost wholly from the ranks of the Bar. The judiciary was represented at the highest levels in the House of Lords by the 'Law Lords', the Lords of Appeal in Ordinary, who were there *ex officio*, the numbers of which had grown over the years, plus some retired Law Lords who had been given peerages to enable them to remain there. They tended to speak and vote on legal matters only.[226] They included the Lord Chief Justice, head of the criminal division of the Court of Appeal and the Master of the Rolls,

---

[226] Drewry, Gavin and Janet Morgan, 'Law Lords as Legislators', *Parliamentary Affairs*, vol 22 (1968-9) pp. 226-239 discuss their history and role extensively. The Law Lords had been there since the Appellate Jurisdiction Act of 1876 to enable them to perform their judicial functions as the ultimate court of appeal, as well as to take part in debate. By virtue of the Constitutional Reform Act, 2005 the powers formerly exercised by these Law Lords have been transferred to a newly created Supreme Court, which began to operate in October 2009.

head of the civil division thereof. The lower ranks of the judiciary are represented by the Association of Circuit Judges and other kindred bodies which naturally tend to have the ear of the Home Office.

The judiciary was the most conservative of all the institutions involved in the capital punishment debate. Historically they had time and again frustrated efforts by reform-minded legislators in the House of Commons to restrict the death penalty to the most heinous offences and to take lesser offences such as petty theft outside the ambit of the gallows altogether. Lord Chancellors such as Eldon and Lord Chief Justices such as Ellenborough typified the reactionary cast of mind of the judicial bench in the early nineteenth century. The Bench maintained its deep antipathy to abolition and to judicial reform generally well into the twentieth century.[227] In the immediate post-war era this antipathy was personified by the Lord Chief Justice, Goddard, who declared all-out war on the criminal from the Bench and who was a relentless foe of all efforts at reform of the criminal justice system.[228] Notoriously, he characterized the Attlee government's Criminal Justice Bill of 1947-8 as a 'Gangster's Charter' and railed against the abolition of the birch from his platform in the Upper House and from the Bench. In the 1950s he repeatedly called for the re-introduction of corporal punishment.

But there appears to have been a very marked sea-change from the immediate post-war generation of judges, personified by Goddard, to the generation that emerged in the later 1950s and 1960s, which was in the main reconciled to abolition if not warmly in favour of it.[229] A similar liberalization seems to have overtaken the judiciary as had occurred within the episcopacy at about the same time, though it was perhaps less marked and somewhat harder to account for in terms of intellectual fashion. Parker, Goddard's successor as Lord Chief Justice, was a rather half-hearted convert to abolitionism and remained a supporter of corporal punishment. It is difficult to account precisely for this

---

[227] Gardiner, Gerald and Nigel Curtis-Raleigh, 'The Judicial Attitude to Penal Reform', *Law Quarterly Review* (April 1949) pp. 196-219. The authors heap scorn on the view expressed by Lord Chancellor Jowitt in the Lords debate on the Criminal Justice Bill of 1948 to the effect that the judges had proved themselves to be in the forefront of reform, given that they had opposed every attempt to restrict the death penalty.

[228] Rayner Goddard, Baron Goddard of Aldbourne in the County of Wiltshire (1877-1971). Lord Chief Justice 1946-1958. Called to the Bar 1899, KC 1923, appointed to the Bench 1932, Lord Justice of Appeal 1938, Lord of Appeal in Ordinary 1944, first 'non-political' LCJ (a position usually given to the Attorney-General). Trial judge in the libel action of Harold Laski 1946, and in the Craig and Bentley murder trial, 1952. Independent Conservative candidate in the 1929 general election (finished bottom of the poll). Alleged by his valet to reach orgasm whilst pronouncing the death sentence, see Spencer, Colin, *Homosexuality: A History* (London: Fourth Estate, 1995) p. 364

[229] Hubert Lister Parker, Baron Parker of Waddington (1900-1972), LCJ 1958-1971. A similar 'non-political' appointment but much less controversial than his predecessor, though he jailed journalists in the Vassall case in 1963.

change but it probably reflects both the increasingly liberal temper of the epoch and, at least according to Blom-Cooper, the effect of the war (either as a liberalizing agent or more likely as something that gave them an aversion to violence of all kinds).[230] It may have reflected also the slightly broader range of social and educational backgrounds from which they were later drawn, though they still came predominantly from public school and Oxbridge. Later generations of judges, mounting the Bench when abolition was a *fait accompli* and hanging becoming a distant memory, have tended to be deeply averse to any suggestion of its return.

Goddard was certainly the last out-and-out hanger to be Lord Chief Justice.[231] His zeal for hanging carried him away to such an extent that his 1948 speech in the Lords included the dubious statement that the whole of the King's Bench was united in its opposition to abolition, which assertion he was forced subsequently to qualify. His successor, Parker, appointed in 1958, was a belated convert to abolitionism and all of his successors were abolitionist to a greater or lesser degree. Widgery was probably an uncertain abolitionist but not one who would have wished to revert to hanging.[232] The anti-hanging views of Parker, and his successors, were very influential not only with regard to the judicial benches but to the whole of the Lords, and played a large role in the conversion of the Upper House to abolitionism.[233] Even Dilhorne became, after 1965, reconciled to abolition together with judicial discretion in sentencing.[234] Parker's conversion was due primarily to the Homicide Act which was the most powerful agency for abolition; 'utterly friendless' as Parker put it. On the 1969 vote in the Lords (on the Dilhorne motion advocating the continuance of suspension) the judicial benches were split with three – Dilhorne himself, Reid and Simonds -voting for the amendment and three others - Denning, Master of the Rolls, Morris of Borth y Gest and Wilberforce voting against.[235]

The criminal Bar has tended to be more liberal than the Bench, at least as regards hanging. Perhaps this stems partly from a reluctance (as a prosecuting counsel) to be held responsible for an execution where a miscarriage is subsequently proved, and a similar fear on the part of defence counsel that such an outcome might be perceived as a result of incompetence. There does not seem to have been a 'conscience' clause (comparable for example to that which exists in the medical and nursing professions to the carrying out of abortions)

---

[230] Louis Blom-Cooper - interview, op cit.

[231] Bresler, Fenton, *Lord Goddard: A Biography of Rayner Goddard, Lord Chief Justice of England* (London: Harrap, 1977). See also Grimshaw, Eric and Glyn Jones, *Lord Goddard: His Career and Cases* (London: Allan Wingate, 1958); and Smith, Arthur, *Lord Goddard: My Years with the Lord Chief Justice* (London: Weidenfeld and Nicolson, 1959)

[232] All according to Morris and Blom-Cooper, interview, op cit.

[233] Again Morris and Blom-Cooper are strongly of this view, interview, ibid

[234] Formerly Sir Reginald Manningham-Buller, Conservative Attorney-General.

[235] *The Times*, 20th December 1969

applicable to a barrister who objected to prosecuting in a capital case, but it is very unlikely that one who did so object would have been obliged to prosecute under the so-called 'cab rank' principle. There has, apparently, never been a united Bar position on the death penalty, and the Bar Council does not appear ever to have promulgated any doctrine on it. Barristers have always been extremely well-represented in the House of Commons, and in all parties, and have taken a wide range of positions on hanging from full support to outright opposition, again demonstrating that there has never been a clear consensus view from the Bar.

Solicitors tended to follow a similar line in regard to capital punishment, as with policy generally, to their brethren at the Bar. Again a conscience clause does not seem to have operated but would not have been very necessary. The Law Society does not seem ever to have debated the question and, like the Bar Council, has never had a collective view.

In addition to the official bodies representing the judges, barristers and solicitors there are other, more ideologically based, organizations of lawyers. Some were linked to the major political parties including the Society of Labour Lawyers; others were independent such as the Haldane Society of Socialist Lawyers, founded in 1930.[236] The latter included amongst its senior figures in the early years Sir Stafford Cripps (President 1937-49), D N Pritt, Clement Attlee, Sir Frank Soskice, John Platts Mills, Gerald Gardiner and Sydney Silverman, and thus contained some of the most prominent abolitionists of the time. It split from the Society of Labour Lawyers in the late 1940s because of its increasingly left-wing stance and the suggestion that it had become too heavily infiltrated by Communists. Gardiner had originally been a member of the Haldane Society and was chairman from 1945-7 but left to join the Society of Labour Lawyers, restricted to accredited Labour Party members, of which he became chairman.

The Haldane Society was strongly abolitionist though its legal/political campaigns tended to focus more on the industrial and social front. In its *Law Reform Now* pamphlet, published in 1947, it advocated, *inter alia*, that the abolition of both capital and corporal punishment should be included in a forthcoming government criminal justice bill and asserted that flogging and capital punishment 'panders to the sadistic impulses in human beings'- 'the state should set a good example.'[237] The Society of Labour Lawyers was also strongly abolitionist, and at its annual meeting of 1956 unanimously passed a resolution protesting against the government's inactivity and failure to act on the recommendations of the Gowers Commission.[238] The resolution regretted

---

[236] Blake, Nick and Harry Rajak, *Wigs and Workers: A History of the Haldane Society of Socialist Lawyers 1930-80* (London: Haldane Society, 1980)

[237] Haldane Society, *Law Reform Now: a programme for the next three years* (1947) See Blake and Rajak, ibid. p. 28

[238] *The Times*, 23rd January 1956

the refusal of the government to state 'Whether or not it concurs in the unanimous recommendations of the Royal Commission that the law of murder relating to constructive malice, provocation, suicide pacts, mental deficiency and provisions of the Capital Punishment Amendment Act 1868, ought to amended.'

Whilst the bodies representing the lawyers were becoming somewhat more liberal no such transformation was overtaking those in the frontline of the war against crime.

The Police

The police were represented by at least three organizations; the Association of Chief Police Officers (ACPO) for the highest ranks, the Superintendents Association for the middle ranks and the Police Federation for the lower ranks up to chief inspector. In addition there were cognate bodies for the Scottish police forces.

ACPO tended to take a moderately hard line on capital punishment. Being close to the Home Office with which it liaised on administrative matters it was less forthright in public expressions of its views by comparison with the bodies representing the lower ranks. It had, however, been invited to give its views to the Gowers Commission, and, in common with other police bodies, took a pro-hanging line. Thereafter its advice to Home Secretaries tended to remain shrouded, but can be assumed to be fairly strongly pro-retention. It decided against making any representations to the Home Secretary in regard to the 1964-5 Abolition Bill, unlike the Federation.

The Superintendents Association represented the middle ranks of the police, the Superintendents and Chief Superintendents. Like ACPO, but unlike the Federation, it made no representations to the Home Secretary regarding the 1964-5 Abolition Bill but its outlook was nonetheless as strongly retentionist as that of the lower ranks. In response to a request from the restorationist Sandys campaign for its views it asserted that recent District Meetings had found they were 'almost unanimous' in wanting capital punishment reintroduced for all forms of murder, because, it was stated, 'the ordinary citizen should have as much protection as the police.'[239] Only a 'very small percentage' was in favour of the present position (that is to say abolition). Thus the superintendents appeared to be even more pro-hanging than the Federation, although these utterances referred merely to statements of opinion expressed at meetings rather than resolutions, and the true position was probably that there was little or no

---

[239] Harry Staples, chairman, Superintendents Association to Bernard Braine, MP, 17th October 1966. Duncan Sandys papers, Churchill College, Cambridge University, DSND 12/1.

difference between them and the Federation.

The Police Federation represented the 80,000 rank and file policemen in England and Wales, from the rank of constable up to that of chief inspector. The Federation had always been strongly pro-hanging, reflecting the fact that it saw capital punishment as the only effective deterrent to the murder of policemen in the execution of their duty. Without capital punishment, it argued, there was every incentive for a cornered criminal to shoot his way out of trouble since the penalty for murder would not be significantly greater than that for some lesser offences.

The Federation had lobbied successive Home Secretaries for the retention (and subsequently restoration) of capital punishment, publicly and privately. The evidence submitted to the Royal Commission from police bodies had been for retention. The Federation opposed abolition in 1955-6, and shortly before the second reading of the 1964 Silverman Bill, in December 1964, representatives of the Federation had 'a full and frank discussion' with the Home Secretary (Soskice). Its Joint Central Committee also circulated a memo to all MPs, headed 'Capital Punishment and the Police' signed by R J Webb (chairman) and A C Evans (secretary).[240] It declared that they: '…firmly request the retention of capital punishment for the murder of a police officer acting in the execution of his duty or any person coming to his assistance' and though there were differences of opinion and some policemen 'hold that capital punishment is against the very foundations upon which our civilisation is based others will hold directly contrary views.' They were 'aware of statistics which indicate that abolition in other countries did not result in more police murders, but this is not a safe comparison for the policeman in Great Britain is unique amongst most forces in carrying out his duties unarmed and alone.' It was 'a matter of pride that they are unarmed and wished for it to remain so.' They believed that capital punishment 'deters the professional criminal though we have no proof. Life imprisonment may not deter because he knows he would eventually be released. The fact is that very few police are murdered and few criminals carry firearms.' This reflected another aspect of Federation policy that came increasingly to be articulated thereafter to the effect that if capital punishment were to be abolished then the police would have to be armed as a *quid pro quo*, though they would prefer to remain unarmed but with the protection, as they saw it, of capital punishment as the invisible shield.

At its annual conference in May 1965 the Federation unanimously endorsed a motion deploring: 'the publication of a bill to abolish capital punishment without the substitution of an adequate alternative deterrent in so far as it relates to the murder of police officers while in performance of their

---

[240] Police Federation Joint Central Committee memo, 'Capital Punishment and the Police', December 1964. Gardiner, Add 56462A. Also Police Federation Newsletter, January 1965, vol V, no 1

duties.'[241] It rejected the view of the Home Secretary, Soskice, who had addressed them, that the stringent provisions contained in the new Firearms Bill would be an adequate deterrent. A spokesman for the Federation said that Parliament was flying in the teeth of public opinion and that the police were losing the battle against violent crime, pointing out that twelve policemen had been killed on duty since the war.[242]

It was unfortunate from the point of view of the abolitionists and their relations with the police that there were a number of murders of policemen in the period during and immediately after the passage of the Abolition Bill. In particular three were killed by escaping prisoners in Shepherds Bush in August 1966, and it was not difficult to imagine that this was attributed to abolition, or at any rate cited as a stark illustration of the dangers of abolition, by the police and others who supported hanging. Arthur Evans of the Federation declared that the police were in a war against crime when they are weak in numbers and 'with one arm tied behind their backs...It is vital to restore capital punishment for the murder of a policeman or to arm them, preferably the former.'[243] Several Home Secretaries, especially Roy Jenkins, received rough treatment at the hands of Federation conferences. Jenkins had already incurred the ire of the Metropolitan Police (for whom as Home Secretary he was directly responsible) after his rejection of their call for the reintroduction of capital punishment after the murder of three policemen in Shepherds Bush in 1966. At the annual meeting of the Metropolitan Police Joint Branch Boards in Central Hall, Westminster in 1966 there were plans for a walk-out of which he had been forewarned. In the event he characterized it as a 'rough and disagreeable meeting though exacerbated by many factors.'[244] Other factors included a pay dispute, but there is little doubt that Jenkins' antipathy to the reintroduction of capital punishment was a major cause.

Roy Jenkins was again reminded of the posture of the police (and the prison officers) when they joined forces with the nascent Duncan Sandys campaign for restoration later that year. He agreed to meet a joint deputation of Sandys and his Parliamentary supporters and the chairmen and secretaries of the Police Federation, the Police Federation of Scotland and the Prison Officers Association at the House of Commons in November 1966 at which their concerns were thrashed out.[245] The Federation was hardly impressed by Jenkins' argument that it was too soon after abolition to make sense of the statistics and that 1966 had been no worse in respect of police murders than 1961, and the attempt to buy them off with the promise of improved pay and conditions was

[241] Notes by Gardiner on amendments by the House of Lords to the abolition bill. Gardiner, Add 56461B
[242] The Times, 21st May 1965
[243] The Times, 13th August 1966
[244] Jenkins, Roy, A Life at the Centre (London: Macmillan, 1991), pp. 200-201
[245] Sandys papers, op cit, DSND, 12/2.

seen as poor recompense. They continued to lobby for abolition and liaised closely with the Sandys campaign.[246] Its annual conferences, too, continued to pass resolutions for the reintroduction of the rope for the murder of police.[247]

Prison Officers

Prison officers, and their representative organizations, have, like the police, always been strongly pro capital punishment, especially for the murder of prison officers in the execution of their duty. The Prison Officers Association argued, logically enough, that for a prisoner already serving a life sentence (whether for murder or not) there was no effective deterrent to murdering a prison officer in an attempt to escape since no greater sanction existed than to impose another life sentence. This was becoming especially true given the abolition of hanging on the one hand and, on the other hand, the trend towards imposing very long sentences for lesser offences, and against the background of an epidemic of prison escapes, many of them highly professional and often successful. Of course the second life sentence might, in practice, be much longer than the first and a prisoner who had murdered a prison officer would doubtless find his life behind bars extremely unpleasant, but this could appear a feeble argument against restoration.

The POA had given evidence to this effect before the Royal Commission, and had lobbied consistently against abolition thereafter. As abolition started to become a distinct possibility, or even probability, so their concern increased. The chief organ of the POA was *The Prison Officers Magazine*, which discussed the question frequently. In March 1956 an editorial noted the recent Commons vote on abolition and argued for the retention of hanging, even if only for the worst murderers.[248] A memo had been sent to the Home Office explaining the special difficulty that 'lifers' presented, and that since there could be no additional penalty they were free, it argued, to kill with impunity. Consequently hanging should, it argued, be retained for those convicted of a second murder.

The following month the problem was extensively dealt with in an article which endorsed the prompt action of the POA Executive in conveying to the Home Secretary the serious disquiet in their ranks over the prospect of abolition.[249] So

---

[246] Scotland had its own police bodies equivalent to the above, whose stance was much the same. The Scottish Police Federation had joined with their English confreres at the meeting with Roy Jenkins at the House in November 1966.

[247] *The Times*, 24th May 1969

[248] Editorial 'Capital Punishment', *Prison Officers Magazine*, March 1956, vol 46, no 3

[249] 'Serious Disquiet' by J Swainston (prize article) *Prison Officers Magazine*, April 1956, vol 46, no 4

far as the merits of hanging were concerned the writer noted that the Home Secretary had said he was satisfied that never in living memory had an innocent man been sent to the gallows, and moreover, to say that capital punishment was not a unique deterrent was 'stuff and nonsense'. Recidivists did not fear a long sentence but did fear the rope, he asserted, and argued that the criminal code was never to carry a gun, but that this would change if abolition came.

The revival of the abolition question in 1964 sparked afresh the disquiet within the ranks. The January 1965 issue of the *POM* contained the text of a letter from Fred Castell, the general secretary, to the editor of the *Sunday Citizen* of 15th December 1964.[250] Alluding to the column by Hugh Delargy (a Labour MP) which had claimed that there had been only two cases of a prison officer being killed in the last twenty years and that this did not provide sufficient justification to hang all murderers, Castell argued that this missed the point because the POA was not arguing that all murderers should hang but merely explaining the exposed position in which prison officers would find themselves. 'A second conviction for murder would presumably carry a second sentence of life imprisonment – to run concurrently with the first!' This point was reinforced by a letter in the following issue which chided MPs for failing to consult their constituents.[251]

As before, in 1956, there was an exchange of correspondence between the POA and the Home Secretary, except that this time around the Home Secretary was less sympathetic to their views. Castell wrote to the Home Secretary, Soskice, that: '...members hold a variety of views as individuals and citizens... but will be responsible for the safe custody of those...sentenced to life imprisonment...men for whom it doesn't appear that there can be any further deterrent. What indeed is to be the protection against such inmates who offer violence which may prove to be fatal to the officer?'[252] Soskice replied that: '...the Bill, if it passes into law, will create no new problem in principle...365 prisoners serve sentences of life imprisonment...additional burden likely to be small... since 1920 three officers have been murdered on duty...none of these was killed by a prisoner serving a life sentence.' He went on to quote the findings of the Royal Commission that the experience of countries where capital punishment has been abolished was that there was no increase in murderous attacks on prison staff by prisoners. Moreover, he proposed to create an 'allocation centre' for all long sentence prisoners with a special wing for murderers identified as presenting extra custodial difficulties which would have a higher staffing ratio, outstanding external security and facilities in respect of work, recreation and accommodation designed for the violent and reckless.[253]

---

[250] Castell to *Sunday Citizen*, 15th December 1964, *Prison Officers Magazine*, January 1965, vol 55, no 1

[251] Letter from B S Jeram, *Prison Officers Magazine*, February 1965, vol 55, no 2

[252] Castell to Soskice, 28th January 1965. *Prison Officers Magazine*, April 1965, vol 55, no 4

[253] Soskice to Castell, 22nd February 1965. *Prison Officers Magazine*, April 1965, vol 55, no

The March issue was even more hard-hitting. An article entitled 'A Licence to Murder?' by Castell was essentially the letter sent to Soskice in January, with perhaps some additional points made in response to Soskice's reply.[254] Lest they be thought a bunch of reactionaries he was keen to stress the progressive outlook of the service, and that the Association's recently published *The Role of the Modern Prison Officer* had made it clear that it was anxious to see and even pioneer new 'aims and methods' in the penal system. However, that did not mean that they would 'stand quietly by and see safeguards in respect of their own safety whittled away.' It may be true that no prison officer had been killed by a convicted murderer (the few such killings of prison officers had been by those convicted of offences other than murder) but the 'vicious type of professional criminal who kills has, in the past, usually suffered the loss of his own life…It would be a strange commentary on the present Bill if by prohibiting what has sometimes been called judicial murder it should provide an avenue whereby the murder of Prison Officers could be undertaken with impunity.'

Matters came to a head when in March officials of the POA including Castell, the national chairman, N Cowling and their adviser, Charles Smith met Soskice, Minister of State Alice Bacon and senior officials at the Commons to discuss a wide range of problems, and the POA spoke 'frankly' about the dissatisfaction and frustration of members over pay and conditions, though curiously there was no mention of abolition.[255]

Their annual conference in Belfast in May inevitably featured a resolution on the matter. A Mr Goodair (Aylesbury) moved a resolution asking the Association to do everything in its power to retain the death penalty for the murder of a prison officer by an inmate.[256] The resolution was carried unanimously and the assistant general secretary, Mr Daniel, said in reply that the Executive fully endorsed it and that it had from the outset lobbied hard to retain hanging under these circumstances by way of approaches to MPs by HQ and from branches, and pledged that they would continue to do so.

This feeling intensified when, right on cue, a prison officer, Derek Lambert, was killed in the line of duty by a Borstal inmate in November 1965 (literally days after the Bill had become law). The POA was not slow to make political capital out of it. The December issue of the *POM* claimed that this provided 'incontrovertible evidence which we would have preferred to do without' of the need for provision along the lines of the resolution unanimously adopted by conference.[257] The Association issued a statement to the press to the

---

4

[254] 'A Licence to Murder?' by Fred Castell, *Prison Officers Magazine*, March 1965, vol 55, no 3

[255] General Secretary's column, *Prison Officers Magazine*, April 1965, vol 55, no 4

[256] Report on Annual Conference, *Prison Officers Magazine*, August 1965, vol 55, no 8

[257] Editorial - *Prison Officers Magazine*, December 1965, vol 55, no 12

effect that coming so soon after the passage of the Bill it must have an effect on the conscience of MPs. The January 1966 issue of the magazine carried a prominent article on the murder of Officer Lambert, including a front page photograph of the funeral.[258] The article pointed out that the murderer, Maxwell, had recently been involved in disturbances and had been sentenced to six strokes of the birch which could not be administered without the Home Secretary's confirmation, and that if Maxwell had committed another murder there was little that could be done. The sense of outrage and frustration was palpable. *Corrigenda,* writing in the March issue boldly asserted that the Abolition Bill was construed in criminal circles as 'ALL SIGNALS GO'.[259]

From late 1966 onwards the POA became strongly associated with the Duncan Sandys campaign to restore hanging for the murder of police and prison officers, and their campaigns were closely co-ordinated. Castell corresponded frequently with Sandys regarding the campaign. The murder of three police officers at Shepherds Bush in the summer of 1966 was the subject of another editorial that referred to the campaign by some MPs to amend the law and stated that they would have the full support of the Association. It stressed that police and prison officers alike were embroiled in a common war against the violent criminal and carried a letter of condolence from Castell on their behalf to A C Evans of the Police Federation.[260] The failure of the Home Secretary (by now Roy Jenkins who had replaced Soskice in December 1965) to confirm the corporal punishment of an inmate at Maidstone, who had been convicted of the murder of Officer Lambert, merely added to the sense of anger and frustration that seemed to be boiling up within the service at this time.[261] In November 1966 there was a deputation from Sandys, the POA and the Police Federation to see Jenkins about the question.[262] The failure of the Sandys campaign, with the defeat of his motion in the Commons in November, and the obvious unlikelihood of revising the legal position at least until the confirmatory votes were due in 1970 caused the issue to die down somewhat, at least within the pages of the *POM*, though it would not have taken much to re-ignite it.

The annual conference of 1968 again carried unanimous resolutions calling for the reinstatement of hanging and corporal punishment for prison offences. The annual conference of 1969 carried another such resolution, again adopted unanimously.[263] The failure to re-introduce hanging in December 1969 led to the question once again going into abeyance to some degree, but the June 1970 issue returned to the attack with an editorial that discussed it in the context

---

[258] *Prison Officers Magazine*, January 1966, vol 56, no 1

[259] 'All Signals Go' by Corrigenda, *Prison Officers Magazine*, March 1966, vol 56, no 3

[260] Editorial – *Prison Officers Magazine*, September 1966, vol 56, no 9

[261] Flogging, and corporal punishment in general, was soon to be abolished as a prison punishment, having already been abolished as a judicial punishment in 1948.

[262] 'A Question of Morals' – *Prison Officers Magazine*, November 1966, vol 56, no 11

[263] Annual conference report, *Prison Officers Magazine*, August 1969, vol 59, no 8

of the upcoming general election.[264] It noted that the Executive had urged at conference that members, their wives and families should try to secure assurances from Parliamentary candidates that they would support re-introduction for the murder of prison officers. The annual conference of 1970, held a month earlier, had contained the by now ritual motion for re-introduction and expressed doubts as to the efficacy of the protection measures announced by Home Secretary Callaghan in a recent letter to the Association, particularly in the light of recent events at Parkhurst (where a riot had occurred).[265] Despite this relentless activity by the Executive, lobbying Home Secretaries and MPs, liaising with pro-hanging movements in Parliament and using the pages of the magazine for propaganda, and the repeated passage of restorationist motions at annual conferences it was completely unsuccessful. Its influence was too small for it to have any real impact.

The Medical and Psychiatric Professions

Another professional group involved, if only marginally, in the hanging process was the medical and psychiatric. A doctor had to be present at the execution to certify death and to oversee the proceedings. Professional ethics in the form of the Hippocratic Oath precludes a doctor from doing harm and therefore a doctor may only assist in the purely passive sense of certifying death, but it could be argued (and may have been by some) that the mere fact of being present to perform that function constituted assistance, in the sense that if they were not present it would be procedurally impossible to carry out the execution. Did this lead to voices within the profession calling for such a boycott as a means of bringing about abolition? What was the view of the medical profession generally about hanging?

The British Medical Association (BMA), the main representative body of the medical profession, was invited by the Royal Commission, in August 1949, both to submit written evidence and to give live evidence. To this end a 'Capital Punishment Committee' was set up by the then Deputy Secretary, Dr A Macrae, in late 1949 to examine aspects of the debate that were relevant to the profession, particularly the McNaghten rules governing criminal insanity and whether they should be extended to embrace lesser degrees of mental incapacity.[266] There were overtures from the Howard League who may have seen the BMA as potential allies in the abolition campaign, but if so they must

---

[264] 'The General Election and the Death Penalty' – *Prison Officers Magazine*, June 1970, vol 60, no 6

[265] Annual conference report, *Prison Officers Magazine*, August 1970, vol 60, no 8

[266] BMA policy file on the Royal Commission (1949-), BMA Archive, Box 502, 20/2/11.

have been disappointed.[267] The BMA's evidence was duly submitted in December 1949, and concentrated heavily on the McNaghten rules and suggested their extension to cover something approximating to the Scots law defence of diminished responsibility. BMA representatives, including a barrister, gave oral evidence to the Commission in February 1950, to enlarge on their submission. Whilst desiring to extend the ambit of the existing defence of insanity and considering the possibility of using alternative, more humane, methods of execution such as lethal injection the general tenor of its evidence, both written and verbal, was not overtly hostile to capital punishment *per se* and certainly did not go so far as to recommend any reduction or mitigation of it beyond the aforementioned, much less its abolition.

There does not appear to have been much debate within the profession in the years immediately following about the continuance of capital punishment, and the participation of prison doctors, other than in respect of the question of introducing into the law the defence of diminished responsibility, a subject with which they were in correspondence with the Home Office.[268] Much more recently, however, subsequent to the abolition of capital punishment in Britain, the profession has undergone a major evolution in that respect, and has passed a number of resolutions at its Annual Representative Meeting (ARM) in recent years opposing capital punishment.[269]

These of course, being of fairly recent origin, pertain only to the medical profession in those countries where capital punishment is still practised. There does not seem to have been any unequivocal resolution prior to those dates, and opinions doubtless differed amongst individual doctors. Certainly there does not seem ever to have been any difficulty in finding a doctor to act at executions, though generally these were prison doctors whose work was based entirely at the prison and who might be presumed to have taken up that position in the knowledge of what the job entailed and who thus might be assumed not to have conscientious or ethical objections to capital punishment.

What of the psychiatric profession? Was there a parallel dilemma with that of the doctors? In some cases a defendant pleading insanity would have had to submit to psychiatric examination. This may even have been so where there was a plea, post-Homicide Act, of diminished responsibility. What was the position of a psychiatrist who was called upon to make an assessment of insanity (or diminished responsibility) knowing that if he deemed the defendant sane he was effectively condemning him to death? Did this create problems from the point of view of professional ethics, and was there a call (or a

---

[267] Howard League to Dr Macrae, October 1949, offering their library services to the BMA. BMA Archive, ibid.

[268] BMA policy file, Box 502, 20/2/11, Home Office to Dr Macrae, 28th September 1956. BMA Archive, ibid.

[269] BMA database of ARM resolutions, BMA Public Information Unit. BMA Archive, ibid.

temptation) to declare all such defendants insane (or suffering from diminished responsibility) to save them from the rope? Or was the defendant to be regarded merely as a subject rather than a patient?

The Council of the Royal Medico-Psychological Association (RMPA) gave evidence to the Royal Commission in 1950, and did not take an abolitionist stance. Indeed it made the point that it had not, and did not think it desirable, to canvass the opinions of psychiatrists individually. The general tenor of its evidence was that it thought the existing system satisfactory. More recently, however, the Royal College of Psychiatrists, the chief representative body, has taken a much more abolitionist stance. It has affirmed that it supports the World Medical Association's 'Declaration on the Participation of Psychiatrists in the Death Penalty' agreed in Athens in 1989 and that it should support the position of psychiatrists working in countries where the death penalty is still in operation. In particular it affirms that a psychiatrist may, in some circumstances: 'refuse to give an expert opinion on criminal responsibility and like matters, if they feel that such an opinion would make it more likely that the person concerned would be found guilty and executed.'[270] As with the medical and legal professions there seems to have been a strong movement towards abolitionism in recent years.

Conclusion

It is difficult to generalize about the role and significance of these various bodies and associations. The Police Federation was vociferous in its opposition to abolition from the outset and argued its case powerfully. After abolition it liaised closely with the Sandys campaign to re-introduce the rope, as well as making formal representations to the Home Secretary of the day. The bodies representing the more senior ranks were perhaps slightly less adamant, but tended to take the same view albeit that they expressed their concerns through the official channels open to them rather than to campaign openly. It was likewise for the Prison Officers Association. Yet for all the 'insider' status they enjoyed, the level of public support that was apparent and the close links they forged with retentionist elements, they made no real impact, and were compelled to watch impotently as abolition duly took place. As with public opinion, it weighed remarkably little in the final analysis, given the overwhelming abolitionist consensus in elite circles and the determination to see abolition through.

The legal, medical and psychiatric professions were rather more restrained, and were less directly affected. Nonetheless the balance of judicial opinion tended to be retentionist initially, but to give way to a cautious

---

[270]*Psychiatric Bulletin*, 1992 (16), p.457

abolitionism especially after the passage of the Bill, whilst the Bar was perhaps rather more abolitionist to start with. Any representations here to government would have tended to be through the official channels, as the judiciary was an insider group *par excellence*, with very close contact with the organs of government, though Goddard was very outspoken in his condemnation of both abolition and the moratoria sometimes applied. His successor, Parker, was a cautious and pragmatic convert to abolition. The medical and psychiatric professions tended to avoid taking a definite stance in the early years of the controversy, but latterly have moved to a strongly abolitionist position.

CHAPTER 6

THE CAMPAIGN CONTINUES - THE HOMICIDE ACT AND AFTER, 1957-64

This chapter takes up the narrative of events from the passage of the Homicide Act of 1957, described at the end of Chapter Two, up to the general election of 1964 and the inception of a Labour government. The period from 1957 to 1964 was one of relative inactivity on the abolition front after the high drama of the campaign during the previous two years, though it was by no means without incident. The NCACP continued its campaign as previously described, but there was little or no movement on the political front, notwithstanding the efforts of a variety of backbench guerilla warriors - both pro and anti. There was a solid Conservative majority in the Commons (greatly enhanced after the general election of 1959) and a Home Secretary, Butler, who was unshakeable in his determination 'to let the Homicide Act work' and in his refusal to countenance any amendment to it. Each capital case and prospective hanging that came along led to attempts, both inside and outside Parliament, for a stay of execution or even to win a reprieve, and the ghost of Timothy Evans continued to haunt proceedings.

The passage of the Homicide Act briefly exhausted the energies of the campaigners on both sides of the debate, but it was not long before hostilities were resumed with renewed vigour.[271] It was the view of some observers that the Act had retarded progress towards complete abolition. For example, the penal reformer Margery Fry commented that the legislation 'indeed went far enough towards abolition: far enough to set back total abolition for another span of years.'[272] Sir Ernest Gowers himself, however, commented that the Act represented 'a search for the chimera', and that the attempt to legislate classes of murder was misconceived.[273] Butler, too, admitted that by the end of his tenure of the Home Office he had begun to see that the system devised by the Act could not continue.[274] His widow, Mollie, has stated that by the end of his

---

[271] This chapter draws heavily on Block and Hostettler, op cit, pp.199-269

[272] Huws Jones, Enid, *Margery Fry - The Essential Amateur* (York: William Sessions, 1990), p.236, quoted in Hodgkinson and Rutherford, op cit, p.263. Rutherford cites a similar utterance by Leon Radzinowicz (a member of the Gowers Commission) at Cambridge in 1961, p.273.

[273] Remarks to Louis Blom-Cooper and Terence Morris, *Crime and Criminal Justice since 1945* (Oxford: Blackwell, 1989), p.81.

[274] Butler, R A, *The Art of the Possible* (London: Hamish Hamilton, 1971) p.202, quoted in Hodgkinson and Rutherford, op cit, p.264; Howard, Anthony, *Rab: The Life of R A Butler* (London: Jonathan Cape, 1987) p. 253. He had in fact, notwithstanding his liberal instincts, sent more condemned prisoners to the gallows than any other post-war Home Secretary, although this was largely a function of his having been in place for longer than most.

tenure of office he had become an abolitionist as a result of his experiences.[275] He had been deeply exercised by both the Evans/Christie and the Craig/Bentley cases, though, despite his misgivings, he had chosen not to re-open the Evans case.[276] The abolitionists continued their Parliamentary guerrilla tactics by concentrating on a series of cases that came before the courts in the immediate aftermath of the Act, focussing upon the way in which the anomalies inherent in the Act were resulting in what they saw as injustices (see also the chapter on murder cases and miscarriages).

The first such case was that of Vickers. On 23 May 1957 John Willson Vickers was convicted of capital murder and sentenced to death, the first such conviction and sentence since the passage of the Act (which had received the Royal Assent and had come into effect on 21st March 1957). His appeal was dismissed and the Attorney General, Sir Reginald Manningham-Buller, refused him leave to appeal to the House of Lords.[277] Silverman asked the Attorney-General by private notice why he had not exercised his fiat so to do.[278] Manningham-Buller asserted that he could only do so if the case involved a matter of law of exceptional importance and that it was in the public interest for a further appeal to be brought, and that those conditions were not fulfilled in the Vickers case. Pressed further by Silverman to the effect that there *was* an important point of law involved the Attorney-General stressed that the Lord Chief Justice (presiding over the Court of Appeal) had convened a full bench of five judges to decide the case - superseding the original bench of three members which had been unable to agree.

Silverman persisted in his argument that the conviction of Vickers of capital murder (he had struck an old lady a relatively mild blow in the course of a theft, from which she had died) went clean contrary to the repeated assurances of both Manningham-Buller and Butler that the effect of Section 1 of the Act was that a man could not be convicted of murder who had had no intention to kill. Silverman argued that the decision of the Court of Appeal was thus a misconstruction of the Act. He was supported in this by Leslie Hale, Labour MP for Oldham West, who argued that the Act had not really abolished the doctrine

---

[275] Lamb, Richard, *The Macmillan Years 1957-1963: The Emerging Truth* (London: John Murray, 1995) pp. 407-410 Lamb's interview with Mollie Butler.

[276] In a question for written answer Fred Willey 'asked the Home Secretary whether he will hold a further enquiry to determine whether there is any ground for thinking that there may have been any miscarriage of justice in the conviction of T J Evans.' Butler replied 'I have carefully considered this case, but I do not think that a further enquiry would serve any useful purpose. All the relevant facts are on record and there is no reason to believe that any new information would be forthcoming.' HC Deb, vol 574, col 246 (written answers), 1st August 1957

[277] Sir Reginald Edward Manningham-Buller, 1st Viscount Dilhorne (1905-1980) Conservative politician, MP for Daventry 1943-50, MP for Northants South 1950-62, Solicitor-General 1951-54, Attorney General 1954-62, Lord Chancellor 1962-64.

[278] HC Deb, vol 573, col 1142, 17th July 1957

of constructive malice, whatever its proponents might have said to the contrary.[279] Manningham-Buller re-iterated that this was nonsense and that the Act *had* expressly abolished constructive malice. Reginald Paget, Labour member for Northampton and another ardent abolitionist, joined the fray by pointing out that the medical evidence in the trial was that the blows struck were not of a nature to maim or kill, and that therefore the Court of Appeal was interpreting the Act in a way different from the government.[280]

The Attorney-General stood fast and Silverman then asked for leave to move the adjournment of the House under Standing Order No 9, to call attention to a matter of urgent public importance, namely: 'the refusal of the Attorney-General to grant his fiat to enable John Willson Vickers now lying under sentence of death to appeal against his conviction to the House of Lords as provided for by the Criminal Appeal Act 1907.'[281] The Speaker ruled that it was a matter for the operation of the law and not for him. Silverman was adamant that it was an administrative duty for which the Attorney-General was responsible to the Commons, and that as such it was right for the House to discuss it under the standing order. The Speaker, however, would not give way.[282]

The following day Silverman and sixty other Labour MPs tabled a motion of censure on Manningham-Buller, deploring his failure to seek a reference to the Lords, especially given that such a reference might have elucidated some of the ambiguities inherent in the Homicide Act relating to the abolition of constructive malice.[283] Home Secretary Butler, during questions relating to the Business of the House, refused the House the chance to debate the motion.[284] Silverman argued that precedent dictated that a motion of censure on a minister was always debated, but the Speaker ruled that the scheduling of debates was a matter for the government and would not be moved by Silverman's implorings. Vickers was executed on 23 July 1957, almost two years since the last execution.[285]

A week later Silverman withdrew the motion criticizing the Attorney-General but tabled a new motion regretting the execution of Vickers and again

---

[279] HC Deb, ibid, col 1144

[280] HC Deb, ibid, col 1145

[281] HC Deb, ibid, col 1146

[282] HC Deb, ibid, col 1147-8

[283] 'That this House deeply deplores the refusal of Mr Attorney-General to grant his fiat to enable John Willson Vickers to appeal against his conviction to the House of Lords, so as to establish on the highest judicial authority whether or not section 1 of the Homicide Act effectively abolishes the doctrine of constructive malice and prevents a man from being liable to be convicted of murder who had no intention to kill or to do grievous bodily harm, as the Government assured the House was its purpose during the debate on the Homicide Act'

[284] HC Deb, ibid, col 1344-5, 18th July 1957

[285] Block and Hostettler, op cit, pp.199-200

attacking the Attorney-General.[286] Silverman moved this motion by saying that he couldn't recall the last occasion when such a motion had been moved, but that it was fully justified.[287] He noted that there was a three-line whip against the motion on the government side. He began by saying that the motion was partly a criticism of Home Secretary Butler for failing to reprieve Vickers despite the fact that every factor was present that would have tended to favour one. He said that the factors influencing Home Secretaries on the question of a reprieve were well-known because the Home Office had on two occasions in recent times told Commissions of Inquiry what they were, and he proceeded to enumerate them. What, he wondered, were the compelling reasons for not then granting a reprieve?[288] Silverman then went on to re-iterate his argument that there appeared to be a contradiction between the decision of the Court of Appeal in the Vickers case and the oft-repeated statements of the government as to the effect of the Homicide Act. He quoted the then Home Secretary (Gwilym Lloyd George) on second reading on 15th Nov, 1956:-

> We propose to take out of the category of murder those homicides about which opinion has long been uneasy: homicides which are murder only by virtue of the doctrine of constructive malice; homicides by people who though not insane are gravely abnormal; homicides under severe provocation by words alone; and homicides in pursuance of a suicide pact.[289]

Silverman then elaborated his argument at considerable length. He was seconded by Leslie Hale, who bracketed the case of Vickers with that of Dunbar.[290] Manningham-Buller replied that Silverman's argument was misconceived because in fact the first instance court had decided that Vickers had had intent to cause grievous bodily harm, and that his conviction was not therefore on the basis of constructive malice. Thus no point of law of grave importance arose to justify him in referring the matter to the House of Lords.[291] Finally the question was put and negatived.

The following year, 1958, there was more controversy surrounding a murder conviction, this time that of John S Spriggs.[292] Again a Labour backbencher, Denis Howell (Birmingham, All Saints) asked the Attorney-

---

[286] 'That this House regrets the execution of John Willson Vickers, is of opinion that his conviction of capital murder is contrary to the declared intention of Her Majesty's Government when they recommended the Homicide Act to Parliament, and deplores the failure of Mr Attorney-General to grant his fiat to enable Vickers to bring a further appeal to the House of Lords'

[287] HC Deb, ibid, vol 574, col 1617, 1st August 1957

[288] HC Deb, ibid, col 1619

[289] HC Deb, vol 560, col 1148, 15th November 1956, quoted by Silverman, HC Deb, ibid, col 1621

[290] HC Deb, ibid, col 1632-6

[291] HC Deb, ibid, cols 1637-1649

[292] Block and Hostettler, op cit. p.201

General by private notice question to exercise his fiat to refer the case of Spriggs to the Lords. When he refused Howell persisted on the basis that the conviction had been deeply unsatisfactory due to its centring on the question of diminished responsibility, and the supposedly inadequate direction given to the jury by the trial judge, the Lord Chief Justice.[293] Again, as with Vickers, the Attorney-General was adamant that no grave question of law was involved, and that therefore there was no valid reason for referring the matter to the Lords. Other Labour MPs such as Patrick Gordon Walker (Smethwick) and Leslie Hale sought to persuade the Attorney-General of the merits of a referral to the Lords but to no avail. The fact that this had been the first case centring on diminished responsibility did not in his view make it *ipso facto* a point of law of exceptional public importance, and he did not in any case accept that there had been any form of misdirection by the trial judge. Spriggs was in fact subsequently reprieved by the Home Secretary.

Retentionist Activity

There was activity too on the retentionist side of the debate with some retentionist Conservative MPs such as Sir Thomas Moore (Ayr) and R Graham Page (Crosby) highlighting the apparent increase in the murder rate since the passage of the Homicide Act. This was often done by means of questions, whether oral or written, to the Home Secretary. Cyril Osborne (Louth) an inveterate opponent of abolition, easily characterized as a reactionary blimp, asked the Home Secretary on 18th July 1957 how many murders were known to the police since the Act came into force, and what were the numbers for the same period in each of the preceding three years. Not surprisingly the figures were not very conclusive of anything.[294] On 1st August 1957 Sir Thomas Moore asked the Home Secretary for the number of murders committed since 31st May.[295] On 14th November 1957 he asked the Home Secretary: 'How long Her Majesty's Government propose to retain the Homicide Act on the statute book, in view of the fact that crimes of murder have so substantially increased since it was passed.'[296]

Brigadier Sir Terence Clarke (Portsmouth, West) another inveterate reactionary and opponent of abolition asked: 'if in view of the increased number of murders he will re-introduce the death penalty for all murders.' Butler gave a table of figures in response to these and various other similar questions, which did not really demonstrate any significant increase. He said, not surprisingly, that it was too soon to assess the effect of the Act or to contemplate a further change in the law. Moore was unimpressed: 'Doesn't this increase clearly show

---

[293] HC Deb, vol 580, col 1256-8, 23rd January 1958
[294] HC Deb, vol 573, col 143, 18th July 1957
[295] HC Deb, vol 574, col 246, 1st August 1957
[296] HC Deb, vol 577, col 1129-32, 14th November 1957

that the death penalty was a deterrent? How many more murders must be committed before the government realise that in this case they made a grave mistake?' Butler re-iterated that the number of murders obviously fluctuated, and that it was too soon to draw any conclusions about the effectiveness of the Act. Silverman intervened to point out that between the passing of the second reading of his Death Penalty (Abolition) Bill and the coming into force of the Homicide Act the death penalty had in effect been in suspension, and that the effect of the Homicide Act was to end that suspension and to partly restore the death penalty.

In February 1958 Brigadier Clarke was on the attack again, asking Butler for the numbers of murders and murder convictions in 1957 as compared to 1956 and asking him if, in view of the increase, he would consider hanging and flogging.[297] In a question for written answer Sir Thomas Moore asked Butler for details of murders from April to December 1957 and how they compared to the same months for 1956, and asked the Secretary of State for Scotland (John Maclay) for the equivalent figures for Scotland.[298] In May Moore asked the Home Secretary whether he had any information as to his intentions regarding a revision of the Criminal Justice Act, 1948 and the Homicide Act. Butler replied in a written answer that the report of the study of the 'Cambridge Department of Criminal Science' into crimes of violence in the Metropolis (to which he assumed Moore was referring) was not yet available. He also stated that the monthly figures for murders known to police in England and Wales in the six months from September 1957 to March 1958 were considerably lower than for the months immediately after the passing of the Homicide Act. The indications therefore, he suggested, did not require any amendment.[299]

In April 1958 R Graham Page (Crosby) presented a petition to the Commons calling on the government to amend the Act to allow for the execution of those convicted of murdering a female or young male.[300] The annual conference of the Scottish Unionist Association overwhelmingly condemned the Act and demanded the restoration of the death penalty for all murders. At the 1958 Conservative Party conference Butler, the Home

---

[297] HC Deb, vol 581, col 1336, 6th February 1958

[298] HC Deb, vol 581, col 59, 28th January 1958; col 100, 30th January 1958

[299] HC Deb, vol 587, written answers col 112-3, 8th May 1958

[300] Block and Hostettler, op cit, p.202; HC Deb, vol 586, col 495, 18th April 1958. Page presented: 'the humble petition of Councillors Robert Alexander McGeoch and many thousands of signatories residing in and around the Borough of Crosby and the Urban District of Litherland, who call attention to the increase in the number of murders and incidents of wounding which have occurred since the passage of the Homicide Act 1957 and to the fear held by womenfolk and children to walk along the roads and streets for fear of being attacked by some sexual maniac, in the absence of the deterrent effect of a possible death sentence. The Petition concludes with the Prayer that the Homicide Act 1957 be repealed or so amended that those persons found guilty of murdering a female or young male person shall be sentenced to death.'

Secretary, rejected calls for the repeal or amendment of the Act, and suggested that there would be no further legislation on the subject for some time.[301]

Calls for the restoration of capital punishment for all classes of murder as per the status quo ante the Act were often linked, both logically and ideologically, with demands for the restoration of corporal punishment for crimes of violence in general.[302] For example, in July 1958 Sir Thomas Moore drew the Home Secretary's attention to the fact that three recent women's conferences had demanded the restoration of corporal punishment for crimes of violence and capital punishment for all crimes of murder, and invited him to give statutory effect to this. David Renton, a junior Home office minister, replied to the effect that the Home Secretary was monitoring the situation carefully but that the figures gave no grounds for suggesting that there should be any amendment to the Act so recently passed. He also said that the Home Secretary did not see fit to re-introduce corporal punishment, unless there was evidence that it was an especially effective deterrent, and that the Departmental Committee that had studied the question before the War did not consider it to be so. Moore was unimpressed by this and insisted that the figures showing a decrease in the murder rate were not convincing, and that the British people were apparently demanding action. Marcus Lipton (Labour, Brixton) however, took the opportunity to ask Renton to convey the thanks of 'enlightened opinion' to Patricia Hornsby-Smith (Conservative, Chislehurst and Parliamentary Under-Secretary at the Home Office) for her 'vigorous handling of one of the more bloodthirsty of the conferences referred to in this question?'[303]

Cyril Osborne (Conservative, Louth) asked the Home Secretary in April 1959 if, in view of the increase in the number of murders, he would introduce legislation to restore hanging for the murder of women, children and old people. Butler insisted that, allowing for natural fluctuations, the murder rate had not increased significantly (the monthly average for September 1958 to February 1959 was 14.3 as against 14.2 for the five years 1952-56). Osborne was undeterred by mere facts, and pointed out that there had been two recent examples of child murders, and that he must do something about it, whatever the 'softies' opposite may feel.[304] In May 1959 Jo Grimond, the Liberal leader, and an abolitionist, asked Butler if he would have an enquiry into the working of the law relating to capital punishment, but Butler replied that the Act had

---

[301] Block and Hostettler, ibid p.202

[302] Corporal punishment as a judicial sentence had been abolished by virtue of the Criminal Justice Act, 1948, a measure passed by the previous Labour government, though corporal punishment as a prison sentence for breaches of discipline still existed and was only abolished by the Criminal Justice Act, 1967, a measure passed by a later Labour government.

[303] HC Deb, vol 591, col. 1423-4, 17th July 1958

[304] HC Deb, vol 603, col. 1124, 16th April 1958

been in force for too little time to contemplate an enquiry.[305] Grimond and others also raised the question of the public announcement of the exact timings of executions, presumably in the light of public demonstrations that had taken place outside prisons at recent executions. Butler said that he was required by the Act to announce the date and place.[306]

Further Capital Cases

In early 1959 Ronald Henry Marwood was arrested for the murder of a police constable in the course of an affray in Seven Sisters Road in North London in December 1958.[307] In due course he was convicted of murder and sentenced to death at the Old Bailey. His appeal was heard before the new Lord Chief Justice, Lord Parker of Waddington, together with Justices Donovan and Salmon, in April 1959, and it was duly dismissed. 150 MPs, mostly Labour, signed a petition against his hanging but to no avail. The Home Secretary said he saw no grounds for a reprieve and the execution duly took place at Pentonville in the midst of a large demonstration from about a thousand people. The inadequacies of the Homicide Act were again highlighted by the case, and Canon Collins, Dean of St Pauls delivered an attack on the execution of Marwood from the pulpit, and in the Commons Silverman was again on the attack demanding the complete abolition of capital punishment on the grounds that the operation of the Homicide Act was deeply anomalous, discriminating between capital and non-capital murders on the basis of criteria which bore no relation to the actual wickedness of the crime or the degree of culpability of the offender. On the other side Sir Cyril Osborne countered the Silverman motion with a wrecking amendment that effectively called for the re-introduction of capital punishment for murder by poisoning and the murder of old people and young children.

In July 1959 Reginald Paget raised the case of Guenther Podola, another man under indictment for capital murder, asking the Home Secretary what had happened to him during his six hours at Chelsea police station which necessitated his hospitalisation. Patrick Gordon Walker called for an enquiry. Butler stonewalled by saying that an enquiry would prejudice the case.[308]

Meanwhile hangings continued sporadically, with a fair share of convicted murderers being reprieved. Everyone, it seems, thought the Homicide Act a disaster. Abolitionists obviously felt it did not go far enough and saw it as at best a stepping stone on the road to total abolition. Retentionists thought it allowed too many murderers to go unhanged, and that its categories were too restrictive. Legal and 'neutral' opinion generally and almost universally

---

[305] HC Deb, vol 605, col. 167, 14th May 1959
[306] HC Deb, vol 605, col. 168-9, 14th May 1959
[307] Block and Hostettler, op cit., pp.202-205
[308] HC Deb, vol 609, col. 873-882, 20th July 1959

regarded the Act as riddled with anomalies and unjust in its operation. There was dissatisfaction all round and yet there was no sign of any movement in the foreseeable future on the political front, with Home Secretary Rab Butler taking the view that the Act should be given a fair period of time to operate before any decision was taken as to its replacement or amendment. In September 1959 even the Lord Chief Justice himself, Lord Parker, delivered a stinging attack on the Act and its numerous anomalies and said that complete abolition was preferable to the continued operation of the Act.

The Conservatives under Macmillan were returned to office with a greatly increased majority of nearly a hundred in the general election of October 1959. The implications of that for the abolition campaign were that Butler remained at the Home Office, pursuing a resolutely 'neutral' line on capital punishment and the workings of the Homicide Act. The Commons contained fewer Labour MPs and therefore, notwithstanding a probable increase in the number of abolitionist Conservatives, probably a smaller majority for outright abolition than before. The Parliamentary guerilla campaigns continued much as before.

In November Tom Iremonger (Conservative, Ilford North) asked Butler to what extent he had 'given consideration in the light of public opinion to the introduction of further legislation to extend or limit the penalties for homicide and treason.' Butler gave his usual reply to the effect that things were under review and that there were no proposals for further legislation.[309] The question of the publicity given to the timing of executions was again raised by Osborne in view of demonstrations that had accompanied recent hangings, and Butler again re-iterated that he was required by section 11(2) of the Act to publish the time and place of hangings.[310]

Sir Thomas Moore again called upon the Home Secretary to reconsider his policy in view of public opinion poll findings that 78% of the population was in favour of the restoration of corporal punishment for crimes of violence against the person, and 74% in favour of capital punishment for all types of murder. Butler re-iterated for the umpteenth time that he was not prepared to consider a change in the law at this stage, and pointed out that the question of corporal punishment had been referred to the Advisory Council on the treatment of offenders and that he awaited their report.[311] In a philosophic aside Moore implored Butler to yield to the opinion of the majority to which Butler replied that he was a disciple of J S Mill. Dr Donald Johnson (Conservative, Carlisle) asked how many persons originally charged with murder had been found guilty and had had the charge reduced to one of manslaughter on the basis of diminished responsibility. Butler replied that the figure was sixty-six - a

---

[309] HC Deb, vol 612, col. 66, 5th November 1959
[310] HC Deb, vol 613, *col. 61*, written answer, 12th November 1959
[311] HC Deb, vol 621, col 1464-5, 14th April 1960

surprisingly high number as Butler conceded.[312]

Controversial murder cases continued to hit the headlines. In April 1960 'Gypsy' Joe Smith was convicted of the capital murder of a PC Meehan in Woolwich at the Old Bailey in front of Donovan. He appealed before Byrne, Sachs and Winn on the grounds of misdirection of the jury and the appeal was allowed and a verdict of manslaughter and a sentence of ten years was substituted. The Director of Public Prosecutions (DPP) then applied for, and was granted, a certificate to appeal to the Lords against the decision of the Appeal Court. The appeal to the Lords was heard by the Lord Chancellor Kilmuir (Sir David Maxwell Fyfe, former Home Secretary), Lord Parker (LCJ), Goddard (former LCJ), and Denning and Tucker. They overturned the Appeal Court's quashing of the original conviction and restored the capital murder conviction (and therefore the death sentence that went with it). The Home Secretary then commuted the sentence.[313]

This case was followed by another deeply contentious one involving the convictions of four men (Norman Harris, Christopher Darby, Francis Forsyth and Terrence Lutt) for a murder (three of them for capital murder) in September 1960 before Mr Justice Winn, the convictions resting again on the doctrine of constructive malice.[314] The case provoked another spate of debate and newspaper correspondence, with a clutch of public figures writing to the *Times* to plead for clemency in the case of one of the defendants (Forsyth) who was only eighteen; a petition signed by 2,000 handed to the Home Office calling for the reprieve of both the men sentenced to death (the third was under eighteen and thus immune); and a telegram to the Queen from the mother of one of the men. Both youths were hanged in November 1960. Silverman took the opportunity to tackle Butler over the case on the day of the executions and asked him to explain to the House why he had chosen not to issue a reprieve in respect of Forsyth and Harris. Butler declined to give an explanation 'in accordance with tradition'. Silverman then railed against the iniquity of being unable to question the Home Secretary on these questions until after an execution had taken place.[315]

There were calls in Parliament from both Christopher Mayhew (Labour, Woolwich East) and Elwyn Jones (Labour, West Ham South) regarding the decision of the Lords in DPP v Smith ('Gypsy Joe Smith') for the Act to be amended so as to redefine murder to exclude cases where there was no intent to kill, but only an intent to cause grievous bodily harm, but these calls were rejected by Butler.[316] The NCACP which had suspended its activities after the

---

[312] HC Deb, vol 623, col 1460, 19th May 1960

[313] Block and Hostettler, op cit, pp.207-208

[314] Block and Hostettler, ibid, pp.209-211

[315] HC Deb, vol 629, col. 1223-4, 10th November 1960 (Business of the House)

[316] HC Deb, vol 630, *col. 122*, 24th November 1960 (Mayhew); vol 633, *col. 47*, 26th January 1961 (Jones) - both written answers

passage of the Act three years previously, now resumed its activities, calling for the complete abolition of capital punishment.[317]

Parliamentary activity continued apace. Whilst Silverman pressed for complete abolition, others on the Tory backbenches petitioned for an extension of the scope of the offence of capital murder, especially to embrace murders committed in the course of sexual attack, and the repeal or amendment of the Act to restore the status quo ante. Butler remained steadfastly neutral, arguing for the Act to be given longer to work before a definite judgment be made as to its effectiveness. Silverman then took up the case of George Riley, recently convicted and sentenced to hang, and he once again challenged the ruling of the Speaker upholding the tradition that no matter affecting a pending capital sentence could be discussed in the House until after the sentence had been carried out.[318] Victor Yates (Labour, Birmingham Ladywood) also raised the case of Riley with Butler to ask if he would have an enquiry to see if there had been a miscarriage of justice, but Butler stated that there had been no miscarriage and that there would be no enquiry.[319] In a written answer two weeks later to the same questioner he agreed to place a transcript of the case in the Commons library.[320]

Bryant Godman Irvine (Conservative, Rye) presented a petition on behalf of a constituent for the repeal of the Act and the restoration of capital punishment for all murders of women.[321] There were further calls for revision of the Act from Commander John Kerans (Conservative, The Hartlepools) and Roger Gresham-Cooke (Conservative, Twickenham) who demanded capital punishment for all murders committed in the course of criminal sexual acts; Sir Thomas Moore who asked for murder with rape to be brought within the ambit of capital punishment; and Jo Grimond calling again for an enquiry into the operation of the Act. Kerans, Gresham-Cooke and Moore all emphasized what they believed to be the rising level of anger in the community at the government's failure to act. Another MP, Eric Fletcher (Labour, Islington East) stressed to Butler the widespread level of dissatisfaction with the working of the Act, both on the part of abolitionists and retentionists. Butler yet again stressed

---

[317] Block and Hostettler, op cit. p.211

[318] HC Deb, vol 635, cols 1745-6, 2nd March 1961

[319] HC Deb, vol 635, col 1745-6, 2nd March 1961

[320] HC Deb, vol 636, *col 142-3*, 16th March 1961 - written answer

[321] Petition presented on behalf of Clifford Francis Winterson for the repeal of the Homicide Act 1957: *Wherefore your Petitioner prays that the said law known as the Homicide Act 1957 may be utterly revoked or so amended in Parliament as to restore fully the aforementioned deterrent protection of the penalty of capital punishment for each and every female person against any crime of murder that might be committed against any one of these persons, which protection they had and cherished before the law known as the Homicide Act 1957 deprived and took away from them this ancient and well-established protection in law.* A very good petition commented Gerald Nabarro (Conservative, Kidderminster). HC Deb, vol 634, col. 1729, 16th February 1961

the need for the Act to be given longer to work.[322]

Silverman was suspended from the PLP in March 1961, along with four other MPs as a result of rebelling against the party line on the defence estimates (he voted against the government whereas the party policy was to abstain).[323] This, however, did not noticeably affect his conduct of the abolition campaign.

Despite his outward implacability all of this Parliamentary activity had had its effect on Butler, and on 8th February 1961 he submitted a memorandum to the Cabinet pointing out that he was under pressure to do something about capital punishment.[324] The Howard League and the NCACP had obtained a lot of publicity *vis a vis* the Ruth Ellis, Derek Bentley and Timothy Evans cases, and on the other hand there were a lot of Conservative MPs who wanted hanging restored for all categories of murder because the murder rate had risen since 1957. Butler argued that he either had to abolish hanging altogether or revert to the position ante 1957. It was, he felt, neither practical nor desirable to alter the existing categories of murder - and he proposed therefore to leave the law unchanged for the moment. On 12th February the Cabinet endorsed Butler's recommendations and the issue was not debated again by the Cabinet during Macmillan's premiership.[325] Norman Brook, Cabinet secretary, minuted to the Prime Minister in regard to the question following on from Butler's submission to Cabinet on 8th February:-[326]

> There is a growing recognition that the Homicide Act 1957 was a mistake. It was inherently unsound to distinguish between capital and non-capital murder - and experience is emphasising the anomalies to which this gives rise.
> On the other hand if the law is to be changed there are only two alternatives - to restore the death penalty for all murders or to abolish it altogether. And on this public opinion is pretty evenly divided. The pressures on the home secretary come from both sides - from the people who want capital punishment extended and from those who want it abolished.
> As there is unlikely to be a clear majority support for either course of action the Home Secretary favours taking none: he suggests that he should play this long. But there is one difficulty which will have to be watched. The Home Secretary says that "it has always been in view" that the Act should have a five years run. The Act came into force in March 1957 and a five year experiment would end in March 1962. If we do nothing until then it may be necessary to set up some form of enquiry in order to prevent this from becoming an issue at the next election. A further enquiry might be

---

[322] HC Deb, vol 634, col 1730-1, 16th February 1961

[323] The other four were William Baxter (W Stirlingshire), S O Davies (Merthyr Tydfil), Michael Foot (Ebbw Vale) and Emrys Hughes (S Ayrshire). The rebellion was a protest over the government's nuclear weapons policy (and the official opposition's stance in relation to that policy). The whip was restored to all five in May 1963 under the party leadership of Wilson.

[324] Lamb, *The Macmillan Years*, op cit, p.410

[325] Lamb, ibid. See The National Archives (TNA): CAB 129/104 and CAB 128/35.

[326] TNA: PRO, PREM 11/4690 Class 1960-1964 Criminal - Item 1 - memo from Norman Brook to PM - 10th February 1961 CP (C(61) 20)

something of an embarrassment. It may be wiser therefore in any future reference to an experimental period to speak in terms of at least five years.

The Home Secretary's paper raises two subsidiary issues. One is the Evans case. If it cannot now be positively established that Evans was innocent of the murder of his child there can be no question of giving him a free pardon, and no point in having a further enquiry. Mr Charles Pannell will on Tuesday seek leave under the ten minute rule to introduce a bill to provide for the transfer of Evans remains to his next of kin. If the bill passed it would be tantamount to Parliament declaring in favour of Evans innocence. The legislation committee have agreed that the government should not oppose the motion seeking leave to introduce the bill but should block it on second reading.

The second point is the pressure under which the Home Secretary comes on decisions on capital cases. Cabinet will no doubt endorse his view that he should continue to resist demands for debates on these.

This was telling stuff, although of course confidential to the Cabinet, but it was clear that nothing was going to happen on the legislative front for a while yet. There was, however, a criminal justice bill going through the House.

Criminal Justice Bill 1961

In April 1961 Labour MP Alice Bacon tabled an amendment to the Criminal Justice Bill, then in passage through the Commons, to prohibit sentence of death being passed on anyone under the age of twenty-one (as against the then minimum age of eighteen). It gave an opportunity to the House for a general debate on the hanging question for the first time since the passage of the Homicide Act, and was duly seized upon by the protagonists of the abolitionist and retentionist causes. The clause had been defeated in committee by 16-15, and was tabled again at report stage by James MacColl (Labour, Widnes).

Notably, the Conservative abolitionist Peter Kirk (Gravesend) abstained, taking the view that whatever one's opinion of capital punishment it would be wrong to distinguish between eighteen and twenty-one year olds.[327] Michael Foot said that he couldn't follow Kirk's reasoning; surely any abatement was better than none. Sir Douglas Glover (Conservative, Ormskirk) who was convinced of the deterrent value of hanging, felt that people were more mature at eighteen than they had been in the past, and that there might even be a case for lowering the age limit, not raising it. Victor Yates, on the other hand, supported the clause, and felt that those under twenty-one were still emotionally immature. Sir Peter Rawlinson (Conservative, Epsom) also felt that eighteen year olds were more mature than before and opposed the clause. In practice members' attitudes to the clause were conditioned by their attitude to capital punishment generally whatever the specific nature of the clause. Silverman was of course vocal in support, pointing out the inconsistency of hanging people at

---

[327] HC Deb, vol 638, col 165-203, 11th April 1961 - Criminal Justice Bill, report stage

eighteen though at that age they were not able to vote. Sir Henry d'Avigdor-Goldsmid (Conservative, Walsall South), an abolitionist, supported the clause, saying that deterrence couldn't be measured, and that it may have been a positive attraction.

The debate was summarized by Butler who said that the Royal Commission had considered the matter and had come down in favour of twenty-one as against eighteen by one vote. The government, however, felt unable to accept the clause, re-iterating the mantra that it was too soon to amend the Homicide Act. Moreover, the number of people aged between seventeen and twenty-one who had been convicted of crimes of violence had continued to rise from 1,635 in 1957 to 2,084 in 1958 and 2,366 in 1959. In 1951 there were seven murders committed by those aged between eighteen and twenty-one, in 1955-6 the number fell to five, rose to nine in 1957 and to fifteen in 1958 and in 1960 to ten. He did not consider that those under twenty-one were necessarily immature. They were often the ringleaders, and raising the age to twenty-one might give out the wrong signals. The prerogative of mercy still existed, and of the four men under twenty-one who had been convicted of capital murder since the coming into operation of the Homicide Act, two had been hanged and two reprieved. David Weitzman (Labour, Hackney North and Stoke Newington) queried why it was right in some cases to hang those under twenty-one, but not under any circumstances to send them to prison. Michael Foot queried whether age was a factor in the decision to reprieve the two under twenty-ones mentioned, and Butler replied in the affirmative.

Alice Bacon summed up for the Opposition and announced that there would be a free vote on that side of the House. She felt unable to congratulate the Home Secretary on his speech, and expressed the view that if he had been a backbencher then he would probably have supported the clause. The fact that Butler felt it too early to amend the Homicide Act had nothing whatever to do with the present clause, she argued, given that the Act made no mention of the minimum age, and that the last change in that regard had been in 1908 when it had been raised from sixteen to eighteen. The Select Committee of 1930 had recommended that no-one should hang under twenty-one. The clause was defeated on second reading by 229-144, with two Conservatives, Peter Kirk and Barnaby Drayson (Skipton) defying the whips to vote with Labour for the amendment.[328] On the other side there was one Labour MP, Alan Brown (Tottenham), who was soon to resign the Labour whip and sit as an independent, who voted against the clause.

Tangentially, there was also an amendment tabled to the bill to reinstate flogging for violent offences, defeated by 259-67, with all 67 supporters, including the two tellers, coming from the Conservative Party, and including Sir

---

[328] Jackson, Robert J, *Rebels and Whips: An Analysis of Dissension, Discipline and Cohesion in British Political Parties* (London: Macmillan, 1968) p.166. HC Deb, vol 638, col 266 and 350. *The Times* 13th April 1961.

Beverley Baxter (an abolitionist respecting capital punishment though evidently not for corporal), Cyril Osborne, Graham Page, Sir Thomas Moore and Margaret Thatcher (Finchley).[329]

Up until that time there had been twenty-nine people convicted of capital murder from the inception of the Homicide Act, of which sixteen had been hanged, ten reprieved, and of whom three had had their convictions reduced to manslaughter on appeal.[330]

A few days later Frederick Harris (Conservative, Croydon North-West) asked Butler if he would arrange for a national referendum to ascertain public opinion regarding a revision of the Homicide Act to permit the full restoration of capital punishment for murder. Butler baldly told him no, and that referenda were not part of our constitutional practice, and that he would prefer the House to express its opinion.[331] Sir Thomas Moore asked him about his analysis of recent murders. Butler replied that the analysis by the Home Office Research Unit was continuing and that the results would be made public when available.[332]

The Timothy Evans Case

In the meantime there were steady rumblings about the Evans case, which, by 1961 had once again come to a head, partly as a result of the publication of another book on the case, by Ludovic Kennedy. Early that year Leo Abse (Labour, Pontypool) pressed Butler to institute a public enquiry into the case to see if there had been a miscarriage, George Rogers (Labour, Kensington North) asked Butler if he had received any new evidence and Silverman asked him if he would grant a posthumous pardon. Butler stonewalled but said that he had been examining new material including the book on the case by Kennedy.[333] Reginald Paget asked if the Home Secretary would grant permission for Evans' remains to be removed from prison and re-interred in consecrated ground, and Jo Grimond asked if he would grant a free pardon, but both to no avail since Butler said he was not yet in a position to add

---

[329] HC Deb, vol 638, col 145-8, 11th April 1961 New clause (corporal punishment for young offenders on second and subsequent conviction): 'Magistrates Courts and the superior courts shall have the power to pass a sentence of corporal punishment as an alternative to a sentence of detention in remand homes, detention centres, Borstal institutions or prison on young male offenders convicted of crimes of violence for whatever purpose committed, such punishment to be with the cane up to the age of 17 years and with the birch for offenders of more than 17 years but less than 21 years of age: Provided that no such sentence of corporal punishment shall be passed on such offender except in the case of a second or subsequent conviction for such a crime.' [Sir T Moore]

[330] Block and Hostettler, op cit, p.212

[331] HC Deb, vol 638, col. 1356-7, 20th April 1961

[332] HC Deb, vol 638, col. 1371-2, 20th April 1961

[333] HC Deb, vol 633, *col. 49*, 26th January 1961 - written answer

to his previous reply.[334]

Charles Pannell (Labour, Leeds West) tabled a motion that leave be given to bring in a bill to provide for Evans' remains to be transferred to his next-of-kin, observing that if the House concurred then it would be accepting that he was wrongly convicted. He quoted Lord Birkett as saying that, 'If the facts as they are now known had been known in 1950 no jury could possibly have said that the case against Evans was proved beyond all reasonable doubt.' He also said that one of the co-sponsors of the bill was Chuter Ede (South Shields), the Home Secretary at the time of the Evans case, who had said that if he had known then what he knows now he would have stopped the execution. The original Scott Henderson enquiry into the case was now worthless, he argued, having been far too rushed.[335]

On 16th February 1961 Butler was bombarded with more questions on Evans by Michael Foot, Reginald Paget and Richard Marsh (Labour, Greenwich) but was unmoved.[336] Two weeks later Michael Foot, Silverman and William Deedes (Ashford, a Conservative retentionist) all asked whether Butler would make a further statement. He said that he had read *10 Rillington Place* (the book on the case by Ludovic Kennedy) with 'great care', but that he didn't think that a further enquiry would bring new information to light. He said he had also read the correspondence in the *Sunday Times* from Dr Teare and Kennedy on the 5th and 12th March. There was, however, no precedent for a posthumous free pardon and the legal powers to do so were doubtful, and in view of the Capital Punishment Amendment Act 1868 he was unable to agree to the proposal that Evans' remains should now be removed from Pentonville Prison.[337]

But the Evans case would not go away and a few months later, on the next supply day when the Opposition chooses the topic of debate, Patrick Gordon Walker opened a debate on the case.[338] He argued that there had been a terrible miscarriage of justice, which was being increasingly recognized, and Lord Birkett had said as much in an article in the *Observer* on 15th January 1961. He pressed for an enquiry to be set up to deal with two key questions: was he wrongly convicted and should his remains be returned to his parents for burial. He said that if Evans were to be regarded as guilty then it was necessary to accept a fantastic coincidence - namely that there were two murderers residing in the same house at the same time but operating independently of each

---

[334] HC Deb, vol 633, col. 148, 2nd February 1961
[335] HC Deb, vol 634, col. 1245-8, 14th February 1961. The Bill was given a first reading, to be read a second time on 24th February. Its sponsors were:- Charles Pannell, Alice Bacon, James Boyden, James Chuter Ede, Cledwyn Hughes, Bob Mellish, Ted Redhead and Sydney Silverman, all Labour MPs.
[336] HC Deb, vol 634, col. 1752-3, 16th February 1961
[337] HC Deb, vol 636, *col. 141-2*, 16th March 1961 - written answers
[338] HC Deb, vol 642, col. 649-711, 15th June 1961 - Supply Day debate

other and in ignorance of each other.

The Scott Henderson enquiry, Gordon Walker argued, had accepted that Evans was guilty because he had known facts that only the murderer could have known, and that Christie's confession to the murder of Mrs Evans was false. These points were stubbornly clung to, argued Gordon-Walker, by Maxwell Fyfe, the then Home Secretary, in the debate on the Scott Henderson enquiry on 29th July 1953, but in fact Evans had probably been told these things at some point in the investigation. Scott Henderson had concluded that Christie's confession to the murder of Mrs Evans was false because he thought that the more murders he confessed to the better were his chances of being found insane. The present Home Secretary (Butler) had refused to grant an enquiry in a written answer on 16th March, 'on the grounds that it was unlikely that any new evidence would come to light and that the passage of time would have caused memories to dim and to be affected by speculation.' But, Gordon Walker continued, that argument would have stopped the pardon and release of Oscar Slater (a *cause celebre* of pre First World War vintage).[339] Scott Henderson had been very rushed and a new enquiry could examine the documents in an unhurried way. If Evans had been still alive he would long ago have been freed, pardoned and compensated. Why cannot justice be retrospective and posthumous, he concluded?

Sir Hugh Lucas-Tooth (Conservative, Hendon South) who had been Under-Secretary of State at the Home Office at the relevant time, pointed out that if Evans had been tried today he would have had the defence of diminished responsibility under section 2 of the Homicide Act and would have been convicted of manslaughter not murder. Scott Henderson had been perfectly satisfactory, and was carried out in private because some material would not have come out if it had been public; some people would have been reluctant to answer certain questions. No further enquiry was necessary, he asserted. Chuter Ede rejected the idea that there had been no impropriety regarding Scott Henderson. Leslie Hale (Labour, Oldham West) said that the evidence had been given in the absence of legal advice for Evans. Silverman said he doubted there was any justification for Scott Henderson being in secret, but anyway the people involved had not been given any right to cross-examine. Lucas-Tooth said there could only be a justification for a new enquiry in the event of new evidence.

Chuter Ede, who had been Home Secretary in the Attlee government at the time of the Evans trial, said that the then Prime Minister had told him, 'You understand that we are not bound to support any decision that you give in capital cases and you are not entitled to come to us and to ask for our view. You must make the decision yourself and you must bear the responsibility yourself.' Chuter Ede quoted from the book *10 Rillington Place* and said that he had had

---

[339]Toughill, Thomas, *Oscar Slater: The Mystery Solved* (Edinburgh: Canongate, 1993)

conversations with the author, Ludovic Kennedy. He quoted passages dealing with Scott Henderson that demonstrated that Bernard Gillis, QC, counsel for Mrs Probert (Evans' mother) had not been allowed to see evidence taken from previous witnesses and to cross-examine them; had not been given access to copies of Evans' original statements and other relevant documents and had not been allowed to examine a number of witnesses of his own. He had been allowed to call them but had to submit questions for them to be asked and Scott Henderson reserved the right to decide whether or not to ask them. Chuter Ede derided the enquiry, conducted in that fashion, as a travesty. He had corresponded with Butler and had received a reply saying, 'I am advised that I cannot say that this man Evans was innocent.' Birkett had said that:-

> If the facts as they are now known had been known in 1950 no jury could possibly have said that the case against Evans had been proved beyond all reasonable doubt. This is the real ground of complaint against the Scott-Henderson Report. The Report was honest and painstaking enough and contained more cogent reasons for the conclusions it contained; but there are equally cogent reasons for believing these conclusions to be wrong.

Sydney Silverman dealt with another aspect of the case. Lucas-Tooth had said earlier in the debate that Evans would not have hanged had he been tried today because of the defence of diminished responsibility under section 2 of the Homicide Act, but he was mistaken in this because, Silverman argued, the Act provided that a man who commits murder on more than one occasion is guilty of capital murder. The terms of reference of the Scott Henderson enquiry were to decide whether there may have been a miscarriage of justice in the conviction of Evans for the murder of Geraldine Evans and he reported that in his opinion there were no grounds for so supposing. I say, Silverman declared, that no honest man, on the evidence before Scott Henderson could have made the report he made. It was just not true that there were no grounds. Scott Henderson must have known it was not true. Lucas-Tooth had suggested that people's view on the Evans case was influenced by their view on capital punishment, but I cannot follow that, he said, for everyone including the most convinced supporter of hanging (perhaps especially the convinced supporter) has an interest in seeing that an innocent man is not hanged. People can tolerate mistakes, but what undermines confidence in our judicial system is that when a mistake is made all the forces of the State are used not to uncover it but to conceal it. He could not understand the stubbornness of the Home Secretary. If another enquiry were to be held, let it be open and let all the evidence be heard, he concluded.

Tom Iremonger (Conservative, Ilford North) criticized Silverman's imputation of dishonesty against Scott Henderson. He argued that it was constitutionally undesirable for the Committee of Supply to set itself up as a judicial body by arranging a pardon. We should not set up an enquiry with, in effect, a directive to arrive at a certain finding, he argued. George Rogers

(Labour, Kensington North), technically Evans' and Christie's MP at the relevant time, said he had been the first person to be convinced of Evans' innocence, when Evans' mother came to see him after his appeal had been turned down. Scott Henderson was secretive and hurried, and he was only once allowed to see Christie, briefly, in his cell. Reader Harris (Conservative, Heston and Isleworth) argued for a new enquiry or perhaps even an outright pardon. Sir Frank Soskice (Labour, Newport) also argued for a new enquiry. Scott Henderson's conclusions and the process of reaching them did not carry any conviction and a new public enquiry by a High Court judge was needed, he declared.

Butler replied that he had studied all the books on the case with great care, including Kennedy's, but that Kennedy did not add any new facts, and the facts as they are did not point conclusively to Evans' innocence. A new enquiry would not bring us any closer to the truth. There was no precedent, as he had said previously on 16th March, for granting a posthumous free pardon and the power to do so was doubtful. It may be, he argued, that if the facts as they are now known were known then that the jury would not have convicted, but that is not a basis on which a pardon can be granted. There is a difference between granting a reprieve in a capital case, and granting a free pardon. If there is any doubt about guilt then that is a basis for a reprieve, but not a pardon which can only be granted where there is a certainty, which is not the case here. Therefore, he said, he could not authorize the removal of the remains, nor under the Capital Punishment Amendment Act 1868 remove the body. Legislation would be necessary.

A week after the Evans' debate there was an attempt to introduce a bill to that effect, but the second reading was objected to by Dudley Williams (Conservative, Exeter) and got no further.[340] Matters regarding Evans were thus still in abeyance.

The issue of capital punishment was being debated everywhere. It was the subject of a debate by the Lower House of the Convocation of Canterbury in October 1961. The Conservative Party Annual Conference at Brighton that year debated a motion to extend capital punishment to all murders where the insanity of the defendant was not proven. The House of Lords debated a motion on the pamphlet 'Murder', promulgated by the NCACP, that turned into a debate on the whole question of capital punishment.

The Hanratty Case

In August 1961 there occurred the so-called A6 murder for which James Hanratty was charged, tried and convicted in February 1962. His appeal was rejected in March 1962, and despite widespread misgivings about his guilt he

---

[340] HC Deb, vol 642, col 1934-5, 23rd June 1961 - Timothy John Evans Bill

was hanged on 4th April. This case, too, provoked a torrent of Parliamentary activity. Tom Driberg (Labour, Barking) raised the case with Butler in a written question, querying what reports on Hanratty's mental history he had studied before refusing to exercise the prerogative, and whether he would publish these reports. Butler said he had studied all the medical reports, from three experienced doctors, and saw no grounds for a reprieve, and that he would not publish a summary of these, in accordance with usual practice.[341]

A year later Fenner Brockway (Labour, Eton and Slough) called for an investigation into the case, but the new Home Secretary, Henry Brooke, declined.[342] The following day there was a debate on the Hanratty case.[343] Brockway said that he had thought long and hard as to whether to initiate the debate. He had been investigating the case for a year since having been approached by a Slough journalist (a Mr Mason) and a businessman and barrister who had followed the case. Mason had approached him before Hanratty had been hanged. Brockway reprised the case: at the trial he had disastrously presented a phoney alibi; the evidence had been regarded as insufficient and there was surprise that there wasn't a reprieve (from Butler). He had known, as the jury hadn't, that Hanratty had been certified as mentally defective – he had had a brain operation after an accident after which character deterioration was marked. Refusal of a reprieve to a mental defective seems inexcusable. He had sent a memo to the Home Secretary and other MPs containing a confession by another man made orally to a barrister and handed in written form to him (Brockway) in May 1962. It contained points additional to those adduced in the trial. The man – Mr X – had been to see Hanratty's father and had confessed to him, but said that he didn't think Hanratty would be hanged.

Peter Kirk (Conservative, Gravesend) said that he had been contacted by Hanratty's solicitor after the conviction but before the execution and sent some papers. A case like this is always bedevilled by the arguments for and against hanging, he went on. The two previous cases like this, where serious doubts were raised about guilt after execution (Evans and Rowland) saw people line up with abolitionists arguing for a reversal of the verdict, and retentionists for no change. I think, he said, that if the present evidence had been before the jury they would not have convicted, and that there should be a public enquiry (public in view of the criticisms of Scott Henderson regarding the Evans case). Eric Fletcher (Labour, Islington East) agreed with Kirk that there should be an enquiry given the unsatisfactoriness of the evidence (especially the ID parade), and the new evidence that had come to light. He had always thought that the strongest argument for abolition was not that there was something wrong in capital punishment for a deliberate, clearly proven murder, but that there is the

---

[341] HC Deb, vol 657, *col. 87*, 9th April 1962 - written answer
[342] HC Deb, vol 682, col. 129, 1st August 1963
[343] HC Deb, vol 682, col. 795-832, 2nd August 1963

risk that a completely innocent man may be hanged.

Dr Donald Johnson (Conservative, Carlisle) concurred that there should be an enquiry – though he was not himself an abolitionist. He said that he had had grave doubts about both this and the Evans case, and that of a constituent of his, John Armstrong, sentenced to death in 1956 but reprieved by the then Home Secretary (Butler) though he had refused an enquiry. The case had come to his notice in 1958 and a very good *Observer* article in January 1961 argued the merits of the continental inquisitorial system as against our adversarial system. The Home Secretary should look at our whole system of justice, he continued. Those of low intelligence are often convicted before they start unless they have clear proof of innocence – e.g. Hanratty, Evans and Armstrong (who though intelligent had an inept pattern of behaviour) – whilst the guilty often tend to escape, e.g. Donald Hume.

Niall MacDermot (Labour, Derby North) urged the Home Secretary not to refuse an enquiry, given the mounting number of criticisms of the jury system. He believed that an innocent man was less likely to be convicted by a jury than by any other tribunal, except where the evidence is ID – because juries for some reason were extraordinarily distrustful of this defence. The ID evidence against Hanratty was not at all convincing, but he had constructed two false alibis – perhaps as a function of his mental defectiveness. Though I am reluctant to argue, he said, that the Home Secretary should re-open the matter, yet he should not refuse an enquiry upon the ground's that the jury's verdict must not be questioned – it is unfortunate that the Court of Appeal is so reluctant to do so. Chuter Ede (Lab, South Shields) followed previous speakers in calling for an enquiry in order to restore public confidence in the judicial system, which was no longer seen as infallible.

Henry Brooke (Home Secretary) recognised Brockway's tremendous effort, but said that false confessions were common, and that it had not been the only one received by his predecessor in relation to the Hanratty case. He had never been certified mentally defective, and the question had been carefully considered before his being denied a reprieve. Brooke said that he felt lucky that he had had to deal with only two such cases in his year as Home Secretary. Traditionally Home Secretaries do not give the reasons for their decision as to whether to issue a reprieve. Brooke said that Butler had carefully examined the confession by 'Mr X' but had dismissed it as groundless since it contained inconsistencies. The memorandum from Brockway did not contain much that had not already been brought to his or his predecessor's (Butler's) attention. If I thought there was anything in the memo, he said, I would appoint a public enquiry – but I do not doubt that the conviction was right and that every point in Hanratty's favour was dealt with, and I cannot believe that the confession by 'Mr X' can be valid.

Unease over the case may well have assisted the abolitionists cause, though the first book about the case did not appear until 1963 and serious doubts about Hanratty's guilt didn't surface until at least 1965 by which time abolition had almost been realized.[344]

Further developments

There was a renewed thrust from the NCACP, reinforced by the pamphlet 'Murder', and drawing on the vote of the Lower House of Convocation and the recent decision of New Zealand to abolish capital punishment, and supported by several bishops as well as Julian Huxley, Compton Mackenzie, Henry Moore and Leonard Woolf. Mervyn Stockwood, Bishop of Southwark, announced his intention to introduce a bill into the Upper House for complete abolition, and was supported by the Archbishop of Canterbury, Dr Michael Ramsey. The executive committee of the Society of Friends (the Quakers) came out for total abolition in February 1962.

Butler was having exchanges with several representative backbench supporters of abolition such as Silverman, Chuter Ede, Jeremy Thorpe, Peter Kirk and Julian Critchley in which he indicated he was sympathetic but in which he clearly ruled out further legislation in the present Parliament.[345] The British Council of Churches resolved to press the government for abolition at about this time. In March 1962 Carol Johnson (Labour, Lewisham South) asked Butler if, in view of the recent change in public opinion, he would review the Act, but he again refused.[346] Tom Driberg (Labour, Barking) asked Butler if he had completed his review of the Act, and whether he would make a statement regarding the proposal that there should be longer actual terms served by those sentenced to life imprisonment.[347] Butler replied that the Act was under continuous review, and that at present a life sentence meant about nine years, though in the light of large numbers being sentenced to life for non-capital murder they may have to be detained for longer than hitherto. Driberg suggested that it was opportune to make a special review given that the Act was now five

---

[344] The burgeoning literature on the Hanratty case embraces the following:- Blom-Cooper, Louis *The A6 Murder: Regina v James Hanratty - The Semblance of Truth* (Harmondsworth: Penguin, 1963); Justice, Jean *Murder vs Murder: The British Legal System and the A6 Murder Case* (Paris: Olympia, 1964); Lord Russell of Liverpool *Deadman's Hill - Was Hanratty Guilty?* (London: Martin Secker and Warburg 1965, Icon 1966); Foot, Paul *Who Killed Hanratty?* (London: Cape, 1971, revised London: Panther 1973, revised Harmondsworth: Penguin 1988); Simpson, Keith *Forty Years of Murder* (London: Harrap 1978, London: Grafton 1980); Foot, Paul *A Break in the Silence* Guardian newspaper 25th February 1995; Woffinden, Bob *Miscarriages of Justice* (London: Hodder and Stoughton 1987, London: Coronet 1989); Woffinden, Bob, *Hanratty: The Final Verdict* (London: Macmillan, 1997) and Miller, Leonard, *Shadows of Deadman's Hill: A New Analysis of the A6 Murder* (London: Zoilus, 2001)
[345] Block and Hostettler, op cit, pp. 225-6
[346] HC Deb, vol 655, *col. 179*, 15th March 1962 - written answer
[347] HC Deb, vol 656, col. 1535-8, 29th March 1962

years old, and especially in view of the unsatisfactoriness of it. Butler said there had been no undertaking to have a review after five years. Sir Thomas Moore intervened to say whatever the illogicality of the Act there should be no revision until the country had expressed a view, supported surprisingly by Silverman.

In July 1962 Henry Brooke replaced Butler at the Home Office as part of Macmillan's drastic reshuffle (the 'Night of the Long Knives'), and amongst other changes Manningham-Buller, the Attorney General, replaced the sacked Kilmuir as Lord Chancellor, becoming Viscount Dilhorne. Sir Peter Rawlinson, the Solicitor-General, addressing the City of London Young Conservatives at around that time, supported the Act's distinction between capital and non-capital murder, said that the Act was working as intended and that the Act would not be reviewed for a substantial period of time.[348]

The Campaign from 1962 to 1964

In January 1963 Hugh Gaitskell, leader of the Labour opposition, died and was replaced by Harold Wilson, a passionate supporter of abolition. Wilson's attitude to abolition was made clear at the annual meeting of the Society of Labour Lawyers that year when he said, *inter alia*, that he was sure that the first private members bill to abolish capital punishment would get through the House and be made law. Diarist and shadow cabinet member Anthony Wedgwood Benn observed that this was very dear to Gerald Gardiner's heart, and that the comments were generally taken as an invitation to him (Gardiner) to join any future Labour government (presumably in the capacity of Lord Chancellor).[349] Henry Brooke, the new Home Secretary, re-affirmed the government's support for the continuation of the Act.

The events of 1963, especially the Profumo affair, severely shook the Conservative government and led ultimately to the fall of Macmillan in October 1963 and his replacement by Sir Alec Douglas Home (Lord Home). Brooke and Dilhorne retained their positions as Home Secretary and Lord Chancellor, respectively, in the new Cabinet. On the Labour side Gerald Gardiner, QC, chairman of the NCACP, was elevated to the peerage at the end of 1963, on the nomination of Harold Wilson, and was seen as Labour's Lord Chancellor in-waiting.[350] It was widely rumoured that at the Bar he had refused an appointment to a High Court judgeship in the late 1950s because he was unprepared to pass the death sentence which he might have had to do in that capacity.[351] In fact the appointment was to the Chancery Division, but even

---

[348] Block and Hostettler, op cit, p.227

[349] Benn, Tony, *Out of the Wilderness: Diaries 1963-1967* (London: Arrow, 1987) p.36

[350] Wilson, Harold, *The Labour Government 1964-70: A Personal Record* (Harmondsworth: Penguin, 1974) p.89

[351] Block and Hostettler, op cit, p.229 (reporting a personal communication from Her Honour Jean Graham Hall)

there he would have had to have accepted collective responsibility with his brother judges for the enforcement of capital punishment, and was unprepared so to do.[352]

There were echoes of the Craig/Bentley case when Marcus Lipton asked the Home Secretary why he had decided to release Christopher Craig that coming May. Brooke said that by May he would have been detained for ten and a half years. Lipton questioned the basis on which lifers were released, given that Craig and Frederick Emmett-Dunne were both to be released, though both involved in murder, yet Joseph Doyle was kept in prison for being implicated in a raid on a military unit. Brooke said he was keeping the Doyle case under review.[353]

On 17th December 1963 Russell Pascoe was hanged at Horfield Prison, Bristol. The protests in the city 'reached an enormous volume' according to Wedgwood Benn (whose constituency was in Bristol) and he opined that it would probably be the last hanging to take place there given that capital punishment, 'is on the way out and in the new Parliament it will certainly be abolished.'[354]

In January 1964 Harold Wilson made clear in a current affairs programme, *This Week,* (produced by Associated Rediffusion and then ITV's flagship current affairs show) that if and when a Labour government was returned it would allow a free vote on the issue of capital punishment, and that he had little doubt what the outcome would be given a Labour majority in the House.

The prominence of the issue at that time is indicated by a play *Hang down your head and die* on the topic of capital punishment that was due to be presented by the Oxford University Experimental Theatre Club (see the chapter on cinema and theatre). The Lord Chamberlain (the official theatre censor, whose post and function would soon be abolished anyway) demanded certain cuts in the play. The producer, Braham Murray, contacted Lord Gardiner, to protest and Gardiner, Lord Ted Willis and Kenneth Robinson, MP successfully urged the Lord Chamberlain to rescind his decision and to restore the cuts to the play on the grounds that by excising arguments against capital punishment the Lord Chamberlain was effectively exercising political censorship.[355]

In April 1964 Harold Wilson, addressing the Society of Labour Lawyers, again re-affirmed the intention of a new Labour government to allow a free vote on the question of capital punishment and he attacked the Homicide Act as being indefensible on both rational and moral grounds.[356] In his speech entitled 'Liberty and the Law' which ranged over many legal issues he said: 'I think that

---

[352] Wilson, Harold, op cit, p.89
[353] HC Deb, vol 671, col. 654, 7th February 1963
[354] Benn, op cit, p.83
[355] Block and Hostettler, op cit, p.230
[356]*The Times*, p.10, 21 April 1964, quoted in Block and Hostettler, ibid. p.230

it is generally agreed now that the Homicide Act has neither a rational nor a moral basis and few can be found to defend the present law. We feel that as this is an issue on which people have strong views and which is to some extent a matter of conscience it should be left to a free vote of the House and we are prepared to find government time for it...'

It seems that in September 1964 Prime Minister Sir Alec Douglas-Home and Home Secretary Henry Brooke discussed the issue and agreed that the 1957 Act was unworkable following a civil service minute that the distinction between capital and non-capital murder was 'inherently unsound'.[357] Nonetheless they decided to let the matter rest, but the note of the conversation concluded that: 'The next Home Secretary of whatever party will have to abolish the death penalty.'(!)

After delaying the calling of a general election until almost the last legal date, in the hope of an improvement in the position of his party in the polls, Douglas-Home went to the country on 15th October 1964. The Labour manifesto made no mention of the issue of capital punishment. Labour won the election with an overall majority of just four, and Wilson became Prime Minister. As expected he appointed Gardiner to the Woolsack, with Sir Frank Soskice going to the Home Office, Elwyn Jones becoming Attorney-General and Dingle Foot Solicitor-General. With the advent of a Labour government the abolitionists could finally see the finishing tape in sight.

Conclusion

The period from the passage of the Homicide Act in March 1957 to the general election of October 1964 was characterized by sustained but relatively low-intensity activity on both sides of the debate, inside and outside of Parliament. Abolitionists in the Commons, mainly on the Labour side of the House, sought to keep the question alive by assailing the Home Secretary and Attorney-General on each and every capital sentence that was passed, raising the matter of reprieves and referrals and the construction of the Act as they applied to the case in hand. They also kept up pressure on the Home Secretary to review the working of the Act, and to narrow further the ambit of the capital sentence, such as by seeking to raise the minimum age at which one could hang from eighteen to twenty-one. Outside the House abolitionists, particularly the NCACP, kept up the campaign, reviving it every so often when a particularly contentious case came along. On the retentionist side there was also activity. An assortment of Conservative backbenchers made repeated attempts to widen the scope of capital murder, such as to embrace the murder of children or murder by poisoning, and in some cases to seek the restoration of the pre-Homicide Act

---

[357] TNA: PREM 11/4690 Class 1960-64 Criminal, Item 2, memo from 'DJM' 22nd September 1964. Quoted by Lamb, op cit, p.410

position.

The Conservative government of the day was steadfast in seeking to maintain the status quo, and in resisting attempts to push it one way or the other. Butler repeated the mantra-like formulation that the Act had to be given a chance to work so that one could assess its merits in practice. In reality he was increasingly of the view that the Act and the distinction between capital and non-capital murder was illogical and unsustainable, and that in the long term hanging would almost certainly go. The irrationality of the two tier system was plain for all to see on both sides of the debate and within 'disinterested' legal opinion, and there was a growing consensus that things could not continue indefinitely. Judicial and clerical opinion was beginning a seismic shift towards abolitionism, reflecting the liberal tide in both of those institutions. Nonetheless, until a change of government were to occur, there would be no change in the legal position.

CHAPTER 7

THE CHURCHES

G iven the ostensibly 'ethical' nature of the capital punishment debate the role of the churches was, arguably, central to the success or failure of the campaign. Yet few churches took an unambiguous line on the issue. Most churches were vaguely abolitionist in outlook but were careful to avoid taking too firm a stance, partly perhaps because they feared alienating members if they became too heavily mired in political controversy. Moreover, the debate occurred at a time when, arguably, the churches were losing influence and when the Christian ethic was under attack from many quarters. This chapter examines, chiefly, the role played by the Church of England, the Roman Catholic Church (in England), the Quakers, the nonconformist denominations and the Jewish religion.

The Church of England

The Church of England was central to the debate given that it was the established church and still carried great moral authority, even as late as the mid twentieth century, notwithstanding the trend towards secularization that had marked the previous decades of the century. Moreover, it commanded a substantial block of votes in the House of Lords. Down the ages it had consistently buttressed and sanctified the institution of hanging, and conferred upon it a scriptural legitimacy without which it could scarcely have survived.[358] Throughout the era of the *Bloody Code* and well into the nineteenth century the hierarchy of the Church had unerringly supported hanging by speaking against and voting down bills to restrict hanging in the Upper House. For example, in 1810 the Archbishop of Canterbury and six other bishops voted down a bill passed in the Commons that would have abolished hanging for stealing property to the value of five shillings from a shop.[359] The Church had consistently preached the righteousness of capital punishment from pulpit and pamphlet.
The attitude of the Anglican Church to capital punishment did not change substantially or at all until the emergence of William Temple, a radical intellectual, who took a strongly abolitionist line in the 1920s and onwards. In

---

[358] Potter, Harry, *Hanging in Judgment: Religion and the Death Penalty in England from the Bloody Code to Abolition* (London: SCM Press, 1993) passim
[359] Potter, ibid, Introduction vii

1924 socially concerned Christians of all denominations met in Birmingham for a conference on Christian Politics, Economics and Citizenship (COPEC) under Temple's chairmanship, and though the executive was divided on the question of capital punishment the conference voted for abolition by a large majority. As Archbishop of York and then of Canterbury Temple was hugely influential but nonetheless the great majority of the bishops and the Anglican clergy remained opposed to abolition. His premature death in 1944 and the elevation of the conservative Geoffrey Fisher to the see of Canterbury (rather than the progressive Bell) set back the cause of abolitionism considerably.[360]

In the 1948 abolition debate in the Lords there were mixed views expressed by the prelates and few were outright abolitionists, and one bishop - Truro - wanted not merely to retain capital punishment but to extend it to other crimes that resulted in severe injury such as attempted murder and rape.[361] Most significantly the new Archbishop of Canterbury, Fisher, spoke in rather ambiguous terms which neither supported the abolition clause nor opposed it outright but hoped that it might be amended: 'so that while it is tempered to meet the exigencies of our present situation it may still be a step forward to that goal which every Christian must desire even if Christians may still differ as to the rapidity of the pace with which it can be approached.' In other words he appeared to desire abolition, but not just yet. Fisher's evidence to the Gowers' Commission echoed the retentionist views he had expressed in the Lords debate to the effect that the death penalty had a quasi-religious and sacral quality to it which expressed society's revulsion against the offence of murder and, moreover, this effect was diluted by the large number of reprieves that took place. In his view the death sentence should not be invoked if it were likely that it was going to be commuted.[362] Other Anglican witnesses to the Commission tended to take a retentionist stance. Bell became the main proponent of abolition within the episcopacy as the campaign started to hot up again in 1955, and he attempted to rally support among his fellow bishops, as well as acting as the conduit between the church and the NCACP.[363] He was also in contact with

---

[360] Geoffrey Francis Fisher, Baron Fisher of Lambeth, GCVO (1887-1972). Headmaster of Repton 1914, Bishop of Chester 1932, Bishop of London 1939, Archbishop of Canterbury 1945-1961. Regarded as a conservative and negative Primate, although it is hard to go all the way with Potter's assessment that had it not been for the succession of Fisher then capital punishment would have been abolished much sooner than it was and perhaps as early as 1948.

[361] Potter, op cit, pp.146-152. Dr Joseph Wellington Hunkin, Bishop of Truro 1935-1951

[362] Minutes of evidence to the Royal Commission (14), 3rd February 1950. His evidence was interrupted by an outburst from the gallery by Mrs van der Elst who had to be removed. Potter, ibid, p.157

[363] He was in frequent contact with the NCACP and other abolitionists concerning the balance of opinion within the episcopacy, e.g. Bell to Gardiner 23rd June 1956 saying that York, Sheffield, Liverpool and Manchester were supporters, as were Birmingham and Chelmsford (not yet in the Lords). Bell papers, vol 218, ff.241. Lambeth Palace Archives.

Gowers, who by then had become an abolitionist.[364]

Outside the ranks of the episcopacy the most prominent Anglican abolitionist was Canon Collins. Christian Action (CA), as noted, was closely associated with the NCACP.[365] Collins preached against hanging at St Paul's and received many abusive letters from 'church people who felt that it was an essential safeguard of the British way of life.'[366] Capital punishment was an issue about which the Christian Action Council had been thinking for a long time and it felt it 'can no longer remain passive in the face of repeated representations from many of our members and of present public interest.' It noted that several recent cases (especially Evans, Bentley and Ellis) had aroused deep concern and that with an average of twelve executions a year there could be no excuse for 'Christian men and women refusing to face this question seriously.' It recognized 'that not all Christians are yet of one mind on this problem' and stated that 'we think on both sides there are those who base their arguments on prejudice rather than factual evidence, on emotion rather than clear thinking, and this, we believe, is particularly true of some who are in favour of retention and, though probably quite unconsciously, are moved by the human desire for vengeance.' Thus in the eyes of CA the conversion of all Christians to abolitionism was merely a matter of time, and the tendency towards irrationality was perhaps rather more on one side than the other.

This ferment within the Church was reflected in the correspondence columns of *The Church Times*, the main organ of the Anglican Church. Diana Collins, wife of Canon Collins, wrote to the paper early in 1956 concerning a letter from a Canon Symon which had attacked the emotional tone of much of the abolitionist thinking within the church.[367] Symon replied the following week sneering at her views and citing the Nuremberg trials and asking whether she thought that all that was required was the use of time 'to bring about a real conversion and amendment of life?'[368] H B Vaisey cited the views of the late Bishop Seaton of Wakefield, who as a chaplain, had started out as an abolitionist but became a supporter of hanging because so many men recognized the justice and appropriateness of their sentence and in some cases

---

[364] Gowers to Bell, 26th February 1957 in which he says he thinks Fisher has been reading his book and has got himself into a position untenable for a Christian. The Homicide Bill was a bad one, he said, in that it is both completely unreasonable and utterly dishonest – a striking and apparently unsuccessful attempt to 'fool all the people some of the time'. Bell papers, ibid, ff.263-4.

[365] He proposed to a Christian Action council meeting as early as 1954 that they should undertake a campaign against hanging which should concentrate on changing opinion within the Church where most of the bishops were on the 'wrong side' and where 'the vast majority of church people of all denominations thought that the retention of capital punishment was necessary, and that it was compatible with Christian insights.' Collins, op cit. pp. 246-7

[366] Potter, op cit. p.174; Collins, ibid, pp. 246-7.

[367] Letter from Diana Collins, *The Church Times*, 6th January 1956

[368] Letter from Rev Dudley Symon, Ham Common, *The Church Times*, 13th January 1956

didn't want to go on living.[369] Another correspondent cited Article 37 of the Thirty-Nine Articles which laid down that: 'The laws of the realm may punish Christian men with death for heinous and grievous offences.'[370] He found it unedifying that bishops, of all people, were telling highly emotional meetings that capital punishment was morally indefensible when they had sworn soberly in church that it is agreeable to the word of God.

Collins wrote to Bell offering to help him in the forthcoming Lords debate in 1956 on the Abolition Bill if he were to speak for abolition. Members of Convocation lobbied the Bishops in the Lords and a group of clergy started up a petition to Fisher urging him to support abolition himself in the Lords.[371] By the mid-1950s the episcopacy was rapidly coming round to an abolitionist stance. The bishops of Sheffield, Manchester and Liverpool rallied to Bell, as did Birmingham and Chelmsford who were not yet in the Upper House. Another wholehearted supporter was the new Archbishop of York, Michael Ramsey, but he was reluctant to speak in the forthcoming debate.[372] Fisher himself, however, remained essentially a qualified retentionist as he had been eight years before. He wrote a memorandum at this time, possibly in response to the considerable postbag he had on the subject, re-iterating his belief that the state had the right to retain capital punishment for the offence of murder, and that Christian faith did not forbid capital punishment though neither did it necessarily require it.[373]

Abolition was once again defeated in the Lords, but the balance of voting on the episcopal benches had changed dramatically by comparison with that of only eight years earlier. Whereas in 1948 Bell was the only bishop in the abolitionist lobby this time both archbishops were there. Fisher reluctantly voted for it on the basis that he wanted to keep the Bill alive so that it could be amended later on – 'to re-found the death penalty on its only secure foundation' - plus eight other bishops, and only one (Chavasse of Rochester) voted against.[374] Ramsey made his maiden speech to support the Bill, and though arguing that capital punishment was not necessarily contrary to New Testament

---

[369] Letter from H B Vaisey, *The Church Times*, 20th January 1956

[370] Letter from O L Willmoth, *The Church Times*, 20th January 1956

[371] Petition from various clergy including Richard Acland (lay reader), Canon Edward Carpenter (Canon of Westminster) and Dudley, Bishop of Colchester, 4th July 1956. Archbishop Fisher papers, Lambeth Palace Library, ff.217

[372] Arthur Michael Ramsey, Baron Ramsey of Canterbury (1904-1988). Bishop of Durham 1952-56, Archbishop of York 1956-1961 and 100th Archbishop of Canterbury 1961-1974. A former pupil of his predecessor as Primate, Fisher, when he was at Repton. Chadwick, Owen, *Michael Ramsey: A Life* (Oxford: Clarendon Press, 1990) p. 157

[373] Fisher - note on capital punishment, 8th March 1956. Fisher papers, vol 167 (1956). ff.200-203

[374] Christopher Maude Chavasse, OBE, MC (1884-1962) Competed in the 1908 London Olympics in the 400 yards together with his twin brother; served as a chaplain in the First World War and decorated (as was his twin). Bishop of Rochester 1940-60.

teaching he felt that the balance of the argument was now in favour of abolition given that hanging no longer 'has the moral dignity of representing ...the will of the community to inflict an unspeakable penalty for an unspeakable crime.'[375] Fisher was a keen supporter of the Eden government's Homicide Bill which proposed degrees of murder very much as he had advocated in the past. He felt the proposal was more in tune with the mood of the general public and devoutly hoped that if the Bill passed 'this long distressing controversy [would be] allowed to pass for a good time into oblivion.'[376] Both Bell and Ramsey, however, took the opposite view that there was no moral justification for the distinction between capital and non-capital murder.

Nonetheless, complete abolition was not far off and the Church of England was at the forefront, having undergone a startling revolution in its attitudes in the space of less than a decade. As Potter records: 'the accepted norms of centuries were discarded almost overnight.'[377] The momentum for change was overwhelming within the Church hierarchy, and this was accentuated by the accession of Ramsey to the see of Canterbury in May 1961 (which Fisher opposed, seeing Ramsey as too radical). The ranks of the bishops were undergoing something of a metamorphosis also, as a new generation of bishops was consecrated replacing a much older generation that had been in place for decades. Of the twenty-nine diocesan bishops in the province of Canterbury twenty-one had been appointed between 1956 and 1962 and of these sixteen were newly consecrated; and of the fourteen bishops in the York Province eight had been appointed in that same period of which six were new bishops. Again to quote Potter: 'the change in atmosphere was extraordinary. No longer were abolitionists the vociferous minority among the episcopate; retentionists, rather, were the moribund dinosaurs.'[378]

Typical of the new breed were the Bishop of Southwark, Mervyn Stockwood, and his suffragen John Robinson, Bishop of Woolwich, both ardent abolitionists and radicals.[379] Stockwood was a keen supporter of the Labour Party and knew that the return of a Labour government was an essential precondition of the abolition of the death penalty. Robinson preached on the topic for his sermon at Great St Mary's on Trinity Sunday, 1961.[380] Capital

---

[375] HL Deb, vol 198, cols 595-6, 9th July 1956. Quoted in Potter, op cit., p.175

[376] Potter, ibid. p.179

[377] Potter, ibid. p.193

[378] Potter, ibid. pp. 193-4

[379] Arthur Mervyn Stockwood (1913-1995) Bishop of Southwark 1959-80. Socialist and Labour councillor. Campaigner on many things including racism. Most famous for his appearance on *Saturday Night and Sunday Morning* in 1979 attacking *The Life of Brian* as blasphemous. John Arthur Thomas Robinson (1919-1983) Bishop of Woolwich. Liberal theologian. Author of *Honest to God* 1963 and scholarly works on the dating of the Gospels. Defended publication of *Lady Chatterley's Lover*. Left the Labour Party for the Liberals over the Commonwealth Immigrants Bill in February 1968.

[380] Robinson sermon at Great St Mary's, 28th May 1961. Robinson papers, Lambeth Palace

punishment was the 'most stinging of all nettles and the most gingerly way in which as a society we are at present trying to pluck it is a classic example of how not to cope with a nettle.'

The previous week a junior clergyman of his diocese, Reverend F P Coleman, had successfully introduced a motion into the Lower House of Convocation to suspend capital punishment for five years, the first time that the Church had officially declared on the question (according to Robinson).[381] In November 1961 the Bishop of Exeter, Mortimer, hitherto a retentionist, pressed in the Lords for abolition.[382] Letters to the church press (such as *The Church Times* and *The Catholic Herald*) were evenly balanced for and against. The BBC documentary *The Death Penalty* was transmitted in October 1961 including contributions from both Ramsey and Godfrey (Cardinal Archbishop of Westminster) as spokesmen for their respective confessions, both of which had been recorded some time earlier. Both contributions were somewhat non-committal, whatever their personal views may have been.

Shortly after the passage of the abolitionist motion in the Lower House Stockwood took the issue to the Upper House of Canterbury Convocation in January 1962, proposing an experimental period of abolition, seconded by Exeter.[383] The debate, he said, had raged for 150 years but the end may be in sight. Much had been achieved and all that was left was for government to write the final paragraph. The Homicide Act, he argued, was illogical and led to the worst of both worlds. The main reason for maintaining capital punishment was vengeance and that was not a word that should be found in a Christian vocabulary. It was a *tour de force* of the classic argument for abolition.

Ramsey, as President of Convocation, summed up the debate by associating himself with the string of speeches in favour of the motion, and said that he had voted in favour of abolition in 1956 and would do so again. The Homicide Act in its present form could not last. He wished, however, that there had been something about punishment as well as treatment in clause two of the resolution, for though vengeance was an utterly evil thing retribution was an essential ingredient of punishment and a criminal or sinner begins to amend when his conscience tells him that he has deserved to suffer. His comments led to an amendment to clause two to include the word 'punishment', which in its slightly amended form was passed unanimously.[384]

Library, ff 102-103

[381] This came shortly after Ramsey had recorded his statement for the BBC documentary *The Death Penalty* in which he said that the church had never officially pronounced on the issue. The Chief Information Officer of the Church, Col. Hornby, asked for the BBC to add a rider to that effect. Ramsey papers, Lambeth Palace Library, ff 264. It is indicative of the speed with which events were moving.

[382] HL Deb, vol 235, cols 446-449, 9th November 1961

[383] Proceedings of Convocation, 17th January 1962: Chronicle of Convocation (Canterbury) vol 100 (1962), pp.105-124 Lambeth Palace Library.

[384] Potter, op cit. pp. 194-5; Proceedings of Convocation, ibid

A similar motion was debated in York Convocation at the same time, moved by Charles Claxton, Bishop of Blackburn, an old ally of Stockwood's with whom he had co-ordinated his campaign. The Archbishop of York, Donald Coggan, was another firm abolitionist.[385] The Lower House of York Convocation passed the motion also, with only sixteen members voting against.[386] With both Houses of both Convocations having passed an abolition motion a few months later in May 1962 a joint synod of the Church (Canterbury plus York) met and passed another abolition resolution moved again by Claxton by a large majority, with only the Bishop of Durham (Maurice Harland) voting against, in the Upper House. It was passed with sixty voting against in the much larger Lower House.[387]

By 1965 with the Silverman Abolition Bill working its way though Parliament Ramsey was invited by Longford (Leader of the House of Lords), Gardiner (now Lord Chancellor) and Silverman to pilot the bill through the Lords, on the grounds that it stood a much greater chance of success with the authority of the established church behind it.[388] Ramsey was reluctant to undertake such an onerous task on the grounds that he was not an experienced Parliamentarian, but allowed himself to be persuaded for what he saw as the greater good, having by this time, according to Potter, become a totally convinced abolitionist.[389] His private secretary, Beloe, had minuted him about the bill and the role of the bishops in the coming Lords debate, and he was being primed by Gardiner with statistics on murder rates etc.[390]

However, this did not meet with the approval of the former Conservative Lord Chancellor, Dilhorne, who wrote to Ramsey urging him in very strong, if amicable, terms not to go ahead with this plan on the grounds that it would be 'unwise and inappropriate' for the head of the church to take sides on so controversial an issue which would inevitably, he argued, damage the standing of the church.[391] He said:-

> It is a most controversial measure on which feelings run high. While of course it is
> right that the views of the Archbishops and the Bishops should be made known, it is a

---

[385] Frederick Donald Coggan, (1909-2000) Baron Coggan of Canterbury and Sissinghurst. Bishop of Bradford 1956-61, Archbishop of York 1961-1974, 101st Archbishop of Canterbury 1974-80

[386] Potter, op cit. p.198

[387] *Daily Telegraph* report, 16th May 1962, Ramsey papers, op cit, ff 154

[388] Potter, op cit, p.199. Silverman to Ramsey, 17th February 1965, Ramsey papers, ibid, ff.172

[389] Ramsey was at first strongly minded to pilot the Bill but later changed his mind from a mixture of reasons. Chadwick, op cit, pp. 160-1

[390] Robert Beloe to Ramsey (nd), Ramsey papers, vol 76 (1965), ff.145. Gardiner to Ramsey, 13th January 1965, Ramsey, ibid. ff.147

[391] Dilhorne to Ramsey, 26th February 1965. Ramsey papers, ibid, ff.174

> very different thing for an Archbishop to take charge of the conduct of the Bill. The Gallup polls show that the majority of the population are against the Bill...and a very great number of church people will think it most inappropriate...I am myself opposed to the Bill but I should feel precisely the same about this if I was in favour of it...I have no doubt that if you do it, it will give rise to very strong criticism both in the House and outside which is bound to impair your position and that of our church...

It is difficult to assess how much of an impact this had on Ramsey's thinking, but there was an undeniable force to Dilhorne's argument that whatever Ramsey's (and other bishops') personal beliefs on capital punishment it was unwise for the established church to involve itself so heavily in so controversial a matter. It would inevitably have split and weakened the church at a time when organized religion was in general decline and may have placed some communicants in an invidious position if their beliefs did not accord with those of the hierarchy.

Dilhorne's was not the only voice urging circumspection. Ramsey's secretary, Beloe, met House of Lords officials (including the clerk of the table dealing with public bills) in March to discuss the Bill and Ramsey's role in its passage.[392] They warned him that piloting a bill was very time-consuming; that the Bill was acquiring a partisan flavour as a result of the shenanigans in the Commons; and that he would be up against very adept Parliamentarians during the tricky committee stage who would 'give no quarter'. The fact that it was the Archbishop of Canterbury piloting the bill would probably 'embitter the atmosphere rather than reduce the tension' and they doubted Ramsey's expertise.

Ramsey eventually decided to withdraw from leading the Bill, probably from a mixture of motives. Most likely he concurred with the Parliamentary advisers that he lacked the time and expertise for the task but he probably also privately recognized the validity of Dilhorne's view that it would be damaging for the Church to become too strongly associated with such an emotive political question; one moreover which had partisan overtones given the tacit support being lent to it by the government. Though he had decided against leading the Bill he nonetheless resolved to give it strong support by speaking in its favour. Ramsey argued in the Lords debate that capital punishment was wrong because it did not allow the possibility of reclamation and that it devalued human life. He might have been swayed, he said, by convincing proof of its unique deterrent value but this was absent.[393] There was nothing to be said, he went on, for the capital/non-capital distinction introduced by the Homicide Act which had led to intolerable moral dilemmas for successive Home Secretaries.

The Bill passed easily through the Lords on second reading by 204-104

---

[392] Note by Beloe on meeting with David Stephens and Peter Henderson, 12th March 1965. Ramsey papers, ibid, ff.181-2
[393] HL Deb, vol 268, col 607, 20th July 1965

with Ramsey and nine other bishops voting for it and none against in stark contrast with the voting only seventeen years earlier. According to Potter Ramsey had arranged for Harland (Durham) to be engaged elsewhere on the relevant day.[394]

In the Lords debate on the confirmatory resolution in December 1969 Ramsey again spoke against hanging, and voted for the resolution along with Coggan and seventeen other bishops. Only Mortimer of Exeter rather surprisingly voted against (or at any rate acted as teller for the Noes) on the slightly paradoxical grounds that he wanted a further delay so as to try to carry public opinion with the church.

Thus within the space of a few years and a single generation of bishops the established church had turned almost 180 degrees in it's position on one of the most contentious ethical and political issues of the day; one moreover on which it could and did claim a special interest and expertise. In the debate on the abolition clause in the Lords in 1948 only one bishop could be found to vote for abolition whilst several argued strongly against it, and yet only seventeen years later not a single bishop could be found to vote against abolition in the comparable debate of 1965. The church which had once preached strenuously for the retention of hanging for the most petty offences now wanted it swept away even for the most heinous. And this change was echoed right down the church hierarchy and in the Anglican communion overseas, and in other churches.

How could this be? The view of the church was, after all, supposed to be based on Scripture, and Scripture had not changed for two thousand years (or considerably longer in the case of the Old Testament). Of course a younger, more radical cohort of prelates had come to the fore in the late 1950s at roughly the same time but that is a question-begging answer because the generations had changed hands countless times before over the centuries without it producing any dramatic change of doctrine. Was there something about this generation of bishops that made them significantly more liberal than their predecessors? They had been born, in the main, in the period from about the turn of the century to the First World War and there was no reason to suppose that anything in their upbringing and life histories would have caused them to turn out so differently. And even those such as Ramsey and Bell had only moved gradually to an outright abolitionist position from a slightly qualified one. But though Scripture had not changed their interpretation had and this was not cause but effect, in that many of the bishops had come to an abolitionist stance for political rather than religious reasons - for even they could not be immune from intellectual fashion and social trends. In the nature of things they sought scriptural authority to rationalize their change of heart, which, given the infinitely flexible nature of the Scriptures was not hard to achieve. To quote Potter again:-

---

[394] Potter, op cit. p.202

The trends within society were more secular, and within the church more liberal. Increasingly Christology took centre stage in theological enquiry, and all knowledge of God was refracted through Christ. There was a greater stress on the social gospel, a rediscovery of the vital ethic of Jesus' teaching, which although it did not condemn the death penalty as such rendered it impossible in practice for anyone to execute it...These factors coupled with the growing unease at the practice of the death penalty...in that the whole process gave a fake religiosity to what was after all the killing of a human being, all created a change in opinion within the church which ultimately bore fruit in the 1960s...[395]

The Roman Catholic Church

The position of the Roman Catholic Church in relation to capital punishment was somewhat more complex than that of the Church of England. Its official line on the matter was, in essence, that the State had the right to take life in defence of the community but that equally it had the discretion not to exercise that right. So far as the individual Roman Catholic was concerned he could personally oppose the death penalty but could not deny the right of the State to possess the sanction. This slightly contorted formulation remained the position for the duration of the controversy, but in practice the position of many leading Catholics became more abolitionist as the debate progressed. The Catholic Bishops in England and Wales (who met twice-yearly) never took the path of the Anglican Convocation and pronounced formally on the issue but then they had no power to do so, whatever their personal inclinations, given that doctrine and policy was handed down from Rome. Again it seems likely that there was a substantial move on their part towards abolitionism though never officially expressed, and certainly never preached.

The preaching of political sermons was frowned upon, especially if the politics was not of the approved brand. The Catholic Church tended to view askance the growing trend within the Anglican Church for clerics to pronounce on political questions such as capital punishment, and especially for them to do so in such a way as to suggest that certain views were the only really Christian option. An editorial in *The Catholic Herald* of 1956, in the course of a diatribe against what it evidently saw as the politicization of the Anglican Church, attacked Canon Collins for preaching his political message as if were binding on all Christians: 'Next we have "capital punishment". This is a matter on which Christians differ for sound reasons, and it is really intolerable presumption on the part of the Precentor of St Paul's to dictate to the Archbishop or any other leading churchman his own doubtless sincerely held view as an individual

---

[395] Potter, ibid. pp. 206-7

Christian.'[396]

It was not only the editor who was annoyed by this presumption. The letters page a few months later saw a contribution from a reader who felt that 'the air of superiority assumed by some abolitionists throughout the hanging debate in Parliament, in the Press, and even in private conversation gives me the right of talking about "the intellectual pride of certain do-gooders" in this connection.' The writer went on to rubbish the murder rate figures that had been quoted by 'Secular Priest' in the newspaper, purporting to show that abolitionist countries did not have a higher rate than the United Kingdom. He finished up by saying that he did not 'object to prayers being offered for the souls of executed criminals, but I did protest against the idea of keeping churches open all night for their sake. While the wretches certainly deserve our pity, there is no justification whatever for according a demonstrative "special treatment" to them.'[397]

The main organ of the Catholic Church, *The Tablet*, tended to take a strongly retentionist line. An editorial of February 1956 argued that the government was in too great a hurry to promise legislation in the wake of that month's vote, which as a free vote subject to the chance composition of the House, should not necessarily have been elevated into legislation.[398] It loftily declared that: 'There is a world of opinion and feeling common to Labour members of Parliament, in which they live, which is not wholly shared by those who vote for them, and not shared at all by the vast majority of the nation.' Though the abolitionists had made much headway since 1948 they should not think that they had converted the country, and the Lords would be much more representative. The five year experiment was pointless, the piece continued, because statistics proved nothing, and it was characteristic of the 'pseudo-scientific spirit of the age.' It declared grandly: 'Looking broadly at human history...no fact is surely better attested than that all those who have been concerned with the government of men have acted on the belief that the death penalty was the great deterrent to prevent people from doing whatever their rulers were most anxious they should not do – whether it was betraying their country, deserting from arms, or murdering or robbing their fellows.' The effects of a more lenient policy may not, it thought, be apparent for a long time and so a five-year experimental period was insufficient.

A few months later, after the Bill's third reading, *The Tablet* returned to the attack, criticizing the government for abandoning its responsibility, as it saw it, to the judgment of the House, and claiming that the low turnout on the third reading precluded Silverman from claiming a majority.[399] The Commons was flouting the expressed views of a majority and of those most closely associated

---

[396] *The Catholic Herald*, 6th January 1956 - editorial
[397] *The Catholic Herald*, 13th April 1956 - letter from George A Floris, London NW1
[398] *The Tablet*, 25th February 1956 – 'The Fate of Murderers'.
[399] *The Tablet*, 7th July 1956 'Now for the Lords'

with law and order - the police, the legal profession and the prison officers - and it hoped that the Lords would reject or heavily amend the Bill.

A few years later and *The Tablet* had not resiled from its opposition to abolition, noting in the wake of the second reading of the new Silverman Bill of 1964-5 that the Lords would be reflecting the general consensus of opinion if it were to again turn it down.[400] It subsequently noted the Lords passage of the Bill rather grudgingly, admitting that the Homicide Act was anomalous, but pointing out that it was, in their view, effective because although robberies had escalated, murder in the course of robbery (still capital) had not.[401]

A third organ of Catholic opinion, *The Universe*, was of a similar mind to *The Catholic Herald* and *The Catholic Times* in that it leant, albeit with apparent reluctance, towards retention. Its 'Notes and Comments' column of February 1956 said that though: 'Hanging in itself is a horrible business – as is vouched for by the chaplains and prison officials who must be present...There can be no doubt that the death penalty is morally lawful and there is a strong case for its retention as long as the temptation to commit murder is so strong.'[402] This was not a matter on which the 'nation can be stampeded by rhetoric but it should proceed gradually and cautiously.' Referring to the recent abolition motion it said that the government should not take a free vote of the Commons as finally settling the question, and that it should take as least as much account of public opinion as of Parliamentary opinion. After the defeat of the Silverman bill in the Lords in July 1956 an article noted that there were few Catholic peers in support of abolition and that of the fifteen Catholic peers who voted on the second reading eleven were against the Bill.[403]

By the 1960s the general tone of the Catholic press, and certainly that of *The Herald*, had softened somewhat. Norman St John-Stevas, the recently elected Conservative MP and a prominent Roman Catholic who had written prolifically on moral questions, had a regular column in the paper from which he sounded off. His position was liberal on capital punishment, and he evidently supported the recently introduced Silverman Abolition Bill which he characterized as: 'a notable secular advance.' He noted that the Bill's prospects in the Commons were excellent and that the real test would be in the House of Lords where:-

> the peers would be unwise to reject a recommendation of the elected House on this question. The House of Lords has a suspensory veto but it should only be used where there is clear evidence that public opinion is strongly against the elected House on a particular issue. Many of the public undoubtedly favour the retention of capital punishment but a substantial number have in recent years changed their minds on the

---

[400] *The Tablet*, 19th December 1964
[401] *The Tablet*, 24th July 1965
[402] 'Notes and Comments' 'Death Penalty', *The Universe*, 24th February 1956
[403] *The Universe*, 20th July 1956

issue. To provoke a clash between the two Houses on capital punishment would therefore not be justified and in the long run would only weaken the position of the hereditary chamber still further.[404]

Of course his views did not necessarily reflect those of the paper as a whole but on the other hand they were not contradicted by anything in the editorial column, which was conspicuously silent on the matter during the whole period. Again *The Herald* was not the same thing as the Catholic Church but it was generally regarded as the voice of the church in England and Wales, and thus it may not be speculating too wildly to surmise that the church hierarchy had tacitly moved to a more abolitionist stance than hitherto. An article on the Lords vote on the Abolition Bill noted the high proportion of Catholic peers who supported the Bill, in marked contrast with the position nine years previously, in that ten voted for the Bill and only three against.[405]

But *The Universe* (now amalgamated with the *Catholic Times*), by contrast with *The Herald,* still came down against abolition. The 'Talking Point' column of Father Gordon Albion of March 1965 clove to the traditional view that the 'State has the right to call for the death penalty.'[406] He opined that he could 'work up no enthusiasm for doing away with capital punishment for murder' (and neither could the general public) which, referring to the 1964 Silverman Bill, would now be 'pushed through by a minority pressure group, one of whom has stated publicly that, we, the public, are incapable of appraising and assessing the reasons for abolition...' The commandment 'Thou shalt do no murder' was no arbitrary discipline, and preventive punishment was imperative, which, moreover, must be such as to deter others. His arguments were challenged by a correspondent who, referring to Albion's invocation of public opinion suggested that he (Albion) could not be serious in suggesting that majority opinion should, by numbers alone, be the right one.[407] He doubted whether Albion would be prepared to put any great moral question to a referendum and abide by the majority decision.

By 1969 and the approach of the vote on the confirmation of abolition the Catholic press was still not of one voice, though by now more favourably disposed towards the abolitionist side than hitherto. *The Catholic Herald* of 19th December 1969, just before the critical vote, had an editorial on the matter headed 'A Matter of Life and Death'. It noted that whatever was decided in the next few days the debate would inevitably continue, and that its attitude to the

---

[404] 'New Views on Hanging' - Norman St John Stevas. *The Catholic Herald*, 11th December 1964

[405] 'Catholics Say "No Hanging" in Lords Vote' by Kevin Aspell, *The Catholic Herald*, 30th July 1965

[406] 'Talking Point' by Fr Gordon Albion, *The Universe and Catholic Times*, 5th March 1965

[407] 'Case Against Hanging', letter from Robert H S Flynn, Stoke on Trent, *The Universe and Catholic Times*, 26th March 1965

question was that '...capital punishment is objectionable because it implicitly seems to doubt the power of God and man to help a shipwrecked soul re-shape itself. It should not be invoked unless it is essential for the saving of innocent lives.'[408] It felt that the possibility of executing an innocent man was a weighty but not decisive consideration, and that it was ultimately impossible ever to draw the unequivocal conclusion that hanging does or does not deter the would-be killer. They were inclined to believe that where it did deter was in the case of 'the professional criminal setting out on a well-planned job and deciding whether or not to take a gun'. This, it admitted, was also something that eludes statistical proof but 'would seem to be a reasonable assumption.' Moreover, 'the mere fact of the capital penalty being attached to murder must surely act as a sign of the horror society has of it, and thus create within the group consciousness a running additional bias against the taking of life. We do not assert these things dogmatically but suggest they should be considered before minds are fully closed.' Thus the death penalty was still, one might infer, justifiable and perhaps necessary.

The *Universe* was also rather of two minds by this stage. Its edition of the same date carried a lengthy piece on the question containing two views of the issue – 'Hanging – Two Views'.[409] 'Some may find it strange, but Catholics are obviously as divided about the issue as the rest of the population' it declared. 'The Church has always in the past upheld the state's right to execute criminals, though there is some difficulty in discovering what precisely is its present attitude to capital punishment.' The following week, after the crucial vote had taken place, there was a headline story 'Relief that the Hangman is now made redundant' by a 'Universe reporter'.[410] It boldly declared that 'A majority of Catholics, it is believed, will have been relieved that the hangman has been made redundant in Britain...All arguments in favour of its retention - that hanging is a deterrent, a justifiable act of punishment for murder – were of no avail as first the Commons...and then the Lords...voted for abolition.' This was a surprisingly partisan assertion considering the sedulously even-handed treatment that the debate had received the previous week, and maybe the paper's abolitionist faction had been let off the leash that week in the wake of the Parliamentary victory.

One gains the impression from all of this that the Roman Catholic hierarchy was uncomfortable with the issue for a number of reasons. For one thing Catholic teaching did not point clearly one way or the other, unlike with issues such as abortion and euthanasia, and it was difficult for church leaders therefore to give a clear lead, thereby perhaps conveying a sense of weakness and equivocation. And yet, being ostensibly a moral question it was an issue where it was generally felt they had to speak out. Then again it was an issue

---

[408] *The Catholic Herald*, Friday, 19th December 1969 – editorial 'A Matter of Life and Death'
[409] *The Universe*, Friday, 19th December 1969 – 'Hanging – Two Views'
[410] *The Universe*, 26th December 1969. 'Relief that the Hangman is now made redundant'

where a great number of communicants had strong views, one way or the other and where the hierarchy was acutely conscious that a clarion call from the pulpit, whatever it may have been, would not have secured the total acceptance of all parishioners. The issue was poised uneasily between, on the one hand, those such as abortion, euthanasia, contraception, divorce and many others where the Church could and did take an unyielding stance dictated by Scripture, and on the other hand those more mainstream political questions pertaining to economic policy, etc. where the Church would not necessarily have been expected to speak out.

The Quakers

The Quakers, or the Society of Friends to give them their formal name, was the only Christian denomination to come out unequivocally for abolition. Their history and beliefs predisposed them to a strongly pacifist position on all questions and the issue of capital punishment was no exception. E Roy Calvert, the early pre-war champion of abolition, was a prominent Quaker, as were others in the movement. Their revised statement of Christian practice of 1925 declared that: 'We believe that a considerate and Christian treatment of the offender is as possible in cases of murder as in the case of other crimes, and we urge Friends to do all in their power to create a public opinion which will demand the abolition of the death penalty.' They were always closely associated with the work of the NCADP and the Howard League.

The revival of the abolition movement in the mid-1950s met with an immediate response from the Quakers. Their penal reform committee was heavily committed to abolition along with other measures of penal reform. Gardiner attended one of their meetings in 1955 at which he outlined the objects of the Campaign, and stressed that the campaign would be conducted in 'a reverent and indeed religious spirit' and that 'disruptive and sensational action would be avoided.'[411] The Committee expressed itself in sympathy with the aims and nature of the Campaign and pledged support in the organization of meetings. Their yearly meeting of 1956 welcomed its report: 'We can record our satisfaction that the work so zealously initiated by our late Friend Roy Calvert...may well be reaching a successful climax in the virtual abolition of the death penalty...and we earnestly pray that the Bill at present before Parliament may soon be passed into law. We, as Quakers, are united in our conviction that Capital punishment is an offence to the Christian conscience...'[412]

---

[411] Minutes of the Penal Reform Committee of the Society of Friends, 1st September 1955. Gardiner Add 56463B
[412] Proceedings of the Yearly Meeting of the Society of Friends, 1956: Reports and Minutes,

A statement prepared for public consumption was even more strident:-

> The Society of Friends in Great Britain in its annual meeting welcomes the Bill now before the House of Commons for the removal of the death penalty for murder...declare unwavering opposition to capital punishment. The sanctity of human life is one of the fundamentals of a Christian society and can in no circumstances be set aside...The sanctioning by the State of the taking of human life has a debasing effect on the community, and tends to produce the very brutality which it seeks to prevent...We fervently hope that the Bill will be passed by Parliament without limitation.[413]

The statement was sent to the Home Secretary and the press, and Friends were encouraged to make it known to their own MPs and local press and to make what use of it they thought fit.

A few years later, at a Meeting for Sufferings (i.e. a meeting of the Executive) a formal statement on capital punishment was issued.[414] It declared itself deeply concerned about the continuance of judicial hangings; expressed its 'abhorrence of what is to us a barbarous and debasing act', said that 'no murderer, however depraved, is beyond the possibility of God's redemption', 'hope that a majority of fellow citizens will unite with us in urging the government to free society from its communal guilt' and whilst stressing that their objections sprang from Christian convictions 'nevertheless share the views of those who base their advocacy on ethical and practical considerations.'

The Friends Meeting House in Euston Road became a focal point for abolitionists where often vigils were held on the eve of executions, attracting a broad spectrum of supporters of abolition extending beyond adherents of the sect itself.

Other Protestant Churches

Most of the nonconformist churches, including the established Scottish Presbyterian Church, like the Anglicans and the Roman Catholics, were officially uncommitted on the question, though several of its leading churchmen took an abolitionist stance. This section concentrates on the attitude of two of the most prominent English nonconformist sects, the Methodists and the Baptists, which were, arguably, very typical of the non-Anglican Protestant

---

minute 38, pp. 140-1
[413] Proceedings of the Yearly Meeting, ibid, minute 39. Also Gardiner, ibid.
[414] Meeting for Sufferings, 2nd February 1962. In Proceedings of the Yearly Meeting of the Society of Friends, pp. 20-21.

position at this time.

Donald Soper, the most prominent Methodist of the era, was very much to the fore in the abolitionist movement. *The Methodist Recorder*, its chief organ, was mildly abolitionist according to Potter, but the Methodist Church Executive took a stronger line communicating a resolution to every Methodist MP welcoming the Silverman clause in 1948.[415] By the mid-1950s the Church was becoming more strongly abolitionist. For example the *Methodist Peace Fellowship* of Victoria College, Manchester, prompted by the forthcoming Parliamentary vote declared in January 1956 that: 'Our Fellowship is convinced that the death penalty is contrary to the teaching of Jesus Christ and to perpetuate such a law is against the will of God.'[416] A month later and the paper printed two views of the question.[417] The Reverend Richard Pyke of Bristol argued for abolition: 'We have moved on, and far ahead, of the barbarity and disgrace of public executions; the time has now come for us to take the further step of dealing with murder by such a form and measure of justice as does not involve the deliberate destruction of a life which God gave, and which only He should take away.' But the Reverend Ernest G Kitchin of Lincoln took the contrary view, asking what the alternative was? 'This is a matter upon which emotions can easily be stirred, but in the stirring let us not be unmindful of those who are maimed in mind and body as a result of unprovoked attack...'

The Commons motion of February 1956 was covered in the issue of 23rd February which noted the sober and restrained character of the debate, contrasting it with some of the more colourful statements made in the press and in public debate, and it lamented the fact that some speakers tried to claim that Christians could hold only one view of the matter: 'This method of trying to bulldoze the opposition is characteristic of would-be dictators.'[418] It noted that opinion everywhere was sharply divided and that: 'many have reached conclusions after almost agonising consideration' and that it was generally hoped that 'the abolition of the death penalty will fulfil all the desires, and avoid all the dangers of so momentous a decision.' The paper seemed to be hedging its bets very carefully on the matter at that stage. Clerical opinion in the Methodist Church was evidently very divided.

Nonetheless, the Methodist Annual Conference of that year produced a large majority for a resolution approving the Commons decision on abolition, noting that the unique deterrent effect of the death penalty cannot be substantiated and affirming that the aim of penal sanctions should be reform rather than retribution.[419] The resolution's proposer, Mr Greet, said that the feeling of the Church was surely behind the reform which had been so largely

[415]*The Methodist Recorder*, 11th December 1947. Quoted in Potter, op cit, p.146
[416]*The Methodist Recorder*, 19th January 1956, George Wakefield and Barrie G Cooke
[417]*The Methodist Recorder*, 16th February 1956 – 'Capital Punishment: Two Opinions'
[418]*The Methodist Recorder*, 23rd February 1956 – 'Notes of the Week'
[419]*The Methodist Recorder*, 12th July 1956 - Report on Annual Conference.

inspired by the Gospel, whereas the Reverend Walter Edwards of Sheffield argued that the police would suffer most from the effect of abolition, based on his experience as a chaplain of life behind bars. But Dr Soper said that he had been satisfied by the Royal Commission and the Commons that there was no widespread fear on the part of the police if the death penalty were to go. Nonetheless, the defeat of the Bill in the Lords very shortly afterwards was not regretted by the *Recorder* which described the debate as, 'in the best tradition' and felt that it '...is a good thing that a breathing space has been given in which both members of the House of Parliament and the public can consider all the arguments presented on both sides.'[420] It suggested instead a compromise measure retaining the death penalty for 'special and extreme cases' which it felt would command a high level of support. Evidently the Annual Conference and the *Recorder* were not quite singing from the same hymn sheet.

By 1964, however, as with many of the other churches, they were singing a different tune. The *Recorder* welcomed the advent of the Silverman Bill in December, which it felt would probably get a smooth passage owing to government support, on the grounds that the Homicide Act had proved an unsatisfactory compromise, perhaps forgetting its previous support for 'degrees of murder' legislation.[421] The same column recalled that the Church had supported the previous Silverman Bill of 1955/6, had been 'distressed' when the Bill fell in the Lords and had felt the 'half-way house' measure of 1957 'profoundly unsatisfactory'. Finally, in November, the *Recorder* trumpeted the passage of the Bill, citing it as a '...refreshing illustration of what can still be accomplished by the dogged persistence of a backbencher.'[422]

By 1969, on the eve of the renewal debate, the *Recorder* was perhaps slightly less stridently abolitionist in tone than it had been four years before. A leader column danced delicately around the question:-

> Here again decision must be made on balance of judgments rather than on absolute conviction of rightness...The alternative is a return to the 1957 Act...The only certain thing is that there is a strong emotional public reaction against abolition. But we believe that the government has chosen the better course and is right to ask for an early decision. To hang or not to hang should not be a General Election issue.[423]

The 'Notes of the Week' column in that issue noted the fact that the Blom-Cooper and Morris Report on murder showed a higher figure than the corresponding Home Office report, and that there was a steep rise in malicious

---

[420] *The Methodist Recorder*, 19th July 1956 – Notes of the Week

[421] *The Methodist Recorder*, 10th December 1964 – Notes of the Week

[422] *The Methodist Recorder*, 4th November 1965 – Notes of the Week, 'Parliament Ahead of People? No Hanging Bill Approved.'

[423] *The Methodist Recorder*, 18th December 1969 'Vietnam, Nigeria and the Rope'

woundings, but that the level of murders, manslaughters and infanticides had remained remarkably consistent, and concurred with the authors conclusion that three years was too short a period from which to draw any firm conclusions.[424]

The Baptists, the other most numerous nonconformist church in England and Wales, took a similar path to the Methodists, moving from a fairly retentionist position to a strongly abolitionist one in the period from 1948 to 1969 with 1955/6 being the watershed moment. The controversy within the Baptist Church really caught light in the pages of the *Baptist Times*, its chief organ, in late 1955 just as the campaign was gaining momentum. An article argued forcefully for abolition, prompted by the unopposed introduction into the Commons of the Silverman Bill, the rapid growth of the NCACP campaign and the publication of Gollancz's slim volume on the controversy: 'For those who believe that no civilised country can long continue to be both civilised and retain any method of punishment by death, there was a brief moment of hope last week.'[425] This was soon followed by a letter on behalf of the *Committee of the Baptist Pacifist Fellowship* appealing to all the Churches to support the campaign: '...We would claim that the whole Gospel of Jesus condemns the death penalty as an outworn barbarity offensive to God and injurious to the human race.'[426] Though it briefly rehearsed the other arguments for abolition the letter anchored its case firmly within the teachings of the Gospel.

There was an uncompromising rejoinder a few weeks later from another correspondent, the Reverend Chown, who asserted that he hoped that the law would be left as it is: 'Has not bitter experience proved that even the advancement of the age from 16 to 18 as regards execution was of doubtful wisdom. I consider that any well-ordered society is within its rights in retaining the death penalty.'[427] The Reverend Chown's letter provoked a whole spate of correspondence. The Reverend Trent, wrote in to take issue and express his apparent dismay at the fact that a Christian minister should champion such an '...outmoded and barbaric form of punishment.'[428] Moreover, to use Scripture as a weapon '...is surely a sword which he grasps by the blade!'

The intensity of debate, both in the pages of the organ and within the Church generally, led to an article in February 1956 which adumbrated the current position of *The Moral and Social Questions Committee* of the Church, representing as they put it, the 'highest possible measure of agreement among

---

[424] *The Methodist Recorder*, 18th December 1969 - Notes of the Week

[425] *The Baptist Times*, 24th November 1955 – Behind the Headlines 'Abolish Capital Punishment' by 'Rover'

[426] *The Baptist Times*, 1st December 1955 – Letter from L Worsnip (Loughborough), general secretary of the Baptist Pacifist Fellowship

[427] *The Baptist Times*, 22nd December 1955 – Letter from Rev J Leslie Chown (Wolverhampton)

[428] *The Baptist Times*, 5th January 1956 – Letter from Rev H W Trent (Gt Shelford, Cambs)

the group.'[429]

> Murder is a terrible crime...By taking the murderer's life in a solemn and deliberate way society declares its abhorrence of the crime and justice is seen to be done against the offender. The punishment is made to fit the crime. The Christian objection to this may be at various levels, including the condemnation of any punishment which is not at the same time remedial...Christian opinion, however, is divided...We earnestly plead that one of two alternatives be found to the present law. If capital punishment is not to be abolished altogether as in other European states...Either (1) a period of ten years trial should be set, during which no criminal is hanged. The period to be carefully studied with regard to any increase of crimes of violence Or (2) the present system of various degrees of murder should be greatly extended to reduce to a bare minimum those types of murder which cannot be answered in any other way than by hanging.

This statement of policy was signed by J W Beaumont, W H Benewith, C H Cleal, R E Cooper and E H Robertson. This was fairly unequivocal stuff, though there seemed to be some confusion in assuming that there were already in existence degrees of murder, and was presumably a strong indicator of the way that the Baptist Church as a whole was moving on the issue during this critical period of the debate.

By 1964 the *Baptist Times* (perhaps reflecting the views of the Church as a whole) had become unequivocally abolitionist. The advent of the new Silverman Bill met with its whole-hearted approval. Capital punishment was deemed simply morally wrong and 'All the waves of passionate argument calling for extreme retribution or for society to protect itself break on this rock.'[430] But this fervour for abolition within the Church did not extend to all of its clergy, many of whom still took a contrary view, and the editorial sparked a renewed epistolary battle within its pages. One stated that he had recently interviewed three people convicted of non-capital murder, none of whom had shown the slightest remorse or concern.[431] 'The taking of human life is regarded in the Bible as so serious that he who with malice aforethought takes a life must forfeit his own as a deterrent to others.' This view was condemned by another letter-writer as 'appalling' and 'hard to understand in a Christian and contrary to the teaching of our Lord.'[432]

Moving forward four years and the approach of the confirmatory votes inspired a renewal of the debate. Jamie Wallace in his column hoped that the vote at the Tory party conference presaged their intention to restore capital

---

[429]*The Baptist Times*, 16th February 1956 – 'Capital Punishment'
[430]*The Baptist Times*, 10th December 1964 - Editorial 'No More Hangings'
[431]*The Baptist Times*, 17th December 1964 – letter from Reverend Herbert Burgess (Battersea)
[432]*The Baptist Times*, 31st December 1964 – letter from J W Lee Palin (Plymouth)

punishment.[433] He was repudiated the following week by the Reverend Donald Black, chairman of the Baptist Union Christian Citizenship department, citing the findings of the Royal Commission and asserting that any killing had the effect of cheapening life: 'You cannot kill anywhere without cheapening life everywhere.'[434] The British Council of Churches voted overwhelmingly in 1969 to re-affirm their support for abolition and the Baptist Union Council was requested by its Christian Citizenship Committee to urge the government to proceed with complete abolition.[435] The Baptist Union Council duly resolved, by a large majority (only five against), to declare its opposition to the death penalty, and to recommend the government: 'to provide now for the continued suspension or abolition of the death penalty', though it stressed that the alternative to hanging must protect the community and reflect society's condemnation of violent crime.[436]

But the debate within the Baptist Church didn't end there by any means. A few weeks later, after the Commons had voted to make abolition permanent, the Reverend David Pawson wrote a lengthy piece in which he asserted that: 'The abolition of capital punishment has been welcomed as evidence that Britain is still moving her barbaric past in a Christian direction. It is at least arguable that the opposite was true and that this decision was only possible because the Bible no longer controls our national thinking.'[437] Unsurprisingly this met with a rapid rebuttal from correspondents. One pointed out that since the Reverend Pawson had based his argument on Exodus he would presumably attach equal weight to the other laws enunciated in Exodus, such as chapter 21, verses 22-25: 'When men strive together and hurt a woman with child, so that there is a miscarriage, and yet no harm follows, the one who hurt her shall be fined, according as the woman's husband shall lay upon him. If any harm follows, then you shall give life for life, eye for an eye, tooth for tooth, hand for hand, foot for foot, burn for burn, wound for wound, stripe for stripe.'[438]

This trend towards abolitionism was observable across most of the Christian churches according to roughly the same time pattern. For example some of the Welsh Congregational churches had passed a motion calling on Parliament to end hanging in 1948.[439] In Scotland the established church, the Presbyterian Church of Scotland, had tended not to commit itself on the

---

[433]*The Baptist Times*, 16th October 1969 – 'The One Way We Can Say No To Murder' Talking Point by Jamie Wallace

[434]*The Baptist Times*, 23rd October 1969

[435]*The Baptist Times*, 13th November 1969 'Say No to Hanging' Baptists Urged

[436]*The Baptist Times*, 20th November 1969 – 'Council Says No to Hanging'

[437]*The Baptist Times*, 15th January 1970 – 'Second Thoughts on the Death Penalty' by David Pawson

[438]*Baptist Times*, 22nd January 1970 'Further thoughts on the death penalty' W D Ford (London)

[439]*The Cardiff Western Mail*, 23rd January 1948. Quoted in Potter, op cit, p.146

question until very recently when it, too, has become declaredly abolitionist but it was noticeably silent on the matter in the period in question. It was discussed at the 1956 General Assembly, but then only in the context of the prison reform which might be necessary if very long sentences were to be handed down as the alternative to hanging. Dr Davidson of Glasgow Cathedral said that there was a big cleavage of opinion in the church as in the country at large, but that since the matter had been decided in the Commons *(sic)* there was no need for an announcement of approval or disapproval, though he felt that much of the discussion had been superficial 'and without sufficient reference to the deeper theological implications.'[440] Since then it has never been high enough up the agenda for any clear decision to be made.[441]

But this remarkable conversion on the part of many of the Dissenting churches to a progressive stance on capital punishment was, unsurprisingly, not shared by all nonconformists. In particular the Free Presbyterian Church of Scotland (the Scottish Free Kirk or 'Wee Wee Frees') was adamantly retentionist, basing its support for capital punishment on the Old Testament, and resenting the suggestion that capital punishment was unchristian as being based on a misconception of Scripture, confusing the requirement for the individual to love his neighbour with the right of the state to administer law and justice. It had condemned the Commons action in passing the Silverman clause in 1948 as 'unscriptural'.[442] Their synod had met in 1962 and had 'noted with disfavour the impression given by various religious bodies such as the Convocation of Canterbury and York and the British Council of Churches that capital punishment is unchristian' and that it resulted from:-

> confusion between scripture that governs relations between man and man and that to do with the administration of law by the courts...The government should not be persuaded to depart from Holy Writ on this particular matter by those who have no clear understanding of the scriptural principles involved...The Synod therefore appeals to the British government to retain the death penalty for the crime of murder, as the abolition of capital punishment would be an insult to the Majesty of Heaven and the cause of bringing Divine displeasure upon our beloved land.[443]

Such apocalyptic language indicated that for some Christians capital punishment was not merely acceptable or justifiable but mandatory, and that its abandonment by the state was almost a sin which would invoke divine

---

[440] *The Times*, 29th May 1956

[441] Rob Whiteman, Associate Secretary, Church and Society Council, Church of Scotland, personal communication 26th May 2008. The 2007 General Assembly

[442] Potter, op cit. p.146

[443] Resolution on capital punishment by the Synod of the Free Presbyterian Church of Scotland, 23rd May 1962. Quoted in the Westminster Standard (pamphlet), in Gardiner, Add 56463B.

retribution of some unspecified nature. This was of course an extreme position that was taken by very few Christians who supported capital punishment.[444]

The British Council of Churches, an ecumenical body representing a broad range of Christian denominations within the United Kingdom but which did not then include the Roman Catholics, also played an active part in the debate at this time.[445] Its 'Social Responsibility Department' produced a statement on the topic, as a result of a canvass of its constituent bodies.[446] It noted the extraordinarily high suicide rate before arrest of those suspected of having committed murder and the very high proportion of those convicted who were found guilty but insane, and that the Royal Commission had thought the McNaghten Rules too rigid. It concluded that deterrence was a red herring because it was impossible to prove either way and that the real issue was retribution and reform: 'I am personally convinced that capital punishment could and should be abolished. I would suggest that the Social Responsibility Department would do well to concentrate its attention on the question of retribution or reform rather than in wandering through the statistical maze of deterrence.' The general secretary of the SRD wrote to the *Times* shortly afterwards stating that at their recent meeting they had expressed the earnest hope that Parliament will take the opportunity to abolish the death penalty, or at least to suspend it.[447] The BCC view probably represented the mainstream of Christian thinking on capital punishment at the time.

Summarizing the position of the Christian churches it may be said that they generally moved strongly towards abolitionism in the mid-1950s onwards as the abolition campaign gained momentum, from having generally been, with the definite exception of the Quakers and the possible exception of a few others, largely retentionist prior to that. A major caveat is that of course this generally applied to the position of the church hierarchy and not necessarily to the lower ranks of its clergy, and certainly not to the broad mass of its communicants who may or may not have shared the conversion to abolitionism. In fact the likelihood is, given that one might reasonably assume that church membership was fairly typical, in that regard, of the general population, that most ordinary church members were somewhat less abolitionist than their senior clergy. A further qualification is that, as mentioned, some churches clung to the view that capital punishment was divinely ordained as the penalty for murder and that it

---

[444] It remains the position of the Free Presbyterian Church today. Donald Ross, 28th May 2007, personal communication

[445] Now known as 'Churches Together in Britain and Ireland'

[446] 'Statement on Capital Punishment' by Reverend E Rogers of the Social Responsibility Department of the BCC, 2nd February 1956. Canon John Collins papers, Church of England Research Committee, BCC/SRD/7/1/6/6

[447] General Secretary of the SRD of the BCC to the Times, 13th February 1956. Collins papers, ibid

was wrong for the state to dispense with it *de jure*, even though they might reduce its application to the point of abolition *de facto*. This was certainly the view of the Roman Catholic Church, and also of the Free Presbyterian Church of Scotland.

Viewing the churches on a high church/low church dimension it is noticeable that the churches at the extremes of the spectrum, the Catholic and the Calvinist were both retentionist, whilst the majority of others in between, especially the *via media* of the Church of England, were or came to be abolitionist. However, one may speculate as to how significant all of this was in terms of influencing the opinions of people on this or any other political question. Few people would have changed their opinion to secure conformity with the position of their church, however religious they might have been, and one might re-emphasize that religious people tend to seek religious justification for their views, rather than the religion dictating the view.

Judaism

The Jewish religion, like most of the Christian churches, had no official stance on the question. However, though neither the Board of Deputies (the secular body representing the Jews) nor any of the Chief Rabbis took an official stance it was very striking that early opinion polls showed a large majority of Jews opposed to capital punishment; the only religious group, and indeed almost the only demographic group of any sort, to show an abolitionist majority (though the polling organizations discounted the statistical significance of the results because of the relatively small number of Jewish interviewees involved). One may speculate as to the reasons, but the Holocaust, all too horribly fresh in their minds, may have created a mood of revulsion against the state using its powers of violence against the individual. On the other hand there is nothing specific in the Old Testament against capital punishment, and much that can be interpreted to sanction it; in particular Genesis: 'whoso sheddeth man's blood by man shall his blood be shed' chapter ix, verse 6, and the Mosaic law: 'an eye for an eye' but it tended to be Christian fundamentalists rather than Jews who cited these as the authority for their beliefs.

The traditional Judaic view of capital punishment can be gauged from an article in *The Jewish Chronicle* from 1982 by the Chief Rabbi, Sir Immanuel Jakobovits. He recalled that the Talmud said that: 'A Sanhedrin that puts a man to death once in seven years is called a murderous court...' and pointed out that Jewish law had suspended the death penalty early in the first century – the first legislature in history to do so.[448] He noted that, paradoxically, though Jewish

---

[448] '...And Death' Article by Sir Immanuel Jakobovits, Chief Rabbi, on hanging from *The Jewish Chronicle*, 11th June 1982

law prescribed the death penalty for over thirty offences ranging from murder to kidnapping, adultery and incest, forms of rape, idolatry, etc, the death sentence was hedged in by so many conditions that it could hardly ever be carried out in practice. Circumstantial evidence was inadmissible in capital trials and there had to be at least two independent eye-witnesses (Deuteronomy 17:6; 19:15) and they had to warn the offender before he committed the crime, and he had to acknowledge their warning, and the witnesses had to become the executioners! Thus the death penalty was in practice never carried out, and yet stayed on the statute book as an indicator of the heinousness with which these crimes were viewed by the community. The article suggested, however, that there were exceptions for those who threatened society as a whole.

At about this time Jakobovits issued a statement about the death penalty that largely followed the contours of the aforementioned article.[449] He lamented that crime flourished in a climate which had lost its abhorrence of crime, and noted as before that Jewish law had all but abolished capital punishment, except for cases where the individual threatened society. He felt that: 'The death penalty should exist in principle to ensure that the public horror of crime is greater than the horror of meting out just punishment. But out of respect for the sanctity of life and to prevent any possible miscarriage of justice it should not be carried out, except in cases of deliberate threats to innocent lives and in any attempt to subvert the rule of law and order on which the security of society depends.' This, like many of the utterances of the Christian clergy of the time, seems a masterpiece of obfuscation and ambivalence. *The Jewish Chronicle*, the main organ of the Jews, seems to have been curiously silent on the controversy, with little or no editorial comment and little mention beyond a brief report of the advent of the NCACP campaign, noting that its two leading figures were both Jewish - Silverman and Gollancz.[450] There were occasional reports of the Parliamentary debates, a few book reviews of some of the early works by the abolitionists, and a profile of Silverman on the occasion of his seventieth birthday, which described him as in the tradition of great individualist and rebel MPs such as Wilberforce and Plimsoll.[451]

So far as the non Judaeo-Christian religions were concerned their numbers and the extent of their influence were too small at that time for them to have any significant impact upon the debate.

---

[449] 'The Death Penalty: A Jewish View' 1982 (?) In Jakobovits papers, ACC/2805/07/21/008, London Metropolitan Archives

[450] *The Jewish Chronicle*, 25th November 1955, 'Incidentally' column

[451] *The Jewish Chronicle*, 8th October 1965, 'Silhouette' column. It might be noted that the state of Israel abolished capital punishment in 1954, only six years after its inception, and that special legislation was needed to enable Eichmann to be hanged in 1961

The Churches and Politics

The churches generally were loath to intervene too strongly in matters of political controversy. For one thing they risked alienating much of their membership if they did, and the Church of England, in particular, as the established church would have been in danger of being perceived as abusing its position, and thereby jeopardizing its special status. For another they could have incurred the displeasure of the government of the day, and possibly the official opposition too. Party political matters were very much off bounds but matters of conscience were rather more the province of the churches, both because of their 'ethical' nature and the fact that they tended to be the preserve of private members bills and therefore not regarded officially as 'party' questions. Nonetheless, as we have seen, there was a strong tendency for opinion on many of these issues to split along party lines to a marked degree, and thus there was still a danger that if a church took too strong a stand it would be seen as too closely aligned with a particular party. Moreover, attitudes among the communicants of these churches varied widely, and any official stance taken by the church hierarchy would necessarily have offended or alienated a substantial proportion of its membership. There was also a difficulty in evaluating the level of authority to be ascribed to any such official pronouncement. Were communicants obliged to sign up to that position as a matter of theological necessity, or were they free to differ, in which case could they differ on other more fundamental matters? Thus the churches, particularly the Anglican Church, tended to be very careful in their public utterances and to stress, in the standard formulation, that different views were possible, even when clearly favouring one side of the debate rather than the other.

On capital punishment this dilemma was strongly apparent in the case of Archbishop Ramsey personally, who had become fully converted to the abolitionist cause, but who was very reluctant to nail his colours too firmly to the mast. Despite being heavily prevailed upon to lead the Abolition Bill in the Lords in 1965, he decided ultimately, and probably wisely, to decline that role. The Catholic Church was in a slightly different position, in that it was governed by the Vatican, and the English hierarchy had no power to make authoritative decisions on any matter, whether theological or secular. It tended to adopt the somewhat Delphic position that the State should have the power to inflict the death penalty, but be not obliged to use it, and that communicants may campaign for or against the death penalty but may not argue that the State should be denied the authority to inflict it. The nonconformist churches tended to differ sharply between themselves over both the death penalty and other conscience issues. The Methodists and Baptists, for example, the two biggest Dissenting churches in England and Wales, were both fairly abolitionist in tone, but as with both the Anglicans and the Catholics they were reluctant to adopt an official stance or to seek to constrain their members in their expression of opinion on these matters.

On other issues, particularly 'conscience' issues, there were again very considerable differences both between and within the various churches. The Roman Catholic Church was, of course, very strongly opposed to both abortion and divorce law reform, and moderately opposed to homosexual law reform (stressing that homosexuality was a sin even if it should no longer be a criminal offence). The nonconformist churches tended to support most or all of these measures, though some were chary of supporting homosexual reform. On the other hand the Catholics were relatively liberal on the question of sabbatarianism, whereas the nonconformists, given their traditions, tended to be more hard-line.

In all of these things the Church of England was somewhere in the middle but tended to incline to a liberal position, certainly from the 1960s onwards, when, as we have seen the church 'liberalized' itself under Ramsey and others of his cast of mind. On the issue of homosexuality the Church had adopted a moderately liberal position from as early as the 1950s when its 'Moral Welfare Council' issued *The Problem of Homosexuality* in 1954 and together with the Howard League was instrumental in urging the Home Secretary to institute an enquiry into the whole question. On divorce the Church took a progressive stance with its report *Putting Asunder* in 1965 which advocated the relaxation of the divorce laws to allow divorce where the marriage had broken down irretrievably. On abortion it was again fairly liberal, its Social Responsibility Board promulgating *Abortion: An Ethical Discussion*, in 1966; one of a series on moral questions including suicide, artificial insemination and sterilization, which was basically a statement of middle of the road Anglican opinion.[452] By the middle 1970s, however, the Church had to a certain extent revised its position as regards abortion, and in *Abortion Law Reform* it regretted the large numbers of abortions then being performed, supported the James White Bill of 1974/5 and said that the Steel Bill had gone too far.[453] It did not, however, resile from its positions on divorce and homosexuality. Attempts by anti-abortion clergy to enlist their parishioners against reform were generally unsuccessful. An ALRA poll taken in 1966 showed 80% of Protestant clergy in favour of reform and that the Methodists and Congregationalists were usually more liberal than the Anglicans. So far as the bishops were concerned they tended not to vote on abortion in the Lords, and when they did they were split with a tendency to support reform but to oppose the more radical clauses. On the other hand on Sunday Observance it was still very conservative.

All of which simply illustrates the difficulties that the churches

---

[452] Hindell, Keith and Madeleine Simms, *Abortion Law Reformed* (London: Peter Owen, 1971)

[453] Marsh, David and Joanna Chambers, *Abortion Politics* (London: Junction Books, 1981) p.72

experienced in the 1960s, when confronted with a rapidly changing social climate and the demands for the radical reform of old laws, and the difficulty they experienced in seeking to reconcile their traditional beliefs with the demand for change that was emanating from so many quarters. Too rigid a stance would leave them in danger of drifting so far away from mainstream opinion as to leave them isolated and irrelevant, whilst too strong a support for progressive causes may have left them looking meretricious and too eager to appease the *avante garde* in their ranks so as to maintain their secular influence. Ultimately it was a difficulty which the churches resolved in different ways, with the Anglicans tending to be in the forefront of reform under the influence of its new generation of reform-minded clerics.

Conclusion

Summarizing the role of the churches in the controversy it is difficult to assess precisely the extent of their influence. Theoretically that influence was very considerable given that, even in the post-war era, the great majority of Englishmen would have considered themselves to be adherents of one church or another, as measured by census and opinion poll data. On the other hand, only a small and declining number of people actually attended church services with any degree of regularity, and few would have been governed in their everyday lives and their political opinions by the views of their church leaders. Religion was, by all accounts, a declining force and had been for most of the twentieth century. Views on capital punishment generally did not seem to be conditioned to any significant degree by the utterances of the clergy, with polls showing that religious affiliation apparently had little or no bearing on whether one was pro- or anti-hanging. Not that it would have been easy for most people to have followed the urgings of their clergy in this respect because most church leaders were chary of nailing their colours too firmly to the mast for fear of alienating their membership. Moreover, one must distinguish between the hierarchy, the lower clergy and the ordinary member. Generally the lower down the ladder the more conservative the views were, on capital punishment and other issues.

CHAPTER 8

PUBLIC OPINION

Public support was of course important to the success of the campaign, though ultimately not absolutely crucial to it. Opinion polls showed that there was still a majority against abolition even in the period 1964-5 when it was being enacted and a much bigger majority against it when it was re-affirmed in 1969.[454] Nonetheless, public opinion had been moving in the right direction from the abolitionists' viewpoint for some time (ever since the mid-1950s) and the retentionist majority had been steadily reduced. This was not vital to the success of the campaign but was probably a big help, particularly in persuading a substantial number of Conservative MPs to switch to the abolitionist camp in the crucial votes (who might have found it otherwise almost impossible in the face of an overwhelming popular consensus - especially given the hostility to it of their constituency associations in many cases). As we shall see public opinion moved back in the opposite direction very rapidly (and may have been a major factor in causing some cautious Conservative abolitionists to reconsider) but by then abolition was a Parliamentary *fait accompli* which had become almost impossible to reverse.

Opinion can be, and was, measured in a variety of ways but by far the most prevalent and the most scientific were the findings of the public opinion polls carried out by the professional polling organizations.[455]

Opinion poll findings

Unsurprisingly in view of the intense controversy that raged over the issue of capital punishment and the frequency with which the matter came up in Parliament there was a plethora of opinion poll surveys conducted by the various polling organizations, though usually confined to the times when the matter was up for debate. This chapter looks at the history of these poll findings, their accuracy and meaning and the effect they had on the course of the debate, if any.

Opinion polling on a large scale only really got going in the 1930s with Mass Observation and the Gallup organization. The earliest British poll on the issue appears to have been in November 1938 which asked the basic question, 'Should the death penalty be abolished?' and found that 49% were against

---

[454] Teer, Frank and James D Spence, *Political Opinion Polls* (London: Hutchinson, 1973) p.138. As they comment this was one of the two outstanding issues of the 1960s, together with British entry to the (EEC) Common Market, in which public opinion was consistently out of kilter with government action.

[455] Teer and Spence, ibid, passim.

abolition and 40% were for it with 11% undecided; a surprisingly high proportion for abolition considering that the issue had scarcely registered on the political radar at that time - though it was due to be debated as an amendment to the government's Criminal Justice Bill.[456] The next polls to be conducted on the issue were in the 1947-8 period, commissioned by the press in the light of the fact that the matter was being seriously considered and was up for debate in the form of the Silverman amendment to the Criminal Justice Bill of 1947-8. All the early polls showed large majorities for the retention of capital punishment, with typically at least twice as many in favour of retention as for abolition. One of the first was a Gallup, i.e. British Institute of Public Opinion (BIPO) Survey conducted in June 1947 (results below).[457]

Table 3: Views on Capital Punishment by Party Political Preference (%)

Party	Favour hanging	Oppose hanging	Don't Know
Conservative	75	18	7
Labour	65	29	6
Liberal	58	34	8
Other	66	20	14
Non-voters	70	22	8

334   123   43

Table 4: Views on Capital Punishment by Religious Affiliation (%)

Denomination	Favour hanging	Oppose hanging	Don't Know
Church of England	74	19	7
Nonconformist	65	27	8
Roman Catholic	70	22	8
Scottish Churches	72	24	4
Others	58	31	11
None	55	40	5

---

[456] SOC (Social Survey (Gallup Poll) Ltd, London. Cited in Erskine, Hazel, 'The Polls: Capital Punishment' *Public Opinion Quarterly*, no 34 (2) 1970-1, pp.290-307. It is unclear if and where this poll was published but it was clearly prompted by the fact that capital punishment was due for debate in the House of Commons.

[457] British Institute of Public Opinion (BIPO) - the Gallup organization - Survey 150, 5th June 1947. Cited in Christoph, op cit, p.44. The question posed was, 'In this country most people convicted of murder are sentenced to death. Do you agree with this or do you think that the death penalty should be abolished?' Of course a sentence of death may not be carried out so that the alternatives posed by the question did not exhaust the possibilities, as pointed out by Christoph.

This poll was very typical in its findings in that there were large majorities for the retention of capital punishment across all groups surveyed, though the breakdown by party preference and religious affiliation showed that the size of the retentionist majority varied somewhat but was always large.

Another poll of six months later, conducted by the same body but breaking down the sample differently, showed 65% in favour of the retention of capital punishment, 25% for abolition and 10% 'don't knows'.[458] This was roughly the balance of opinion irrespective of sex, age group and socio-economic status. That balance of opinion and its consistency across a variety of independent variables was very typical of poll findings on the issue at the time. Also striking were the very small percentages of 'don't knows', much smaller than was usual on public policy questions.

These findings were approximately replicated in three polls conducted a few months later in the immediate aftermath of the April 1948 Commons vote to approve the Silverman amendment, and relating specifically to that vote. A *Daily Express* poll asking if respondents approved of the Commons' decision found 14% approved, 77% disapproved and 9% didn't know. Broken down by party allegiance 85% of Conservatives disapproved, 69% of Labour supporters, 76% of Liberals and 76% of those expressing no political preference.[459] Another Gallup poll showed 26% approving and 66% disapproving with 8% don't knows, again with very little differentiation by sex, age group and social class, and with party preference again showing a smaller but still considerable majority for retention amongst Labour and Liberal supporters as compared to Conservatives.[460]

A Mass Observation poll of over 6,000 Britons, using an open-ended and unstructured interviewing technique unlike the other polling organisations, found 69% disapproving of the vote and 13% approving, but with another 18%, comprising 7% for recognizing degrees of murder, 4% with mixed feelings, 2% 'miscellaneous answers' and 5% don't knows.[461]

---

[458] BIPO Survey 158, 5th November 1947. Cited in Christoph, ibid, p.43. The wording of the question was as for the previous survey.

[459] *Daily Express*, 29th April 1948. Cited in Christoph, p. 53. Its sampling techniques are unknown and the question it posed was inaccurate because it implied that the Commons had voted for total abolition rather than mere suspension.

[460] BIPO survey 167, 10th May 1948, appearing in the *News Chronicle*. Cited in Christoph, p. 54

[461] Mass Observation, 28th May 1948, published in the *Daily Telegraph*. Cited in Christoph, p. 55. This survey was published by MO as a pamphlet 'Capital Punishment: A Survey' (London, 1948)

Table 5a: Breakdown by Sex[462]

Opinion	Males	Females	Total
Approval	15	12	13
Disapproval	69	69	69
Degrees of murder	8	6	7
Mixed responses	3	4	4
Miscellaneous	2	2	2
Don't Know	3	7	5

Table 5b: Breakdown by Age[463]

Opinion	16-24	25-44	45+	Total
Approval	18	14	11	13
Disapproval	60	69	71	69
Degrees	9	7	7	7
Mixed	3	3	4	4
Miscellaneous	1	2	3	2
Don't Know	9	5	4	5

Table 5c: Breakdown by Income[464]

Opinion	under £4 p.w.	£4-7 p.w.	£7-12 p.w.	£12-20 p.w.	£20+ p.w.
Approval	14	12	15	16	14
Disapproval	63	69	66	69	73
Degrees	6	8	9	7	6
Mixed	5	3	4	4	4
Misc	9	2	2	3	2
Don't Know	3	6	4	1	1

Table 5d: Breakdown by Education[465]

Opinion	Elementary	Secondary (up to 16.5)	Secondary (over 16.5)
Approval	11	14	21
Disapproval	71	68	63
Degrees	7	9	7
Mixed	3	4	5
Misc	6	2	2
Don't Know	2	3	2

---

[462] MO archives, Record ID 2996 – May 1948 – Appendix A

[463] MO archives, ibid

[464] MO archives, ibid. The effects of inflation make the income categories look absurdly low (even at the top end).

[465] MO archives, ibid. The categories betray the fact that few went on to higher education at the time.

Table 5e: Breakdown by Geographical Region[466]

Opinion	London	Wales&SW	Scotland	NW	Midlands	SE	NE
Approval	16	11	17	13	12	12	12
Disapproval	66	70	64	71	71	68	71
Degrees	7	6	4	7	8	9	9
Mixed	6	3	3	4	3	3	3
Misc	1	3	3	2	2	2	1
Don't know	4	7	9	3	4	6	4

Table 5f: Breakdown by Religion[467]

Opinion	None	CE	RC	Noncon.	Jewish	Scot.	Other
Approval	16	10	15	17	40	12	30
Disapproval	65	72	66	66	42	70	50
Degrees	8	8	7	7	8	3	5
Mixed	4	3	5	4	2	4	7
Misc	2	2	2	2	2	2	4
Don't know	5	5	5	4	6	9	4

Table 5g: Breakdown by size of town[468]

Opinion	London	Conurbations	Large Towns	Other Towns	Rural
Approval	16	15	15	11	9
Disapproval	66	68	67	71	69
Degrees	7	8	6	6	8
Mixed	6	3	5	4	3
Misc	1	2	2	2	3
D/K	4	4	5	6	8

Again there was very little effect of any of the usual variables such as sex, age, income level, area and size of town. Religious affiliation was a slight influence with Anglican and Church of Scotland affiliates being a little more retentionist than the others. Level and length of education showed a marked tendency for the better educated to be more abolitionist than the less well educated. And as with other polls Labour and Liberal supporters were markedly more abolitionist than Conservatives though still very much in the minority within their respective parties. Striking, though, is the unusual inclusion of Communist supporters in the survey, and the fact that they, uniquely among political groups, showed a majority approving and a large majority at that.[469]

---

[466] MO archives, ibid. The regions are of necessity drawn somewhat arbitrarily.

[467] MO archives, ibid

[468] MO archives, ibid. Again the categories are somewhat arbitrary.

[469]That might have been expected given the left-right orientation of the debate and the fact that Labour and Liberal supporters were more abolitionist than Conservatives but nonetheless it is striking in that Communist regimes at the time were none too averse to the use of capital punishment for political as well as criminal activity and illustrates to a remarkable degree that Communists in western countries were often vastly more dovish in their attitudes than the regimes they supported. See, for example, Brittan, Sam, *Left or Right: The Bogus Dilemma* (London: Secker and Warburg, 1968)

Table 5h: Classification by Party Political Preference[470]

	Con	Lab	Lib	Comm	Other	None	Total
Approve	8	19	16	57	25	14	13
Disapprove	76	63	65	27	59	62	69
Degrees	7	9	7	8	6	7	7
Mixed	4	3	6	4	6	4	4
Miscellaneous	2	1	3	4	2	3	2
Don't Know	3	5	3	0	2	10	5

Another notable point is that the survey was started immediately after the Commons vote and the responses logged by date. There appeared to be no variation between an earlier and a later sample.

The results of the poll were published in the *Daily Telegraph*; the first such survey ever published in that august organ, under the headline, 'Public Opinion Approves the Death Penalty' with an accompanying article by J C Johnstone written in a tone of hearty endorsement of the findings, which illustrated the way in which newspapers tended to use poll findings as political propaganda:-

> It is now as certain as anything can be that an overwhelming majority of the people of this country is opposed to the experimental abolition of the death penalty for murder. This fact is so decisively proved by the result of the MO enquiry…that Parliament if it persists in the measure will be openly belying its character as a representative institution…[471]

Conversely the liberal and moderately pro-abolitionist *News Chronicle,* which had published the BIPO/Gallup poll, gave its survey results a different spin:

> If over a period public opinion tests have shown that a particular aspect of government policy is unpopular with the mass of the people the government should certainly tread cautiously for in a democratic society the voice of the people must be the ultimate arbiter. It is precisely as an index to the public mind and not as a substitute for leadership that the Gallup poll should be regarded. If a government perpetually veered course according to the changing winds of public opinion it would be its own leadership, not the public survey, which would be at fault.[472]

These three poll findings are summarized below.[473]

---

[470] MO, Capital Punishment survey 1938-1956 (TC72), Box 1 File 1/C. The results were published in the *Daily Telegraph* of 28th May 1948
[471] *Daily Telegraph,* 28th May 1948
[472] *News Chronicle,* leading article, 3rd June 1948
[473] Cited in Christoph, op cit, p.56

Table 6: Summary of Polling Results

Response	Daily Express poll	BIPO (Gallup)	Mass Observation
Approve vote	14	26	13
Disapprove vote	77	66	69
Favour degrees	*	*	7
Mixed feelings	*	*	4
Misc.	*	*	2
Don't Know	9	8	5

A comparison of these three polls shows that there is a fairly high degree of consistency, with all three showing very large majorities against abolition. Nonetheless, there is some variation with the *Daily Express* figures showing easily the largest majority for retention and the other two showing roughly the same balance of opinion. Taking the BIPO and MO figures there is a striking similarity. If one includes, logically enough, those 'favouring the creation of degrees of murder', those with 'mixed feelings' and 'miscellaneous' in the MO survey as being on the 'approve' side then the percentage in favour is identical at 26% and the percentage disapproving only differs by three points because of a difference in the percentage of 'don't knows' (higher in the BIPO survey perhaps because the MO open-ended techniques may have drawn out half-forgotten memories from respondents). It may be significant that these latter two surveys were conducted by professional polling organisations whereas the *Express* poll is of unknown provenance and may have used less exacting sampling techniques and thus may have less statistical validity. Also the *Express* and BIPO polls used dichotomous questions unlike MO which was open-ended. The MO report speculates that on an issue such as capital punishment where opinion was in flux the precise wording of the question may be influential. The *Express* survey question failed to clarify that the Parliamentary vote was on a motion proposing merely an *experimental* period of abolition, whereas the BIPO survey was very specific on that point. Thus the 11% who favoured degrees of murder or who had mixed feelings in the MO survey would probably have come down as 'disapprovers' in the other two surveys. MO concluded that their open-ended techniques were a more sensitive indicator of public opinion.[474] These similarities and differences are worth exploring.[475]

The *Daily Express* stated that their sample was between 3,000 and 4,000, BIPO 2,000 and MO 6,000, with the stratifications appearing to be similar. All

---

[474] MO archives, Record ID 3001 May 1948.
[475] MO archives.

three surveys showed that political affiliation was an important factor with Conservative supporters far more opposed than Labour supporters. BIPO and MO by direct statement and *Express* by implication all showed that age, sex and income differences cause only small variations in attitude.[476] This was consistent with most subsequent poll findings on capital punishment especially as regards age and sex. Opinions on the death penalty may be vehemently held but not deep-seated, as noted by MO, and thus be subject to rapid change.

One might mention that a Conservative MP, Stanley Prescott (Darwen, Lancs), who had voted for the Silverman amendment conducted a private poll of his constituents shortly afterwards using reply-paid postcards and found an overwhelming majority disapproving of his action; 13,736-718.[477] Interestingly the majority for retention was vastly higher than even any of the public polls demonstrated and may have reflected that the retentionists were more likely to have replied and that Darwen was a very Conservative seat. Prescott never again voted for abolition and the result was flaunted by the retentionists in the House of Lords debate. However great was the reforming zeal of the campaigners it was not embraced by the bulk of the population.

This remained the state of opinion in the country at large until the mid-fifties when a cautious and sluggish move in the abolitionist direction was perceptible, maybe partly as a function of the assorted *causes celebre* of the era, possibly because of the liberalizing climate. Opinion in the period from 1953 (when the Gowers Commission reported) to 1955 (when abolition gained renewed impetus) can be summarized by three BIPO polls as below:-

Table 7a: Views on Capital Punishment[478]

Date	Retain	Abolish	Don't Know
October 1953	73	15	12
July 1955	50	37	13
Dec. 1955	61	25	14

The surge of abolitionism evident in the July 1955 poll may have been heavily affected by the very recent hanging of Ruth Ellis with its heavy emotional charge and, if so, the dwindling of it by the end of the year suggests that its impact was rather ephemeral. The survey also ascertained respondent's reasons for disapproving of abolition.

---

[476] MO archives, Record ID 3001, May 1948
[477] Reported in the Times, 12th and 24th May 1948. cited in Christoph, op cit. pp. 56-57
[478] Taken from the files of BIPO. The question in each case was:- 'In this country most people convicted of murder are sentenced to death. Do you agree with this or do you think that the death penalty should be abolished?', cited in Christoph, op cit. p.109

Table 7b: Reasons for Disapproval of Abolition[479]

Reason	1948	1955
Security, danger to individual and community	40	42
Life for a life (revenge)	26	22
Time not yet ripe	11	1
Danger to children	4	2
Menace from released prisoners	4	2
Special danger to police	2	1
Will entail arming police	1	0
Miscellaneous reasons	12	20
Capital punishment abolished elsewhere with bad results	0	9

However, the trend towards abolitionism was manifest in a Mass Observation poll of January 1956.[480] This used the same number of respondents (6,000) as its predecessor of 1948 and the same open-ended interviewing techniques, though unlike that of 1948 it was conducted just before rather than just after a Commons vote. It found 49% against the abolition of capital punishment in principle and 18% for its abolition, with the other 33% either undecided or favouring the recognition of degrees of murder. However, 34% approved a five year experimental period of abolition (the traditional Parliamentary formula) and 45% disapproved. Thus the percentage favouring suspension had increased from 13% to 34% by comparison with the 1948 MO survey and the figures opposing it had dropped from 69% to 45%. The breakdowns by assorted variables showed the familiar pattern but the majorities for retention were consistently smaller than in the 1948 Survey, across all religious, political, sex, age and class groups.

Table 8a: Views on trial suspension of hanging by sex[481]

Men	1948	1956
Approve of trial suspension	15	36
Disapprove of the trial suspension	69	48
Degrees of murder should be recognised	8	2
Mixed feelings	3	4
Miscellaneous replies	2	5

---

[479] BIPO survey 1955, MO archives, ibid

[480] Published in the *Daily Telegraph*. Taken from *Capital Punishment: A Survey* (1948), op cit, and *A Report on Capital Punishment* (1956) both by Leonard England of Mass Observation. Cited in Christoph, op cit. pp. 116-124. MO, Capital Punishment survey 1938-1956 (TC72), ibid, Box 2, file 72/2/A: MO survey no 290

[481] Cited in Christoph, ibid, p.118. It is unclear why the figures quoted do not add up to 100%.

Don't know	3	5
Women		
Approve of trial suspension	12	33
Disapprove of trial suspension	69	42
Degrees of murder should be recognised	6	2
Mixed feelings	4	6
Miscellaneous	2	5
Don't know	7	9

Clearly both sexes had moved by about the same amount in an abolitionist/suspensionist direction.

Table 8b: Views on trial suspension of hanging by age group[482]

Age group	16-24	25-44	45-64	65+
Approve trial suspension				
1948	18	14	11*	–
1956	38	36	33	28
Disapprove trial suspension				
1948	60	69	71*	–
1956	41	45	45	47
Degrees of murder				
1948	9	7	7*	–
1956	2	2	2	2
Mixed feelings				
1948	3	3	4*	–
1956	4	4	6	7
Miscellaneous replies				
1948	1	2	3*	–
1956	5	5	5	5
Don't know				
1948	9	5	4*	–
1956	12	8	9	11

*The earlier poll had used a single classification of 45 and over

---

[482] Cited in Christoph, ibid, p.118

Table 8c: Views on trial suspension of hanging by school leaving age[483]

School-leaving age	Up to 15	Up to 16½	Over 16½
Approve trial suspension			
1948	11	14	21
1956	34	35	40
Disapprove trial suspension			
1948	71	68	63
1956	45	44	42
Degrees of murder			
1948	7	9	7
1956	1	2	2
Mixed feelings			
1948	3	4	5
1956	5	5	5
Miscellaneous replies			
1948	6	2	2
1956	5	5	6
Don't know			
1948	2	3	2
1956	10	9	5

Table 8d: Views on trial suspension of hanging by religious persuasion[484]

Religion	None	CE	RC	Church of Scotland	Noncon.	Jewish*	Other*
Approve suspension							
1948	16	10	15	12	17	40	30
1956	36	32	45	30	35	39	40
Disapprove suspension							
1948	65	72	66	70	66	42	50
1956	42	48	35	44	42	37	37
Degrees of murder							
1948	8	8	7	3	7	8	5
1956	22	2	1	2	1	2	-
Mixed feelings							
1948	44	3	5	4	4	2	7
1956	55	5	4	5	6	5	6
Misc.							
1948	22	2	2	2	2	2	4

[483] Cited in Christoph, ibid, p.119. Interesting that this should be the only index of educational attainment used. Later polls would tend to classify by higher education versus non higher education, reflecting the much greater numbers that went on to university. In 1956 those numbers were probably still too small for the results to be meaningful.

[484] Cited in Christoph, ibid, p.119

1956	55	4	7	5	6	5	7
Don't know							
1948	55	5	4	9	4	6	4
1956	10	9	8	10	10	12	10

*sample too small to be statistically significant

Table 8e: Views on trial suspension of hanging by party preference[485]

Party	Con	Lab	Lib	Undecided	None
Approve suspension					
1948	8	19	16	14	14
1956	30	38	39	33	35
Disapprove suspension					
1948	76	63	65	64	62
1956	50	42	43	43	39
Degrees of murder					
1948	7	9	7	10	7
1956	1	4	2	2	1
Mixed feelings					
1948	4	3	6	4	4
1956	6	2	6	4	5
Miscellaneous					
1948	2	1	3	2	3
1956	5	5	4	7	5
Don't know					
1948	3	5	3	6	10
1956	8	9	6	11	15

Table 8f: Views on trial suspension of hanging by newspaper usually read[486]

	Approve suspension	Disapprove suspension	Degrees of murder	Mixed feelings	Other answers	Don't know
Daily Telegraph	32	48	3	6	7	4
Daily Mirror	35	45	2	5	4	9
Daily Express	35	44	2	5	6	8
Daily Mail	31	50	2	5	4	8
Daily Herald	37	45	1	4	6	7
News Chronicle	41	39	1	5	7	7
Daily Sketch	37	47	*	5	3	8
The Times	35	42	2	4	9	8
Manchester Guardian	51	24	1	3	17	4
Other**	32	45	1	7	5	10
None	32	40	1	4	6	17
Total	34	45	2	5	5	9

[485] Cited in Christoph, ibid, p.120
[486] Cited in Christoph, ibid, p.121

* less than one percent; ** Includes some evening papers

These findings were more or less replicated in another BIPO survey of February 1956.[487] The evidence of these polls was that although the retentionists were still in the majority the general trend across all demographic, political and religious groups, by the mid-fifties, was evidently towards the abolitionist position, at least to the extent of a preparedness to accept an experimental period of suspension. Sex appeared to have little effect despite the supposed emotional impact upon women of the Ruth Ellis case. Age was significant with younger respondents being somewhat more abolitionist, as might have been expected, but length of education was not as significant a predictor as it had been in 1948. Religious persuasion showed that Anglicans and Church of Scotland affiliates were somewhat less abolitionist than were the others, and striking was the three-fold increase in the percentage of Roman Catholics favouring suspension; hard to explain given the silence of the church hierarchy on the question. Also notable was the fact that Jews were significantly more abolitionist than other religious groupings, though the pollsters were anxious to stress that the sample was too small to be statistically significant. One might speculate as to the reasons, which lay probably more in the recent experiences of state violence against them rather than in any scriptural or cultural factors. Politically as always Labour and Liberal supporters were significantly more abolitionist than were Conservatives, although the configuration of opinion among the general population was still markedly different from that at Westminster where the Labour and Liberal parties had become overwhelmingly abolitionist. The breakdown by newspaper preference rather confounds any notion of public opinion being shaped by editorials given that only the *Manchester Guardian* and *News Chronicle* readers were significantly different from the average.

Interesting also in the Mass Observation survey were the explanations given by respondents who said that certain things had recently helped them make up their mind on the issue.

Table 8g: Issues helping respondents to make up their minds[488]

Issue	Approving of capital punishment	Disapproving of capital punishment	Total
Ruth Ellis murder case	11	27	16
Bentley/Craig case	4	11	6

---

[487] BIPO files, poll s.457a, cited in Christoph, ibid, p.125f

[488] MO Capital Punishment survey (TC72), Box 2, file 72/2/A op cit. The figures do not add up to 100% because not all respondents gave a particular reason (and some may have given more than one). The zero figures in the 'murder cases generally' category do not appear to make complete sense.

Evans/Christie case	2	7	3
Other named murder cases	3	6	3
Other unnamed murder cases	16	10	14
Murder cases generally	0	0	37
A general increase in crime	8	-	5
Dangers to children and old people	15	1	10
Miscarriages of justices	1	12	4
Activities of 'Teddy Boys'	4	1	3
Effect on those who are left	1 (-)	1 (1)	1
Miscellaneous answers	4 (6)	11 (9)	6
Total number of respondents	333 (670)	150 (328)	541

Clearly the specific *causes celebre* of the mid-fifties, and especially that of Ruth Ellis, were influential factors in regard to undecided respondents who moved towards abolitionism, but those on the retentionist side or those shifting in that direction were more influenced by murder cases in general and by the supposed threat to the more vulnerable members of society. A further MO survey, or an extension of the earlier survey, published by MO in 1956 showed the following reasons cited by respondents as causing them to make up or alter their opinion.

Table 9a: Reasons that may have helped respondents to make up their mind [489]

Reason	Approve	Disapprove	Total
Ruth Ellis case	8	24	14
Bentley/Craig case	2	9	4
Evans/Christie case	1	9	4
Other named cases	4	3	4
Other unnamed cases	21	10	18
Cases generally	38	43	40
General increase in crime	8	-	5
Dangers to children and old people	19	2	13
Miscarriages	-	12	5
Effect on those left	-	1	1
Miscellaneous	6	9	8
Total	670	328	1130

As before, it is evident that specific miscarriages tended to be cited by

---

[489] MO Archive, ibid. Also cited in Christoph, op cit., p. 123 based on L England, op cit.

abolitionists or those who had moved in that direction, whereas crime and murder in general and the supposed danger to the young and old are the things that animated the retentionists. Of course these latter reasons are always apparent, whereas the spate of miscarriages was of recent origin and accounted to a considerable extent for the surge in abolitionism. The breakdown showed that, unlike formerly, men were now slightly more abolitionist than women and that thus sex had apparently become a factor, though it is unclear why. Age had also become a factor with younger respondents, especially those in the 16-24 category, more likely to approve of experimental abolition. Politics was an important factor as before, with only 30% of Conservatives supporting abolition as against 38% of Labour supporters. So far as religion was concerned Anglican and Church of Scotland communicants were least in favour. By comparison with the 1948 survey the proportion of Roman Catholics favouring abolition had trebled. Education, by contrast, was no longer a significant factor. Habitual newspaper was still a factor with 51% of *Manchester Guardian* (as it then was) readers in favour, higher than for the readership of any other national paper. Only 31% of *Daily Mail* readers were in favour.

Of those favouring abolition the reasons given were as below:[490]

Table 9b: Reasons that may have helped abolitionists to make up their minds

Reason	1948	1955
Experiment worth a trial	36	71
Humanitarian/ethical	29	4
Death penalty not a deterrent	8	2
Religious feelings/principles	6	1
Successfully abolished elsewhere	6	3
Dangers of judicial errors	3	1
Frequency of extenuating circumstances	1	3
Miscellaneous	11	12
Says death penalty abolished with good results	-	1

There was a steep rise in the percentage feeling abolition was 'worth a trial', i.e. that 'the time was ripe', and a consequent decline in the percentages citing more specific reasons. Even the proportion citing the possibility of judicial miscarriage had declined, notwithstanding recent events, but again this is probably accounted for by its subsumption under the head of 'experiment worth a trial'.

One might mention some of the more humorous responses given:-[491]

I would be against it because it is a deterrent. Prison has no terror now. All my mates

---

[490] MO archives, ibid
[491] MO archives, ibid, cited in Christoph, op cit, p.125

have been in from time to time. Although I haven't been – when they come out they are fit and strong – not like me who is always working. 48 year old maintenance engineer foreman, Camberwell.
No, I think it had better stay as a detergent. 47 year old wife of a cashier.
Its hanging I don't like. They should have elocution as in America.

As a coda to these results MO mentions replies given by police officers (this is in relation to the 1956 survey I think). Out of 79 respondents who were serving policemen only 4% approved of abolition, 72% disapproved, 5% favoured degrees of murder, 13% had mixed feelings and 6% gave miscellaneous replies or were 'don't knows'.[492] It is unclear whether these were selected because they were policemen or were just part of a more general sample. Those disapproving gave their reasons in order as being:- security, danger to life etc; 'the time not ripe'; 'a life for a life'; the danger to police; the menace from released prisoners; 'entail need to arm the police'; and miscellaneous other reasons. The majority stressed that the job would be made less easy after abolition, as the following typical responses illustrated.[493]

It won't be much help to us chap. I don't think they should have given it up' was a typical response (policeman aged 30, rank not stated).
You can guess what our opinions are, can't you? There is no deterrence now. If a man shoots a policeman he knows twelve and a half years is the most he'll do. It makes you think twice about tackling a man when you know he's armed. I think they're making a great mistake. (policeman aged 36, rank not stated)

Such responses were characteristic though not entirely accurate in their premises in that they tended to read as if abolition were already a reality which it certainly wasn't in 1956. One might imagine that most of the police respondents were of low rank and probably not totally cognizant of the finer points of Parliamentary procedure, and one might also make allowance for stereotypical police pessimism which tended to presuppose the inevitability of what they feared.

Opinion polls continued to be conducted over the years, usually at times when the issue was under debate in Parliament. There was never an abolitionist majority and the 1955-57 period may, in retrospect, have been the high-water mark for the abolitionists in public opinion terms, notwithstanding that Parliament and elite opinion moved increasingly in that direction. The passage of the Homicide Act probably assuaged the abolitionist sentiments of many and the apparent rise in the murder rate and of violent crime in the years following (whether a function of abolition or otherwise) may well have driven many late or cautious converts to the abolitionist cause to revert to their former stance. Though the issue had died down somewhat in Britain in the immediate post-

---

[492] MO archives, ibid, Supplement no 2
[493] MO archives, ibid

Homicide Act period a poll was conducted by INRA (International Research Associates Inc.) of New York in December 1958 which examined the state of opinion internationally, and is thus useful in enabling a comparison of British opinion with that in other countries.[494] The question was simply 'Are you for or against capital punishment?'

Table 10: Are you for or against capital punishment?

	For	Against	Don't know
Britain	79	11	10
West Germany	78	12	10
Mexico City	70	24	6
Austria	64	24	12
Australia	58	30	12
Rio de Janeiro and Sao Paulo (Brazil)	56	38	6
Japan	49	28	23
Bogota (Columbia)	41	56	3
Belgium	32	59	9
Buenos Aires (Argentina)	28	68	4
Caracas (Venezuela)	25	73	2
Norway	11	82	7

One might have expected some uniformity of opinion given the transcendent nature of the debate but the results were quite stunning in demonstrating huge divergences in the state of opinion world-wide. Britain was the most pro-death penalty country of those surveyed, just ahead of West Germany and well ahead of most other countries in all continents. The differences almost certainly reflected, at least partly, the fact that many of these countries had abolished capital punishment either *de jure* or *de facto*. The balance of opinion in Norway for example, which had dispensed with capital punishment many decades before, was almost exactly the obverse of that in Britain! Nonetheless, abolition does not necessarily cause public opinion to follow suit, as was to be emphatically demonstrated in Britain a few years later and so explanations for the British fondness for the death penalty must be sought in deeper cultural and social terms. Moreover, West Germany was by then an abolitionist country. This American survey did not apparently include the USA itself, though all polls there had long confirmed that there was a large pro-capital punishment majority roughly comparable with that in Britain.

Moving forward to the 1960s when full abolition was imminent there was

---

[494] INRA poll, published 13th December 1958. Cited in Erskine, Hazel, op cit.

a further flurry of British polls. An SOC poll (of which there seem to have been a welter) of July 1964 found 67% for the retention of hanging and only 21% for complete abolition with 12% don't knows.[495] Another set of SOC polls asked not only whether the death penalty should be abolished altogether but also, if the answer was in the negative or a don't know, whether it was applied in too many cases or in too few. In July 1962 81% either favoured retention or had no opinion as against 19% for abolition, and that majority consisted of 4% who thought there were too many executions, 58% who considered there were too few and 19% don't know.[496] By November 1964 those figures had changed very little with 79% still favouring retention, composed of 4% again who thought there were too many executions, 51% who though too few and 24% don't knows.[497] The following year yet another SOC poll found 77% for retention. In answer to the follow-up question of whether with some murders there are 'extenuating circumstances so that the case does not call for the death penalty' 58% thought that sometimes there were, 13% thought not and 6% didn't know.[498] A 1966 SOC poll found 76% for restoring hanging as against 18% against and 6% don't know.[499] As regards the expected effects of abolition the January 1965 SOC poll asked respondents whether they thought murders would go up, down or be unaffected. 70% thought they would go up, 2% thought down, 22% thought they would stay the same and 6% had no opinion.[500] A June 1966 poll queried respondents as to whether there had been more cases of murder since abolition, less cases [sic] or exactly the same. 56% thought more, 8% thought fewer cases, 18% thought the same number and 18% had no opinion.[501] Finally the January 1965 poll additionally asked pro-hanging respondents whether they favoured hanging chiefly because it was the punishment most fitting the crime or because it was a possible deterrent stopping others from committing such crimes. 25% said it was the former, 42% the latter and 10% didn't know the reason.[502]

In November 1964, on the eve of the Silverman bill's appearance, there was a Marplan poll in the *Times* which showed a large majority for keeping hanging.[503]

---

[495] SOC poll - July 1964, cited in Erskine, ibid.
[496] SOC poll - July 1962, cited in Erskine, ibid.
[497] SOC poll - November 1964, cited in Erskine, ibid.
[498] SOC poll - January 1965, cited in Erskine, ibid
[499] SOC poll - July 1966, cited in Erskine, ibid
[500] SOC poll - January 1965, cited in Erskine, ibid.
[501] SOC poll - June 1966, cited in Erskine, ibid
[502] SOC poll - January 1965, cited in Erskine, ibid
[503]*The Times*, 18th December 1964. The fieldwork was done 5th-8th November 1964. Cited in Block and Hostettler, op cit, p.237. The question was 'Would you like to see the death penalty kept or abolished?'

Table 11: Views on capital punishment

	All voters	Conservative	Labour	Liberal
Keep	65.5	73	62	64
Abolish	21.3	17	26	26
Don't know	13.2	10	12	10

This was fairly typical of polls in the period. A nationwide NOP poll was conducted on 17th and 18th December 1964 from a quota sample of 1,000 people over 21 (by contrast with the Mass Observation surveys which had included 16-21 year olds) for publication in the *Daily Mail*. Unsurprisingly the figures are very similar to the poll above showing little movement in public opinion in the period leading up to the critical Commons vote.[504]

Table 12a: Would you like to see the death penalty kept or abolished?

	8th November 1964	18th December 1964
Kept	66	67
Abolished	21	26
Don't know	13	7

It is slightly unclear as to whether the earlier, November, poll was an NOP poll or not since it is apparently identical to the Marplan poll published in the *Times* and cited in Block and Hostettler. Maybe they had shared resources. Evidently as opinions crystallized in the approach to the Commons vote there was some shift of the 'don't knows' in the proportion of 5 to 1 in favour of the abolitionist camp.

Sixty percent of those interviewed thought that hanging deterred people from committing murder. Notably 21% of those wanting to keep hanging did not hold that opinion on those grounds, but conversely 21% of abolitionists took the view that hanging is a deterrent.[505]

Table 12b: Do you think that fear of the death penalty prevents people from committing capital murder?

	All	Keeping	Abolishing
Yes	60	76	21
No	36	21	74
Don't Know	4	3	5

56% thought that abolition would cause an increase in murder. This view was taken by 76% of those for keeping hanging, whereas 78% of abolitionists thought it would have no effect.

---

[504] NOP Special Supplement 1964, courtesy of Nick Moon of NOP.

[505] NOP report 1964, ibid.

Table 12c: If capital punishment is abolished, do you think this will cause an increase in murder, a decrease in murder, or have no effect?

	All	Keeping	Abolishing
Increase	56	76	7
Decrease	4	3	8
No effect	34	16	78
Don't know	6	5	7

Majorities of both abolitionists and retentionists agreed that innocent people might be hanged, though the majority is much greater in the former category as might have been expected.

Table 12d: Do you think that on occasions innocent people are hanged?

	All	Keeping	Abolishing
Yes	60	53	80
No	28	35	12
Don't know	12	12	8

All of those who answered yes to the previous question were then asked:-

Table 12e: Do you think this is a necessary price to pay for the protection of society?

	All	Keeping	Abolishing
Yes	32	40	14
No	23	9	61
Don't know	5	4	5
Question not asked	40	47	20

It is curious that even 14% of abolitionists thought that the occasional miscarriage was a price worth paying which, as the report comments, indicates either that they were in favour of abolition only in an ideal world or a measure of confusion on their part.[506]

Table 12f: At the moment, murderers can be hanged for some types of murder, but not for others. Do you think that this is just or unjust?

	All	Keeping	Abolishing
Just	33	38	21
Unjust	61	57	75
Don't know	6	5	4

It is somewhat difficult to interpret these results. Presumably the 57% of the keepers thought that hanging should be extended to cover all murders as before the 1957 Act, or at least a wider range than provided for by the Act, but the 21%

---

[506] NOP special Supplement on Hanging 1964, ibid

of the abolitionists might have been split between those who felt that no murderers should hang and those who felt that the current dispensation was satisfactory if hanging were to stay. The NOP report concluded that people tended to think in highly emotional terms since many respondents were illogical or inconsistent in their responses.[507]

Less than two years later, in September 1966, NOP returned to the question - perhaps sparked by the impending 'Sandys' vote in the Commons - and found that there was a considerably larger majority for hanging than just prior to abolition, 82%-15%. In fact the pro-hanging majority was perhaps larger than at any time before or since. This was very likely as a result of some of the high profile murder cases that had occurred in the intervening period and which were very fresh in respondent's minds (especially the Moors murders and the Shepherds Bush killings) and which were attributed, rightly or wrongly, to the effects of abolition, or which at any rate excited a desire for revenge.

Table 13a: Some people think hanging should be brought back as the punishment for murder. Do you agree with this or not?

	All	Con	Lab	Lib
Agree	82	87	81	74
Disagree	15	11	16	23
Don't know	3	2	3	3

Those who answered yes were asked whether they thought that all murderers should hang or only some.

Table 13b: Do you think that all murderers should be hanged or only some?

	All	Con	Lab	Lib
All	40	44	40	30
Some	41	42	40	43
Don't Know	1	1	1	1
Total	82	87	81	74

Those answering 'some' or 'don't know' to that question were then asked:-

Table 13c: Do you think that people who murder policemen should be hanged or not?

	All	Con	Lab	Lib
Should	38	39	37	40
Should not	2	2	3	3
Don't know	2	2	1	1
Total	42	43	41	44

Clearly if only some were to hang this was very much one of the desired categories. The freshness in the memory of the Shepherd's Bush murder of

---

[507] NOP, ibid

three police officers in the previous month by a gang of robbers was almost certainly a potent factor (and probably the main reason for the pollsters asking the question or for framing it in that way).

Moving forward again a few years to the time when the confirmatory votes were due to be held in late 1969 there was another set of polls.

Table 14: Views on capital punishment[508]

	All voters	Con	Labour	Liberal	Other
All types of murder	38	38	37	34	31
Certain types only	47	51	45	45	52
Not at all	12	8	16	19	7
Don't know	3	3	2	2	10

This again was fairly typical of responses found in polls of the period and reflected, most likely, that the rising crime and murder rate (irrespective of its actual causes) was widely attributed to the ending of capital punishment a few years earlier. It was striking that the percentage of those opposing restoration altogether was down to only 12% from the 21.3% favouring abolition of five years previously and the 37% of July 1955! It is debatable to what extent one can make a direct comparison between these polls and others because of the widely different circumstances in which they were conducted. That of 1955 came at a time when hanging was the norm and abolition may have seemed far off, whilst that of 1964 was when abolition seemed (and was) imminent, whilst that of 1969 was when capital punishment had been in abeyance for five years. Nonetheless, the atavism of public opinion was remarkable.

NOP conducted a poll in December 1969, published in the *Daily Mail* asking respondents which law they would most like to pass, and which produced the restoration of hanging as, marginally, the most popular response. It is unclear whether the timing of the poll (immediately prior to the debate on the requisite confirmatory motions) was intentional since it did not deal specifically with hanging, but the coincidence is remarkable. The framing of the question was presumably prompted by the *Daily Mail* (then still fairly pro-hanging) by whom the poll was commissioned, and may have been designed to elicit precisely that response given the known state of public opinion, and may have been thought of as a more effective demonstration of opinion by giving it the appearance of spontaneity.

---

[508] Marplan poll, *The Times*, 24th October 1969. cited in Block and Hostettler, op. cit. p.261. The question was 'Do you think the law should allow hanging for all types of murder, for certain types only, or not at all?'

Table 15: If you could pass a law in Britain now, what would it be?[509]

Suggested law	
Bring back hanging	26
Stricter punishment/bring back the birch	25
Control student demonstrations	3
Abolish hanging	3
Condemn strikes	4
Cut taxation	3
Tighten up welfare benefits	5
Overhaul the legal system	1
Stronger laws on dogs	2
Laws regulating drivers	2
Stop immigration	5
Other	21

It is interesting that the runner-up in the poll is also concerned with penal policy (capital punishment's natural partner corporal punishment) and that all other competitors are way behind the front-runners, even immigration, which was then as now a very hot political potato (coming only a year and a half after Enoch Powell's 'rivers of blood' speech). It is interesting also that 'abolish hanging' gets 3%, presumably from the hard-core abolitionists who wanted the imminent confirmatory votes passed. It is unclear whether the responses were completely spontaneous and unprompted or whether respondents were invited to choose from a selection, but probably the former. That the return of capital punishment gets top billing way ahead of hardy perennials such as restricting the right to strike, cutting taxation and restricting immigration speaks volumes for the intensity of feeling on the issue.

There were numerous attempts to restore capital punishment in the years and decades that followed, and big Parliamentary debates on the topic often prompted a fresh spate of opinion polls. NOP conducted an elaborate one in the run-up to the Commons debates of June 1983 (when there were votes on a whole range of options proposing restoration for a variety of types of murder in the wake of the Conservative landslide in the general election of that year).

---

[509] NOP poll, December 1969. NOP archive, op cit. The fieldwork was done with a representative sample of 1,742 electors, from 10th-15th December 1969, finishing the day before the crucial Parliamentary debates on the confirmation of abolition.

Table 16a: Are you in favour of bringing back capital punishment?[510]

	Total	Conservative	Labour	Liberal/SDP Alliance
For all murders	32	32	35	23
For some types	55	61	43	58
Totally against	13	8	20	18
Don't know	-	-	1	1

Once again, even eighteen years after abolition and fourteen years after the entrenchment of that abolition, there was still an overwhelming majority for restoration, with 87% favouring it either for all or only some types of murder and only 13% against. This was a staggeringly high figure, and probably higher even than those obtained in 1966 in the immediate aftermath of abolition. And once again this held true for both sexes, all age groups, all political allegiances, all regions and all classes though there was a clear trend for older voters to be more pro-hanging than younger, for women to be slightly more pro-hanging than men and for the lower socio-economic classes (C2DE) to be more pro-hanging than the higher (ABC1). In regard to political allegiance once more Conservative voters were more pro-hanging than either Labour or Alliance (Liberal–SDP) voters, though even among Labour and Alliance voters there was an enormous majority for restoration, and in fact there was a higher percentage for restoration for all types of murder among Labour voters than among Conservatives, a finding which is hard to interpret.

Those in favour of reintroduction were then asked whether they thought capital punishment should be brought back for each of three different types of murder.

Table 16b: Which of these do you think it should be possible to punish by death?[511]

	Total	Con	Lab	Alliance
Terrorist murder				
Yes	93	94	91	92
No	31	3	4	3
D/K/depends	36	3	6	5
Child Killer				
Yes	90	88	94	90
No	3	3	3	3

[510] Summary of NOP/9492 poll on Capital Punishment, June 1983 (Omitting data on sex, age, region and socio-economic class). NOP archive, ibid. The fieldwork was done on 16th June 1983

[511] NOP/9492 – Capital Punishment, June 1983, ibid. For full results see Appendix.

D/K/depends	7	9	4	7
Killers of policemen				
Yes	85	87	86	80
No	6	5	5	8
D/K/depends	9	8	9	12

Those in favour of reintroduction were then asked if a murderer should be executed even if proved insane.

Table 16c: Do you still think a murderer should be punished by death if he is proved insane?[512]

	Total	Con	Lab	Alliance
Yes	30	30	37	25
No	50	52	45	55
D/K/depends	20	18	18	20

Intriguingly a higher proportion of Labour supporters than of Conservatives thought that a finding of insanity should not have saved a murderer from the rope. Of course Labour supporters overall were more abolitionist than Conservatives, as we have seen, but this question was asked only of those who supported restoration. It would have been very interesting to know the interaction between political allegiance and socio-economic class (and indeed other variables generally).[513] Certainly the poll findings were that ABC1 (higher class) respondents were rather more likely to accept insanity as entitling a defendant to be spared the rope – 58%/22% as against a split of 46%/34% for the C2DE group.

The poll went on to ask another intriguing question - one rarely asked by pollsters - as to whether people thought crimes other than murder should be punishable by death (asked of all respondents).

Table 16d: Are there any crimes other than murder which you think it should be possible to punish by death?[514]

	Total	Con	Lab	Alliance
Yes	24	26	21	18
No	69	67	72	73
D/K	7	7	7	9

---

[512] NOP/9492 – Capital Punishment, June 1983, ibid. For full results see Appendix

[513] This is a weakness with the reporting of poll results in general (but especially on this question where political allegiance and class almost certainly interact) in that they often examine a wide range of independent variables but rarely show the interactions. This poll in fact does show the breakdown by age and sex combined but not for any other combination of variables. Indeed there is no statistical analysis at all to show whether there are statistically significant effects.

[514] NOP/9492, ibid. For full results see Appendix.

The offences for which some respondents wanted hanging brought back included rape and sexual assaults on adults (7%), sexual assaults on children (9%), drug-pushing (1%), violent mugging (3%), causing death by drunken driving (1%), armed robbery (1%) and treason/betraying state secrets (5%). Overall a surprising 24% of respondents wanted hanging brought back for something other than murder. Of course the desire to bring back the rope for offences other than murder went well beyond anything that was, or was ever likely to be, on the political agenda (though treason still technically carried the death penalty) and indicated that the 'punitiveness' of the general public was much greater than that of 'informed' (i.e. establishment) opinion. In line with other findings there was a clear tendency for Labour and Alliance supporters to be less favourable to this than Conservatives (across all suggested offences).

All respondents were then asked which method of execution should be used, irrespective of whether they favoured capital punishment. There was a plurality for lethal injection (42%) as against hanging (28%) with other methods attracting relatively little support. This was slightly surprising given that hanging was so traditional and deeply embedded in the national psyche, but it probably reflected the fact that lethal injection was widely seen as more humane and efficient.

The poll did not break down the results by pro/anti capital punishment but one might assume that the bulk of those favouring injection were anti-capital punishment, whereas the hangers were mainly pro, though there must have been a lot of pro-capital punishment respondents who favoured injection. There was little effect of political allegiance or any of the usual variables:- sex, age, region or class.[515] A final question asked of all respondents was whether there should be a member of the public present at an execution to see that it was carried out properly which showed that a majority did (58%-35%).[516] As with the previous question the results were not broken down by pro/anti capital punishment. Labour and Alliance supporters were slightly more in favour of this than Conservatives. There was little effect of other variables.

The next Parliamentary attempt to re-introduce hanging (after the surprisingly heavy defeat that it suffered in 1983) was in 1987, and this was attended by more opinion polls. NOP carried out a survey concurrent with a debate on the topic at the Conservative Party conference later that year which found once again that there was a large majority for re-introduction (73%-23% with 5% don't knows).[517]

---

[515] NOP/9492, ibid. For full results see Appendix
[516] NOP/9492, ibid. For full results see Appendix
[517] NOP poll conducted between 30th September and 2nd October 1987 with a representative sample of 1,083 adults aged 18 and over, reported in the NOP Political Social and Economic Review No 67, October 1987

Table 17a: Capital punishment has been abolished in this country for twenty years now. Do you think capital punishment should be re-introduced, or should the situation be left as it is?

	Total (1083)	18-34 (391)	35-54 (341)	55+ (351)
Reintroduced	73	64	74	81
Left	23	30	23	14
Don't know	5	6	4	4

Approval of its reintroduction was correlated somewhat with age with the oldest group being most in favour, a finding which is slightly at odds with most earlier polls which found little or no effect of age. This may well be because the poll was conducted a long time after abolition - twenty-two years - and a belief in hanging (even among the pro-hanging respondents) was probably strongest among those who remembered it best and who took its existence for granted. Even the oldest members of the youngest age-group (18-34) would have been only eleven when the last hangings were carried out and would not have regarded hanging as the norm. This, however, does not fully explain the difference between the middle and oldest age groups which is nearly as great, although of course the same observations may be made in regard to the youngest members of the middle group as to the oldest members of the youngest group.

Similarly there was a marked effect of social class, again contrary to the contours of previous poll findings which had found no significant effect of class.

Table 17b: Question as before[518]

	Total (1083)	AB (182)	C1 (260)	C2 (332)	DE (308)
Reintroduced	73	64	67	76	80
Left	23	31	28	20	16
Don't know	5	5	5	4	5

As with age social class as a variable seemed to have acquired a predictive capacity which it lacked before with a very marked trend from the top group to the bottom. This is harder to account for since the 'lapse of time' argument doesn't afford a ready-made explanation.

This poll, as for the previous one mentioned, then asked all respondents whether they thought that judges should be able to pass a death sentence for a variety of types of murder and/or for certain other offences. Predictably enough this found very large majorities favouring reintroduction for terrorist murder (80%), the murder of policemen (75%) and the murder of children (83%) but only a minority favouring reintroduction for all murder (42%), for rape (34%), but a surprising, though very small, majority for major drug dealing (52%).

[518] NOP poll, Sept/Oct 1987, ibid.

Among those supporting reintroduction 97% favoured hanging for child murder as a judicial option.[519] This view was strongest in the oldest age group and the lower social classes, consistent with the other findings of this poll. The report comments that it is interesting that even for those favouring re-introduction the figures for 'all murders' is only 54%, but though the wording implied that the death sentence should be available to sentencing judges as an option it may have been misinterpreted as implying mandatoriness, hence the low figure. Similarly they comment on the fact that a larger majority favoured capital punishment for drug dealers than for murderers in general, but here the reverse strictures apply in that the exact wording suggested giving courts the option of the death sentence. It may be that more people favoured giving courts the option in the case of drug dealers than for murderers in general, but that fewer would have actually wanted to see drug dealers hang than murderers in general.

Finally all respondents were asked if they thought there ought to be a referendum on the question of reintroduction to which, again unsurprisingly, a very large majority answered in the affirmative. Probably the recent refusal of Parliament to vote for re-introduction, along with all of its previous refusals, prompted both the question and the answer. Referenda had acquired a higher saliency in the light of the government referendum on British membership of the EEC in 1975.

Table 17c: Do you think the government should hold a referendum, so the public can say what they think about capital punishment, or should Parliament decide whether or not to bring back hanging without a referendum?[520]

	Total (1083)	Reintroduce (788)	Leave (245)
Pro-Referendum	85	91	65
Anti-referendum	14	8	33
Don't know	1	1	2

The huge majority for a referendum no doubt reflected a degree of public frustration at the failure of Parliament to reflect the overwhelming view of the electorate on the issue, with numerous attempts to achieve reintroduction thwarted, rather than devotion to the principle of referenda as a tool of government. It is nonetheless interesting that while the majority for a referendum is massive among pro-capital punishment respondents it is very large even for anti-capital punishment respondents.

---

[519] The wording of the question implied that hanging should be an option for the sentencing judge but not mandatory, though of course some respondents may have misinterpreted the question as implying the latter.
[520] NOP survey, Sept/Oct 1987, ibid

Yet another poll was conducted by NOP, this time for the *Sun* newspaper (rather than the *Daily Mail*, its usual client) in 1990. Once again there was a huge majority for reintroduction.

Table 18: Do you personally think that capital punishment should be brought back for all murders, or brought back for some murders, or should capital punishment not be used at all?[521]

	Total	18-34	35-54	55+	AB	C1	C2	DE
All	32	25	32	39	17	25	37	40
Some	49	53	46	47	51	51	50	44
Not	18	21	21	13	31	22	13	14
D/K	1	1	1	2	1	1	1	2

Overall the majority for reintroduction for some or all murders was again very large (81%-18%). As with the NOP survey of three years previously, but unlike those of an earlier vintage, there was a marked trend for the older age groups to be more strongly in favour of reintroduction and for the lower social classes to be more strongly in favour. As before, one can account for the age effect more easily than for the class effect. Those who favoured reintroduction for some but not all murders were asked for which category of murder they favoured it. As usual the murder of children came out top (94%), followed by terrorist murder (85%), rape and murder (84%) and then the murder of policemen (75%).[522]

Those who favoured reintroduction for some or all murders were asked if they were still in favour even if there was a danger of hanging someone who was innocent. This found that 60% as against 18% were still in favour but with the rather high figure of 23% not sure, a slightly odd result given that the possibility of hanging the innocent is implicit in supporting capital punishment and not usually something that presents too much of an obstacle to justifying it in the eyes of most of its supporters. There was also a striking sex difference here with men splitting 69%-16% with 15% unsure but females dividing 51%-19% with the very high figure of 30% unsure. Why females should be disproportionately concerned with this feature of the debate is unclear.[523]

As before, the most favoured method of execution was lethal injection (45%), followed by hanging (24%), the electric chair (13%), firing squad (4%), gas chamber (3%) and 2% for some other method.[524] Intriguingly, whilst there was a large overall plurality for lethal injection there was actually a small plurality for hanging among those who favoured reintroduction for all murders (38%-32%). For those who opposed reintroduction hanging came a very poor second to injection (46%-8%). No doubt the supposedly benign nature of

---

[521] NOP survey, 23rd May 1990 conducted with 1,148 adults across the country. Reported in the NOP Political, Social and Economic Review, no 81, May 1990.
[522] NOP survey, May 1990, ibid
[523] NOP survey, May 1990, ibid
[524] NOP survey, May 1990, ibid

injection recommended itself to the abolitionist but the favouring of hanging by the restorationist may be accounted for by its appeal to tradition.

Finally, respondents were asked whether, if capital punishment were brought back, the courts alone should decide whether it should be imposed on a particular defendant or whether the Prime Minister or the Home Secretary should have to approve.[525] A smallish majority (53%-42%) favoured the latter option, though abolitionists favoured it by a big majority (65%-24%) and those who favoured hanging for all murders were for the courts alone deciding (57%-40%). Presumably the anti-capital punishment respondent felt that the requirement for the approval of the PM or the Home Secretary would either make it less likely to occur or that it would be more likely to ensure that the innocent did not hang. For the out and out hanger, however, the intervention of the politician would not recommend itself for more or less the same reasons in that it would make it less likely that a given defendant would hang.

Taking the whole history of opinion polling on the topic into account one may ask how accurate all these findings were as a measure of public opinion in Britain? Nearly all of the polls were carried out by professional polling organizations, and though the newspapers that commissioned them undoubtedly had their political agendas the organizations themselves were strictly impartial in their conduct and reporting of results. The sampling techniques of the polling organizations were fairly sophisticated and there is no known reason to fault them. Of course the only ideal way of measuring opinion is by taking a completely random sample of the population but randomness is almost impossible to achieve in practice and representative sampling is in effect far more accurate.[526] Nor is there any reason to suppose there were any serious flaws in their method of conducting interviews or interpreting responses or analysing the results. Thus one can reasonably assume that they were an accurate reflection of public opinion.

If so public opinion on capital punishment was curiously volatile, with poll results veering from overwhelming majorities for the retention of hanging (as in most of the early 1948 polls) to fairly slender majorities for retention in the mid-fifties back again to quite large majorities in the polls of the sixties.

---

[525] NOP survey, May 1990, ibid. It is unclear whether 'the courts' was meant to imply the judge alone or the jury alone or both in conjunction. It is also uncertain whether the approval of the PM or Home Secretary meant one or the other or both.

[526] The most famous example of an inadvertently non-random 'random' sample occurred in the American presidential elections of 1936. *The Literary Digest* (a journal that specialized in mass polling based on postal ballot returns) predicted a victory for the Republican Alfred Landon over the incumbent Democrat Franklin Roosevelt on the basis of a huge sample derived from telephone directories and car registration lists - failing to allow for the fact that possession of a telephone or a car was then highly correlated with income and wealth, themselves major predictors of voting intention, and thus seriously skewing the result. Such errors of method were soon eliminated and superseded by the Gallup method that used quota samples, but it illustrates the point. See Teer and Spence, op cit., pp.12-15

This may well have reflected the tendency of public opinion on the question to be strongly influenced by the emotional impact of contemporary cases, with a particularly brutal or horrific murder, or the murder of a police officer, causing a rise in the demand for the retention (or restoration) of the rope and, conversely, a particularly controversial hanging where a miscarriage was suspected or a reprieve felt strongly indicated (as with Bentley or Ellis) leading to a swelling of the ranks of the abolitionists. Thus short-term factors may have played an unduly significant role in the formation of public opinion. Equally, however, this was an issue where most people had strong opinions and there were very few 'don't knows' as evinced by all the polls. How well does that notion sit with the apparent volatility of opinion?

The most likely explanation is that the distribution of opinion was 'camel-like', i.e. bi-polar, with a majority being strongly retentionist, a fairly small but unyielding minority being abolitionist and a relatively small number of people somewhere in the middle or undecided. As the abolitionists gained ground in the fifties due to the success of the fledgling NCACP, the crop of acutely controversial cases and a liberalizing climate so those in the middle moved towards the abolitionist side, reaching a peak in the 1955-57 period between the execution of Ellis and the passage of the Homicide Act (a period of moratorium). With the passage of the Act (and the consequent halving of the numbers hanged), the steady rise in the murder rate and of violent crime generally and the widespread belief that there was a causal link between the two so the floating vote moved back towards the retentionist side in the sixties. This reached a high point in the late sixties and thereafter, which paralleled the configuration of opinion in the late forties. Thus in the twenty year period of the abolition campaign's serious bid for success, between 1948 and 1969, as the Parliamentary tide turned more or less consistently in favour of the abolitionists and establishment opinion likewise so public opinion followed its own entirely independent and divergent course coming full circle. It is very striking also that the majority for re-introduction seemed if anything to increase in the seventies and early eighties, arguably reaching a zenith in or about 1983, some eighteen years after its abolition, possibly subsiding somewhat thereafter as capital punishment started to become a distant memory.

The shifting sands of public opinion were affected also by the wording of the question asked and the availability to them of middle options, such as the suggestion of creating categories or degrees of murder and of suspending, but not abolishing hanging, for an experimental period; thereby providing a refuge for the undecided and for the confirmed retentionist or abolitionist who may have been reluctant to admit as much to the pollster. One might also note the fact that the earlier polls - those of the late forties, fifties and sixties - showed that most demographic variables had no effect on opinion, but the later polls of the eighties and after showed an effect of both age and class. The former is easier to account for in that as hanging receded into the past so an ever larger proportion of the population had no memory of it and would have been socialized into a Britain in which it did not exist. This in turn may have made it harder for them to envision or support its re-introduction. The increased significance of class is harder to explain.

What was the significance of the polls and what use was made of them by the campaigners and politicians? It almost goes without saying that the state of public opinion on capital punishment was a tool to be utilized or discarded according to need by the partisans on both sides. The retentionists were keen to play up the widespread popular attachment to hanging, especially when the polls were going strongly their way. This was certainly so in the 1948 debate when more than one MP and peer commented on the BIPO and other polls that had appeared, and it was true again in the sixties when there was a strong attempt by Sandys and others to mobilize public opinion through petitions and the like. The abolitionists were anxious to stress the pre-eminence of Parliament and to appeal to the 'Burkean' independence of MPs, though of course acknowledging that cognizance should be taken of the trend of public opinion on the occasions when it might have seemed to be moving their way, as in the mid fifties.

In the final analysis it is unlikely that public opinion counted for all that much on the issue! The capital punishment debate, more than any other in recent times, exemplified the mechanics of an indirect, Parliamentary democracy. On a free vote, when members are freed from the constraints of party diktat, they are generally minded to follow their own conscience and judgment rather than the promptings, however vociferous, of the multitude. In a sense, on capital punishment, Parliament defeated the people.

Other expressions of public opinion

Of course public opinion could and did express itself in numerous ways other than through the agency of official polls, such as by means of letters to the newspapers, whether national or local, or more forcefully through meetings, marches and demonstrations. It is fair to say that the balance of opinion in the letters pages tended to be on the side of retention, whereas those engaged in more active propaganda were doing so predominantly in the abolitionist cause. The private constituency poll conducted by Prescott in 1948 has already been mentioned. Another straw in the wind was an Oxford Union debate of 1955 that showed a majority of 378-161 for abolition compared with a majority of only forty in a similar debate two years earlier.[527] All of these things were of course merely indicators of the strength of opinion in certain quarters, rather than precise measures of the balance of opinion overall, and as such do not tell us

---

[527] Reported in *The Spectator*, 195, 11th November 1955, p.618. Cited in Christoph, p.116.

much.

But at least one other relatively empirical source exists in the form of a BBC audience research survey. Such surveys were conducted on a regular basis by the BBC to measure the impact and popularity of various programmes and types of programming. As it happens one such survey was conducted on the documentary 'The Death Penalty' transmitted in October 1961 (see the chapter on television for details of the programme) and provides interesting information on the state of opinion at a moment in time when no other polls were being conducted, being in-between periods when the matter was subject to Parliamentary debate.[528] It supplements the data supplied by the normal opinion polls in an intriguing way because it measured the balance of opinion both before and after a specific event (namely the watching of the documentary) - something that went beyond the scope of the official opinion polls which at most could only ask respondents what things had influenced their opinion *ex post facto*.

This survey was naturally concerned primarily with the impact of the programme rather than with viewers' opinions on capital punishment, but to assess the effect of the programme it was necessary for the researchers to ascertain respondent's views on the matter both before and after the programme had been transmitted. The report presented the results of a study of the effects of the programme on:- (1) viewers' interest in further programmes of that kind (2) their knowledge of some of the facts about the murder rate and (3) their attitudes towards murder and capital punishment. The BBC used a national sample of 6,000 viewers selected from amongst those already interviewed in the above Survey, and sent them a questionnaire before the broadcast and after it. Respondents were not told when sent the first that a second would follow and the second was sent in such a way as to conceal that the main purpose was to examine differences between responses on the two occasions. A total of 1,522 people saw the programme and responded to both questionnaires and the survey is based on these responses.

Firstly, viewers were asked about their interest in television programmes about crime and punishment in general. The survey suggested that there was no significant change as a result of watching the broadcast.

---

[528] BBC Written Archives, file R9/10/9: Audience Research: Special Reports: TV Chronological 1962. 'The Death Penalty'. The Effect of this Broadcast upon Viewers' Knowledge of and Attitudes towards Murder and Capital Punishment, VR/62/74 - February 1962.

THE POLITICS OF THE ROPE

Table 19a: Viewers' Interest in Television Programmes about Crime and Punishment

	Before programme (%)	After programme (%)
Very interested	18	15
Interested	62 (80)	66 (81)
Not interested	12	9
Not at all	2 (14)	1 (10)
No reply	6	9
Total	100	100

Source: BBC Written Archives: Audience Research Survey. Figures in brackets are the percentages of those who gave the same answer before and after.

A second question dealt with the level of knowledge of facts which had been presented in the programme to do with the murder rate over the previous century. Twice as many people got the correct answer after watching than before, though this was still only a small percentage of the total.

Table 19b: Question: Do you happen to know if the number of murders per head of the population has increased or not in Britain in the last hundred years?

Answers:	Before (%)	After (%)
I have no idea at all	10	8
I think it has increased	69	59
I think it has remained the same*	13	26
I think it has decreased	7	6
No reply	1	1
Total	100	100

(*correct answer) Source: BBC Written Archives: Audience Research Survey

There was a similar increase in the number of correct responses from both abolitionists and retentionists, but both before and after the former group was twice as well informed as the latter (a later question had enabled respondents to be assigned to one or other category).

A third question dealt with another issue of fact that had been presented.

Table 19c: Question: Quite a number of countries have abolished capital punishment. Do you know what effect this has had on the murder rate?

Answers	Before (%)	After (%)
I have no idea	28	16
Increased	22	19
I don't think much difference*	41	60
Decreased	8	4
No reply	1	1
Total	100	100

THE POLITICS OF THE ROPE

(*correct answer) Source: BBC Written Archives: Audience Research Survey

There were no significant differences in the answers given by men and women, nor by different age groups. However, both before and after, the more abolitionist the outlook of the respondent the better informed he was. The percentage of 'strong retentionists' giving the correct answer rose from 25% to 38% while the percentage of abolitionists doing likewise rose from 57% to 81%.

Another question dealt with the changes in the law as a result of the Homicide Act (i.e. the restriction of the death penalty that had occurred four to five years previously). Viewers were told to examine eight kinds of murder and to say which might now be punished by death.

Table 19d: Question: Which of the following may be punished by death?

	Before (%)	After (%)
Murder of police officers*	88	90 (96)
Murder with theft*	66	76 (90)
Murder while resisting arrest*	61	76 (90)
Premeditated(e.g. poisoning)	71	55 (70)
Murder with extreme cruelty	54	47 (77)
Murder of children	50	43 (78)
Murder of members of the government	38	40 (76)
Murder with rape	46	27 (56)

*capital murder, i.e. punishable by death. Figures in brackets are the percentages giving the same answer before.
Source: BBC Written Archives: Audience Research Survey

More correct than incorrect answers were given after the broadcast than before, with the percentages of those identifying capital murders as such rising and the percentages of those misidentifying non-capital murders as capital falling – but this was no more marked in any sub-group of respondent's than another. But once again abolitionists were better informed than retentionists. There was some evidence of wishful thinking (on both sides) in that 'retentionists', and especially 'strong retentionists', were much more likely than 'abolitionists' to say that all eight kinds of murder listed were capital; whereas the 'abolitionists', both before and after, were much more likely to say that none was capital.

The next question dealt with attitudes toward murder and capital punishment. Viewers were asked for their reactions to six statements:-

A: Murder is a dreadful thing and all murderers should be hanged.
B: The whole question of capital punishment should be carefully examined. As the law stands at present it is very unfair, some murderers being reprieved and others

hanged.
C: All the evidence points to an immediate abolition of capital punishment.
D: For certain sorts of murder there is no alternative to capital punishment.
E: There is some evidence in favour of abolishing capital punishment but this does not really prove that things would not be much worse without it.
F: Nowadays when hanging is scientific and humane no-one can object to this form of capital punishment for convicted murderers.

Table 19e: Responses to six statements about murder and capital punishment

Statement	A	A	B	B	C	C	D	D	E	E	F	F
Before or after	B	A	B	A	B	A	B	A	B	A	B	A
Agree strongly	29	29	49	45	6	6	36	34	11	12	23	23
Agree	118 (47)	118 (47)	339 (88)	444 (89)	99 (15)	110 (16)	337 (73)	441 (75)	339 (50)	444 (56)	443 (66)	443 (66)
Not sure	8	9	2	2	112	112	7	7	115	113	8	8
Disagree	330	229	6	5	336	442	111	110	221	119	114	113
Disagree strongly	113 (43)	113 (42)	3 (9)	2 (7)	336 (72)	228 (70)	77 (18)	66 (16)	111 (32)	88 (27)	110 (24)	111 (24)
No reply	2	2	1	2	1	2	2	2	3	4	2	2
Answers same	73		666		665		553		553		668	

B = before watching; A = after watching
Source: BBC Written Archives: Audience Research Survey. Figures in brackets are the combined percentages for 'agree strongly' and 'agree' and for 'disagree strongly' and 'disagree'.

To summarize these figures roughly three-quarters were for retention for 'certain sorts of murder' (statement D) and nearly as many were against abolition (statement C); less than half were for the imposition of capital punishment in all cases (statement A); two-thirds thought hanging should not be objected to as a method; and more than half did not consider the evidence against capital punishment as a deterrent a convincing answer to those who said abolition would not be followed by an increase in murders (statement E) - though the awkward wording of the statement with two double negatives made it hard to grasp and requires one to treat the answers with caution. But most unanimity was secured by the proposition that the law was unsatisfactory and needed re-examination (statement B).

The distribution of answers given before viewing and after were more or less the same - which may have indicated that the programme had had little effect or that substantial numbers had changed their view but that these had cancelled out. Opinion was most stable in regard to statement A which was the most categorical and absolute. The least stable responses were elicited by statements D and E with nearly half replying differently, though as before the obscurity of the wording of statement E may have been partially responsible for that effect. There was no apparent effect of age or sex or of whether people followed news of crime.

The data were used to create five categories of respondent based upon the replies to four of the statements (A, C, D and F). This yielded three degrees of 'retentionist', one 'undecided' group and one 'abolitionist', and these were then used in the analysis of the responses to the preceding questions. The five groups were:-

Very strong retentionist (<u>R</u>) – strong agreement with A, D and F and strong disagreement with C

Strong retentionist (R) – agreement (not necessarily strong) with A, D and F plus disagreement with C

Retentionist (r) – As for strong retentionist except for one abolitionist answer

Undecided (U) – frequent use of 'not sure' answer. Definite answers both retentionist and abolitionist.

Abolitionist (A) - all definite answers favouring abolition.

Viewers were assigned on the basis of their answers to the first questionnaire and then re-assigned according to their answers to the second.

Table 19f: Responses to question 5

	Before (%)	After (%)
R	8	9
R	35	29
r	17 (60)	24 (62)
U	24	23
A	16	15
Total	100	100

Source: BBC Written Archive: Audience Research Survey. Figures in brackets are percentages assigned to the same category after/before.

The only significant change was a diminution in the strong retentionist category (R) to the benefit of the retentionist (r), i.e. while the retentionist/abolitionist dichotomy was not significantly altered, the strength with which the retentionists adhered to their view was reduced.

Table 19g: Post-broadcast regrouping of viewers in each category

category after	category before (R)	category before (R)	category before (r)	category before (U)	category before (A)
(R)	68	8	1	2	0
(R)	26	64	12	9	0
(r)	5	18	65	28	2
(U)	0	9	20	54	20
(A)	1	1	2	7	78
Total	100	100	100	100	100

Source: BBC Written Archive: Audience Research Survey

Of course those in the outer categories could only move towards each other, if they were to move at all. Those in the middle categories showed a movement from 'very strong retentionism' to merely 'strong retentionism' and 'abolitionism' to 'undecidedness'. Thus, to quote the conclusion of the survey, most viewers' attitudes toward capital punishment remained the same but when attitudes changed they tended to be of degree rather than of kind.

Conclusion

Summarizing all of this it confirms the findings of the opinion polls to the effect that there was a large majority against total abolition. There was a considerably larger majority in fact than those obtained in the polls taken in the 1955-6 era and later in the 1964-5 period. If anything the BBC research was somewhat more subtle and sophisticated than that of the pollsters in that it attempted to gauge opinion by asking for responses to a series of statements exploring the issue from slightly different angles and thus it was able to calibrate opinion in a rather more nuanced way than hitherto. Moreover, unlike any other poll it was able to examine opinion before and after respondents had been exposed to an event, namely a broadcast containing a battery of information and propaganda (balanced but conflicting) that might have been assumed to wring some change. Actually very little change seems to have occurred and where it did this was to moderate opinion but not to convert it. Certainly exposure to information improved the level of knowledge of the viewer but still left many abysmally ignorant of basic facts. It may also have undermined to some extent the somewhat elitist assumption of many abolitionists that support for hanging was based on ignorance and that increased knowledge would automatically favour their cause. The categorization of opinion (admittedly very arbitrary) showed a trend towards a moderating of opinion from the 'before' to 'after', but this was on both sides. Not only did the more extreme retentionists become less extreme, but the abolitionists too moved slightly towards the middle, becoming more 'undecided'. Ultimately all of this is intriguing but inconclusive. One must reiterate the caveat that public opinion was a major consideration but not in the final analysis a decisive one.

CHAPTER 9

EVENTS IN THE COURTROOM:
MISCARRIAGES AND *CAUSES CELEBRE*

This chapter examines the various murder cases and possible miscarriages that occurred during the currency of the campaign and examines the effect that they may have had on public opinion and Parliament, and how they shaped the debate.

The abolition campaign had been given added impetus in the 1950s by the series of apparent miscarriages and *causes celebre* that had emerged, rather providentially from the viewpoint of the abolitionists. The Evans/Christie travesty vividly illustrated the possibilities of error or misfeasance in the investigative and judicial process as, arguably, did that of the much less well known case of Rowland.[529] Walter Graham Rowland was hanged in February 1947 for the murder of a prostitute in Manchester by battering her to death with a hammer, on the basis of forensic evidence that linked him to the crime scene, although he had a good alibi. After his conviction for murder another man, David John Ware, confessed to it, but a Home Office enquiry dismissed the Ware confession as a fabrication and Rowland was not reprieved. In 1951 Ware was convicted of the attempted murder of a woman by battering her with a hammer, was found guilty but insane and institutionalized, committing suicide in his cell in 1954. Rowland had previously been convicted of the murder of his child in 1934, sentenced to hang but reprieved and released after serving several years imprisonment.[530]

And the Craig/Bentley and Ruth Ellis cases ruthlessly pinpointed the inanities and shortcomings of the law as it then stood which failed to allow for a defence of diminished responsibility (under which the emotionally unstable Ellis could surely have sought refuge) and permitted a conviction via the preposterously contorted legal doctrines of constructive malice and common purpose (as per Bentley). The latter two cases also highlighted the capriciousness with which successive Home Secretaries exercised the power of reprieve. The fate of Derek Bentley is especially noteworthy in this respect, given that his youth and mental sub-normality, the jury's recommendation of mercy, the highly technical nature of his guilt, the dubiousness of the evidence against him, the manifestly biased conduct of the trial judge (Lord Chief Justice Goddard), and not least the public outcry against his impending execution

---

[529] See Paget, R and S Silverman, *Hanged and Innocent?* (London: Gollancz, 1953) op cit; and Cecil, Henry, *The Trial of Walter Rowland* (Newton Abbot: David and Charles, 1975).

[530] Silverman concluded that Rowland was innocent of the later murder, and that the enquiry was prejudiced in favour of sustaining the original conviction at all costs.

The Home Secretaries

1a. Sir Samuel Hoare (Viscount Templewood): An abolitionist after being Home Secretary but not during.
1b. James Chuter Ede: An abolitionist before and after being Home Secretary but not during. Refused a reprieve
for Timothy Evans.
1c. David Maxwell Fyfe (Lord Kilmuir): Never an abolitionist. Refused a reprieve for Derek Bentley.
1d. Gwilym Lloyd George: An abolitionist before being Home Secretary but not during. Refused a reprieve for Ruth Ellis.

The Home Secretaries (cont.)

1e. R A Butler: Never openly an abolitionist. Refused to re-open the Timothy Evans case.
1f. Henry Brooke: An abolitionist after being Home Secretary but not during.
1g. Frank Soskice: A cautious abolitionist before, during and after being Home Secretary. Abolition Act passed
under his stewardship of the Home Office. Refused to grant a posthumous pardon to Timothy Evans.
1h. Roy Jenkins: A strong abolitionist but not Home Secretary at the relevant times. Granted a posthumous pardon to Timothy Evans.
1i. James Callaghan: A strong abolitionist before, during and after being Home Secretary. Oversaw the confirmation of abolition in 1969.

The Judges and the Lawyers

2a. Lord Goddard: Lord Chief Justice 1946-1958. Vehemently pro-hanging. Opponent of most measures of legal reform. Trial judge of Craig and Bentley.
2b. Lord Parker: Lord Chief Justice 1958-1971. Reluctant convert to abolition.
2c. Christmas Humphreys, QC: Prosecuted in all three of the great *causes celebre* of the 1950s: Timothy Evans; Craig/Bentley; and Ruth Ellis.
2d. Sir Reginald Manningham-Buller (Viscount Dilhorne), QC: Attorney-General and Lord Chancellor; chief architect of the Homicide Act, 1957.

The Hangmen

3a. Thomas Pierrepoint: Brother of Henry and uncle of Albert.
3b. Henry Pierrepoint: Brother of Thomas and father of Albert.
3c. Albert Pierrepoint: Chief hangman for many years. Hanged
Timothy Evans, Derek Bentley and Ruth Ellis, *inter alia*, and a total
perhaps in excess of 600. Much later a convert to abolition!
3d. Harry Allen: The last hangman. Assisted Pierrepoint and later
hanged Hanratty and the last two to hang in 1964.

The Gallows

3e. The Gallows: The gallows at Rutland County Museum. One of
the last surviving of the "New Drop" design, used in the nineteenth
century. After 1868 all executions were within prison walls.

The Churchmen

4a. Archbishop William Temple: Abolitionist
4b. Archbishop Geoffrey Fisher: Moderate retentionist.
4c. Bishop George Bell: Abolitionist, but never got the top job.
4d. Archbishop Ramsey: Abolitionist. Urged to pilot the Abolition
Bill through the Lords.
4e. Bishop Stockwood: Abolitionist

The Journalists and Writers

5a. David Astor: Editor of *The Observer* and campaigner for
Timothy Evans.
5b. Ian Gilmour: Editor of *The Spectator* and campaigner for
Timothy Evans.
5c. Ludovic Kennedy: Campaigner for Timothy Evans and author of
Ten Rillington Place.
5d. Nigel Nicolson, MP: Conservative MP and journalist. Forced
out of his seat due to his stance on abolition and Suez.
5e. CH Rolph: Former policeman and journalist.
5f. Sir Ernest Gowers: Civil servant and author. Chaired Royal
Commission and subsequently wrote book advocating abolition.

The Campaigners

6a Sydney Silverman, MP: Left-wing Labour backbencher and
leading Parliamentary campaigner for abolition.

6b. Victor Gollancz: Co-founder of the NCACP and all-round campaigner.

6c. Arthur Koestler: Polymath and journalist. Co-founder of the NCACP

6d. Canon Collins: Radical Anglican churchman. Co-founder of the NCACP and of CND.

6e.Gerald Gardiner: lawyer and subsequently Lord Chancellor in the Wilson government who oversaw abolition. Co-founder of the NCACP.

The Campaigners (cont.)

6f. Peggy Duff: All-round left-wing campaigner and secretary to the NCACP.

6g. Earl of Harewood. Cousin of the HM the Queen and chairman of the Committee of Honour of the NCACP.

6h. Violet van der Elst. Lone campaigner against hanging and all round eccentric.

6i. Sir Cyril Osborne, MP: Right-wing conservative backbencher and leading Parliamentary opponent of abolition.

6h.Sir Duncan Sandys, MP: Conservative Cabinet minister and subsequently the leading Parliamentary campaigner for the restoration of hanging.

The Miscarriages?

7a Walter Rowland: Convicted of murder twice! Innocent twice?

7b.Timothy Evans: Almost certainly innocent.

7c. John Christie: Almost certainly guilty of the murder for which Evans hanged.

7d. Derek Bentley: Guilty, but only technically?

7e. Ruth Ellis: Guilty, but deranged?

7f. James Hanratty: Guilty after all?

1a. Sir Samuel Hoare (Viscount Templewood)

1b. James Chuter Ede

1c. David Maxwell Fyfe (Lord Kilmuir)

1d. Gwilym Lloyd George

1e. R A Butler

1f. Henry Brooke

1g. Frank Soskice

1h. Roy Jenkins

1i. James Callaghan

. Lord Goddard

2b. Lord Parker

. Christmas Humphreys, QC

2d. Sir Reginald Manningham-Buller
(Viscount Dilhorne), QC

3a. Thomas Pierrepoint

3b. Henry Pierrepoint

3c. Albert Pierrepoint

3d. Harry Allen

3e. The Gallows

4a. Archbishop William Temple

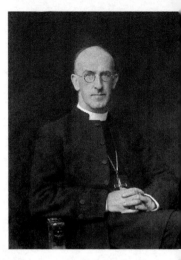

4b. Archbishop Geoffrey Fi[

4c. Bishop George Bell

4d. Archbishop Ramsey

4e. Bishop Stockwood

a. David Astor

5b. Ian Gilmour

c. Ludovic Kennedy

5d. Nigel Nicolson, MP

. CH Rolph

5f. Sir Ernest Gowers

6a Sydney Silverman, MP

6b. Victor Gollancz

6c. Arthur Koestler

6d. Canon Collins

6e.Gerald Gardiner

. Peggy Duff

6g. Earl of Harewood

6h. Violet van der Elst

Sir Cyril Osborne, MP

6h.Sir Duncan Sandys, MP

7a Walter Rowland

7b.Timothy Evans

7c. John Christie

7d. Derek Bentley

7e. Ruth Ellis

7f. James Hanratty

might, in practice, have led under ordinary circumstances, to a reprieve.

That neither David Maxwell Fyfe nor Gwilym Lloyd George saw fit in the cases of Bentley and Ellis, respectively, to grant reprieves may have cast serious doubt in the public mind as to the satisfactoriness of the Crown's prerogative of mercy as a means of determining who should hang and who shouldn't. Certainly the opinion poll evidence (see the relevant chapter) strongly indicated that the occurrence of specific miscarriages weighed on some respondents as a factor. It is apparent that Maxwell Fyfe refused a reprieve to Bentley on the grounds that it would have antagonized the police, the judiciary and the Conservative Party, and that it was part of a campaign to counter what was seen as the sharp rise of violence and gangsterism.[531] But if Bentley was executed *pour encourager les autres,* as Yallop would have it, then it was a spectacular own goal by the political and judicial establishment, because no case so enraged the abolitionist movement and none gave them so much ammunition in their attempt to enlist the support of the public for whom the hanging was very widely seen as unjust and capricious.[532]

It is difficult to gauge the precise effect of these events on the balance of public opinion as regards the death penalty issue, but it is very likely that they contributed to the slow but sure trend towards abolitionism, or at least partial abolitionism, and gave succour to the abolitionist campaigners. Certainly opinion polls showed that some respondents cited these cases as a factor that influenced them (though sometimes prompted by the pollsters). The Homicide Act had addressed some of these areas of concern by importing into English law (from Scots law) the partial defence of diminished responsibility, and by abolishing the doctrine of constructive malice. It had also, of course, introduced a distinction between capital and non-capital murder. But the basis of the distinction (grounded as it was chiefly in government fears for public order

---

[531] John Parris says that he, Desmond Donnelly and Barbara Castle had been to see Maxwell Fyfe at his office in the Commons just before the execution, when Maxwell Fyfe admitted on terms of strict confidentiality that he would have had the whole of the judiciary led by Goddard at his throat; the whole of the Cabinet led by Churchill at his throat; and an insurrection in the police force if he had granted a reprieve. He also rebutted the suggestion (made later by Goddard) that Goddard expected a reprieve, and that on the contrary he had urged the opposite course, both in writing and personally in conversation. Parris, John, *Scapegoat: The Inside Story of the Trial of Derek Bentley* (London: Duckworth, 1991) pp. 136-139. Maxwell Fyfe himself concedes that he was influenced in his decision by the possible effects upon the police 'by whom the murder of a police officer is justly regarded as the most heinous of crimes'. David Maxwell-Fyfe, Earl of Kilmuir, *Political Adventure: The Memoirs of the Earl of Kilmuir* (London: Weidenfeld and Nicolson, 1964) p. 206. Berkeley, op cit. describes the scene at the Carlton Club on the morning of the execution when Maxwell Fyfe entered looking pale and exhausted and was instantly embraced by a shoal of club members who applauded his steadfastness in the face of the reprieval campaign – a display that repelled Berkeley and (he suggests) Maxwell Fyfe too, pp. 126-7

[532] Yallop, David, *To Encourage the Others* (London: W H Allen, 1971; London: Corgi, 1990) passim. Parris, op cit, passim

rather than in any attempt to grade the heinousness of the murder or the moral turpitude of the defendant) had come to be seen as ever more anomalous. It was discredited in many eyes almost as soon as it was promulgated. It contrasted oddly, for example, with the division into first and second degree murder based on the question of premeditation which was prevalent in the USA. The Act was widely perceived as an awkward half-way house and did nothing to still the clamour for complete abolition.

Meanwhile, back at the courthouse, murder cases continued to be tried, but from 1957 forwards, as a result of the Homicide Act, they were now indicted as either 'capital murder' or 'murder' simpliciter. Those convicted of capital murder were still subject to the death penalty, which continued to be carried out, albeit with reduced frequency. There seems to have been a lingering misconception (among pro-hangers and anti-hangers alike) that hangings would not be resumed at all, and that those convicted of capital murder would automatically be reprieved. The Home Office was anxious to dispel any such misunderstanding and took the step of announcing that this was very definitely not so. The effect of partial abolition was to cut the number of capital convictions and consequently the number of executions in half, from roughly a dozen a year to a half dozen. Of course Home Secretaries could still exercise the prerogative of mercy, and the reprieval rate stayed about the same as before the Act, which was perhaps slightly unexpected given that it was ostensibly only the worst murderers who were now subject to the death penalty, thus implying a reduction in the proportion of reprieves.

Hangings followed at regular intervals thereafter, all of them fought over frenetically by the abolitionists, some more controversial than others. Most were legally and factually straightforward, though a few, such as Marwood and Podola, were more contentious and aroused stronger campaigns for a reprieve and provoked very noisy demonstrations outside the prison.

The first murder case to come before the courts after the passage of the Act (which received the Royal Assent and came into effect in March 1957) was that of Ronald Dunbar who was convicted of capital murder in May 1957 and sentenced to hang but then had his conviction for murder reduced to manslaughter on appeal.[533] The second such case was that of John Willson Vickers who was convicted of capital murder a week later and also sentenced to death. He had battered an old woman to death whilst committing a burglary on her grocery shop in Carlisle, and was thus guilty of capital murder under section 5 of the Act, dealing with murder in the course or furtherance of theft.[534] His appeal was dismissed by the Court of Criminal Appeal and the Attorney General, Sir Reginald Manningham-Buller, refused him leave to appeal to the

---

[533] Block and Hostettler, op cit. p.199
[534] Block and Hostettler, op cit. pp. 199-200. Eddleston, John J, op cit. p. 878

House of Lords.[535] The Parliamentary struggle that ensued over the Vickers case is described in detail in chapter six, and so will not be reprised here. Vickers was duly executed in July 1957, the first hanging for capital murder under the new Act, nearly two years after the last hanging under the old law of murder.

The following year, 1958, there was more controversy surrounding a capital murder conviction, this time that of John S Spriggs.[536] Again a Labour backbencher, Denis Howell (Birmingham, All Saints) asked the Attorney-General by private notice question to exercise his fiat to refer the case of Spriggs to the Lords and again he refused. When he refused Howell persisted on the basis that the conviction had been deeply unsatisfactory due to its centring on the question of diminished responsibility, and the supposedly inadequate direction given to the jury by the trial judge, the Lord Chief Justice.[537] Again, as with Vickers, the Attorney-General was adamant that no grave question of law was involved, and that therefore there was no valid reason for referring the matter to the Lords. The fact that this had been the first case centring on diminished responsibility did not in his view make it *ipso facto* a point of law of exceptional public importance, and he did not in any case accept that there had been any form of misdirection by the trial judge. Spriggs was in fact subsequently reprieved by the Home Secretary.

In early 1959 Ronald Henry Marwood was arrested for the murder of a police constable in the course of an affray in Seven Sisters Road in North London in December 1958.[538] A police officer had been stabbed after attempting to arrest someone and Marwood, who was considerably inebriated, had intervened on behalf of the arrested man. Though he initially denied being the perpetrator of the attack on the officer he eventually made a partial confession claiming that he had merely pushed the officer and may have had a knife in his pocket at the time. In due course he was convicted of murder and sentenced to death at the Old Bailey. His appeal was dismissed. 150 MPs, mostly Labour, signed a petition against his hanging but to no avail. The Home Secretary said he saw no grounds for a reprieve and the execution duly took place at Pentonville in the midst of a riot inside the prison and a demonstration from about a thousand people outside. The inadequacies of the Homicide Act were again highlighted by the case, and Canon Collins, Dean of St Pauls delivered an attack on the execution of Marwood from the pulpit, and in the Commons Silverman was again on the attack demanding the complete abolition of capital punishment on the grounds that the operation of the Homicide Act was deeply anomalous, discriminating between capital and non-capital murders

---

[535] Sir Reginald Edward Manningham-Buller, 1st Viscount Dilhorne (1905-1980) Conservative politician, MP for Daventry 1943-50, MP for Northants South 1950-62, Solicitor-General 1951-54, Attorney-General 1954-62, Lord Chancellor 1962-64.
[536] Block and Hostettler, op cit, p.201
[537] HC Deb, vol 580, col 1256-8, 23rd January 1958
[538] Block and Hostettler, op cit, pp.202-205; Eddleston, John J, op cit. p.888

on the basis of criteria which bore no relation to the actual wickedness of the crime or the degree of culpability of the offender. On the other side Sir Cyril Osborne countered the Silverman motion with a wrecking amendment that effectively called for the re-introduction of capital punishment for murder by poisoning and the murder of old people and young children.

The next controversial murder case was that of Guenther Podola, another man sentenced to hang for capital murder, after having allegedly shot dead a police officer who was in pursuit of him for a burglary.[539] Podola claimed to have no memory of the events surrounding the shooting as a result of a blow to the head sustained during his subsequent arrest. In the House Paget intervened to enquire of the Home Secretary the causes of Podola's blow to the head and the reasons for his subsequent hospitalization. Patrick Gordon Walker called for an enquiry, but Butler stonewalled by saying that an enquiry would prejudice the case.[540] Podola was eventually convicted of capital murder, becoming the last man to hang for the murder of a policeman in the execution of his duty. Podola's defence and appeal on the basis that he had no recollection of the incident did not avail him.

Controversial murder cases continued to hit the headlines. In April 1960 'Gypsy' Joe Smith was convicted of the capital murder of a PC Meehan in Woolwich, after the officer had clung onto Smith's car as it sped away, and was then thrown into the road and run over by another vehicle.[541] He appealed on the grounds of misdirection of the jury by the trial judge, in that the test of whether he had intended to cause grievous bodily harm should have been a subjective one, not the 'reasonable' man test that the judge (Donovan) had suggested to the jury. In other words did Smith actually appreciate at the relevant time that his actions were likely to cause grievous bodily harm, not was it objectively likely that that was so. The appeal was allowed and a verdict of manslaughter and a sentence of ten years was substituted. The Director of Public Prosecutions (DPP) then applied for, and was granted, a certificate to appeal to the Lords against the decision of the Appeal Court. The appeal to the Lords was heard by the Lord Chancellor Kilmuir (Sir David Maxwell Fyfe, former Home Secretary), Lord Parker (LCJ), Goddard (former LCJ), and Denning and Tucker. They overturned the Appeal Court's quashing of the original conviction and restored the capital murder conviction (and therefore the death sentence that went with it). The Home Secretary then commuted the sentence.

This case was followed by another deeply contentious one involving the convictions of four men (Norman Harris, Christopher Darby, Francis Forsyth and Terrence Lutt) for a murder (three of them for capital murder) in September 1960, the convictions resting again on the doctrine of constructive malice.[542]

---

[539] Eddleston, John J, op cit., p. 892
[540] HC Deb, vol 609, col 873-882, 20th July 1959
[541] Block and Hostettler, op cit. p. 207-8
[542] Block and Hostettler, op cit, pp.209-211; Eddleston, John J, op cit. p.895

Here a gang of four young men had set upon the victim battering him to death as part of a robbery. This case raised again the knotty question of the interpretation of the Act in respect of constructive malice, in that three of the four men were convicted of capital murder on the basis that they were engaged in a joint criminal enterprise, and therefore equally guilty irrespective of who had actually struck the fatal blows. The case provoked another spate of debate and newspaper correspondence, with a clutch of public figures writing to the *Times* to plead for clemency in the case of one of the defendants (Forsyth) who was only eighteen, a petition signed by 2,000 handed to the Home Office calling for the reprieve of both the men sentenced to death (the third was under eighteen and thus immune), and a telegram to the Queen from the mother of one of the men. Both Harris and Forsyth were hanged in November 1960. Silverman took the opportunity, as so often before, to tackle Butler over the case on the day of the executions and asked him to explain to the House why he had chosen not to issue a reprieve, but as so often before, Butler declined to give an explanation 'in accordance with tradition'. Silverman then railed against the iniquity of being unable to question the Home Secretary on these questions until after an execution had taken place.[543]

There were calls in Parliament from both Christopher Mayhew (Labour, Woolwich East) and Elwyn Jones (Labour, West Ham South) regarding the decision of the Lords in DPP v Smith – 'Gypsy Joe Smith' for the Act to be amended so as to redefine murder to exclude cases where there was no intent to kill, but only an intent to cause grievous bodily harm, but these calls were rejected by Butler.[544] Naturally, not all capital cases at around this time were as contentious as these and there were quite a few others that proceeded in a manner that was relatively free of controversy and legal complexity, though nonetheless invariably provoking an outcry from the abolitionist camp, if only because of the fact of their being capital.

Whilst these battles were being fought over the procession of capital cases as and when they appeared they were dwarfed in significance by the Timothy Evans case which continued to hover over the whole controversy like a storm cloud threatening to break. The passions of the abolitionists and the campaigners against miscarriage peaked every so often with the publication of each new book on the case or the revelation of new evidence. And, as described in chapter six, there was a full scale debate in the Commons in mid-1961, at the instigation of the Opposition, to examine the new evidence examined in Ludovic Kennedy's book on the case. There were renewed calls for a public enquiry into both the case and the subsequent, and, arguably flawed, Home Office enquiry under Scott Henderson and for a free posthumous pardon, though yet again the plangent cries for action were unavailing.

---

[543] HC Deb, vol 629, col 1223-4, 10th November 1960 (Business of the House)
[544] HC Deb, vol 630, *col 122*, 24th November 1960 (Mayhew); vol 633, *col 47*, 26th January 1961 (Jones) - both written answers

Moreover, the litany of celebrated miscarriages was soon to be supplemented by another.

The Hanratty Case

The cases of Walter Graham Rowland; Timothy Evans and John Christie; Derek Bentley and Christopher Craig; and Ruth Ellis all fell into the *causes celebre* class and were grist to the abolitionists' mill insofar as they raised key questions about the possibility of hanging the innocent, and of the way in which liability to hang could often depend upon abstruse legal technicalities or the caprice of Home Secretaries. Subsequent cases, post Homicide Act, such as that of Vickers, Marwood, Podola *et al* were again fiercely contested in Parliament and the media as well as in the courtroom because of the points of law they raised, though never achieving the iconic status of the earlier cited cases.

But one case, however, attracted, at least in retrospect, such a measure of media attention that it equalled and perhaps surpassed that of the *causes celebre* of the 1950s and grew increasingly controversial with the passage of time. So famous did the case become, and so much did it overshadow other murder cases of the same era, that there is a widespread misconception that it was the last hanging to take place in Britain. James Hanratty was hanged on 4th April 1962 for the murder of Michael Gregsten at Deadman's Hill on the A6 the previous August.[545] The case was replete with points of interest, and the crime, investigation, trial, execution, and subsequent controversy about the case (which has continued unabated for over forty years) bear examination in detail.

On the evening of 22nd August 1961 Michael Gregsten and Valerie Storie, who had been conducting a clandestine affair, were abducted from their car by an unidentified gunman from where it had been parked at Dorney Reach in Berkshire. A few hours later, in the early hours of 23rd August, the gunman shot and killed Gregsten, and raped and shot Storie, leaving her for dead at Deadman's Hill, a stretch of the A6 in Bedfordshire. As a result of a lead a man called Peter Alphon was arrested shortly afterwards on suspicion of being the

---

[545] The burgeoning literature on the Hanratty case embraces the following: Blom-Cooper, Louis, *The A6 Murder: Regina v James Hanratty - The Semblance of Truth* (Harmondsworth: Penguin, 1963); Justice, Jean, *Murder vs Murder: The British Legal System and the A6 Murder Case* (Paris: Olympia, 1964); Lord Russell of Liverpool, *Deadman's Hill - Was Hanratty Guilty?* (London: Martin Secker and Warburg 1965, Icon 1966); Foot, Paul, *Who Killed Hanratty?* (London: Cape, 1971, revised London: Panther 1973, revised Harmondsworth: Penguin 1988); Simpson, Keith *Forty Years of Murder* (London: Harrap 1978, London: Grafton 1980); Foot, Paul, *A Break in the Silence* (Guardian newspaper, 25th February 1995); Woffinden, Bob, *Miscarriages of Justice* (London: Hodder and Stoughton, 1987, London: Coronet, 1989); Woffinden, Bob, *Hanratty: The Final Verdict* (London: Macmillan, 1997) and Miller, Leonard, *Shadows of Deadman's Hill: A New Analysis of the A6 Murder* (London: Zoilus, 2001)

murderer, but was not identified by Storie at an ID parade, and was consequently ruled out. Hanratty then came under suspicion, and was eventually arrested by police at Blackpool on 11th October. He was picked out by Storie in another ID parade, though one conducted under very unsatisfactory conditions, and was duly charged with the murder. On 5th December he was committed for trial at the Old Bailey, though the case was re-located to Bedford. Despite having a strong alibi based on his presence in Rhyl at the material time he was convicted on 17th February 1962 of the capital murder of Gregsten and sentenced to death. His appeal was dismissed in early March 1962, on 2nd April the Home Secretary, Rab Butler, turned down an appeal for him to be reprieved and on 4th April Hanratty was hanged at Bedford Prison.

This was merely the beginning of the story, which was to drag on and on for decades thereafter with a barrage of articles in the press, questions in the House, books and even television documentaries, highlighting the mounting evidence that Hanratty may have been innocent. Not the least of this evidence was that Alphon, the original suspect, confessed to it himself voluntarily. The matter acquired huge publicity, attracting the attentions amongst others of Jean Justice, effectively a professional campaigner against miscarriages, who became increasingly immersed in the case. In August 1963 there was a debate in the Commons on the case, instigated by Fenner Brockway (Labour, Eton and Slough) and in the Lords in August 1966.[546] In November 1966 there was a *Panorama* programme on the case, and in December 1966 a *Sunday Times* investigation by Brian Moynahan and Peter Laurie.[547] The pressure for the matter to be re-opened led to Home Secretary Roy Jenkins ordering a police enquiry into Hanratty's Rhyl alibi. In May 1967 Alphon again publicly confessed to the murder both in a press conference and on an ITN news programme. In November 1967 the *Frost* programme re-examined the case, following the decision of the Home Secretary not to order an enquiry into the case. In 1971 Paul Foot published his celebrated book on the case.

There were repeated calls for an enquiry until finally, in June 1974 Lewis Hawser, QC was ordered by the Home Secretary (Roy Jenkins again in his second stint in that office) to conduct an enquiry, which failed to conclude that there had been a miscarriage. In 1992 there was a *Granada* television documentary on the case, repeated in 1994 and again in 1995. In April 1996 the *News of the World* announced that a Metropolitan Police enquiry into the case had concluded that Hanratty was innocent. In 1997 the matter was referred to the newly created Criminal Cases Review Commission. In 1997 Bob Woffinden's book was published re-affirming the innocence of Hanratty and the guilt of Alphon, and hinting unmistakeably at the identity of the figure who had instigated the murder.[548] The referral to the CCRC led to a further Appeal which

---

[546] HC Deb, vol 682, cols 795-832, 1st August 1963
[547] *Panorama*, 7th November 1966, see Woffinden, op cit, pp. 277-8
[548] Woffinden, op cit. passim

as a result of examining the DNA evidence was dismissed. The most recent book on the Hanratty case by Leonard Miller radically re-interprets the evidence and comes to the conclusion that Hanratty was guilty, that his alibi was weak and obviously concocted, that he had acted alone and not as part of a conspiracy, that he was motivated by revenge, jealousy and the lust for power, and moreover that his champions such as Foot were blinded by prejudice to the possibility of his guilt.[549]

Conclusion

A succession of notable and controversial cases from the late 1940s onwards had begun to undermine public confidence in the integrity and infallibility of the judicial system. The cases of Walter Rowland in 1947, and of Timothy Evans in 1950 and the associated case of John Christie in 1953, all raised the spectre of an innocent man being hanged – a possibility ridiculed in a Commons debate on the abolition clause in 1948 by a supporter of the death penalty – but which was now seen to be all too real a possibility. The case of Derek Bentley highlighted the way in which the law could work to deliver a capital sentence on someone who manifestly should not have hanged, and the Ruth Ellis case arguably demonstrated the shortcomings of the English law in failing to recognise a defence of diminished responsibility. The combined weight of these cases, and others less celebrated, began to unseat a hitherto unshakeable consensus about the righteousness of the death penalty amongst the British public. The very large majorities in favour of the retention of the rope that were evident in the opinion polls of the late 1940s began to lessen somewhat by the mid-1950s, and there was evidence of a growing feeling that the law ought to exhibit greater flexibility, with provision for degrees of murder and for defences, or partial defences, of diminished responsibility.

These cases were undoubtedly providential from the point of view of the abolitionist movement which started to gather heavy momentum in the mid-1950s, and were cleverly exploited by them in meetings, publications and media events to strengthen their case. The campaign was generally careful to stress that it based its case upon the lack of proof of the deterrent effect of the death penalty and upon its inhumanity and 'immorality', but the possibility of error was a very useful back-up weapon. Public opinion would probably have moved to some extent in an abolitionist direction with or without the efforts of the NCACP, and the NCACP would unquestionably have campaigned vigorously for abolition had none of these cases occurred, but the confluence of the two was serendipitous.

Whatever the contribution of these *causes celebre* to the campaign the net result was the Homicide Act, after which hangings continued - though many

---

[549] Miller, L, op cit

murders were now classified as 'non-capital' and no longer attracted the death penalty. This, however, did not still the controversy, but to some extent re-ignited it because of the arbitrariness of the distinction that had now been erected between capital and non-capital murder. The NCACP renewed its efforts, particularly when it became apparent that hangings would continue on a regular basis. Each capital case that came before the courts was seized upon by the abolitionists inside and outside Parliament, and Parliamentary guerilla warfare continued, with questions fired at the Home Secretary or the Attorney-General about points of law raised and refusals to grant reprieves. None of these subsequent cases attracted the same degree of media attention as the earlier ones, and public opinion stubbornly refused to shift any further, if anything starting to move back in the opposite direction. Pro-hangers on the Conservative backbenches mirrored the activities of the abolitionists by calling for the widening of the scope of capital murder or even the restoration of the position ante- Homicide Act. The Hanratty case was the last of the great *causes celebre* of the hanging era, though it had little or no effect on the hanging question.

CHAPTER 10

THE CAMPAIGN 1964-1965

This chapter chronicles the events from the general election of October 1964 up to the passage of an abolition bill in November 1965, bringing the focus to bear almost wholly on the Parliamentary theatre to where the great weight of the struggle had now once again shifted.

The general election of 1964 was one of the true watershed elections of twentieth century British political history, bringing not only a change of government, but heralding a change of mood and style, and not least infusing the Commons with a new generation of politicians – 'the class of "64"' - which formed much of the bedrock of the Labour Party over the next twenty to thirty years.[550] In came a cohort of Labour members, often working class, left-wing, in their early to mid-thirties, representing in many cases the new upwardly mobile grammar school and university educated working class of the immediate post-war era. The election had been long-awaited, having been delayed to almost the last moment legally permissible by Prime Minister Alec Douglas-Home in the desperate hope of seeing the Conservatives position in the polls improve further. There was thus a palpable sense of the release of long built up tension, and of fresh air blowing through the nation.

The election was fought primarily on the economy and the usual raft of domestic issues. Capital punishment was scarcely a major issue in the campaign, though it can hardly have escaped the notice of the more percipient voters that a great many Labour candidates were declared abolitionists and that a Labour victory would yield a big majority for abolition and create the momentum for a renewed and probably successful push to the campaign. Few candidates would have included any mention of the issue in their election addresses, though doubtless the question arose in constituency campaigns on the doorstep and in meetings. It is difficult to gauge the effect that the issue had given its low salience in the campaign, though possibly, given the state of public opinion which was still deeply hostile to abolition amongst Labour voters as well as Tory, Labour candidates may have lost a few votes because of the issue.[551]

---

[550] Butler, David and Anthony King, *The British General Election of 1964* (London: Macmillan, 1965)

[551] Stan Newens, successful Labour candidate for Epping, says that the issue was undoubtedly a vote-loser for him and for other Labour candidates up and down the country, both in 1964 and in subsequent elections. It was raised on the doorstep by voters and there were erstwhile supporters who told him that they wouldn't vote for him because of his stance. It would, he felt, be impossible to quantify the extent of vote-loss but it was probably only a very minor vote-loser given that few people would have decided their vote on the issue. Interview with Stan Newens, MEP, 9th April 1999.

The Queen's Speech duly, and uniquely, included mention of the government's intention to allow a free vote on the issue of capital punishment early in the new Parliament.[552] Though the government, and especially Prime Minister Wilson and Lord Chancellor Gardiner, had expressed sympathy with the principle of abolition it would not itself introduce legislation, in accordance with the established precept that abolition was a matter of personal conscience. It would, however, support and give time, if necessary, to a backbench measure to abolish capital punishment - anticipated to be a Ten Minute Rule Bill (to be introduced probably by Silverman).[553] It was considered fairly certain that the prospective bill would pass through the Commons but it was more debatable whether it would get through the Lords, the composition of which was not vastly different from when it had struck down the 1956 abolition bill (though of course infused by the accretion of a number of life peers under the Life Peerages Act of 1958). Once again the two sides of the debate girded themselves for battle, with a certain amount of shadow boxing going on even before the anticipated bill had been promulgated.

In the debate on the Queen's Speech Edward Gardner (Conservative, Billericay) said that the matter should have been referred to a committee such as the Barry Committee that dealt with corporal punishment. Since the Gowers Commission had specifically been precluded from considering the question there was no authoritative guidance for MPs.[554] Tom Iremonger (Conservative, Ilford North), noting the reference to capital punishment, said that it was pregnant with great danger. Capital punishment was 'a ritual deeply cherished by the English people though perhaps they may be weaned off it without undue screams soon'. The government side should, he thought, not be so glib in their acceptance that the Homicide Act was a foolish measure - it provided for the execution of the professional criminal who carried a gun and was prepared to use it. Having a free vote on capital punishment without considering life sentences is distressing - the Home Secretary should consider legislating on life sentences for wilful killers before abolishing capital punishment.[555]

The question of life imprisonment, and its real meaning, assumed ever greater importance as the prospect of abolition loomed ever closer. Paul Channon (Conservative, Southend West) questioned the length of time served by lifers, and was told by Alice Bacon, junior Home Office minister, that prisoners sentenced to death and reprieved before the Homicide Act had come into force served on average nine years. Of those convicted after the Act only three out of 202 prisoners convicted of non-capital murder by the end of 1963 had been released, i.e. 1.5%. Channon said that there was grave disquiet that

---

[552] HC Deb, vol 701, col 40, 3rd November 1964, 'Facilities will be provided for a free decision by Parliament on the issue of capital punishment.'
[553] Wilson, Harold, op cit. pp.88-89
[554] HC Deb, vol 701, col 101-2, Queens Speech debate, 3rd November 1964
[555] HC Deb, ibid, col 136-7

some persons convicted of murder were serving less time than those convicted of lesser crimes.[556] Both Silverman and Sir Edward Boyle (Conservative, Birmingham, Handsworth) intervened to say that these figures may be misleading, and Bacon said that it varied between four and fourteen years in the period 1959-63.

The Murder (Abolition of Death Penalty) Bill

The new Silverman abolition bill, the 'Murder (Abolition of Death Penalty) Bill', was duly introduced in the Commons and received its (unopposed) first reading on Friday, 4th December 1964.[557] The government had placed a moratorium on hanging at least for the duration of the passage of the bill, and it was felt that the two hangings of the previous August (Allen and Evans) would turn out to be the last. There were, as it happened, no prisoners awaiting execution at that moment. The long title of the bill was:-

> A Bill to abolish capital punishment in the case of persons convicted in Great Britain of murder or a corresponding offence by court-martial and, in connection therewith, to make further provision for the punishment of persons who are convicted. Further provisions will be a proposal to allow judges to prescribe long sentences.

Supporting Silverman as sponsors of the bill were Labour members Bessie Braddock (Liverpool, Exchange), Michael Foot (Ebbw Vale), Sir Geoffrey de Freitas (Kettering), Leslie Hale (Oldham, West), Stan Newens (Epping), Reginald Paget (Northampton), Emanuel Shinwell (Easington) and Shirley Williams (Hitchin); Conservatives Humphry Berkeley (Lancaster) and Chris Chataway (Lewisham North); and Liberal Jeremy Thorpe (North Devon). The bill proposed that life imprisonment should be the mandatory sentence for murder, but that the actual length of a life sentence should be decided by the Home Secretary on the basis of an assessment programme. It was welcomed by Hugh Klare, secretary of the Howard League.

Both abolitionists and retentionists rallied their forces inside the Commons and outside. There would be a free vote on the issue in all the parties, but on the government side Wilson advised any ministers who might have opposed the bill to abstain rather than vote against.[558] Moreover, he cautioned ministers to advise junior ministers and Parliamentary private secretaries accordingly with the caveat that they should not be pressed to act against their

---

[556] HC Deb, vol 702, col 612-3, 19th November 1964

[557] HC Deb, vol 703, col 927-8, 4th December 1964, 'A Bill to abolish capital punishment in the case of persons convicted in Great Britain of murder or convicted of murder or a corresponding offence by court martial and in connection therewith to make further provision for the punishment of persons so convicted.'

[558] TNA: CAB, 128/39, CC (64), minute 1, 15th December 1964. Cited in Block and Hostettler, op cit, p.237

consciences.[559] It is an open question to what extent this had an influence on the voting of the Cabinet and on that of junior ministers and PPSs. Certainly none voted against the bill, but given the composition of the Parliamentary party there were few who would have been inclined to have done so. Did Wilson's Cabinet injunction cause a few ministerial retentionists to abstain? It is difficult to say but probably unlikely. To what extent was the Wilson injunction proper in Cabinet on an issue of conscience? Was there any precedent for a PM to urge fellow ministers (in Cabinet) to vote a certain way on a conscience issue? Maybe not. All of which arm-twisting may have indicated Wilson's strength of feeling on the question. Meanwhile section 6 of the Homicide Act was invoked for the first time to pass sentence of death on Peter Dunford for conviction for murder, he having already been convicted of murder on a previous occasion.[560]

In the country MPs were subject to pressures from constituents and bodies. Stan Newens, a prominent abolitionist and co-sponsor of the Silverman bill was lobbied by local police officers who felt strongly on the issue, partly because of a local case where two policemen had been killed by a man called Roberts who went to ground in the Bishops Stortford area. Both a deputation from the Police Federation and individual officers had harried him on the issue.[561]

Second Reading

The second reading of the bill took place on Monday, 21st December 1964, with time provided for it by the government.[562] Sydney Silverman opened the debate by claiming the unique distinction of being the only member whose private member's bill was mentioned in the Queen's Speech. He argued, rather ingeniously (or perhaps disingenuously) that Parliament had in effect already abolished capital punishment by virtue of the Homicide Act and that it was now simply a question of deciding whether to get rid of the few exceptions to abolition that that Act had enshrined, and which had proved to be so unsatisfactory in practice.[563] He declared, in response to an interruption from Sir Alexander Spearman (Conservative, Scarborough and Whitby), that he was opposed to having a trial period of abolition since they had had that in effect as a result of seven years experience with the Homicide Act, and that anyway Parliament was still sovereign and could vote to reinstate capital punishment at

---

[559] TNA: ibid.

[560] Block and Hostettler, op cit, p.237

[561] Newens, interview April 1999, op cit. They were, he says, 'extremely angry when they found I was not prepared to give way on the issue' and the discussions were acrimonious. The police were very passionate on the issue, and Newens says he never met an officer on the beat who supported him in his stance.

[562] Hughes, Emrys, op cit p.172

[563] HC Deb, vol 704, col 877-883

any time it wanted to.[564] He said that he did not believe 'that we have any right to pursue and carry out this callous, brutal, cold-hearted ritual unless we are satisfied that a useful social purpose is thereby attained. I do not believe that it is attained.'

He was opposed by Sir Peter Rawlinson, (Conservative, Epsom), Solicitor-General in the previous administration. Rawlinson defended the Homicide Act, and said that there were bound to be anomalies where a border is erected artificially but that the basic rationale of the distinction was to preserve the Queen's Peace.[565] He wanted to retain the status quo, because he felt that capital punishment shouldn't be abandoned for 'something that is nebulous and uncertain, and can never carry the effectiveness of a sentence of capital punishment.' With the rise of violence and the operations of organized gangs of criminals he feared that the removal of capital punishment would encourage more use of guns and pose a greater risk to the public. 'Terrible and ugly as we recognise the punishment to be I believe there is a right and a duty on the State to say "for this deliberate act you will lose you life". I believe that such warning can and does deter certain men...'

Sam Silkin, (Labour, Dulwich) in his maiden speech, supported the bill and attacked capital punishment as a purely retributive sentence. He said that at the end of the Second World War he had been responsible for trying and sentencing to death a number of Japanese soldiers for crimes against Allied captives. There was no question he said of them being deterred from their crimes by the thought of capital punishment. He was very sceptical as to whether the professional criminal was really deterred, and as to whether hanging was such a unique deterrent as to justify its continued use. He cited the 1930 Select Committee and Gowers Commission findings to the effect that hanging was no more an effective deterrent than other sentences.[566]

The big surprise was that Henry Brooke, (Conservative, Hampstead), the former Tory Home Secretary, announced his conversion to the abolitionist cause. He said that he had become disenchanted with the Homicide Act as a result of his experiences at the Home Office from 1962-1964, and felt that the attempt to divide murder into two types had merely created anomalies and that any attempt to rectify these anomalies would merely create further ones. It had resulted in the death sentence being passed on people for capital murders which were less serious than others for which capital punishment was not available.[567] Though he did not believe that capital punishment was immoral he was not convinced of its deterrent value and thought that a five-year trial period of abolition was desirable. He was thus the fifth former Home Secretary to become an abolitionist, after Templewood, Samuel, Morrison and Chuter Ede (and like

---

[564] Hughes, Emrys, op cit. p.173-4
[565] HC Deb, vol 704, col 890-899
[566] HC Deb, ibid, col 900-903
[567] HC Deb, ibid, col 905-915; Hughes, Emrys, op cit. p.174-6

all of these he waited until he had vacated the office before undergoing his conversion).

William Wilson, (Labour, Coventry South) in another maiden speech, argued for abolition on the grounds that he was not convinced of the deterrent value of hanging and that as a solicitor he had had some experience of defending men charged with murder. He was conscious of the burden that guarding a condemned man had on the prison staff.[568] Mark Carlisle, (Conservative, Runcorn) in another maiden speech, supported the bill and said that it was wrong for the state to take life and that the experience of other countries where abolition had taken place showed that the murder rate had not increased thereafter.[569] Home Secretary Frank Soskice (Labour, Newport) spoke in favour, concurring with his predecessor, Brooke, that the evidence did not support the notion that hanging was a unique deterrent.[570] Dr Wyndham Davies (Conservative, Birmingham Perry Barr) in yet another maiden speech argued against abolition on the grounds that public opinion was too much against it.[571] He referred to psychiatric opinion, and said he was sceptical about alleged miscarriages of justice, but felt that there should be a more humane form of capital punishment. Leo Abse (Labour, Pontypool) argued for abolition in a characteristically quirky contribution which alluded to pickpockets who attended hangings in the eighteenth and early nineteenth centuries at a time when pickpocketing was still a capital offence.[572] Murderers were psychopathic types who were not deterred by the threat of punishment.

Brigadier Terence Clarke (Conservative, Portsmouth, West) made a resounding defence of hanging.[573] There was no mandate for abolition. He had solicited the views of the general public through his local newspaper and found 200 against abolition and only two for it. He claimed that no innocent person had ever been hanged and that miscarriages were illusory and made up by people to sell books. Even if there had been the occasional miscarriage it was a small price to pay for the deterrent effect that hanging had. He made a vitriolic attack on Silverman, whom he said he would blame personally for the death of any murdered child that occurred in the next few years. Dr Shirley Summerskill (Labour, Halifax) argued for abolition and felt that hanging was morally wrong, and that it brutalised and degraded the prison officers and the public.[574] Bettie Harvie Anderson (Conservative, Renfrew East) said that she was an abolitionist but (somewhat confusingly) she would not support the bill because there was an

---

[568] HC Deb, ibid, col 915-917
[569] HC Deb, ibid, col 918-920
[570] HC Deb, ibid, col 922
[571] HC Deb, ibid, col 932-935
[572] HC Deb, ibid, col 936-941
[573] HC Deb, ibid, col 944-948
[574] HC Deb, ibid, col 949-950

element of deterrence in the law at present.[575] Raphael Tuck (Labour, Watford) thought that hanging was no deterrent.[576] Tom Iremonger (Conservative, Ilford North) opposed the bill because there was no effective provision for an alternative punishment.[577] Life imprisonment was an uncertain concept and not an effective deterrent. Michael McGuire (Labour, Ince) was for the bill and thought that hanging was degrading.[578] Emlyn Hooson, (Liberal, Montgomery) was for the bill and said that the 1957 Act was 'the sorriest, shabbiest compromise in the history of Parliament.'[579]

John Hynd (Labour, Sheffield Attercliffe) was for the bill.[580] Sir Richard Glyn (Conservative, Dorset North) was against the bill and thought that capital punishment was a deterrent, citing the lack of rise in capital murders as against crimes of violence in general in the same years.[581] Dr David Kerr, (Labour, Wandsworth Central) supported the bill.[582] Sir Edward Boyle (Conservative, Birmingham Handsworth) supported the bill and said that hanging was inexpressibly horrible and that juries might be tempted to acquit if they thought a defendant might be hanged.[583]

The debate was wound up by Reginald Paget (Labour, Northampton), a consistent supporter of abolition, in uncompromising terms.[584] He said that Rawlinson's argument that capital punishment was a deterrent was fatuous. That had been said about every move to abolish capital punishment for what were formerly capital crimes such as forgery and sheep-stealing. Capital murders were not the preserve of the professional criminal. He contrasted France and Belgium, where the former still had the death penalty and the latter (in practice) didn't, and pointed out that in France many criminals carried guns whereas in Belgium very few did. He believed very strongly in the principle of representative democracy and that: 'On great questions, on the security of the Realm, on the taking of life of human beings, there we betray the whole system which we represent and which we created if we seek for popularity rather than follow our own judgment as to what we believe to be right'. He was against capital punishment: 'because I know in my heart that it is wrong. I know that I would not hang a man because I would know that it would be an evil thing to do, and nearly all of us feel that, and I would not do by another that which I would not do by myself.'

The bill received its second reading by 355-170, a majority of 185, on a

---

[575] HC Deb, ibid, col 954
[576] HC Deb, ibid, col 958
[577] HC Deb, ibid, col 959
[578] HC Deb, ibid, col 965
[579] HC Deb, ibid, col 967-972
[580] HC Deb, ibid, col 973
[581] HC Deb, ibid, col 977
[582] HC Deb, ibid, col 980
[583] HC Deb, ibid, col 983-984
[584] HC Deb, ibid, col 992-1000

free vote. Eighty Conservatives (including two Ulster Unionists who then still took the Conservative whip at Westminster) voted for the bill, as well as eight out of the nine Liberals, and 267 Labour MPs. Only one Labour MP, Frank Tomney (Hammersmith) and the remaining Liberal, Alasdair Mackenzie (Ross and Cromarty) voted against it, together with 168 Conservatives and Ulster Unionists.[585] At this point the Conservatives put the whips on - perhaps owing to a promise made to their backbenchers as Harold Wilson suggests - and voted as a party that the bill, instead of being sent to a Standing Committee upstairs (as would normally be the case), should have its Committee stage on the floor of the House. With the help of the Liberals this was defeated by only eighteen votes, 247-229.[586]

Initial Committee Stage

In the Committee stage retentionists put down amendment after amendment to delay its passage onto the statute book, and used every device to delay and obstruct.[587] Equally, on the abolitionist side, Silverman's supporters were under instruction from him to keep as quiet as possible so as to speed the passage of the bill.[588] Silverman was not keen for others to emulate his own prolixity. Amendments included those to retain the death penalty for murder by shooting or by causing an explosion or in the furtherance of theft, or for those convicted of murder after a previous murder conviction, and for the murder of police and prison officers in the execution of their duty. After proceeding on its way in Committee for seven mornings it suddenly became de-railed when on a motion from a Conservative back bencher Forbes Hendry, moved on a Friday afternoon, 5th March 1965, when the House was debating private motions selected by ballot, the House voted by 128-120 to discharge the Standing Committee and instead commit the bill to a committee of the whole House.[589] This was plainly a planned Conservative ambush, carefully whipped, launched on an unsuspecting government, and designed to disrupt Parliamentary business, especially the contentious Iron and Steel Nationalisation Bill, given that the whole House would now be enmeshed in the details of the legislation. Either the bill would have had to be dropped or other important government business would be lost. The government had to consider its options.

Six days later Lord President and Leader of the House of Commons Herbert Bowden informed the Cabinet that there were four courses of action:- a) to accept the decision of the House, thus devoting four or five days of Commons time to the Committee stage and possibly a further three days to the

---

[585] HC Deb, ibid, col 1001-6
[586] HC Deb, ibid, col 1005-10; Wilson, Harold op cit p.89
[587] Hughes, Emrys, op cit p.177
[588] Newens - Interview, April 1999, op cit.
[589] Wilson, Harold, op cit, p.89

remaining stages; b) to send the bill back to the Standing Committee by resolution of the House, though the motion to do this would have occupied a day and (since the opposition had indicated that they might table a number of amendments at report stage) a further three or four days for the remaining stages; c) to accept the decision of the House but secure a resolution to enable the House to sit on Wednesday mornings for the consideration of the Committee stage. (If all amendments could be defeated the government could dispense with a report stage - but they might then be subject to pressure to accord similar treatment to other private members bills); d) to abandon the attempt to secure passage of the bill in the current session.[590]

The balance of advantage appeared to favour the third course. It was generally agreed that the bill should if possible be passed in the current session. Bowden argued that if they took that course they might be better able to secure the attendance of their supporters and moreover it might dissuade the opposition from using the same tactic with other bills. On the other hand to adopt a novel means of dealing with the bill might suggest that the government attached disproportionate importance to a measure which didn't command widespread public support, and that therefore it might be preferable to deal with the bill during normal Parliamentary hours and then use the Wednesday mornings for the Committee stages of other bills. It was suggested that some government supporters might move an amendment to the bill to provide for the establishment of an independent body to advise the Home Secretary on the exercise of his discretion to release prisoners subject to life imprisonment. The PM summed up the discussion by saying that the Cabinet was agreed that option three was the least objectionable course of action, and that provided the principle of a free vote was preserved arrangements should be made to prevent the adoption of any amendments to the bill. The Cabinet duly invited the Lord President to make the necessary arrangements.[591]

Committee Stage Redux

The Committee stage thus had to start afresh.[592] The same set of amendments as the first time around were duly debated and defeated. The Police Federation unsurprisingly condemned the rejection of the amendment to retain the death penalty for the killing of a policeman.[593] Brooke and five other Conservative back-benchers moved an amendment to the effect that the Act, if passed, would continue in force until July 1970 (five years hence) and would then expire unless Parliament decreed otherwise by an affirmative resolution of both Houses (what would now be called a sunset clause). If no action were

---

[590] TNA: CAB 128 series, vol 39(2) cc(65) 15th conclusions, minute 2, 11th March 1965
[591] TNA: CAB 128, ibid
[592] Block and Hostettler, op cit, p.241
[593] Block and Hostettler, ibid, p.243

taken to prolong the Act then the law relating to murder would simply revert to its present (1965) state. The Brooke amendment was accepted by 176-128.[594] This was the only amendment that managed to get through in Committee.

Meanwhile Home Secretary Soskice had done a *volte-face* over the Timothy Evans case and the findings of the Scott Henderson enquiry, refusing to set up a new inquiry into the case, despite his previous pronouncements on the subject.[595]

Silverman wrote to all MPs on 22nd June in connection with the sunset clause:-

Dear Member,

Many members, including abolitionists, have found extremely attractive the new clause whereby the Murder (Abolition of Death Penalty) Bill shall cease to operate in July 1970 unless both Houses before that date pass resolutions to the contrary. I fully appreciate the tactical advantage of this proposal. But the clause involves such a constitutional absurdity that no democratic parliament should accept it, and I propose on Report to move to delete the clause. My reasons are:-
1) There is no obligation on any government to move such a resolution.
2) There is no obligation on any government to provide time for such a resolution to be moved by a private member.
3) Any government which desired the Act to lapse or merely to avoid embarrassment need merely sit back and do nothing.
4) If it did nothing then the Homicide Act with all its anomalies would *automatically* be restored, not merely without the people being consulted, but without Parliament being consulted either.
5) If Parliament sees reason to change its mind, it can always do so. It need not wait five years.
6) The anomalies of the 1957 Act are rejected by everybody, abolitionist and retentionist alike. It cannot possibly be right that they should all be automatically re-enacted without Parliament having a say in the matter at all.
I hope that for these reasons you will support me in getting rid of this clause.

Sydney Silverman, 22nd June 1965[596]

The extent to which the fate of the bill was in doubt in its later stages is indicated by the fact that Benn (by now Postmaster-General) cancelled a trip to Germany in June 1965 so as not to miss a crucial vote. Silverman had indicated to him that he was afraid it wouldn't get carried with so many abolitionists going away unpaired, and Benn felt that 'I could never forgive myself for missing this vote if it were to lead to the defeat of the Bill.'[597] Home Secretary Soskice, also, was not convinced that the bill would be passed, and commented to an appalled

---

[594] Block and Hostettler, ibid, p.243
[595] *The Times* 20 May 1965, p.18
[596] TNA: PREM 13/2552 - Letter from Silverman to MPs 22nd June 1965
[597] Benn, op cit p.279

Benn on 1 July 1965 that if the bill fell 'I shall have to start hanging again.' Benn was shocked at the thought and observed that such a thing would provoke the resignation of Gardiner and a major revolt.[598]

Behind the scenes the Home Office was on the case. The Home Secretary had sought advice from his civil servants on what would happen if the bill failed in the present session and had to be carried over to the next session.[599] A Home Office memo canvassed the options. There were two methods. One was a carry-over motion in which one would have to move a resolution providing:-

(a) that further proceedings on the bill should be suspended until the next session
(b) that on any day in that session a motion might be made to be disposed of without amendment or debate that proceedings on the bill be resumed and
(c) the Speaker to call upon the sponsor of the bill to present the bill in a form in which it stood when proceedings thereon were suspended and that thereupon the bill shall be deemed to have had a second reading.

There was, however, no precedent for this being done in the case of a public bill. Alternatively, the government could announce its intention of re-introducing the bill in its present form as a government bill. The occasion for the use of either method would be the desirability of affording some basis on which the present practice as to reprieves could reasonably be continued by giving public notice that the proceedings on the bill were to be resumed in the next session and brought to a conclusion either way without undue delay.[600] In other words the moratorium on hangings would be enabled to continue so long as the bill was still deemed current in the sense of being capable of being revived at short notice.

The Cabinet had been informed that the Commons was to take the remaining stages of the Abolition Bill on 13th July but that there was no possibility of finding further time if the bill failed to secure a third reading on that occasion.[601] Cabinet considered the question again on the eve of the third reading. It was felt that half a day would be sufficient to dispose of the amendments and, if the Speaker were prepared to accept a closure motion, to secure the third reading by a reasonable hour.[602] However, it was considered that there was a serious risk of losing the bill if time were spent on an amendment by Silverman to remove the clause (inserted at Committee stage) limiting the operation of the bill to five years. Silverman, it was agreed, should

---

[598] Benn, ibid. p.284
[599] TNA: HO 291/1550 - Sir Charles Cunningham - memo on the Murder (Abolition of Death Penalty) Bill - 30th June 1965.
[600] TNA: ibid
[601] TNA: HO 291/1550 Home Office - Abolition of the Death Penalty - Programme for Report and later stages of the Bill, consideration after House of Commons Committee Stage. CABINET Extract from the Minutes of a Meeting held on 1st July 1965.
[602] TNA: CC(65), 35th Conclusions, minute 1 - 1st July 1965.

be informed that while the government was prepared to allow half a day for the remaining stages they were not prepared to jeopardise their own legislation in order to secure its passage. Government time was to be made available on condition he withdrew his amendment. The Bill's sponsors should be persuaded to keep their speeches short.[603]

On 13th July 1965 the third reading was finally arrived at, and moved by Silverman. It was opposed by Sir John Hobson (Conservative, Warwick and Leamington), Attorney-General and Solicitor-General in the previous administration, and Edward Gardner (Conservative, Billericay), and supported by Henry Brooke. It was passed by 200-98, a majority of 102, with twenty-three Conservatives, including nine former ministers, going into the abolition lobby. The nine were former Cabinet ministers Henry Brooke, Sir Edward Boyle, Sir Keith Joseph and Enoch Powell, and former junior ministers Sir Hugh Fraser, Chris Chataway, Sir Hugh Lucas-Tooth, Miss Mervyn Pike and Peter Thomas. Eight Liberals voted for the bill.[604]

House of Lords Stage

The bill went forward to the Lords where the debate was opened by Baroness Wootton of Abinger and opposed by Viscount Dilhorne, the former Conservative Attorney General (as Manningham-Buller) and Lord Chancellor.[605] Significantly the Lord Chief Justice, Lord Parker, supported the bill, subject to a strengthening of the provisions regarding the alternative penalty of life imprisonment. He felt that the Homicide Act had been a failure and that it was now a choice between going back to the position prior to that or opting for complete abolition.[606] Also in favour of the bill were the Earl of Harewood, a leading figure in the NCACP, (speaking for the first time in eighteen years in the Lords), Lord Chuter Ede (former Labour Home Secretary) and the Archbishop of Canterbury (Dr Michael Ramsey), who felt that capital punishment devalued human life. The fact that the heads of both the judicial and episcopal benches in the Lords were in favour of the bill must have been deeply influential in shaping opinion in the Upper House. But Lord Kilmuir (as David Maxwell Fyfe, a former Conservative Home Secretary) opposed it, criticizing the way that public opinion was being swept aside and arguing that if the Homicide Act was inadequate then it should be amended. The debate was wound up by a brilliant speech from Lord Gardiner, and was given a second reading by 204-104.[607] The Lords generally gave the bill a much easier ride than was anticipated, with most of the bishops and the judges giving it support.

---

[603] TNA: ibid
[604] HC Deb, col. 463-466 - 13th July 1965
[605] HL Deb [268] col 153 - 14th July 1965.
[606] HL Deb [269] col 480.
[607] HL Deb, ibid. cols 711-714 - 20th July 1965.

In the Committee stage in the Lords the Brooke amendment was affirmed (the requirement for another vote in five years time) and an amendment from Parker was carried abolishing the fixed penalty of life imprisonment, and substituting complete judicial discretion. Other amendments were defeated in the Committee stage, including those moved by Lords Conesford and Ilford which were essentially to retain capital punishment for two of the five categories which were presently capital (resisting arrest and the murder of police officers), i.e. para (c) and (d) of section 5(1) of the Homicide Act. Conesford, who had voted for the bill, had indicated in the second reading debate that he intended to put down such an amendment because he regarded these murders to be in a different class from other capital murders. It was of course wholly arbitrary to regard some types of murder as worse or in a 'special class' and anyway the Home Office Research Unit report, 'Murder' showed that there had been no convictions for capital murder under section 5(1)(c) of the Act in the period 1957-60, and there had not been any since then (i.e. 1960-65).

The amendment may well have been motivated in part by recent high-profile escapes of convicted prisoners, e.g. Ronnie Biggs and Charles Wilson, 'the Great Train Robbers' (albeit that they were not murderers). There was undoubtedly a strongly held view that the police believed that hanging was a deterrent to the murder of a police officer, and that that was certainly the view of the Police Federation. Lord Ilford had moved a very similar amendment regarding the murder of police and prison officers, based on the assumption that a prisoner serving a life sentence would have nothing to lose by murdering a prison officer (though it neglects the point that his actual sentence could have been enormously lengthened from maybe nine or ten years to actual life). Another Parker amendment dealt with the setting up of a Judicial Review Tribunal to which the Secretary of State would have to refer.

A slightly bizarre amendment moved by Viscount Stuart of Findhorn proposed that the prisoner convicted of murder be given the right to choose execution rather than life imprisonment or as he put it 'rather than suffer the decay of soul and body resulting from long-term imprisonment.' This was effectively state-sanctioned suicide for which there was no precedent, and there were numerous objections, such as what would happen if a prisoner changed his mind at the last moment, and what of the position of non-murderers sentenced to life. Lord Burton had moved an amendment to restrict the operation of the Act to England and Wales, i.e. to exclude Scotland. That was deemed anomalous. Northern Ireland had been excluded from the bill, but that was because the Stormont Parliament was competent to legislate regarding the criminal law.

There were further moves at about this time over the Timothy Evans case with a committee being set up including Ludovic Kennedy and Chuter Ede to press for a re-consideration of the case.[608] Soskice conceded an enquiry under Mr Justice Brabin whose terms of reference were to re-examine the evidence given in the Evans and Christie trials and to hear any other information relating to the question of whether Evans did or did not kill his wife and baby.[609]

The third reading of the Abolition Bill passed without a division in the Lords in October 1965.[610] The bill went back to the Commons with the amendments agreed to and on Monday, 8th November 1965 the Murder (Abolition of Death Penalty) Act 1965 received the Royal Assent and became law.[611] It had required thirteen sittings in government time, including nine morning sessions.[612]

Three days later, on 11th November 1965, Ian Brady and Myra Hindley were charged with the murders of two children on Saddleworth Moor.

---

[608] *The Times*, 22 July 1965, p.10

[609] Block and Hostettler, op cit, pp. 247-8

[610] HL Deb [vol 269] cols 550-557 - 26th October 1965

[611] Block and Hostettler, op cit. p.249

[612] Wilson, Harold, op cit, p.229

CHAPTER 11

THE MURDER RATE AND CRIME STATISTICS

It may be fruitful to look at the statistical trends in the murder rate and those of other crimes, especially violent ones, in the period under study, comparing and contrasting the rates before, during and after the Abolition Act of 1965. Of course it would be misleading to suggest that a general rise in the murder rate is automatically a result of the abolition of capital punishment or, for that matter, that other trends in the crime figures are necessarily a consequence of changes in the penal system. These things are conditioned by numerous social, economic and political factors. Equally one cannot discount the notion that there may be certain things which are a matter of cause and effect. There is no question, however, that the statistical trends were used by both sides in the debate over capital punishment to bolster their case or to discredit their opponents' case, and on that basis alone it is useful to examine the statistical evidence. Moreover these figures were an integral part of the public perception of the effects of abolition and may have intensified the public clamour for the restoration of the rope.

The abolitionists were anxious to deploy murder figures from a variety of countries where abolition had taken place to demonstrate that there was no significant rise in the murder rate thereafter. In this they were reinforced by the findings of the Gowers Commission which had scrutinized the figures from abolitionist countries far and wide, especially Scandinavia and states of the USA and had concluded that in general abolition had not been followed by more murders. Also there did not seem to be any significant difference in the murder rate between comparable countries (or adjoining states of the USA) where one was abolitionist and the other not.

For the retentionists on the other hand it was self evident that the rope acted as a deterrent, and a uniquely efficacious one at that, and that to abandon it would be an act of foolishness and irresponsibility on the part of Parliament and government. This was apparent from the evidence given to Gowers by such as Lord Goddard, LCJ, and others representing the judiciary, the legal profession, the police force and the prison service. They were scathing about the apparent lack of any ill-effects suffered by abolitionist countries and argued that 'England was different' and that to abandon the rope would be a dangerous and unnecessary experiment designed only to appease the demands of sentimentalists and effete intellectuals.

Thus the abolitionists had the powerful but relatively unwieldy weapon of statistics on their side whereas the retentionists had the overwhelming weight of history, tradition and public opinion on theirs. In the short term it was an unequal contest. The response of the retentionists to the statistics brandished by the abolitionists was either to ignore them, or to suggest that 'statistics can be made to prove anything', and though certainly the figures may have appeared to support the abolitionist case they were open to a multiplicity of interpretations.

After abolition in 1965, however, the terms of the debate changed somewhat, with the abolitionists now slightly on the defensive over the figures which may, at least superficially, have given credence to the hangers' claim that abolition would be followed by a rise in the murder rate. It has to be stressed, though, that the figures were far from presenting a clear picture in the years immediately following, and that any long-term trends were hard to discern at that stage. But, embarrassingly for the abolitionists, there occurred a few especially heinous and high-profile cases such as the Moors murders and the Shepherds Bush killings of police officers which aroused the ire of the general public and led to a clamour for the restoration of the rope in the right-wing press and kindred circles. These cases naturally dominated the headlines and overshadowed the small print of the statistics.

There were a host of complicating factors which made the figures hard to interpret and thus liable to recruitment by both sides. Firstly, there had been in Britain, and the western world generally, a slowly rising tide of violent crime ever since the end of the Second World War, though this ebbed and flowed, and the murder rate was but a feature, though an especially prominent one, of this underlying trend. Thus murder had been on the rise well before abolition had come to pass, and indeed before it had even been seriously mooted, and an examination of the very long- term trends over the whole period from 1945 to 1969 and beyond would show an irregular but palpable increase. This appeared to be wholly independent of, and not susceptible to any and every change in the penal system during those years, whether it was the abolition of capital or corporal punishment, the imposition by judges of shorter or longer sentences or the innovation of new and more flexible court punishments such as suspended sentences, probation and community service. None of this prevented the law and order brigade from latching on to any apparent rise as evidence of the deleterious effects of 'soft' sentencing and the abandonment of the birch and the rope.

Secondly, the first wave of the abolitionist campaign had, as discussed, resulted in the Homicide Act 1957 which, apart from creating two categories of murder only one of which was capital, made a variety of other changes to the law of murder. In particular it provided, under section 2, for the partial defence of diminished responsibility which was raised by a large number of defendants in murder trials in the years succeeding, and resulted in a lot of cases where the defendant was convicted of manslaughter where otherwise he would surely have been found guilty of murder and liable to hang. This defence cut right across the artificial division into capital and non-capital murder since it related to the state of mind of the culprit, not the nature or means of committing the murder. It meant that the figures produced annually showing 'Murders known to the police in England and Wales' were subject to constant retrospective amendment in the light of the outcome of murder trials where diminished responsibility was successfully raised (and murder thus legally reduced to manslaughter). Of course these police figures had always been provisional and liable to downwards adjustment for many reasons such as suspicious deaths turning out to be accidents or suicides. But that was more a matter of adjustment to an objective reality whereas the diminished responsibility defence was highly subjective and only resolvable by a court perhaps many years later if and when someone was tried, and even then resolvable only in law but not in fact. Therefore the police figures were constant from year to year but appeared to be more inflated than they had been in the past, but this inflation was partly illusory. It might be added that the Homicide Act had also enlarged the law of provocation and introduced another partial defence in the form of a failed suicide pact, and that these too increased the number of cases where a murder indictment might result in a manslaughter conviction.

Thirdly, it was not often appreciated (either at the time or subsequently) that from February 1956 to the passage of the Homicide Act in March 1957 there was a complete moratorium on hangings brought about largely by the progress through Parliament in those two successive sessions of the first Silverman Bill and then the Homicide Bill, and in accordance with the accepted practice of Home Secretaries not to allow hangings while the matter of abolition was under active Parliamentary consideration.[613] Conversely there was a widespread misconception at the time that the effect of the Homicide Act would be to put an end to hangings altogether, at least in practice if not in principle, to the extent that the government found it necessary to make it clear that this was not the case.[614] Thus, by a curious paradox, the coming into effect of the Act caused hangings to recommence and not to cease as was commonly supposed.

---

[613] In fact there had been no hangings at all for nearly two years from August 1955 (that of Alec Wilkinson at Leeds) until that of Vickers at Durham in July 1957. Eddleston, op cit. Sentences were always commuted and executions never merely stayed to await the outcome of legislative deliberation since tradition and propriety were felt to demand that executions take place strictly according to custom and precedent within a prescribed timetable from the date of sentencing. A 'Death Row', as in the USA, was felt to be an intolerable burden on all concerned.

[614] For example, in Agatha Christie's *4.50 from Paddington*, published in 1957 (and presumably written shortly prior to that), Miss Marple proclaims at the end of the book, after having nailed the murderer, that it was such a pity that they had abolished the death penalty because he really deserved to hang. In fact the nature of the murder (strangulation for the purposes of an elaborate deception) meant that the murder was (under the terms of the Homicide Act which became law in March 1957) non-capital but that is not the import of Miss Marple's words. Did Miss Marple speak for Miss Christie, and if so, did even such an apparently knowledgeable author misapprehend the change in the law that had taken place, or was about to take place? Of course the book may well have been written some time before the passage of the Act and maybe while the earlier Silverman abolition bill was still under consideration and not 'corrected' before publication to take account of events.

This makes any interpretation of the murder rates for the relevant years, even assuming a direct causal relationship, extremely problematic and confounds some of the arguments that were brought forward about the effects of the Act.

Fourthly, the creation of degrees of murder by virtue of the Homicide Act made it possible to compare the trends in the murder rate of capital and non-capital murders respectively, and thereby offer a crude measure of the deterrent effect of the rope, for if it were a deterrent one might imagine that the increase in the rate of non-capital murder would be steeper than that for capital murder. The figures tended to show that there was no clear increase in either and that there was no significant difference in the rate of increase as between the two categories of murder. On the other hand a truly comprehensive analysis would require an assessment of the very long term trends, taking into account both the period well before 1957 and well after 1965.This was very hard to achieve in practice in regards to the pre-1957 period because the criteria that differentiated capital and non-capital murder were a function of issues of fact that were often not tried or resolved during the investigation or the trial because they were of no relevance. Before the Homicide Act it would have been utterly immaterial whether a murderer stole his victim's wallet after beating him to death, but after the Act it became crucial to his prospects of dodging the gallows.

These and other factors muddied the waters of statistical interpretation and provided plentiful ammunition for the arsenals of both sides in the debate. All of the foregoing illustrates a methodological conundrum in that for figures to be truly meaningful they had to be analysed over a very lengthy period of time, so as to ensure that any increase or decrease was not merely a short-term fluctuation. But if the figures were taken over a very long period then inevitably other factors obtruded such as changes in the criminal justice system, the penal system and even long-term changes in the nature of society.

Table 21: Murders Known to Police 1957-1971

Year	England and Wales		Scotland		Total	
1957	135	(+2)	12	(−14)	147	(−12)
1958	114	(−19)	18	(−8)	132	(−27)
1959	135	(+2)	14	(−12)	149	(−10)
1960	123	(−10)	16	(−10)	139	(−20)
1961	118	(−15)	14	(−12)	132	(−27)
1962	129	(−4)	27	(+1)	156	(−3)
1963	122	(−11)	16	(−10)	138	(−21)
1964	135	(+2)	27	(+1)	162	(+3)
1965	135	(+2)	32	(+6)	167	(+8)
1966	122	(−11)	30	(+4)	152	(−7)
1967	154	(+21)	41	(+15)	195	(+36)

1968	148	(+15)	41	(+15)	189	(+30)
1969	119	(−14)	31	(+5)	150	(−9)
1970	135	(+2)	29	(+3)	164	(+5)
1971	173	(+40)	45	(+19)	218	(+59)
Total and mean	1,997	(133)	393	(26)	2,390	(159)

Source: Home Office press release on the report of the Criminal Law Revision Committee (January 1973). Figures in brackets are the numbers above or below the mean for the overall period (rounding to whole numbers)

Several points need to be made about these figures. Firstly they are subject to retrospective amendment in the light of further investigation where, for example, a suspected murder may turn out to have been an accident or suicide or the other way about, and also because other murders may be discovered. They are also liable to revision because of the outcome of trials where a murder indictment may result in a manslaughter conviction for whatever reason.

The figures for Scotland are roughly proportional given its relatively small population and demonstrate a similar trend to England and Wales though of course there are years where the numbers go up in England and Wales and down in Scotland, or vice-versa. Over the whole period which extends from the year of the passage of the Homicide Act in 1957 up to two years after the confirmation of the Abolition Act there is relatively little fluctuation or long-term trend, certainly not for England and Wales, except for the final year where there is a sharp increase. In Scotland there does appear to be something of a long-term increase. Strikingly, the total of 135 murders for England and Wales in 1970 is the same as that for 1957 and for the 'middle' years of 1964 and 1965 when the Abolition Bill was making its passage through Parliament.

These figures do not, however, take account of the distinction between capital and non-capital murder that was current between 1957 and 1965, and fail to address the question of whether there was a significant increase in one or the other that may have been masked by the overall constancy of the totals. If the death penalty were truly a deterrent one might expect that, from 1964/5 onwards the figures for capital murder would have increased more sharply than that for non-capital murder which might not have increased at all (or may even have decreased to offset the increase in the other). This was the argument put forward repeatedly by the Sandys restoration campaign. Unfortunately the data is lacking on this point because the legal distinction no longer existed and therefore was not provided for in the Home Office statistics. Of course it would have been possible to ascertain in a majority of cases whether the murder *would have been capital* had the distinction still existed but not always because often the critical facts to determine that question were not tried because not relevant. For example, if a police officer were murdered in the execution of his duty, or a person were shot dead then it would clearly have been capital, trial or no trial.

But on the other hand if a person were clubbed to death for unknown reasons then only a trial could resolve the matter of whether it were done for theft, and therefore capital, and maybe not even then. No definitive study seems to have been made of this intriguing question.

Then again one has to consider the nature of deterrence and how it works on the individual. It might seem axiomatic that deterrence works in a very short-term way and that if hanging had the deterrent effect ascribed to it by its proponents then its removal would bring about an almost immediate rise in the behaviour that it was designed to deter. But this may not necessarily be the case. It may be that it works on the community as a whole rather than on the individual and takes time to seep into the collective consciousness to work its magic. On this view murder is a bad thing because it is punishable by a uniquely awful penalty rather than being punishable by a uniquely awful penalty because it is a bad thing. After a lengthy period the absence of the uniquely awful penalty reduces society's perception of the awfulness of the crime. This would suggest that rather than any short-term increase being evident in the murder rate it would be a very long-term phenomenon, which it has been. But this of course does not prove the validity of the proposition.

All of this has to be seen against the background of the manifold changes in British culture evident in the period from the mid-1950s onwards.[615] As stated before long-term statistics have to take account of long-term trends in other variables and this period probably witnessed greater and more wide-ranging change than any other. There were undoubtedly huge increases in crime generally, and especially violent crime, though these were not subject to capital punishment (though they may have been subject to corporal punishment which was abolished in the late 1940s). There was much less reluctance on the part of the professional criminal, or even the casual one, to carry firearms and thus a much greater prospect of a fatal shooting taking place.

Another point that is frequently overlooked in the discussion of crime statistics for this period (and of socio-cultural trends generally) is that there was a startling change in the demographic profile of the country because the ratio of very young adults (18-23) to older groups increased dramatically. The post war baby-boom of 1945-1950 resulted in massive cohorts of eighteen year olds in the period 1963-1968. This is of course precisely the age group most liable to commit violent crime. It is also the age-group most liable to commit capital murder, but not non-capital murder, as studies have shown.[616] If there were actually a sharper rise in the former compared to the latter this is a factor that may partially account for it.

---

[615] See, for example, Booker, Christopher, *The Neophiliacs: The Revolution in English Life in the Fifties and Sixties* (1st ed. London: William Collins, 1969; 2nd ed. London: Pimlico, 1992)
[616] See for example Morris, Terrence and Louis Blom-Cooper, *A Calendar of Murder: Criminal Homicide In England since 1957* (London: Michael Joseph, 1964) p. 376, Table E

Conclusion

Crime and murder statistics have to be treated with great caution, especially if one wishes to draw conclusions from them about the effects of particular changes in the law, because there are numerous political, legal, social and cultural factors that have to be taken account of. Politicians, anxious to draw succour from the statistics to support their particular stance, were often highly careless in their use of them, bandying them about as if they constituted incontrovertible proof of the efficacy of capital or corporal punishment, or the futility of capital or corporal punishment. In truth the relatively short time span of the statistics available during the currency of the abolition campaign described here did not really permit any firm conclusions to be drawn, and even long-term statistics, now in the public domain, have to bear the weight of all the transformations in British society that have occurred within that time frame.

CHAPTER 12

THE PRINT MEDIA

This and the following chapters examine the way in which the debate over abolition was reflected in the mass media; the influence the mass media may have had on public opinion; the extent to which the media were enlisted in the cause of abolition (or against it), and the success or otherwise of this form of propaganda. This chapter examines the print media (newspapers, magazines, periodicals and books) and the next two chapters look at radio and television, and the cinema and the theatre, respectively.[617]

The Press

For the purposes of the following discussion it should be appreciated that 'the press' connotes essentially the editorial view of newspapers, which is habitually explicit in its partisanship, and which tends to some degree to carry its editorial partisanship through to its news columns and general coverage of events.[618] Of course there may be differences of opinion between the editor and columnists, and between different columnists.

Generally a newspaper's stance on the death penalty was consistent with that of the majority view of the party it habitually supported, with the Labour-supporting or left-leaning papers favouring abolition and the Conservative-supporting and right-leaning papers being retentionist, though the latter tendency was more qualified. This section looks in turn at daily newspapers, Sunday newspapers, London evening newspapers, the provincial press and the political press.

Daily newspapers

In the 1960s there were eight mass circulation national dailies, disregarding the small circulation and specialist *Financial Times* and the *Daily Worker/Morning Star*. Of these eight, two were strongly Labour supporting, the *Daily Mirror* and the *Herald/Sun* (a very different paper in format, content and outlook from that of today), while the *Guardian* abandoned its traditional Liberalism to support Labour. Four were strongly supportive of the

---

[617] For the impact of the mass media generally see Seymour-Ure, Colin, *The Political Impact of the Mass Media* (London: Constable, 1974); and the same author's, *The British Press and Broadcasting since 1945* (Oxford: Basil Blackwell, 1991)

[618] Butler, David and Donald Stokes, *Political Change in Britain: The Evolution of Electoral Choice* (London: Macmillan, 2nd ed, 1974), p.116

Conservatives; the *Daily Express,* the *Daily Mail,* the *Daily Telegraph* and the *Daily Sketch,* whilst the *Times* was more cautiously and qualifiedly Conservative. On the whole their readership shared the partisan preferences of the newspapers. Prior to that, in the 1950s, there had been one other mass circulation daily, the *News Chronicle,* a Liberal paper that met its demise in 1960 and was absorbed into the *Daily Mail.*

On capital punishment the *Daily Mirror* and the *Guardian* came out early and strongly for abolition, whereas the *Daily Telegraph* and the *Daily Mail* were hostile to it. Nonetheless there were some deviations from the expected line. The *Daily Telegraph,* by late 1964, came out for abolition, albeit somewhat reluctantly so, to the delight of the abolitionists (and probably the dismay of much of its Conservative voting and pro-hanging readership). Notwithstanding the right-wing bias of the press the balance of opinion may have been somewhat for abolition, indicating a tendency for some Conservative papers to take a fairly liberal line on the matter, and the Labour-inclined papers to be strongly abolitionist. In this respect the press followed the lines of the party configuration, given that a considerable minority of Conservatives were abolitionist. Thus the press did not altogether reflect the overall state of British public opinion, given that the total readership of the abolitionist papers was probably rather greater than the size of the minority of public opinion that favoured abolition. This fact, however, did not seem to exert any influence on public opinion which was steadfastly pro-hanging, largely irrespective of paper read.

Of all of the national newspapers the most prestigious and influential, then as now, was the *Times.* Its position in the 1950s was moderately but consistently retentionist. Typical was a leader of January 1956 which said that moderate supporters of the gallows would wish to see it rarely used 'but would keep it standing to mark society's extreme horror of the greatest crime, except treason, known to the law in the hope that they may thus foster such an instinctive aversion from the act that no normal person will ever commit it.'[619]

By the 1960s it had modified its views to the point of teetering over the brink into outright abolitionism. It accounted for the renewal of the abolition drive by the 'obvious inadequacies of the Homicide Act', and it conceded, moreover, that any attempt to redefine categories of murder was a waste of time:-[620]

> ...it can hardly be maintained that a system which results in an average of four executions a year has any real effectiveness as a deterrent. Neither can that system be justified as a denunciation of what society regards as the most detestable crime, when the authors of the most detestable crimes, do not, in most cases, pay the final penalty. In such circumstances execution has degenerated into a totem and totems have no place in adult societies. Legislative opinion has moved closer towards abolition in the

---

[619] Leader - *The Times,* 19th January 1956
[620] Leader - *The Times,* 18th December 1964

past ten years. It is now time to take the last step.

By 1969, however, it had retreated somewhat from that advanced position, asserting that hanging may have acted as a deterrent for some organized criminals carrying a firearm and committing murder in the course of crime.[621]

Whilst the *Times* was the voice of the Establishment, the *Guardian* (the *Manchester Guardian* prior to 1959) was the authentic voice of the liberal intelligentsia, and took a consistently left of centre line on most issues. On hanging it was predictably supportive of abolition from an early stage, and in 1956 urged support of the abolition amendment, albeit in fairly restrained terms.[622] 'Perhaps a five-year suspension would best represent the views which have been making headway in this country. For the rising tide which threatens to swamp the gallows is not so much one of outrage against its wickedness (though this element is there) as of scepticism about its usefulness.' By the 1960s its abolitionism was more enthusiastic and confident: 'This is a momentous step, though the first step only...we ought to pay far more attention to the reformative possibilities of prisons than we do, and not only on the deterrent effect.'[623] By 1969 it had become even more stridently abolitionist, and its opposition to reinstatement was ferocious in its intensity:-[624]

> Capital punishment is state murder...nor should statistics be used to cloud the issue...They are not the main factor...Until its abolition capital punishment was a unique survival from an earlier and more brutal age...The death penalty admits of no error. It admits of no repentance either...cases of reprieved men who have reformed themselves are not uncommon. As long as this is so...the arguments in favour of hanging have to be overwhelming. But they are not.

Whilst the *Guardian* was the quality newspaper of the political left, its counterpart of the right was the *Daily Telegraph*. Its brand of conservatism was strongly paternalist and socially traditional, and unsurprisingly this predisposed it to a stout defence of hanging, at any rate in the earlier days of the controversy in the 1955-7 period, basing its defence solidly on its deterrent effect, the need for some form of retribution and the unpreparedness of the general public for abolition: 'It is re-assuring to find so large a proportion of the public still unconvinced by the emotional and often irrelevant arguments with which they have been assailed.'[625]

By the mid-1960s however, it had modified its views, perhaps simply in recognition of the inevitable. In an editorial that surprised many on both sides of the debate it declared that:-

---

[621] Leader - 'Politics of debate' *The Times*, 15th December 1969

[622] Leader - 'Day of Decision', *The Manchester Guardian*, 16th February 1956

[623] Leader - *The Guardian*, 22nd December 1964

[624] Leader – 'A Decision of Conscience', *The Guardian*, 9th December 1969

[625] Leader – 'Penalty of Death', *The Daily Telegraph*, 6th February 1956

> If, as seems certain, the Government promptly fulfils its election pledge by finding time early in the new Parliament for the introduction of a Private Member's Bill abolishing hanging, all but the most fanatical retentionists will breathe a sigh of relief. The argument has gone on ad nauseum. What is certain is that the law as it stands...cannot conceivably be maintained. To restore hanging as the uniform punishment for murder would equally run counter to increasingly strong currents of opinion.[626]

By the end of the decade the *Daily Telegraph* had more or less maintained its quasi-abolitionism, and its coverage of the confirmatory votes in 1969 centred, as did that of much of the Conservative press, on the side issue of the government's alleged chicanery in seeking to suppress the Blom-Cooper/Morris report which, it erroneously claimed, showed a significant increase in the murder rate.[627]

The only other quality paper then in existence was the *Financial Times*, which was dedicated to economic affairs. In the 1950s, as for most of its history, it had little or no coverage of non-financial matters, and even by 1964 the non-economic coverage was minimal. By 1969, however, it had expanded to embrace some reportage of politics and other areas. Politically it was regarded as centrist, notwithstanding its obvious support for and embrace of free market capitalism. Its columnist, 'Justinian', discussed the hanging question and though ambivalent in tone seemed to come down on the abolitionist side.[628] A leader just before the crucial vote came down clearly against re-introduction.[629]

Thus of the four quality broadsheets then on offer all were, by the 1960s, abolitionist to a greater or lesser extent, though the degree of zeal varied according to the paper's general political line, with the right-wing *Telegraph* the least enthusiastic and the centre-left *Guardian* the most. When it came to the mid-market papers, however, the two titles on the market throughout the period were both right-wing and populist, often strongly so, and this tended to be reflected in their stance on hanging. The *Daily Mail* did not stress the issue all that heavily, though a front page murder story of February 1956, just after the successful abolition vote, was headlined *First 'I Can't Hang' Murderer*, illustrating the tendency of the more down-market press to put an editorial gloss on news stories and to attempt to exploit popular misconceptions to achieve the desired spin, given that many readers, as it suspected, would not have appreciated that the Parliamentary vote did not, of itself, have any legislative

---

[626] Leader – 'Exit the Gallows', *The Daily Telegraph*, 26th October 1964

[627] 'Censorship Protest on Hangings' by John Kemp (social services correspondent). *The Daily Telegraph*, 11th December 1969. This proved to be rather a non-story because the report's authors said that it was their decision not to publish it.

[628] Justinian 'Crime and Punishment – the hangman's dilemma', *The Financial Times*, 15th December 1969

[629] Leader – 'Politics and Conscience', *The Financial Times*, 17th December 1969

effect.[630] An editorial a few days later approved the government's decision not to legislate on its own account and urged that MPs should 'think twice' before exercising their judgment it if were contrary to that of the people and stating that the House had gone far ahead of public opinion.[631]

By 1964 its hostility to abolition had mellowed to the point of reluctant acquiescence, if not avid acceptance, though it gave prominence to an NOP poll that showed that 67% of those sampled wanted hanging retained.[632] Five years on and its editorial line did not seem to have resiled from that position, though it published an article by Conservative MP Jock Bruce-Gardyne, explaining why he had changed from being abolitionist in 1964 to retentionist now, chiefly because he felt MPs must not flout the will of the people.[633]

But if the *Daily Mail* was ambivalent on the question its mid-market rival the *Daily Express* had no such doubts. The *Express*, with its unerring instinct for the lost cause, was the most strongly retentionist of all the mass circulation papers. On the eve of the key vote of February 1956 an editorial, headed 'Keep Murder Risky', opined that: 'A long and wearisome agitation reaches its climax today...' and dismissed the recent case in which three men had been released on appeal after being wrongly convicted of the wounding of a policeman as an irrelevance.[634] Unlike the *Daily Telegraph* and the *Daily Mail* which had softened their retentionist stance by the mid-1960s, almost to the point of becoming abolitionist, the *Express* maintained its hardline position. A feature on hanging discussed it from the point of view of the family or friends of the victims in several murder cases, some high profile, some not.[635] By 1969 it had to concede that the verdict of Parliament was beyond doubt, but emphasized that future Parliaments were not bound by this one.[636]

The *News Chronicle* was traditionally a Liberal supporting paper, and correspondingly liberal in its social outlook. Predictably therefore it strongly supported abolition. It welcomed the government's desire to reform the law of murder in 1956, which it caricatured as a 'practically medieval system', and approved its proposed recognition of 'diminished provocation' [sic] and revision of the law of constructive malice, but argued that: 'what is needed to bring Britain into line with other civilised countries is the suspension of the

---

[630] 'First 'I Can't Hang' Murderer', *The Daily Mail*, 20th February 1956

[631] Leader – 'To Hang or Not?', *The Daily Mail*, 24th February 1956

[632] 'Hanging: Most want to keep it' by Walter Terry, political correspondent, *The Daily Mail*, 21st December 1964

[633] Jock Bruce-Gardyne, 'Do MPs take enough notice of the people?', *The Daily Mail*, 16th December 1969

John (Jock) Bruce-Gardyne, Baron Bruce-Gardyne, (1930-1990), Conservative MP for South Angus and the Mearns 1964-74, Knutsford 1979-83

[634] Leader – 'Keep Murder Risky', *The Daily Express*, 15th February 1956

[635] Magnus Linklater 'Verdict on Hanging. By people who really know', *The Daily Express*, 16th December 1964

[636] Leader – 'Setting a Dangerous Pattern', *The Daily Express*, 19th December 1969

death penalty.'[637] The *Daily Herald* was the only Labour supporting mid-market paper. Its stance, too, was strongly abolitionist. In 1956 it regretted that the government had seen fit to put forward proposals intended to retain the 'barbarism and savagery' of hanging, which did not address the problem that 'innocent people can hang – and some have almost certainly done so.'[638] In 1964 the *Herald* metamorphosed into the *Sun*, still a mid-market, Labour-supporting broadsheet, and in its new guise it maintained its stance against hanging. In 1969, a week or so before the key vote, it carried an article on a reprieved murderer 'Frank X' who had been recently released after having been convicted in 1958.[639] On the substance of the issue the paper was unequivocal: 'Hanging People is Wrong' it stated, and this was not a matter of statistics, or popular opinion, or party advantage.[640]

There were two down-market tabloids in the 1950s, the *Daily Mirror* which was Labour supporting and the *Daily Sketch* which was Conservative and populist. The *Mirror* was abolitionist and declared in January 1956 that: 'The sooner Parliament decides for or against hanging the better.'[641] Its legendary columnist, 'Cassandra', was all for abolition, having penned a controversial article denouncing the execution of Ruth Ellis the previous year.[642] The *Daily Mirror* continued its opposition to hanging into the 1960s, though giving little coverage to the issue during the 1964 vote, probably regarding it as a foregone conclusion. In 1969 it had, curiously, a feature on Harry Allen, the leading hangman, though perforce idle for several years, who naturally favoured re-introduction.[643] The *Daily Mirror's* tabloid competitor, the *Daily Sketch*, took the opposite line from the 1950s, though its tone was generally not quite as uncompromising. A February 1956 editorial was fairly neutral but the paper organized its own postal ballot, using a cut-out and return coupon on the front page.[644] Two days after that the result of the ballot was announced which showed that 65% wanted to retain the death penalty as now, 16% wanted to hang only the worst cases and 19% wanted to abolish hanging altogether; a result that was perhaps in line with other polls, though the compromise option found curiously little favour. Despite having had only one day in which to respond before its announcement the poll was apparently very large, though no

[637] Leader – 'Change This Law!', *The News Chronicle*, 10th February 1956
[638] Leader – 'What we think' - 'Doubt and the Hangman', *The Daily Herald*, 13th February 1956
[639] 'I was only Twenty...I didn't Want to Hang' - Frank X talks to Elizabeth Prosser, *The Sun*, 10th December 1969
[640] 'The Sun Says' – 'Hanging People is Wrong', *The Sun*, 15th December 1969
[641] Leader 'Hangman's Holiday', *The Daily Mirror*, 25th January 1956
[642] William Neil Connor (1909-1967). Columnist for *The Daily Mirror* from 1935 to 1967. Author of many controversial articles, including one on the 'treachery' of P G Wodehouse.
[643] Harry Allen, the executioner-in-waiting 'Hanging: A Few Harsh Words', *The Daily Mirror*, 10th July 1956, *The Daily Mirror*, 11th December 1969
[644] 'Would you Hang a Killer', *The Daily Sketch*, 14th February 1956

figures were given.[645] A leader a month later came out clearly for retention citing the poll result, as if such legitimation were crucial to its calculations, and ascribing the success of the abolitionists to the efforts of an 'intensive pressure group.'[646]

By 1964 the *Sketch*, along with most of the right-wing press, had moved with the tide to the extent of muting its enthusiasm for hanging. Five years later it took the view that hanging should not be brought back, conceding, as many former pro-hangers did not, that there was no significant rise in the number of murders committed by professional criminals against whom the death penalty was chiefly directed, though the available figures were 'too meagre to be conclusive.'[647]

The only other national newspaper was the *Daily Worker* (later the *Morning Star*), a Communist supporting paper which specialized heavily in political and industrial news and, like the *Financial Times*, cannot be regarded as an ordinary mass circulation newspaper. Its stance, too, was strongly abolitionist. Llew Gardner, in his regular column, declared in ringing tones that, 'The death penalty must go' and dismissed the government compromise as an obvious attempt to confuse the issue.[648] The victory of the Bill on second reading a month later was lauded on the front page.[649] The paper maintained its support into the 1960s, being favourable to abolition in 1964. In 1969 its front page declared 'Good Riddance to Britain's Hangman.'[650]

Sunday newspapers

A similar tendency was evident with the Sunday newspapers, with the more right-wing papers tending to favour retention and the more left-wing favouring abolition, especially in the earlier period of the controversy in the 1950s. This cut right across the market position of the papers. The *Sunday Times*, not originally associated with the *Times*, came out against abolition in 1956, declaring that the death penalty ought to be retained because 'in an imperfect world' it was necessary as the 'last instrument of human justice and social order.'[651] By 1964 it had moved, along with most Conservative papers, to a more neutral position. On the eve of the crucial second reading vote it gave space for proponents of both sides to put their case; Sir John Hobson, former Tory attorney-general, for the retentionists and Reginald Paget, QC, MP for the

---

[645] 'Hanging Must Stay: The People's Verdict', *The Daily Sketch*, 16th February 1956

[646] Leader – 'Listen to the People', *The Daily Sketch*, 12th March 1956

[647] The Sketch Says: 'Why Hurry on Hanging', *The Daily Sketch*, 16th December 1969

[648] Llew Gardner – 'To Hang or Not to Hang', *The Daily Worker*, 16th February 1956

[649] *The Daily Worker*, 13th March 1956

[650] 'Good riddance to Britain's hangman', *The Daily Worker*, 19th December 1969

[651] Editorial – 'The Death Penalty', *The Sunday Times*, 12th February 1956

abolitionists.[652] By 1969 it was more or less abolitionist, conceding that there was little statistical evidence for its supposed unique deterrent effect, notwithstanding the efforts of Sandys and the hanging lobby to find some.[653]

The other chief Sunday broadsheet in the 1950s was the liberal *Observer*, whose proprietor and editor from 1948-75, David Astor, was a strong abolitionist. It came out early and strongly for abolition, giving wide coverage to the movement and providing a regular platform for polemicists such as Koestler, whose *Reflections on Hanging* was serialized in the paper in 1956. In February 1956 it argued for MPs to be guided by conscience because if Parliament had waited for public opinion then few penal reforms would ever have got through.[654] The *Observer* maintained its liberal outlook and unsurprisingly continued to support abolition into the 1960s, acclaiming the vote of December 1964 as a 'resounding condemnation of an odious practice.'[655] In 1969 it argued that Callaghan was right to push ahead with the abolition vote because there was nothing immoral in allowing political considerations to dictate the timing and 'there should be no holding back in such a reform which humanity and reason plainly recommend.'[656]

The quality end of the Sunday market was monopolized by the *Sunday Times* and the *Observer* until the founding of the *Sunday Telegraph* in 1961 as the complement to the *Daily Telegraph*. It took a similarly Conservative line, though, like its weekday sister, by 1964 it was not hostile to abolition. In 1969, however, the paper seemed to revert to type. Charles Curran, a Conservative MP who had penned a piece opposing abolition many years before in the *Evening News*, attacked the premature vote and stressed that public opinion was on the opposite side from the 'talking classes'.[657]

The *Sunday Express* took the same hardline position against abolition as its weekday equivalent. In 1956 Anthony Fell, Conservative MP, denounced abolition, saying that: 'Once again the sentimentalists are in full cry...' and asking what is the alternative given that genuine life imprisonment would be intolerable?[658] The tone had not changed by 1964. Percy Howard argued that in order to win over the judges such as Parker, the then Lord Chief Justice, the abolitionists had become enthusiastic supporters of life sentences.[659] In 1969 it gave a platform to Duncan Sandys for him to denounce the government for

---

[652] Editorial – 'Out of its time', *The Sunday Times*, 13th December 1964

[653] Editorial – 'Politics of the Rope', *The Sunday Times*, 14th December 1969

[654] Comment, *The Observer*, 12th February 1956

[655] Editorial - *The Observer*, 27th December 1964

[656] Editorial 'Going against the views of the public', *The Observer*, 14th December 1969

[657] Charles Curran, 'Who Should Decide on Hanging?', *The Sunday Telegraph*, 14th December 1969

[658] Anthony Fell, 'If Hanging Goes – These are the Fearful Choices that We Face', *The Sunday Express*, 29th January 1956

[659] Percy Howard, 'Abolish the Death Penalty? The answer must be NO', *The Sunday Express*, 6th December 1964

trying to bounce Parliament, as he saw it, into confirming abolition, because abolition was an 'unwritten article of Socialist policy.'[660] Of the newspapers that were still extant in the 1950s but disappeared in the early 1960s under the impact of television and rising costs notable was *Reynolds News* which supported Labour and the Co-operative movements.[661] As a left-wing paper it predictably supported abolition and dismissed the government compromise as a bad idea. Hanging should be abolished not reformed.[662]

The right-wing, populist *News of the World* was the most prominent of the down-market Sundays. It took a cautious position in the 1950s, noting that many had changed their minds and that the debate centred on the deterrent value: 'in these days of the gangster with the gun and the cosh.'[663] It argued for a period of suspension, after which 'the results would speak for themselves.' By 1964 its position was still unclear, arguing only that in the event of abolition the actual length of a life sentence should be fixed by the judge at trial rather than decided by the Home Secretary of the day given that judges were the ones in the best position to assess the murderer.[664]

After the slaying of three police officers in the summer of 1966, however, all caution and equivocation was thrown to the winds as the paper launched a virulent campaign to restore hanging for the murder of police and prison officers (at least). The story dominated the front page (as it did with all of the national press) under a headline that announced the start of a 'bring back hanging' campaign.[665] This was accompanied by a front page opinion piece which called for 'Tough Action Now' against violent crime, and an inside page article by a former head of Scotland Yard CID, Sir Richard Jackson, who argued that the police shootings were an inevitable consequence of the repeal of the Homicide Act the previous year[sic].[666] Next week the paper carried another front page article asking readers if hanging should return for the murder of police and prison officers, and, in a familiar device, carried a cut-out and return coupon for readers to vote on the question.[667] The next edition announced that there had been an 'amazing response' to the ballot, and reprinted the coupon, while an editorial declared that they would keep the campaign going.[668] The next week's front page gave the result of the poll, and, to the surprise of no-one,

---

[660] Duncan Sandys 'Before Callaghan Jumps the Gun', *The Sunday Express*, 14th December 1969

[661] *Newspaper Press Directory and Advertisers Guide* (London: Benn Brothers, 1956)

[662] Editorial 'Why Cling to the Rope?' *Reynolds News and Sunday Citizen*, 12th February 1956

[663] Editorial 'Hanging: The Vital Question', *The News of the World*, 12th February 1956

[664] Editorial 'Let the Judges decide', *The News of the World*, 13th December 1964

[665] 'The Fury Grows 'Bring back hanging' Campaign begins', *The News of the World*, 14th August 1966

[666] Sir Richard Jackson, CBE, 'A Licence to Kill', *The News of the World*, 14th August 1966

[667] 'Should we bring back HANGING?', *The News of the World*, 28th August 1966

[668] Editorial 'Voice of the nation', *The News of the World*, 4th September 1966

there was an overwhelming majority for restoration with 99.4% in favour.[669] The *News of the World* campaign dovetailed neatly with the corresponding movement in Parliament led by Sandys from the Conservative backbenches, which aspired, at least initially, to bring back hanging for the murder of police and prison officers, and which came to a head in November of that year with the failed attempt to get a second reading for a Bill to that effect, and the next edition carried an article by Eldon Griffiths, Conservative MP, about the Sandys Bill.[670]

Curiously though, despite the *News of the World's* zeal for restoration and its stated intention to keep the campaign going, there was little more coverage of either its own campaign or that of Sandys once the furore over the Shepherds Bush killings had died down. It may well be that for all its ardour it recognized that the campaign was not going to be successful, at any rate not in the short-term, and that there was really nowhere else for the campaign to go. By 1969 its enthusiasm had died away altogether and there seems to have been little or no coverage of that year's vote, except for Auberon Waugh's column which praised Edward Heath for having the courage to vote for abolition.[671]

Another down-market Sunday newspaper still extant in the 1950s was the *Sunday Pictorial*. Its strapline was the 'Newspaper for the Young in Heart' whatever that was supposed to mean, and it was basically a left-leaning paper. Wilfred Fienburgh, Labour MP, had a regular column, which damned the government compromise in 1956, and praised Chuter Ede for having the courage to admit he had been wrong about hanging.[672] The *Pictorial* disappeared in the 1960s and was reborn as the *Sunday Mirror* in 1963. The *Sunday Mirror* was, like its weekday sister paper the *Daily Mirror*, a Labour supporting and left-leaning paper. It supported abolition in 1964 declaring that Britain was 'catching up with civilization' and that 'HANGING IS WRONG' and 'HANGING MUST GO'.[673] In 1969 it declared that abolition was a triumph and that society was now more civilized and more humane.[674]

The *People*, another down-market Sunday, was the only other paper existing in the 1950s that survived into the 1960s and beyond. Hannan Swaffer used his column to argue that the prospects for abolition were bright and wondered whether the peers would use their veto to obstruct the Commons

---

[669] *The News of the World*, 11th September 1966. The actual figures were 127,384 for and 680 against, and of the 680 antis 150 voted that way because they wanted restoration for all murders.

[670] Eldon Griffiths, *The News of the World*, 18th September 1966

[671] Auberon Waugh, *The News of the World*, 21st December 1969

[672] Wilfred Fienburgh, 'Beyond the News', *The Sunday Pictorial*, 12th February 1956. Some of the figures he quoted about the numbers of persons convicted and reprieved were so off beam that it seems likely that he had little knowledge of the question.

[673] Editorial – 'The End of Vengeance', *The Sunday Mirror*, 20th December 1964

[674] Editorial – 'Epitaph for the hangman', *The Sunday Mirror*, 21st December 1969

again and thereby hasten their own end.[675] The paper came out very strongly for abolition in its editorials.[676] In 1964 there was little or no coverage of the question, but in 1969 it was still pro-abolition and dismissive of the whole controversy as a dangerous waste of time, while the nation should focus on other matters.[677]

London evening newspapers

There were in the 1950s three London evening newspapers:- the *Evening News,* the *Evening Standard* and the *Evening Star* (absorbed into the *Evening News* in 1960). Each was associated with one of the daily nationals, and their politics tended to reflect that of the sister paper, though generally they avoided being too avowedly partisan. The *Evening News,* owned by Associated Newspapers Ltd that owned the *Daily Mail* and the *Daily Sketch* and the *Sunday Dispatch*, was predictably right-wing. On hanging it was, in 1956, editorially neutral and fairly even-handed in its coverage, giving space to articles by both Charles Curran against abolition and Sir Ernest Gowers in favour. In the 1960s, by which time the paper had absorbed the *Star*, there was little prominence given in its pages to the abolition controversy.

The *Evening Standard* was associated with the *Daily Express* and the Beaverbrook group and was also a right-wing paper, though it characterized itself as 'independent' (as did most of the Conservative press). The *Standard* was rather more retentionist than the *Evening News*, as might have been supposed given the attitude of the *Express*, though relatively even-handed. An editorial of February 1956 urged MPs to keep calm and do their best on the evidence, but warned that they should not 'lightly cast away a penalty which the majority of the public and the Government earnestly believe offers the best protection the law can devise against calculated murder.'[678] By the 1960s ownership had changed hands and it was no longer associated with the *Express*. This may have altered its political outlook. In 1964 it ventured only a rather neutral piece which urged better prison security in the light of the greatly increased number of lifers and the recent spate of escapes, but had nothing to say on the substance of the question.[679] But by 1969 the paper had become strongly abolitionist, saying that legislators should be supported unequivocally in voting away hanging, and only criticizing the government for rushing the vote.[680]

---

[675] Hannan Swaffer, *The People*, 5th February 1956

[676] Editorial – 'Stop it!', *The People*, 12th February 1956

[677] 'The Voice of the People' (editorial) 'An Old Man's Row', *The People*, 14th December 1969

[678] Editorial – 'The Last Barrier', *The Evening Standard*, 16th February 1956

[679] Editorial – 'A Long Stretch', *The Evening Standard*, 22nd December 1964

[680] Editorial – 'No more hanging', *The Evening Standard*, 15th December 1969

The third London evening of the 1950s was the *Star*, self-described as independent progressive and associated with the Liberal *News Chronicle*. Like the *Chronicle*, and unlike its two London rivals, it took a strongly abolitionist line. It exulted in the anti-hanging vote of February 1956, declaring it to be a great day for the abolitionists and deriding the idea that there should be an experimental trial period.[681] In 1960 the paper was swallowed up by the *Evening News*.

Thus the London evening papers mirrored the tendencies of the national daily and Sunday press in that their stance on hanging was a function of their general political outlook, at any rate in the 1950s, with the one progressive paper, the *Star*, taking a strongly abolitionist line and the others not. By the 1960s the two papers remaining, both moderately right-wing, tended to follow most of the Conservative press in acceding to abolition. This shadowing is scarcely remarkable given the common ownership and close associations existing between them.

Provincial and local newspapers

The provincial press was numerous, but generally did not take a strong line on politics in general or capital punishment in particular, though there were exceptions, and certainly the regional papers tended to be more partisan than strictly local papers. As with the national press the general tendency was for Labour or Liberal supporting papers to favour abolition and for Conservative supporting ones to oppose it, though far from universally so.

The *Daily Record*, for example, the largest circulation Scotland-wide newspaper, and Labour supporting, took an abolitionist line in 1956: 'The Daily Record believes the gallows should go. We declare that from the experience of abolitionist countries the deterrent value of hanging is at least doubtful.'[682] It maintained this line into the 1960s, declaring in December 1964 that the abolition bill marked 'An End to Savagery' but insisting that punishment for murder must be 'hard and long'.[683] The other major Scots newspaper, the *Scotsman*, a more upmarket paper and Conservative supporting, was largely silent on capital punishment in 1956, though the issue featured prominently in its correspondence columns. By 1964 it had moved from silence to neutrality but by 1969 it gave extensive coverage to the debate and signified its cautious welcome of abolition.[684]

The *Yorkshire Post,* then as now, was one of the largest circulation regional newspapers with national news coverage and national distribution, and

---

[681] Editorial – 'No Undue Delay – We Hope', *The Star*, 17th February 1956
[682] 'Verdict on Hanging' - editorial, *The Daily Record* (Scotland), 16th February 1956
[683] 'An End to Savagery' – editorial, *The Daily Record*, 22nd December 1964
[684] 'Death Penalty' – editorial, *The Scotsman*, 22nd December 1964; 'The Hanging Debate' part 1, 16th December 1969, part 2, 19th December 1969, *The Scotsman*.

like the two Scottish papers mentioned above it was daily. It was a staunchly Conservative paper from its inception and was rather hostile to abolition. In 1956 its editorials consistently supported the government compromise proposals, opposed outright abolition and favoured the retention of hanging for the murder of police officers especially.[685] It was, if anything, more strongly opposed to abolition by 1964, arguing that if hanging went the police would have to be armed and that the gallows was an essential deterrent. If abolition were to be enacted it urged that it should be subject to annual review and renewal.[686] By 1969 it took the standard Conservative line that the government should not have hastened the decision, but it seemed to have softened its stance on the principle by conceding that there was little hard evidence of hanging's deterrent value but that commonsense suggested that some professional criminals would be less likely to carry firearms.[687]

It is unlikely that the provincial press had any more influence on public opinion than had the national press. Their circulation and area of distribution were generally very restricted, and though there may have been a slight tendency for people to identify with a local paper rather more than with a national because of its local associations it is unlikely that this would have offset their basic lack of political weightiness.

Political and specialist periodicals

Amongst the political periodicals the position was rather different with a very heavy consensus for abolition, even and perhaps especially among the right-wing ones. This may be partly because, catering to a more high-brow readership, it did not feel the need to pander to what it saw as populist sentiment, or perhaps simply that the proprietorship and editorship of these organs happened to be in the hands of abolitionist minded people at the relevant time. The *Spectator* and the *Economist* were as strongly abolitionist in tone as were the *New Statesman* and *Tribune*, if not more so.

Certainly the right-wing *Spectator* was in the vanguard of the abolitionist campaign under the proprietorship of the very liberal Conservative, Ian Gilmour, from 1954-67 and the editorship of Gilmour himself (1954-59), Brian Inglis (1959-62), and Iain Macleod (1963-65). As early as 1955 Gilmour was penning leaders condemning hanging as judicial barbarism and pouring scorn on Home Secretaries for their continued support of it and their failure to grant reprieves when they were clearly indicated. Maxwell Fyfe's failure to reprieve

---

[685] 'The death penalty' – editorial, 16th February 1956; 'Momentous decision' – editorial, 17th February 1956; 'Protect the police' editorial, 13th March 1956, *The Yorkshire Post*
[686] 'If Hanging Goes: Must the Police Be Armed?' by J P Eddy, QC; 19th December 1964; 'Thugs Charter?' – editorial, 22nd December 1964. *The Yorkshire Post*
[687] 'Unfinished' – editorial, *The Yorkshire Post*, 17th December 1969

Bentley was the 'worst decision since the hanging of Mrs Thompson.'[688] Unsurprisingly, this attitude did not find favour with all of the *Spectator's* subscribers, and one letter attacked the 'wholesale indictment of the last three home secretaries' and described it as a 'scurrilous article' and 'a disgrace to journalism.'[689]

This rather intense campaign by the *Spectator* tended to fall away somewhat after 1957 with the failure of the Silverman Bill, and Gilmour's decision to hand over the editorship to others, though his successors in the chair were also liberal Tories and abolitionists in the form of Brian Inglis and Iain Macleod. By 1964, and the revival of the issue, the paper had, however, more or less maintained its abolitionist stance, though perhaps slightly less virulently so. After Macleod the editorship passed to Tories of, perhaps, a slightly less liberal stamp such as Nigel Lawson and George Gale, though both were nonetheless inclined to abolitionism. A leader penned by Lawson in 1969 argued that the Lords would have been perfectly justified in frustrating the government's attempt to 'bounce' Parliament into making abolition permanent.[690] Why had such a right-wing journal been so consistently abolitionist? It almost certainly did not reflect the views of the bulk of its Conservative readership, as evidenced by the apoplectic reaction of some of them, and neither was it in tune with most of the Conservative press of the time. It undoubtedly reflected the views of its then proprietor/editor, Ian Gilmour, and of others who wrote for the paper such as Christopher Hollis and John Grigg, both liberal Tories and prominent members of the newly-formed NCACP.

The other chief right-wing periodical, the *Economist,* was, curiously, also strongly abolitionist at this time, though this was perhaps less surprising given that historically it had been socially liberal, and its conservatism was chiefly of an economic *laissez-faire* variety. As with the *Spectator* it was the Ruth Ellis case that fired up its indignation over capital punishment. 'Does anybody suppose that this hanging will have done anything to discourage murderesses of this woman's type and her state of mind?'[691]

On the left the *New Statesman* was predictably abolitionist, though arguably less violently so than its right-wing competitor, the *Spectator*, and it tended to give the question less coverage. One of its contributors was C H Rolph, a prominent member of the NCACP, who was the chief progenitor of articles on the matter in its pages. He argued that the death penalty must be abolished 'boldly and totally – not as a negative step in the amelioration of the law but as the beginning of a new approach to the entire problem of crime in the

---

[688] 'Judicial Barbarism' – leading article (Gilmour), *The Spectator*, 11th February 1955

[689] E H Cobb, Basingstoke to editor, *The Spectator*, 18th February 1955

[690] 'Murder is not a party game' – leading article (Nigel Lawson), *The Spectator*, 20th December 1969

[691] 'The Ellis Case', *The Economist*, 16th July 1955, vol 176, no 5838

20th century.'[692] The *New Statesman's* left-wing rival *Tribune*, a more down-market and concentratedly political publication, was also abolitionist, though as with the *New Statesman* it did not give great prominence to the issue, possibly because it was conscious that the issue did not necessarily play all that well with some of its working-class and trade union supporters. After the February 1956 victory for the abolitionists Mervyn Jones declared in its pages that: 'The vote to end capital punishment is a triumph of civilisation over the dark forces in men's minds and in society.'[693] However, not all its readers were as enamoured of abolition as its writers. One letter-writer questioned why so much energy was devoted to the question which was not a political one. 'How ironical it is to find the ranks closed and the whole body of Labour so unitedly and dutifully sinking their differences in one grand gesture to inaugurate THE MURDERERS CHARTER!'[694] A few years later and Silverman was given the freedom of *Tribune's* pages to write a stirring defence of his abolition bill on the eve of its second reading.[695] In 1969 it celebrated the victory of abolition in the confirmatory vote: 'Despite the frenzied retentionist campaign the Lords finally ensured that hanging will never come back.'[696]

Of all the mass circulation magazines the one that went most strongly with the issue, at any rate in the critical mid-1950s phase of the campaign, was the weekly *Picture Post*, which announced it as 'the moral issue of the year', i.e. 1956, in its final edition of 1955.[697] It pulled no punches in its coverage, declaring melodramatically that: 'We believe that human life is sacred: that for any man acting for the ordinary men and women of Britain, coldly and grotesquely to end a human life, is a desecration of the law of humanity and the law of God.' The demise of the Abolition Bill was followed not too long afterwards (in July 1957) by the demise of the magazine itself due to falling circulation. It is not too clear why it took such a strong stand on capital punishment, though it had the reputation of being a fairly left-wing publication, and it was possibly looking for an issue upon which to take a stand and recapture its former reputation as a campaigning organ.

Clearly there was a very heavy consensus for abolition amongst the mass circulation periodicals and magazines, on the right as embodied by the *Spectator* and the *Economist* as much as on the left, as embodied by the *New Statesman*, *Tribune*, and perhaps *Picture Post* (though the last was more a general interest magazine than a political one). However, these publications had relatively small circulations compared to the national dailies and Sundays, and,

---

[692] Rolph, C H, 'Abolition and After', *New Statesman and Nation*, 24th March 1956, vol 51, no 1306

[693] Jones, Mervyn, 'Hanging: Watch Out for the Lords', *Tribune*, 24th February 1956

[694] Letter to editor, E Lesels (Salford), *Tribune*, 9th March 1956

[695] Silverman, Sydney, *Tribune*, December 1964

[696] 'Hanging – an end to barbarity', *Tribune*, 26th December 1969

[697] 'The Moral issue of the Year', *Picture Post*, 31st December 1955

in the case of all except *Picture Post*, a rather untypical readership. The dailies were probably less influential than they supposed themselves to be, and it is difficult to think that the weeklies had much impact on the general public or the government of the day.

The most striking thing about the stance taken by a newspaper on the issue was the way that it seemed largely conditioned by the general political position of the paper, with the Conservative supporting and more right-wing papers usually taking a fairly retentionist stance and the Labour supporting and more left-wing papers adopting an abolitionist stance. This of course merely reflected the balance of opinion within the parties themselves nationally and, probably, the feelings of the bulk of the readership of the paper concerned. This was especially true in the 1950s when the Conservative Party 'house journal' the *Daily Telegraph*, the Conservative-leaning *Times* and the right-wing *Daily Express, Daily Mail* and *Daily Sketch* all came out for retention and the Labour supporting *Daily Herald* and *Daily Mirror*, and the Liberal *Manchester Guardian* and *News Chronicle* came out decidedly for abolition. This also roughly matched the balance of opinion in the country because the right-wing papers tended to have a wider circulation than their competitors, though the *Mirror* probably outsold the *Sketch* at the bottom end of the market. On the other hand there was no correlation with position in the market, with quality broadsheets, mid-market and down-market papers all split. This again reflected the political realities where attitudes to hanging showed no effect of social class, but some effect of party preference. There was clearly a symbiotic relationship between the newspapers, the political parties, pressure group activity and informed public opinion, with the different actors feeding off each other and reinforcing their respective viewpoints. Leading abolitionists were often given a platform in the liberal papers to expound their views and advertise their activities, such as Koestler at the *Observer*, and the same was true to a lesser extent on the other side of the debate.

Did the press have any great influence on the course of the debate and the ultimate victory of the abolition movement? This seems unlikely, notwithstanding the huge amount of newsprint devoted to the topic at different times. As mentioned a newspaper did not seem to possess much capacity to influence its readership on this, or any other question, and it had little traction on Parliament and the government despite Herculean efforts, particularly on the part of the retentionist papers, at seeking to convince these bodies that they articulated the outrage of vast swathes of popular opinion. On hanging Parliament seemed largely indifferent to public opinion.

To what extent, if at all, did the views of a newspaper, whether those of the editor or a columnist, influence the reader? As with political questions generally there is little evidence to support the contention that the press wields any great influence over its readership, and considerable evidence to suggest that it does not.[698] Views on capital punishment were usually too deeply entrenched to be susceptible to conditioning by the press. It may have reinforced views but not changed them. Generally also it is often the press that follows its readership rather than the other way about. As Trenaman and McQuail have observed on the basis of their study of the influence of press and the media campaign generally during the 1959 general election:-

> Personal political prejudices create a barrier. They are of such a nature that the individual selects what he wants to select. The only appreciable effect of the mass media on political attitudes is to reinforce or to crystallise them, but not to alter them...No medium or source of propaganda, or combination of sources had any ascertainable effect on attitude changes. And attitude changes were certainly large enough to be susceptible of effect...what is established here is not merely an absence of cause and effect, but a definite and consistent barrier between sources of communication and movements of attitude in the political field at a General Election.[699]

What applies to a general election campaign surely applies to a more specific political campaign also.

Books and Pamphlets

The literature on the question of capital punishment and its abolition was profuse and tended naturally to emanate chiefly from the abolitionists since it was they who were seeking to change the status quo. It tended to fall into two categories; polemical works (often merely pamphlets) inveighing against capital punishment, or works that highlighted and sought to rectify specific miscarriages of justice, real or alleged.

Of the polemical works much of the early literature was promulgated by E Roy Calvert and the NCADP, such as *Capital Punishment in the Twentieth Century* (1927); and *Death Penalty Enquiry: Being A Review of the Evidence Before the Select Committee on Capital Punishment* (1930) and *Capital*

---

[698] The consensus view is that the press, and the media in general, have very little effect on the political views, and voting patterns, of the public. 'Teeming shoals of votes do not lie ready to be trawled by press magnates', Seymour-Ure (1974), op cit. p. 203. Though there may be a considerable correlation between the views of a newspaper and those of its readership this is just as likely to be the result of the readership's influence on the newspaper as the other way about. Papers seldom persist with a policy view or a campaign if it realizes that it does not chime with the bulk of its readership. Anyway studies have demonstrated the widespread ignorance of many readers about their preferred newspaper's political allegiances. See Butler, David and Donald Stokes, op cit, pp.115-119.

[699] Trenaman, Joseph and D McQuail, *Television and the Political Image* (London: Methuen, 1961) Quoted in Finer, S E, *Anonymous Empire* (London: Pall Mall Press, 1958; 2nd ed 1966) pp. 119-20

Punishment (1936).[700] In the same vein was G D Turner's *The Alternative to Capital Punishment* (1938); John Paton's *This Hanging Business* (1938) and Theodora Calvert's pamphlet *Capital Punishment: Society Takes Revenge: An examination of the necessity for capital punishment in Britain today* (1946).[701] Also notable was Violet van der Elst's *On the Gallows* (1937) written by an indefatigable opponent of hanging. Notable here also was the celebrated satirical squib, *A Handbook on Hanging* written by a barrister, linguist and translator, Charles Duff, and published originally in 1928 which remorselessly and devastatingly ridicules the whole hanging trade in a mock antiquated style which superficially purports to laud it.[702]

In the immediate post-war era the most notable piece was Templewood's *The Shadow of the Gallows* (1951), a fairly remarkable one in that it announced the conversion (or re-conversion) of a former Conservative Home Secretary to the abolitionist cause and therefore had a somewhat greater impact than that of 'career abolitionists' such as the Calverts.[703] He agued that he was instinctively drawn to the abolitionist cause but that he dared not include it in his Criminal Justice Bill of 1938 for fear of endangering the Bill, but that the time was now ripe for a renewed effort 'to re-establish and reinforce the dignity of human life.'

The next significant book was that of another convert to the abolitionist cause, Sir Ernest Gowers with *A Life for A Life?: The Problem of Capital Punishment* (1956), and as with Templewood's it probably carried somewhat greater weight than many others.[704] He declared in his foreword that before he had taken up the chairmanship of the Commission he had given no great thought to the question and would probably have described himself as in favour of the death penalty and was 'disposed to regard abolitionists as people whose hearts were bigger than their heads. Four years of close study of the subject gradually dispelled that feeling. In the end I became convinced that the abolitionists were right...and that so far from the sentimental approach leading into their camp and the rational one into that of the supporters, it was the other

---

[700] Calvert, E Roy, *Capital Punishment in the Twentieth Century* (London: Putnam, 1927); Calvert, E Roy, *Death Penalty Enquiry: Being a Review of the Evidence Before the Select Committee on Capital Punishment* (London: Gollancz, 1930); and *Capital Punishment* (London, NCADP, revised edition, 1936).

[701] G D Turner, *The Alternatives to Capital Punishment, Roy Calvert 5th Memorial Lecture* (London: NCADP, 1938); John Paton, *This Hanging Business* (London: NCADP, 1938). Paton succeeded Calvert as general secretary. Theodora Calvert, *Capital Punishment: Society Takes Revenge: An examination of the necessity for capital punishment in Britain today* (London: NCADP, 1946). Theodora Calvert was Roy's widow.

[702] Duff, Charles, *A Handbook on Hanging: Being a Short Introduction to the Fine Art of Execution* (London: Cayme, 1928; revised and enlarged ed. London: Putnam, 1961; revised ed. Stroud: The History Press, 2011)

[703] Templewood, Viscount (Samuel Hoare), op cit.

[704] Gowers, Sir Ernest, op cit.

way about.'

From the mid-1950s the NCACP took up the baton and became responsible for the bulk of the polemical literature. Of the oeuvre of the NCACP and its membership first and foremost was Arthur Koestler's *Reflections on Hanging* published in 1956, a classical statement of the abolitionist case.[705] Koestler had of course been one of the three founders of the movement.[706] It is a brilliant piece of invective to which it is difficult to do justice without extensive quotation. Though factual in tone the book is infused with the author's passionate detestation of hanging. As he states in the preface: 'My intention was to write in a cool and detached manner, but it came to naught; indignation and pity kept seeping in...Fair pleading requires that one's facts and figures should be right...it does not exclude having one's heart and spleen in it.'[707] The book reads as a passionate denunciation of capital punishment in all its forms and a scathing indictment of hanging in practice in England down the centuries. This was the masterpiece of the abolitionist canon, though much of it has now dated badly, not only because the abolition of capital punishment has rendered much of its polemic redundant but also because of the transformation in the landscape of the English judicial system in the intervening decades. The impact of Koestler's work was doubtless considerable, though as with the polemics of the press and much of the rest of the media it is likely that most of that impact was on his fellow abolitionists. The work of Templewood and Gowers by contrast was influential, more so probably than that of Koestler, since they, unlike him, had not been dyed-in-the-wool abolitionists from the outset, and their conversions doubtless carried weight in establishment circles.

Two other leading figures in the Campaign also produced books at about this time. Gardiner published *Capital Punishment as a Deterrent and the Alternative* shortly before Koestler (with a revised second edition taking account of developments published in 1961).[708] This was a more prosaic rehearsal of the arguments for and against than Koestler's as befitted a lawyer rather than a philosopher. It was couched in self-consciously 'rational' terms and purported to deal objectively with the arguments for hanging followed by his refutation of them.

At about the same time Gollancz published *Capital Punishment: The*

---

[705] Koestler, Arthur, *Reflections on Hanging* (London: Gollancz, 1956)

[706] Arthur Koestler, 1905-1983. Hungarian born but British naturalized polymath, political writer, journalist, novelist, philosopher, scientist etc. One-time communist he became passionately anti-communist in response to Stalin's show trials and was one of the foremost opponents of Soviet expansionism in the post-war era. Founder member of the NCACP in 1955. Supporter of Lamarckianism, investigator of the paranormal and instigator of controversial theories of the origins of the Ashkenazi Jews such as himself. Committed suicide as part of a suicide pact with his third wife.

[707] Koestler, ibid, preface

[708] Gardiner, Gerald, *Capital Punishment as a Deterrent and the Alternative* (London: Gollancz, 1955) (2nd ed NCACP 1961)

Heart of the Matter, a very brief pamphlet and an impassioned and emotional treatise.[709] It pulled no punches. 'I am convinced, for my own part, not indeed that no single murder has at any time been prevented by fear of the death penalty... but that on balance the existence of the death penalty is devoid of preventive value, and may even tend in the opposite direction.'

After this initial burst of literary activity by members of the NCACP and the enactment of the Homicide Act a year or two later it became apparent that full abolition would have to wait. The abolition movement lost momentum and their literary efforts likewise started to dry up, though books and pamphlets continued to appear more sporadically. At the end of the 1950s came Roy Jenkins' *The Case for Labour* (1959), one of three Penguin 'Specials' brought out just prior to the general election of that year to argue the case for their respective parties. It included a chapter entitled *Is Britain Civilized?* in which he argued strongly for penal and social reform including abolition and castigated the record of recent Tory Home Secretaries (whom he felt the most reactionary since the 1920s) in that regard. He deprecated the fact that, though the system was operated with 'moderate humanity' by the current Home Secretary, Rab Butler, 'the ghastly apparatus of the gallows continues to exist, and is used much more often than was thought likely when the Homicide Act was passing into law.'[710]

A couple of years later came Koestler and Rolph's *Hanged by the Neck* and *Hanged in Error* by Leslie Hale, MP, both Penguin Specials published in 1961, and favourably reviewed in the *Spectator* of 15th September.[711] *Hanged by the Neck* was basically an update of Koestler's *Reflections* with additional material from Rolph including the 'police view' which was scathing about police procedures for electing representatives to the Federation and ascertaining the opinions of serving officers. A Howard League pamphlet was *The Working of the Homicide Act* by Glanville Williams. This was followed by another pamphlet *Murder in Microcosm* by Dr Terence Morris and Louis Blom-Cooper (1961) which consisted of a general discussion of murder cases that had led to hangings in the period after the passage of the Homicide Act.[712] From the same two authors came *A Calendar of Murder: Criminal Homicide in England since 1957* (1964) being a statistically based account of murder cases since the passage of the Homicide Act. That year saw the publication of Christopher

---

[709] Gollancz, Victor, *Capital Punishment: The Heart of the Matter* (London: Gollancz, 1955)

[710] Jenkins, Roy, *The Case for Labour. Why Should You Vote Labour?*, (Harmondsworth: Penguin, 1959) pp.135-146

[711] Koestler, Arthur and C H Rolph, *Hanged by the Neck: An Exposure of Capital Punishment in England* (Harmondsworth: Penguin 1961); Hale, Leslie, *Hanged in Error* (Harmondsworth: Penguin, 1961)

[712] Terence Morris and Louis Blom-Cooper, *Murder in Microcosm* (London: The Observer 1961); Terence Morris and Louis Blom-Cooper, *A Calendar of Murder: Criminal Homicide in England since 1957* (London: Michael Joseph, 1964)

Hollis' *The Homicide Act* (1964), another dispassionate account by a leading abolitionist.[713] Few if any works argued the case for retention since this was the status quo and was felt to need no defending, though Fenton Bresler's *Reprieve: A Study of a System* (1965) is a detailed study of one aspect of capital punishment which tended, if anything, to suggest that the present system was satisfactory enough.[714]

Much later came Albert Pierrepoint's *Executioner Pierrepoint* (1974), a biography in which he declared that he thought hanging 'did no good and was merely a matter of revenge.'[715] This was a staggering assertion from the man who had executed more murderers than anyone else, though it came very late in the day, eight years after abolition and seventeen years after his slightly premature retirement – ostensibly on financial grounds - and thus could not be said to have influenced the debate in any way. Nonetheless it represented the most remarkable of all the Damascene conversions (following on from those of Templewood and Gowers many years earlier). It is difficult to asses the impact and effectiveness of these many and various publications since they were very much preaching to the converted and had a small circulation.

The literature on wrongful convictions from the 1950s onwards was almost as profuse, reflecting perhaps both the steady accumulation of perceived miscarriages and the growing strength of the abolition movement which drew sustenance from these miscarriages and gave rise to the closer inspection of capital cases. Thus the campaign was both cause and effect of the miscarriage canon. Unlike the general polemical works mentioned above several of these books on specific miscarriages were highly influential and almost certainly, in their combined effect, led to the posthumous exoneration of both Timothy Evans and Derek Bentley.

There were at least four on the Timothy Evans case:- Silverman and Paget's *Hanged - and Innocent?* (1953) was an early collaboration between two leading lights of Parliamentary abolitionism which dealt with three alleged miscarriages, those of Rowland in 1946, Evans in 1950 and Bentley in 1953; Michael Eddowes' *The Man on your Conscience* (1955) followed; and Ludovic Kennedy's book on the subject *Ten Rillington Place* (1961) which was perhaps more influential than its two predecessors because published later and with the benefit of additional evidence exonerating Evans. There was also a *Spectator* pamphlet by Lord Altrincham (John Grigg) and Ian Gilmour in 1956.[716] Several

---

[713] Hollis, M Christopher, *The Homicide Act: The First Thorough Examination of how the Homicide Act has been working in Practice* (London: Gollancz, 1964)

[714] Bresler, Fenton, op cit., foreword by Chuter Ede

[715] Pierrepoint, Albert, op cit.

[716] Silverman, Sydney and Reginald Paget, *Hanged – and Innocent?* (London: Gollancz, 1953); Eddowes, Michael, *The Man on your Conscience: An Investigation of the Evans Murder Trial* (London: Cassell, 1955); Gilmour, Ian and John Grigg, *Timothy Evans: An Appeal to Reason* (Spectator pamphlet, 1956); Kennedy; Ludovic, *Ten Rillington Place*

other lesser books on the case, sometimes in conjunction with other notorious cases, were published. These were ultimately triumphant in that Evans was posthumously pardoned.

The Derek Bentley travesty arguably produced more works than any other miscarriage, partly because it took much longer for it to produce any tangible result. Foremost among these was David Yallop's *To Encourage the Others: Startling New Facts on the Craig/Bentley Murder Case* (1971) - the basis for both a BBC play of that title in 1973 and of the film *Let Him Have It* (1993). Yallop's book probably had as big an impact upon that case as had Kennedy's on the Evans case ten years earlier, leading to questions in the Commons and a debate in the House of Lords. Others books followed, most notably *Scapegoat: The Inside Story of the Trial of Derek Bentley* by John Parris in 1991, a scathing account of the trial, the judicial system, Goddard, Maxwell Fyfe and much else written by the barrister who had defended Craig. *Let Him Have It, Chris* by M J Trow (1990) was another fairly sensational account which suggested that there was another police officer on the roof who was never asked to give evidence, because his evidence would have blown the prosecution case apart! *Gangland: The Case of Bentley and Craig* by Francis Selwyn (1988) and *Dad, Help Me Please: The Story of Derek Bentley* by Christopher Berry-Dee and Robin Odell (1993) are other recent contributions to the canon. Much earlier Bentley's father had published *My Son's Execution* by William George Bentley (1957), and later his sister Iris published *Let Him Have Justice* (2001).[717]

The Ruth Ellis case was similarly productive of books. Foremost were *Ruth Ellis: A Case of Diminished Responsibility?* (1990) by Laurence Marks and Tony Van Den Bergh; *Ruth Ellis* by Robert Hancock (1963); and Kenneth Harper's *Dance with a Stranger* upon which the film of the same name was based.[718]

Somewhat later (1961-2) came the Hanratty case which has probably produced more written words than any other, with at least half a dozen books by Louis Blom-Cooper, Jean Justice, Lord Russell of Liverpool, Paul Foot, Bob Woffinden and Leonard Miller. Recently adduced DNA evidence seems to indicate fairly conclusively that Hanratty was guilty and thus he is the odd one out in being a *cause celebre* who may have been guilty.[719] The last two

---

(London: Simon and Schuster, 1961)

[717] Bentley, William G, *My Son's Execution* (London: W H Allen, 1957); Yallop, David, *To Encourage the Others* (London: W H Allen 1971; London, Corgi, 1990); Parris, John, *Scapegoat: The Inside Story of the Trial of Derek Bentley* (London: Duckworth, 1991); Trow, Michael J, *Let Him Have It, Chris* (London: Constable 1990); Bentley, Iris, *Let Him Have Justice* (London: Picador 2001)

[718] Hancock, Robert, *Ruth Ellis* (London: Arthur Barker, 1963); Marks, Laurence and Tony van den Bergh, *Ruth Ellis: A Case of Diminished Responsibility?* (Harmondsworth: Penguin, 1990); and Harper, Kenneth, *Dance with a Stranger* (London: HarperCollins, 1985)

[719] The full list is:- Blom-Cooper, Louis, *The A6 Murder: Regina v James Hanratty – The*

executions, those of Allen and Evans, were the subject of *The Last Two to Hang* (1960) by Elwyn Jones, a prolific crime-writer and television script-writer. There was no question of that case being a miscarriage and it was notable simply for being the last hangings.[720] Miscarriages in general have been covered in many books such as Bob Woffinden's *Miscarriages of Justice* (1987) and *Blind Justice: Miscarriages of Justice in Twentieth Century Britain?* by John Eddleston (2000).

Whilst these books on miscarriages were sometimes successful in bringing about the rectification of an injustice, or at least bringing it to popular attention, it is debatable to what extent if at all they contributed to the success of the abolition campaign. Of course the possibility of a miscarriage in a capital case was one of the main planks in the abolitionist platform, and some of the perceived injustices of the 1950s almost certainly had a considerable impact on public opinion on the capital punishment issue. Moreover, though one can theoretically be a campaigner for the innocence of a hanged man and yet be a supporter of hanging, in practice the most vociferous investigators of miscarriages were often keen abolitionists and no doubt saw their work as not merely the rectification of injustice but as ammunition in the abolition campaign.

One might also mention fiction, whether literary or popular, but whilst there were of course numerous crime thrillers about which one might say, as with crime films, that the shadow of the gallows loomed behind them, there were few that dealt explicitly with the question of capital punishment. One such was *Yield to the Night*, the novel upon which the film of the same name was based. Written by Joan Henry and published by Gollancz in 1954 it is a short but gut-wrenchingly powerful story, written in first person narrative, of a condemned woman (Mary Hilton) convicted of the murder of her ex-lover's new mistress, whom she blames for his suicide.[721] It consists largely of an account of her last few weeks in prison awaiting execution, and of the daily routines through which she is put by the authorities, a mixture of tedium and torment, interspersed with flashbacks of her life and the events that led up to the murder, her trial and conviction. Though the events suggest the case of Ruth

---

Semblance of Truth (Harmondsworth: Penguin, 1963); Justice, Jean, *Murder vs. Murder: The British Legal System and the A6 Murder Case* (Paris: Olympia, 1964); Lord Russell of Liverpool, *Deadman's Hill – Was Hanratty Guilty?* (London, Secker and Warburg, 1965 and London: Icon, 1966); Justice, Jean, *Le Crime de la Route A6* (Paris: Robert Laffont, 1968); Foot, Paul, *Who Killed Hanratty?* (London: Cape 1971; London: Panther 1973; revised Harmondsworth, Penguin 1988); Woffinden, Bob, *Hanratty: The Final Verdict* (London: Macmillan 1997); and Miller, Leonard, *Shadows of Deadman's Hill: A New Analysis of the A6 Murder* (London: Zoilus 2001). See also Simpson, Keith, *Forty Years of Murder* (London, Harrap 1978, London, Grafton 1980) and Woffinden, Bob, *Miscarriages of Justice* (London, Hodder and Stoughton 1987; London, Coronet 1989).

[720] Elwyn Jones, *The Last Two to Hang* (London: Macmillan, 1966)

[721] Henry, Joan, *Yield to the Night* (London: Gollancz, 1954)

Ellis in certain aspects the book was written and published a year or so before that case and any resemblances were thus coincidental (though the film came out after the Ellis case and therefore tended to reinforce the misconception that it had been quasi-biographical).

Conclusion

The impact of the print media, particularly the press, is, like so many of the other institutions examined, difficult to assess, but probably generally less influential than commonly supposed, and certainly less influential than its own *amour propre* would like us to suppose. Its influence on political questions generally is debatable, and such evidence as exists tends to confirm the impression that the press reinforces existing opinions but does not change them to any significant extent. The press tended to take a rather abolitionist line on the whole, with the more left-leaning and Labour or Liberal supporting newspapers invariably taking an abolitionist stance while the right-wing and Conservative supporting papers were rather more divided between those which favoured a cautious acceptance of abolition, even if only provisionally, and others which were very hostile to it. The evidence, in the form of opinion polls and much else, suggests that the press had little effect on either public opinion or political opinion, but merely reflected the debate. When, for example, the *News of the World* in the late summer and autumn of 1966 launched a 'bring back hanging' campaign it was largely ineffectual, and was eventually quietly dropped by the paper which was thus tacitly forced to accept its own impotence in the face of events.

Books, even the tide of intensely propagandistic and missionary efforts designed to raise public awareness of the issue and to rectify perceived miscarriages, were probably even less influential than their journalistic equivalents, since their readership was very limited and confined largely to those who had an interest in the subject, and therefore probably a fixed view, to start off with. Rather more influential, even if only on the face of it, were the 'live' media of radio, television, film and theatre.

CHAPTER 13

RADIO AND TELEVISION

This chapter looks at radio and television and examines the way in which they presented the capital punishment controversy and evaluates the extent and nature of their influence on the debate.

Radio

By the middle to late 1950s television was already overtaking radio as the chief source of news and information for the average household but radio nonetheless maintained a high level of output in the news, current affairs and documentary field (which was of course its speciality) and the question of capital punishment received much more of an airing there than it did on television.[722] This section examines the role of radio.

The report of the Royal Commission in 1953 was the occasion for a whole slew of programmes across its various stations, such as editions of *Press Conference* with Ernest Gowers on 24th September and *Topic for Tonight* with Ernest Watkins also on 24th September. The following year came *Reflections on the Report of the Royal Commission* by Professor H L A Hart on the Third Programme in September 1954.[723] The revitalization of the controversy in 1955 and the advent of the Silverman Abolition Bill led to more programmes; for example an item in November 1955 by H R Cummings on *Home Affairs*. February 1956 was a bumper month for the question because of the Commons debate which produced another rash of programmes such as an edition of *London Commentary* with Michael Davie and *Topic for Tonight* with Paul Leach covering the Commons debate.

This profusion of news and current affairs coverage naturally led to rather more expansive treatment. In late 1955 a full-length documentary on capital punishment was aired, perhaps the first. *Capital Punishment* was an hour-long programme written and presented by Nesta Pain and transmitted on 13th December 1955 on the Home Service. It was based largely on the evidence adduced by the Gowers Commission, which had reported a couple of years before. Laurence Gilliam had memoed to the Head of Features asking for the

---

[722]It should be mentioned that during the whole of the relevant period the BBC had a monopoly on lawful radio broadcasting for, though its monopoly on television had been broken in 1955, independent commercial radio did not come into being until the 1970s. Pirate radio existed of course but its output was devoted almost exclusively to pop music.

[723] BBC Written Archives, index of radio programmes on 'Punishment'

go-ahead for Pain to do the programme saying: 'to my mind this is a most important matter for public airing. Each fresh execution leads to public and Press debate...'[724] Pain, having been given the nod, memoed to the Head of Features suggesting that the programme be composed chiefly of verbatim extracts from the evidence given to the Royal Commission with linking narration, concentrating on whether hanging has a unique deterrent value, whether executions have an undesirable effect on the public, whether hanging was the most effective, speedy and humane method, and whether life imprisonment was more or less merciful to the condemned man.[725] A slight nervousness at handling such combustible material was evident in the higher ranks, as the Controller of the Home Service memoed, stressing the need for absolute impartiality.[726] It seems that alterations to the programme were requested at some stage but what these were and whether they were acceded to is unclear.[727]

Shortly after this came a talk given by H L A Hart, Professor of Jurisprudence at Oxford University, on the Third Programme (as it then was) transmitted on 6th January 1956 entitled *Capital Punishment - a review of the arguments*.[728] This was a fairly bland discussion of the issue that tended to shade towards abolition though scrupulously avoiding any hard conclusion. A discussion programme on the Home Service between Gardiner, Hailsham (a Conservative retentionist) and Frank Byers (a Liberal abolitionist) recorded on 2nd February 1956 and planned for broadcast on 9th February was apparently cancelled because of concerns about the fourteen day rule.[729] This was an agreement between the broadcasters and the political parties which prohibited the discussion of issues that were due to be debated in Parliament within the next fortnight.[730]

The earlier Nesta Pain project was evidently deemed a success because not long afterwards the Head of Features was again writing to her saying that the DSB (Director of Sound Broadcasting) had agreed that the Light Programme do a sixty minute programme on capital punishment with the suggested title *Life and Death*, which unlike her earlier effort need not confine

---

[724] Laurence Duval Gilliam, (1907-1964) radio producer. Gilliam to Head of Features, 20th July 1955. BBC Written Archives, File R71/582. Significantly or not this memo was written seven days after the hanging of Ruth Ellis which had re-ignited the controversy.

[725] Pain to Head of Features, 2nd August 1955. BBC Written Archives, ibid.

[726] Controller, Home Service, 3rd August 1955. BBC Written Archives, ibid.

[727] Nesta Pain, memo 29th September 1955. BBC Written Archives, ibid.

[728] BBC Written Archives, File T32/518/3 *The Death Penalty* (scripts and research).

[729]*The Times*, 10th February 1956

[730] This absurd rule was blown out of the water a few months later when Granada Television (which had the independent television franchise for the north of England) ignored it by devoting extensive coverage to the ongoing Suez crisis, which otherwise could not have been discussed at all. Once breached the BBC and other independent companies followed suit and the rule was abandoned.

itself to the Royal Commission.[731] As before there was a flurry of memos emphasizing the need for balance. The outcome was a dramatized documentary, *Life and Death: The Case For and Against Capital Punishment* broadcast in March 1956.[732] This was written and produced by Nesta Pain, and seems to have been a very similar, but perhaps more elaborate, production to her earlier Home Service effort. Notwithstanding the licence to go beyond the findings of the Royal Commission the programme was devoted exclusively to that aspect of the debate, focussing on the testimony of some of its distinguished witnesses. In addition there were studio interviews with a couple of experts; Dr Keith Simpson, a prison doctor who had dealt with post-mortems of executed prisoners, and Dr Clive Stafford-Clark, a psychiatrist who discussed some of the more macabre murder cases of recent years. The format had the evidence of the Commission witnesses read out by actors (or so it appears), with a linking narration spoken by an actor, John Slater, seemingly in the persona of 'the common man'. This led into highlights from the testimony of several of the leading witnesses including that of Albert Pierrepoint, then still the chief hangman, with both the witnesses and the chairman's (Gowers') lines spoken by actors. We hear Pierrepoint's view that hanging was 'quick, certain and humane...I think it's the fastest and quickest in the world bar nothing. It's quicker than shooting and cleaner.'

This was almost certainly the most comprehensive treatment of the issue on radio to date. As with her previous effort there were accusations of bias towards retention. One correspondent, a solicitor, wrote to the 'Director of Talks' complaining that most of the 'speakers' were pro-hanging and that the information given about the length of time from 'cell to drop' was misleading.[733] Pain replied that the programme was factually accurate and that the information had been taken from governors, prison officers, hangmen, chaplains etc. from their evidence to the Royal Commission.[734] The fact was that since the programme was centred almost wholly on the Royal Commission evidence and the bulk of that evidence was from witnesses (Home Secretaries, judges, policemen, prison officers, hangmen etc.) who were retentionist by profession, trade or inclination, there was almost bound to be something of a pro-hanging bias if considered strictly in terms of the apportionment of time. But the overall impression was that the show strove hard to be fair and impartial by canvassing all shades of opinion and all arguments for and against.

In addition to all this factual programming a play was transmitted, *Murder Story*, by Ludovic Kennedy sometime in 1956, having been produced

---

[731] Head of Features to Pain, 26th January 1956. BBC Written Archives, op cit.

[732] *Life and Death: The Case For and Against Capital Punishment* written and produced by Nesta Pain. Transmitted on the Light Programme at 9.00pm on Wednesday, 28th March 1956. Transcript, BBC Written Archives, RP, Ref. No. DLO 68A

[733] Leonard A Bird to Director of Talks, 10th April 1956. BBC Written Archives, ibid.

[734] Pain to Bird, 26th April 1956. BBC Written Archives, ibid.

for the stage a couple of years earlier. After the defeat of the Silverman Bill in the Lords the debate ebbed away somewhat and there was something of a hiatus in radio coverage of the issue. Thereafter the treatment of the controversy was somewhat sporadic.

Victor Gollancz, talking to Margaret Lane and George Scott, was the subject of *Frankly Speaking* on the Light Programme in January 1959, in which he touched on his antipathy to capital punishment and said that as a boy he had wanted to become Home Secretary so as to bring in an abolition bill, and at Oxford he had written a play on that theme.[735] In May 1959 there was a discussion on the Home Service's *At Home and Abroad* chaired by George Scott with Labour MP Kenneth Younger and Conservative MP Cyril Osborne entitled *Amendments to the Homicide Act* debating the merits of the Act. Victor Gollancz took part in an edition of *Out of the News* on the Home Service in 1960.[736] Interviewed by George Scott about his part in the abolition movement he was characteristically uncompromising as this extract indicates:-

> Scott: 'Mr Gollancz, why do you feel so strongly that capital punishment should be abolished?'
> Gollancz: 'Because I simply loathe cruelty, and I think that capital punishment is, without any exception, the greatest cruelty in the world. To kill a man is one thing - its an appalling thing - but to deliberately put an end to a life at three weeks notice; the agony of the waiting is one of the most horrible things I can possibly conceive, and in no possible circumstances do I regard such cruelty as tolerable, just as I regard the torturing of a baby as in all circumstances inadmissible.'

The Earl of Harewood (George Henry Hubert Lascelles), chairman of the Committee of Honour of the NCACP, was interviewed about his life on *Frankly Speaking* in April 1961, and mentioned his antipathy to capital punishment.[737] An edition of the Home Service's *What's the Idea?* had a discussion between Bernard Levin, Bernard Williams and Conservative MP Gerald Nabarro on crime and punishment in June 1961.[738] The format was for Levin and Williams as journalists to grill Nabarro the politician about his hard-line views on capital and corporal punishment, but the argument tended to go round in circles and the debate was not very illuminating. On 13th April 1962 Gardiner gave a talk on capital punishment for the BBC North American service.[739] There was a BBC

---

[735]*Frankly Speaking*, Light Programme, 12th January 1959. BBC Sound Archive, DD04567021. The programme may have been repeated on 1st February 1959.

[736]*Out of the News* (*Womans' Hour*) BBC Home Service, 8th December 1960. Gollancz, op cit. MS/157/3/BR/8/76; BBC Written Archives index of radio programmes on 'punishment'.

[737]*Frankly Speaking*, Light Programme 9th July 1961. British Library Sound Archives (27356). It was repeated on 1st June 1968 in the *It's Saturday* slot. BBC Sound Archives, 31879.

[738] Crime and Punishment in *What's the Idea?*, BBC Home Service, 16th June 1961. Microfilm transcript, BBC Written Archives.

[739] BBC to Gardiner, 11th April 1962. Gardiner, Add 56459B.

Home Service programme on the Hanratty case presented by James Mossman on 2nd August 1963 after the case had been raised in the Commons as a possible miscarriage.[740] *An End to Hanging* was presented by the abolitionist Donald Soper in September 1963 on the Light Programme.[741] A more offbeat offering was *A Question of Inheritance* on the Home Service presented by Paul Stephenson about Barry Trenowell whose father had been hanged.[742]

The advent of the Silverman Abolition Bill and its crucial second reading in December 1964 was the spur to another rash of programmes. A programme on the Home Service on 13th December 1964 went out which some members of the NCACP thought weighted in favour of hanging.[743] Silverman himself was interviewed both on the Light Programme and on *Today* on 22nd December in the immediate aftermath of his Commons victory.[744] He said he had not been surprised by the size of the majority. Henry Brooke, the former Home Secretary, who had supported the Bill was interviewed the same day.[745] He explained his conversion to abolitionism by reference to the report he had commissioned, as Home Secretary, on the Homicide Act whose anomalies were hard to remove. Asked about the burden of recommending the death sentence he said that he always gave a reprieve when he possibly could, and only recommended the law take its course if there were no mitigating circumstances at all. He had had only six or so such decisions to make a year, whereas before the Homicide Act there had been twenty or thirty per year.

Instead of Hanging – What? was a discussion with the writer Giles Playfair in the *Womans' Hour* slot in June 1965.[746] Ex-hangman Harry Allen was interviewed on the Light Programme in April 1968 (former hangmen were prominent in the media at this time!).[747] There was a discussion programme with Leslie Smith, Sir Donald Finnemore, Professor Terence Morris and the playwright James O'Connor in March 1969 on Radio 4 (the successor to the Home Service).[748] The approach of the necessary confirmatory votes in Parliament was the occasion for interviews with Edward Heath (Leader of the Opposition and a mild abolitionist) and Teddy Taylor (pro-hanging

---

[740] Transcription of recording, 2nd August 1963. Gardiner, ibid.

[741] This may have been *Hanging Must Go* according to the British Library Sound Archive

[742] BBC written archives, index of radio programmes on 'punishment'

[743] Letter to the DG of the BBC. Gardiner, op cit.

[744] Silverman interview, 22nd December 1964, *Today*, BBC Home Service. BBC Sound Archives (29094)

[745] Henry Brooke interview, *Ten O'Clock*, 22nd December 1964. Light Programme. British Library Sound Archives (29094).

[746] BBC Written Archives, index of radio programmes on 'punishment'

[747] Interview with Harry Allen, Light Programme, 30th May 1968. British Library Sound Archives catalogue

[748] BBC Written Archives, index of radio programmes on 'punishment'

Conservative MP) in June 1969 on the Light Programme.[749] Heath re-affirmed that he was an empirical abolitionist who wanted hanging abolished but would regrettably have it back if proved essential. Lady Wootton, who had piloted the 1964-5 Abolition Bill through the House of Lords, was the interviewee on an edition of an occasional series called the *Bow Dialogues* recorded and transmitted on 25th November 1969. This was a half hour dialogue with Joseph McCulloch, rector of St Mary-le-Bow (hence the title) over moral questions. The first part of the programme was taken up with the question of capital punishment. Wootton was adamant that there was no evidence of the deterrent effect of hanging, the murder rate being unaffected by abolition both in England and elsewhere, though she stressed that her stance was very much a moral one because she believed that no-one had the right to take life.

The forthcoming Parliamentary vote in December 1969 was the occasion for another round of programmes. There was a special edition of *Radio 4 Reports* on 11th December which dealt with the subject in great depth.[750] Presented by Robert Kee, it 'cleared the airwaves' for the issue, possibly regarding the imminent vote as portending a greater degree of finality than actually proved to be the case. This programme included interviews with a wide range of people from politicians, campaigners and professionals to the mothers of murdered children. The balance here was clearly for restoration and that may have been designed to reflect the division of opinion in the country. Amongst the politicians, campaigners and professionals there were the inevitable Duncan Sandys, his associate in the petition movement Charlotte Hurst and a Lieutenant-Colonel Bartlett (who had organised a 'bring back hanging' petition in Brighton). Also interviewed were Reg Gale of the Police Federation and Fred Castell of the Prison Officers Association, both of whom stressed the strong feelings within their organizations that hanging should be brought back for the murder of police officers and prison officers respectively. The balance was redressed somewhat with a Dr Leopold Field, a prison psychiatrist, who opined that hanging did not have the deterrent effect claimed for it, neither with the 'normal' nor the 'abnormal' murderer, though his views would have been as tiresomely predictable to the restorationists as would the views of Gale and Castell and their like to the abolitionists. People generally played to their stereotypes.

Several editions of *Ten O'Clock* a few days later, also on Radio 4, featured items on the prospective vote. There was a short debate between Tom Iremonger, Conservative MP and pro-hanging, Willie Hamilton, Labour MP and John Pardoe, Liberal MP, both anti-hanging, on the 16th December.[751]

---

[749] Interview with Rt. Hon Edward Heath, MP. BBC Sound Archive, 32587. Interview with Teddy Taylor, MP Light Programme, 24th June 1969. British Library Sound Archives.
[750] Radio 4 Reports, *Capital Punishment – proposed abolition*, (BBC Radio 4). TX 11.12.69 BBC Sound Archives, CD111388 (32735)
[751] *Ten O'Clock*: *Debate on Hanging*, BBC Radio 4, 16th December 1969. BBC Sound

Pardoe argued that if the vote went against the government (thereby causing the Act to expire automatically in July) then Callaghan, the Home Secretary, would let the Act run until that date and then introduce a new measure. Hamilton pointed out that if so the ridiculed capital/non-capital distinction provided by the Homicide Act would be revived, but Iremonger said that that Act was not as bad as it was painted.

Radio thus dealt extensively with the topic, and indeed intensively when the matter was up for debate. Though radio had by the later 1950s become very much the junior partner to television it still enjoyed a very large audience, especially for news and current affairs coverage. Nonetheless, as with the print media, it is unlikely, for all the welter of programming that took place, that it had much influence on opinion, either at the elite level or that of the general population. Television as a medium had by then overtaken and outgrown its older brother, and had a rather greater potential for impact.

Television

Of all of the media television is probably the most influential, combining pervasiveness, accessibility and impact (and had been so from as early as the late 1950s). By the mid-1950s it was rapidly overtaking radio as a source of information and the cinema as a means of entertainment, whilst its reputation for political impartiality lent it a degree of legitimacy denied to the often highly partisan press. By the end of the 1950s most households possessed a television set. Television was of course governed, then as now, by a statutory requirement to display impartiality on all questions of political controversy, an injunction that applied equally to the BBC and ITV (which came into existence in 1955 just as the capital punishment debate was hotting up). That did not, of course, preclude it from discussing the matter so long as it provided for balance. The prominence of the issue was evident in news and current affairs coverage but occasionally in documentaries and drama output. To what extent, if at all, did television influence the debate?

Television coverage may be divided into news, current affairs, documentary and drama. Of these drama was the least prominent though arguably, insofar as it dealt with capital punishment at all, the most influential, precisely because drama was not in practice subject to any rigorous requirement of impartiality and therefore propagandistic efforts could 'slip by'. In the entire period there seems to have been only one serious contemporary drama concerned wholly or primarily with capital punishment, Ken Loach's *Three Clear Sundays* (1965), and the indications from audience research are that it may have had some influence on public opinion. This is dealt with below. Documentary treatments, too, were thin on the ground given the relative paucity

---

Archives, CDA 32751

of this form of programming, especially on ITV, though the BBC only transmitted one major documentary devoted to the topic, *The Death Penalty* (1961). This, too, is discussed below. News and current affairs coverage, by contrast, was fairly considerable. Any important trial or execution tended to attract the news cameras particularly if, as happened often in the later years, there were demonstrations or scuffles outside the prison gates on the day of a hanging.[752] News coverage of Parliamentary debates on capital punishment was also plentiful, especially in the years after abolition when restorationist bills and motions were frequent.[753] Current affairs programmes tended to deal with the issue somewhat fitfully, with *Panorama* on the BBC and *This Week* on ITV devoting the occasional edition to it, or more often including it as a brief item. Lighter magazine programmes such as the BBC's *Tonight* tended not to touch it, neither, more surprisingly, did Granada's trailblazing flagship current affairs strand *World in Action*.

From a very early stage of the abolition controversy there were efforts to recruit television to the abolition cause, or at any rate to interest the medium in the topic. The NCACP lost no time in wooing television executives. Gerald Gardiner wrote to Sir Ian Jacobs, the director-general of the BBC, within a few months of the founding of the NCACP trumpeting the success of the Campaign to date and that it was a worthy topic for a programme.[754] He wrote the same day to Sidney Bernstein, founder of the Granada media empire, urging a documentary on the topic which might be shown in cinemas.[755] The reply from the latter was not encouraging, but the reply on behalf of the former was rather more so. It is likely that a similar approach was made to the other ITV companies, as and when they gained their respective franchises.[756]

Given its public service remit it is natural that the BBC should have devoted considerable air-time to news, current affairs and documentaries, and certainly more so than its commercial rivals. The BBC had certainly been toying with the idea of capital punishment as promising documentary material from 1955 onwards, as evidenced by internal memoranda, quite independently

---

[752] By the late 1950s demonstrations were almost invariable and these sometimes erupted into violence as with for example the hangings of Marwood in 1959 and Podola in 1960.

[753] For examples of such news items see www.bbc.co.uk/catalogue/infax and www.itnsource.com

[754] Gardiner to Jacobs, 4th January 1956. Gardiner, op cit. Add 56455B.

[755] Gardiner to Bernstein, 4th January 1956. Gardiner, ibid.

[756] Granada initially held the franchise for the whole of the north of England, though later only the north-west with Yorkshire and Tyne Tees entering the market for their respective areas. Associated-Rediffusion and ATV shared the franchise for London and the South-east and ABC won the franchise for the Midlands. New ITV regions rapidly came into being in the late 1950s to the early 1960s with the franchises being widely dispersed among several companies. This remained the position until a big shake-up in 1968. ITV franchisees were naturally very conscious of the need to attract audiences and advertisers and so the output tended to be downmarket of the BBC.

of any approach from the NCACP. Indeed radio had already found it a fruitful source of material for its output. In October 1955 producer Gilchrist Calder wrote to the 'HD Television' on the topic of 'Future Programmes' (based upon discussions with Colin Morris) suggesting three hour-long documentaries on the theme of: 'we are supposed to be civilised in Britain, but in 1955 we are still barbaric.'[757] He proposed capital punishment as one of the topics, together with the colour bar and prison life:-

> We would argue for abolition whilst naturally providing all the pros and cons as research would bring out...the angle would be 'You tolerate capital punishment, because you don't know what goes on. Well this is what goes on. Do you still want it?' – the billing and presentation of this subject would have to be done in such a way that it removed the onus of the argument from BBC policy as obviously the BBC cannot state an opinion...But of course to have any guts, the show must have a viewpoint.

Bold stuff, though it seemed to be tying itself into knots over whether the programme would be neutral or otherwise. The reply by the 'Controller, Prog TV' was predictably equivocal, stating that capital punishment was an excellent subject but that the BBC, 'just could not start such a project on the basis that "we would argue for abolition"...We must approach this subject cautiously – are there any existent BBC rulings...' and much in this vein.[758]

Nonetheless, the project managed to get off the ground to the extent of Colin Morris writing to the Home Office to 'discuss issues'.[759] He received a rather dusty reply to these overtures, however, to the effect that the topic was very controversial; was about to be debated in the Commons; that no Home Office official would be permitted to discuss the question and that any such person would be precluded from providing any assistance in the preparation of the programme.[760] Just for good measure the Home Office spokesman added that he understood that Morris had arranged a discussion with an official from the Prison Commission and that he had cancelled it as they were subject to the same strictures as the Home Office! It seems that the approach had been squelched at the highest level by Sir Frank Newsam, the permanent secretary, who was a strong retentionist, and whose veto effectively precluded any further discussions between the BBC and the Home Office on the matter.[761] Morris

---

[757] Calder to 'HD (Tel)' memo on 'Future Programmes' 5th October 1955. BBC Written Archives, File T16/542 TV policy (programme policy – capital punishment 1955-61)

[758] Cecil McGivern to Calder, 2nd November 1955. BBC Written Archives, ibid.

[759] Colin Morris to D M Edwards (Public Relations) Home Office, 19th December 1955, BBC Written Archives, ibid.

[760] Public Relations Office, Home Office to Morris, 21st December 1955, BBC Written Archives, ibid.

[761] Sir Frank Newsam. Permanent Under-Secretary (i.e. civil service head) for the Home Office, 1948-57.

decided, after consulting with Hugh Klare of the Howard League, that it was useless to continue with the project.[762]

The matter did not rest there, however, and it was felt that they shouldn't be deflected by the Home Office's refusal to co-operate and that it had been a mistake to approach them formally.[763] Unfortunately the Howard League was powerless to provide access to the condemned cell and was reluctant to violate the privacy of reprieved murderers with whom they were in contact. On the other hand it was known that the film of Joan Henry's *Yield to the Night* was due for release in May or June (1956) and was to be strongly abolitionist in tone, while the 'Gollancz campaign' was gathering momentum. Capital punishment was up for debate in the Commons in February (1956) but there would not be time for a bill until April and hence there should not be difficulties with the fourteen-day rule (which precluded discussion of matters due to be debated in Parliament within the next fortnight). Thus, it was argued, the time was ripe for the topic to be properly aired. But this optimistic outlook was not shared by everybody and some thought that the non co-operation of the Home Office made it impossible to do a dramatized documentary.[764] The necessary information could be obtained in other ways but there would be no guarantee that it would be accurate and up-to-date, and moreover since one was dependent in the documentary field on organizations coming under the Home Office it would be 'inviting trouble'. As an alternative to the documentary treatment it was suggested they consider an adaptation of Frank Tilsley's novel, *Thicker than Water,* dealing with the effect of capital punishment on a condemned man's family which by contrast would 'not cause trouble with the authorities.'

This led to an approach to Nesta Pain, a writer-presenter who had already done one radio documentary on capital punishment and was about to do another, to write a programme on the subject.[765] She reluctantly refused.[766] This rebuff seemed to mark the end of capital punishment as a potential television topic for the time being, at least as far as the BBC was concerned, notwithstanding its high political salience, and it was several more years before it resurfaced. A great deal of preparation and planning had petered out into nothing, partly as a result of the lack of co-operation from the Home Office which effectively precluded in-depth treatment of the topic, but it speaks also of the over-cautiousness that characterized the BBC at that time.

Whilst the BBC had backed away and been baulked in its more ambitious projects an ITV company, ATV (weekend franchisee for London and the south-east) transmitted a half hour programme on capital punishment *Death or*

---

[762] Memo from Michael Barry, Head of Drama to Mary Adams, 9th January 1956, BBC Written Archives, op cit.

[763] Mary Adams to 'HD, Tel', 10th January 1956, BBC Written Archives, ibid.

[764] Arthur Swinson to HD Tel, 28th January 1956, BBC Written Archives, ibid.

[765] (Florence) Nesta Kathleen Pain (nee Taylor) 1905-1995. Broadcaster and author.

[766] Nesta Pain to Mary Adams, 30th January 1956, BBC Written Archives, ibid.

Redemption in late 1960.[767] Gerald Gardiner was a participant along with several notables such as Sir John Wolfenden (who was to appear in another programme on the topic a year later) but the programme was not very inspiring, being a late-night discussion in which the participants did little but exchange platitudes.[768] Capital punishment did start to feature as an occasional item on *Panorama*, the BBC's flagship current affairs show from the early 1950s, from 1960 onwards. The first such outing on *Panorama* seems to have been in February 1960 with an item about the execution in the USA of Caryl Chessman which appears to have been used as a handle to examine the American judicial system in general and contained a contribution from Dr Terence Morris, the noted criminologist.[769] The question of capital punishment in Britain featured as an item in another edition later that year, prompted possibly by the renewal of the NCACP campaign, and was presented by Robert Kee, who began by giving a series of examples to illustrate the anomalies inherent in the Homicide Act. Capital punishment was to become a topic on at least two other editions of Panorama over the next decade, but it became the subject of something rather more ambitious from the BBC the following year with the production of the first (and perhaps only) major television documentary devoted to the question.

The Death Penalty was transmitted by the BBC in October 1961. Early in 1961 Gardiner, at the suggestion of Wayland Young, had approached the BBC about the making of a documentary on capital punishment and the Corporation seemed amenable to the idea. Whether these promptings led directly to the making of the programme is unclear, but certainly by mid 1961 a well-known BBC producer, Anthony de Lotbiniere, had started to formulate plans for a documentary that would tackle the festering controversy head-on, whilst of course being mindful of the need for balance and impartiality.[770] It was clear that this would be a fairly major undertaking, certainly by the standards of the time and the budgetary limitations then in place. Filming was done in Norway, Denmark and the USA so as to give a world-wide perspective and a very broad spectrum of distinguished contributors and interviewees had been lined up including Gardiner as the main proponent of the abolition case and Sir Thomas Moore, MP as the chief spokesman of the retentionists, with Sir John Wolfenden to sum up. Also to be included were the new Archbishop of

---

[767] *Death or Redemption*, ATV, transmitted 18th November 1960.

[768] Apart from Wolfenden the other participants were Field Marshal Lord Harding, Sir Linton Andrews (chairman and editor of the Yorkshire Post), Rev Dr Leslie Weatherhead (minister of the City Temple), Gerald Gardiner and Edward Glover (penologist). Rolph, op cit, 1/4/2s

[769] BBC Written Archives, Panorama 22nd February 1960. Chessman (1921-60) gained celebrity/notoriety as a death row inmate for twelve years during which time he wrote several books and essays and became the focus of the American anti-capital punishment movement before finally being executed at San Quentin after defying numerous execution deadlines.

[770] BBC Written Archive Centre, files T32/518/1-5, *The Death Penalty* (TX 24.10.61).

Canterbury, Michael Ramsey and the Cardinal Archbishop of Westminster, Godfrey, to give the Christian viewpoint; Ludovic Kennedy (on Timothy Evans); Albert Pierrepoint, former chief hangman; the Chief Constable of Birmingham and many others. It was written and narrated by Patrick O'Donovan, a journalist for the *Observer*. The final product ran for sixty minutes and went out at 9.25pm (preceded by a warning that the content was unsuitable for children).[771]

The programme begins starkly with a minatory drum-roll over a logo of a gallows with a question mark hanging from it and the main title. The introductory monologue is played over a backdrop of scenes of everyday life in England; Punch and Judy shows, Madame Tussauds, queues outside the Old Bailey and newspaper kiosks with sensational headlines to illustrate the point that 'we take our violence vicariously', but that 'we retain a violent and ignoble death for our convicted murderers' against a shot of the drawing of a hanged man. The programme ends with a summary of the debate from Sir John Wolfenden which was impeccably balanced.[772] He concludes that:-

> Whether or not to hang men in England for murder and treason has become an emotional problem in this country...an enormous number of statistics have been produced to prove that the death penalty serves no useful purpose...nonetheless those statistics are not decisive...the future of the death penalty in this country is a political matter...Objectively it must be said that in Britain the reformers usually get their way in the end...neither public opinion nor politics stand still in a democracy...but in this case the reformers still have a long way to go. They have got to get more public opinion on their side. They have to recruit more support in Parliament...In the end it depends on the voter – me and you.

Overall the show comes across as slightly staid and conventional, and yet, despite its obvious technical limitations, it is remarkable for its time. The show inevitably looks somewhat dated with its contributors delivering their pieces straight to camera in somewhat stilted fashion and the absence of any debate between contributors or hard questioning from an interviewer. But there is a surprising degree of licence involved containing, as it did, interviews with a professional criminal, a reprieved murderer, and a whole posse of Death Row inmates, none of which might have been permitted by the powers that be at a later and supposedly more liberal date. Though the pace is rather sluggish it packs a considerable punch and there has probably not been anything quite like it before or since.

---

[771] The considerable advance publicity the programme attracted led to approaches from would-be contributors including a bizarre one from a Victor Soanes who had constructed a working model of the gallows which he thought might be useful! Soanes to de Lotbiniere, 15th October 1961. BBC Written Archives T32/518/5

[772] Sir John Frederick Wolfenden, KB, CBE, Baron Wolfenden of Westcott (1906-1985), educationalist and civil servant, Vice Chancellor of Reading University. Chairman of the Home Office Committee on Homosexuality and Prostitution which reported in 1957.

The programme went out on 24th October 1961.[773] It seems to have provoked a reaction from Silverman who wrote to Hugh Carleton-Greene, the Director-General, about the way that MPs had been presented on the programme; specifically that the only MPs had been pro-capital punishment.[774] This was technically true since Sir Thomas Moore was the only MP to appear, but there were plenty of eminent abolitionists on show and Silverman may have over-estimated the esteem in which politicians were held in the eyes of the general public. He may also have been slightly miffed that, as a longstanding champion of the abolitionist cause, he had not been invited onto the programme himself. Gollancz was certainly happy with the programme telling Gardiner that he thought it was 'superb'.[775]

The BBC Survey of Viewing and Listening showed that the programme had an estimated viewership of eight million, which was 16% of the population aged five and over. Most had been favourably impressed with the programme and asked to rate it 31% gave it A+, 43% A, 20% B, 5% C, and 1% C- yielding a high 'reaction index' of 75. It was probably the most significant programme made on capital punishment before or since, but how influential was it? Some objective evidence exists in the form of the standard audience research carried out by the BBC which seems to suggest that it may have modified the views of those who held strong views on either side without actually *changing* anyone's view.[776] Moreover, though it increased people's knowledge of the issue there was still widespread ignorance of basic points that had been stressed within the programme. This seems to have been generally true across sex, age, level of interest in crime etc. The BBC research is of considerable interest because it represents probably the only example of research dealing with opinion on capital punishment as affected by a specific event, both before and after that event. For a detailed analysis of the research see the chapter on public opinion.

Only a couple of weeks earlier ITV had again ventured into the controversy with an edition of its current affairs strand *This Week* dealing with the issue.[777] Capital punishment featured again on *Panorama* in March 1962, marking the fifth anniversary of the passage of the Homicide Act.[778] This was a relatively short item (about a quarter of an hour) which consisted very largely of a studio discussion chaired by Robin Day between the Bishop of Exeter (Dr Mortimer) and Sydney Silverman (pro-abolition) and Peter Rawlinson, MP, QC

---

[773] de Lotbiniere to Gardiner, 6th October 1961. Gardiner, op cit.

[774] Silverman to Carleton-Greene October 1961; Carleton-Greene to Silverman 24th October 1961. Gardiner, ibid.

[775] Gollancz to Gardiner, 31st October 1961. Gardiner, ibid.

[776] BBC written archives, File R9/10/9 Audience Research: Special Reports: TV chronological 1962, *The Death Penalty*. This was one of several programmes or classes of programme to have been made the subject of the BBC's audience research.

[777] *This Week* (Rediffusion), transmitted 6th October 1961. BFI, TV Curator (Phil Wickham). However, the programme recording seems not to have survived.

[778] BBC Written Archives, T32/1,290/1, Panorama TX 62.03, 19th March 1962

and Edgar Lustgarten (anti).[779] It was a good, if rather brief, airing of the main arguments which would have been unlikely to alter anyone's opinion on the matter. As with previous *Panorama* pieces the format was staid and studio-bound and typical of the television of the time. This was to change with the coming of more imaginative treatments of current affairs as the decade progressed. The BBC's next serious venture into the hanging debate came with an edition of *Man Alive* in 1968.

Man Alive was the flagship documentary series of the fledgling BBC2 channel and ran from 1965 until 1982. It dealt with a range of current affairs topics in an innovative way, but was often criticized for dealing too flippantly with serious issues and for striving too hard to adopt a populist approach. Its edition on hanging, *Bring Back the Rope?,* epitomized that approach and seems to have provoked a strong reaction.[780] The decade of the 1960s had witnessed something of a revolution in programme formatting as with so much else. The 'three men around a desk' approach of Panorama had been superseded, or at least supplemented, towards the end of the decade with an audience participation format in which the studio was crammed with participants all of whom were expected to make a contribution. Since the programme was made more than two years after the suspension of hanging the thrust of it was whether hanging should be brought back and the focus was very much on the restoration campaign of Duncan Sandys, and more specifically on the 'Bring Back Hanging' petition that he was organizing to that effect. There was an introductory film report by co-presenter Jeremy James:-

> For two and a half years there has been no capital punishment in this country. In 1970 at the end of a five-year 'no-hanging' trial period Parliament is going to review the situation...In 1966 Duncan Sandys tried to reintroduce hanging for the murder of policemen and prison warders but Parliament rejected his bill by 122 votes. Duncan Sandys may deny he started the present move to bring back the rope but he is certainly its leader. The campaign is run from Duncan Sandys office in the Houses of Parliament and has a full-time organiser whose ambition it is to collect a million signatures in its support.

The ensuing studio discussion brought together many interested parties to the debate, but if it was hoped that it would be enlightening and intellectually nourishing it almost certainly fell far short. It appears from the transcript to have been rowdy and incoherent with several guests talking over each other, and that the participants were generally inarticulate and failed to make their points effectively.

This BBC foray into capital punishment was followed a few months later

---

[779] Edgar Marcus Lustgarten (1907-1978) Broadcaster and crime writer. Hosted television series *Scotland Yard* and *Scales of Justice*

[780] BBC Written Archives, T14/2, 568/1; Man Alive TX 68.01.30 *Bring Back the Rope?* Tuesday, 30th January 1968

on ITV. *Frost on Friday* was one of the mainstays of the London Weekend Television schedule and had more or less invented the audience participation format used by *Man Alive*.[781] The presenter David Frost was one of the pioneers of the hard-hitting television interview, now commonplace, and presented a trio of programmes on LWT, of which he was a founding director. *Frost on Friday* was the current affairs strand, complemented by the lighter *Frost on Saturday* and *Frost on Sunday*.[782] *Frost on Friday* devoted an edition to capital punishment in October 1968, very early in the programme's history (it began in August 1968 when LWT took up the franchise).[783] It was directed by Derek Bailey and produced by Geoffrey Hughes. The format of the show, which was transmitted live and ran for about forty minutes, pitched a guest or (as here) a small panel of guests, representing different sides of a debate against an audience which might include those with a direct interest. Frost would alternate between grilling members of the panel and seeking reactions from the audience. The panel consisted on this occasion of Duncan Sandys (no programme on capital punishment at that time was complete without his presence) and David Ensor (Labour MP for Bury) for restoration, and Canon Collins and Humphry Berkeley against.[784] However, despite what one feels were the aspirations of Frost and the programme-makers to galvanize panel and audience into producing something memorable the show obstinately refused to take flight, and little but platitudes and clichés flowed forth from the participants.

A year later and it was the turn of the BBC again to pick up the capital punishment baton, once more with *Panorama* as the vehicle, and with the forthcoming confirmatory votes as the prompt. The edition of 15th December 1969 devoted the whole programme to a discussion of the following day's

---

[781] London Weekend Television (LWT) was the franchisee for ITV in London and the South-east at weekends from 1968-2002, in succession to ATV.

[782] Sir David Paradine Frost (b.1939), found fame as presenter of the satirical *That Was the Week That Was* on BBC, and later *The Frost Report* before transferring to ITV. Co-founder of LWT. Presenter of the *Frost On...* shows which included famous encounters such as that with Emil Savundra, the first supposed instance of trial by television. 'He rose without trace' according to Kitty Muggeridge.

[783] *Frost on Friday*, 11th October 1968. Videotape of programme viewed at the BFI National Film and Television Archive.

[784] Alick Charles Davidson Ensor (1906-1987) Lawyer and Labour MP for Bury and Radcliffe 1964-1970. He seems to have had a brief career as an actor who played, almost exclusively, judges as for example in *The Trials of Oscar Wilde* (1960). One of a very small group of Labour MPs who voted for the Silverman Bill in 1964, but then became an advocate of restoration, despite having been writing and speaking against the death penalty for years. By 1969 he was arguing for the use of some form of electronic stunning prior to despatch as per poultry. Humphry John Berkeley (1926-1994), Conservative MP for Lancaster 1959-1966. Treasurer of the NCACP 1965. Promoted the Homosexual Reform Bill, 1965. Joined Labour Party in 1970, SDP in 1981, rejoined Labour 1988. Author of the Rochester Sneath letters.

debate in the Commons.[785] The main speakers on the pro-death penalty side were, one might say, the usual suspects and included Duncan Sandys, Peter Rawlinson, David Ensor (thereby balancing the hanging ticket somewhat with the inclusion of a Labour MP to complement the two Conservative MPs), Fred Castell (general secretary of the Prison Officers Association), Inspector Reg Gale (chairman of the Police Federation), Reverend Donald Pateman, K Harvey Proctor (of the Monday Club), Mrs Charlotte Hurst (a supporter of the Sandys petition campaign who had also appeared on the *Man Alive* programme *Bring Back the Rope?)* and Harry Allen (former hangman, who had also appeared on the *Man Alive* programme). On the anti-death penalty side there were some equally familiar names with Leo Abse, MP (Labour MP and supporter of a range of progressive causes, especially homosexual law reform) and Professor Rupert Cross (Vinerian Professor of Law, Oxford University) as the main speakers, supported by Louis Blom-Cooper (barrister and by then prominent member of the NCACP), Margaret Drabble (novelist); Dr Alistair Macrae (professor of forensic medicine, Edinburgh University) and Ludovic Kennedy (writer and broadcaster). The format of the programme, innovative for *Panorama* and for television in general (though subsequently much imitated) was that of a Parliamentary debate with a studio set designed like the House of Commons with speakers on either side of the floor arranged into front and back-benches. Though the format may have been innovative the overall effect may have been somewhat stodgy. It is uncertain how effective this treatment was and how entertaining or illuminating the show may have been.[786]

Though the capital punishment debate was covered in numerous small items on news and current affairs shows over the years, especially when the matter was up for Parliamentary debate, as in the periods 1955-7, 1964-5 and 1969, rarely was it dealt with in depth. Full-blooded documentaries on the topic, as per *The Death Penalty* or *Man Alive's Bring Back the Rope?* were few and far between. Though a fascinating subject and politically contentious it may have been regarded by many television executives as just too morbid for extensive treatment.

During this whole period (1955-1969) there seems to have been remarkably little in the way of drama bearing directly on the question, maybe because it was deemed too controversial or too disturbing. The only significant

---

[785] BBC Written Archives, T58/414/1, Panorama TX 69.12.01, 15th December 1969

[786] It might be noted that the show was subject to the attentions of the Conservative Party's Monitoring Service which scrutinises programmes for bias, real or supposed, and which concluded that the programme was excellent with all issues covered, and that the pro-hanging lobby probably won the day. Norman St John Stevas, it felt, was particularly good for the anti-hangers and Reg Gale of the Police Federation for the pro-hangers. Day was thought to be an excellent chairman. Conservative Party Archives, op cit. CRD 3/19/1 - Monitoring Service Report by Sally Moussa, 20th December 1969

television drama work was *Three Clear Sundays*, a segment of the BBC's ground-breaking drama strand, *The Wednesday Play*, transmitted in April 1965. It was directed by Ken Loach, controversial pioneer of British televisual social realism, produced by James MacTaggart (the strand's regular producer) and written by Jimmy O'Connor.[787] It starred Tony Selby, Rita Webb, Glynn Edwards and George Sewell amongst a very large cast, and the story centred on a young prisoner (Selby) convicted of a minor offence who is inveigled by his cell-mates into attacking a warder who dies of his injuries. The rest of the play centres on the sequence of events leading up to his trial, conviction and execution for murder. At the end it lists a series of hangings that had gone wrong and were bungled in some way. The title referred to the legal formula, then obtaining, for the time that had to elapse between conviction and hanging.

It is a powerful and moving piece, and, like nearly all of Loach's work, unrelentingly polemical. Neither Loach nor O'Connor were reluctant to load the dice, and here the audience is manipulated ruthlessly into sympathizing with the plight of the hapless and unworldly Danny, wrongly convicted, poorly defended and generally ill-served by the system and by life, brought down by a succession of unfortunate occurrences over which he has little control. It was full of cameo performances from quirky characters in scenes that were peripheral to the plot but conveyed the realities of life in prison, and the nature of the relationship between prisoner and 'screw'. It was semi-autobiographical, or an 'emotional autobiography' as its writer put it, O'Connor having spent two months in the condemned cell in 1942 for a murder which he had ever after strenuously denied committing, though a pardon was never forthcoming. Though the play seems dated and clichéd in some respects, it was fresh and pioneering for its time, and innovative in its technique.

The BBC's audience research indicates that it may have had a significant impact on public opinion.[788] It showed the size of the audience to be 20% of the population of the UK, ITV attracting a 9% share at the same time. The audience reaction, based on a questionnaire completed by a sample of 322, which was 15% of the BBC1 viewing panel which saw all or most of the broadcast, showed that 28% gave it an A+; 35% an A; 23% a B, 8% a C and 6% a C-; giving a reaction index of 68 (above the average of 56 for the earlier *Wednesday Plays* which included a score of seventy-two for *A Tap on the Shoulder* in week

---

[787] Kenneth Loach (1936-). Television and film director noted for social realism, a naturalistic style of film-making and a strongly left-wing stance. Director of several of the *Wednesday Play* series which first brought him to prominence, especially *Up the Junction* (1965), *Cathy Come Home* (1966) and *The Big Flame* (1969). Moving to film he directed *Poor Cow* (1967), *Kes* (1969) and many others. Winner of numerous awards including the Palme D'Or at Cannes for *The Wind that Shakes the Barley* (2006). James (Jimmy) O'Connor (1918-2001) convicted murderer who was reprieved and became a professional writer. Author of several dramas in the *Wednesday Play* strand, usually with a crime theme, including the first, *A Tap on the Shoulder* (1965).

[788] BFI screen-online, www.bfi.org.uk

one).[789] It is open to question what political effect the play had, for though many viewers said they were affected by the play, one must take this with a measure of scepticism. Unlike the BBC's previous effort, *The Death Penalty*, whose audience research included an assessment of how people's views had changed as a consequence there was nothing comparable to that here. And yet it may have had as strong, if not an even stronger impact. If so it may be telling that a work of drama had more of an impact and more effect on opinion than did a whole series of factual programmes.

Though the debate over hanging rumbled on for many years in Parliament and elsewhere, after 1969 television devoted relatively little attention to it, presumably on the basis that the issue had effectively been settled and that there was little more mileage to be had out of it. Nonetheless several more programmes appeared in the post 1970 era, as well as it being a staple item on news and current affairs programmes at any time that the reintroduction of capital punishment was up for debate in the Commons, which was frequently. One might compare and contrast the televisual treatment of the capital punishment issue with its treatment of other issues of political controversy in general, and with 'conscience issues' in particular, and ask to what extent if at all it was ever influential?[790] The various conscience issues were of course treated in news, current affairs and documentary programmes from time to time, as well as occasionally being the subject of, or at any rate a plot device in, dramas, thrillers and other non-factual programming. Most notably in this regard, abortion was the subject matter of *Up The Junction* (BBC *Wednesday Play*, directed by Ken Loach and written by Nell Dunn, 1965), which was subsequently remade for the cinema two years later. As with much of Loach's work it was highly innovative in style, and created considerable controversy upon its transmission (as did several of his plays and as did much of the *Wednesday Play* strand) but it cannot be conclusively demonstrated, notwithstanding Loach's avowedly political motivation, that it had any significant influence on the abortion debate then raging. Though the law was reformed in 1967, this was very much the product of Parliamentary and pressure group activity and it would be hard to ascribe its success in any measure to public opinion having been softened up by plays such as this.

Topics such as homosexuality and divorce were often dealt with in television drama though usually simply as a plot device, and rarely did expressly propagandistic efforts emerge. Other issues of more general political

---

[789] Audience research, (week 14, VR/65/185), file TS/659/1, BBC Written Archives.

[790] The term conscience issue refers in practice to a set of controversies that emerged onto the political agenda in the 1950s and 1960s concerning, in addition to the death penalty, abortion, divorce and homosexual law reform, and to a lesser extent, theatre censorship and Sunday entertainments. Matters that have risen to prominence in more recent years such as euthanasia, embryo research and gay marriage, might also be subsumed under this rubric.

controversy were frequently the basis of drama, for example industrial relations and trade unionism (*The Lump*, Jack Gold, 1967; *The Big Flame*, Ken Loach, 1969 - both *Wednesday Plays*) being key examples; immigration and race relations (*Fable*, Christopher Morahan, 1966, another *Wednesday Play* offering); nuclear war and deterrence (*The War Game*, Peter Watkins, 1965 – though never transmitted until the 1980s); but far and away the most contentious drama to emerge and the one that clearly did have a big political impact was *Cathy Come Home* (Ken Loach, again, 1966, yet another in the *Wednesday Play* strand) which dealt with issues of poverty, unemployment, homelessness and family separation. It is fair to say that this was the most controversial television drama (and perhaps the single most controversial television programme) ever produced and transmitted, and almost certainly did produce significant results in the form of the setting up of 'Shelter', the charity for the homeless, and led to much greater public awareness of the problem of homelessness.[791] It is interesting though that this dealt with what might fairly be characterized as a mainstream issue rather a conscience one, and may have prompted greater governmental action rather than private members bills.

Notwithstanding the extensive treatment that the capital punishment controversy received and the high-impact, all-pervasive nature of the television medium there is little evidence of a substantial effect on opinion. The audience reaction research of the BBC in respect of *The Death Penalty* is interesting, but indicates that the programmes' effect was minimal. Comparing and contrasting the welter of factual programming with drama one might note the apparently greater impact on the viewing public of *Three Clear Sundays*, and speculate on whether this was due to the greater impact of drama in general, or a function of the show's heavily exploitative technique. As with the other media discussed opinion was too deeply entrenched and largely impervious to modification for even the medium of television to have much effect.

---

[791] Though it has been denied that the inception of Shelter was a function of the play, and that the timing was largely coincidental. But there is no question that the programme burned through the public consciousness and helped the success of the charity.

CHAPTER 14

CINEMA AND THEATRE

This chapter explores the role of film and the stage in the debate.

Cinema

Few films have dealt exclusively or chiefly with the question of the death penalty, though in a sense the shadow of the gallows loomed over all the murder mysteries, courtroom dramas, whodunits, etc. made during the currency of the death penalty. Many British melodramas and thrillers had the spectre of the gallows as a backdrop (so to speak) to the plot, and many films, of course, dealt more generally with themes of crime and prison life.[792] None of these, however, could be described as tackling in any way the rights and wrongs of capital punishment, and the intentions of the film-makers were plainly artistic and commercial rather than polemical. Wrongful conviction was often a theme but this was essentially a plot device not a political statement.

The only major films made in Britain in that period (mid-fifties to late-sixties) that dwelt substantially on the question were *Yield to the Night* (1956), *Time Without Pity* (1957) and *The Quare Fellow* (1962). Both *Yield to the Night* and *The Quare Fellow* dealt largely with the languors and torments of prison life and the prospect of a hanging, and both may be seen as anti-capital punishment because the morbid concentration on the imminent prospect of hangings within the prison walls inevitably brought home the barbarity of hanging as an institution. *Time Without Pity*, was a murder thriller that dealt with the attempt to save a convicted man from the gallows, and may be read as anti-capital punishment only in the limited sense that it concerned the perennial theme of an innocent man facing execution.

Yield to the Night (UK, 1956) was directed by J Lee Thompson, written by John Cresswell and Joan Henry from the latter's book (and released in the USA with the misleadingly titillating title of *Blonde Sinner)*. It is a highly effective downbeat drama about the forthcoming hanging of woman convicted of murder, set within the prison walls, but ranging over the events that led up to the murder. It was widely but wrongly assumed to be based, albeit very loosely, on the Ruth Ellis case of the previous year but the book from which the screenplay was drawn was written and published a year or more before the Ellis case hit the headlines. The film makes no secret of its political dimensions, and opens with a caption stating that the death penalty has currently been suspended

---

[792] See Crowther, Bruce, *Captured on Film: The Prison Movie* (London: Batsford, 1989)

pending the decision of the House of Lords on the abolition bill recently passed by the Commons and that: 'Whatever the outcome the permanency of this law will depend ultimately on public opinion.' The ensuing drama doesn't pull its punches and may be read as an unashamedly emotional plea to for abolition, though it is not clear that this is the film-makers intention.

It opens with the heroine Mary Hilton (Diana Dors in a powerful performance) setting off from a pigeon cluttered Trafalgar Square to a mews cottage in the West End. On the arrival of a wealthy young woman at the cottage she shoots her dead with a hail of bullets from a revolver, and stands gazing with steely-eyed resolution at her handiwork. The film shifts to the prison where she is now incarcerated awaiting her execution, due in a couple of weeks, subject to any reprieve. The daily routine of her prison life is explored in convincing and sombre fashion, whilst we are given a series of flashbacks to the events that had led her to her present pass with her voice-over narrating the flashback scenes. She meets a young man, Jim Lancaster (Michael Craig), falls in love with him, leaves her husband for him, but he is still seeing a rich young woman Lucy Carpenter, with whom he seems obsessed. After various ups and downs in their relationship he is found dead, having gassed himself in his bedsit, apparently as a result of having been spurned by Lucy. Mary is shattered and, blaming Lucy for his death, decides to kill her using a revolver she had taken from Jim some time previously.

The flashbacks are interspersed with scenes from prison life; the visits from the doctor, the chaplain, the governor, her mother and brother, and her husband from whom she is separated, and the daily excruciatingly regulated routine. In accordance with the conventions of condemned prisoners there are two warders in the cell with her the whole time, the light is always on even throughout the night so as to ensure that nothing befalls her such as a suicide attempt, and she is given close medical attention so that the hangman isn't cheated by a premature death. There is constant badinage with the rota of prison warders, sympathetic on their part, sometimes sour on hers. The tension is built slowly and remorselessly as the execution date approaches, and as she learns that there is to be no reprieve. The mixture of tedium and tension in the condemned cell is convincingly evoked, and by the end of the film it has been racked to an excruciating pitch of intensity: 'I know every mark and blemish in this cell...the door at the foot of my bed - the door without a handle - I know it better than any room I have ever lived in...the light, the light, why don't they ever put out the light.' She rails against her fate, though unremorseful about her crime: 'If they are going to do it why don't they do it quickly.' She feels as if she is on, 'a drug that slows down time and heightens emotions and sensations - is it because I am near to death?'

The tenor of the blandishments given to her by the authorities is to accept the inevitable. Reading from a book the chaplain had given her: 'For the night is already at hand and it is well to yield to the night' she resiles from these attempts to lull her to a complaisant death with, 'Perhaps it is but I want to live, I want to live more than ever', (a phrase that strangely harbingers the title of another film of a year later, *I Want To Live!*, which could be regarded as in many ways the American companion piece to this). The morning of the execution dawns and we see her go into the execution cell adjacent, through the door with no handle. The camera doesn't follow her, and fades to black. We return to the condemned cell to see the fag end of her cigarette about to drop into the ashtray.

This is one of the more explicitly anti-capital punishment films of the era, and can be read as a crudely exploitative piece of propaganda, the more so because there is no question about her guilt, or that her crime was premeditated, done in cold blood, and that she is largely unremorseful. But its evocation of the sustained gloom of the condemned cell is masterly. It does not, however, address itself to some of the deeper questions surrounding the death penalty, which are aired in the film by a few colloquial exchanges such as where one warder says, 'Of course I feel sorry for her but you mustn't forget the other one - the one that was murdered' and another replies, 'Oh, I don't but another death won't bring her back' *Halliwell* assesses it as: 'gloomy prison melodrama making an emotional plea against capital punishment', while *Time Out* concurs that it is, 'decidedly anti- capital punishment... but it never, however, attempts to explore in any depth the relationship between the legal practice of hanging and society's attitudes to crime.'[793]

A year later came *Time Without Pity* (UK, 1957) directed by Joseph Losey (his first film in Britain after having been blacklisted in his native USA), written by Ben Barzman, from the play *Someone Waiting* by Emlyn Williams. This is an overblown and vaguely absurd British thriller about the efforts of an alcoholic writer to save the life of his son who is due to be hanged in twenty four hours, by uncovering some new evidence that will clear him. The film is ludicrously overacted all round, and the direction is melodramatic to breaking point, whilst the plot is obscure at times to say the least.

It opens in an ultra-dramatic sequence with a murder being committed, full of portentous imagery. It moves to the arrival in London from Canada of David Graham (Michael Redgrave) an alcoholic writer who has come to see his son Alec (Alec McCowen) who is about to be hanged for the murder. He hopes to come up with some last minute evidence that will clear him, but Alec's lawyer Clayton (Peter Cushing) tells him that the case against him is overwhelming. We see him race around London, seeing all and sundry in a desperate effort to save Alec. He visits Alec in prison who rejects him, goes to see the murdered girl's sister, goes to see the family who had been putting his

---

[793] Pym, John (ed), *Time Out Film Guide*, seventh edition (Harmondsworth: Penguin, 1999) p.1026; Walker, John (ed) *Halliwell's Film and Video Guide*, twelfth edition (London: Harper Collins, 1996) p.841

son up prior to the murder, keeps an appointment with a Home Office minister in an unavailing effort to get a further stay, etc. He goes to the House of Commons where an MP is giving a press conference to publicise his campaign against capital punishment, using the Alec Graham case as the immediate cause. Graham is also fighting a personal battle against alcoholism; at several points in the film resisting the impulse to drink, but giving way at other times. Eventually, after a good deal of somewhat opaque clue-chasing he concludes that his son's erstwhile protector Robert Stanford (Leo McKern) is the murderer and confronts him with the accusation at a race-track. Going back to Stanford's office he pulls a gun on him, and engineers a struggle in which he deliberately arranges for Stanford to shoot him dead in the tussle. Stanford's wife and son conveniently arrive on the scene at that moment to see Graham lying dead with Stanford having apparently killed him. Stanford pleads that it was an accident, while Stanford's son phones Clayton to instruct him to tell the Home Office to stop the execution since Stanford has killed Graham. The film abruptly ends there.

The film is deeply unsatisfactory in many respects. Its direction is overblown, there is very heavy-handed use of symbolism such as the incessant and obvious use of clocks (particularly in one scene where he goes to a house full of madly ticking timepieces), the incidental music hammers you remorselessly, and the acting is very over the top with Graham's alcoholism a tiresomely incessant theme. From the point of view of narrative logic it is far from clear how Graham arrives at the conclusion that Stanford is the murderer, and it is difficult to comprehend how he thinks that framing Stanford for his own murder/suicide is going to save his son from the rope. The film seems to take this point for granted, with the final line of the film being Stanford's son's telephone injunction to Clayton to tell the Home Office to stop the hanging. Though the hanging might well have been halted in the light of these events it is debatable to say the least what effect it might have had on the case.

From the point of view of the capital punishment controversy the film's impact is questionable. There are several references in the film to the barbarity or outmodedness of the rope, and the distress of the son at the prospect of his imminent execution is evident (though not entirely convincing in view of his earlier apparent indifference to his fate). More importantly the brief scene in which the politician argues his case against the rope is presented as little more than a cheap stunt on his part designed for self-publicity, and his professed unconcern with the guilt or innocence of Alec Graham leaves him as incidental to the plot. A newspaper editor, and former friend of David Graham's, contemptuously dismisses Graham's appeal to him to do something by querying why he had not seen fit to do anything about any of the other hangings that had taken place. He seems anyway to be quite satisfied about the prospect of executing murderers. The Home Office junior minister who rejects Graham's appeal for a further stay is portrayed sympathetically, having apparently carefully explored all the evidence before allowing matters to proceed. Notwithstanding the film's occasional references to the hanging controversy it is essentially a thriller rather than a political polemic. It centres on the wrongful conviction theme, and not on the rights and wrongs of hanging. Critical judgments again vary with *Time Out* describing it as: 'an undeniably powerful film...conceived with raw-edged brilliance', while *Halliwell* is less complimentary calling it a 'heavy-going, introspective, hysterical downbeat melodrama which takes itself with a seriousness which is almost deadly.'[794]

A few years later *The Quare Fellow* (UK, 1962) was released, written and directed by Arthur Dreifuss from the stage play by Brendan Behan. This is a quirky British/Irish Republic co-production, released in the year of Hanratty's hanging, both gloomy and jocular at the same time, informed by a puckish Irish humour that relieves the gloom.

The film follows life in a Dublin prison (Mountjoy) through the eyes of a new, young prison warder, Crimmin (played by Patrick McGoohan). There are two hangings pending in a couple of weeks, 'Silvertops' and 'the Quare Fellow' (Irish slang for a condemned man), both of whom have been convicted of murder. Crimmin is assigned to assist Regan, a veteran warder, who has charge of the hangings. Regan is cynical and world-weary but distinctly unhappy about the merits of hangings. Crimmin seems to have few such doubts. The film follows the daily routine of prison life, and the interaction between the warders and the prisoners. Though the action is realistic, the characters are in the main stereotypical Irish types, who seem to conform to an Anglo-Saxon view of the Irish as rascally and loveably conniving alcoholics.

Crimmin meets the wife of the 'Quare Fellow', Kathleen, who happens to be his landlady's niece. Her initial hostility to him, on account of his being a prison officer, mellows to the point where she explains to him the reason for her husband's crime, which had never been given in court. He had discovered her in bed with his brother and hacked him to death in the proverbial fit of jealous rage. He had not revealed any of this in court, and had not allowed her to, so as to preserve her reputation against charges of adultery. Crimmin tells Regan the story, who tries to tell the governor. Kathleen tracks down the governor at a social function and tells him the story. He in turn informs the minister by phone. The hangman and his assistant (based very loosely on the English hangmen Thomas and Albert Pierrepoint who had carried out several hangings at Mountjoy in the 1940s when Behan was a prisoner there) arrive in Dublin and there is a sub-plot involving the hangman losing his 'box of tools' containing the rope etc., after a pub-crawl. The box is eventually found and there is a punch-up in the bar.

There is no word of a reprieve and the preparations for the hanging go ahead under the supervision of Regan and Crimmin with the prisoners digging

---

[794] Pym, John (ed), ibid, p.920; Walker, John (ed), ibid p.762

his grave. The hours leading up to the execution are dwelt on with a lengthy scene showing the 'Quare Fellow' being led into the execution cell with the hood over his head, having the rope placed around his neck, and the lever being pulled by the hangman releasing the trap. The scene switches at that instant to the bar nearby and the solemn reactions of the customers, and then back to the cell showing the taut rope, with an ashen-faced Crimmin looking on.

As with *I Want to Live!* (an American film released a few years previously) there is considerable detail about the grim mechanics of the execution itself, although in this case of course a hanging rather than the gas chamber. There is skilful evocation of the atmosphere of tension pervading the prison in the hours leading up to the awful moment. Thus the film's message stands or falls by the rights and wrongs of the rope. As Dreifuss himself is supposed to have said of the film, comparing it to *I Want to Live!*, where that film had been about whether society had hanged the wrong person, 'this one is about whether society has a right to hang the right person - guilty or not doesn't come into this - we really are making this film on faith, spit and belief. We can't believe that the judicial process it describes can go on ad infinitum.'

There was apparently considerable difficulty in getting the finance for the film, since according to Dreifuss it 'scared the hell out of the movie magnates' and he had to struggle to get it made both at Columbia and in the British studios. He was rewarded by it winning the prize for the Best Film of 1962 by the British Producers Association. There is much good dialogue in the film and some mildly amusing moments, presumably inherited from the Behan stage-play, though there is an irritating tendency for it to descend into stage 'Irishness'. When Silvertops learns of his reprieve and the substitution of a sentence of life imprisonment he exclaims, 'Life!'. 'Better than death', is the reply. When an official is being shown round the prison he argues about hanging with Regan and says in reply to the latter's jaundiced view of hangings that, 'some of them die holier deaths than if they had lived a natural span', to which Regan rejoins, 'We can't advertise that or they would all be at it - they take religion seriously in this country'.

In fact the screenplay had altered Behan's original play in several respects, opening it out to include the city of Dublin beyond the narrow confines of the prison in which the play had been exclusively set. It also altered the plot by introducing a greater measure of justification or mitigation for the Quare Fellow's actions, a concession perhaps by the film's makers to the backers insofar as a justification represents a softening of the film's anti-capital punishment message.[795] Moreover, in the stage original Silvertops is a very camp homosexual, no doubt felt to be far too controversial for a British audience of the time. Halliwell, perhaps for this reason, calls it, 'a watered down version of a rumbustious stage tragi-comedy with not much but the gloom

---

[795] Crowther, op cit. p. 155

left.'[796] Its impact is debatable, though Alexander Walker in the *Evening Standard* called it: 'The best argument yet against hanging', and the *Times* described it as, 'One of the most sombre and uncompromising indictments against capital punishment ever to be drawn up on the screen.'

Given that the death penalty was far more prevalent in the USA than in Britain it is perhaps not surprising that there were rather more American films dealing, expressly or otherwise, with the topic than there were British. Possibly the outstanding film dealing with the question of capital punishment at this time was *Twelve Angry Men,* Sidney Lumet's stunning directorial debut, released in 1957 in the USA, a gripping jury-room drama, dealing with the struggle of the liberal Henry Fonda to convince his fellow jurors of the innocence of the accused. Wrongful conviction as an argument against the death penalty is more explicitly covered in *Beyond a Reasonable Doubt,* directed in the USA by Fritz Lang and released in 1956. Here the plot ingeniously has the hero faking his own complicity in a murder in order to get himself charged and convicted so as then to produce the exculpatory evidence at the last moment, all designed to undermine confidence in the judicial system. Needless to say, the plan backfires. Other outstanding American films of the period are *I Want to Live!* (Robert Wise, 1958) and *Paths of Glory* (Stanley Kubrick, 1957). The latter is a cinematic masterpiece dealing with a court-martial in the French army during the First World War, and its message is pre-eminently anti-war rather than anti-capital punishment. These American films would of course have made their way across the Atlantic and been seen in British cinemas, but whatever their commercial success in Britain their political impact may have been muted by the American context and lack of applicability to the British judicial system.

One might mention that, in more recent years, long after abolition, several films have appeared dealing with the events and the *causes celebre* of the period. *10 Rillington Place*, released in Britain in 1970, directed by Richard Fleischer, and starring Richard Attenborough as Christie, deals with the Evans/Christie imbroglio and was based on Ludovic Kennedy's masterly account of the cases. *Dance with a Stranger*, released in Britain in 1984, directed by Mike Newell, was an account of the Ruth Ellis case, and *Let Him Have It*, released in 1991 and directed by Peter Medak, was an account of the Craig/Bentley case. As yet no feature film has appeared dealing with the Hanratty case, although several television documentaries have been made on the subject. British *causes celebre* of the post-capital punishment era have been explored in films such as *In the Name of the Father* (the Guildford pub bombing case). And executioner Albert Pierrepoint, has been the subject of a biographical film, *Pierrepoint* (2005), directed by Adrian Shergold and starring Timothy Spall in the title role.[797] All of which may demonstrate that British

---

[796] Walker, John (ed), op cit, p.608

[797] Albert Pierrepoint (1905-1992). A member of a family of British hangmen - following his father Henry and uncle Thomas into the business. The most prolific hangman of the twentieth

cinema has become bolder, and less shy of dealing with political controversy than in former years, though on the other hand it could be argued that there is little controversial about the depiction of long-ago cases which are now universally recognized as miscarriages.

To what extent are these films anti-capital punishment? In the sense that many of them deal with the possibility of wrongful conviction, a major strand of the abolitionist case, they may be said to be so, but one has to exercise great caution in rushing to such conclusions. Wrongful conviction, especially in capital cases, with the innocent party being saved from the gallows (or the electric chair or the gas chamber) in the nick of time by the hero who identifies and nails the real culprit is very much a staple of the thriller (cinematic and otherwise), employed (in endless subtle variations) in innumerable films. Hitchcock's *Dial M for Murder, The Wrong Man,* and *Witness for the Prosecution* spring to mind. Wrongful conviction is often merely a plot device, not a political statement, and should not be too hastily construed as an anti-capital punishment polemic on the part of the makers.

Nonetheless some of these films clearly were intended as such by the director/screenwriter/producers etc. If so, were they successful in bringing about any change in the public mind, or were they just dismissed as entertainments, devoid of political content? It is easy to believe that in the climate of the fifties and early sixties, with opinion moving slowly but discernibly in an abolitionist direction, some of these films may have chimed with the public mood and hardened the focus of a growing, albeit vague, unease about the death penalty, but it is doubtful if any of them, taken individually or collectively, would have changed anyone's views about the death penalty. They were products of their times, but it is very unlikely that they had any significant effect on either public opinion or government policy. Interestingly most of the relevant films seem to have appeared either in the mid to late fifties when the controversy was at its height rather than later in the sixties. Maybe the politically committed cinema had by then become pre-occupied with other issues and the capital punishment battle felt to be won in all but name. By contrast with the British cinema the American film industry has continued to turn out capital punishment oriented fare continuously, doubtless reflecting the fact that it is still a matter of intense controversy there.

---

century, in office 1932-1956, he hanged 433 men and 17 women including over 200 Nazi war criminals and 6 US servicemen at Shepton Mallet. Carried out executions at various English and Scottish prisons, at Mountjoy Prison, Dublin, various colonial locations and at Hameln, Germany and Graz, Austria. Hanged William Joyce (Lord Haw-Haw), John George Haigh, Timothy Evans, John Christie, Derek Bentley and Ruth Ellis among numerous others. After resigning from the lists in 1956 he eventually became an advocate of abolition! Published his autobiography in 1974 in which he re-iterated his conversion to abolition, questioning the deterrent value of hanging and claiming that it was little more than organized revenge.

One might compare and contrast this with the part played by film in other reform campaigns of the time, and its use as a medium for the expression of political views in general. Film has not infrequently been utilized as a propaganda weapon but rarely if ever has it had a significant or decisive effect on the success of political campaigns. The most obvious comparison is with cinema's treatment of the other conscience issues paramount in the period from the mid 1950s to the late 1960s.

Abortion, for example, was the subject of, or played a significant role in, several films of the era, most notably *Look Back in Anger* (Tony Richardson, 1958 - based on the play by John Osborne), *Saturday Night and Sunday Morning* (Karel Reisz, 1960 - based on the novel by Alan Sillitoe), *The L-Shaped Room* (Bryan Forbes, 1962 - based on the novel by Lynne Reid Banks), *Alfie* (Lewis Gilbert, 1966 – based on the play by Bill Naughton) and *Up The Junction* (Peter Collinson, 1968 from the novel by Nell Dunn, and already and more famously a television play). These, certainly the first three, could be classified as 'kitchen sink' dramas, typical of the British New Wave of the late 1950s and early 1960s, whilst the latter two might be characterized as 'swinging sixties' films which evolved from the former, typical of the middle to late 1960s. These films were all very much products of their time. Whilst these films often had a big impact artistically and stylistically it would be difficult to say that they were self-consciously polemical or that they significantly accelerated the pace of social change, rather than their being merely indicative of the direction in which society was moving. In none of them was the question of abortion really pre-eminent, except perhaps the last.

Homosexual law reform, to take another key example of a social issue, was also occasionally the subject matter of films of the period, though homosexuality (and lesbianism) was sometimes a plot device, and political axe-grinding was usually subordinate to the aims of the film-makers to entertain rather than lecture. Key British films here include *Victim* (Basil Dearden, 1961), *A Taste of Honey* (Tony Richardson, 1961 from the novel by Shelagh Delaney), *The Leather Boys* (Sidney J Furie, 1964) and *The Killing of Sister George* (Robert Aldrich, 1968), in addition to American films such as *Advise and Consent* (Otto Preminger, 1962).

On the other hand the potentially explosive question of coloured immigration and race relations, which emerged onto the political agenda in this era, became the topic of several British films such as *Sapphire* (Basil Dearden, 1959), *Flame in the Streets* (Roy Ward Baker, 1961 with a screenplay by Ted Willis), *A Taste of Honey* (Tony Richardson, 1961), and *The L-Shaped Room* (Bryan Forbes, 1962) though of course it was treated far more extensively in the American cinema of the period. These films, too, explored the question though rarely if ever altered minds or shaped government policy. Other political hot potatoes that were dealt with in the British cinema of the epoch were nuclear weapons: *The Day The Earth Caught Fire* (Val Guest, 1961) and *Dr Strangelove* (Stanley Kubrick, 1964); and industrial relations in the satirical *I'm All Right Jack* (John Boulting, 1959) and *The Angry Silence* (Guy Green, 1960). Whilst the British cinema did not treat extensively of the hanging question, and then not clearly with any propagandist voice, attempts at which may have been curtailed anyway by the film censor, the theatre was on the whole even less enamoured of the subject.

Theatre

As with the cinema few plays have dealt expressly with the topic, the British stage being not very receptive to strongly political or polemical works, either then or now.

Easily the most famous is *The Quare Fellow*. Written by the Irish dramatist, poet, novelist and critic Brendan Behan in 1954, and already alluded to in the film section, *The Quare Fellow* was originally performed in 1954 at the Pike Theatre in Dublin (co-incidentally the year of the last hanging in the Irish Republic) and was Behan's debut as a dramatist.[798] In 1956 it was staged by Joan Littlewood's Theatre Workshop at Stratford East, London to considerable acclaim. The play is a tragi-comedy, showing the grim realities of prison life and the events leading up to a pair of hangings due to take place, and is based in part of his own experiences of imprisonment in Mountjoy Prison, Dublin for terrorist-related activities. The style is Brechtian with the use of song and dance and direct addresses to the audience to make its points. Whilst the first half of the play is largely comic the second half is slow, melancholic and tragic. It can be viewed as an attack on the institution of capital punishment, or as a satire on prison life. Whilst a very celebrated play and by a famous author, it is probably fair to say that its impact on the debate over capital punishment was little or non-existent, its themes perhaps too particular to Behan's own experiences, and altogether too 'highbrow'.[799]

Arguably of somewhat greater direct relevance, though much less national impact, was *Hang down your head and die*. This was a satirical revue somewhat along the lines of *Oh, What A Lovely War!* (then still a Joan Littlewood theatre production and not filmed until several year later) which

---

[798] Brendan Francis Behan (1923-1964). Irish poet, playwright and novelist. One-time IRA member, imprisoned for republican activities the period 1939-1946, serving time in Mountjoy. *The Quare Fellow* was his first play to be produced and was based on his own experiences of prison.

[799] Incidentally, the film version changes the play very considerably in both plot and atmosphere, because in the play one or both of the condemned men have been convicted of a homosexual offence, something probably deemed too controversial for the film-makers of 1962.

gave the same dramatic treatment to the gallows that *Oh, What A Lovely War!* gave to the First World War. It was originally produced for the Oxford University's Experimental Theatre Club, an essentially undergraduate body, in February 1964, having been written over the preceding few months, and was staged at the Oxford Playhouse.

It was produced by Braham Murray, devised by David Wright, designed by Michael Ackland and written by a collection of people, chiefly undergraduates, including David Wright, Robert Hewison, Michael Palin and Terry Jones, the last two of whom went on to fame as one third of the Monty Python team.[800] It was very much a collaborative effort with most of the writers also amongst its cast of seventeen including both Palin and Jones. It had an eleven day run at the Oxford Playhouse starting on 11th February 1964 to packed houses and rave reviews before achieving enough critical approbation to transfer briefly to Stratford and then to the Comedy Theatre in the West End in March/April 1964 where it ran for six weeks at the Comedy Theatre still under the auspices of Braham Murray.[801]

Like its theatrical precursor, *Oh What A Lovely War!*, it deployed the Brechtian conceit of using a light-hearted and innocuous setting (though with vaguely sinister undertones), in this case a circus, which then transforms to other more sombre settings (the courtroom, the condemned cell, the gallows) throwing into much sharper relief the horrors of its real subject matter. By the same token the characters start out as those appropriate to the circus; ringmasters, clowns, jugglers, a strongman, bareback riders, lion-tamers, tumblers etc and then metamorphose with the changes of scene. Thus the ringmasters become judges or figures of authority in general, and most tellingly the strongman becomes the hangman and the white-faced clown (played apparently by Terry Jones) becomes the condemned man. Like the *Quare Fellow*, its theatrical precursor, it is in two parts, with the first light and jocular and the second grave and melancholy following the course of a murder case from judgment to hanging.[802] The tone of the whole piece was darkly ironic throughout and was clearly designed to heap scorn on hanging as an institution by subjecting it to sustained mockery. There is no doubt that the sympathies of the show's creators were deeply hostile to capital punishment and that their

---

[800] Attested to by various websites such as *http://movies.yahoo.com;*
http://www.pbs.org/hemingway/palin; http://www.dailyllama.com/spam/audio; and
www.geocities.com/fang_club/Jones_biog.html
[801] *http://www.royalexchange.co.uk.* Michael Elwyn, an actor in the production said that, unusually for a provincial student production, it was watched and reviewed by Harold Hobson of the *Sunday Times*, amongst others, who described it as brilliant. Michael Codron, a London impresario, saw it and was so impressed by it that he offered to take it to Stratford and the West End of London complete with the whole cast., virtually unchanged in content. Michael Elwyn, personal communication, 28th September 2006
[802] I am grateful to David Wood, one of the writer/performers, for giving me a copy of the transcript of the play, along with other valuable and interesting material.

intentions in staging it were essentially polemical.

The bulk of the material consisted of parodic comedy, song and dance routines, interspersed with mimed sketches and set speeches presenting the 'official view' delivered po-faced by an onstage 'Narrator' often against the backdrop of comic routines illustrating his words. Thus, for example, early in the show the Narrator reads out the words of the Gowers Commission dealing with the method of execution to be preferred; the options being hanging, shooting, electrocution and the gas chamber. Behind him the circus performers act out these methods with the clown being the condemned man. A band at the rear of the stage were got up like circus musicians; there was a screen upon which slides were projected depicting quotations from the proceedings of the Gowers Commission; and one heard occasional offstage voices, representing the opinions of the general public such as: 'Why pay £14 a week for a man who is no use to himself or anyone else?'; 'I don't think it's worth keeping them alive and feeding them and everything if they do things like that.'

The songs centred around different aspects of capital punishment; for example the best method of execution - with an Elvis Presley type singing to a rock-and-roll rhythm about how, if given the choice, he would prefer gas:

> When I was first convicted
> On that gloomy fateful day
> The judge he said to me have you anything to say
> I said - give me gas for can't you see
> That hanging, shooting, electric chair aren't
> Good enough for me.
> Do you wanna be hanged - no, no,
> Do you wanna be shot - no, no,
> Do you wanna be electrocuted my friend?
> I said no, no, no, that's not the way to end -
> I want gas zzz zzzz
> I want gas zzz zzzz
> I want something with class - gas has -
> I want gas…

Or 'the British way to die' (sung in the style of Noel Coward):

> Throughout our history
> It's been no mystery
> Why Englishmen have reigned supreme
> We stand on our dignity
> And spread no malignity
> And by all other nations are held in high esteem
> The British way of living
> Has a quality that's rare
> But the British way of dying is quite beyond compare…

And how the hangman decided on the length of the rope:-

> When I applied to do this job
> I didn't realise
> The technicalities involved
> To attain true expertise
> but thanks to Hangman Berry
> its easier by far
> Its simple to get good results - just use his formula...

And much else in that vein.

It was contentious enough, even on paper, to attract the attentions of the Lord Chamberlain, Lord Cobbold, who then still possessed powers of pre-production censorship over every theatre in the land. He initially demanded large cuts in the revue, amounting to about two-thirds of the whole piece, before it had even started its Oxford run, on the basis of the transcript only, though it is difficult to see what legitimate concern he may have had given that it contained no sex, overt violence or swearing.[803] Nonetheless, the transcript was returned heavily laden with blue pencil. A protest by the producer Braham Murray to Lord Gardiner (in his capacity as a leading light of the abolition movement) led to Murray, writer-in-chief David Wright, Gardiner, Lord (Ted) Willis (in his capacity as secretary of the executive committee of the League of Dramatists) and Kenneth Robinson, Labour MP for St Pancras (at that time shadow minister for health) interceding with the Lord Chamberlain on the grounds that he was effectively seeking to exercise political censorship on a question of acute topical concern.[804]

A meeting was arranged with the Lord Chamberlain's representative, the Assistant Comptroller, a Lieutenant-Colonel Eric Penn (the Lord Chamberlain himself, one assumes, being too august a figure to be required to deal personally with writers and politicians) at his offices off Trafalgar Square sometime in late January 1964.[805] The arguments raged to and fro in which in essence Penn voiced the objections (whether emanating from him or the Lord Chamberlain himself is not clear) which were numerous: anything remotely controversial;

---

[803] Braham Murray, the producer, felt that the cuts demanded (which were about two-thirds of the play!) were essentially a matter of political censorship in that the Lord Chamberlain objected to anything that smacked of criticism of capital punishment as an institution, even where the material was no more than a statement of fact. Braham Murray, *personal communications*, 28th September and 1st October 2006. Michael Elwyn, op cit, thinks that it was the overall impact of the piece that attracted the Lord Chamberlain's concern, i.e. the tendency of it, 'to make the audience laugh and then to chill them into silence'. Both Elwyn and Murray recall that a scene depicting the execution of the Rosenbergs was especially disliked for its presumed shock effect (in every sense!).

[804] Block and Hostettler, op cit, p 230. *The Times*, 8th February 1964.

[805] Murray, ibid. The date of the meeting was probably 27th January.

any direct quotes even from the Royal Commission; anything that might have offended living persons, or relatives of dead persons; anything to do with ladies underwear (evidently something in the revue involved this) etc, etc. Gardiner and co. argued out the merits of the play and the unfairness of the cuts that were being demanded.[806]

Finally, an exasperated Gardiner, who had hitherto been quiet, told the Assistant Comptroller in no uncertain terms that there would soon be a Labour government; that he would be Lord Chancellor in it; and that the office of Lord Chamberlain (and that of Assistant Comptroller presumably) was an anachronism and that he would, as Lord Chancellor, abolish the powers of theatre censorship that it conferred.[807] Certainly Gardiner's prediction came true in most respects because within a few years the powers of the Lord Chamberlain to censor the theatre were, like the gallows, swept away. Whatever the effect of Gardiner's intervention the Lord Chamberlain was persuaded to rescind his decision and shortly after Murray received notification that the revue could go ahead almost as originally written, with the exception of a piece about the Rosenbergs which was still deemed just too shocking (literally as well as figuratively!).

Whatever the actual merits of the cuts demanded (and certainly there would have been numerous heads under which such a production might have been caught) it is difficult to escape the suspicion that the chief reasons were political in that the Lord Chamberlain (possibly in consultation with the Home Office) was reluctant to have anything depicted on the stage that smacked of contemporary controversy in such a way that might pre-empt Parliamentary deliberation, and particularly if it was felt designed to mock hallowed institutions.

However, the Lord Chamberlain affair gave huge favourable publicity to what might otherwise have been an obscure provincial student play and probably added to whatever impact it might anyway have had.[808] The whole affair certainly attracted the attention of the press with the *Daily Telegraph* for example reporting on the matter of the cuts and whether the Lord Chamberlain would relent.[809]

Critical comment was almost unanimously favourable, mostly strongly so, from reviewers in the local and University press to the national press, both in its initial run and in its later West End incarnation. Harold Hobson in the *Sunday Times*, whilst lamenting somewhat the explicitly political motives of the show's creators, described it as, 'like the "white" chapter in *Moby Dick* is both

---

[806] Murray, ibid

[807] Murray, ibid

[808] Murray, ibid. It was not the only occasion that Murray suffered censorship at the hands of the Lord Chamberlain having two further plays subject to the dread blue pencil including his production of Joe Orton's *Loot*

[809] *Daily Telegraph*, 11th February 1964

horrible and beautiful...Terrible as Greek tragedy, it has tragedy's effect of purgation.'[810] The *Stage* described it as, 'a vividly attacking, swift-moving, bitterly witty and on the whole polished piece of imaginative entertainment'.[811] On its transfer to London the reviews were equally effusive. Milton Shulman in the *Evening Standard* said that, 'we are entertained in the best sense of the word and at the same time pummelled into thinking...The nightmare sequence of a condemned man about to die with a particularly eerie representation of a Punch and Judy show about hanging is one of the most imaginative single strokes of theatre I have seen in a very long time.'[812] Bernard Levin in the *Daily Mail* described it as, 'brilliant, passionate, hilarious and staggeringly professional...a surpassingly moving, funny and relentless marriage of theatre and theme.'[813] It also came top in a London theatre critic's poll for the best new revue of the year according to the *Sunday Telegraph*.[814]

During its London run it numbered several Cabinet ministers in its audience including Home Secretary Henry Brooke, not to mention other luminaries such as Princess Margaret and Lord Snowden. Whether this had any effect on Brooke's views of hanging is highly debatable, though he subsequently moved from being a strong hanger to being a cautious abolitionist to the extent of voting for the Silverman abolition bill a few months later (though he allowed a further two hangings - the last two - to take place in August of that year).

It then transferred to Broadway to the Mayfair Theatre in New York for one night only, though with a completely new and professional cast, where it received mixed reviews. Of course the production (as well as the cast) may have undergone substantial changes in the transition from Oxford and London to Broadway but one might suppose that English undergraduate humour did not translate well to the American theatre, and probably also that American theatre audiences were even less enamoured of political productions than were their British counterparts. Undoubtedly the show struck a chord with the English theatre-going public, which it probably did not with the American public, being perhaps less receptive to the heavy irony and bemused by some of the cultural references.

Other plays of the period on the English stage that at least touched on capital punishment included *Now Barabbas* by the prolific William Douglas-Home, though it deals only tangentially with the subject.[815] It was first performed at the Bolton's Theatre in Kensington in 1947 and was filmed in

---

[810] *The Sunday Times*, 16th February 1964

[811] *The Stage*, 20th February 1964

[812] *The Evening Standard*, March or April 1964

[813] *The Daily Mail,* March or April 1964 (?)

[814] *The Sunday Telegraph*, 22nd March 1964

[815] www.doollee.com

1949. This was a prison drama featuring a group of inmates, one of whom is a convicted murderer awaiting the gallows and hoping for a reprieve. There was a one-act play called *The New Hangman* by Laurence Housman that had a run in or about 1948 and may have been written partly to accompany the 1948 abolition drive, and to which reference is made by the NCADP.[816] A play by Ludovic Kennedy, an abolition campaigner and later chronicler of miscarriages, *Murder Story* was staged at the Cambridge Theatre in 1954 and then on radio in 1956. One might also mention R G Gregory's *Death at the New Year* first performed at Scarborough in 1962 which tells the story of a murder for which the perpetrator is eventually hanged and explores the law on capital punishment as it then was.

It is striking that during the period in question, when the controversy over the death penalty was at its height, only two (major) plays on the English stage dealt specifically with the topic; *The Quare Fellow* roughly at the start of the period (its 1956 London debut occurred the year before the passage of the Homicide Act) and *Hang down your head and die* towards the end of it (a year before the enactment of the Abolition Act). Behan's work was the more celebrated and has been frequently revived, partly because of the universality of its themes which transcend the issue of capital punishment, and because of the posthumous celebrity that Behan has gained. *Hang down your head* by contrast was very much a product of its time and place and though a great critical and popular success has not been revived.

Both were poignant and powerful works that doubtless animated their audiences and provoked public debate, reflecting as they did major contemporary concerns. But it is questionable whether either play had any significant impact upon the balance of public opinion or the course of political events. Theatre audiences were, then as now, minuscule and drawn pre-eminently from a small metropolitan, intellectual elite wholly unrepresentative of the general population. The two plays' polemical messages would likely have served only to confirm prejudices not shake them, notwithstanding the understandable but somewhat naïve belief of some of the progenitors of *Hang down your head* that it put a stop to hangings in the short-term (pending the enactment of abolition in the longer term).

Comparing theatre and cinema it is notable that the former produced a couple of works more poignant and polemical on the subject of capital punishment than anything managed in the latter during the relevant period. This reflects perhaps the greater focus of the theatre on social issues in the late fifties and early sixties, by comparison with the much more commercially driven cinema which tended to bypass political controversy and featured capital

---

[816] NCADP letter to members, February 1948, Gardiner papers, op cit. Laurence Housman, (1865-1959), a socialist and pacifist campaigner and the younger brother of the poet A E Housman, was a prolific author of plays and poetry. *The New Hangman* seems to have been published originally in 1930, and may or may not have had an earlier run. It is unclear where its 1948 run was or for how long it ran, and whether it was revived as part of a propaganda campaign to accompany the abolition movement of that year.

punishment only as plot device if at all. In the period in question the British cinema produced only *Yield to the Night* and the film version of *The Quare Fellow* as significant contributions (and the latter was an Anglo-Irish co-production that somewhat changed Behan's original).

CHAPTER 15

ABOLITION AND AFTER (1965-1969)

This chapter looks at the immediate post-abolition phase from 1965 to 1969, and focuses particularly on the political manoeuvring to ensure the passage of the confirmatory vote required by the Abolition Act.

After a prolonged Parliamentary battle a private members bill to give effect to abolition, introduced by Silverman in December 1964 shortly after the election of a Labour government, was successfully steered through both Houses. Its passage was certainly not without incident, and included an attempt by the Conservative Party to wreck the government's timetable by forcing the Abolition Bill back onto the floor of the Commons at Committee stage, obliging the government to allow morning sittings rather than to give up its own time to the Bill. The Murder (Abolition of Death Penalty) Act received the Royal Assent in November, 1965. A moratorium on hangings had been in force from October 1964, and the hangings of Allen and Evans in August 1964 were to prove to be the last in English criminal history. It had been a gargantuan struggle and though undoubtedly a triumph for the abolitionist cause the one fly in the ointment from their point of view was that an amendment (moved by Henry Brooke) had been tacked onto the Bill at the Committee stage which required that, by July 1970, the Act had to be confirmed by a vote of both Houses. In default of this or in the event of it being defeated in either or both Houses the Act would expire and the status quo ante would be revived; i.e. the Homicide Act's division into capital and non-capital murder would be revived, with the former subject again to the death penalty.

Most abolitionists were confident of surmounting that obstacle when the time came, but few could have been under any illusions that there would be a big effort by the supporters of hanging to re-introduce it and that they would not necessarily wait the full five years. Much depended, in the short-term, on the murder rate and the effect that that might have on public opinion, which in turn could influence some of the fainter-hearted or more cautious abolitionists within the Conservative Party, not to mention some of the more unconvinced Labour MPs. Also much depended on the party balance in the Commons. It was impossible to predict at that juncture whether there would still be a small Labour majority in five years time, or a much larger one, or a Conservative majority.

In December 1965 Wilson had re-shuffled his Cabinet and Soskice was replaced at the Home Office by Roy Jenkins, who inaugurated a reformist era during his two year tenure of that office.[817] Wilson went to the country for a renewed mandate in March 1966 and was duly rewarded with an overall majority of nearly a hundred. Though the issue of capital punishment did not feature prominently in that election (and it would have been unusual if it had given that economic and industrial questions predominated as usual) the most interesting feature from the capital punishment viewpoint was the intercession of an explicitly pro-hanging candidate in Silverman's constituency. Silverman was challenged at Nelson and Colne by Patrick Downey, the uncle of Lesley Anne Downey, one of the victims of the notorious Moors murderers, Myra Hindley and Ian Brady (murders committed very recently and very near to the constituency).[818] The Conservative candidate, Peter Davies, was a lukewarm retentionist who appeared to have made a belated conversion to the hanging cause as a matter of electoral expediency, and it was far from clear whether Downey would take more votes from the Conservative candidate or from Silverman, given that he declared himself to be a Labour supporter on most issues. While some felt Silverman was in danger of losing the seat he himself was confident of retaining it.[819] In the event, Downey polled over 5,000 votes, the largest vote until then ever achieved by a genuinely independent candidate (who was not a former MP) in a general election since 1945. It was indicative of the strength of public feeling on the matter, at least in Nelson and Colne. Nonetheless, Silverman doubled his majority to four and a half thousand, and the national swing to Labour was replicated. It may well have been that Downey took more votes from the Conservative than from Silverman, and it is difficult to interpret the full significance of the result.

After that the question of restoration died down somewhat for a period as both sides waited to take stock of the effects of abolition, though there were intermittent demands from various sources for restoration and Conservative MP and former minister Duncan Sandys was soon mobilizing the Conservative backbenches in support of restoration. In November 1967 James Callaghan replaced Roy Jenkins at the Home Office in a straight swap, having resigned from the Chancellorship after devaluation. Though a less liberal figure than Jenkins he was a firm supporter of abolition, and had always voted for abolition in the House from 1948 onwards.[820]

---

[817] A widespread fallacy is that Jenkins was Home Secretary at the time of abolition. Despite his fervent support for it he was not in position, neither in 1964-5, nor again in 1969 when the confirmatory votes were held, having by then swapped offices with Jim Callaghan.

[818] Hughes, Emrys, op cit, pp.182-192

[819] Hughes, Emrys, ibid. p.183

[820] Callaghan, (Leonard) James (Lord Callaghan of Cardiff) 1912-2005.Labour MP for Cardiff South East 1945-1983, Chancellor of the Exchequer 1964-67, Home Secretary 1967-1970, Foreign Secretary 1974-76, Prime Minister 1976-1979. Wrote the foreword to Block and Hostettler, op cit, p.viii - October 1997.

The Affirmative Resolutions

The question of whether abolition was to be made permanent was due to come up in July 1970 under the terms of the Abolition Act, but the government decided to settle the issue in advance, chiefly so as to get it out of the way well before the next general election. There was some anxiety at the official level within the Home Office, which was inevitably concerned with the legal complications that might arise about both the timing of the resolutions and the consequences of their rejection. A Home Office internal memorandum showed official thinking at the time.[821] It was argued that if the statistical trend (regarding the murder rate) were to continue there would be a growing demand for the return of capital punishment, at least for some categories of murder, and argued that there was no point seeking ministerial authority for contingency planning since even, 'hypothetical reintroduction of the death penalty might well be repugnant to some ministers and could, moreover...give rise to embarrassment.' It wasn't easy to see what the fall-back position would be and the Homicide Act demonstrated the unsatisfactoriness of legislating for categories of murder. It suggested that contingency planning should not be mentioned in submissions to ministers or should be mentioned only in order to be dismissed. In a further memo of January 1969 the previous points are re-iterated.[822] It argued that matters should not be left as late as June 1970 and that the government should take the initiative.

Callaghan and Wilson sounded out opinion to see whether it was feasible to bring the affirmative vote forward. Callaghan says he became convinced of the wisdom of disposing of the issue sooner than had been originally envisaged when he learned that the leaders of the other two parties, Edward Heath and Jeremy Thorpe, were both in favour of immediate abolition.[823] The Cabinet had considered the question over the summer and autumn of 1969 and had decided in November 1969 to settle the matter before the Christmas recess.[824] It was felt by many in the government to be unhealthy for capital punishment to be made an election issue by candidates of any party, though according to Wilson that was not the primary consideration.[825]

Callaghan and the Scottish Secretary of State (William Ross) had drafted a memorandum in January/February 1969 on the permanent abolition of capital punishment for murder for the consideration of the Parliamentary committee of

---

[821] TNA: HO 291/1552, Item 4 - Review of Murder (ADP) Act 1965 (nd). Comment on policy - contingency planning for a fall-back position.
[822] ibid - memo of 15th January 1969
[823] Callaghan (in Block and Hostettler) op cit, p.viii-ix
[824] Wilson, Harold, *The Labour Government: A Personal Record* (Harmondsworth: Penguin, 1974) p.924
[825] Wilson, Harold, ibid, p.924

the Cabinet.[826] They invited their colleagues to agree that the government should take the initiative in making abolition permanent and that they should decide on tactics and timing. Section 4 of the Abolition Act caused the Act to lapse after five years. They assumed that colleagues needed no convincing to make abolition permanent - the case was essentially a moral one - capital punishment was a 'barbarous penalty which the community has no right to exact however heinous the crime.' Other arguments were subsidiary, they argued, such as the Timothy Evans case and the unsatisfactoriness of the Homicide Act. The case should not stand on statistics – it was unfortunately true that recent murder statistics lent more support to restoration than to abolition. There was clearly a majority in the Commons for abolition. It pointed out that the Sandys motion (to amend the Abolition Act so that it expired automatically in 1970 with or without a renewal vote) was coming up and it was desirable to brief a backbencher to oppose. Parliament was 'ahead of public opinion' and from the political angle abolition needed careful handling. On tactics and timing they felt that it was for government initiative not for a backbencher, but that it should clearly be subject to a free vote. The matter had to be dealt with by July 1970, and there was a strong case for taking the matter early since the murder figures for 1969 wouldn't be available and the interim figures might be inflated. To wait for the corrected figures for 1969 would mean waiting until May/June 1970 which might be awkward given the imminence by then of a general election. If we forgo the 1969 figures, it argued, the vote could be brought forward. A debate in spring 1970 might lead to demands for the disclosure of the uncorrected (and inflated) figures for 1969, and therefore we should, they argued, aim for a debate in autumn 1969 - which may relieve the restlessness on both sides.

In February 1969 another Home Office memorandum reprised the situation, examining possible difficulties.[827] It concluded that if the resolutions were tabled in the current session (1968-9) and passed by the Commons but rejected by the Lords (a definite possibility) then the resolution could be presented to the Lords again in the next session (1969-70), the Commons resolution staying valid. If both Houses rejected the resolutions they could be presented again in the following session, though this was 'questionable', and it might be better to introduce fresh legislation. If they were tabled in the 1969-70 session initially and rejected in either House the rules of procedure would not permit them to be tabled again in that session and they would be lost. It was debatable whether the rules would then permit the introduction in the same session of legislation in the sense of a rejected resolution.

In May 1969 Callaghan and Ross presented their memorandum to

---

[826] TNA: HO 291/1551 *Capital Punishment - Abolition of Death Penalty* - Memo by Home Secretary and Scottish Secretary for the Parliamentary Committee of the Cabinet January/February 1969.
[827] TNA: HO 291/1551 *Murder (Abolition of Death Penalty) Act*, February 1969.

Cabinet dealing comprehensively with the whole vexed question.[828] Callaghan argued for abolition in that there was no conclusive evidence that hanging was a unique deterrent, though he felt the case was largely a moral one. If Cabinet was of that mind then it should be the government that took the initiative. The available figures had to be taken with caution because changes in the law relating to murder, especially the diminished responsibility defence, meant that comparisons between relevant periods had to be based on estimates of a jury's decision on matters that were not actually put to them. It was possible that abolition increased both the willingness of defendants to confess and the willingness of juries to convict. Moreover, while there had been an upward trend in the number of recorded murders there had been an increase before abolition and this increase was therefore not necessarily attributable to it.[829]

Callaghan argued that though the resolutions did not have to be moved until July 1970 there was no reason why they could not be timetabled earlier, and there was certainly a case for the autumn of 1969. If the two Houses came to a different decision there was no way that they could be asked to reverse that decision in the same session. Rejection by one House at the beginning of the 1969-70 session would leave time for legislation to rectify the position by, for example, continuing the effects of the Act temporarily. But to move the resolutions at the end of the present session (1968-69) would allow the government to ask either House to reverse its decision in the following session. Both ministers urged the government to table the resolutions in autumn 1969.

There was general agreement in Cabinet to their taking the initiative, but there was a suggestion that in order to remove the controversy from the next general election there should be an extension of the operation of the Act for a further three years rather than a resolution for permanent abolition. In further discussion it was suggested that the government should not rely too heavily on the argument that the case against hanging was a moral one. It was still in existence for treason and other offences and its appropriateness as a penalty was to some extent dependent on the seriousness of the offence. The Prime Minister summed up by saying that Cabinet agreed with the proposals put forward in the memorandum and that the resolutions should be moved in the spillover of the present session. The decision should be kept confidential for the time being.[830]

Cabinet again considered the matter in July 1969. Callaghan told the Cabinet that the timing required further consideration.[831] By September 1969 the question was becoming a matter of urgency. Callaghan informed Cabinet on 25th September that the murder statistics for 1968 had now become available and showed a substantial rise in capital murders (i.e. those that were estimated

---

[828] TNA: CC (69) volume 44, 24th Conclusions, minute 7 - 22nd May 1969. Memo C(69)48.

[829] TNA: ibid.

[830] TNA: ibid. Also TNA: HO/291/1551 Cabinet Office memo, 23rd May 1969.

[831] TNA: Vol 44, Part 2, CC(69) 39th Conclusions - 30th July 1969, minute 1 Parliamentary Affairs.

would have been capital murders had the distinction, nullified by virtue of abolition, still been operative), though only a slight rise in murders in general by comparison with 1967.[832] Cabinet discussion centred on whether to hold the resolutions in the spillover (i.e. the period after Parliament reconvened at the fag end of the present session) which would have had the advantage of getting the issue out of the way as soon as possible. Delay could strengthen the resistance to abolition. The Law Officers had advised that if the resolutions were defeated in either House it would not be possible to introduce a bill on the same subject in the same session. There was widespread support for the idea of publishing the Home Office analysis in October and to move the resolutions early in the following month.

On 23rd October Cabinet was informed that the Home Office Statistics Unit had prepared or were about to publish an evaluation of statistical evidence relevant to abolition. As Heath, Leader of the Opposition, had recently proposed (at his party conference) that a committee of three impartial experts, under the chairmanship of a judge, and with a former Home Secretary and a criminologist, should be appointed to evaluate the evidence there might be an advantage in informing him of the impending publication. On balance it might be better to publish and await reactions.[833] A Cabinet memo commented that Heath's proposals, though superficially attractive, presented difficulties. It was desirable to devise a tactic to outflank the Opposition and avoid party conflict.[834]

While Cabinet agonized over these decisions the Conservative Shadow Cabinet (technically the Leader's Consultative Committee) was also taken up with them, albeit with much less pressure attached and with much greater freedom of action, though without the benefit of civil service briefings. In November 1969 it considered the Home Office report *Murder 1957-68* in the light of the question of whether the government was going to bring the confirmatory debate forward from July 1970.[835] Quintin Hogg (shadow Home Secretary) argued for an extension to the experimental period for anything up to eighteen months, and said that at least five years crime figures should be available for consideration before a decision were made, and that anything less than that would be a breach of faith on so serious a matter.

At another Shadow Cabinet meeting two weeks later Sir Peter Rawlinson (shadow Attorney-General) said that he thought the government was about to move on the matter and that he had been approached by Duncan Sandys (then on the backbenches) who wanted to forestall matters by putting down a motion that there should be no decision until the complete 1969 figures were available

---

[832] TNA: CC (69) 45th Conclusions, 25th September 1969, minute 3 - Permanent Abolition of Capital Punishment.
[833] TNA: CC(69) 51st Conclusions, 23rd October 1969, minute 1.
[834] TNA: HO 291/1551 Cabinet memo, 23rd October 1969.
[835] Conservative Party papers, op cit. LCC 1/2/18. minutes (69) 320-339, 327th meeting, 5th November 1969, item 3.

and had been analyzed by an independent commission.[836] Hogg felt that no decision should be made by this Parliament. He didn't agree with Sandys that the only question was whether to wait for the 1969 figures, because when the five-year trial period was debated (in 1965) it was not foreseen that it would be due for review at the 'fag-end' of a Parliament. Heath decided to write to the Home Secretary to that effect.

Lord Chancellor Gardiner indicated that he would not be happy for the matter to be put off until after Christmas. He felt the nettle ought to be grasped. What is there to argue about he said.[837] Clearly he was jittery. Callaghan agreed but said he had failed to mention public opinion. In November Cabinet again returned to the question, and was informed that it was proposed to table a motion on 8th December and to debate it on 17th December.[838] It was important also that the matter be debated in the Lords before the Christmas recess.

There was a meeting between Callaghan and Quintin Hogg, at the latter's behest, on 26th November.[839] Hogg informed him that there was great opposition within the Conservative Party to any action that would truncate the five-year experiment, and thought that they would vote as a party against any resolution tabled before Christmas. Callaghan was careful not to give any hint to Hogg as to the government's plans but Hogg had of course seen the rumours in the press, and he suggested to Callaghan that the government introduce a short bill to extend the five years by another eighteen months so as to clear the forthcoming general election. He proposed a debate on a general motion in which he would say that capital punishment should not be made a party issue and that he would be prepared as Home Secretary to operate a system of capital punishment without a reprieve board to advise him. Callaghan responded by saying that a temporizing bill would not prevent capital punishment becoming an election issue, and would not be attractive to the Labour Party. It would also place him in an exposed position *vis a vis* Duncan Sandys and his ilk. Callaghan put it to Hogg that he was attempting to walk down the middle of the road and was liable to be knocked over, to which Hogg retorted that if he wasn't allowed to walk in the middle he would walk on the right. Callaghan said he doubted that any compromise would work and that in the last resort it was a matter of conscience. Temporizing measures were only going to lead to greater confusion and to greater awkwardness for candidates in a general election. Hogg said that in the absence of a temporizing measure he would be bound to say that the government was acting wrongly.

At the next Cabinet Callaghan reported on the meeting with Hogg.[840] In the ensuing discussion there was general agreement that they would want to

---

[836] LCC 1/2/18 ibid. minutes (69), 331st meeting, 19th November 1969.
[837] TNA: HO 291/1551 letter from Gardiner to Callaghan 19th November 1969.
[838] TNA: CC (69) 55th Conclusions, 20th November 1969 - minute 1 - Parliamentary Affairs.
[839] TNA: PREM, 13/2552, memo from Callaghan to PM, 26th November 1969.
[840] TNA: CC (69) 57th Conclusions - 27th November 1969, minute 1 - Parliamentary Affairs.

consider the terms of any Opposition motion before taking a final decision about the introduction of the resolutions. A week later Cabinet returned once again to the matter in hand and the Parliamentary tactics envisaged for the debate on the resolutions, which was by now hardening up for the 17th December.[841] A final decision would have to be taken by the Cabinet of 8th December and it was felt, notwithstanding any inconvenience to the Lords, that no indication should be given to the Opposition in either Lords or Commons until after the meeting about the government's intentions in relation to the tabling and timing of the debate.

On 8th December the Home Secretary duly informed Cabinet that there were overwhelming arguments for the early introduction of the resolutions.[842] There was, he argued, no need to wait for further figures to become available, while too much significance should not be attached to the statistics when such small numbers were involved. The figures published in the Home Office Research Study, *Murder 1957-1968*, would not support the argument that the suspension of capital punishment had resulted in a substantial increase in the number of murders. To extend the five year period by eighteen months as Hogg had suggested would not in his view prevent capital punishment from becoming an election issue, and he could see no merit in extending the period for another five years since at the end of this further period the issue was likely to be just as controversial as now. If the resolution were to be defeated in the Lords there might be a case for introducing a short bill extending the operation of the Act for a further period of years, and it would be open to the government so to do. Cabinet agreed in discussion that it would be undesirable to postpone a decision on the matter else it would undoubtedly become a subject of controversy at the next general election. It was suggested that no reference should be made in the debate to the possibility that the government might introduce new legislation if the resolutions were defeated. It would be better to confront Parliament with a straight choice between permanent abolition on the one hand or a return to the Homicide Act.

At the Shadow Cabinet meeting that day (8th December) Rawlinson reported that Sandys was enquiring about the possibility of amending the government motion.[843] At their next meeting, after the government's intentions had been made known, they were still considering whether to put down a procedural motion or a substantive one.[844] Hogg was still very critical of the government for having decided to take matters before the Christmas recess and before the 1969 figures were available. Francis Pym thought that the Chair

---

[841] TNA: CC (69) 58th Conclusions - 4th December 1969, Item 1 - Parliamentary Affairs.

[842] TNA: CC (69) 59th Conclusions - 8th December 1969 - Item 2.

[843] Conservative Party papers, op cit. LCC 1/2/18 ibid. Minutes (69) 336th meeting, 8th December 1969

[844] Conservative Party papers, ibid. LCC 1/2/18 ibid. Minutes (69) 337th meeting, 10th December 1969

might not accept a dilatory motion. Henry Brooke, now Lord Brooke, who was in attendance purely for this item on the agenda, said that he had tabled a motion in the Lords with Jellicoe and St Aldwyn on the lines that, 'this House declines to come to a decision until the 1969 figures are available.' He didn't think there would be any difficulty in carrying that but unfortunately there was a complication because Dilhorne had wanted to table an amendment to the effect that the Act would not expire until 1973. It was agreed to go with the Brooke amendment in the Lords and to put down a motion of censure comparable to that in the Commons.

The government duly tabled the resolutions for debate in both Commons and Lords on 15th-16th December and Callaghan made it clear that he would resign if the motions were not passed.[845] Both parties decided they would allow a free vote on the substantive question, but the Conservatives put down a censure motion deploring the government's decision to make a decision there and then before the figures for 1969 were yet available. On a whipped vote this motion was easily defeated, the vote being on party lines.[846] On 16th December 1969 Callaghan opened the debate on the substantive motion, and outlined the legal position.[847] He argued that there had not been a significant increase in the numbers of murdered police officers or prison officers, or of sexually motivated murders of children in the relevant period, and that he was unconvinced that hanging was a necessary protection for the forces of law and order. He said he was aware that public opinion was overwhelmingly against abolition but felt that this was a case where, as before, Parliament should take a lead on the issue. Hogg, leading for the Opposition, opposed the motion, but did not make it entirely clear whether he favoured abolition or not.[848] The government won the debate on the substantive motion by 343-185, a majority of 158.[849] All three party leaders voted to make abolition permanent, as did a total of 278 Labour MPs, fifty-two Conservatives, ten of the thirteen Liberals and three others.[850] 180 Conservatives, two Labourites, two Liberals and one Independent voted against. It was debated in the Lords the next day, 17th December. An amendment moved by Lord Brooke that would have delayed a decision until 1973, was not put, and the Lord Chancellor's motion was passed, after an outstanding speech by him, by 220-174.[851] All the bishops and almost all of the judges were on the abolitionist side. The Archbishop of Canterbury, Dr Michael

---

[845] Block and Hostettler, op cit, p.263

[846] HC Deb, vol 793, col 893 - 15th December 1969

[847] HC Deb, vol 793, col 1149 - 16th December 1969

[848] Block and Hostettler, op cit, p.265

[849] HC Deb, vol 793, cols 1293-1298, 16th December 1969

[850] Block and Hostettler incorrectly give the figures as 51 Conservatives and 'all nine Liberals'.

[851] Wilson, Harold, op cit, p. 925-6. Block and Hostettler, op cit, p. 267 incorrectly assert that there was no division on the Lords debate.

Ramsey, commented after the debate that the abolition of capital punishment once and for all would help to create a more civilized society in which the search for the causes of crime and experiments in penal reform could be continued. As Block and Hostettler comment, 'Perhaps he expected too much.'[852]

Conclusion

It was inevitable that there would be some anxiety in the ranks of the Labour government and the abolitionists generally over the timing and the outcome of the affirmative resolutions necessitated by the terms of the Act. However, the government appreciated that it was expedient to hold the votes at the earliest reasonable opportunity for several reasons; partly to minimize the number of years of murder statistics that would be available given the propensity of the retentionists to make tendentious and, arguably, misleading use of them; partly to ensure that the matter was dealt with well before the next election when it might prejudice the Labour Party's chances, given that they were the 'party of abolition'; and partly to obviate any possibility that the votes might have to be held *after* an election in which there might be a large Conservative majority in the Commons that could threaten to defeat the resolutions. In the event the government went for the vote when there was still six months to spare, and were predictably heavily criticised by the Conservatives for so doing, but the outcome of the vote was never in doubt in either House given the continuing large abolitionist majorities as in 1965.

Matters were resolved for the time being, though it was evident to all that the retentionists would return to the attack at a later date, given their refusal to accept the outcome, and their attribution of rising crime figures to abolition. Moreover public opinion was becoming increasingly restive over the issue with polls showing ever larger majorities favouring restoration, and there was grave disquiet within the ranks of the police force and the prison service in particular. Matters were far from settled.

---

[852] Block and Hostettler, ibid, p.267

CHAPTER 16

THE RETENTIONISTS STRIKE BACK

Whereas the cause of abolition spawned numerous bodies to propagandise for it, there were very few dedicated specifically to the opposite cause of retention (or restoration). This may have been because, prior to abolition, they represented the status quo and saw no need to mobilise to defend an institution they regarded as self-evidently necessary and justifiable. Such bodies as did emerge tended to advocate retention/restoration as part of a wider agenda dealing with the maintenance of law and order and the preservation of traditional values. They were, more or less by definition, conservative, at least with a small 'c' if not a large. The serious opposition to abolition up to 1965 had come from pre-existing representative and professional bodies, especially the Police Federation and the Prison Officers Association; legal and judicial bodies; the Conservative Party and the House of Lords and the right-wing press. This tended to inhibit the emergence of specifically pro-capital punishment bodies. Only after hanging had been abolished, or with the spectre of abolition becoming an imminent reality, did retentionist bodies become more prominent and start to organize themselves.

The only significant retentionist lobby organization prior to 1965 was the 'Anti-Violence League'. This curiously-named body seems to have been formed sometime in the very early sixties with the declared aim of 'preserving the British way of life'. Its headquarters was in Lower Grosvenor Place, Victoria, its general secretary was Paull Hill and its National Council boasted, *inter alia*, the names of Sir Percy Sillitoe, Sir Thomas Moore and the Countess of Dartmouth.[853] Its executive committee consisted of T C L Westbrook, Moore, J Mulcahy, M Bilmes and Hill. Its objectives were proclaimed to be:-[854]

> 1. To provide a specific channel through which public dissatisfaction with the present state and administration of the criminal law, with particular emphasis on crimes of violence against the person and property, can be forcibly directed to Parliament.

---

[853] Its other National Council members were T C L Westbrook, CBE; Lady Colwyn; H Cobden-Turner, JP; Rev W Stanhope-Lovell; J Mulcahy; M Bilmes; W P Potts; A J Scammell; and Paull Hill, the general secretary. Sir Percy Joseph Sillitoe, KBE, CBE (1888-1962), policeman, Chief Constable of Glasgow and later head of MI5 1946-1953. Sir Thomas Cecil Russell Moore (1888-1971), Conservative MP for Ayr Burghs 1925-1950 and Ayr 1950-1964. Indefatigable campaigner on Tory backbenches for law and order and against abolition. Raine Legge (nee McCorquodale), (1929-) wife of the 9th Earl of Dartmouth, daughter of Barbara Cartland, subsequently Countess Spencer. GLC councillor (Con, Richmond-upon-Thames).

[854] Labour Party general secretary's papers (Labour Party archives, Museum of Labour History, Manchester) GS/DP/5vii

2. The reform of the Homicide Act of 1957 and the re-introduction of the death penalty for such crimes as murder by poisoning, sex murders and accessories to murder in all crimes of violence, irrespective of the weapon used.

3. Improvement of relations between police and public.

4. To counteract the activities of psychiatrists and so-called reformers who advocate reform before punishment for the criminal, and to investigate the extent of their influence on Government committees, Radio, Television and similar public media. Also to set up a special committee to investigate and report upon the present extent and future influence of paid Agitators in industry and other National Institutions.

5. To provide a medium through which the great mass of teenagers and responsible young people can express their feelings.

6. To press for a system of government compensation for victims of criminal attacks on the basis of "Third-Party" damages for motorists, irrespective of the financial means of the victim.

7. To assist financially victims or their dependents who have suffered injury or loss...

8. To build up an organisation with a target of at least 5 million members, so that direct pressure can be brought to bear on MPs in their constituencies.

9. The League to be completely non-political and non-sectarian.

10. Any other objects that may be approved by the Committee.

Hill wrote to Morgan Phillips, general secretary of the Labour Party, in 1961, asking the party to nominate a member to its national committee and enclosing literature.[855] According to Hill it had definite views on the 'vital need to change the present provisions of the Homicide Act 1957, with all its anomalies.' He continued:-

> Whether 12 or 24 - or any - murderers are hanged annually is, of course, a matter of grave concern, but it is the thoroughly unsatisfactory working of the criminal justice in all its aspects that has aroused the intense feelings of our members in particular and the public in general. The citizen has surrendered his power to exact retribution to the State and the State, in our opinion, has let him down, irrespective of party. The Law of Diminished Responsibility has indeed provided a haven of refuge for those criminals who have no real answer to the charge. In our opinion, except in a small percentage of cases, the criminal is bad not mad despite what the psychiatrists would have us believe. The AVL is NOT a pro-flogging body. It unashamedly campaigns for the Judge or Magistrate to be given discretion to order corporal punishment by birching for delinquents under 21... The shocking rise in crimes of violence on the one hand, and the undermining of good labour relations by paid agitators on the other has now reached a point beyond any Party solutions...'[856]

Phillips' deputy gave a non-committal reply merely asking for clarification of whether Hill was asking for the Party to associate itself with the AVL in which case, he pointed out, only the NEC could make the decision.[857] Given the long

---

[855] Labour Party general secretary's papers (Labour Party archives, Museum of Labour History, Manchester), GS/DP/1-6, letter from Hill to Phillips, 25th May 1961

[856] ibid

[857] ibid, deputy general secretary to Hill, 7th June 1961

opposition of the Labour Party to corporal punishment it would have been surprising had it elected to associate itself with such a body but one can presume that Phillips or his deputy were unsure of the real nature of the AVL and reluctant to appear to be too hostile to the notion of maintaining law and order.[858] At any rate there seems to have been no further correspondence between the two organisations and there is no evidence that Labour seriously considered associating with it. Hill and the AVL probably realised that their overtures were falling on stony ground and abandoned the attempt to interest the party in their activities. The AVL probably made similar overtures to the other parties, and one would certainly have imagined them approaching the Conservative Party given that it might have been expected to be rather more sympathetic to its aims.

Hill gave an interview in *Time and Tide* (an influential literary magazine published from the 1920s but now defunct) in 1961 outlining his views: 'We all agree that life imprisonment must mean imprisonment for life or at any rate 25 years – without remission.'[859] The present position regarding life sentences, 'is completely ineffective for public protection.'

It was fairly clear from the tenor of the literature that its agenda embraced a broad spectrum of contemporary right-wing concerns about law and order, industrial unrest and the erosion of traditional values. Moreover, it seems to have been highly vexed by what it saw as the excessive influence of psychiatric theories on government policy and judicial sentencing; a recurrent theme of right-wing critiques of public policy in succeeding decades. The incorporation into the Homicide Act of the diminished responsibility defence was, it seemed convinced, a manifestation of this tendency and something highly subversive of the need for 'tough' sentencing. This, as much as the partial abolition of capital punishment, was central to its platform.

Despite its protestations to be 'non-political' (meaning as is often the case non-partisan) its objectives unmistakably identified it as both highly political and essentially conservative, if not Conservative (given the membership on its National Council of two elected Conservative politicians). There seems little evidence of the organization's activities besides a brief scathing reference to it (paired rhetorically with the 'hangers and floggers of the Conservative Party conference') in a review by Dennis Potter (in pre-playwright days) of a book on criminology in the Daily Herald in 1961.[860] It gained a fleeting prominence when the BBC documentary *The Death Penalty* produced in late 1961 had a contribution from Sir Thomas Moore who was a member of its executive, but

---

[858] The Attlee government had abolished corporal punishment as a judicial penalty in 1950 and had supported the Macmillan government's abolition of it as a prison penalty in 1961 against the opposition of a clutch of hard-line Tory backbenchers including Margaret Thatcher.

[859] *Time and Tide*, 13th July 1961. Quoted in Gardiner, op cit., Add 56463B

[860] *Daily Herald,* 9th October 1961 - see www.yorksj.ac.uk/potter/61_10_09

although he had intended originally to deliver his statement from the AVL's offices he ended up doing so from his own home. The AVL seems to have had little influence on the course of events and it probably dwindled away within a few years.

The AVL was by no means the only organization of its type to wax and wane in the relevant period. As mentioned in the chapter on political parties the Downey challenge to Sydney Silverman in Nelson and Colne in the 1966 general election seems to have been backed by a pro-hanging organization of businessmen in the Manchester area, though here again there seems to be little trace of its existence beyond that event, and no evidence that it had any influence on government policy.

Another very small organization that seems to have flickered briefly into life and may in fact have been nothing more than a one-man show was the 'Campaign for the Retention of Hanging' whose secretary was M G Walker of Croydon, Surrey. Little or nothing is known of this body and the only material emanating from it was a single foolscap sheet written and produced by Mr Walker outlining his arguments against abolition.[861] His name as secretary was the only one on the letterhead and it seems to have been produced from his home address. The circular adopted a sneering tone about leading abolitionists whom he dismissed as soft-headed and misguided intellectuals, and it argued strongly for keeping the gallows as the only really effective deterrent: 'It has never been known for a corpse to commit murder' and because public opinion was overwhelmingly for it. Moreover, he argued that execution was preferable to lengthy imprisonment because it was less of a strain on the public purse. The general tone can be gauged from this passage, under the heading of misplaced sympathies:-

> After sentence all public sympathy is …focussed on the prisoner in the condemned cell…You never hear of the real victim of the crime. The mother and father of an innocent person viciously attacked…Oh no, nothing so humane as this. After all they are dead and done with. But the cruel killer must not die. It would be unjust to take his life.

The remedy lay squarely on the shoulders of the public rather than with, 'the be-cardiganed intellectuals with fat state grants bulging from their pockets' who should write to their MPs. He signed off with the rallying cry that, 'the fight is on; let us fight to, and for, the death.' He had been approached by Anthony de Lotbiniere to take part in his BBC documentary *The Death Penalty* but after apparently giving an initial acceptance he had had to decline (and to discontinue his activities as secretary) due to 'changed circumstances' and 'purely professional reasons'. He indicated to de Lotbiniere that he would inform him of his successor but there is no indication that he did, or whether

---

[861] Circular of 11th April 1961. BBC Archives, T32/518/5

indeed he had a successor. Other such bodies no doubt existed on a very small and localised basis but their agenda was usually somewhat broader than merely the retention of the death penalty.

This changed somewhat in the immediate post-abolition period. From 1965 there rapidly developed various campaigns to restore capital punishment at the earliest opportunity, or at the very least to ensure that when the matter came up for renewal in 1970 it was decisively reversed. Hitherto, support for hanging had been chiefly institutionalised, emanating from bastions of the establishment such as the judiciary, the police, the House of Lords, the Conservative press and much of the Conservative Party. As some of these bastions began to falter in their enthusiasm for hanging, and as they were in any case proved ineffectual in stopping the abolition juggernaut, so thereafter it tended to emanate from more non-institutional sources, developing a momentum of its own comparable with the NCACP a decade earlier (though less influential). Much of this activity was spontaneous and localised and reflected a concern with the steady rise in violent crime and the use of firearms, which tended to be attributed at least partly to abolition (justifiably so or not). Moreover, particular crimes shocked the nation, especially the horrifying revelations surrounding the Moors murders in late 1965, and the deaths of three police officers in the shoot-out at Shepherds Bush in 1966, the timing of both of which were unfortunate for the abolitionists (though only the latter could rationally have been perceived as connected in any way with the end of hanging).

The activities of the Downey campaign in the 1966 general election have been mentioned, though it appeared to be narrowly-based and ephemeral. More substantial was the campaign launched by Duncan Sandys in 1966.[862] This aimed at the reintroduction of hanging, initially, at least, only for the murder of police and prison officers, and the marshalling of public opinion to that end. He introduced a Bill into the House using the Ten Minute Rule in November 1966 to bring back hanging for the murder of police and prison officers in the execution of their duty, but this was decisively defeated. His speech introducing the Bill argued that, 'we have no right to save our consciences at the expense of other people's lives', and though he admitted that there was no conclusive evidence that the death penalty was a deterrent he felt it was hard to believe that it was not.[863] The recent shootings of three police officers by escaped convicts and the murder of a prison officer gave added impetus to his campaign, and it

---

[862] Duncan Edwin Sandys, Baron Duncan-Sandys of the City of Westminster, CH, PC (1908-1987). Son-in-law of Winston Churchill. Founder of the European Movement 1947. Conservative MP for Norwood 1935-45; Streatham 1950-1974. Minister of Defence 1957-59, Minister for Aviation 1959-60, Secretary of State for Commonwealth Relations 1960-64. Sacked by Heath from front bench over Rhodesia 1966.

[863] Notes for speech. Duncan Sandys papers, DSND 12/1. Churchill College Archive, Cambridge University.

was matched by a number of motions at the Conservative Party conference that autumn. Close confederates in the campaign were Conservative MPs Peter Rawlinson, Bill Deedes and John Boyd-Carpenter. Deedes was able to supply him with information about the various opinion polls on capital punishment over the years.[864] Rawlinson supplied him with information on criminal statistics such as the rise in fire-arm offences.[865]

His Bill was co-ordinated with a deputation to the Home Secretary, Roy Jenkins, in November, led by himself accompanied by Conservative MPs John Boyd-Carpenter, Betty Harvie Anderson, Peter Rawlinson and Sir David Renton and pro-hanging Labour MPs Harold Boardman, J T Price and Frank Tomney. The same day there were two other deputations with the same request from the Police Federation and the Prison Officers Association, with whom Sandys had been liaising, and the meeting with Jenkins was attended by members of all three since also present were Reginald Webb (chairman) and Arthur Evans (secretary) of the Police Federation, Inspector John Black (chairman) and Daniel Wilson (secretary) of the Scottish Police Federation and Norman Cowling (chairman) and Fred Castell (secretary) of the Prison Officers Association.[866] Sandys argued that the record number of police murders, gaol-breaking on a large scale, the views of the PF, POA and public opinion were all factors that the Home Secretary should take into account in considering whether to re-introduce capital punishment for the murder of police and prison officers. The movement, he argued, was a spontaneous one that had sprung up in the country with many local petitions being organized. Moreover morale was declining in the police and prison services with a concomitant rise in resignations and retirements and a fall in recruitment. He admitted that there was no conclusive evidence that capital punishment was a unique deterrent but neither was there evidence of the reverse.

There was really no chance of Jenkins, an arch-abolitionist, ever acceding to their entreaties or concurring with their arguments. He attempted to smooth away their concerns by pointing out that it was too soon to make anything meaningful out of the statistics and that anyway 1966 had been no worse, qualitatively, than 1961 when hanging was still in operation. In the case of one of the police murders, that at Gateshead, the perpetrator was only fourteen and too young to hang under the old law anyway, and the other instance, that at Shepherds Bush was one not three for deterrent purposes. The spate of gaol-breaking was disturbing but hardly relevant. There was, he went on, a misconception about life sentences and the worst murderers would not be released after nine or ten years as was previously the norm. Rawlinson and Boyd-Carpenter raised the matter of the increased use of firearms and argued

---

[864] Deedes to Sandys, 19th September 1966. Sandys papers, ibid.

[865] Rawlinson to Sandys, 21st November 1966. Sandys papers, ibid

[866] Note of meeting between Roy Jenkins and deputation at House of Commons, 14th November 1966, by a Mr Chilcot (Home Office). Sandys papers, ibid.

that capital punishment would reduce the likelihood of their being used as a threat but Jenkins argued that that rise pre-dated abolition. Moreover the rise in the murder rate was not nearly as high as the rise in crime generally. There was simply insufficient evidence to say capital punishment should come back and it was not, he felt, in the long-term interests of the police and prison officers themselves for them to be singled out for special treatment under the law. Sandys and company could scarcely have been satisfied with the outcome of the meeting but they could not have expected anything else.

Sandys' correspondence with other MPs showed that he was not sanguine about the prospects of success for his Bill, given the large Labour majority in the House as a result of the March 1966 general election. He also admitted, in some of his correspondence with supporters in the country who wanted hanging brought back for a wider range of murders, that his decision to limit the bill to the murder of police and prison officers was essentially tactical; i.e. more likely to attract the support of wavering MPs, particularly on the Labour side, than a more general measure of reintroduction, though he was careful not to make this point explicit. In that respect fortune was on his side because the murder of three police officers in August 1966 and the murder of a prison officer later that year highlighted the risks faced by the police and prison staff. It also meshed with the strong campaigns being mounted at the same time by the Police Federation and the Prison Officers Association.

The bill was trailed by an Early Day Motion of October 1966 in the names of Sandys, Rawlinson, Deedes and Michael Jopling (Conservative), Tomney, Albert Roberts and Robert Woof (Labour) and Alasdair Mackenzie (Liberal) and called for the restoration of capital punishment for the murder of police and prison officers 'mindful of the special dangers to which they are exposed.'[867] It attracted the signatures of 171 MPs (162 Conservative, seven Labour and two Liberal). Sandys calculated that this was over two-thirds of the Conservative Party if one were to exclude the Shadow Cabinet who did not sign EDMs.[868] Moreover, thirteen on the list had voted for the Silverman bill on second reading and nine on the third reading, indicating that a fair measure of re-consideration was going on. The EDM was undercut slightly by an 'amendment' to the above in the names of Conservative MPs Michael Heseltine, John Nott, Patrick Jenkin, Nicholas Scott; Liberal MP John Pardoe and Labour MPs David Owen and Eric Ogden which effectively negated it by saying that: 'it would be premature to re-introduce capital punishment...before the expiry of the 5-year review period or the emergence of clear evidence of the deterrent effect of the punishment.'

The Sandys campaign was co-ordinated to some extent with that of the *News of the World,* a right-wing Sunday tabloid that could be relied upon to

---

[867] House of Commons EDM no 211, 26th October 1966
[868] Sandys papers, op cit., 19th October 1966

take a rabidly populist stance on most issues. Eldon Griffiths, a fellow Conservative MP, penned a pro-hanging article in the *N.O.W.* in September 1966 which included a statement from the Police Federation about the recent murders of policemen in Shepherds Bush and Gateshead which drew attention to the dangers they faced. The statement from the Joint Central Committee of the Federation firmly and specifically called upon Parliament to reintroduce capital punishment for the wilful murder of police officers and those coming to their assistance.[869]

Parallel to these Commons activities Sandys led a grass-roots campaign to re-introduce hanging, chiefly by organizing a monster petition to present to Parliament. This aimed at achieving at least a million signatures of ordinary men and women and was clearly intended to be such a powerful demonstration of grassroots feeling as to break down the resistance of the House of Commons. The campaign was orchestrated from his Commons office by Louis Fitzgibbon and Charlotte Hurst. It may well have attained its projected figure but its presentation did not have the desired effect. Moreover, their method of collecting signatures came in for some criticism because potentially misleading.[870]

Sandys himself was prominent on public platforms advocating restoration and no television or radio programme on the issue in the period from 1966-70 was complete without his presence. He liked to emphasize that he was not the initiator of the restoration campaign but merely a channeller of the efforts of local bodies, though this was not wholly convincing, and it is likely that without his organizational skills and Commons experience the local campaigns extant would have fizzled out as with others. He was in very frequent correspondence with constituents and other members of the public over the campaign, especially policeman's wives. Many of the letters urged him to expand the campaign to include other categories of murder and were often coupled with the desire for the return of corporal punishment, and sometimes with other more general right-wing concerns of the time, especially that of race and immigration.[871] His frequent television appearances, especially on the *Man Alive* programme *Bring Back the Rope?*, attracted a lot of favourable comment from supporters in the country.[872] Unsurprisingly, few letters were opposed to his stance. Though most were from private individuals some were from corporate entities such as the 'Scottish Housewives Association' and a branch of the 'Old Age Pensioners Association'. Often there were invitations to speak at a local meeting or to debate at a university debating society (such as that at Aberdeen) or to contribute an article, usually refused for lack of time. One of the few letters that

---

[869] Eldon Griffiths, *News Of The World* article, 15th September 1966

[870] See the section on television and specifically the *Man Alive* documentary of 1968, *Bring Back the Rope?*

[871] One such letter actually was written in green ink.

[872] Sandys papers, op cit, 12/2

was not wholly supportive came from a Dr Morris Markowe of the 'Royal Medico-Psychological Association' regarding Sandys (somewhat controversial) use of statistics.[873]

From mid-1966 he was in frequent communication with Louis Fitzgibbon, a private citizen from Hampshire, who was calling for action to restore the rope, the birch and the cat and complaining that, 'pseudo-psychiatric nonsense had been allowed to cloud reason and common-sense.'[874] Fitzgibbon had been in touch with his MP, Ian Lloyd (a Conservative abolitionist), and had written to the *Portsmouth Evening News*. Within a few months he was able to write to Sandys announcing the formation of the 'Society for the Restoration of Capital Punishment' of which he was chairman and advertising its first meeting in the Portsmouth Langstone constituency, to be followed by other public meetings to which the local MPs had been invited.[875] He had distributed the campaign literature to all local MPs, candidates, newspaper editors and police chiefs and was trying to organize a local referendum on the issue. He had enclosed a letter from a confederate of his, Arthur Hill, who was critical of Ian Lloyd for being unsympathetic to their campaign, and a reference to the *News of the World* poll which showed that out of 128,000 replies, 127,384 were for hanging.

There was going to be a big recruitment drive in Portsmouth, Fitzgibbon said, which had a conservative tradition due to its long association with the armed forces. Sandys was invited to speak at the inaugural meeting.[876] Sandys replied giving him encouragement but declining to speak at or attend the meeting because he felt it better for it to appear to be a spontaneous expression of public opinion rather than something which might appear to be inspired by MPs.[877] In a further communication now on letter-headed paper the 'Society' had apparently recruited Brigadier Terence Clarke (the recently defeated Conservative member for Portsmouth, Langstone and an avid retentionist) as president, with a Lady Antrobus (Fitzgibbon's aunt) as vice–president, Fitzgibbon as chairman, Arthur Hill as vice-chairman, Christopher B Thompson as treasurer, Roger A Carter as honorary secretary and Kenneth R Groves as assistant honorary secretary.[878] Fitzgibbon congratulated Sandys on his stand and urged him to expand it to include all murders.

There was a discussion between Sandys and Fitzgibbon about the future course of the campaign in December 1966 at Sandys' house in Vincent Square.[879] It is clear from Fitzgibbon's note of the meeting that Sandys had a

---

[873] Sandys papers, op cit,12/2
[874] Fitzgibbon to Sandys, 15th August 1966. Sandys papers, DSND 12/1
[875] Fitzgibbon to Sandys, 4th November 1966. Sandys papers, ibid
[876] Fitzgibbon to Sandys, 14th September 1966. Sandys papers, ibid.
[877] Sandys to Fitzgibbon, 23rd September 1966. Sandys papers, ibid.
[878] Fitzgibbon to Sandys, 21st October 1966. Sandys papers, ibid.
[879] Fitzgibbon to Sandys, 10th December 1966. Sandys papers, ibid

realistic appreciation of the difficulties inherent in reversing abolition given the Parliamentary arithmetic, and that he expected that it would take about four years to bring the campaign to a successful conclusion (i.e. roughly as long as the 'experimental' period was due to last and maybe as long as the Labour government would last). Even the name of the organization, which was felt by Fitzgibbon to be unwieldy, was up for discussion, though his suggested alternatives such as the 'National Society to Reduce Crime', the 'Crime Deterrent Society', the 'Citizens Safety Association' and the 'Anti-Murder League' (!) were little easier on the tongue. Sandys felt that the public meeting approach was unpromising and that they should concentrate on lobbying MPs using the weight of public opinion as expressed through local as well as national polls. A Central Committee should be set up and pro-hanging Conservative MPs, candidates or agents should be made chairmen of local branches who should then conduct a poll within the constituency gaining at least a thousand signatures. These should then be presented to the local MP who should be asked to state his position. This way, Sandys felt, it might be possible to swing Labour supporters to the Conservatives. Charlotte Hurst was to be the major organizer of the petition campaign.[880] Fitzgibbon planned to spread the campaign and meetings to all places where the local MP was known to be anti-hanging. Sandys admitted in a reply to him that he favoured the return of capital punishment for all murders but for tactical reasons felt it better to confine himself to the question of policemen and prison officers.[881]

Despite this frenetic activity in late 1966 Fitzgibbon informed Sandys early the next year that the SRCP was now 'on ice'; that he was handing over all his files to Hill, the vice-chairman; and that he was going to Portugal for a year. The correspondence file was being handed to Charlotte Hurst, who had already corresponded directly with Sandys regarding the petition campaign she was organizing, as had another such organiser, Athlene O'Connell.[882] Another such correspondent, Mrs Marjorie Arnold of Wood Green, wrote to him regarding her own petition (which she enclosed) saying that, 'If only Mr Heath would say he would bring back the birch and capital punishment he would win the next election hands down.'[883] It was evident that there was a great deal of grass-roots activity on the petition front that was clearly not being orchestrated from the top by Sandys and his ilk, but it was debatable to what extent these efforts had any proper organizational basis or sustainability.

The tendency of these localized campaigns to draw in some rather odd bedfellows was evident from another letter from Hurst to Sandys at this time in which she enclosed a letter to her from F D W Tye of the 'National Cleansing

---

[880] Fitzgibbon to Sandys, 31st October 1966. Sandys papers, ibid.

[881] Sandys to Fitzgibbon, 2nd November 1966. Sandys papers, ibid.

[882] Hurst to Sandys, 29th October 1966. O'Connell to Sandys, 9th October 1966. Sandys papers, ibid.

[883] Arnold to Sandys, 19th August 1966. Sandys papers, ibid.

Crusade', asking how to respond.[884] This body indicated from its letterhead that it was for not only the restoration of capital punishment but the outlawing of sodomy (which was still against the law anyway) and stiffer penalties to fit the crime including recompense and corporal punishment. Tye went on to suggest the amalgamation of the two bodies (the SRCP and his own) so as to make them more powerful. It seemed that she was not averse to the idea but there is no indication of Sandys' reply on this matter.

Though the Sandys campaign had started out specifically to reintroduce capital punishment solely for the murder of police and prison officers (admittedly for tactical reasons) by late 1967 it had evolved into a more generalized campaign for the reintroduction of the death penalty for all murders. This was no doubt partly because the original narrow approach had failed but also because it grass-roots sentiments were for a wider attack. The demands from correspondents for restoration often broadened the categories to include the murder of children, which was understandable from an emotive point of view but scarcely logical. Given the failure, at least in the short-term, to achieve the restoration of hanging for the murder of police and prison officers it may have been felt that they might just as well agitate for restoration across the board because that was, in the main, what his supporters really wanted. By late 1967 there appears to have been some friction between Fitzgibbon (who must by then have re-entered the fray after his previously announced absence) and Hurst, with the latter complaining that he was treating her in too high-handed a fashion and was more interested in his campaign to get selected as a Tory MP.[885]

Fitzgibbon, on Sandys' behalf, was making overtures to various people and in November 1967 met the entertainer, Hughie Green, to canvass his views and enlist his support.[886] Green, according to Fitzgibbon, was passionate about the restoration of capital punishment and promised to help by getting someone on his show who was sympathetic to it, though it is not clear which show and how and in what way this person would assist the cause. Green felt that this was often a more effective way of getting a message across than by more conventional means, though he had been 'warned off' the subject of capital punishment (presumably by television executives). He also conveyed a warning to Sandys for him not to appear on the David Frost programme due to Frost's handpicking of the audience and 'rigging' unless Sandys was able to send out half the ticket allocation himself. This may have been prompted by overtures

---

[884] Tye to Hurst, 15th October 1966. Hurst to Sandys, 9th November 1966. Sandys papers, ibid.

[885] C Hurst to Sandys, 12th November 1967. Sandys papers, 12/2

[886] Fitzgibbon to Sandys: report on meeting between himself and Hughie Green, at Chiltern Court, Baker St. 15th November 1967. Sandys papers, 12/2. Hughie Green (1920-1997), actor, presenter and producer. Host of long-running shows *Double Your Money* and *Opportunity Knocks* on ITV (Rediffusion)

that Fitzgibbon was already making to the producers of the then *Frost Programme* on Rediffusion.[887]

A year later Sandys did indeed appear on the Frost Programme (by then *Frost on Friday* on the newly-formed LWT) to debate capital punishment (see the chapter on television). Whether he had been allowed to select part of the audience on that occasion is unclear but a large majority of the audience was definitely pro-hanging. Green also seemed to think that there might be a concerted BBC/ITV effort to denigrate the Sandys campaign.[888] Whilst an appearance on Frost was a long way off Sandys and his campaign was going to feature in an edition of *Man Alive* due to be transmitted in January 1968 (see television chapter again) and Fitzgibbon was in touch with the producers of that show regarding the filming of himself, Sandys, Hurst and the petitioners in Manchester.[889]

Another line of attack for the campaign was a mailshot to bank managers who were presumably felt ripe for conversion (and a possible source of funds) given their line of work. Likewise security firms were felt to be likely donors and Sandys wrote to Lord Alexander of Tunis in his capacity of 'Governor' of Securicor.[890] Another person approached with a view to donating funds to the cause was Lord Sieff.[891] A third was Robert McAlpine who was asked for funds in the sum of £10,000.[892] Whilst it is unclear what success these entreaties had the 'Licenced Victuallers Association' (the UK pub landlords association) was much more forthcoming in its support. The affiliated 'Licenced Victuallers Protection Society of London' came out firmly in support of the Campaign and urged members (i.e. publicans) to display their posters and petitions for signing.[893] The National Consultative Council of the 'Retail Liquor Trade' was also sympathetic.[894]

The press, especially the popular press, was another avenue. Sandys wrote an article in the *News of the World* in July 1967, and in November 1967 the *Sun* had a feature by Allan Hall on Duncan Sandys and the petition campaign.[895] The local press was targeted also and letters would go out to

---

[887] Nicola Mellersh of Rediffusion TV Ltd to Fitzgibbon, 17th November 1967 re his 'fruitless journey', but saying that they were keen to deal with the capital punishment campaign in the near future and would be in touch again. Sandys papers, 12/2

[888] Green also seemed to have some strange idea about the government seeking to amalgamate BBC and ITV (prefigured in his view by the translation of Lord Hill from the one to the other).

[889] Fitzgibbon to Adam Clapham, 8th December 1967. Sandys papers, 12/2

[890] Sandys to Alexander, 11th October 1967. Sandys papers, ibid

[891] Sandys to Sieff, 12th September 1967. Sandys papers, ibid

[892] Sandys to McAlpine, 8th December 1967. Sandys papers, ibid

[893] LVA to Fitzgibbon, 12th January 1968. Sandys papers, ibid

[894] Aide-memoire from Fitzgibbon to Sandys, 23rd October 1967. Sandys papers, ibid

[895] 'Allan Hall talks to the Duncan Sandys Hanging Ladies'. *The Sun*, 13th November 1967. This was a reference to the Manchester petition campaign which seems to have been

newspapers in localities where murders had been recently committed via the Direct Mail Group. He also gave consideration to upcoming by-elections and Fitzgibbon seems seriously to have considered whether an independent pro-capital punishment candidate should stand at Manchester Gorton, given that Manchester was believed to be a strongly pro-hanging area of the country (the precedent of Downey at Nelson and Colne in 1966 was encouraging). Fitzgibbon seems even to have wondered whether he might be such a candidate, though it would have scuppered his chances of being selected as a Conservative candidate.

In September and October 1967 there was an exchange of correspondence between Sandys and Roy Jenkins, still Home Secretary, over the murder statistics in which Jenkins was adamant that there was no significant rise whilst Sandys was equally adamant that there had been. In particular Sandys was fond of asserting that there had been a rise in 'capital murder' (i.e. those murders that would have been capital by virtue of the Homicide Act had it not been for abolition) which he said had gone up from 35 in the two years prior to abolition to 71 in the two years after. As ever with debates over the statistics it was all a matter of interpretation (see the chapter on murder and crime statistics) and neither party could get the other to concede an inch.

Sandys attempted to introduce another bill in 1969, pursuant to standing order no 13, that would have amended the 1965 Abolition Act in such a way that it would have expired automatically in July 1970 rather than be subject to renewal, but this too failed to get anywhere in the House.[896] In any event his campaign lost impetus after the failure of his legislative efforts and the petition proved to be a damp squib. Further attempts to legislate for reintroduction after the 1970 election were the work of other backbench Conservatives such as Teddy Taylor, Jill Knight and Eldon Griffiths. Sandys himself stood down from his seat at the February 1974 election. Grassroots desire for restoration continued to be articulated but thereafter lacked cohesion. It is perhaps surprising that the Sandys campaign was not more effective than it was, given that it had wide popular support, good organization and a prominent figure-head, but ultimately it was banging its head against the brick wall of a solid abolitionist majority within Parliament which could not be shaken.

No really effective single-issue pro-capital punishment organization ever developed or gained significant traction on the body politic, though several briefly waxed and waned, and no significant electoral challenge to the main parties was ever mounted by a pro-capital punishment party other than the

---

exclusively female for some reason.

[896] 'That leave be given to bring in a Bill to delete the provisions in the Murder (Abolition of Death Penalty) Act 1965, which enables the suspension of capital punishment to be prolonged beyond the five-year experimental period by Resolutions of both Houses of Parliament'. HC Deb, vol 785, col 1228-1236, 24th June 1969. It was defeated by 256-126, a majority for the Noes of 130 (division no 284).

isolated instance of Downey at Nelson and Colne in 1966. Given the level of public opposition to abolition that grew thereafter and the relative success of Downey's candidacy it is perhaps more than a little surprising that this did not happen. It is likely that there was a widespread, but ultimately mistaken, belief within the retentionist camp that Parliament would reverse its actions through the agency of the existing parties and especially the Conservative Party.

It is instructive to compare and contrast the two movements as embodied by the main pressure groups, the NCACP on the abolitionist side and the Sandys movement on the retentionist. The former was extraordinarily successful, attracting the support of large numbers of what might be termed the great and the good, especially in the world of the media, the arts and the liberal intelligentsia generally, as well as considerable numbers of the general public. Its membership expanded dramatically within a few months of its inception and it gained prominent adherents relatively easily. It was powerfully led by some very eminent figures, in some cases already well-known to the public from other campaigns, such as Victor Gollancz, Canon Collins and Arthur Koestler. It was well-funded thanks largely to Gollancz, though it did very well in subscriptions and donations. It was well organized, though there was evidently discord between some of the leading figures which, however, did not seem to hamper its progress. It was able to achieve widespread publicity, stage large meetings and rallies, spread its literature far and wide and get the abolition question thrust onto the political agenda. It was infused with a passion for its cause and sometimes exhibited an almost evangelical moral fervour which frequently outshone the more defensive postures of its opponents. And it was remarkably successful, not merely in propagating its cause but in translating that cause into Parliamentary action very rapidly to the extent that within a couple of years a Conservative government had put onto the statute book a measure that partially vindicated its aims.[897]

It is difficult to think of any parallel in modern times for a contentious measure of social reform, not explicitly backed by a major political party and opposed by formidable institutions such as the police, the judiciary and the right-wing press, to achieve that rate of success. Though its progress stalled somewhat after 1957 it was really just a matter of time before it achieved the completion of its objectives. Thus by November 1965 total abolition had been enacted, just over ten years from the formation of the movement in September 1955. Moreover, despite repeated and intensive efforts to reverse its achievements the death penalty in this country appears to have been ended for perpetuity.

The campaign to restore the death penalty led by Sandys also enjoyed

---

[897] Collins has said that it was one of the most efficient and effective campaigns of its type ever seen, and that 'we can now look back with wonder at what the Campaign achieved'. Collins, op cit, p 247

very widespread support, in fact far wider amongst the general populace than its competitor movement. On the other hand it did not attract high-profile adherents to the same extent that the NCACP did, and those who were inclined to offer their endorsement did not enjoy the approval of the *bien pensant* classes. Opinion polls though, and the monster petitions it organized and set such great store by, attest to the popularity of its aims. Events in the pubic domain, especially the apparent increase in the murder rate, the killing of policemen in the line of duty, the revelation of some especially horrific murders, and the increase in violent crime in general all seemed to work in its favour. Like the NCACP it was well-funded, with some wealthy backers such as the victuallers associations and leading businessmen. It was well organized both within Parliament and outside (though its leadership perhaps did not enjoy quite the same intellectual cachet as that of the NCACP) and many of its supporters exhibited a similar degree of crusading zeal for its cause, sometimes of a biblical inspiration which brooked no argument (though it made no converts). Yet it failed utterly to prevent the confirmation of abolition in 1969, nor did it manage ever to come close to restoring hanging at any time thereafter despite public opinion moving ever more strongly for it. Nor, incidentally, did it halt the liberalization of the criminal justice system in other ways.

Why then, in a democracy, did a movement which had the support of a large majority of the people fail? The obvious answer is that there was by the 1960s, and thereafter, a large and immovable majority in both the Commons and the Lords for abolition that was impervious to the entreaties of public opinion. In the absence of a plebiscitary system of government there is simply no mechanism for translating popular will into law if it is opposed by a large and intractable majority of legislators. But at a deeper level the movement failed because it could never quite present itself as intellectually sound or morally respectable. It was too easy to caricature as atavistic and reactionary, and too easy for it to be outdone in argument by the superior debating skills of its opponents. This was underlined by the wholesale conversion to abolition, in the early 1960s, of the hierarchy of the Church of England, as of that of most of the other Christian denominations, and of much of the judiciary and the legal profession too. Progressive opinion had by then hardened to the view that not only was capital punishment unjustifiable on both moral and rational grounds but that it was simply out of date. Parliament was strengthened in its determination to resist public opinion by the conviction that it was moving with the tide of history, and there can be no stronger motive than that.

CHAPTER 17

THE ABOLITION CAMPAIGN IN CONTEXT

It may be fruitful to examine the abolitionist campaign in the context of other political campaigns, particularly those for social reform, that were in progress at or about the same time, and to compare and contrast their methods and degree of success, to see what light it throws upon the process of attitude change and political decision making. Abolition was one of several so-called 'conscience' issues that bubbled just above the surface of British politics in the 1950s and 1960s, and which, like abolition, were able to crown their efforts with success in the period 1965-69. Chief among these were the campaigns to liberalize the divorce laws and legalize abortion and homosexuality, and, in a similar reforming vein though of lesser importance, the attempts to abolish theatre censorship and ease the Sunday Observance laws pertaining to sport and entertainment. Each had their own pressure groups to co-ordinate their campaigns and articulate their case to government and Parliament; each rose to a crescendo of activity in the middle to late 1960s; each was deemed to be a non-partisan question and a matter for private members bills not government bills; and each met with success (with the partial exception of the Sunday Observance campaign) in the sense that legislative change was brought about largely in accordance with their objectives.[898] The course of these campaigns is briefly summarized below.

Homosexual Law Reform

Homosexuality had been an offence from time immemorial, denounced in the Bible.[899] It ceased to be a capital offence by virtue of the Offences Against the Person Act, 1861 and instead became punishable by legal servitude for life. There was little or no change in the position during the twentieth century until the 1950s when the Church of England Moral Welfare Council produced a

---

[898] This was something of a Golden Age for the private members bill with five contentious pieces of legislation passed this way in the space of four years. See, particularly, Bromhead, P A, *Private Members' Bills in the British Parliament* (London: Routledge and Kegan Paul, 1956); Richards, P G, *Parliament and Conscience* (London: Allen and Unwin, 1970); Pym, Bridget, *Pressure Groups and the Permissive Society* (Newton Abbot: David and Charles, 1974); Marsh, David and Melvyn Read, *Private Members' Bills* (Cambridge: Cambridge University Press, 1988); There was something of a reaction against the private member's bill as a vehicle for important legislation after 1970 and the Heath government refused to give time or assistance to any of them. Burton, Ivor and Gavin Drewry, *Legislation and Public Policy: Public Bills in the 1970-74 Parliament* (London: Macmillan, 1981).

[899] 'Though shalt not lie with mankind, as with womankind; it is an abomination' Leviticus, chapter xviii, verse 22. King James Authorized Bible. Quoted in Richards, ibid, p.63

report, *The Problem of Homosexuality,* published in 1954. Both they and the Howard League urged the Home Secretary to initiate an official departmental enquiry which was duly set up under the chairmanship of Sir John Wolfenden, and which reported three years later in 1957. The tone of the latter's report was surprisingly liberal. It regarded homosexuality as being neither more nor less harmful than heterosexuality, and found no justification for the existing law. It argued that it was not the business of the state to interfere in the private conduct of the individual, and said that homosexual acts in private between consenting adults should cease to be criminal and that the age of consent should be fixed at seventeen: 'We do not think it is proper for the law to concern itself with what a man does in private unless it can be shown to be so contrary to the public good that the law ought to intervene in its function as the guardian of the public good.'[900]

The Homosexual Law Reform Society (HLRS) was set up in 1958 emerging out of the correspondence generated by a letter to the *Times* by an academic Tony Dyson, which was co-signed by Lord Attlee, A J Ayer, Isaiah Berlin, Trevor Huddleston, Julian Huxley, J B Priestley, Bertrand Russell, Donald Soper, Angus Wilson and Barbara Wootton and which called for the implementation of the Wolfenden proposals. The HLRS included among its founders Victor Gollancz, Sir Stephen Spender and Kenneth Younger, MP. Parliament gave slowly increasing attention to the subject. There were Parliamentary debates on the question in 1957 (Lords) and 1958, 1960 and 1962 (Commons) but the Parliamentary campaign only really got going after the election of a Labour government in 1964 (as with capital punishment). In May 1965 the Earl of Arran (Liberal) moved in the House of Lords for action and introduced a private members bill to implement Wolfenden which was passed by 94-49, but it was unable to progress in the Commons.[901]

Several other attempts were made but it was not until the 1966-7 session that the measure finally came to fruition. Leo Abse re-introduced a previous Bill in the Commons under the Ten-Minute Rule which was supported by 244-100, partly due to the enhanced Labour composition of the Commons after the 1966 general election.[902] Abse persuaded the government (or, more precisely, Leader of the House of Commons Richard Crossman and Home Secretary Roy Jenkins) to find time for the legislation.[903] He obtained a second reading for the Bill without a division in December 1966 (partly because the leading Conservative

---

[900] Wolfenden Committee Report, 1957, paragraph 52, quoted in Richards, ibid, p.70
[901] HL Deb, 1965, vol 266, cols 631-712, cited in Richards, ibid, p.76
[902] HC Deb, 1967, vol 731, cols 259-68, cited in Richards, ibid., p.77
[903] TNA: HO 291/198 'Note of a meeting with the Lord President of the Council', 6th September 1966, cited in Dorey, Peter, *Homosexual law reform,* In: Dorey, Peter (ed.) *The Labour Governments, 1964-70* (Abingdon: Routledge, 2006) p. 349

opponent of the Bill was allegedly too drunk to stand up and object).[904] After the government was persuaded to give it further time it finally received a third reading by 99-14.[905] The Lords gave it a second reading by 111-48, the committee and report stages were formalities and *The Sexual Offences Bill* received the Royal Assent on 27th July 1967.[906] It had taken only ten years from the publication of the Wolfenden Report for its recommendations to be translated into law.

Abortion Law Reform

Abortion became a statutory offence in 1803, and a capital offence in 1828, though the latter was repealed in 1837. It was re-enacted in the Offences Against the Person Act, 1861 which then formed the basis of the law for the next century. The Infant Life (Preservation) Act, 1929 partially legalized it by providing that it was not an offence when done to preserve the life of the mother.[907] A leading case of 1938, *R v Bourne,* effectively legalized abortion where giving birth might be seriously injurious to the general health (physical and mental) of the mother, and/or where the pregnancy occurred as a result of rape, so as to avoid consequent distress to the mother in continuing the pregnancy and in giving birth.[908] The Birkett Committee (a Home Office departmental committee) was set up in 1937 and reported in 1939, and recommended the legalization of 'therapeutic' abortion in line with the Bourne case which occurred while the Committee was sitting. However, it rejected the proposals of the Abortion Law Reform Association (ALRA), the pressure group for law reform in that area founded in 1936, for legalization of abortion for social, economic and personal reasons.

The first real step on the Parliamentary road to reform came with a private members bill introduced in June 1965 under the Ten-Minute Rule by Renee Short (Labour, Wolverhampton North East).[909] It proposed that abortion be made legal on four grounds:- a) to preserve the life of the mother; b) where giving birth would impose a grave risk to the mother; c) where there was a risk of serious deformity to the child; and d) where pregnancy was as a result of a sexual offence. The Bill wasn't debated or voted on and made no further progress. In November 1965 Lord Silkin (Labour) introduced a similar bill in

---

[904] Ponting, Clive, *Breach of Promise: Labour in Power 1964-70* (Harmondsworth: Penguin, 1990) p. 265 and Castle, Barbara, *The Castle Diaries, 1964-76* (London: Macmillan, 1990) p.100, 20th December 1966

[905] HC Deb, 1967, vol 749, cols. 1403-1525 cited in Richards, op cit., p.79

[906] HC Deb, 1967, vol 275, cols. 146-77 cited in Richards, ibid, p.79

[907] Again the account is taken largely from Richards, ibid, pp. 85-112. See also Hindell, Keith and Madeleine Simms, *Abortion Law Reformed* (London: Peter Owen, 1971)

[908] (1938) 3 AER 615; (1939) IKB, 687 Cited in Richards, ibid, p. 87

[909] HC Deb, 1965, vol 714, cols 254-8, cited in Richards, ibid, p. 98

the Upper House which received a second reading by 67-8.[910] It passed through the Lords just as Parliament was dissolved for the 1966 general election. Another private members bill was introduced in the Commons under the ballot system by Simon Wingfield Digby (Conservative, Dorset West) in February 1966 but the Speaker refused to allow it a second reading because the debate had been too short and it was talked out by Peter Mahon (Labour, Preston South).[911] But the ground had been set as with homosexual law reform for a bill in the new Parliament.

After the 1966 election David Steel, the recently elected Liberal MP for Roxburgh, Selkirk and Peebles, got third place in the ballot for private members bills, and after consultation with ALRA he introduced a Bill which received a second reading by 223-29.[912] Home Secretary Roy Jenkins explained the government's position as one of neutrality but offered drafting assistance for the later stages. The Steel Bill was similar to previous ones and allowed for 'therapeutic' and 'eugenic' abortion and included a social clause that permitted abortion where a woman's capacity as a mother would be severely overstrained. This and a clause covering rape were dropped at committee stage. Again, as with both homosexual law reform and the abolition of capital punishment the government awarded the Bill extra time, and two more whole days were required to complete the Bill's passage.[913] Twenty-eight divisions were needed on report and there was an element of deliberate time-wasting. A sunset clause allowing for the Bill to expire in 1973 (shades of capital punishment again) was heavily defeated. Opponents of the Bill were split between those opposed on principle and those who wanted it more tightly drawn. It was passed on third reading 167-83.

Theatre Censorship

Censorship of the theatre had a very long history going back to the sixteenth century and to an Act of 1543 concerned with the 'advancement of true religion and the abolishment of the contrary'. The Master of the Revels was the first official to be responsible for the enforcement of censorship, succeeded by the Lord Chamberlain in the late seventeenth century. Walpole in the eighteenth century attempted to extend censorship in the light of theatrical attacks on him and his administration, and though his motives were political it was disguised as being concerned with morals. This resulted in the Licensing Act of 1737 which enlarged the powers of the Lord Chamberlain. By the early twentieth century censorship was under strong attack, especially in the light of

---

[910] HL Deb, 1965, vol 270, cols 1139-242, cited in Richards, ibid. p. 98

[911] HC Deb, 1966, vol 725, cols 837-56, cited in Richards, ibid, p. 99

[912] HC Deb, 1966, vol 732, cols 1067-1166

[913] HC Deb, 1967, vol 749, cols 895-1102; and vol 750, cols 1159-1386 cited in Richards, ibid., p. 101

the number of plays by distinguished playwrights such as Wilde, Ibsen and Shaw for which the Lord Chamberlain had refused a licence, but the edifice of censorship stood, though there were private theatre clubs outside the scope of the censorship laws.

In 1949 a private members bill proposed the abolition of theatre censorship and was carried on second reading by 76-37 but made no further progress due to lack of Parliamentary time.[914] In the theatre itself barriers were rapidly being broken down irrespective of the attentions of the Lord Chamberlain who grew increasingly permissive anyway. The campaign to end his powers really got underway in 1958 with the formation of the Theatre Censorship Reform Committee (TCRC) including Noel Annan, Roy Jenkins, Wayland Young and representatives of the League of Dramatists and Equity. Dingle Foot (Labour, Ipswich) introduced a Ten-minute Rule Bill in 1962 to make the submission of a play to the Lord Chamberlain for licensing optional, but it was rejected by 134-77.[915] As with the other conscience issues it was the advent of the Labour government in 1964 which re-invigorated the Parliamentary campaign. Senior figures of the TCRC were now in positions of authority. Roy Jenkins became Home Secretary in December 1965 and Annan and Young were now in the Lords. In the Commons another Ten-Minute Rule Bill was moved by Michael Foot (Labour, Ebbw Vale) to abolish stage censorship altogether, but neither of these initiatives got anywhere due to the imminence of the 1966 general election.[916]

But early in the new Parliament the Commons accepted the Lords proposal without a debate.[917] It took evidence from a range of witnesses and produced a report unanimously in favour of the abolition of censorship.[918] George Strauss (Labour, Vauxhall) won tenth place in the ballot for private members bills that year (1967-8) and approached the Home Office for assistance in drafting a bill to give effect to the Committee's proposals, which

---

[914] HC Deb 1949, vol 463, cols 713-798 cited in Richards, ibid., p. 119

[915] HC Deb, 1962, vol 668, cols 1321-34 cited in Richards, ibid, p. 124

[916] HC Deb, 1966, vol 725, cols 2053-60; cited in Richards, ibid, p. 125

[917] HC Deb, 1966, vol 729, col 419, cited in Richards, ibid, p. 125. The membership of the resultant Joint Committee was from the Lords: - The Earl of Scarborough, ex Lord Chamberlain, Earl of Kilmuir (Conservative ex Lord Chancellor who died while the committee was sitting and was replaced by Lord Brooke, Conservative ex Home Secretary), Viscount Norwich, Lord Tweedsmuir, Baroness Gaitskell, Lord Lloyd of Hampstead, Lord Annan, Lord Goodman, Chairman of the Arts Council; and from the Commons: - Andrew Faulds (Labour, Smethwick) ex actor, Michael Foot (Labour, Ebbw Vale), Emlyn Hooson (Liberal, Montgomery), Hugh Jenkins (Labour, Putney) ex officer of Equity, Sir David Renton (Conservative and National Liberal, Huntingdonshire) ex Under Secretary at the Home Office, Norman St John Stevas (Conservative, Chelmsford), George Strauss (Labour, Vauxhall) Minister of Supply 1947-1951 and William Wilson (Labour, Coventry South). St John Stevas had been a keen supporter of Roy Jenkins Obscene Publications Act, 1959. Wilson was a sponsor of the Divorce Reform Bill in the 1967-8 session.

[918] HC 503 and HL 255 (1966-7)

was duly forthcoming. It received a second reading in February 1968 without a division.[919] Only one division was required at Committee stage when a new clause proposed by St John Stevas (Conservative, Chelmsford) to safeguard the Royal Family was rejected by 9-2. The Bill went to the Lords where it received almost unanimous support.[920] After debate on some points of detail in committee and at report, it won a third reading and received the Royal Assent as the Theatres Act, 1968.

Divorce Law Reform

Divorce had been a statutory matter from the end of the seventeenth century, having previously been a matter for the ecclesiastical courts. It was not until 1836 that civil marriage ceremonies were permitted. In 1857 the Matrimonial Causes Act instituted a secular 'Court for Divorce and Matrimonial Causes' which took on the divorce work of the ecclesiastical courts, following on from the recommendations of a Royal Commission on the Law of Divorce.[921] The Divorce Law Reform Union (DLRU) was established in 1906 to campaign for further liberalization. A further Royal Commission of 1909-1912, under the chairmanship of Gorell, failed to come to a unanimous view and the outbreak of war in 1914 prevented further legislation. The granting of the vote to women immediately after the war led to an equalization of the grounds for divorce as between the sexes, but it was not until the 1930s and the campaign led by A P Herbert that the Gorell proposals became law in the Divorce Act, 1937.[922] This was a private members bill under the ballot procedure and was thus a trailblazer for the much later campaigns on divorce and other issues in the 1960s. After the Second World War Eirene White (Labour, East Flint) promoted a Bill in 1950-51 which sought to allow divorce where the couple had lived apart for seven years, even if one party objected, and introduced the concept of 'irretrievable breakdown' of marriage rather than fault on one side or the other.[923] The Bill was carried easily on second reading. However, she withdrew her Bill in return for a promise of another Royal Commission. This duly laboured for four years under Lord Morton but produced an anodyne report.[924]

There was no further action until 1963 when Leo Abse (Labour,

---

[919] HC Deb, 1968, vol 759, cols 825-74 cited in Richards, op cit, p. 128

[920] HL Deb, 1968, vol 292, cols 1044-1104

[921] 1852-53 [1604], xl cited in Richards, op cit, p. 133

[922] Herbert, A P, *The Ayes Have It* (London: Methuen, 1937) is his own account of the campaign.

[923] HC Deb, 1951, vol 485, cols 1017-20

[924] Report of the Royal Commission on Divorce 1955-56, Cmnd 9678, xviii. Cited in Richards, op cit, p. 137 For a critique see McGregor, O R, *Divorce in England* (London: Methuen, 1957)

Pontypool - subsequently a promoter of homosexual law reform and an opponent of abortion law reform) introduced a bill under the ballot procedure which sought to provide for reconciliation between estranged couples but also to allow divorce after seven years separation. This received a second reading without a vote.[925] However, such was the opposition to the divorce element of the Bill that he had to drop it to permit the Bill to pass with the reconciliation element. Nonetheless, this re-activated discussion of the issue. In 1967 another bill incorporating the idea of irretrievable breakdown as the basis of divorce was introduced by William Wilson (Labour, Coventry South) who won fourth place in the ballot. It received a second reading by 159-63 in February 1968. It had a difficult committee stage requiring thirteen meetings and by the time it got back to the floor of the House there was insufficient time to debate the report stage and, since the government refused to give it extra time, the bill was lost. There was dissatisfaction with the situation from the bill's supporters, especially Leo Abse, and this resulted in the government giving support to a similar bill in the following session of 1968-9. Alec Jones (Labour, Rhondda West) was persuaded by Abse to adopt a divorce bill, which was almost identical to the Wilson bill, and which received additional time in a morning session to enable it to receive a second reading by 183-106.[926] Finally the bill received a third reading by 109-55.[927] In the Lords it received a second reading by 122-34. The bishops were split with five in favour and three against with the Archbishop of Canterbury abstaining. In October 1969 the Commons accepted the Lords amendments and the bill finally received the Royal Assent.

Sunday Entertainment

The Lord's Day Observance Society (LDOS) was founded in 1831 to oppose commercial encroachments upon the Sabbath. In practice it has concerned itself with sport and entertainment rather than trade and employment given that it accepted that essential services have to be maintained on the Sunday. Much Sunday Observance legislation was archaic and had become a dead letter, such as the Acts of 1625 and 1677 which were repealed in 1969 as part of the Statute Law (Repeals) Act. The controversy centred on an Act of 1780 which stipulated:-

> that...any house, room, or other place, which shall be opened or used for publick entertainment or amusement, or for publickly debating upon any subject whatsoever, upon any part of the Lord's Day... and to which persons shall be admitted by the payment of money, or by tickets sold for money, shall be deemed a disorderly house

---

[925] HC Deb 1953, vol 671, cols 806-84 cited in Richards, ibid, p.137

[926] HC Deb 1968, 17th December 1968, vol 775, cols 1045-8

[927] Richards, op cit, p.154

or place...[928]

The coming of the cinema in the twentieth century added to the anomalies by opening on a Sunday. The London County Council, which like all local authorities was required to licence cinemas, required that the profits from Sunday screenings be paid to selected charities. The Labour government of 1929 sought to legalize the status quo and a bill was given a second reading on a free vote by 258-210 but the government was overwhelmed by economic difficulties before proceeding any further. The National Government passed the Sunday Entertainments Act effectively legalizing the status quo in relation to cinema, concerts and lectures, though theatre, variety and dancing were still prohibited. Inevitably these were sidestepped in sometimes bizarre ways and clubs were exempt. During World War Two there was a free vote on whether theatres should be allowed to open for the benefit of servicemen on leave. It was defeated by 144-136, indicating the strength of Sabbatarian feeling.

Lord (Ted) Willis introduced a bill into the Upper House in November 1966 covering only sport and entertainment which passed through all stages, but there was no time to debate it in the Commons and it therefore lapsed. In the following session William Hamling (Labour, Woolwich West) sponsored the Willis bill and its second reading was carried by 29-18, after a nifty piece of Parliamentary gamesmanship by John Parker (Labour, Dagenham) who allowed himself to be portrayed as talking the bill out when in fact he was talking it in![929] The bill was talked out at report stage, however, by Sir Cyril Black (Conservative, Wimbledon) amongst others. In the 1968-9 session effectively the same bill was introduced again by Parker who had won third place in the private members' ballot, and it narrowly received a second reading, by 104-95.[930] But the bill was talked out in committee.

A Comparison of the Campaigns

Of the five campaigns outlined above (taken together with that for abolition) there are many striking similarities, and a few key differences. In terms of general support there was a tendency for the leadership to be drawn from the ranks of fairly high-profile and moderately liberal establishment figures, whether from politics, the law, medicine, the churches and even from the world of sport, the arts and entertainment, though supplemented (and sometimes handicapped) at grassroots level by more extreme or outlandish figures. Given the tendency for support to come from the establishment, and from wealthy figures such as Gollancz, they tended to be well funded, though

---

[928] Quoted in Richards, ibid, p.161
[929] HC Deb, vol 755, cols 1931-2, cited in Richards, ibid, p.167
[930] HC Deb, vol 778, cols 2069-174, 28th February 1969 cited in Richards, ibid, p.169

funding was not necessarily an issue. Given also the high intellectual calibre of their leadership they were able to articulate their respective cases very effectively in the press and the media generally. They also tended to have rather good access to Parliament and to government, usually because they were assiduous in cultivating Parliamentary support, and because anyway the world of the campaigners on the one hand and that of Parliament on the other intertwined so closely. Moreover, there was usually a smattering of support for their causes within the ranks of the government of the day, whatever its complexion.

Each of these campaigns, initially loosely-based, developed well organized pressure groups to co-ordinate their activities and act as a conduit to Parliament.[931] Sometimes there was only one such body; sometimes there were several to start off with which eventually coalesced into one, the better to co-ordinate their efforts; and sometimes there was a breakaway at some point in their history. The HLRS was formed in 1958 to agitate for homosexual law reform and more specifically the implementation of Wolfenden, and was for a long time effectively the only major lobby group. But, after the passage of the Sexual Offences Act in 1967, there was a breakaway by a more radically-minded group from its north-west branch in 1969, which agitated for a more strenuous campaign to achieve equality rather than mere toleration and which evolved into the *Campaign for Homosexual Equality (CHE)*. Other, even more radical groups, emerged in their wake by the 1970s such as *The Gay Liberation Front*. ALRA was founded in 1936 to argue for the legalization of abortion, at least in certain circumstances where there was a danger to the life or health of the mother or where pregnancy had occurred as a result of rape or incest, and was active before the Second World War, contemporaneously with the sitting of

---

[931] For an analysis of pressure groups see particularly Stewart, J D, *British Pressure Groups* (Oxford: Clarendon Press, 1958); Finer, S E, *Anonymous Empire* (London: Pall Mall, 1958); Potter, A, *Organized Groups in British National Politics* (London: Faber, 1961); Kimber, R and J J Richardson (eds), *Pressure Groups in Britain: A Reader* (London: J M Dent, 1974); Richardson, J J and A G Jordan, *Governing under Pressure: The Policy Process in a Post-Parliamentary Democracy* (Oxford: Martin Robertson, 1979); Jordan, A G and J J Richardson, *British Politics and the Policy Process: An Arena Approach* (London: Allen and Unwin, 1987); Baggott, Rob, *Pressure Groups Today* (Manchester: Manchester University Press, 1995); and Grant, Wyn, *Pressure Groups, Politics and Democracy in Britain* (Hemel Hempstead: Harvester Wheatsheaf, 2nd ed, 1995). For case studies of particular groups and/or particular campaigns see, for example, Eckstein, H, *Pressure Group Politics: The Case of the BMA* (London: Allen and Unwin, 1960); Wilson, H H, *Pressure Groups: The Campaign for Commercial Television* (London: Secker and Warburg, 1961); Self, Peter and H Storing, *The State and the Farmer* (London: Allen and Unwin, 1962); Driver, Christopher, *The Disarmers: A Study in Protest* (London: Hodder and Stoughton, 1964); Hindell, Keith and M Simms, *Abortion Law Reformed* (London: Peter Owen, 1971); Ryan, M, *The Acceptable Pressure Group: A Case Study of the Howard League and RAP* (Farnborough, Saxon House, 1978); and Marsh, David and J Chambers, *Abortion Politics* (London: Junction Books, 1981)

the Birkett Committee, and was for a very long time the only real advocacy group for abortion law reform. With legislation imminent an anti-abortion group was founded in the form of SPUC (the Society for the Protection of the Unborn Child), and given the continuing Parliamentary trench warfare a whole series of other groups have subsequently emerged, on both sides of the debate. The DLRU was founded as early as 1906 to lobby for a relaxation of the divorce laws, specifically for the concept of irretrievable breakdown of the marriage as valid grounds. The TCRC was formed in 1958 to campaign for the abolition of theatre censorship. On the other hand there was no single pressure group to agitate for a relaxation of the Sunday Observance laws, and it may or may not be coincidental that this was the only campaign that was unsuccessful.

Usually the executive committees of these pressure groups contained at least a few Parliamentarians among their number, sometimes from each of the three main parties, so as to emphasize the breadth and diversity of their support and to facilitate liaison with each of the parties separately. The NCACP had Silverman and Paget (Labour, left and right wings respectively), Peter Kirk, Julian Critchley and Christopher Hollis (Conservative) and Jeremy Thorpe (Liberal). The TCRC had Roy Jenkins. The HLRS had Kenneth Younger (Labour). Their tactics were carefully crafted to eschew unlawful or eccentric activities, and they were mindful to exclude from their ranks and their counsels the mavericks (such as Mrs Van der Elst from the NCACP). They were anxious to avoid alienating the establishment and popular opinion, confident in the knowledge that diligent campaigning in the right quarters would bring eventual success.

Most of these campaigns enjoyed a fair measure of popular support, with the obvious exception of the abolition of capital punishment, usually amounting to a majority of the population (at any rate as measured by opinion poll data), though the sizes of these majorities varied over time and between the different issues. Divorce law reform probably had the highest level of consistent public support, amounting to a large majority, with abortion law reform some way behind and homosexual law reform someway behind that. Theatre censorship was too esoteric a matter to attract strong opinions from the bulk of the (non theatre-going) populace, and may never have been the subject of a poll, while the question of the Sunday Observance laws was too multi-stranded to provide a clear picture of the level of support.

The campaigns tended to enjoy, at least potentially, the support of a majority of the House of Commons and the House of Lords, though the bulk of that support tended almost invariably to come from the Labour and Liberal Parties, with a smattering of reformist Conservatives. The level of Parliamentary support tended to grow over time with an initially very small group of Conservatives tending to become a substantial minority, and a majority of Labourites and Liberals eventually becoming an overwhelming majority. Nonetheless, a majority of Conservative MPs was always opposed to most or all of these reforms, as was likewise a small minority of Labour MPs, drawn preponderantly from the ranks of socially conservative, working class members, often northern and often Roman Catholic, of which the Mahon brothers, Simon and Peter, were archetypical. There was a good deal of overlap between those supporting and those opposing reformist measures in both major parties, and support for one of these measures was fairly highly correlated with support for another, lending credence to the notion of an underlying variable of liberal/conservative that, to some extent, cut across the party divide. This is discussed more fully in the chapter on the political parties. There were, inevitably, some exceptions. Leo Abse, for example, was a prominent supporter of both homosexual and divorce law reform, and of the abolition of the death penalty, and an equally prominent opponent of abortion law reform.

All of these campaigns had had a fairly long history of extra-Parliamentary campaigning before becoming the material of private members bills in the 1960s, and often there had been a succession of Royal Commissions, or committees of enquiry of one description or another, which had promulgated reports advocating reform, and which foreshadowed the bills actually passed. Capital punishment had been the subject of Royal Commissions in the 1860s and the 1950s (Gowers) and a Commons Select Committee in 1929-1931; abortion a Home Office committee in the late 1930s (Birkett); homosexuality a Home Office committee in 1954-7 (Wolfenden); divorce a Royal Commission in the Edwardian era (Gorell) and again in the 1950s (Morton). These bodies tended to sit for a long time and to produce very little in the way of recommendations, and their reports tended to gather dust on the shelf for a long time before taken up by politicians. All these issues were the subject of several abortive attempts at private members legislation, before finally one of them managed to make it through the meat-grinder to the statute book.

However, all of these campaigns were able to crown their efforts with success at some point in the 1960s – in fact within a space of four years between 1965 and 1969, with the exception of the Sunday Observance laws (and even here there was a clear indication that the law would eventually be relaxed or would simply be defied with impunity). The Death Penalty (Abolition) Act was passed in 1965, less than twenty years since it had become a seriously debated question and only ten years after the formation of the NCACP. The Sexual Offences Act was passed in 1967, only ten years after Wolfenden had reported and nine years after the HLRA was formed. The Abortion Act was passed the same year, some thirty-one years after the formation of ALRA, but only a few years from the first real attempts to legislate for legalization. Abolition of theatre censorship went through with extraordinary ease in 1968, only ten years after the initiation of the TCRC. And the Divorce Reform Act was passed in 1969, after a slightly longer and rather more convoluted process than the others, though again only a few years after the first serious attempt to reform the law in 1963.

Unquestionably none of these measures could have been passed as swiftly as they were (or in fact at all) had it not been for the support, or at least benevolent neutrality, of the government of the day, which was prepared to offer Parliamentary time, assistance with drafting and tactics, and moral support. Invariably the benevolence was more apparent than the neutrality. That in turn was because the Wilson government was, on the whole, favourable to these reforms, though by no means all of its members favoured all of the reforms. Harold Wilson and Lord Gardiner were passionate advocates of the abolition of the death penalty, as was Roy Jenkins, though he did not arrive at the Home Office until after it had been accomplished. Jenkins was, nonetheless, unshakeable in his resistance to the demands for reintroduction that emanated from the police force and the prison service in particular, orchestrated by Duncan Sandys from the Conservative backbenches. He was also a keen supporter of the other reforms, all of which he had advocated in his influential book *The Case for Labour*, published during the 1959 election campaign, and he had been responsible for the passage of the Obscene Publications Act, 1959, arguably the only other significant piece of private members legislation of the post-war era. He was also, as mentioned, on the executive committee of the TCRC. Richard Crossman, Leader of the House and the government's Parliamentary manager, was another keen advocate of these reforms. However, not all members of the Wilson Cabinet were so favourably disposed. George Brown and James Callaghan, for example, were opposed to homosexual law reform and Anthony Greenwood voted against the Abortion Bill, to which Lord Longford, Ray Gunter and William Ross were all opposed to a greater or lesser extent. Harold Wilson himself was unenthusiastic, to say the least, about both homosexual and abortion law reform, and was only persuaded by Jenkins of the desirability of giving government assistance so as to get the matters out of the way before the next election.

Nonetheless, the government was generally extremely well-disposed to reform, and was accused in some quarters of seeking to promote its own liberal agenda by the back door of private member's bills, thereby sidestepping the ensuing controversy and evading responsibility for the consequences of the measures. Another frequent Conservative accusation was that these measures were a sop to its vociferous and discontented left-wing which was angry with Wilson for his economic, industrial and foreign policies. This, suggestion, however, fails to take fully into account the fact that the reforms tended to be supported across the whole spectrum of PLP opinion from extreme left to extreme right, and that the party's left-wing was consistently and unremittingly hostile to the government throughout the whole period during which they were being enacted.

The various pressure groups that sprang up were classic examples of the promotional rather than sectional type, in the sense that their membership was not drawn from any particular sphere of employment nor had anything in common other than their desire to see the reforms enacted, and the membership could not personally benefit from the reforms in any direct material sense. Generally speaking, as promotional groups, they did not enjoy the insider status of, for example, sectional groups such as the trade unions or the CBI; they had no regular access to government ministers or senior civil servants and had no regular forum with which to exchange views with government. They did, of course, contribute and give evidence to the various Royal Commissions and departmental committees of enquiry which were set up. Certainly the Howard League and the NCADP gave evidence to Gowers, ALRA gave evidence to Birkett and the DLRU gave evidence to Gorell and Morton. But they tended to make their input and exert their influence at the level of the Parliamentary backbenches rather than government, because the very nature of the reforms made them candidates for private members bills, and the relevant government departments tended to disavow responsibility for legislation, even when favourably disposed towards the reforms.

On the other hand, the membership of the executives of several of these groups was often very high profile, and in the nature of things there may have been a great deal of networking with frequent informal, social contacts between these figures and government ministers and senior civil servants, and a commonality of outlook would have been fostered even if it did not already exist, which would have conduced to the gradual erosion of resistance to reform. Moreover, some promotional groups, especially the Howard League, were of long standing, were highly respected within their respective Departmental circles and had institutionalized contact with that Department (the Home Office in the case of the League and most of the other groups). In respect of the League this was partly because of their fact-gathering function, which was useful to government, and the breadth of their agenda was such as to necessitate regular and frequent contact. They were able to lobby for abolition, in addition to their more general objective of penal reform, but were also prominent in lobbying for homosexual law reform.

This contrasts with the position of the NCACP, which had been set up specifically to lobby for abolition, but who could thus use the League as a conduit to government, given the commonality of their aims and the overlap of their membership. In fact the two bodies were complementary in their methods and objectives. Whilst the League acted as the classic insider group, meeting regularly with Home Office officials to lobby for their cause and to exchange information they rigorously eschewed any overt criticism of the government of the day, and avoided any sort of public display of dissent in the form of demonstrations, petitions and so on. They had acted as host and adviser to the earlier Calvert led NCADP, and both bodies lobbied Home Secretary Chuter Ede in the late 1940s to include abolition within the forthcoming criminal justice bill.[932] From October 1948, after the defeat of the abolition clause in the Lords and before the inception of the Royal Commission the NCADP effectively wound itself up and agreed to continue under the auspices of the League, with members transferring their subscriptions from the NCADP to the League, but on the understanding that in due course a League committee dedicated to abolition would be formed. It duly was and it was this body which prepared the League's evidence to the Royal Commission in 1949.[933]

After the formation of the NCACP in August 1955 the League was slightly wary of forming too close an alliance with the new Campaign, and initially rejected Gollancz's proposal that the League secretary, Hugh Klare, should join the executive.[934] This was partly because, as before, they did not want to compromise their excellent working relationship with the Home Office (then still institutionally hostile to abolition under the aegis of its permanent secretary, Frank Newsam) and did not want to become too closely identified with a single issue campaign that formed only one aspect of their multi-faceted penal reform work. Moreover, it was immediately evident that the NCACP wanted to engage in very public and overt displays such as mass rallies, petitions and propaganda directed at the media which would again have jeopardized their relations with the Home Office. The League was jealous of its reputation for building its case on the dispassionate presentation of factual information with a view to persuading officialdom of its merits. Nonetheless it assisted the NCACP unofficially, and Klare did eventually join the executive, whilst Gardiner, also a member of the League's executive, was allowed to join the Campaign. There may have been justification for the League's wariness, given that some of the Campaign's more vigorous antics did cause offence to the League's official contacts in the police force and the prison service. The two groups complemented rather than competed with one another, and the resultant division of labour may have been beneficial, with the League providing the research, contacts with government, officialdom and the world of criminology and a reputation for integrity, whilst the NCACP supplied the wider membership, finances and propaganda. This symbiosis was necessary because the League was not equipped for, or desirous of, engaging in a large scale campaign.

The passage of the various reform measures can, and have been, cited as triumphs for their respective lobby groups, but it is debatable to what extent this was really so. The passage of the bills could not have happened had there not been receptive Parliamentary soil, backed up, as we have seen by the tacit support of the government of the day. There were plenty of supporters of these measures on the backbenches, particularly on the Labour side, straining at the

---

[932] Howard League, executive committee minutes, July 1947, quoted in Ryan, Mick, op cit. p.39

[933] Howard League, executive committee minutes, April 1948. Quoted in Ryan, Mick, ibid

[934] Howard League, executive committee minutes, October 1955. Quoted in Ryan., ibid

leash to introduce bills or propose amendments to give effect to them, and they needed no extra-Parliamentary organization to thrive. On the other hand, all of the extra-Parliamentary lobbying in the world would never have enabled the bills to pass had not pre-existing Parliamentary majorities been there.

Generally the reforms have been consolidated since their enactment, with public acceptance of their legitimacy, and often further progressive legislation has been enacted, building on the earlier Acts. Most have been largely proof against repeal or regressive amendment. The divorce laws have been further liberalized and there has been no attempt to legislate in the opposite direction notwithstanding the huge rise in the divorce rate (and the claim in some quarters that this is a factor contributing heavily towards social breakdown). Homosexual law reform has advanced dramatically in the intervening years with the passage of legislation equalizing the age of consent, the removal of the ban on homosexuals in the armed forces and the diplomatic service (the former as a result of a European directive), acceptance of the right of homosexual or lesbian couples to adopt and the inception of 'civil partnerships'. Significant also has been the repeal of the one piece of regressive legislation passed in the intervening period in the form of section 28 of the Local Government Act, 1988, which banned the promotion of homosexuality by local authorities.

By contrast, both abortion law reform and the abolition of the death penalty have been repeatedly subject to attempts at reversal and/or regressive amendment. Though there has been no attempt to repeal the Abortion Act there have been numerous attempts to water it down, chiefly by seeking a reduction in the period of time after which a termination may not be performed from the twenty-eight weeks specified in the Act. There were no fewer than nine private members' bills in the period between 1967 and 1981 designed to de-liberalize the Act in one way or another, culminating in the Corrie Bill of 1979-80, and only one such bill designed to liberalize it.[935] And though no attempt has been made to repeal the Act the attempts to restrict its application may be seen as a tactical move in that direction. There were many reasons for this retrogression. SPUC had been to an extent superseded by a more radical group in the shape of LIFE. In 1974 a book was published which made a variety of allegations (subsequently proved false) that placed the practice of abortion in a very unfavourable light.[936] By 1979 there was a bewildering array of pressure groups operating in the field – nine on the pro-abortion side, including ALRA, and seven on the anti-abortion side.[937] Moreover, as Marsh and Chambers argue, the abortion issue was a very complex one morally in that the characterization of it as a 'liberal' measure is far from clear-cut. The supporters of abortion always

---

[935] Marsh, David and Joanna Chambers, *Abortion Politics* (London: Junction Books, 1981) and Marsh, David and Melvyn Read, op cit

[936] Lichfield, Michael and Susan Kentish, *Babies for Burning* (London: Serpentine Press, 1974)

[937] Marsh and Chambers, op cit, p. 40

saw it as a matter of 'a woman's right to choose'; of freedom versus compulsion; but those on the other side saw it as, at worst, mass slaughter comparable to murder on a massive scale, and would have seen it as 'liberal' only in a highly technical, politicized sense of that word.

Given the extent to which it has come under repeated attack it may be questioned as to why and how an Abortion Bill was able to be passed in the first place. There were many factors. As with the other reforms there was a favourable climate of public opinion, a relatively young and Labour- dominated House, a supportive government and Home Secretary and the fact that the bill's sponsor, David Steel, drew a high place in the ballot. But additional factors were at play such as the recent thalidomide disaster which heavily conditioned public opinion, Steel's adept Parliamentary tactics, wide consultation and willingness to compromise, the hyper-activity of ALRA which had been given a new lease of life in 1963 by the infusion of a new generation of activists, and the relative ineffectiveness of the opposition which was slow to mobilize itself.[938]

The abolition of the death penalty has been, if anything, under even stronger assault than the Abortion Act. Unlike any of the other measures, including abortion, it was opposed by a clear majority at the time of its enactment - a majority which has grown steadily larger over time - and there have been repeated attempts at repeal and the restoration of the death penalty, often for specified categories of victim, particularly police and prison officers, and sometimes for specific types of murder, though none has ever come close to success. There were several reasons why abolition failed to gain general acceptance, but undoubtedly the initial public hostility to the Act denied it the legitimacy granted to the other reform measures. This lack of acceptance encouraged backbench Conservatives to introduce restoration bills or amendments, and the rapid rise in the murder rate, attributed (rightly or wrongly) to abolition, gave them a powerful incentive and a superficially powerful argument. Nonetheless the line held against restoration in Parliament, and for all the public clamour the rope has never looked like making its reappearance.

In many ways the capital punishment issue was the odd man out amongst these five or six conscience issues. It was a penal question, as well as a social and moral one, and by comparison with the other measures it directly affected only a tiny minority of the population, though of course it may be agued (and was by the retentionist camp) that the deterrent effects of the death penalty made the issue one that potentially affected the whole population. It was the one issue that very definitely, and at no stage, had the support of anything like a majority of the population and where, moreover, the majority against it steadily

---

[938] Marsh and Chambers, ibid. They argue, p.41, that ALRA was perhaps the most sophisticated, politically aware and knowledgeable of all non-economic lobby groups operating at that time.

increased after its enactment. With none of the other changes was there a clear majority against, and generally the state of opinion in the immediate aftermath of these reforms was favourable and tended to grow more favourable over time (though arguably the abortion issue may be another partial exception). It was an issue where it was argued, with or without justification, that the effects of the change were immediately apparent and highly deleterious to society in the form of rising murder and violent crime figures. And, perhaps as a function of the previous two points, it was the one issue where there was an almost immediate demand from many for a repeal of the reform and the re-instatement of the status quo ante.

Given all of that it might be queried, as for abortion, how it came to be enacted and how it has withstood the demand for repeal. One obvious answer is that, as with all these measures, the existence of a clear Parliamentary majority, much of it very passionate in pursuit of its objective, was bound to win through given the arrival of a sympathetic government. But other factors worked in favour of the abolitionists that were perhaps not present in the other campaigns. One point is that the very nature of the issue provided a 'built-in' occasion for abolition propaganda in the form of an impending execution, thereby providing a flashpoint which focussed attention on the controversy in a way that was never possible for the other issues which could not supply these moments of high drama. Though the NCACP was essentially an 'outsider' group in the sense that, as a body, it had no routine or institutionalized access to government, its leadership was of such distinction that its chairmen, Gardiner and Gollancz, regularly corresponded with the Home Secretaries of the day over the campaign and particularly over specific upcoming executions usually in order to plead for a reprieve. Moreover, the Howard League, with which the NCACP was closely associated, was very much an 'insider' group by contrast, having regular meetings with Home Secretaries and Home Office officials over a range of penal reform issues, and the NCACP unquestionably benefited from the linkage.

Another aspect of the reforms is the extent to which they were susceptible of compromise. Here again capital punishment was rather the exception in that no real compromise was possible. The state either hanged people or it didn't, though of course the ground had been prepared by the introduction of degrees of murder, and the division into capital and non-capital murder, and of course prior to that the gradual diminution in the number of capital offences during the course of the nineteenth century. There was also the introduction of new defences and the re-definition of existing ones so as to reduce further the chances of being hanged. With most of the other reforms there was much greater scope for compromise, and to that extent a better prospect of getting some sort of reform through. Abortion reform was enacted on the basis of a very restricted set of criteria for its legalization, though the interpretation of these criteria has become so lax as to be almost meaningless. David Steel was very flexible and open to compromise during the passage of the Abortion Bill.

Likewise with the Sexual Offences Bill Leo Abse was very willing to negotiate over the details of the legislation. Homosexual reform went through but with a much higher age of consent than for heterosexual intercourse and with all or most of the restrictions on homosexuality that did not apply to heterosexuality still in place, such as the ban in the armed forces and the diplomatic service (and like abortion it did not apply to Northern Ireland), though most of these anomalies have subsequently been legislated away.[939] But it was clear that without these compromises neither the abortion nor homosexual reforms would have been passed – or certainly that was the view of their protagonists. Abse has admitted that many of the compromises were tactically necessary to get the reforms through. The Divorce Bill, likewise, greatly increased the scope of the grounds on which divorce could be sought and obtained, but still made divorce relatively difficult, though again subsequent legislation has further widened it.

Conclusion

Ultimately these campaigns highlight questions about the whole process of pressure group activity and its relationship with Parliament and government. Do these campaigns distort the democratic process by coming between the peoples' will on the one hand and government on the other, so as to advance the interests of a small subsection of the people, or do they enrich the democratic process by filling in the gap between the electorate and the government in between (necessarily infrequent) elections by providing a process of continuous consultation?[940] As Finer argued the overall effect of lobbying may be to temper the system and to provide a continuous interchange between government and governed. Moreover, as numerous studies have found, propaganda and media campaigns can be very ineffective.[941] Looking at the broad political picture, for example, the Conservative Party vastly outspent the Labour Party in the immediate pre-election periods 1958-9 and 1963-4, and won handsomely in 1959 and lost in 1964. Both parties vastly outspent the Liberals, who did badly in 1959 but who rose dramatically in 1964, at least in terms of votes.[942] *The Aims of Industry* (a private enterprise lobby group), to take another example cited by Finer, conducted a vigorous media campaign against nationalization in the

---

[939] Leo Abse felt obliged to make a large number of concessions to get the Bill through and was hard pressed by the HLRS for doing so.

[940] The latter is the view taken by Finer, op cit., in his seminal work on the topic, arguing that it embodies two basic principles of democratic government:- participation in policy-making and the demand for redress of grievances.

[941] E.g. Trenaman, Joseph and D McQuail, *Television and the Political Image* (London: Methuen, 1961) This studied the effects of the party political campaigns and persuasive communications from various media on groups of electors in two neighbouring constituencies in Yorkshire during the 1959 general election, by comparing their knowledge, views and opinions both before and after and found little or no attitude change.

[942] Finer, S E, op cit, (2nd ed, 1966)

period 1963-4 which appears, to judge by the opinion polls, to have been almost wholly ineffective.[943] As Finer has observed money may be important to help publicize a campaign, but it is only useful up to a point, because there appears to be a ceiling above which extra money fails to bring commensurate results, if indeed any results at all.

---

[943] Finer, ibid, pp.120-1. 'Say NO! to Nationalisation' (Aims of Industry campaign 1963-4) BIPO polls conducted at six monthly intervals of the same set of voters indicated if anything a slight increase in the desire for more nationalization from March 1963 to August 1964 (22% for it at the end as against 18% for it at the beginning). Gallup Political Index, nos. 45, 51, 54 (1963-4)

CHAPTER 18

RETROSPECT

This final chapter assesses the campaign and tries to account for its success, examines various aspects of the process including its legitimacy and asks some questions about the actual course of events and whether things might have been different.

Why Did the Campaign Succeed?

What, ultimately, was the reason for the success of the abolition campaign?

It is plausible to cite the dynamism, indefatigability and resourcefulness of the abolition campaign in the form, chiefly, of the NCACP. Had it not lobbied incessantly for a change in the law in the teeth of public opposition and establishment hostility then capital punishment would still be with us today, they might contend. But there are many such campaigns from the 'Campaign for Real Ale' to 'the Flat Earth Society' that are similarly obsessed and yet whose exertions get them precisely nowhere. For a campaign to bring about a fundamental change in the law as profound as the ending of centuries of judicial custom and practice it required Parliamentary soil receptive to it. Without a doubt abolition could not have happened had it not been for the fact that there were large Parliamentary majorities, in both Houses, at the relevant times to carry through this profound change.

Why had Parliament become favourable? It was not always so, though the Commons had, it is fair to say, a majority for abolition continuously from 1945 onwards, and the Lords had one from the 1960s onwards. Did the mood of Parliament change as a result of the persuasiveness of the abolitionist campaign or because of events in the country or was it simply a natural continuation of the liberal, progressive trend in politics that was so evident in that era? Almost certainly it was the latter. The gradual rise of the Labour Party during the course of the twentieth century gave it an ever larger presence in the Commons, culminating in the massive majorities of 1945 and 1966. In addition the general composition of the Party in the Commons became increasingly middle-class and reflected a progressive liberal intellectual agenda that went way beyond merely a desire for the improvement of the conditions of the working class. Penal reform went with movements for decolonization, social reform, educational egalitarianism, welfare enhancement and numerous other such policies.

On the other side of the House there was a steady influx, especially after 1945, of a more progressive and socially liberal element in the Conservative Party. This was particularly marked after 1955 and 1959 with the intakes of those years being generally more liberal and progressive than their predecessor generations. In fact, paradoxically, it was the change in the composition of the Conservative Party that was more indicative of the changing times than that of the Labour Party which had always been liberal and progressive. In 1948 only four Conservative MPs were prepared to put their heads above the parapet and vote for abolition but by 1964/5 it had swelled to between a quarter and a third of the Parliamentary party. Indeed, without the votes of the large abolitionist minority within the Conservatives abolition would have struggled to get through.

It was likewise with the two Houses of Parliament. It was the more conservative House, the Lords, that exhibited the most marked change in its composition, and that therefore reflected more faithfully the *zeitgeist*. The Commons had always been fairly favourable to abolition but the Lords only became so in the 1960s. This was in large part a function of a variety of constitutional changes that admitted life peers, enabled hereditary peers to renounce and saw a steady increase in the Labour representation. It also witnessed what might be termed the 'progressivisation' of the episcopacy, and then the liberalisation of the judiciary. These changes were in themselves indicative of a change in the temper of the times and the perceived need for reform and re-invigoration that was evident by the late fifties. Both were signposts on the long road to the liberalisation of British society so apparent in the 1960s and after. Again had it not been for this dramatic alteration in the Lords abolition could never have passed through Parliament. It is noteworthy that the Parliament Act of 1949 could not have been invoked in the case of abolition since it was not applicable to private members bills. Of course successive governments, mainly Conservative, didn't change the make-up of the Lords in order to facilitate the passage of controversial progressive legislation but that was clearly one of the effects and one of which those governments could not have been totally unaware.

The paradox, though, is that while society and Parliament was liberalising public opinion remained obstinately and firmly opposed to outright abolition. Though moving somewhat towards abolition by the early sixties it swung back strongly in the immediate aftermath of abolition and the rise in the murder rate that took place in the middle to late sixties.

Given that Parliament, or at least the Commons, had become so receptive to abolition by the late-1940s one might pose another question; namely why it took so long for that inclination to be translated into legislative effect. Here the answer lies in the vagaries of the Parliamentary system. Bringing matters to fruition, if government is not highly favourable, is a long and painstaking business. There is relatively little time to transact private members business and opportunities to get a private members bill rolling do not arise very often. Even when it does it can very easily be de-railed by determined opposition merely by talking it out.

Having had to fight hard to get abolition onto the agenda by 1948 by tacking it onto a government Criminal Justice Bill it then saw it stamped on by the Lords. The government, lukewarm about abolition to put it mildly, kicked the matter into the long grass in the form of a Royal Commission which predictably took years to report and which was not, perversely, even officially permitted within its terms of reference to consider the chief question which had given rise to its inception. It then took several attempts to get the matter raised again seriously at Westminster before a backbench bill was re-launched. Then they again endured the frustration of seeing the Lords squelch the bill for the second time, before the government of the day took the matter up and gave partial effect to it in the form of the Homicide Act. This, however, was deemed a highly unsatisfactory compromise but the need to give the Act time to work and to evaluate its effectiveness (and the large Conservative majority) blocked any further attempt to progress the issue for several more years.

Ultimately it required the election of a Labour government and a Labour Prime Minister highly favourable to abolition for the matter to come to fruition. Even then it was necessary for the government to give the matter a great deal of assistance in the form of time and advice and for it to be forced to accept a pesky amendment requiring a confirmatory vote to take place in order to prevent the re-assertion of the provisions of the old Act. This in turn did not happen until late 1969. Thus the whole campaign took twenty-one years from 1948 to get to its destination. That abolition finally happened in the mid-sixties may superficially suggest an influence of the *zeitgeist* but really reflects the natural length of the cycle of a highly controversial campaign.

Legitimacy

This raises the question of the legitimacy of abolition as enacted, both in terms of the substance of the legislation and the means by which it was passed through Parliament. It might be argued, and was agued by some opponents of abolition, that Parliament had no mandate and therefore no constitutional or moral right to abolish hanging in view of the fact that public opinion as indicated by opinion polls was still strongly opposed to its abolition. As momentous an alteration to the law and judicial custom of the land as that should only be carried through by a government and Parliament that had a clear mandate, as expressed through the ballot box at the preceding general election. This is closely related to the other critique of the Abolition Act (and of the other contentious measures put through by private members bills - abortion, homosexual and divorce law reform) namely that it was carried through by means of a private members bill, i.e. one for which the government disavowed any responsibility whilst actually assisting it by giving it Parliamentary time and moral support. Thus the government was trying to have the best of both worlds by carrying through an unpopular measure which it (or many of its leading members) strongly supported and yet distancing itself from the public opprobrium that might result from its passage. This was very much the burden of the Conservative critique of the method by which abolition and the various other controversial measures in the social and moral sphere were carried through in the 1964 and 1966 Parliaments.

This is part and parcel of a wider critique of private members bills, especially as vehicles for the passage of important legislation.[944] This critique asserts that, apart from the fact that they lack the imprimatur of government, they tend to be passed with insufficient study and debate devoted to the issues involved; that constituents do not necessarily know the views of candidates on non-party issues and thus members cannot claim to have a mandate; that votes are often taken on Fridays or late at night when attendance is low and thus the outcome is to some extent a lottery depending on who is or is not present; and that such bills are badly drafted and do not operate as intended. Indeed the private members bill, as a feature of Parliamentary procedure, had been suspended for nine years from 1939-1948 until the Attlee government re-instated it. But it was not until the 1960s that they became the agents of so much radical and contentious political change.

Supporters of the private members bill would reject all of these arguments. So far as the government's abdication of responsibility is concerned it would be countered that government has to assist controversial backbench legislation or else it would necessarily fail for lack of time. Ultimately it is still Parliament that makes the decision and government cannot force through a backbench measure that the House as a whole opposes. As pointed out by Richards it was suggested by some that the main reason for the Wilson government's encouragement of private members legislation was to divert the crusading energies of its backbenchers unhappy with the performance of the government in other fields. If so it was a spectacular failure! As Richards argues, given that the main political parties in Britain are differentiated primarily by economic and industrial policies rather than by moral and social attitudes, and that electors vote very largely upon that basis, no government could possibly claim to have a mandate for change in the social and moral sphere. Thus if any sort of change is to occur in that area logically it has to be the backbencher who initiates it.

In regard to the suggestion that private members' bills are inadequately researched it might be pointed out that nearly all the issues that formed the subject of backbench legislation had been heavily debated for a long time at

---

[944] Richards, op cit. pp. 197-215 and passim discusses these questions in some depth and this section draws heavily on his work.

every level of society and had been subject to some form of scrutiny by Royal Commission (as with abolition), by departmental committee (homosexuality and Sunday Observance), a Joint Select Committee (theatre censorship) or the Law Commission (divorce). The Church of England had pronounced on homosexuality, abortion and divorce. Naturally debate continued after the passage of these various pieces of legislation, often with renewed vigour, but that was because of the refusal of the anti-reformers to accept the verdict of Parliament rather than because new facts or arguments had suddenly been discovered. In regards to abolition the effect on murder rates and crime figures could of course only be known in retrospect but that did not constitute a failure of research. Moreover the legislation that was repealed by these private members bills was itself not always a model of carefully considered research (the criminalization of homosexuality was for example rushed through late at night without a debate).[945]

With reference to constituents' ignorance of the views of candidates whilst this is undoubtedly true it is arguably irrelevant because very few voters cast their vote on the basis of candidates' views on moral questions, even if they knew what they were. And if a voter considers it important there are various ways for him to elicit this information and to cast his vote accordingly. As noted Sydney Silverman, champion of the abolitionists, whose views on the matter could scarcely have been unknown even to the most ill-informed elector, did not appear to suffer any adverse effects at the ballot box. For though he was opposed by an independent pro-hanger who garnered many votes at the 1966 general election his own majority was increased. If there was any effect at all of the abolition issue it was very slight indeed compared to the pull of party allegiance and the concomitant raft of traditional, mainstream issues.

Taking the point about the timing of important Parliamentary divisions it so happens that, if one looks at five key votes on the various conscience issues, only two out of five were held on a Friday and of the other three only one was late at night. Though there were a very large number of abstentions (or more properly failures to vote) this was down to many reasons and few members could claim that they were simply unable to vote if they had been determined to do so.

Finally, *apropos* the supposed bad drafting of private members bills, it may be said that backbenchers receive the help of Parliamentary draftsmen and that the bill is then subject to often minute scrutiny on the floor of the House and in Committee. Of course the resultant legislation may operate in a way that goes beyond the intentions of its authors or at any rate the strict wording of the Act (almost certainly so in the instance of abortion) but that is a failure of professional administration and law enforcement not of draftsmanship.

Ultimately the arguments against the use of the private members bill as an

---

[945] Criminal Law Amendment Act, 1885, section 11 (the Labouchere amendment)

agent for social change fail, chiefly because without its lubricant effect the machinery of government would atrophy and be inadequate to the task of effecting radical change outside the mainstream of political debate. That abolition was carried through by that means does not undermine or reduce its legitimacy. Legitimacy of course does not necessarily connote wisdom or advisability, but that can only be assessed in terms of its probable effects.

Permanence

How permanent is abolition and could hanging ever be re-introduced?

Though one should never say never in politics it is difficult to envisage the return of the gallows for a variety of reasons. This is certainly not for want of trying on the part of the retentionists who fought bitterly every inch of the way against its enactment, in the Commons and the Lords and outside Westminster in the chamber of public opinion, and who have attempted on numerous occasions thereafter to re-introduce hanging. There has been something like a dozen attempts at re-introduction in the Commons over the years. Scarcely was the ink dry on the parchment of the Silverman Act than forces were mobilising to bring hanging back. Motions to that effect appeared on the order paper, and in 1966 Duncan Sandys tried to re-introduce hanging for the murder of police and prison officers in the execution of their duty. Three years later he introduced a technical motion that would have caused the Silverman Act to expire unconditionally after five years. Throughout the seventies and eighties and into the nineties there have been backbench bills introduced by various means by an assortment of Conservative backbench restorationists, all of which have foundered on the rock of the Commons majorities against. Even in periods of very large Conservative majorities, as in 1983 when there was a very concerted effort to bring back hanging for different forms of murder, there was still a very large majority against re-introduction, mainly because the Labour and Liberal Parties (and its successors) have remained solidly abolitionist and there has consistently been a substantial minority of Tories of the same mind. By the nineties the restorationists had pretty much given up and the gallows seemed to have disappeared permanently and unalterably from the judicial landscape.

Why then the failure of the restorationists? They certainly had public opinion on their side and a lot of important lobbies, especially the police and the prison service and some law and order pressure groups. Crucially however, they did not have the House of Commons on their side, and after the early sixties, nor the House of Lords. Also, and perhaps more surprisingly, they did not, at some point in the sixties, any longer have the judiciary on their side.

There is a limit to which public opinion can make itself felt when Parliament is adamant and hanging has been the most conspicuous example of an issue where public opinion has been consistently and unrelentingly at odds with Westminster. In the final analysis Parliament will get its way if sufficiently determined. There have been many other issues of course where there has been a divergence between Parliament and people, but none is quite comparable. The other conscience issues of the sixties probably enjoyed a measure of popular support, certainly divorce and abortion reform, if not perhaps homosexual law reform. Theatre censorship was never a big issue, and the relaxation of the Sunday observance laws has been a piecemeal affair, which has had a degree of public support. With these questions public opinion always seemed to 'catch up' eventually whatever the initial balance.

Of course government may argue that being a matter of a free vote it is at the mercy of the backbenches. That raises the question of why the people have never elected a Commons more in tune with its own restorationist views. However, the people can only vote for what is on offer, and few electors vote for a party or candidate on the basis of his or her views on an issue as peripheral to the mainstream of political debate as capital punishment. Moreover, few electors, unless they specifically ask for the candidates' views could be expected to know his or her stance on capital punishment. The ignorance of most electors on political questions is, in any case, well-documented. But why has there not been a hanging party to vote for? Such a party has never emerged. There have been pressure groups but not a party dedicated to the business of fighting elections on the issue, unless one counts the instance of Patrick Downey at Nelson and Colne in 1966, backed by a group of businessmen. Though he achieved a striking success, by the standards of genuine independents in general elections, the experiment has never been repeated. It would be difficult to raise the funds necessary to fight a large number of seats, and such a party would be gravely handicapped by having only the one plank in its platform. Thus it is hard for popular opinion to find adequate expression on the question, and people, for all their vociferous clamour for the return of hanging when asked, have tended to acquiesce in the status quo. The passage of time has caused the gallows to recede, subjectively, into the distant past and younger generations of voters though taking an equally tough-minded stance on law and order questions may see hanging as too distant an artefact to resurrect. Thus the restorationists, though often mobilizing public opinion behind their cause, have found it a wasting asset.

The support of the police and prison officers had been an important factor, their professional associations and trade unions having consistently maintained a policy in favour of re-introduction (at least for the murder of police or prison officers), but again their voice has carried relatively little weight in the corridors of power whatever lip service successive Home Secretaries might pay to them. Certainly they have carried less weight than that of the judiciary and the law profession which was becoming increasingly antipathetic to the rope. And though police and prison officers may have been strongly for re-introduction few other bodies were. As mentioned, the legal profession was becoming distinctly lukewarm if not decidedly hostile to hanging, partly a reflection of establishment liberalization, but also, because as people close to the process they were very aware of the shortcomings of the system and the possibility of miscarriage. Moreover the press, even the Conservative press, was becoming increasingly abolitionist, as was the media generally and the churches and much of what might be termed the 'great and the good'. By the mid sixties the bulk of the establishment had been converted and most of it was not going to be converted back again. The social and legal culture was undergoing a sea change.

Nor would the equipment and the expertise to carry out hangings be available any longer since by the late sixties the Home Office had effectively decommissioned the gallows in most prisons in England and Wales, and given most of the regular hangmen their redundancy notices. The business of hanging required a surprisingly large amount of skill and knowledge and only a limited number possessed it, having been handed down from father to son in many cases.

By the late eighties and early nineties there was an ever lengthening catalogue of apparent miscarriages of justice that had come to light, often after decades, from the Hanratty case that would not lie down to more recent miscarriages that had been perpetrated well after abolition, most conspicuously that of the Guildford Four and the Birmingham Six, though there were many others. This was excellent propaganda for the abolitionist side and made it almost impossible for the retentionists to argue, as they long had, that English justice could be relied upon to convict only the guilty. Perhaps the retentionist case was fatally weakened by this, though it could be and was sometimes argued that abolition had caused a decline in standards of justice since it was no longer a matter of life and death. The police, it was argued, had fewer scruples about fabricating or extorting confessions or planting evidence, whilst maybe courts and juries were not quite so fastidious in weighing the evidence as minutely as they had in former days. Nearly all the miscarriages that had come to light in the 1980s onwards were from the period after abolition. None apart from the already known cases had occurred before abolition (apart from Hanratty which had long been hotly contested). Of course it could equally be said that there was little incentive for campaigners to re-investigate the cases of those who had been executed, unlike those who were still screaming their innocence from within the prison system, and that if they had then more miscarriages might have been turned up from pre-abolition days.

Another factor of importance that militated against re-introduction was that much had changed in the legal system since abolition, including the introduction of majority verdicts in the English courts under the Criminal Justice Act, 1967 and the introduction of the juryless Diplock courts in Northern Ireland in the early seventies. The former was to some extent made possible by abolition since it is hard to imagine Parliament sanctioning executions on the basis of anything less than a unanimous verdict, whilst the latter was a response to the widespread intimidation of juries (and witnesses) by the IRA and other terrorist organizations. Again it would have been inconceivable for anyone to be hanged on the verdict of a judge or panel of judges, sitting alone. The political consequences would have been catastrophic, which of course has always been part of the reason for having juries. If hanging had returned would murder cases in England and Wales have been tried under a different system from all other cases (Scotland has always had majority verdicts for all cases), with a requirement for a unanimous verdict re-instated? Would the courts have then operated under a two tier system? Alternatively would a majority verdict have been allowed but to be deemed a powerful or compelling reason for the Home Secretary to grant a reprieve? Or would the majority verdict just have been abolished? Then again if unanimity were re-established as a necessity was there not a danger that some juries would fail to convict even the manifestly guilty defendant because at least one juryman had a conscientious objection to capital punishment? Would it have been necessary then to introduce a system as in some states of the USA to filter out the conscientious objectors, and if so how effective would it have been. And might it have introduced an undesirable bias into the selection of juries since, as some American psychological studies have shown, there is a correlation between support for capital punishment and propensity to convict. All of these are intriguing questions.

Significant also in the long-term was Britain's adherence to the Council of Europe and the European Convention on Human Rights, and its accession to the EEC (as it then was) in 1973, which latter body in the fullness of time required all member states to adhere to the Convention, including its provisions outlawing capital punishment. The culmination of this was the decision of the Blair government in 1998 to incorporate the Convention into English and Scots law, thereby at least technically making it impossible, without repealing the Act, to re-introduce capital punishment, whatever the political climate might be. Europe has thus become, in effect, the abolitionists' goalkeeper, if one were needed.

The Effects of Abolition

What were the consequences of the abolition of the death penalty? The actual effect of abolition on the crime figures is very hard to gauge. Though murder (and violent crime generally) rose steadily in the years after abolition it is fair to say that it had been rising equally steeply in the years immediately before abolition (and indeed in the whole of the post-war period), and the rate of increase after abolition was not significantly greater than it had been before. Also, in the period between 1957 and 1965 when there were two classes of murder it might have been supposed that if hanging had a unique deterrent effect there would have been a significantly steeper rise in the rate of non-capital murder than of capital murder, yet actually they both rose at roughly the same rate. Clearly there were profound changes occurring in the fabric of British society in the 1950s and 1960s which saw a dramatic loosening, if not actual breakdown, of authority of which more crime was partly a function.

This, needless to say, did not prevent politicians on both sides of the debate from drawing conclusions favourable to their case from the statistical evidence. How effective this propaganda was in influencing public opinion is highly questionable, but public opinion didn't need any prompting, especially in the immediate aftermath of a particularly foul or high-profile murder. It would be difficult to argue that hanging had no deterrent effect; intuitively one feels it must. Yet it is equally difficult to identify the class of murderer who would be deterred. The calculating murderer would act on the basis that he would get away with it and thus the penalty would not weigh too heavily in his calculations. The 'spontaneous' murderer would not calculate at all, and the nutcase would be incapable of rational calculation (and indeed might be likely to kill himself either at the time of the murder or sometime afterwards). Perhaps it is the robber who deliberately carries a gun who might think twice about going armed. This is the case often pinpointed by the pro-hangers.

What were the effects of abolition on the political situation? It is doubtful if the issue had much effect on the results of any British general election, or by-election for that matter, despite the amount of publicity it received. Few, if any, elections have been fought primarily, or even significantly, on the issue. Even the Nelson and Colne election in the 1966 general election was fought mostly on the great national questions as elsewhere, notwithstanding the intervention of the pro-hanging candidate who garnered a very substantial vote. Abolitionist candidates in that or any other general election do not seem to have been adversely affected by their stance on the issue since the swing for or against them was generally no different from the average. Nor has the Labour Party, as the party most identified with abolition, appeared to have suffered at any point electorally. The famous case of Nigel Nicolson, the abolitionist Conservative, seems to be the solitary exception to the rule, but even there his de-selection was primarily a function of his position in regard to Suez rather than hanging. It may be that electoral contests (or selection contests) have been influenced by the hanging question, especially within the Conservative Party but no case has been identified. On the Labour side it is unlikely that any sitting candidate has been prejudiced by his stance on hanging, pro or anti. The solitary Labour retentionist of 1965, Frank Tomney, was indeed de-selected by his Hammersmith constituency in the 1970s but that was at a time when many right-wing Labour MPs were under pressure from the left, and Tomney was vilified for his stance on a whole range of issues. Support for hanging was the least of his offences in the eyes of the left-wing of the party. In fact the issue seemed to have united the Labour Party, from Roy Jenkins to Sydney

Silverman, in an era when the party was riven by dissension on just about everything else and when rebellion against the government was rife, certainly after 1966.

So far as the general public was concerned the persistent disregard of its views on the matter by Parliament may have been perceived as indicative, as with so much else, of the contempt in which they were held by politicians and may have contributed to the general disenchantment with politics that became so evident in the period in question.

Counterfactuals

It is intriguing to ponder a number of counterfactuals in regard to the whole campaign.[946]

Suppose that the 1964-5 abolition bill had not succeeded? Would a Labour Home Secretary have resumed authorising hangings? On each occasion that the question of abolition had been considered in Parliament there had been a moratorium on hangings, with convicted prisoners awaiting execution reprieved (notwithstanding the eventual outcome of the debate). This had been challenged by Lord Chief Justice Goddard in 1948 as of dubious constitutional propriety, and for a Home Secretary to have issued a blanket reprieve even when the matter was *not* under direct and immediate consideration would have been even more contentious.[947] And yet would Labour MPs have tolerated the continuation of hangings? Just before the third reading of the Silverman bill in July 1965 Tony Benn queried Home Secretary Frank Soskice on what would happen if the bill failed. Benn was aghast when Soskice informed him that he supposed he would have to start hanging people again.[948] All of this was rendered academic by the carriage of the bill, but it is fascinating to speculate. It is as certain as anything can be in politics that if the bill had failed of passage it would have been re-introduced in the next session or in the next Parliament. After the 1966 general election the very large Labour majority combined with a beefed-up Labour presence in the Lords would surely have seen the bill home, and moreover probably without the awkward provision requiring a subsequent confirmatory vote. But in the interim of maybe a year or two would there have been any hangings? Newens, for one, is adamant that Roy Jenkins, who became Home Secretary in December 1965 (after the bill had reached the statute book) would have stood firm against hangings, whereas Soskice's stance would, he

---

[946] Much of what follows is drawn from my own chapter on the abolition campaign in Dorey, Peter (ed.) *The Labour Governments 1964-70* (London: Routledge and Kegan Paul, 2006) pp. 330-344

[947] This was to exercise a dispensing power unknown since before the Bill of Rights according to Goddard. Christoph, op cit.

[948] Benn, Tony *Out of the Wilderness: Diaries 1963-1967* (London: Arrow, 1987) p.284 - 1st July 1965

feels, have been harder to predict.[949] And Callaghan too, Jenkins' successor as Home Secretary is on record as saying that he would have resigned rather than preside over any more hangings.

Suppose that the Lords had not passed the bill in 1965? Would that have provoked a constitutional crisis? Previous Lords' vetoes on abolition in 1948 and 1956, though intensely controversial, could nonetheless have been viewed as a proper exercise of their watchdog role. In 1948 and again in 1956 there was no government mandate for abolition and on each occasion the government of the day, first Labour and then Conservative, was opposed to abolition. Certainly the Conservatives in the Lords in 1948 did not consider themselves bound by their self-denying ordinance, the Salisbury convention, according to which they did not, as a party, oppose government legislation for which it had a mandate (a convention adhered to partly in the interests of its own preservation). Moreover, on each occasion public opinion was demonstrably opposed to abolition by large margins. All of this was still true, to an extent, in 1964/5. The government didn't have a mandate for abolition (though it *had* included the pledge to allow a free vote on the question in the Queen's Speech); it was a backbench measure in which the government was officially neutral (though its neutrality was in practice highly benevolent); and public opinion was still somewhat hostile to total abolition.

It could be argued that the Lords would not have been acting improperly by again resisting the measure had it been so inclined, and it is difficult to visualise even a Labour government seeking to argue otherwise, however much the ardent abolitionists in their ranks might have gnashed their teeth. If the government had wanted to engineer a confrontation with the Lords it would surely have done so on an issue of its own choosing and certainly not on a backbench issue where the Lords could be seen to be closer to public opinion than the Commons, thereby fatally undercutting any argument based on the democratic legitimacy of the Lower House. On the other hand it might have concentrated the minds of the Cabinet rather more closely on the whole question of the Upper House, its powers and composition, and hastened the reform proposals which did not actually surface until much later in the 1966 parliament.[950]

Suppose again that either the Commons or the Lords had not passed the necessary resolutions in 1969 (or whenever the government had chosen to schedule them).[951] It is inconceivable that the Commons would have undone the

---

[949] Newens, interview, op cit.

[950] Reform of the House of Lords featured in the 1966 Labour manifesto but proposals were so long in the gestation that a bill wasn't presented until the 1968-9 session and then had to be abandoned in the face of backbench recalcitrance. Ponting, Clive *Breach of Promise* (Harmondsworth: Penguin, 1990) pp. 342-349.

[951] This was a very real fear within the ranks of the government and the abolitionists, at any rate in regard to the Lords, as the preceding account of events testifies.

work of only five years previously given the much larger Labour majority, but the Lords was again harder to predict. In fact the balance of opinion in the Lords was still strongly abolitionist and the experience of a very recent attempt by the government to clip its wings may have made it too mindful of self-preservation for it to provoke the government even if so inclined. But if the Lords had voted down the 1969 resolution then the provisions of the Homicide Act relating to murder would have been re-instated and those convicted of capital murder be again liable to hang. It is known that Home Secretary Callaghan would have refused to countenance hangings and would thus have had to issue to issue a reprieve in any and every case or been forced to resign.[952] It is unlikely that any replacement Labour Home Secretary would have acted differently and thus a constitutional impasse would have been reached. Maybe a subsequent Conservative Home Secretary would have resumed hangings but by 1969 most gallows had been de-commissioned. In all probability hanging would have remained in abeyance pending the neutering of the Lords and another abolition bill to follow.

And what of Northern Ireland? The abolition bill did not extend to the Province which of course, at that time, still had an autonomous government at Stormont under the 1921 settlement and which had full responsibility for all criminal and judicial matters. Abolition was not brought into effect there statutorily until 1973 under the Emergency Powers Act of that year. Prior to that reprieves had been issued to convicted murderers by the British Home Secretary in the name of the crown, from 1965-1973, the last hanging in the Province being in 1961. It is hard to gauge the possible repercussions of the hanging of republican or loyalist terrorists in the period from the onset of the 'Troubles' in the late sixties, but the impact of an execution would surely have been incalculable!

One might also ponder an opposite set of counterfactuals. Suppose that abolition had gone through at one of the earlier attempts, say in 1948 or 1956? It is difficult to envisage the Lords, as then constituted, passing an abolition bill but if it had done so (presumably by a very narrow margin and with a five-year renewal clause) would abolition have 'stuck' as it did after 1965? The likelihood is that the murder rate would have been unaffected (i.e. that it would have continued its slow but erratic rise) thereby giving both sides of the argument some ammunition for their views, but with the restorationists having rather more chance of success than was the case after 1965. Thus hanging might have been restored, after five years or so, presumably by the same mechanism of a private members bill (or by the failure of the putative renewal vote), bolstered by public opinion, perhaps passing narrowly through a Conservative-dominated Commons and easily through a traditionally constituted Lords which would have 'recognised its mistake'. However, the issue would scarcely have

---

[952] *The Times*, 3rd November 1969.

gone away and the abolitionists would merely have re-doubled their efforts, having had the cup dashed from their lips after partaking of a hefty draft. One could foresee, *ex hypothesi*, an almost endless series of attempts to abolish/restore the rope, the fate of which would have depended upon the precise configuration of the Commons and Lords at any given time.

But this non-monotonic progression of events seems slightly implausible and relies upon a presumption that other conditions would not change in the way that they actually did. Such great shifts of policy, especially in the judicial area, are awkward, lumbering but inexorable affairs that tend to move uni-directionally. Most likely the coming into office of a Labour administration in 1964 would have 'cured' the question once and for all and led to permanent abolition as per actuality, albeit with a brief interlude of 'failed abolition' in the 1950s. In retrospect the slow and gradual progress of the abolition campaign was to its advantage, giving time for the establishment to acclimatise itself to the idea and for public opinion to reconcile itself to abolition in practice, though continuing to dislike it intensely in principle.

Summary

By 1964 capital punishment had become one of the great unresolved issues of British politics and few doubted that matters would stand still for long. For abolitionists it was very much unfinished business and the return of a Labour government was the long-awaited opportunity to conclude matters in their favour.

As a result of Labour's victory in 1964 the Commons had a large and unequivocal abolitionist majority for the first time since 1951 and for the first time there was a government that was collectively, albeit unofficially, favourable to abolition and prepared to give an abolition bill time and support. Equally the government left the matter to the backbenches and a private members bill so as not to flout the convention that this was a conscience issue that should be subject to a free vote. The bill piloted by the veteran left-winger Sydney Silverman went through the Commons and Lords by sizeable majorities, though not without a few alarums and excursions. This was in the teeth of opposition from several interest groups, most noticeably the police and prison service, and against a backdrop of hostility from a majority of the public. Nonetheless repeated attempts to re-introduce hanging all foundered and the necessary confirmatory vote went through both Houses easily thereby consolidating abolition.

If ever there has been an issue that has divided people and Parliament it was hanging, and the fact of the failure to re-introduce it is better testimony than anything possibly could be that where such a conflict occurs it will be Parliament that will ultimately get its way, especially in the absence of any obvious vehicle for public dissent.

The whole affair is a paradigm public policy-making on a non-party issue. The progress of the campaign, or lack of it at various times, reflects the difficulty of achieving change by backbench means, but equally its ultimate success is indicative of the inexorability of change when the campaign is sufficiently determined and has much of the liberal establishment on its side.

APPENDICES

APPENDIX ONE - CHRONOLOGY OF EVENTS

1810   Romilly commences campaign against the death penalty.

1832   Hanging abolished as the mandatory penalty for the theft of property valued at five shillings or more.

1833-37 Hanging abolished as the penalty for two-thirds of the crimes formerly classified as capital.

1841   Hanging for rape abolished. Death now inflicted, effectively, only for the crimes of murder and treason.

1866   Royal Commission recommends end to public executions and the introduction of degrees of murder. Only the former put into effect.

1868   Murder now to take place only within the prison precincts.

1908   Death penalty abolished for persons under sixteen years of age.

1921   Howard League for Penal Reform founded.

1922   Creation of new statutory offence of infanticide by a mother, taking it out of the sphere of murder.

1925   Formation of the National Council for the Abolition of the Death Penalty.

1930   Parliamentary Select Committee recommends suspension of the death penalty for a trial period of five years. Not adopted.

1931   Execution of pregnant women prohibited.

1932   Age limit for executions raised to eighteen.

1938   Free vote of the House of Commons in favour of abolition of capital punishment. Not adopted.

Nov 1947 Attlee government introduces Criminal Justice Bill, not containing any provision for abolition.

Apr 1948 Commons passes Silverman amendment to Criminal Justice Bill by 245-222.

June 1948 Lords delete abolition clause 181-28

15 July 1948 Commons passes government's compromise clause 307-209

20 July 1948 Lords rejects compromise clause 99-19

22 July 1948 Commons agrees to eliminate death penalty clause from bill 215-34

July 1948 Nat Council for the Abolition of the Death Penalty disbanded
18 Nov 1948 Attlee announces appointment of a Royal Commission on
    Capital Punishment
1949-1953 Royal Commission meets
9 March 1950 Timothy Evans hanged for murder
27 Jan. 1953 Derek Bentley hanged for murder
1 July 1953 Motion for leave to bring in abolition bill defeated 256-195
6-13 July 1953 Scott Henderson enquiry into Evans/Christie cases
15 July 1953 Christie hanged for murder
23 Sept 1953 Royal Commission reports
16 Dec 1953 Lords debate Commission Report
10 Feb 1955 Commons debate on report results in defeat of abolitionist
    amendment 245-214
13 July 1955 Ruth Ellis hanged for murder
August 1955 National Campaign for the Abolition of Capital Punishment
    founded.
8 Nov.1955 Abolitionists lose opportunity to introduce Private Member's
    Bill
10 Nov.1955 Government rejects all major recommendations of Royal
    Commission
15 Nov.1955 Silverman abolition bill given first reading under Ten
    Minute Rule
19 Nov.1955 Silverman bill fails to receive second reading
January 1956 Conservative Inns of Court Society publishes *Murder*
16 Feb.1956 Commons rejects government motion to amend law of
    murder and passes abolitionist motion 293-262
23 Feb.1956 Eden promises government facilities and free vote for all
    stages of Silverman bill
12 March 1956 Commons gives Silverman bill second reading 286-262
Apr-June 1956 Silverman bill passes through committee stage
28 June 1956 Commons gives Silverman bill a third reading 152-133
10 July 1956 Lords rejects Silverman bill 238-95
Summer 1956 Government and constituency pressurises Conservative
    abolitionists
October 1956 Conservative Party Annual Conference passes resolution
    opposing abolition but favouring limiting application of
    death penalty
8 Nov.1956 Government announces its Homicide Bill and refuses
    support for Silverman bill
15 Nov.1956 Abolitionists fare poorly in balloting for private members
    bills

16 Nov.1956   Commons gives Homicide Bill second reading unopposed
January 1957   Homicide Bill passes committee stage unaltered.
1 Feb.1957   Alice Bacon Private Members abolition bill fails to receive
               second reading
6 Feb.1957   Commons gives third reading to Homicide Bill 217-131
19 March 1957 Lords passes Homicide Bill
21 March 1957 Homicide Bill receives Royal Assent and becomes the
               Homicide Act 1957. Creates two classes of murder, capital
               and non-capital; introduces defence of diminished
               responsibility; and abolishes constructive malice.
22/23 Aug 1961 A6 murder committed
6 Oct.1961   James Hanratty arrested and charged with A6 murder
17 Feb.1962   Hanratty convicted of A6 murder and sentenced to death
13 March 1962 Hanratty appeal dismissed
2 April 1962   Home Secretary refuses reprieve for Hanratty
4 April 1962   Hanratty hanged at Bedford Prison
June 1963   Publication of *The A6 Murder* by Louis Blom-Cooper
2 August 1963 First Commons debate on Hanratty case
16 Oct.1964   Publication of *Justice v Justice* by Jean Justice
21 Oct. 1965   Publication of *Deadman's Hill* by Lord Russell of Liverpool
8 Nov.1965   Murder (Abolition of Death Penalty) Act receives Royal
               Assent. Death penalty suspended for five years.
4 August 1966 Debate on Hanratty case in Lords
14 Sept.1966   Publication of first Paul Foot article on Hanratty case in
               Queen magazine
7 Nov.1966   Transmission of Panorama programme on Hanratty case
14 Nov.1966   Publication of *Sunday Times* article on Hanratty case
22 March 1967 Completion of Nimmo report on Hanratty case
December 1969 Death penalty for murder totally abolished by resolution of
               both Houses.
6 May 1971   Publication of *Who Killed Hanratty?* by Paul Foot

Sources: Block, Brian P and John Hostettler, *Hanging in the Balance: A History of the Abolition of Capital Punishment in Britain* (Winchester: Waterside Press, 1997) pp. 271-272; Christoph, James B, *Capital Punishment and British Politics: The British Movement to Abolish the Death Penalty 1945-57* (London: Allen and Unwin, 1962) pp. 198-199; Woffinden, Bob, *Hanratty: The Final Verdict* (London: Macmillan, 1997) pp. 455-467

APPENDIX TWO

THE HOMICIDE ACT 1957

5 and 6 Eliz.2, Ch 11

An Act to make for England and Wales (and for courts- martial wherever sitting) amendments of the law relating to homicide and the trial and punishment of murder, and for Scotland amendments of the law relating to the trial and punishment of murder and attempts to murder.

(21 March 1957)

Be it enacted by the Queen's most Excellent Majesty, by and with the advice and consent of the Lords Spiritual and Temporal, and Commons, in this present Parliament assembled, and by the authority of the same, as follows:-

PART I
AMENDMENTS OF LAW OF ENGLAND AND WALES
AS TO FACT OF MURDER

Abolition of "constructive malice"(marginal note)

1.--(1) Where a person kills another in the course or furtherance of some other offence, the killing shall not amount to murder unless done with the same malice aforethought (express or implied) as is required for a killing to amount to murder when not done in the course or furtherance of another offence.

(2) For the purposes of the foregoing subsection, a killing done in the course or for the purpose of resisting an officer of justice, or of resisting or avoiding or preventing a lawful arrest, or of effecting or assisting an escape or rescue from legal custody, shall be treated as a killing in the course or furtherance of an offence.

Persons suffering from diminished responsibility (marg.note)

2.--(1) Where a person kills or is a party to the killing of another, he shall not be convicted of murder if he was suffering from such abnormality of mind (whether arising from a condition of arrested or retarded development of mind or any inherent causes or induced by disease or injury) as substantially impaired his mental responsibility for his acts and omissions in doing or being a party to the killing.

(2) On a charge of murder, it shall be for the defence to prove that the person charged is by virtue of this section not liable to be convicted of murder.

(3) A person who but for this section would be liable, whether as principal or as accessory, to be convicted of murder shall be liable instead to be convicted of manslaughter.

(4) The fact that one party to a killing is by virtue of this section not liable to be convicted of murder shall not affect the question whether the killing amounted to murder in the case of any other party to it.

Provocation (marg. note)

3. Where on a charge of murder there is evidence on which the jury can find that the person charged was provoked (whether by things done or by things said or by both together) to lose his self-control, the question whether the provocation was enough to make a reasonable man do as he did shall be left to be determined by the jury; and in determining that question the jury shall take into account everything both done and said according to the effect which, in their opinion, it would have on a reasonable man.

Suicide Pacts (marg. note)

4--(1) It shall be manslaughter, and shall not be murder, for a person acting in pursuance of a suicide pact between him and another to kill the other or be a party to the other killing himself or being killed by a third person.

(2) Where it is shown that a person charged with the murder of another killed the other or was a party to his killing himself or being killed, it shall be for the defence to prove that the person charged was acting in pursuance of a suicide pact between him and the other.

(3) For the purposes of this section "suicide pact" means a common agreement between two or more persons having for its object the death of all of them, whether or not each is to take his own life, but nothing done by a person who enters into a suicide pact shall be treated as done by him in pursuance of the pact unless it is done while he has the settled intention of dying in pursuance of the pact.

PART II
LIABILITY TO DEATH PENALTY

Death penalty for certain murders (marg. note)

5--(1) Subject to subsection (2) of this section, the following murders shall be capital murders, that is to say, -
    (a) any murder done in the course or furtherance of theft;
    (b) any murder by shooting or by causing an explosion;
(c) any murder done in the course or for the purpose of resisting or avoiding or preventing a lawful arrest, or of effecting or assisting an escape or rescue from legal custody;
(d) any murder of a police officer acting in the execution of his duty or of a person assisting a police officer so acting;
    (e) in the case of a person who was a prisoner at the time when he did or was a party to the murder, any murder of a prison officer acting in the execution of his duty or of a person assisting a prison officer so acting.

(2) If, in the case of a murder falling within the foregoing subsection, two or more persons are guilty of the murder, it shall be capital murder in the case of any of them who by his own act caused the death of, or inflicted or attempted to inflict grievous bodily harm on the person murdered, or who himself used force on that person in the course or furtherance of an attack on him; but the murder shall not be capital murder in the case of any other of the persons guilty of it.

(3) Where it is alleged that a person accused of murder is guilty of capital murder, the offence shall be charged as capital murder in the indictment, and if a person charged with capital murder is convicted thereof, he shall be liable to the same punishment for the murder as heretofore.

(4) In this Act "capital murder" means capital murder within subsections (1) and (2) of this section.

(5) In this section--

(a) "police officer" means a constable who is a member of a police force or a special constable appointed under any Act of Parliament, and "police force" has the same meaning as in section thirty of the Police Pensions Act, 1921 (as amended by the Police Act, 1946) or, as regards Scotland, the same meaning as in section forty of the Police (Scotland) Act, 1956;

(b) "prison" means any institution for which rules may be made under the Prison Act, 1952, or the Prisons (Scotland Act), 1952, and any establishment under the control of the Admiralty or the Secretary of State where persons may be required to serve sentences of imprisonment or detention passed under the Naval Discipline Act, the Army Act, 1955, or the Air Force Act, 1955;

(c) "prison officer" includes any member of the staff of a prison;

(d) "prisoner" means a person who is undergoing imprisonment or detention in a prison, whether under sentence or not, or who, while liable to imprisonment or detention in a prison, is unlawfully at large;

(e) "theft" includes any offence which involves stealing or is done with intent to steal.

Death penalty for repeated murders (marg. note)

6--(1) A person convicted of murder shall be liable to the same punishment as heretofore, if before conviction of that murder he has, whether before or after the commencement of this Act, been convicted of another murder done on a different occasion (both murders having been done in Great Britain).

(2) Where a person is charged with the murder of two or more persons, no rule of practice shall prevent the murders being charged in the same indictment or (unless separate trials are desirable in the interests of justice) prevent them being tried together; and where a person is convicted of two murders tried together (but done on different occasions), subsection (1) of this section shall apply as if one conviction had preceded the other.

Abolition of death penalty for other murders (marg. note)

7. No person shall be liable to suffer death for murder in any case not falling within section five or six of this Act.

Courts-martial (marg. note)

8.--(1) The foregoing provisions of this Part of this Act shall not have effect in relation to courts-martial, but a person convicted by a court-martial of murder or of an offence corresponding thereto under section seventy of the Army Act, 1955 or of the Air Force Act, 1955) shall not be liable to suffer death, unless he is charged with and convicted of committing the offence under circumstances which, if he had committed it in England, would make him guilty of capital murder.

(2) An accused so charged before a court-martial under the Naval Discipline Act may, on failure of proof of the offence having been committed under such circumstances as aforesaid, be found guilty of the murder as not having been committed under such circumstances.

Punishment for murders not punishable by death, and other consequential provisions (marg. note)

9.--(1) Where a court (including a court-martial) is precluded by this Part of this Act from passing sentence of death, the sentence shall be of life imprisonment.

(2) Accordingly paragraph (a) of subsection (3) of section seventy of the Army Act, 1955, and of the Air Force Act, 1955, and the first paragraph of section forty-five of the Naval Discipline Act, shall each be amended by the addition, at the end of the paragraph, of the words "or in the case of a murder not falling within section eight of the Homicide Act 1957, imprisonment for life".

(3) In section fifty-three of the Children and Young Persons Act, 1933 and section fifty-seven of the Children and Young Persons (Scotland) Act 1937, there shall be substituted for subsection (1)--

"(1) Sentence of death shall not be pronounced on or recorded against a person convicted of an offence who appears to the court to have been under the age of eighteen years at the time the offence was committed, nor shall any such person be sentenced to imprisonment for life under section nine of the Homicide Act, 1957; but in lieu thereof the court shall (notwithstanding anything in this or any other Act) sentence him to be detained during Her Majesty's pleasure, and if so sentenced he shall be liable to be detained in such place and under such conditions as the Secretary of State may direct."

(4) The provisions of the First Schedule to this Act shall have effect with respect to procedural and other matters arising out of sections five to seven of this Act, and with respect to the convictions which may be taken into account under section six.

APPENDIX THREE

Murder Rate (murders known to the police in England and Wales 1957-1968)

Year	Normal Murder	Abnormal Murder	Insane	Total Murders	Sect. 2 Manslaughter	Total abnormal Homicides
1957	57	55	23	135	22	100
1958	47	44	23	114	29	96
1959	57	50	28	135	21	99
1960	51	45	27	123	31	103
1961	54	42	22	118	30	94
1962	56	57	16	129	42	115
1963	59	48	15	122	56	119
1964	76	49	10	135	35	94
1965	77	50	8	135	50	108
1966	88	29	5	122	65	99
1967	90	52	12	154	57	121
1968	96	45	7	148	57	109
1969	80	28	10	118	64	102
1970	112	19	4	135	66	89
1971	118	40	15	173	77	132
1972	113	26	10	149	95	131

Abnormal murder includes cases where the suspect committed suicide.
Sources: Gibson, E and S Klein, *Murder 1957-1968* (HMSO, 1969) table 1, quoted in Block and Hostettler, op cit p. 261; Rolph, C H, *Murder and Capital Punishment in England and Wales* (1973), in Rolph papers, op cit, 1/4/3.

APPENDIX FOUR

Persons Sentenced to Hang 1957-1960 (England & Wales)

Defendant	Age	Date	Result
Ronald Dunbar	24	16.05.57	manslaughter - appeal
John Vickers	22	23.05.57	executed
Franklin Macpherson	22	28.06.57	manslaughter - appeal
Dennis Howard	24	18.10.57	executed
John Spriggs	29	19.12.57	reprieved
Arthur Matheson	52	30.01.58	manslaughter - appeal
Vivian Teed	24	18.03.58	executed
Mary Wilson	66	29.03.58	reprieved
Arthur Bosworth	20	30.04.58	reprieved
George Collier	67	22.05.58	reprieved
Matthew Kavanagh	32	03.07.58	executed
Frank Stokes	44	23.07.58	executed
Brian Chandler	20	29.10.58	executed
Ernest Jones	?	10.12.58	executed
Joseph Chrimes	30	04.03.59	executed
Ronald Marwood	25	19.03.59	executed
Michael Tatum	24	23.03.59	executed
David Di-Duca	21	14.04.59	reprieved
Bernard Walden	33	01.07.59	executed
Gunter Podola	30	24.09.59	executed
(Gypsy) Joe Smith	26	?	Manslaughter - appeal; capital murder conviction restored by House of Lords; then reprieved
Mihaly Pocze	25	01.06.60	reprieved
John Constantine	22	22.07.60	executed
Norman Harris	21	26.09.60	executed
Francis Forsyth	18	26.09.60	executed
John Rogers	20	20.10.60	reprieved

THE POLITICS OF THE ROPE

Persons Sentenced to Hang 1957-60 (Scotland)

Defendant	Age	Date	Result
Peter Manuel	31	29.05.58	executed
Donald Forbes	23	25.09.58	reprieved
Alexander Stirling	24	09.03.60	reprieved

Total: 29 convictions for capital murder in England, Wales and Scotland in the period from the passage of the Homicide Act of 1957 up to December 1960, of which 16 had been executed, 10 had been reprieved and 3 had had manslaughter convictions substituted on appeal.

Source: *The Times*, 12th December 1960; reproduced in Block and Hostettler, *Hanging in the Balance: A History of the Abolition of Capital Punishment in Britain* (Winchester: Waterside Press, 1997) p. 212

APPENDIX FIVE

Key Parliamentary Votes on Abolition and/or Restoration

Vote	Abol	Abol	Abol	Abol	Ret	Ret	Ret	Ret	Maj
	Lab	Con	Other	Total	Lab	Con	Oth	Total	
1948	216 (54.96)	17 (7.83)	14	247	75 (19.08)	146 (67.28)	3	224	2: (A
1953	191 (64.96)	4 (1.24)	2	197	15 (5.10)	243 (75.46)	0	258	6: (R
1955	195 (66.32)	18 (5.59)	3	216	5 (1.70)	241 (74.84)	1	2247	3' (F
1956 (a)	240 (87.00)	49 (14.24)	5	294	3 (1.08)	245 (71.22)	0	2248	4((R
1956 (b)	236 (85.19)	47 (13.66)	5	288	8 (2.88)	256 (74.41)	0	2264	2 (F
1964	268 (84.22)	81 (26.64)	8	357	1 (0.31)	170 (55.92)	1	1172	18 (/
1966	255 (70.44)	30 (11.85)	9	294	17 (4.69)	154 (60.86)	1	1172	1: (/
1969	279 (80.17)	53 (20.00)	13	345	3 (0.86)	181 (68.30)	3	1187	1! (/
1973	238 (82.92)	78 (23.78)	6	322	3 (1.04)	176 (53.65)	1	1180	1: (/
1974	302 (94.67)	52 (18.77)	17	371	3 (0.94)	212 (76.53)	4	2219	1! (.
1975	297 (93.39)	48 (17.26)	18	363	3 (0.94)	216 (77.69)	115	2234	1: (.
1979	256 (95.16)	93 (27.43)	15	364	3 (1.11)	229 (67.55)	112	2244	1. (.
1983	200 (95.69)	141 (35.51)	29	370	0	212 (53.40)	113	2225	1 (.

All figures include tellers. Conservative includes National Liberal and Ulster Unionist up to and including 1969. Thereafter Ulster Unionists are treated as 'Others'. Figures in brackets are the proportion of that party's MPs voting for or against.
1956 (a) = Chuter Ede motion
1956 (b) = Abolition Bill – 2nd reading
1966 = Sandys motion
1969 = Confirmatory vote
1983 = Vote on motion to restore capital punishment for murder in general (there were several other divisions on various classes of murder).
Source: HC Debs

APPENDIX SIX

Summary of some major public opinion poll findings

Year and Poll	For Retention (or restoration)	For Abolition	Other Responses	Don't Knows
1938 (Gallup)	49	40	0	11
1948 (Gallup)	66	26	0	8
1948 (MO)	69	13	13	5
1948 (Daily Express)	77	14	0	9
October 1953 (Gallup)	73	15	0	12
July 1955 (Gallup)	50	37	0	13
December 1955 (Gallup)	61	25	0	14
Jan 1956 (MO)	45	34	0	21
July 1964 (SOC)	21	67	0	12
November 1964 (Marplan)	65.5	21.3	0	13.2
December 1964 (NOP)	67	26	0	7
September 1966 (NOP)	82	15	0	3
October 1969 (Marplan)	85	12	0	3
June 1983 (NOP)	87	13	0	0
October 1987 (NOP)	73	23	0	5
May 1990 (NOP)	81	18	0	1

Figures are percentages. MO = Mass Observation

The abolition column includes those favouring an experimental period of suspension as well as outright abolition. The 'Other Responses' column includes those favouring recognition of degrees of murder and is only applicable to the Mass Observation polls. The precise wording of the question tended to vary across polls.

Sources: Christoph, op cit; Block and Hostettler, op cit; Hazel Irvine, op cit; NOP (Nick Moon)

APPENDIX SEVEN

CABINET MEMORANDUM ON PERMANENT ABOLITION OF CAPITAL PUNISHMENT FOR MURDER (BY HOME SECRETARY AND SECRETARY OF STATE FOR SCOTLAND)

1) In this memo we invite our colleagues to agree that the government should take the initiative in making permanent the abolition of capital punishment for murder and we make proposals for tactics and timing.

2) The Murder (Abolition of Death Penalty) Act was introduced by Sydney Silverman with government help. Section 4 - the renewal clause - was moved by Henry Brooke against government advice and required simple resolutions not a statutory order. The House authorities, surprisingly, take the view that resolutions could provide for temporary extensions. Our advice, however, is that this would not be permissible under the Act and that the only choice is to make the Act permanent or to let it lapse. It seems to us that a temporary extension would be undesirable.

3) We don't think that our colleagues need any convincing that abolition ought to be made permanent.

4) Essentially the case for abolition is a moral one. Capital punishment is a barbarous penalty which the community has no right to exact. Other subsidiary arguments are: rehabilitation; wrongful conviction; no conclusive evidence that it is a unique deterrent. Also if the Act lapsed the Homicide Act would be revived which was widely regarded as unsatisfactory by both sides and was strongly criticised by judges. Though there is support for restoration there is no broad agreement as to the form it should take. Any attempt at categorisation of murders would produce anomalies as unacceptable as those of the Homicide Act.

5) The case does not stand or fall on statistics. The appendix gives murder figures for 1957-1967. The figure for 1967 is 168, the highest since the Homicide Act was passed. The figures for 1968 will not be known until next month but may be a little lower than for 1967, but higher than most for recent years. There seems to be an upward trend though the greatest increase was between 1963 and 1964 when executions were still taking place. Post-abolition estimates of what would have been capital murder must be treated with great caution since it is almost certain that some murders would not have been capital if the issue had been tried. Estimates made now cannot identify cases in which a jury might decide against a verdict of capital murder. Still less can they identify cases where a jury might have returned a perverse verdict in the face of clear evidence. Also estimates for capital murder include those committed by the insane and by suspects who commit suicide. The increase in murder in Scotland, starting from small figures is proportionately greater. As in England and Wales the 1967 figure is the highest. The 1968 figure is likely to be about the same as for 1967.

6) The figures above should be set in the context of the experience of other countries where capital punishment has been abolished. It suggests that abolition does not bring about a permanent upward trend.

7) There have been increases in other forms of serious crime, in particular, in England and Wales, of indictable offences of violence of 33.3% (from 17,601 to 23,407) between 1961 and 1964 and an increase of 23.8% from 23,470 to 29,048 between 1964 and 1967. For robbery the corresponding increases were 30.5% and 48.9% respectively. Abolitionists will say that the increase in the murder rate has to be looked at in the context of the increase of violent crime generally. Restorationists will no doubt attribute some share of the cause of the

increase in violent crime to abolition.

8) There is a majority on the Commons for abolition - the Act was passed by a large majority and attempts to re-introduce it have been heavily defeated. The shift in the political balance of the Commons and the influx of younger members assisted this process. The next occasion when opinion in the commons will be tested will be the Sandys motion on 24th June 1969 when he will seek leave under the Ten Minute rule.

9) There is little doubt that the Commons is ahead of public opinion.

10) Should the government take the initiative? Or should it be left to a private member with government support? We are in no doubt that it is a matter for government initiative but with a free vote.

11) When should the resolutions be taken? The interim murder figures for 1969 are bound to be inflated - but if we wait for the corrected 1969 figures the debate would have to be in May-July 1970 and likely therefore to be conducted in a pre-election atmosphere. We cannot rely on the statistics and we should forgo the 1969 figures so as to have the resolutions debated this year, though perhaps not before the autumn, by which time a revised edition of the Home Office Research Unit Report "Murder" bringing it up to the end of 1968 will be ready.

12) Another argument for taking resolutions early is the slight possibility that they would be rejected by the House. Rejection by the Lords could not be overridden and the Rules of Procedure would not permit either House to be asked either by legislation or by a fresh resolution to reverse a previous decision of the same session. Rejection in the summer of 1970 would leave no room for anything other than a revival of the Homicide Act, at least for a time. Rejection at the beginning of 1969-70 might just leave time for legislation not amounting to a flat reversal - say by extending the Abolition Act for a limited period to be enacted (though not carried through if rejected by the Lords) by the end of July 1970. Rejection in the closing days of the current session would not prevent reversal in the next session.

13) We would welcome the views of colleagues.

14) It is desirable to stimulate informed support for abolition. Sandys will no doubt intensify his nationwide petition for restoration but the committee of the National Campaign for the Abolition of Capital Punishment has been re-activated under Canon Collins. Information might be prepared for backbenchers and suitable outside commentators.

Conclusion

15) We invite colleagues to agree: -

i) that the government should take the initiative.
ii) that the resolutions be taken in autumn 1969.

LJC/WR
6th May 1969

Appendixes

Public opinion

A poll carried out by ORC and published in the Evening standard on 7th March found the following percentages for restoration:-

Child murder   83%
Murder of policemen   78%
Murder with firearms   67%
Murder in the course of robbery   65%
Murder by poison   64%
Murder following a love affair   36%
Don't knows ranged from 2%-7%

Overseas Experience

The evidence of the UN Economic Social Council in 1962 and the Royal Commission was that abolition has little effect.

Source: National Archives: CAB 129 1969 C(69) 48 6th May 1969

APPENDIX EIGHT

Holders of Major Political and Judicial Office 1955-1969

Prime Minister-
Sir Anthony Eden (Con)	6th April 1955-9th Jan 1957
Harold Macmillan (Con)	10th Jan 1957-13th Oct 1963
Sir Alec Douglas-Home (Con)	18th Oct 1963-16th Oct 1964
Harold Wilson (Lab)	16th Oct 1964-19th June 1970

Home Secretary-
Gwilym Lloyd George (Con)	18th October 1954-13th Jan 1957
Richard A Butler (Con)	13th Jan 1957-13th July 1962
Henry Brooke (Con)	13th July 1962-16th Oct 1964
Sir Frank Soskice (Lab)	18th Oct 1964-23rd Dec 1965
Roy Jenkins (Lab)	23rd Dec 1965-30th Nov 1967
James Callaghan (Lab)	30th Nov 1967-19th June 1970

Lord Chancellor-
Viscount Kilmuir (Con) (Sir David Maxwell Fyfe)	18th Oct 1954-13th July 1962
Lord Dilhorne (Con) (Sir R Manningham-Buller)	13th July 1962-16th Oct 1964
Lord Gardiner (Lab)	16th Oct 1964-19th June 1970

Attorney-General-
Sir R Manningham-Buller (Con)	18th Oct 1954-16th July 1962
Sir John Hobson (Con)	16th July 1962-16th Oct 1964
Sir Elwyn Jones (Lab)	18th Oct 1964-19th June 1970

Solicitor-General-
Sir Harry Hylton-Foster (Con)	18th Oct 1954-22nd Oct 1959
Sir John Simon (Con)	22nd Oct 1959-8th Feb 1962
Sir John Hobson (Con)	8th Feb 1962-19th July 1962
Sir Peter Rawlinson (Con)	19th July 1962-16th Oct 1964
Sir Dingle Foot (Lab)	18th Oct 1964-24th Aug 1967
Sir Arthur Irvine (Lab)	24th Aug 1967-19th June 1970

Secretary of State for Scotland-
James Stuart (Con)	30th Oct 1951-13th Jan 1957
John Maclay (Con)	13th Jan 1957-13th July 1962
Michael Noble (Con)	13th July 1962-16th Oct 1964
William Ross (Lab)	18th Oct 1964-19th June 1970

Lord Advocate-
William R Milligan (Con)	30th Dec 1954-5th April 1960
William Grant (Con)	5th April 1960-12th Oct 1962
Ian H. Shearer (Con)	12th Oct 1962-16th Oct 1964
George G. Stott (Lab)	20th Oct 1964-26th Oct 1967
Henry S. Wilson (Lord Wilson)	26th Oct 1967-19th June 1970

Solicitor-General for Scotland-
William Grant (Con)	10th Jan 1955-11th May 1960
David Anderson (Con)	11th May 1960-27 April 1964
Norman Wylie (Con)	27th April 1964-16th Oct 1964
James G. Leechman (Lab)	20th October 1964-11th Oct 1965
Henry S. Wilson (Lab)	11th Oct 1965-26th Oct 1967
Ewan G. F. Stewart (Lab)	26th Oct 1967-19th June 1970

Lord Chief Justice-
Lord Goddard	23rd Jan 1946- 29th Sept 1958
Lord Parker of Waddington	29th Sept 1958-20th April 1971

Director of Public Prosecutions-
Sir Theobald Mathew	1944-1964
Sir Norman Skelhorn	1964-1977

APPENDIX NINE

The Murder (Abolition of Death Penalty) Act 1965

An Act to abolish capital punishment in the case of persons convicted in Great Britain of murder or convicted of murder or a corresponding offence by court-martial and, in connection therewith, to make further provision for the punishment of persons so convicted.

[8th November 1965]

Be it enacted by the Queen's most Excellent Majesty, by and with the advice and consent of the Lords Spiritual and Temporal, and Commons, in the present Parliament assembled, and by the authority of the same, as follows:-

1-(1) No person shall suffer death for murder, and a person convicted of murder shall, subject to sub-section (5) below, be sentenced to imprisonment for life.

(2) On sentencing any person convicted of murder to imprisonment for life the Court may at the same time declare the period which it recommends to the Secretary of State as the minimum period which in its view should elapse before the Secretary of State orders the release of that person on licence under section 27 of the Prison Act 1952 or section 21 of the Prisons (Scotland) Act 1952.

(3) For the purpose of any proceedings on or subsequent to a person's trial on a charge of capital murder, that charge and any plea or finding of guilty of capital murder shall be treated as being or having been a charge, or a plea or finding of guilty, of murder only; and if at the commencement of this Act a person is under sentence of death for murder, the sentence shall have effect as a sentence of imprisonment for life.

(4) In the foregoing subsections any reference to murder shall include an offence of or corresponding to murder under section 70 of the Army Act 1955 or of the Air Force Act 1955 or under section 42 of the Naval Discipline Act 1957, and any reference to capital murder shall be construed accordingly; and in each of the said sections 70 there shall be inserted in subsection (3) after paragraph (a) as a new paragraph (aa)--
      "(aa) if the corresponding civil offence is murder, be liable to

imprisonment for life".

(5) In section 53 of the Children and Young Person's Act 1933, and in section 57 of the Children and Young Person's (Scotland) Act 1937, there shall be substituted for subsection (1)--
"(1) A person convicted of an offence who appears to the court to have been under the age of eighteen years at the time the offence was committed shall not, if he is convicted of murder, be sentenced to imprisonment for life, nor shall sentence of death be pronounced on or recorded against any such person; but in lieu thereof the court shall (notwithstanding anything in this or any other Act) sentence him to be detained during Her Majesty's pleasure, and if so sentenced he shall be liable to be detained in such place and under such conditions as the Secretary of State may direct."

2. No person convicted of murder shall be released by the Secretary of State on licence under section 27 of the Prison Act 1952 or section 21 of the Prisons (Scotland) Act 1952 unless the Secretary of State has prior to such release consulted the Lord Chief Justice of England or the Lord Justice General as the case may be together with the trial judge if available.

3.-(1) This Act may be cited as the Murder (Abolition of Death Penalty) Act 1965.

(2) The enactments mentioned in the Schedule to this Act are hereby repealed to the extent specified in the third column of that schedule.

(3) This Act, except as regards courts-martial, shall not extend to Northern Ireland.

(4) This Act shall come into force on the day following that on which it is passed.

4. This Act shall continue in force until the thirty-first day of July nineteen hundred and seventy, and shall then expire unless Parliament by affirmative resolutions of both Houses otherwise determines: and upon the expiration of this Act the law existing immediately prior to the passing of this Act shall, so far as it is repealed or amended by this Act, again operate as though this Act had

not been passed, and the said repeals and amendments had not been enacted:

Provided that this Act shall continue to have effect in relation to any murder not shown to have been committed after the expiration of this Act, and for this purpose a murder shall be taken to be committed at the time of the act which causes the death.

APPENDIX TEN

Membership of the Committee of Honour of the NCACP (alphabetical order)
(as at July 1963)

Earl of Harewood (chmn); Sir Richard Acland; Lady Allen of Hurtwood; Walter Allen; Lord Amulree, MD; Kingsley Amis; Sir Norman Angell; Noel Annan; John Arlott; Malcolm Arnold; Hon Anthony Asquith; Hon David Astor; Prof A J Ayer; Sir Michael Balcon; Sir Gerald Barry; Leonard F Behrens; Prof Max Beloff; Prof Norman Bentwich; Mrs Norman Bentwich; the Lord Bishop of Birmingham; Prof W Lyon Blease; Lady Violet Bonham-Carter, DBE; Lord Boothby; Miss Phyllis Bottome; Dr John Bowlby; Sir Maurice Bowra; Lord Brabourne; Christopher Brasher; Benjamin Britten CH; Prof D W Brogan; Dr Jacob Bronowski; Anthony Brooke; Prof Max Born, FRS; Ivor Brown; Frank Byers; Mrs Theodora Calvert; Canon Edward Carpenter; Sir Alexander Carr Saunders; Sir Hugh Casson; Sir Lewis Casson; Prof George Catlin; Chris Chataway, MP; the Bishop of Chichester; Dame Harriette Chick; Lord Chorley; the Bishop of Colchester; Norman Collins; Prof C A Coulson, FRS; Dame May Curwen; Clifford Curzon; Dr Glyn Daniel; Helen Darbishire; Colin Davis; Prof Cecil Day-Lewis; Frank Dobson, RA; Lord Douglas of Kirtleside; G H Elvin; Sir Jacob Epstein; Lord Esher; Eleanor Farjeon; Lord Farringdon; James Fitton, RA; E M Forster, CH; Pamela Frankau; John Freeman; Christopher Fry; David Garnett; Sir Philip Gibbs; Sir John Gielgud; Ian Gilmour; Jo Grimond, PC MP; William Glock; Dr Edward Glover; Elizabeth Goudge; Sir Wilfred Le Gros Clarke, FRS; Sir Kenneth Grubb; Sir Alec Guinness; Hamish Hamilton; Gilbert Harding; Lord Harmsworth; Christopher Hassall; Jacquetta Hawkes; Barbara Hepworth; Laurence Housman; Christmas Humphreys, QC; Earl of Huntingdon; Dr Julian Huxley FRS; H Montgomery Hyde, MP; Kenneth Ingram; Eglantine Jebb; Augustus John OM; Cmdr Sir Stephen King-Hall; Sir Allen Lane; Margaret Lane; Lord Layton; Laurie Lee; John Lehmann; Rosamond Lehmann; The Vicar of Leeds; Earl of Listowel; Lady Megan Lloyd George; Sir Ben Lockspeiser; Dame Kathleen Lonsdale, FRS; Col. the Earl of Lucan; Rose Macauley; Derek McCulloch; Sir Compton Mackenzie; Very Rev G F MacLeod; Prof John Macmurray; Miles Malleson; the Bishop of Manchester; Sir Geoffrey Mander; Dr Herman Mannheim; Kingsley Martin; Very Rev W R Matthews; Lord Maugham; Gavin Maxwell; Sir Robert Mayer; Lady Mayer; Lord Merthyr; Sir Francis Meynell; Dame Alix Meynell; the Bishop of Middleton; Bernard Miles; Dr Emanuel Miller; G R Mitchison, QC, MP; Sir Walter Moberley; Hon Lily H Montagu; Henry Moore, CH; Raymond Mortimer; Dr Joseph Needham, FRS; Dr Dorothy Needham, FRS; Ben Nicholson; Sir Harold Nicolson; Lord Pakenham; Rev Dr James W Parkes;

Margery Perham; Lord Pethick-Lawrence; John Piper; Dr J H Plumb; Prof Michael Polanyi, FRS; Dr Karl R Popper; Stephen Potter; Dilys Powell; J B Priestley; Walter Raeburn QC; Canon C E Raven; Ernest Raymond; Sir Herbert Read; Lord Russell of Liverpool; Earl Russell, OM, FRS; Hon Edward Sackville West; Rev Canon C B Sampson; Ronald Searle; Peter Sellers; Lord Shawcross; Moira Shearer; the Bishop of Sheffield; Dame Edith Sitwell; Sir Matthew Smith; Rev Donald Soper; the Bishop of Southwark; Stephen Spender; Howard Spring; Dr Enid Starkie; R R Stokes, MP; Dr E B Strauss; G R Strauss, MP; Graham Sutherland; Dame Sybil Thorndike; Michael Tippett; Prof R M Titmuss; Ann Todd; Dr Arnold Toynbee, CH; Philip Toynbee; Kenneth Tynan; Laurens van der Post; Dame Janet Vaughan; Very Rev C L Warr; Dame Rebecca West; H Graham White; Emlyn Williams; Francis Williams; Glanville Williams; Angus Wilson; Harold Wilson, MP; Prof John Wisdom; Leonard Woolf; the Bishop of Woolwich; Lady Barbara Wootton of Abinger; Diana Wynyard; Kenneth Younger, MP.

* membership was expanded greatly over the years.

Source: The Gerald Gardiner papers (British Library), the Victor Gollancz papers (Modern Record Centre) and NCACP papers (Howard League).

BIBLIOGRAPHY

PRIMARY SOURCES

Interviews
Newens, Stan MEP, St Pancras Town Hall, 9th April 1999
Blom-Cooper, Louis QC, LSE, 6th April 2006
Morris, Professor Terence, LSE, 6th April 2006
Williams, Shirley (Lady Williams of Crosby), Westminster, 10th May 2007
Braham Murray, September 2006 (telephone)
Michael Elwyn, September 2006 (telephone)

Government Papers
Cabinet Conclusions (CC) (The National Archives)
Prime Ministers papers (PREM) (The National Archives)
Home Office papers (HO) (The National Archives)
Report of the Select Committee on Capital Punishment, 1930-1 (HMSO 1931)
Report of the Royal Commission on Capital Punishment, 1949-1953 (Cmnd 8932, HMSO 1953)
Henderson, J. Scott *Report of the Inquiry into the Case of Rex v. Evans and the Case of Rex v. Christie* (Cmnd. 8896, HMSO 1953)
Brabin, Mr Justice *Report of the Enquiry into the Case of Timothy John Evans* (Cmnd 3101, HMSO 1966)
Gibson, E and S Klein, Home Office *Murder 1957-1968* (HMSO 1969)

Parliamentary Records
Hansard - House of Commons Debates
Hansard - House of Lords Debates

Statutes
The Homicide Act, 1957
The Death Penalty (Abolition) Act 1965

Political Parties
The Conservative Party Archives, Bodleian Library, Oxford University, Oxford
The Labour Party Archives, National Museum of Labour History, Manchester
The Liberal Party Archives, London School of Economics

Archives and Collections of Private Papers
The Howard League for Penal Reform (Howard League, Hackney, London; The Modern Records Centre, University of Warwick, Coventry)
The National Council for the Abolition of the Death Penalty (The Modern Records Centre, University of Warwick, Coventry)
The National Campaign for the Abolition of Capital Punishment (Modern Records Centre, University of Warwick, Coventry)
Victor Gollancz papers (Modern Records Centre, University of Warwick, Coventry)
Gerald Gardiner papers (The British Library)
C H Rolph papers (LSE)
Canon John Collins papers (Church of England Research Committee)
The Society of Friends Penal Reform Committee (The Friends Meeting House)
Haldane Society of Socialist Lawyers (The Temple)
The Duncan Sandys papers (Churchill College, Cambridge)
Archbishop Temple papers (Lambeth Palace Library)
Archbishop Fisher papers (Lambeth Palace Library)
Archbishop Ramsey papers (Lambeth Palace Library)
Bishop Stockwood papers (Lambeth Palace Library)
Archbishop Coggan papers (Lambeth Palace Library)
Bishop Bell papers (Lambeth Palace Library)
The BMA Archives, London
The Centre for Capital Punishment Studies, University of Westminster
The Catholic National Library, Farnborough, Hampshire
The Westminster Diocesan Archives (Abingdon St, SW1)
The London Metropolitan Archives, City of London (Chief Rabbi's papers)

Film, Television and Radio
The BBC Written Archive Centre, Caversham Park, Reading
The British Film Institute, London
The British Library Sound Archive, London

Newspapers and Periodicals
The British Library Newspaper and Periodical Section, Colindale

National Dailies:-
The Times
The (Manchester) Guardian
The Daily Telegraph

The Financial Times
The Daily Mail
The Daily Express
The Sketch
The Daily Mirror
The News Chronicle
The Herald
The Daily Worker (The Morning Star)

National Sundays:-
The Sunday Times
The Observer
The Sunday Telegraph
The Sunday Express
The News of the World
The Sunday Mirror
Reynolds News
Sunday Pictorial

Local and regional newspapers:-
Western Mail
Daily Record

London Evening Newspapers:-
Evening Standard
Evening News
Evening Star

Political Magazines and Periodicals:-
The New Statesman
The Spectator
The Economist
Tribune
Picture Post

Religious press:-
The Church Times
The Tablet
The Universe

The Catholic Herald
The Catholic Times
The Methodist Recorder
The Baptist Times
The Jewish Chronicle

Public Opinion Surveys:-
Mass Observation Archive, University of Sussex
The Gallup Organization, London
National Opinion Polls Ltd (NOP) London

SECONDARY SOURCES

Reference works
Butler, David E and Gareth Butler, *British Political Facts 1900-1985* (London: Macmillan, 6th ed. 1986)
Craig, F.W.S., *British General Election Manifestoes 1918-1966* (Chichester: Political Reference Publications, 1970)
Craig, F.W.S., *British Parliamentary Election Statistics* (Chichester: Political Reference Publications, 1971)
Dod's, *Parliamentary Companion* (London: Business Dictionaries Ltd)
Roth, Andrew, *The MPs Chart* (London: Parliamentary Profiles, 1965)
Stenton, Michael and Stephen Lees, *Who's Who of British Members of Parliament: A Biographical Dictionary of the House of Commons, vol IV 1945-1979* (Sussex: Harvester Press, 1981)
The Times Guides to the House of Commons
Vachers Parliamentary Companion 1964 and 1966
Whitakers Almanac
Who's Who

Biographies, autobiographies, memoirs and diaries
Abse, Leo, *Private Member* (London: Macdonald, 1973)
Benn, Tony, *Out of the Wilderness: Diaries 1963-67* (London: Arrow, 1987)
Berkeley, Humphry, *Crossing the Floor* (London: Allen and Unwin, 1972)
Box, Muriel, *Rebel Advocate: A Biography of Gerald Gardiner* (London: Gollancz, 1983)
Bresler, Fenton, *Lord Goddard: A Biography of Rayner Goddard, Lord Chief Justice of England* (London: Harrap, 1977)
Butler, Richard Austen, *The Art of the Possible* (London: Hamish Hamilton, 1971)
Campbell, John, *Edward Heath, A Biography* (London: Jonathan Cape, 1993)

Castle, Barbara, *The Castle Diaries, 1964-70* (London: Macmillan, 1990)

Chadwick, Owen, *Michael Ramsey: A Life* (Oxford: Clarendon Press, 1990)

Collins, Canon John, *Faith Under Fire* (London: Leslie Frewin, 1966)

Dernley, Syd with David Newman, *The Hangman's Tale: Memoirs of a Public Executioner* (London: Pan, 1990)

Dudley Edwards, Ruth, *Victor Gollancz: A Biography* (London: Gollancz, 1987)

Duff, Peggy, *Left, Left, Left: A Personal Account of Six Protest Campaigns, 1945-65* (London: Allison and Busby,1971)

Evans, Harold, *Downing Street Diary: The Macmillan Years 1957-1963* (London: Hodder and Stoughton, 1981)

Faber, David, *Speaking for England: Leo, Julian and John Amery – The Tragedy of a Political Family* (London: Free Press, 2005)

Fielding, Steve, *Pierrepoint: A Family of Executioners. The Story of Britain's Infamous Hangmen* (London: John Blake, 2006)

Fisher, Nigel, *Iain Macleod* (London: Andre Deutsch, Weidenfeld and Nicolson, 1973)

Fisher, Nigel, *Tory Leaders: Their Struggle for Power* (London: Weidenfeld and Nicolson, 1977)

Fisher, Nigel, *Harold Macmillan: A Biography* (London: St Martins Press, 1982)

Gattey, Charles Neilson, *The Incredible Mrs Van der Elst* (London: Leslie Frewin, 1972)

Grimshaw, Eric and Glyn Jones, *Lord Goddard: His Career and Cases* (London: Allan Wingate, 1958)

Heffer, Eric, *Never A Yes Man: The Life and Politics of an Adopted Liverpudlian*(London: Verso, 1993)

Heffer, Simon, *Like the Roman: The Life of Enoch Powell* (London: Weidenfeld and Nicolson, 1998)

Horne, Alistair, *Macmillan, volume 2, 1957-1986* (London: Viking Adult, 1989)

Howard, Anthony, *Rab - The Life of R A Butler* (London: Macmillan, 1987)

Hughes, Emrys, *Sydney Silverman: Rebel in Parliament* (London: Charles Skilton, 1969)

Huws Jones, Enid, *Margery Fry, The Essential Amateur* (York: William Sessions, 1990)

Jenkins, Roy, *A Life at the Centre* (London: Macmillan, 1991)

Kilmuir, Earl of, *Political Adventure: The Memoirs of the Earl of Kilmuir* (London: Weidenfeld and Nicolson, 1964)

Klein, Leonora, *A Very English Hangman: The Life and Times of Albert Pierrepoint* (London: Corvo, 2006)

Macmillan, Harold, *Riding the Storm 1956-1959* (London: Macmillan, 1971)

Macmillan, Harold, *Pointing the Way 1959-1961* (London: Macmillan, 1972)
Macmillan, Harold, *At The End of the Day 1961-1963* (London: Macmillan, 1973)
Maudling, Reginald, *Memoirs* (London: Sidgwick and Jackson, 1978)
Pierrepoint, Albert, *Executioner Pierrepoint: The Amazing Autobiography of the World's Most Famous Executioner* (London: Harrap, 1974; London, Coronet 1977)
Pimlott, Ben, *Harold Wilson* (London: HarperCollins, 1993)
Rawlinson, Peter, *A Price Too High – An Autobiography* (London: Weidenfeld and Nicolson, 1989)
Roth, Andrew, *Enoch Powell: Tory Tribune* (London: Macdonald, 1970)
Shawcross, Hartley, *Life Sentence: The Memoirs of Lord Shawcross* (London: Constable, 1995)
Shepherd, Robert, *Iain Macleod* (London: Pimlico, 1994)
Shepherd, Robert, *Enoch Powell: A Biography* (London: Hutchinson, 1996)
Smith, Arthur, *Lord Goddard: My Years with the Lord Chief Justice* (London: Weidenfeld and Nicolson, 1959)
Thompson, Douglas, *Donald Soper: A Biography* (Nutfield, Surrey: Denholm House, 1971)
Thorpe, D R, *Selwyn Lloyd* (London: Jonathan Cape, 1989)
Van der Elst, Violet, *On The Gallows* (London: Doge Press, 1937)
Weale, Adrian, *Patriot Traitors: Roger Casement, John Amery and the Real Meaning of Treason* (London: Viking, 2001)
Wilson, Harold, *The Labour Government 1964-1970: A Personal Record* (Harmondsworth: Penguin, 1974)

General political works
Barker, A and M Rush, *The Member of Parliament and his Information* (London: Allen and Unwin, 1970)
Barnett, M, *The Politics of Legislation* (London: Weidenfeld and Nicolson, 1969)
Barr, James, *The Bow Group: A History* (London: Politico's, 2001)
Beer, Samuel, *Modern British Politics* (London: Faber, 1965)
Berrington, Hugh B, *Backbench Opinion in the House of Commons 1945-1955* (Oxford: Pergamon Press, 1973)
Birch, A H, *Representative and Responsible Government* (London: Allen and Unwin, 1979)
Blake, Robert, *The Conservative Party from Peel to Thatcher* (London: Fontana, 1985)
Brittan, Sam, *Left or Right: The Bogus Dilemma* (London: Secker and Warburg, 1968)
Bromhead, P.A., *The House of Lords and Contemporary Politics, 1911-1957* (London: Routledge and Kegan Paul, 1958)

Bromhead, P A, *Life in Modern Britain* (London: Longmans, 1966)

Burton, Ivor and Gavin Drewry, *Legislation and Public Policy: Public Bills in the 1970-74 Parliament* (London: Macmillan, 1981)

Butler, David E, *The British General Election of 1951* (London: Macmillan, 1952)

Butler, David E, *The British General Election of 1955* (London: Macmillan, 1955)

Butler, David E and Richard Rose, *The British General Election of 1959* (London: Macmillan, 1960)

Butler, David E and Anthony King, *The British General Election of 1964* (London: Macmillan, 1965)

Butler, David E and Anthony King, *The British General Election of 1966* (London: Macmillan, 1966)

Butler, David and Donald Stokes, *Political Change in Britain: The Evolution of Electoral Choice* (London: Macmillan, 2nd ed, 1974)

Butt, Ronald, *The Power of Parliament* (London: Constable, 1967)

Coombes, D, *The Member of Parliament and the Administration* (London: Allen
and Unwin, 1966)

Copping, Robert, *The Story of the Monday Club – The First Decade* (Ilford, Essex: Current Affairs Information Unit, 1972)

Copping, Robert, *The Story of the Monday Club – Crisis and After* (Ilford, Essex: Current Affairs Information Unit, 1975)

Crick, Bernard, *The Reform of Parliament* (London: Weidenfeld and Nicolson, 1964)

Dorey, Peter (ed.), *The Labour Governments 1964-70* (London: Routledge, 2006)

Epstein, Leon, *British Politics in the Suez Crisis* (London: Pall Mall Press, 1964)

Ewing, K D and C A Gearty, *Freedom under Thatcher: Civil Liberties in Modern Britain* (Oxford: Clarendon Press, 1990)

Finer, S. E., H B Berrington and D J Bartholomew, *Backbench Opinion in the House of Commons, 1955-59* (London: Pergamon, 1961)

Gilmour, Ian, *The Body Politic* (London: Hutchinson, 1969)

Hampton, W, *Democracy and Community* (Oxford: OUP, 1970)

Hansen, A and B. Crick (eds), *The Commons in Transition* (London: Collins, 1970)

Jackson, Robert J, *Rebels and Whips: An Analysis of Dissension, Discipline and Cohesion in British Political Parties* (London: Macmillan, 1968)

Jenkins, Roy, *The Case for Labour. Why Should You Vote Labour?* (Harmondsworth: Penguin, 1959)

Johnson, N, *Parliament and Administration* (London: Allen and Unwin, 1966)

Lamb, Richard, *The Macmillan Years 1957-1963: The Emerging Truth*

(London:
    John Murray, 1995)
Lapping, Brian, *The Labour Government 1964-70* (Harmondsworth: Penguin,
    1970)
Layton-Henry, Zig (ed), *Conservative Party Politics* (London: Macmillan,
    1980)
Lipset, Seymour Martin, *Political Man: The Social Bases of Politics* (New
    York: Anchor, 1963)
Mackintosh, John, *The Government and Politics of Britain* (London:
    Hutchinson, 1970)
McKenzie, Robert T, *British Political Parties: The Distribution of Power within
    the Conservative and Labour Parties* (London: Heinemann, 2nd ed.1963)
McKenzie, Robert T and A Silver, *Angels in Marble* (London: Heinemann,
    1968)
Morgan, Janet P, *The House of Lords and the Labour Government 1964-1970*
    (Oxford: Clarendon Press, 1975)
Morris, A (ed.), *The Growth of Parliamentary Scrutiny by Committee* (Oxford:
    Pergamon, 1970)
Nicolson, Nigel, *People and Parliament* (London: Weidenfeld and Nicolson,
    1958)
Nordlinger, Eric, *The Working Class Tories* (London: MacGibbon and Kee,
    1967)
Norton, Philip, *Conservative Dissidents* (London: Temple Smith, 1978)
Norton, Philip, *Dissension in the House of Commons 1945-1974: Intra-party
    Dissent in the House of Commons Division Lobbies1945-1974*
    (London: Macmillan, 1975)
Norton, Philip, *Dissension in the House of Commons 1974-1979* (Oxford:
    Clarendon, 1980)
Onslow, Sue, *Backbench Debate Within the Conservative Party and its
    Influence on British Foreign Policy, 1948-1957* (London: Macmillan,
    1997)
Parkin, Frank, *Middle Class Radicalism: The Social Bases of the British
    Campaign For Nuclear Disarmament* (Manchester: Manchester
    University Press, 1968)
Ponting, Clive, *Breach of Promise: Labour in Power 1964-1970*
    (Harmondsworth: Penguin, 1990)
Ranney, Austin, *Pathways to Parliament* (London: Macmillan, 1965)
Richards, Peter G, *Parliament and Foreign Affairs* (London: Allen and Unwin,
    1967)
Rose, R, *The Problem of Party Government* (Harmondsworth: Pelican, 1976)
Rose, R, *Do Parties Make a Difference?* (London: Macmillan, 2nd ed. 1984)
Seyd, Patrick, *Factionalism in the 1970s* In Layton-Henry, Zig (ed.)
    Conservative Party Politics (London: Macmillan, 1980) pp. 231-243

Seymour-Ure, Colin, *The Press, Politics and Public* (London: Methuen, 1968)
Seymour-Ure, Colin, *The Political Impact of the Mass Media* (London: Constable, 1974)
Seymour-Ure, Colin, *The British Press and Broadcasting since 1945* (Oxford: Basil Blackwell, 1991)
Taylor, Eric, *The House of Commons at Work* (Harmondsworth: Penguin, 1958)
Teer, Frank and Spence, James D, *Political Opinion Polls* (London: Hutchinson, 1973)
Thompson, Peter, *Labour's "Gannex Conscience"? Politics and Popular Attitudes in the Permissive Society* In Coopey, Richard, Steven Fielding and Nick Tiratsoo (eds), *The Wilson Government, 1964-70* (London: Pinter, 1993)
Treneman, Joseph and D. McQuail, *Television and the Political Image* (London: Methuen, 1961)
Tunstall, J, *The Westminster Lobby Correspondents* (London: Routledge, 1970)
Walkland and Ryle (eds), *The House of Commons in the Twentieth Century* (Oxford: Clarendon, 1979)
Wheare, K.C., *Government by Committee: An Essay on the British Constitution* (Oxford: Clarendon Press, 1955)
Whiteley, Paul, Patrick Seyd and Jeremy Richardson, *True Blues: the Politics of Conservative Party Membership* (Oxford: Clarendon Press, 1994)
Widgery, David, *The Left in Britain 1956-1968* (Harmondsworth: Penguin, 1976)

Pressure group activity and private members bills

Baggott, Rob, *Pressure Groups Today* (Manchester: Manchester University Press, 1995)
Bromhead, P.A., *Private Members' Bills in the British Parliament* (London: Routledge and Kegan Paul, 1956)
Dickens, B, *Abortion and Law* (MacGibbon and Kee, 1966)
Driver, Christopher, *The Disarmers: A Study in Protest* (London: Hodder and Stoughton, 1964)
Eckstein, Harry, *Pressure Group Politics: The Case of the British Medical Association* (London: Allen and Unwin, 1960)
Finer, S.E., *Anonymous Empire* (London: Pall Mall Press, 1958, 2nd ed 1966)
Fryer, Peter, *The Birth Controllers* (London: Secker and Warburg, 1965)
Grant, Wyn, *Pressure Groups, Politics and Democracy in Britain* (Hemel Hempstead: Harvester Wheatsheaf, 2nd ed 1995)
Hindell, Keith and Madeleine Simms, *Abortion Law Reformed* (London: Peter Owen, 1971)
Jenkins, Alice, *Law for the Rich* (London: Gollancz, 1960)

Jordan, A G and J J Richardson, *British Politics and the Policy Process: An Arena Approach* (London: Allen and Unwin, 1987)

Jordan, A G and J J Richardson, Government and Pressure Groups in Britain (Oxford: Clarendon Press, 1987)

Kimber, R and J J Richardson (eds), *Pressure Groups in Britain: A Reader* (London: J M Dent, 1974)

Leonard, Dick and Valentine Herman, *The Backbencher and Parliament* (London: Macmillan, 1972)

Marsh, David and Joanna Chambers, *Abortion Politics* (London: Junction Books, 1981)

Marsh, David and Melvyn Read, *Private Members Bills* (Cambridge: C.U.P., 1988)

Potter, A, *Organized Groups in British National Politics* (London: Faber, 1961)

Pym, Bridget, *Pressure Groups and the Permissive Society* (Newton Abbot: David and Charles, 1974)

Richards, Peter G, *Parliament and Conscience* (London: Allen and Unwin, 1970)

Richards, Peter G, *The Backbenchers* (London: Faber, 1972)

Richardson, J J and A G Jordan, *Governing under Pressure: The Policy Process in a Post-Parliamentary Democracy* (Oxford: Martin Robertson, 1979)

Rush, Michael, *Parliament and Pressure Politics* (Oxford: Clarendon, 1990)

Ryan, Mick, *The Acceptable Pressure Group: Inequality in the Penal Lobby: A Case Study of the Howard League and RAP* (Farnborough: Saxon House, 1978)

Ryan, Mick, *The Politics of Penal Reform* (Harlow: Longman, 1983)

Self, Peter and Herbert J Storing, *The State and the Farmer* (London: Allen and Unwin, 1962)

Stewart, J D, *British Pressure Groups: Their Role in Relation to the House of Commons* (Oxford: Clarendon Press, 1958)

Wilson, H H, *Pressure Group: The Campaign for Commercial Television* (London: Secker and Warburg, 1961)

The history of capital punishment and abolition campaigns

Bedau, Hugo A (ed), *The Death Penalty in America* (Oxford: OUP, 1982)

Bedau, Hugo A, *Death is Different: Studies in the Morality, Law and Politics of Capital Punishment* (Boston: Boston University Press, 1987)

Black, Charles L, Jr, *Capital Punishment: The Inevitability of Caprice and Mistake* (New York: Norton 1974)

Block, Brian P and John Hostettler, *Hanging in the Balance: A History of the Abolition of Capital Punishment in Britain* (Winchester: Waterside Press, 1997)

Blom-Cooper, Louis (ed), *The Hanging Question: Essays on the Death Penalty* (London: Gerald Duckworth, 1969 for the Howard League for Penal

Reform)

Brooke, Alan and David Brandon, *Tyburn: London's Fatal Tree* (Stroud: Sutton, 2004)

Calvert, E. Roy, *Capital Punishment in the Twentieth Century* (London: Putnam, 1927)

Calvert, E Roy, *Death Penalty Enquiry: Being a Review of the Evidence Before the Select Committee on Capital Punishment* (London: Gollancz, 1930)

Calvert, E Roy, *Capital Punishment* (London, NCADP, revised edition, 1936)

Christoph, James B, *Capital Punishment and British Politics: The British Movement to Abolish the Death Penalty 1945-1957* (London: Allen and Unwin, 1962)

Cook, Kimberley J, *Divided Passions: Public Opinions on Abortion and the Death Penalty* (Boston: Northeastern University Press, 1998)

Cooper, David D, *The Lesson of the Scaffold: The Victorian Controversy Over Public Executions* (London: Allen Lane, 1974)

Duff, Charles, *A Handbook on Hanging* (London: Cayme, 1928; revised and enlarged ed. London: Putnam, 1961; revised ed. Stroud: The History Press, 2011)

Duff, Charles, *A New Handbook on Hanging* (London: Andrew Melrose, 1954)

Eddleston, John J, *The Encyclopaedia of Executions* (London: John Blake, 2002)

Fielding, Henry, *An Inquiry into the causes of the Frequent Executions at Tyburn* (1725)

Gardiner, Gerald, *Capital Punishment as a Deterrent: and the Alternative* (London: Gollancz, 1956)

Gardiner, Gerald and Andrew Martin (eds), *Law Reform Now* (London: Gollancz,1963)

Gatrell, V A C, *The Hanging Tree: Execution and the English People 1770-1868* (Oxford: Oxford University Press, 1994)

Gollancz, Victor, *Capital Punishment: The Heart of the Matter* (London: Gollancz, 1955)

Gowers, Sir Ernest, *A Life for a Life? The Problem of Capital Punishment* (London: Chatto and Windus, 1956)

Griffiths, A, *The Chronicle of Newgate* (1884)

Hale, Leslie, *Hanged in Error* (Penguin Special) (Harmondsworth: Penguin, 1961)

Hay, Douglas, Peter Linebaugh, John G Rule, E P Thompson and Cal Winslow, *Albion's Fatal Tree: Crime and Society in Eighteenth Century England* (Harmondsworth: Penguin, 1975)

Heald, Sir Lionel, *Murder: Some Suggestions for the Reform of the Law Relating To Murder in England* (London: Inns of Court Conservative and Unionist Society, 1956)

Hibbert, Christopher, *The Roots of Evil: A Social History of Crime and Punishment* (London: Weidenfeld and Nicolson, 1963)

Hodgkinson, Peter and Andrew Rutherford, (eds), *Capital Punishment: Global Issues and Prospects* (Winchester: Waterside Press, 1996)

Hollis, M Christopher, *The Homicide Act: The First Thorough Examination of How The Homicide Act has been Working in Practice* (London: Gollancz, 1964)

Hood, Roger, *The Death Penalty: A World-Wide Perspective* (Oxford: OUP, 1989)

Hostettler, John, *The Politics of Punishment* (Winchester: Barry Rose, 1994)

Koestler, Arthur, *Reflections on Hanging* (London: Gollancz, 1956)

Koestler, Arthur and C H Rolph, *Hanged by the Neck: An Exposure of Capital Punishment in England* (Penguin Special) (Harmondsworth: Penguin, 1961)

Laurence, John, *A History of Capital Punishment* (New York: Citadel, 1963)

Linebaugh, Peter, *The London Hanged: Crime and Civil Society in the Eighteenth Century* (London: Penguin, 1993)

Morris, Terence and Louis Blom-Cooper, *Murder in Microcosm* (London: The Observer, 1961)

Morris, Terence and Louis Blom-Cooper, *A Calendar of Murder: Criminal Homicide In England since 1957* (London: Michael Joseph, 1964*)*

Paton, John, *This Hanging Business* (London: NCADP, 1938)

Pettifer, Ernest, *Punishments of Former Days* (Bradford: Clegg, 1939)

Potter, Harry, *Hanging in Judgment: Religion and the Death Penalty in England from the Bloody Code to Abolition* (London: SCM Press, 1993)

Rose, Gordon, *The Struggle for Penal Reform: The Howard League and Its Predecessors* (London: Stevens and Sons, 1961)

Scott, George Ryley, *The History of Capital Punishment* (London: Torchstream, 1950)

Templewood, Viscount (Samuel Hoare), *The Shadow of the Gallows* (London: Gollancz, 1951)

Thompson, E P, *Whigs and Hunters: The Origin of the Black Act* (London: Allen Lane, 1975)

Turner, G D, *The Alternatives to Capital Punishment - Roy Calvert 5th Memorial Lecture* (London: NCADP, 1938)

Tuttle, Elizabeth Orman, *The Crusade Against Capital Punishment in Great Britain* (London: Stevens and Sons, 1961)

Windlesham, Lord, *Responses to Crime, volume 2: Penal Policy in the Making* (Oxford: Oxford University Press, 1993)

Wrightson, Thomas, *On the Punishment of Death* (1837)

Criminal cases, *causes celebre* and miscarriages of justice

Altrincham, Lord (John Grigg) and Ian Gilmour, *The Case of Timothy Evans:*

An Appeal to Reason (London: The Spectator, 1956)

Bentley, Iris, *Let Him Have Justice* (London: Picador, 2001)

Bentley, William, *My Son's Execution* (London: W H Allen, 1957)

Blom-Cooper, Louis, *The A6 Murder: Regina v James Hanratty – The Semblance of Truth* (Harmondsworth: Penguin, 1963)

Cecil, Henry, *The Trial of Walter Rowland* (Newton Abbot: David and Charles, 1975)

Eddowes, Michael, *The Man on your Conscience: An Investigation of the Evans Murder Trial* (London: Cassell, 1955)

Foot, Paul, *Who Killed Hanratty?* (London: Cape, 1971; revised ed, London: Panther, 1973; revised ed, Harmondsworth: Penguin, 1988)

Hancock, Robert, *Ruth Ellis* (London: Arthur Barker, 1963)

Hodge, Harry and Hodge, J.J. (eds), *Famous Trials* (Harmondsworth: Penguin, 1984)

Hyde, Montgomery (ed.), *Trial of Craig and Bentley* (London: William Hodge, 1954)

Jones, Elwyn, *The Last Two to Hang* (London: Macmillan, 1966)

Justice, Jean, *Murder vs Murder: The British Legal System and the A6 Murder Case* (Paris: Olympia, 1964)

Justice, Jean, *Le Crime de la Route A6* (Paris: Robert Laffont, 1968)

Kennedy, Ludovic, *Ten Rillington Place* (London: Gollancz, 1961)

Liverpool, Lord Russell of, *Deadman's Hill - Was Hanratty Guilty?* (London: Secker and Warburg, 1965; London: Icon, 1966)

Marks, Laurence and Tony van den Bergh, *Ruth Ellis: A Case of Diminished Responsibility?* (Harmondsworth: Penguin, 1990)

Miller, Leonard, *Shadows of Deadman's Hill: A New Analysis of the A6 Murder* (London: Zoilus, 2001)

Paget, Reginald, Sydney Silverman and Christopher Hollis, *Hanged - and Innocent?* (London: Gollancz, 1953)

Parris, John, *Most of My Murders* (London: Frederick Muller, 1960)

Parris, John, *Scapegoat: The Inside Story of the Trial of Derek Bentley* (London: Duckworth, 1991)

Selwyn, Francis, *Gangland – The Case of Bentley and Craig* (London: Routledge, 1988)

Simpson, Keith, *Forty Years of Murder* (London: Harrap, 1978; London: Grafton, 1980)

Toughill, Thomas, *Oscar Slater: The Mystery Solved* (Edinburgh: Canongate, 1993)

Trow, Michael J, *Let Him Have It, Chris* (London: Constable, 1990)

West, Rebecca, *The Meaning of Treason* (London: Virago, 1982)

Woffinden, Bob, *Miscarriages of Justice* (London: Hodder and Stoughton, 1987; London: Coronet, 1989)

Woffinden, Bob, *Hanratty: The Final Verdict* (London: Macmillan, 1997)

Yallop, David, T*o Encourage The Others* (London: W H Allen, 1971; revised and updated – London: Corgi, 1990)

General legal works
Blake, Nick and Harry Rajak, *Wigs and Workers: A History of the Haldane Society of Socialist Lawyers 1930-80* (London: Haldane Society, 1980)

Blom-Cooper, Louis and Terence Morris, *Crime and Criminal Justice since 1945* (Oxford: Blackwell, 1989)

Bresler, Fenton, *Reprieve: A Study of a System* (London: George G Harrap, 1965)

Cale, Michelle, *Law and Society. An Introduction to Sources for Criminal and Legal History from 1800* (PRO Readers Guide No 14, 1996)

Griffiths, J A G, *The Politics of the Judiciary* (London: HarperCollins/Fontana, fourth edition, 1991)

Pannick, David, *Judges* (Oxford: OUP, 1988)

Radzinowicz, Leon, *A History of English Criminal Law and Its Administration from 1750, 5 volumes* (London: 1948-1986)

Stephen, James Fitzroy, *A History of the Criminal Law of England, volume 1* (London: Macmillan, 1883)

Williams, Glanville, *The Sanctity of Life and the Criminal Law* (London: Faber, 1958)

Criminological, sociological and psychological works
Adorno, T W, E Frenkel-Brunswick, D J Levinson and R N Sanford, *The Authoritarian Personality* (New York: W.W. Norton, 1982)

Christie, R and F. Geis, *Studies in Machiavellianism (*London: Academic Press, 1970)

Davies, Christie, *The British State and the Power of Life and Death* - In Green, S J D and R C Whiting (eds), *The Boundaries of the State in Modern Britain* (Cambridge: CUP, 1996) pp. 341-374

Eysenck, Hans, *The Psychology of Politics* (London: Routledge and Kegan Paul, 1954)

Eysenck, H J and Glenn D Wilson (eds.), *The Ideological Basis of Conservatism* (*Lancaster, MTP Press, 1978)

Nathanson, Stephen, *An Eye for an Eye: The Immorality of Punishing by Death* (Lanham, MD, USA: Rowson and Littlefield, 1987)

Rokeach, M, *The Open and Closed Mind* (New York: The Free Press, 1960)

Secord, Paul F and Carl W Backman, *Social Psychology* (Tokyo: McGraw-Hill, 2nded., 1974)

Sellin, Thorsten (ed), *Capital Punishment* (New York: Harper and Row, 1967)

Sellin, Thorsten, *The Penalty of Death* (London: Sage, 1980)

St John-Stevas, Norman, *The Right to Life* (London: Hodder and Stoughton, 1963)

St John-Stevas, Norman, *Law and Morals* (London: Burns and Oates, 1964)
Wilson, Glenn D (ed.), *The Psychology of Conservatism* (London: Academic
    Press, 1973)

Miscellaneous works
Booker, Christopher, *The Neophiliacs: The Revolution in English Life in the
    Fifties and Sixties* (1st ed. London: William Collins, 1969; 2nd ed.
    London: Pimlico, 1992)
Crowther, Bruce, *Captured on Film: The Prison Movie* (London: Batsford,
    1989)
Davies, Christie, *Permissive Britain: Social Change in the Sixties and Seventies*
    (London: Pitman, 1975)
Hopkins, Harry, *The New Look: A Social History of the Forties and Fifties in
    Britain* (London: Secker and Warburg, 1963)
Levin, Bernard, *The Pendulum Years: Britain and the Sixties* (London:
    Macmillan, 1972)
Litchfield, Michael and Susan Kentish, *Babies for Burning* (London: Serpentine
    Press, 1974)
Marwick, Arthur, *The Sixties: Cultural Revolution in Britain, France, Italy and
    the United States, 1958-74* (Oxford: Oxford University Press, 1998)
McGregor, O R, *Divorce in England* (London: Methuen, 1957)
Melly, George, *Revolt into Style: The Pop Arts in Britain* (Harmondsworth:
    Penguin, 1972)
Morgan, Kenneth O, *The People's Peace: British History 1945-1989* (Oxford:
    Oxford Paperbacks, 1992)
Pym, John (ed.), *Time Out Film Guide*, Harmondsworth: Penguin, 7th edition,
    1998)
Spencer, Colin, *Homosexuality: A History* (London: Fourth Estate, 1995)
Trevelyan, G M, *English Social History: A Survey of Six Centuries from
    Chaucer to Queen Victoria* (London: Longman, 1944)
Walker, John (ed), *Halliwell's Film and Video Guide* (London,
    HarperCollins, 12th ed, 1996)

Journal articles, conference papers and theses
Bailey, Victor, 'The Shadow of the Gallows: The Death Penalty and the British
    Labour Government 1945-51 '*Law and History Review*, vol 18 (no 2),
    (Summer 2000), pp. 305-349
Baker, David, Andrew Gamble and Steve Ludlam, '1846…1906…1996?
    Conservative Splits and European Integration' *Political Quarterly*, vol 64
    (1993), pp. 420-434
Beer, Samuel H, 'Pressure Groups and Parties in Britain' *American Political
    Science Review* 50 (March 1956) pp.1-23
Berrington, Hugh, 'The Conservative Party: Revolts and Pressures 1955-

1961'*The Political Quarterly*, vol 32, (Oct-Dec 1961) pp. 363-373

Blom-Cooper, Louis J, 'Murder (Abolition of Death Penalty) Act 1965' *The Modern Law Review,* vol 29, no 2 (March 1966), pp 184-186

Chorley, Lord, 'Capital Punishment' *Political Quarterly*, vol 25, 1954, pp 4-16

Christoph, James B, 'Political Rights and Administrative Impartiality in the British Civil Service' *American Political Science Review*, 51, March 1957, pp. 67-87

Christoph, James B, 'Capital Punishment and British Party Responsibility' *Political Science Quarterly,* vol 77, no 1 (March 1962), pp 19-35

Cowley, Philip and Mark Stuart, 'Sodomy, Slaughter, Sunday Shopping and Seatbelts: Free Votes in the House of Commons, 1979-1996', *Party Politics* vol 3, (no 1) 1997, pp. 119-130

Cowley, Philip and J Garry, 'The British Conservative Party and Europe: the choosing of John Major' *British Journal of Political Science*, vol 28 (1998) pp.73-499

Cowley, Philip and Philip Norton, 'What a ridiculous thing to say! (which is why we didn't say it): a response to Timothy Heppell', *British Journal of Politics and International Relations*, vol 4, no 2, June 2002, pp. 325-329

Critchley, Julian, 'The Intellectuals', *Political Quarterly*, vol 32, 1961, pp. 267-274

Dickson, A D R, 'MP's Readoption Conflicts: Their Causes and Consequences', *Political Studies*, XXIII, 1975, pp. 62-70

Drewry, Gavin and Janet Morgan, 'Law Lords as Legislators', *Parliamentary Affairs*, vol 22 (1968-9) pp. 226-239

Drewry, Gavin and Jenny Brock, 'Prelates in Parliament', *Parliamentary Affairs,* vol 24 (3), (1970-1), pp. 222-250

Drewry, Gavin, 'Parliament and Hanging: Further Episodes in an Undying Saga',*Parliamentary Affairs*, vol 27, 1973-4, pp. 251-261

Epstein, Leon D, 'British MPs and their Local Parties: The Suez Cases', *American Political Science Review* 54, June 1960, pp. 374-390

Erskine, Hazel, 'The Polls: Capital Punishment', *Public Opinion Quarterly*, 34 (1970), pp. 290-307

Eysenck, H J and T Coulter, 'The personality and attitudes of working-class British Communists and Fascists', *Journal of Social Psychology*, 87, (1972) pp. 59-73

Franklin, Mark N and Michael Tappin, 'Early Day Motions as Unobtrusive Measures of Backbench Opinion in Britain', *British Journal of Political Science*, vol 7 (1), (1977), pp. 49-69

Frasure, Robert C, 'Backbench Opinion Revisited: the Case of the Conservatives', *Political Studies*, Vol XX, no 3, 1972, pp. 325-328

Gallie, W.B, 'The Lord's Debate on Hanging, July 1956: Interpretation and Comment', *Philosophy* 32 (1957) pp. 132-147

Gardiner, Gerald and N Curtis-Raleigh, 'The Judicial Attitude to Penal

Reform', *The Law Quarterly Review*, April 1949, pp. 196-219

Hall-Williams, J.E, 'The Homicide Bill', *Howard Journal* 9 (1957) pp. 285-299

Heppell, Timothy, 'The Ideological Composition of the Parliamentary Conservative Party 1992-97', *British Journal of Politics and International Relations,* vol 4, no 2, June 2002, pp. 299-324

Hibbing, John R and David Marsh, 'Accounting for the Voting Patterns of British MPs on Free Votes', *Legislative Studies Quarterly*, vol 12 (no 2) (May 1987) pp. 275-297

Marsh, David and Melvyn Read, 'British Private Members Balloted Bills: A Lottery with Few Winners, Small Prizes but High Administrative Costs', *Essex Papers in Politics and Government*, no 21, 1985

Marsh, David and Melvyn Read, 'The Government and Private Members Bills: Wolves in Sheep's Clothing', *Essex Papers in Politics and Government*, no 43, 1987

Martin, Laurence W, 'The Bournemouth Affair: Britain's First Primary Election', *Journal of Politics*, vol 22 (Nov.1960) pp. 654-681

Mason, Lisa, 'The Development of the Monday Club and its Contribution to the Conservative Party and the Modern British Right, 1961-1990', *PhD thesis,* University of Wolverhampton, June 2004

McHugh, John , 'The Labour Party and the Parliamentary Campaign to Abolish the Military Death Penalty, 1919-1930', *The Historical Journal*, Vol. 42, No. 1 (March 1999), pp. 233-249

Moyser, George, 'Voting Patterns on Moral Issues in the British House of Commons 1964-69' (*Paper presented to the Political Studies Association conference,* 1980)

Mughan, Anthony and Roger M Scully, 'Accounting for Change in Free Vote Outcomes in the House of Commons', *British Journal of Political Science*, vol 27 (4) (1997) pp. 640-647

Parkin, Frank, 'Working-Class Conservatives: A Theory of Political Deviance', *The British Journal of Sociology*, vol 18, (1967), pp. 278-290

Pattie, Charles, Edward Fieldhouse and R J Johnston, 'The Price of Conscience: The Electoral Correlates and Consequences of Free Votes and Rebellions in the British House of Commons, 1987-92', *British Journal of Political Science*, vol 24 (3), (1994), pp. 359-380

Potter, Allen, 'Attitude Groups', *Political Quarterly*, 29 (January-March 1958) p. 72

Read, Melvyn, David Marsh and David Richards, 'Why Do They Do It? Voting on Homosexuality and Capital Punishment in the House of Commons', *Parliamentary Affairs*, vol 47 (1994) pp. 374-386

Read, M and D Marsh, 'The Family Law Bill: Conservative Party splits and Labour Party cohesion', *Parliamentary Affairs*, vol 50 (1997), pp. 263-279

Rose, Richard, 'The Bow Group's Role in British Politics', *The Western Political Quarterly*, vol 14 (4), December 1961, pp. 865-878

Rose, Richard, 'Parties, factions and tendencies in Britain', *Political Studies*, vol XII 1964, pp. 33-46

Seyd, Patrick, 'Factionalism Within the Conservative Party: The Monday Club', *Government and Opposition*, vol 7 (4), October 1972, pp. 464-487

Uschanov, T P, 'Capital Punishment in Modern British Law and Culture', (*University of Helsinki paper*)

Vincent, J R, 'The House of Lords', *Parliamentary Affairs*, vol 19, 1965-6, pp. 475-485

Walsha, Robert, 'The One Nation Group: a Tory approach to backbench politics and organisations 1950-55',*Twentieth Century British History*, 11 (2), (2000) pp. 183-214

Wilson, Glenn D and A H Brazendale, 'Social Attitude Correlates of Eysenck's Personality Dimensions', *Social Behavior and Personality* 1 (1973) pp. 115-118

Newspaper, magazine and periodical articles
Foot, Paul, 'A Break in the Silence', *The Guardian*, 25th February 1995

Hollis, Christopher, 'The Tactics of Abolition', *The Spectator*, vol 195, 25th November 1955, pp. 706-707

Holway, Peter, 'Hang first, ask questions later', *New Scientist*, 23rd February 1991, pp. 63-4

Rose, Jacqueline, 'Getting away with murder', *New Statesman and Society*, 22nd July 1988, pp. 34-7

Rubinstein, William D, 'The Secret of Leopold Amery', *History Today*, Vol 49 (2), February 1999, pp. 17-23

Websites (miscellaneous)
http://www.imdb The Internet Movie Database
http://www.britmovie.co.uk The Home of British Films
http://www.bfi.org.uk The British Film Institute
http://www.abortionrights.org.uk
http://www.capitalpunishmentuk.org Capital Punishment UK
http://www.stephen-stratford.co.uk Stephen's Study Room – British Military and Criminal history in the period 1900 to 1999
http://innocent.org.uk Fighting Miscarriages of Justice since 1993
http://www.doollee.com Dollee.com (theatre guide)

Index

A

abortion (as an issue): 80, 89, 154, 266, 276, 310, 312, 317-328, 335
Abse, Leo: 116, 209, 264, 311, 315, 316, 320, 326-7
Ackland, Michael: 278
ACPO (Association of Chief Police Officers): 91
Advise and Consent: 276
A Hard Day's Night: 11
Aims of Industry, The: 327
Albion, Father Gordon: 140
Aldrich, Robert: 276
A Life for A Life? The Problem of Capital Punishment: 242
Alfie: 276
Allen, Harry: 230, 253, 264
Allen, Peter Anthony: 12, 206, 246-7, 285
Alphon, Peter: 200, 201
Alexander, Lord: 306
ALRA (Abortion Law Reform Association): 154, 312, 313, 318, 320, 322, 324
Alternative to Capital Punishment, The: 242
Amery, John: 77
Amery, Julian: 77
Amis, Kingsley: 55
An End to Hanging: 253
Angry Silence, The: 277
Anderson, Sir John: 26, 31
Annan, Noel: 314
Antrobus, Lady: 303
A Question of Inheritance: 253
Armstrong, John: 122
Arnold, Mrs Marjorie: 304
Arran, Earl of: 311

Artificial insemination:154
Asquith of Bishopstone, Lord: 31
Associated Newspapers Ltd: 235
Associated Rediffusion: 125
Association for the Reform of the Law on Capital Punishment in Northern Ireland: 61
Association of Circuit Judges: 88
Astor, David: 46, 232
A Tap on the Shoulder: 265
A Taste of Honey: 276
At Home and Abroad: 252
Attenborough, Richard: 274
Attlee, Clement: 26, 34, 46, 61, 66, 67, 90, 311
Attlee government: 66, 88, 118, 332
ATV: 258
AVL (The Anti-Violence League): 295-8
Ayer, A J: 311

B

Bacon, Alice: 39, 96, 114, 115, 205, 206
Bailey, Derek: 263
Baker, Kenneth: 80
Baptist Church: 143, 146-8, 153
Baptist Times, The: 146, 147
Baptist Union Christian Fellowship Department: 148
Bar Council: 90
Barry Committee: 205
Bartlett, Lt Col: 254
Barzman, Ben: 270
Baxter, Sir Beverley: 115-6
Baxter, William: 70
BBC: 188, 193, 252, 254, 256, 258, 261, 262, 265, 266, 298, 306
Beatles, The: 11

Beaumont, J W: 147
Beaverbrook Group: 235
Behan, Brendan: 272, 277, 283
Bell, George (Bishop of Chichester): 28, 129, 131, 132, 136
Beloe, Robert: 134, 135
Benewith, W H : 147
Benn, Anthony Wedgwood: 124, 125, 213, 214, 339
Bentley, Derek: 17, 31, 42, 43, 62, 103, 113, 125, 130, 185, 194, 195, 200, 202, 237, 245, 246, 274
Bentley, Iris: 246
Bentley, William George: 246
Berkeley, Humphry: 75, 76, 206, 263
Berlin, Isaiah: 311
Bernstein, Sidney: 49, 256
Berry-Dee, Christopher: 246
Bessell, Peter: 82
Bevan, Aneurin: 27, 33, 34, 66
Bevin, Ernest: 26, 66
Beyond a Reasonable Doubt: 274
Big Flame, The: 267
Biggs, Ronnie: 216
Bilmes, M: 295
Birmingham Six, The: 336
Bing, Geoffrey: 33
BIPO polls: 163, 167, 187
Birkett Committee: 312, 318, 320, 322
Birkett, Lord: 117, 119
Black, Insp. John: 300
Black, Rev Donald: 148
Black, Sir Cyril Black: 317
Blair government: 337
Blind Justice: Miscarriages of Justice in Twentieth Century Britain: 247
Blom-Cooper and Morris Report: 145, 227
Blom-Cooper, Louis: 244, 246, 264
Blonde Sinner: 268
Bloody Code, The: 19, 128
BMA: 98, 99
Boardman, Harold: 300
Board of Deputies of British Jews: 151
Boothby, Lord: 11
Boulting, John: 277
Bowden, Herbert: 211, 212
Bow Dialogues, The: 254
Bow Group, The: 49, 78
Boycott, Geoffrey: 11
Boyd-Carpenter, John: 300

Boyle, Sir Edward: 75, 76, 206, 210, 215
Brabin enquiry: 217
Braddock, Bessie: 206
Brady, Ian: 286
Bresler, Fenton: 245
Bright, John: 21
Bring Back the Rope?: 262, 264, 302
British Council of Churches: 123, 148, 149, 150
Britten, Benjamin: 35, 48
Brockway, Fenner: 121, 122, 201
Brook, Norman: 113
Brooke, Henry: 84, 121, 122, 124, 125, 126, 208, 212, 213, 215, 216, 253, 282, 285, 293
Brown, Alan: 70, 115
Brown, George: 321
Bruce-Gardyne, Jock: 229
Burton, Lord: 216
Butler, Mollie: 102-3, 108
Butler, R A (Rab): 40, 56, 84, 102, 104, 105, 106-7, 108, 109, 110, 111, 112, 113, 115, 116, 117, 118, 119, 120, 121, 122, 123, 124, 127, 198, 199, 201
Byers, Frank: 250
Byrne, Mr Justice: 111

C

Calder, Gilchrist: 257
Calendar of Murder, A (Criminal Homicide in England since 1957): 244
Callaghan, James: 58, 82, 98, 232, 255, 286, 287, 288, 289, 291, 293, 321, 339, 341
Calvert, E Roy: 23, 44, 142, 241:
Calvert, Theodora: 242
Cambridge Department of Criminal Science: 107
Campaign for Real Ale: 329
Capital Punishment: 241-2
Capital Punishment (radio programme): 249
Capital Punishment: A Review of the Arguments: 250
Capital Punishment as a Deterrent and the Alternative: 243
Capital Punishment in the Twentieth Century: 23, 241

Edwards, Glyn: 265
Edwards, Rev Walter: 145
Eichmann, Adolf: 44, 59
Eighty Club: 83
Eldon, Lord Chancellor: 20, 88
Ellenborough, Lord Chief Justice: 20, 88
Ellis, Ruth: 17, 33, 35, 42, 43, 48, 62, 113, 130, 163, 168, 169, 185, 186, 194, 195, 200, 202, 230, 238, 246, 274
embryo research (as an issue): 80
Emergency Powers Act, 1973: 341
Emmett-Dunne, Frederick: 125
Ensor, David: 263, 264
Equity: 314
Ethical Union, The: 61
European Convention on Human Rights, the: 337
European Parliament, the: 82
euthanasia (as an issue) 80
Evans, A C: 92, 93, 97, 300
Evans, Geraldine: 119
Evans, Gwynne Owen: 12, 206, 285
Evans, Stanley: 70
Evans, Timothy: 17, 32, 34, 42, 43, 61, 67, 83, 84, 102, 103, 113, 114, 116, 117, 118, 119, 120, 121, 122, 130, 194, 199, 200, 202, 213, 216-7, 245, 246, 260, 274, 288
Evening News, The: 232, 235, 236
Evening Standard, The: 235, 273, 274, 282
Evening Star, The: 235, 236
Executioner Pierrepoint: 245

F

Fable: 267
Fell, Anthony: 232
Fellowship of Reconciliation: 61
Field, Dr Leopold: 254
Fienburgh, Wilfred: 234
Financial Times, The: 225, 228, 231
Finnemore, Sir Donald: 253
Firearms Bill, 1965: 93
Fisher, Geoffrey (Archbishop of Canterbury): 28, 51, 59, 129, 131, 132
Fitt, Gerry: 85
Fitzgibbon, Louis: 302-7
Flame in the Streets: 276
Flat Earth Society: 329
Fleischer, Richard: 274
Fleming, Ian: 11

Fletcher, Eric: 112, 121
Fonda, Henry: 274
Foot, Dingle: 60, 126, 314
Foot, Michael: 33, 114, 115, 117, 206, 314
Foot, Paul: 201, 202, 246
Forbes, Bryan: 276
Forsyth, Francis: 54, 111, 198, 199
Frankly Speaking: 252
Fraser, Sir Hugh: 215
Freeman, John: 46
Free Presbyterian Church of Scotland, the (Wee Wee Frees): 149, 151
Friends Meeting House, Euston Road: 143
Frost, David: 201, 263, 305-6
Frost on Friday: 263, 306
Frost on Saturday: 263
Frost on Sunday: 263
Fry, Margery: 102
Furie, Sidney J: 276

G

Gaitskell, Hugh: 34, 67, 86, 124
Gale, George: 238
Gale, Reg: 254, 264
Gallup polls: 11, 135, 156, 157, 158, 161, 162, 163
Gangland: The Case of Craig and Bentley: 246
Gardiner, Gerald: 35, 44, 45, 46, 47, 49, 50, 51, 52, 53, 54, 55, 56, 57, 59, 62, 83, 90, 124, 125, 126, 134, 142, 205, 214, 215, 243, 250, 252, 256, 259, 261, 280,281, 291, 321, 323, 326
Gardner, Edward: 205, 215
Gardner, Llew: 231
Gay Liberation Front, The: 318
Gilbert, Lewis: 276
Gilliam, Laurence: 249
Gillis, Bernard, QC: 119
Gilmour, Ian: 237-8, 245
Glover, Douglas: 114
Glyn, Sir Richard: 210
Goddard, Lord Chief Justice: 28, 38, 51, 88, 89, 101, 111, 194, 198, 218, 246, 339
Godfrey, Cardinal Archbishop: 133, 260
Gold, Jack: 267
Gollancz, Ruth: 46, 47, 50

244-5, 252, 253, 254, 259, 261, 287, 288, 296, 297, 331, 341
homosexuality (as an issue): 80, 154, 266, 276, 310, 317-28, 335
Homosexual Law Reform Society (HLRS): 311, 318, 319, 320
Hooson, Emlyn: 84, 210
Horfield prison: 125
Hornsby-smith, Patricia: 108
Housman, Laurence: 283
Howard League for Penal Reform, The: 16, 21, 23, 29, 30, 35, 44, 45, 60, 62, 98, 113, 142, 154, 206, 244, 258, 310, 322, 323, 326
Howard, Michael: 80
Howard, Percy: 232
Howe, Geoffrey: 49
Howell, Denis: 105, 197
Huddleston, Trevor: 311
Hughes, Geoffrey: 263
Humanity: 62
Hume, Donald: 122
Hunkin, Joseph (Bishop of Truro): 28, 129
Hurst, Charlotte: 254, 264, 302, 304, 305, 306
Huxley, Julian: 123, 311
Hyde, Montgomery: 75, 76, 85
Hynd, John: 210

I

Ibsen, Henrik
identity cards (as an issue): 80
Ilford, Lord: 216
I'm Alright Jack: 277
immigration and race relations (as an issue): 80, 178, 267, 276, 302
industrial relations (as an issue): 277
industrial revolution, the: 20
Infanticide Act, 1922, The: 21
Infant Life (Preservation) Act, 1929, The: 312
Inglis, Brian: 237-8
Inns of Court Conservative and Unionist Society: 35
NRA (International Research Associates Inc): 171
Instead of Hanging – What?: 253
In the Name of the Father: 274
RA, the: 336

Iremonger, Tom: 110, 119, 205, 210, 254, 255
Iron and Steel Nationalisation Bill: 211
Irvine, Bryant Godman: 112
Isaacs, George: 34
It's All Over Now: 11
ITV: 125, 255, 256, 258, 263, 306
I Want to Live!: 270, 273, 274

J

Jackson, Sir Richard: 233
Jacobs, Sir Ian: 49, 256
Jakobovits, Sir Immanuel: 151, 152
James, Jeremy: 262
Jellicoe, Lord: 293
Jenkin, Patrick: 301
Jenkins, Roy: 69, 86, 93, 97, 201, 244, 285, 286, 300, 301, 307, 311, 313, 314, 319, 321, 338, 339
Jewish Chronicle, The: 151, 152
Jewish religion, the: 128, 151
Johnson, Carol: 123
Johnson, Dr Donald; 110, 122
Johnstone, J C: 161
Jones, Alec: 316
Jones, Elwyn, QC, MP (politician): 111, 126, 199
Jones, Elwyn (writer): 247
Jones, Mervyn: 239
Jones, Terry: 278
Jopling, Michael: 301
Joseph, Sir Keith: 215
Jowitt, Viscount: 27
Judicial Review Tribunal: 216
Justice, Jean: 201, 246
Justinian: 228

K

Kee, Robert: 254, 259
Kennedy, Ludovic: 83, 84, 116, 117, 119, 120, 199, 216, 245, 246, 251, 260, 264, 274, 283
Kerans, Comm. John: 112
Kerr, Dr David: 210
Killing of Sister George, The: 276
King's Bench, the: 89
Kirk, Peter: 37, 46, 49, 50, 55, 56, 75, 114, 115, 121, 123, 319

Man Alive: 262, 263, 264, 302, 306
Manfred Mann: 11
Manningham-Buller, Sir Reginald
(Viscount Dilhorne): 89, 103, 104, 105,
106, 124, 134, 135, 196, 215, 293
Man on Your Conscience, The: 245
Margaret, Princess: 282
Markowe, Dr Marcus: 303
Marks, Laurence: 246
Marplan poll: 173
Marwood, Ronald Henry: 54, 55, 109, 196,
197, 200
Marsh, Richard: 117
Mason, Mr: 121
Mass Observation: 35, 156, 158, 162, 163,
164, 168, 169, 171, 174
Master of the Rolls, the: 87
Matrimonial Causes Act, 1857, The: 315
Maude, Angus: 37, 76, 78
Maudling, Reginald: 77
Maxwell: 97
Maxwell Fyfe, Sir David (Lord Kilmuir):
31, 32, 42, 111, 118, 124, 195, 198, 215,
237-8, 246
Mayhew, Christopher: 111, 199
McAlpine, Robert: 306
McCowen, Alec: 270
McCulloch, Joseph: 254
McGoohan, Patrick: 272
McGuire, Michael: 210
McKern, Leo: 271
McNaghten rules, 1843, the: 22, 30, 98-9,
150
Medak, Peter: 274
Medlicott, Sir Frank: 60, 75, 76
Meehan, PC: 111, 198
Methodist Church, the: 143-6, 153, 154
Methodist Peace Fellowship, the: 144
Methodist Recorder, The: 144, 145
Metropolitan Police, the: 93, 201
Middleton, Bishop of: 51
Mill, J S: 110
Miller, Leonard: 202, 246
Millington, Ernest: 67
Miscarriages of Justice: 247
Monday Club, the: 78, 264
Monty Python's Flying Circus: 278
Moore, Henry: 35, 123
Moore, Sir Thomas: 75, 106, 107, 108, 10,
112, 116, 124, 259, 261, 295, 297

Moors murders: 176, 219, 286, 299
Morahan, Christopher: 267
Moral and Social Questions Committee (of
the Baptist Church): 146
Moral Welfare Council (of the Church of
England): 154
Morris, Colin: 257, 258
Morris, Dr Terence: 244, 253, 259
Morris of Borth-y-Gest, Lord Justice: 89
Morrison, Herbert: 26, 34, 66, 208
Mortimer, Dr (Bishop of Exeter): 56, 133,
136, 261
Morton Commission, the: 315, 320, 322
Mossman, James: 253
Moynahan, Brian: 201
Moynihan, Lord: 83
Mulcahy, J: 295
Murder (Abolition of Death Penalty)
Bill/Act, 1964-5: 57, 62, 64, 65, 68, 72,
82, 84, 91, 92, 93, 134, 139, 145, 147, 204,
206, 214-5, 217, 218, 253, 254, 282, 283,
285, 287, 288, 293, 301, 307, 320, 331,
334, 339
Murder in Microcosm: 244
Murder Story: 251, 283
Murray, Braham: 125, 278, 280-1
My Son's Execution: 246

N

Nabarro, Gerald: 252
National Cleansing Crusade, the: 304-5
National Front, the: 85
National Government, the: 21, 43, 317
National Liberal Club: 83
National Liberals, the: 72
National Secular Society: 61
Naughton, Bill: 276
NCACP (National Campaign for the
Abolition of Capital Punishment): 16, 29,
33, 34, 36, 42, 43-60, 61, 62-3, 84, 102,
111-2, 113, 120, 123, 124, 126, 129, 130,
142, 146,152, 186, 202, 203, 215, 238,
243, 244, 252, 253, 256, 259, 299, 308,
309, 319, 320, 322, 323, 326, 329
NCADP (National Council for the
Abolition of the Death Penalty): 21, 23,
25, 29, 44, 45, 65, 142, 241, 283, 322-3
NCCL (National Council for Civil
Liberties): 61

Lightning Source UK Ltd.
Milton Keynes UK
UKOW030734281212

204163UK00002B/51/P